Exam Number	MCSE Course Title	Course Number	MCSE Study Series Title	Required or Elective?
70-59	Internetworking with Microsoft TCP/IP on Windows NT 4.0	688	TCP/IP MCSE Study Guide Bulette, 0-7645-3112-3	E
70-14	Supporting Microsoft System Management Server 1.2	732	SMS 1.2 MCSE Study Guide Bulette, 0-7645-3163-8	E
70-87	Implementing and Supporting Microsoft Internet Information Server 4.0	936	IIS 4.0 MCSE Study Guide Dillon, Linthicum, 0-7645-3118-2	E
70-81	Implementing and Supporting Microsoft Exchange Server 5.5	771	Exchange Server 5.5 MCSE Study Guide Robichaux and Glenn, 0-7645-3111-5	E

Solution Architectures MCSD Study System

Solution Architectures MCSD Study System

Bruce T. Prendergast

IDG BOOKS WORLDWIDE

® IDG Books Worldwide, Inc
An International Data Group Company
Foster City, CA • Chicago, IL • Indianapolis, IN • Dallas, TX

Solution Architectures MCSD Study System

Published by
IDG Books Worldwide, Inc.
An International Data Group Company
919 E. Hillsdale Blvd., Suite 400
Foster City, CA 94404
`www.idgbooks.com` (IDG Books Worldwide Web site)

Library of Congress Catalog Card Number: 99-66367

ISBN: 0-7645-3314-2

Printed in the United States of America

10 9 8 7 6 5 4 3 2 1

1P/QR/RQ/ZZ/FC

Distributed in the United States by IDG Books Worldwide, Inc.

Distributed by CDG Books Canada Inc. for Canada; by Transworld Publishers Limited in the United Kingdom; by IDG Norge Books for Norway; by IDG Sweden Books for Sweden; by IDG Books Australia Publishing Corporation Pty. Ltd. for Australia and New Zealand; by TransQuest Publishers Pte Ltd. for Singapore, Malaysia, Thailand, Indonesia, and Hong Kong; by Gotop Information Inc. for Taiwan; by ICG Muse, Inc. for Japan; by Intersoft for South Africa; by Eyrolles for France; by International Thomson Publishing for Germany, Austria and Switzerland; by Distribuidora Cuspide for Argentina; by LR International for Brazil; by Galileo Libros for Chile; by Ediciones ZETA S.C.R. Ltda. for Peru; by WS Computer Publishing Corporation, Inc., for the Philippines; by Contemporanea de Ediciones for Venezuela; by Express Computer Distributors for the Caribbean and West Indies; by Micronesia Media Distributor, Inc. for Micronesia; by Chips Computadoras S.A. de C.V. for Mexico; by Editorial Norma de Panama S.A. for Panama; by American Bookshops for Finland.

For general information on IDG Books Worldwide's books in the U.S., please call our Consumer Customer Service department at 800-762-2974. For reseller information, including discounts and premium sales, please call our Reseller Customer Service department at 800-434-3422.

For information on where to purchase IDG Books Worldwide's books outside the U.S., please contact our International Sales department at 317-596-5530 or fax 317-596-5692.

For consumer information on foreign language translations, please contact our Customer Service department at 800-434-3422, fax 317-596-5692, or e-mail rights@idgbooks.com.

For information on licensing foreign or domestic rights, please phone +1-650-655-3109.

For sales inquiries and special prices for bulk quantities, please contact our Sales department at 650-655-3200 or write to the address above.

For information on using IDG Books Worldwide's books in the classroom or for ordering examination copies, please contact our Educational Sales department at 800-434-2086 or fax 317-596-5499.

For press review copies, author interviews, or other publicity information, please contact our Public Relations department at 650-655-3000 or fax 650-655-3299.

For authorization to photocopy items for corporate, personal, or educational use, please contact Copyright Clearance Center, 222 Rosewood Drive, Danvers, MA 01923, or fax 978-750-4470.

ABOUT IDG BOOKS WORLDWIDE

Welcome to the world of IDG Books Worldwide.

IDG Books Worldwide, Inc., is a subsidiary of International Data Group, the world's largest publisher of computer-related information and the leading global provider of information services on information technology. IDG was founded more than 30 years ago by Patrick J. McGovern and now employs more than 9,000 people worldwide. IDG publishes more than 290 computer publications in over 75 countries. More than 90 million people read one or more IDG publications each month.

Launched in 1990, IDG Books Worldwide is today the #1 publisher of best-selling computer books in the United States. We are proud to have received eight awards from the Computer Press Association in recognition of editorial excellence and three from Computer Currents' First Annual Readers' Choice Awards. Our best-selling *...For Dummies®* series has more than 50 million copies in print with translations in 31 languages. IDG Books Worldwide, through a joint venture with IDG's Hi-Tech Beijing, became the first U.S. publisher to publish a computer book in the People's Republic of China. In record time, IDG Books Worldwide has become the first choice for millions of readers around the world who want to learn how to better manage their businesses.

Our mission is simple: Every one of our books is designed to bring extra value and skill-building instructions to the reader. Our books are written by experts who understand and care about our readers. The knowledge base of our editorial staff comes from years of experience in publishing, education, and journalism — experience we use to produce books to carry us into the new millennium. In short, we care about books, so we attract the best people. We devote special attention to details such as audience, interior design, use of icons, and illustrations. And because we use an efficient process of authoring, editing, and desktop publishing our books electronically, we can spend more time ensuring superior content and less time on the technicalities of making books.

You can count on our commitment to deliver high-quality books at competitive prices on topics you want to read about. At IDG Books Worldwide, we continue in the IDG tradition of delivering quality for more than 30 years. You'll find no better book on a subject than one from IDG Books Worldwide.

John Kilcullen
Chairman and CEO
IDG Books Worldwide, Inc.

Steven Berkowitz
President and Publisher
IDG Books Worldwide, Inc.

Eighth Annual Computer Press Awards 1992

Ninth Annual Computer Press Awards 1993

Tenth Annual Computer Press Awards 1994

Eleventh Annual Computer Press Awards 1995

IDG is the world's leading IT media, research and exposition company. Founded in 1964, IDG had 1997 revenues of $2.05 billion and has more than 9,000 employees worldwide. IDG offers the widest range of media options that reach IT buyers in 75 countries representing 95% of worldwide IT spending. IDG's diverse product and services portfolio spans six key areas including print publishing, online publishing, expositions and conferences, market research, education and training, and global marketing services. More than 90 million people read one or more of IDG's 290 magazines and newspapers, including IDG's leading global brands — Computerworld, PC World, Network World, Macworld and the Channel World family of publications. IDG Books Worldwide is one of the fastest-growing computer book publishers in the world, with more than 700 titles in 36 languages. The "...For Dummies®" series alone has more than 50 million copies in print. IDG offers online users the largest network of technology-specific Web sites around the world through IDG.net (http://www.idg.net), which comprises more than 225 targeted Web sites in 55 countries worldwide. International Data Corporation (IDC) is the world's largest provider of information technology data, analysis and consulting, with research centers in over 41 countries and more than 400 research analysts worldwide. IDG World Expo is a leading producer of more than 168 globally branded conferences and expositions in 35 countries including E3 (Electronic Entertainment Expo), Macworld Expo, ComNet, Windows World Expo, ICE (Internet Commerce Expo), Agenda, DEMO, and Spotlight. IDG's training subsidiary, ExecuTrain, is the world's largest computer training company, with more than 230 locations worldwide and 785 training courses. IDG Marketing Services helps industry-leading IT companies build international brand recognition by developing global integrated marketing programs via IDG's print, online and exposition products worldwide. Further information about the company can be found at www.idg.com.

1/24/99

The Value of Microsoft Certification

As a computer professional, your opportunities have never been greater. Yet you know better than anyone that today's complex computing environment has never been more challenging.

Microsoft certification keeps computer professionals on top of evolving information technologies. Training and certification let you maximize the potential of Microsoft Windows desktop operating systems; server technologies, such as the Internet Information Server, Microsoft Windows NT, and Microsoft BackOffice; and Microsoft development tools. In short, Microsoft training and certification provide you with the knowledge and skills necessary to become an expert on Microsoft products and technologies — and to provide the key competitive advantage that every business is seeking.

Microsoft offers you the most comprehensive program for assessing and maintaining your skills with our products. When you become a Microsoft Certified Professional (MCP), you are recognized as an expert and are sought by employers industry-wide. Technical managers recognize the MCP designation as a mark of quality — one that ensures that an employee or consultant has proven experience with Microsoft products and meets the high technical proficiency standards of Microsoft products.

As an MCP, you receive many benefits, such as direct access to technical information from Microsoft; the official MCP logo and other materials to identify your status to colleagues and clients; invitations to Microsoft conferences, technical training sessions and special events; and exclusive publications with news about the MCP program.

Research shows that organizations employing MCPs also receive many benefits:

- A standard method of determining training needs and measuring results — an excellent return on training and certification investments
- Increased customer satisfaction and decreased support costs through improved service, increased productivity, and greater technical self-sufficiency
- A reliable benchmark for hiring, promoting, and career planning
- Recognition and rewards for productive employees by validating their expertise

- Retraining options for existing employees, so they can work effectively with new technologies
- Assurance of quality when outsourcing computer services

Through your study, experience, and achievement of Microsoft certification, you will enjoy these same benefits, too, as you meet the industry's challenges.

Nancy Lewis
General Manager
Microsoft Training and Certification

Foreword to the MCSE Series

Certifications are an effective way of "selling your skills" to prospective employers, since they represent a consistent measurement of knowledge about specific software or hardware products. Because of their expansive product line and tremendous marketing efforts, Microsoft certifications have become the gold standard in the exploding certification industry. As a Microsoft Certified Professional, you are recognized as a "Subject Matter Expert" as defined by objective standards. As a training organization, we recognize the value of offering certification-level training. In fact, approximately 55 percent of students in our Microsoft classes are working toward certification, and I expect that number to continue to rise.

Studies have been conducted that show increased productivity among Microsoft Certified Solutions Developers versus noncertified programmers. Additionally, compensation for Microsoft Certified Systems Engineers and Microsoft Certified Solutions Developers averages higher than for those without certification. For individuals looking for a career in these areas, there is no better metric of legitimacy that can be placed on a resume than Microsoft certification credentials.

Information Systems/Information Technology (IS/IT) decision makers for ExecuTrain clients worldwide increasingly require certifications for their IS employees. Often, individuals are required to be certified or find that certification was their competitive edge in landing the job. Conventional wisdom and every study you read indicates these trends will continue as technologies become more a part of daily business in corporations.

Microsoft recently certified the 100,000th Microsoft Certified Professional. I expect this number to balloon as corporations make certification part of IS staff job descriptions. I predict certified candidates can expect better-paying jobs and positions with more technical responsibility to match their hard-won certification. Although the number of MCPs rises daily, that population is eclipsed by the more than 200,000 open IT positions reported today. Microsoft tracks these open positions and would like to fill each of them with an MCP. My bet is that if anyone can make the math work, they can.

Kevin Brice

Vice President/General Manager

Technical Training

ExecuTrain Corporation

Credits

ACQUISITIONS EDITOR
John Read

DEVELOPMENT EDITORS
Martin V. Minner
Jennifer Rowe

TECHNICAL EDITORS
David Hodkinson
Nikolas Landry

COPY EDITORS
Christine Schultz-Touge
Julie M. Smith

PRODUCTION COORDINATORS
Ritchie Durdin
Linda Marousek

BOOK DESIGNER
Kurt Krames

ILLUSTRATOR
Heather Hudson

GRAPHICS & PRODUCTION SPECIALISTS
Mario Amador
Jan Contestable
Stephanie Hollier
Jim Kussow
Ramses Ramirez

PROOFREADING AND INDEXING
York Production Services

QUALITY CONTROL SPECIALIST
Chris Weisbart

COVER DESIGN
Mike Parsons

About the Author

Bruce Prendergast, MCSE and MCSD, has been programming since the 1950s and is an independent consultant in the Los Angeles area. In his spare time Bruce can be found riding either a road bike, a mountain bike, or captaining a Santana tandem. Bruce has started his long awaited novel and another computer book is not immediately planned. Bruce may be contacted by e-mail at `Bruce@Prendergast.com` or on the Web at `http://www.bruce.prendergast.com`.

Please be sure to email Bruce before coming to Los Angeles. For the *hammerdogs* he has spare road and mountain bikes and a Santana tandem. If you're a *hammerette* there is the Santana tandem or he can borrow a bike for you from a friend.

As always, this book is dedicated to dearest Dianna

Preface

This book is a study guide for the Microsoft Certified Solution Developer (MCSD) core exam 70-100, *Analyzing Requirements and Defining Solution Architectures*.

Why You Need This Book

This book is about Exam 70-100, but the certification is useless if you don't have the skills needed to build an application. A paradigm shift is occurring as we enter the era of distributed applications. Very few understand the issues of an n-tiered application, and the performance of an n-tiered application is pitifully poor unless developers understand the technology. COM is now ubiquitous in the Microsoft architecture and is the basis for the new paradigm. This book is a COM cookbook for tiered-component architectures, a survival guide for tiered-component architectures, and a study guide for Exam 70-100.

The book is directed to the lowest common denominator, the Visual Basic developer, however the principles set forth in this book are applicable to any language

The book is divided into four sections. Let's look at the first section.

Component Technologies

The first ten chapters are about the Component Object Model (COM). The approach used in these chapters is to gradually layer COM technology features until ActiveX (OLE) controls are realized in Chapter 10. The illustrations are very comprehensive and you might want to pause here and look ahead at Figures 5-6 and 5-7, which illustrate the complex issue of moniker binding.

I've tried to make the early labs in this book interesting by illustrating fundamental COM technology, which is used later in comprehensive labs. Chapter 1 starts with two Microsoft Visual Basic labs, the first lab illustrates *creating an interface* and second lab illustrates *delegation*.

Components are building blocks of distributed applications. A lab at the conclusion of Chapter 4 illustrates *building a property bag* (**IPropertyBag** interface). Another lab in Chapter 10 illustrates *building a component property page*.

Component communication is essential in a tiered architecture. A lab at the conclusion of Chapter 6 *implements an advisory sink* (**IAdviseSink** interface), which depends upon the Microsoft Visual Basic **RaiseEvent** keyword. Another aspect of component communication is illustrated in Chapter 10 with a lab that implements a *callback function*. Callbacks are relatively easy in Microsoft Visual C++, but they're a bit more work in Microsoft Visual Basic.

Type libraries are a performance issue in a component technology. I introduce type libraries in Chapter 2 where Visual Basic is used to create an ActiveX DLL with an embedded type library. Type libraries are revisited in Chapter 21, DCOM.

Microsoft Visual Basic is not always adequate for the task at hand. Chapter 4 illustrates *writing structured storage streams* using StorageTools 2.0 from Desaware.

Tiered Architecture Building Blocks

We've completed the COM fundamentals. The second section consists of six chapters on database access technologies, which includes ODBC, RDO, and ADO. DAO is not a member of the new distributed application paradigm. The chapter examples in this book are *birdhouse* quality (very simple examples). Not so with the programming labs for the remainder of the book.

Chapters 11 and 12 are dedicated to ODBC, RDO is discussed in Chapters 13 and 14, and ADO is discussed in Chapters 15 and 16. The labs start with Chapter 12 and different database access versions are created for each chapter from the initial Chapter 12 lab. The variations in the different labs are all brought together in Chapter 21 where I build a DCOM application.

The labs are the highlight of the database access technology section. Labs by chapter include:

- **Chapter 12: ODBC Applications Lab** - A tiered architecture approach is used with a generic class driver and an ODBC class, which transparently translates Unicode queries. The concept of a class driver is not new and is commonly used with devices where specific device drivers are subservient to a class device driver. This approach yields reusable code and insulates the application from specific database class changes. This lab also introduces custom marshaling with a piped string. You'll find why we do this in Chapter 21.

- **Chapter 13: RDO Lab** - The ODBC class is converted to an RDO class. The class driver remains the same and custom marshaling is still used with a piped string.
- **Chapter 14: RDO Queries Lab** - This is the last of two RDO chapters. Updates are added to the RDO class.
- **Chapter 15: Active Data Objects Lab** - The lab of Chapter 12 is converted to an ADO class. The class driver is changed slightly since the ADO class returns an ADO **Recordset** object rather than a piped string.
- **Chapter 16: Working with Active Data Objects Lab** - This is the second of two ADO chapters. The Chapter 15 lab is modified to custom marshaling with collections, which is Microsoft sponsored. Microsoft class 1298, which is a recommended course for Exam 70-100, uses collections. Marshaling issues, which includes collections, are discussed in greater detail in Chapter 21.

Designing a Tiered Architecture Application

The third section consists of four chapters that are dedicated to Exam 70-100 issues. At this point in the book the reader should have a reasonable understanding of COM and should understand most of the mechanics of building a tiered-component application. The only problem left is to correctly identify and implement the client (customer) requirements. The 70-100 exam objectives are nearly exhaustive with respect to the enumeration of user requirements. The Exam 70-100 objectives are deficient in that the issue of how to collect user requirements is not addressed.

I reviewed many of the Microsoft white papers relating to Exam 70-100. I found the white papers in general were reprints from material in currently published books. With that in mind, I've tried to communicate the essence of my forty years plus of programming experience. You'll find a lot of experience buried in these pages.

The answers to the labs for Chapters 17, 18, 19, and 20 are all contained in separate appendix that is a bit over one hundred pages. This provides a very succinct study guide for Exam 70-100. There is a discussion laboratory for each 70-100 objective. The chapters are as follows:

- **Chapter 17: Conceptual Design** - Chapter 17 discusses the mechanics of collecting the application requirements. Many models are built that are used to manage the resulting analysis. The models are used later in Chapter 18, which addresses data design issues and in Chapter 19 where the application is designed. The important point of this chapter is that a methodology is introduced for analyzing user requirements.
- **Chapter 18: Logical Data Design** - ERwin from Platinum technology, Inc. is used to illustrate all aspects of data modeling. I am traditional in that I believe that I must understand what I need to do before I can address how to do it. To start with the how is a bottom-up design approach from a process-oriented mindset. This is the reason that logical data design precedes application design in this book. The approach sponsored by Microsoft in Course 491, which is a recommended course for Exam 70-100, is to identify application objects, remove the methods, and map the remaining properties to data entities. I'm in severe disagreement with this and I'm sure that I'll hear from the Microsoft loyalists.
- **Chapter 19: Application Design** - This chapter discusses the various stages of application design. Rational Rose is used for conceptual modeling and the reader is introduced to the basics of the Universal Modeling Language (UML). Conceptual modeling an application with UML lets the developer feedback to the user the system requirements in user and business terms. This doesn't happen with Microsoft Visual Modeler where the developer starts immediately with logical modeling, which puts the project at risk because the user hasn't obtained enough feedback from the developer.
- **Chapter 20: Solution Interface Design** - Chapter 20 addresses the remaining Exam 70-100 objectives. I discuss user interface issues extensively. This chapter repeats commonly known and accepted presentation styles and standards that are well documented in The Windows Interface Guidelines for Software Design from Microsoft Press.

Building a Tiered Architecture Application

This section has only one chapter, Distributed COM (DCOM). I discuss DCOM as an extension of COM. Don't overlook the importance of this chapter, because it addresses the many performance issues associated with DCOM.

This chapter takes a different tack for the labs. This chapter examples contain a create, read, update, and delete (CRUD) class, which is discussed in Microsoft course 491. (Course 491 is a Microsoft recommended course for Exam 70-100.) The CRUD class, which uses DAO, is used in the labs at the conclusion of the chapter. The CRUD class is quite extensive, including transactions, cascading deletes, and parent-child insertions. There is also a method for acquiring unique identifiers.

A lab at the end of the chapter converts the DAO CRUD class to an ADO CRUD class. *State* (persistent data) was intentionally built into the CRUD class. Microsoft Transaction Server components cannot have *state,* and another lab at the conclusion of Chapter 21 suggests two different alternatives for removing *state* from the DAO CRUD class. Even though DAO is not a member of the new distributed application paradigm, DAO was used for the CRUD class because not all readers of this book have access to Microsoft SQL Server.

Chapter 21 concludes the book. Along the way we'll build many classes, each exhibiting different characteristics. You'll learn how to collect user requirements, design a system, and build it. You'll also learn that the new order of distributed applications is not simple and is fraught with peril. Along the way you'll also learn the material necessary for passing Exam 70-100. Passing the exam is important, but you'll need a broader skill set and a firmer foundation in critical thinking if you're going to make it in the real world. That's what I hope to accomplish in this book.

Conventions Used in This Book

The following style conventions are used throughout this book.

Bold - An interface, property, method, or object name is set in bold face. An example is the **Recordset** object of DAO or the **IUnknown** interface of COM.

Italic - Parameters that require values are set in italics. You'll find these frequently used in database access technology when discussing syntax for object methods.

CAPITALS - All capital letters are used for directory names, filenames, and acronyms.

Listings - All listings are in a mono-spaced font.

Several different icons used throughout this book draw your attention to matters that deserve a closer look:

concept link

This icon points you to another place in this book (or to another resource) for more coverage on a given topic. It may point you back to a previous chapter where important material has already been covered, or it may point you ahead to let you know that a concept will be covered in more detail later.

Be careful here! This icon points out information that can save you a lot of grief. It's often easier to prevent tragedy than to fix it afterwards.

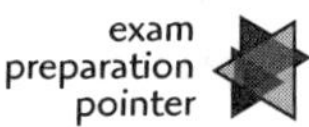

This icon identifies important advice for those studying to pass the three Microsoft Certified Professional exams on Windows NT.

I know this will be hard for you to believe, but sometimes things work differently in the real world than books or software documentation say they do. This icon draws your attention to the author's real world experiences, which will hopefully help you on the job, if not on the Microsoft Certified Professional exams.

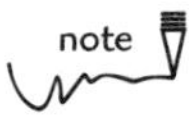

This icon points out an interesting or helpful fact, or some other comment that deserves emphasis.

Here's a little piece of friendly advice, or a shortcut, or a bit of personal experience that might be of use to you.

Acknowledgments

This *is* a good book. How do I know that? It's because the team that worked with me on this book are all experts. A heart-felt thanks to each and every one of them.

Lam Nguyen is my expert on the pedagogic issues. COM is very difficult for those already immersed in computer technology, and correspondingly more difficult for new-comers to the industry. Lam, thanks for making the book readable.

I am blessed with the best technical editor in the industry, David Hodkinson. I've lost count but David has somewhere around thirty Microsoft certifications. David kept me honest in my many lapses with simple questions. Thanks David, your restraint is certainly appreciated.

Martin Minner is my development editor. He too is very patient with me. Marty is the type of editor that every writer needs. When my paragraph leads go astray, he is there with just the right phrasing. Thanks for letting me mooch all those great paragraph leads Marty. My gratitude extends far beyond a mere thank you.

Christine Schutz-Touge is my copy editor and she is very special. Christine did a marvelous job of copy editing this book without losing the idiom. That's very rare for copy editors and truly appreciated. Thank you Christine.

Julie Smith is my IDG copy editor and another one of those special people. Julie's job is to assemble all the small pieces that constitute this book while fighting daily production schedules. She did this professionally and efficiently while dealing with IDG's most difficult author. Thank you for your patience Julie.

The really special person is Jennifer Rowe, my IDG development editor. Her effort during this book is nothing short of Herculean. My acquisitions editor was hired away by the Redmondians in the early stages of the book. Jennifer ended up wearing many hats and managed to keep everything going with grace and style. Jennifer, thanks for going far beyond the call of duty.

A special thanks to all the many members of the MCSDChat forum and especially to Luke Schollmeyer, Matt Mizenko, Waldemar Nowak, Robert Faybrick, Steve Winfough, and all those many others that space does not permit me to name. Lastly I wish to thank my many fans that purchased 0-7645-3123-9, Da BIG WA BOOK. There were a few rough edges, but I did the best that I could, and in the process I acquired thousands of new friends. I thank each and every one of you for the support. I know that many are waiting for this book and I hope it meets your expectations. Your support made this book possible.

Contents at a Glance

Contents

PART I

Component Technologies

The Component Object Model (COM) and Object Linking and Embedding (OLE) are now ubiquitous in the Microsoft architecture. These few chapters offer a birds-eye view of COM, which will provide you with a solid understanding of COM's architectural aspects.

Chapter 1: COM - Discusses historical issues and sets the background for the Microsoft COM implementation.

Chapter 2: Object Interfacing - Deals with the basic interface issues.

Chapter 3: Interface Issues - Continues with COM basics and such issues as global naming, type libraries, and the Registry.

Chapter 4: Structured Storage - Continues the layering of COM technology with the introduction of Structured Storage.

Chapter 5: Monikers - Functionality continues to move upward with the introduction of monikers.

Chapter 6: Uniform Data Transfer - This is our last stop in Component technologies before we build our first functional COM application.

Chapter 7: Document Linking - In this chapter we build the first COM application.

Chapter 8: Document Embedding - Presents COM document embedding, which is surprisingly similar to document linking.

Chapter 9: Automation - Presents Automation, a COM technology that does not support linking or embedding.

Chapter 10: OLE Controls: Using It All (Well, Almost!) - This is the pinnacle of COM, where an ActiveX control uses all COM technologies except embedding.

CHAPTER

1

COM

About Chapter 1

The *Component Object Model* (COM) is an effort to realize reusable components and reduce system costs. Each generation of faster and larger computers fosters seemingly larger and larger programs. COM fosters a component architecture where components are shared between applications, which is not the case for monolithic legacy applications. An example is a spell checker used by both Visio and Microsoft Word. Application errors increase with additional program complexity. Thus, Microsoft developed the component object model to attain these very important goals:

- Build manageable applications with components
- Manage application complexity
- Eliminate any implementation or distribution issues between the client and its object(s)
- Promote the development of systems that are less fragile and easier to extend

Chapter 1 starts a bit before the beginning of COM and provides thumbnail sketches of prior efforts at code reusability. The history section is abbreviated, but it is important to know that COM addresses and solves the issue of interapplication communication, which has existed since the start of the computer age. Microsoft solved the universal-naming problem to make COM a reality. Microsoft didn't define the concept of a *universal unique identifier* (UUID); it borrowed the concept from the Open Systems Foundation's (OSF) *distributed computing environment* (DCE) and made it happen. Without Microsoft's efforts, I am sure the standards committee would still be discussing the relative merits of various technologies.

The remainder of this chapter focuses on Microsoft's unique approach to COM to realize code reusability. COM supports *encapsulation, inheritance,* and *polymorphism,* which are the principles of object-oriented technology. Encapsulation wraps prior technology in a wrapper, and the client accesses the technology indirectly through the outer shell. COM supports interface inheritance and not implementation inheritance. C++ is an example of a language that supports implementation inheritance. With implementation inheritance, a subclass *inherits* executable code from a parent class. COM interface inheritance is more of an attitude than a programming paradigm, and COM interface inheritance places a burden on the developer. The developer must implement all the interface functionality, however, no restrictions are placed on the code generated (see Lab 1.1). This leads directly to the polymorphic nature of COM. Polymorphism occurs when two different code implementations support the same interface. (It's rather fun to hear the programming purists say, "That's not inheritance!") Whether or not COM supports true implementation inheritance is not the issue. The end result is that COM realizes code reuse, and that is the ultimate goal.

In the Beginning

Monolithic applications, such as a large, compiled FORTRAN program, are relics of the past. The new software paradigm is a component architecture, which may be a distributed architecture. Component technologies are not an invention of Microsoft, but rather a natural evolution of computing technology. Early, and certainly primordial, programs are indeed monolithic when compared to a tool with hundreds of components, such as Microsoft Word. The compiled legacy applications of the past are best characterized as an immutable binary mass. This changed over time, however, as the concept of shared code evolved to today's component technology.

The evolution started with system libraries where subroutines were copied into the linked application task. These libraries evolved into specialized application libraries, which were still copied into linked space. By the late 1960s, the UNIVAC 1108 with Exec VIII defined an operating system with shared instruction space and private data space. The evolution continued with RSX from Digital Equipment Corporation (DEC), which begat VAX/VMS, which in turn begat Windows NT.

Libraries, shared I-bank instruction sets, and shared *dynamic link libraries* (DLLs) are all part of an effort to reuse code. Microsoft addressed the age-old problem of code reuse with a universal interface in *object linking and embedding* (OLE). A standard interface is defined in advance, and the application interrogates the standard interface for additional functionality. The interfaces are reasonably complex to implement; however, starting with Visual Basic 5.0, the developer task of creating OLE Controls, which are now called ActiveX controls, was greatly simplified.

The Microsoft infrastructure development language is C++. Knowledge of C++ is not a prerequisite of this book; however, COM borrows some notation from C++. If you are not a C++ developer, don't worry. This book is still for you. If you are a C++ developer, you are already familiar with the C++ *scope resolution operator* (::). This book won't teach you programming, although there are many Visual Basic for Applications examples as well as some C++ examples. Please bear with me while I present a C++ feature that illustrates a notation of COM.

The *scope resolution operator* is a formal name for the class::method syntax, which is a notation often used in discussions of COM. For example, the statement **IUnknown::QueryInterface** is understood to mean, "use the **QueryInterface** method of the class **IUnknown**."

The following C++ example illustrates the class Rectangle with the member function Area:

```
Class cRectangle {
  int width, height;           // private data members
Public:
  cRectangle(int ht, int wd);  // constructor
    {height = ht; width = wd; }
  ~cRectangle();               // destructor
  int area()                   // member function (method)
    { return width * height; }
};
```

I embellished the Rectangle class a little bit to illustrate a simple, but reasonably complete, C++ class. I can compute the areas of a rectangle with a class member function reference to **cRectangle::Area**. This distinguishes between another member function reference, **cSphere::Area** of the class **Sphere**, which is not illustrated. That's all there is to it.

The Roots of COM

Let's enumerate some useful COM facts. We'll address the evolutionary nature of program communication and show how it evolved into the COM of today.

Program communication is a very old issue.

The Microsoft Architecture deals with a classic problem: program communication. Program communication is fundamental to computing, and is an issue that has been with us since the very early days of computing. The difference between the environment today and the environment then is easy to envision. Very early applications did not communicate with other applications, and the application scope was limited to the immediate host computer. This changes today where the application is distributed across more than one system, and the components communicate transparently. For example, I once worked for UNIVAC, a large computer mainframe manufacturer. UNIVAC was a leader in computer technology, yet I remember only one notable accomplishment of the company: NASA used a UNIVAC 1108 multiprocessor system for the 1969 Apollo moon shot. If I recall correctly, only thirty-seven or so of the predecessor UNIVAC 1107 systems were sold. I don't know the actual number of UNIVAC 1100s that were sold, but sales were somewhere in the very low thousands. (I do remember the milestone when the 800th unit was shipped.) These numbers are very low when considering the 60,000,000 plus desktop versions of Microsoft Windows that are installed today. Still, UNIVAC had difficulty supporting fewer than one thousand clients using the UNIVAC Exec VIII operating system. Today, Microsoft supports millions of customers. This volume has forced Microsoft to consider standards and code reuse as a matter of corporate survival. The initial push for a component architecture with OLE 1.0, the predecessor to COM and OLE 2.0, came only after Windows 3.1 was a resounding success.

Software libraries enhanced computing and program communication. Libraries were often limited to a specific development language.

Traditional software libraries were specific to one language, but they came in many flavors. Modules that your application required were automatically linked to your executable, giving you your own private copy of the module. System libraries were common, with literally hundreds of modules available to FORTRAN and COBOL developers.

What if you had your own copy of a library? That was an entirely different matter. The concept of a system installation of application-oriented libraries came later on the evolutionary computing timeline. The library-install technique began with the very early RSX-class systems from Digital Equipment Corporation, which evolved into a fine science in VaxVMS (known today as OpenVMS). This technology is carried forward to Microsoft Windows NT. (Dave Cutler, who today is the chief architect of Windows NT, was an architect of RSX and all its progeny that eventually evolved into OpenVMS.)

A COM interface permits client-server interrogation of services available.

Traditional libraries have unique interfaces. The interfaces were usually well documented and could be used very readily, but only if you read the documentation. Contrast that with COM. Client legacy applications interface the services available, but this is only possible with proper documentation. COM is different in that the client object interfaces with a universal and generic interface, even when the services available are known. The required interface for all COM-compliant components is the **IUnknown** interface. **QueryInterface** is a method of this interface through which a user interrogates a server that returns available interface information. This is a universal interface, which is only a binary specification. As I explain later, an interface may be implemented in any language, which results in platform independence. I discuss this interrogation mechanism in a detailed discussion of COM in the Chapter 2.

A published COM object interface is rigid. Published interfaces cannot be modified, and new services can be added without affecting existing services. New COM services, however, are not published.

As with traditional libraries, the COM interface is rigid. The issue at hand is of maintenance at a later date. A COM interface is never modified and is considered a contract between the client and the interface. New features are implemented as a new interface. Adding a new parameter results in the creation of a new interface, while at the same time inheriting functionality from the prior interface. The existing client is not aware of the new functionality.

Compare that to a traditional library when a new parameter is added to an interface. This cannot be done without significant client expense.

COM provides a negotiation tool with the **IUnknown::QueryInterface** interface. **IUnknown::QueryInterface** is a rigid COM interface where the client tells the server object, "I want to use this feature. Where is it?" COM publishes a universal interface but not client services, whereas the legacy model publishes client services and specifications. If you think about this for a minute, you'll realize that this feature significantly reduces code complexity because specific functionality is never published. New functionality can be added, but the older client is not aware of the new functionality because of the contract between the client and the interface.

The advantage of not publishing services is that new services may be added at a later date (through delegation or aggregation) without informing the client. In other words, new features can be added with zero impact. The client won't use them because the client is requesting a service it needs, a service it knows is there, and a service with which it has a contract. This is very different from strict object-oriented implementations where the smallest change in the base class forces the recompilation of all subclasses. New functionality may be added to a COM component through aggregation and delegation with no effect on the client. At least, that's the theory, and it works except when the newly implemented feature has a bug. COM solves what is known as the *fragile base class problem,* which was a major selling point when COM was first introduced.

Implementing **IUnknown** in C++ is illustrated by the following code:

```
interface IUnknown
{
  virtual HRESULT QueryInterface(IID& iid, void ** ppvObj) = 0;
  virtual ULONG AddRef() = 0;
  virtual UNLOG Release() = 0;
}
```

Implementing **IUnknown** in Visual Basic 5.0 is illustrated by the following code:

```
Implements IUnknown
```

Actually, the **Implements** statement isn't needed for the **IUnknown** interface because it is automatically included with every Visual Basic 5.0 object method.

QueryInterface, AddRef, and Release are also automatically implemented with any Visual Basic 5.0 component. The implemented class accepts COM QueryInterface calls for the specified interface identifier (IID).

Late binding is a feature of COM. Users have additional flexibility and a wider range of choices available.

Traditional libraries are always linked at object-time, as opposed to run-time. The developer, not the user, binds the object. Note that late binding requires COM server-object interrogation with IUnknown::QueryInterface. The user is given a choice of services available.

COM gives the user the choice of linking (binding) the objects of choice, whereas the traditional library model delegates all linking responsibility to the developer.

Program name space has evolved from private, to departmental, to corporate, to worldwide. The Internet has turned us into a world community; binding to an object now requires a unique name. A UUID names COM objects and their interfaces.

Traditional libraries have name spaces generic to library usage. These libraries were (and are) used in a heterogeneous environment. The usage is not universal; however, the client has the responsibility of avoiding name-space collisions.

Within a *Visual Basic for Applications* (VBA) event subroutine, the scope of the variables is limited to the event subroutine. Variable scope (domain) has some semblance of a name-space, but it is not an accurate model. The difference is that name-spaces have territorial and jurisdictional constraints. A manufacturing plant has many departments. Rules that exist between the departments within a plant do not apply to relations with other plants of the same corporation. Name-space is not an issue of name collisions within an application, a local area network (LAN), or a wide area network (WAN). The name-space rules- are relatively simple. Without a universal naming convention, the rules of the host governed—something akin to "My house, my rules!"

Name-space has evolved from internal names within an application, to departmental name-space, to corporate name-space, and, thanks to the Internet, to a universal name-space. This is a far cry from the traditional developer tasked to create a department library. The traditional developer had no global naming problems because one department controlled all application development and the software had no external interfaces. The Internet reinforces the fact that we are one very large community. Naming standards must be global, not departmental.

Microsoft solves the naming problem by borrowing the UUID from the Open Software Foundation's DCE. A UUID identifying an object is known as a *class identifier* (CLSID) and a UUID identifying an interface is known as an *interface identifier* (IID).

COM supports emulation, preserving an investment in older software.

As stated previously, COM is a contract between an interface and a client. This contract is immutable and does not change. Even though new features with new interfaces are added, prior services are still available. It is possible to implement the latest version with no impact on existing applications—if there are no bugs in the latest version.

This is not true with traditional libraries. New libraries inevitably crash applications. There is always a lengthy evaluation period to assess the impact on productions. Reworking the applications can be quite expensive, and the applications may still crash.

It has always been difficult to decide when and if to upgrade an application. If you didn't upgrade to the new library, your application became an orphan without vendor support. The problem compounded if you were more than one library release behind—you were eventually forced to upgrade your application at a considerable expense.

Emulation assumes the characteristics of an object of another type while maintaining its name and original format. The opportunity for emulation exists with older-version client software. Emulation is a retro operation, because only older versions, and not newer versions, are emulated. Historically, the client software is modified to conform to the newer server specifications, and this isn't always possible or feasible. COM avoids this problem by emulating prior versions or features unique to the older version by using COM library features such as **CoTreatAsClass**. **OleSetAutoConvert** automatically upgrades an existing component to the newer version level.

Automatic object conversion is the other user option. **OleSetAutoConvert** and **OleDoAutoConvert** are COM library features that support automatic conversion. This option however, should be used with some caution, as the conversion is not always backward-compatible.

Reusable components can reduce development costs.

Traditional libraries are reusable; their use, however, is often limited to one language. Subroutine libraries for specific languages were quite common. Developers used assembly language hacks to access library subroutines of other languages. COM is a binary specification, and is not limited to any particular language. The only real requirement is that a language supporting COM must have the necessary programming constructs and support the COM library, the interface **IUnknown,** and the methods **QueryInterface, Release,** and **AddRef.** Every COM implementation must have a COM library, and must support these three methods. Of course, there are other interfaces, but this is the minimal COM implementation.

COM generalizes component interfaces and is a natural step in the evolution of software development. The future of COM is very promising.

Benefits of COM

The benefits of COM are:

- COM supports code reuse between diverse development systems, which implies platform interoperability. COM components are independent of the language or operating system. Microsoft Visual Basic components communicate freely with components developed in other languages, such as Microsoft C++ and Microsoft Visual FoxPro. Digital Equipment Corporation (now Compaq) FORTRAN and Fujitsu COBOL also communicate with COM components. COM is a binary specification and is language-independent. Yes, an older language might have used a library component of a different language, but that was only with great difficulty and only if the developer knew the proper incantations. It wasn't always possible to share library components.
- COM is an accepted standard. The COM specification states three basic standards for interoperability: how an object will be instantiated from a class, how a client accesses features of the object, and the client responsibilities for managing the instantiated object. How these responsibilities are to be implemented is not stated in the COM specification. This makes COM language-independent.
- The component developer controls application installation. If you recall, earlier in the computing evolution timeline, the developer had control, but it was a private copy of a library. Library installations eventually evolved to an operating system-level function. It has now moved back to where it should be: developer-controlled installation of components.
- COM objects support distributed applications with the use of a UUID. Applications are no longer limited to a departmental or a locale solution. Enterprise-wide and worldwide applications are now possible. (This is a benefit of the new distributed COM.)
- COM supports a client interrogating a server. Users now have a choice of services. Every COM object is required to support the **IUnknown::Query Interface**. The client object interrogates this interface of the server with an IID identifying the requested service. A COM client object can build and present a palette of services. The user selects from the available services.

- COM reduces code complexity. Although it is true that application complexity increases slightly when developing a COM server, the overall complexity should reduce with Microsoft Visual Basic 5.0 and later versions. There is only one instance of the server, but many instances of server usage by clients. The payoff can be huge. The common code can be developed or purchased and then plugged into the architecture.
- COM supports code reuse with emulation. The COM object can emulate an older server version when an older application version is present. This protects software investments. Contrast this with a legacy application for which existing software must be modified whenever a newer client library is installed.
- Interfaces are rigid in that as new features are added, the original interface remains intact with no loss of functionality. An existing client object is unaware of new server services. This is done through either delegation or aggregation. *Delegation* occurs when an interface delegates a client service request to another interface. This is often called a *wrapper* function. *Aggregation* is the binding of two different interfaces. Methods of the first interface can be accessed by the second interface and the functionality appears to be owned by the second interface. The converse is also true, and methods of the second interface may appear to be owned by the first interface. Microsoft Visual C++ supports both aggregation and delegation; however, Microsoft Visual Basic only supports aggregation.
- COM objects are integrated with a consistent interface. A COM implementation must support a COM library, and all COM objects must support the **IUnknown** interface with the methods **QueryInterface, Release,** and **AddRef**. The COM object does not publish services. It publishes universal and generic interfaces to the server object for client use. The client determines the actual services available with an interrogation process.
- COM supports location transparency. A client calls a service, which may be located in the client process, located on the same system in a different process, or located on a remote system. A service is always called in the same manner independent of location.

- COM objects are extensible. New features added to an existing COM object do not impact existing client code. COM has an immutable law that all existing interfaces cannot change. This is known as a contract between the client and the server.

  The immutable interface contract is a major pillar of COM; however, the Microsoft Visual Basic design team circumvented those rules, to the consternation of the COM purists, and the circumvention simplifies application development. A Microsoft Visual Basic project may be assigned *No Compatibility, Project Compatibility,* or *Binary Compatibility.* Binary Compatibility assures that the COM contract is not broken.

- The global model of COM supports localization and the UNICODE character set, which is the default character set of Microsoft Windows NT. The UNICODE character set supports foreign languages where the locale identifier is used to designate specific language regions, such as France.
- COM is manageable. Type libraries are created form the older *object description language* (ODL) file or the newer *interface description language* (IDL) file. The program `MKTYPLIB.EXE` is used to create a type library with a `.TLB` extension. The information is moved to the Registry at component registration time. The Registry is a central repository of available and active COM components.

COM and the Windows Architecture

That's enough of extolling the virtues of COM for now. Let's discuss COM and the Windows architecture. I'll begin with an historical perspective and the forces in motion. I want to take you back in time to that period I call the CORBA Wars. I think that I can rightly call the CORBA Wars an internecine war: There were zealots on all sides and the salvos were epistles grandly stating the virtues of the respective technology. For those of you who recall the period, there were (and still are) different competing technologies, COM, *Common Object Request Broker* (CORBA), and IBM's *System Object Model* (SOM). I won't venture an opinion as to which technology is the best, but simply point out that Microsoft supports millions of customers and couldn't wait for negotiated standards from a committee.

For more information about CORBA, visit its Web site at `http://www.omg.org`.

DESIGNED BY COMMITTEE IS NOT ALWAYS AN ATTRACTIVE SOLUTION

I have seen standards that were beneficial. I've also seen languages in which the standards committee lost sight of the original value of the language and added features that tried to mimic other languages. Not all problem solutions are or should be the domain of one language—some problems are better suited to another language. But you couldn't tell the standards committee that. The standards committee language had to do everything, but not everything can be done in one language. I'm certain there are more than a few of you who shudder when you hear the phrase "Designed by Committee."

These technologies were inspired by the OSF DCE specification mentioned earlier. The DCE specification was an attempt to reduce computational complexity with respect to heterogeneous networking. It identified several key issues, but some of the specifications were in error. For example, a DCE *remote procedure call* (RPC) was synchronous. Could that work today? Certainly not; loading an image from the Internet is one example, and there are countless others. Microsoft's solution was to implement COM as an object layer over DCE, as shown in Figure 1-1. Thus, Microsoft implementations are DCE-compliant when possible.

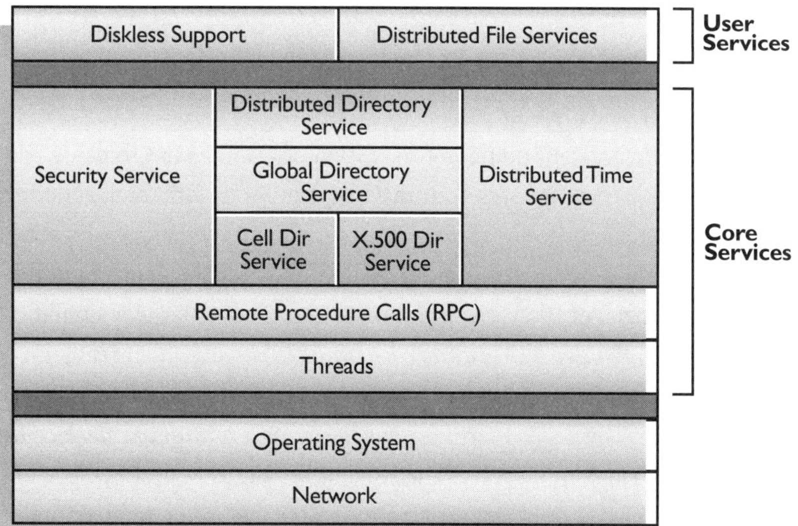

FIGURE 1-1 The DCE over which COM is implemented as an object layer

You see some familiar Windows NT features in DCE services. The architecture is not quite the same, because threads and RPCs are features of the Windows NT operating system, rather than functions in their own right.

COM has evolved from a desktop architectural tool to a tiered application component architecture. Creating enterprise software is not a simple task. Remember that Microsoft was initially a provider of desktop systems and services. Microsoft has developed a very rich infrastructure to support the desktop, and new ventures in that area can be highly leveraged. Microsoft is slowly accumulating software at the enterprise level that can be leveraged. Microsoft Transaction Server (MTS) and Microsoft Message Queue (MSMQ) are both recent examples of component tools. When necessary, Microsoft purchases or licenses the necessary tools. Microsoft Visual Modeler (VM) is an example of an enterprise tool that is licensed from Rational Rose Corporation. VM is a limited version of Rational Rose 98 (formerly Rational Rose 4.0) and I look under the hood of Rational Rose in Chapter 19.

The rules of the game will change once Microsoft builds enough enterprise software that can be leveraged. Leverage will enable Microsoft to quickly eclipse competitors who currently have technological leads in specific areas.

Microsoft is able to leverage technology. An example is the relatively small amount of time it took for Microsoft to convert *OLE Controls* (OCXs) to ActiveX controls. This wasn't just a renaming of the technology. It is true that ActiveX controls have less capability than the older OCX technology, but ActiveX controls have a distinct advantage on the Internet: quicker response time. ActiveX looks like a winner (see Chapter 10).

Before continuing my discussion of COM, I want to pause and look at the application interface architecture. COM is only one facet of the Microsoft architecture, but note how the abstraction of these different models appears to be successful.

There are several terms used to describe the application interface architecture; many of these terms, however, may be seen as oversimplifications. The first term is *Windows Operating System Extensions,* which really is correct, but does not effectively convey the complexity of what can be accomplished with this architecture. The second term is *application programming interface* (API). This is too much detail and involves the student of Microsoft architecture in needless minutiae, which is not necessary for an understanding of architectural issues.

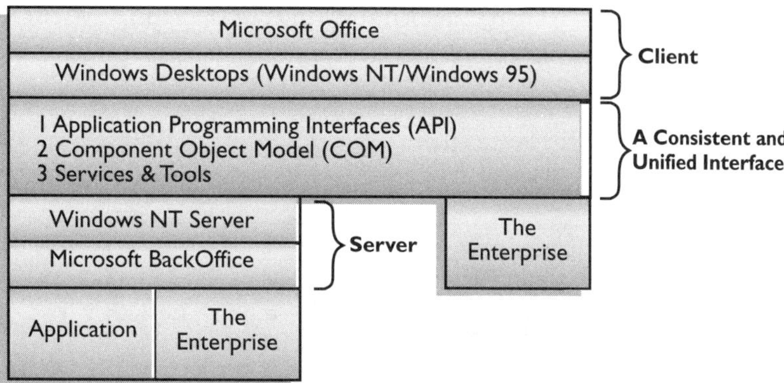

FIGURE 1-2 Microsoft's client-server architecture in a heterogeneous environment

You can see from Figure 1-2 why an API is called a Windows Operating System Extension. An API is an application portal to services. Any language may use an API. It is language-independent if the language has the constructs necessary to support an API call.

COM is at the same logical level as an API and appears to serve the same purpose, but it does more than provide an interface. The position of COM in the overall architecture belies the rich functionality available. It is the cornerstone of a new component-based architecture, while at the same time it can be used as a wrapper function for legacy code. I believe that the most important contribution COM can make to the computing community is to provide wrapper functions for legacy code. (I'm certain my perspective is different because much of the adult population appears to have Internet fever.) Desktop systems require access to legacy data and moving legacy data to the desktop is unreasonable.

An API is not the only component of the Microsoft Windows architecture. Microsoft defined a *service provider interface* (SPI) as an abstraction level. A SPI is a compartmentalization of API functions reserved for use by the service provider as illustrated in Figure 1-3, and Figure 1-4 identifies specific service providers. Not all APIs have a companion SPI; only those involving architectural issues do. As an example, internal APIs do not have a companion SPI. The best example of a service provider interface is the *messaging application program interface* (MAPI). Well-known MAPI service providers include Microsoft's MSMail, IBM's Profs, and Digital Equipment's All-In-One.

Figure 1-3 is a restatement of Windows Operating System Extensions. The consistent and unified interface in Figure 1-2 illustrates the relationship between an API and SPI. Only two APIs are shown, *Open Database Connectivity* (ODBC) and MAPI, but there are others.

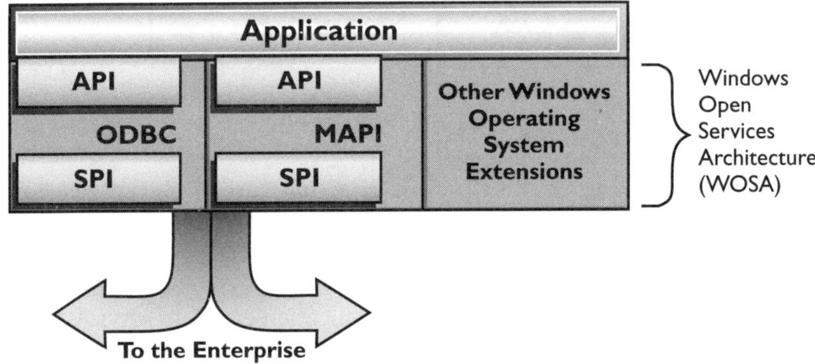

FIGURE 1-3 The API and SPI relationship in Windows architecture

A generic feature of all Windows Operating System Extensions is the API and SPI interface architecture. Microsoft calls this architecture *open,* as third-party vendors are free to provide services using the SPI. COM supports a client and server architecture with the server functioning as a service provider.

I close this discussion of Microsoft architecture with Figure 1-4, a functional API/SPI model. This discussion is not about MAPI; however, the MAPI architecture is the best representation of the relationship between an API and a SPI. MAPI supports **IUnknown** and is a COM-based technology.

OLE/ActiveX and COM do nothing more than what we have always done as developers, but now we can do it with a little élan. COM allows code reuse, it is extensible, its interfaces are negotiated, older versions can be emulated, and all of its components have a standard interface. Application complexity can be reduced. COM is also a tool for salvaging legacy code.

Microsoft demonstrated wrapping a COBOL CICS transaction within an ActiveX control in spring 1997. This was a major step forward in salvaging legacy software. Rather than rewrite or convert legacy applications, encapsulate them, and use remote automation to control them.

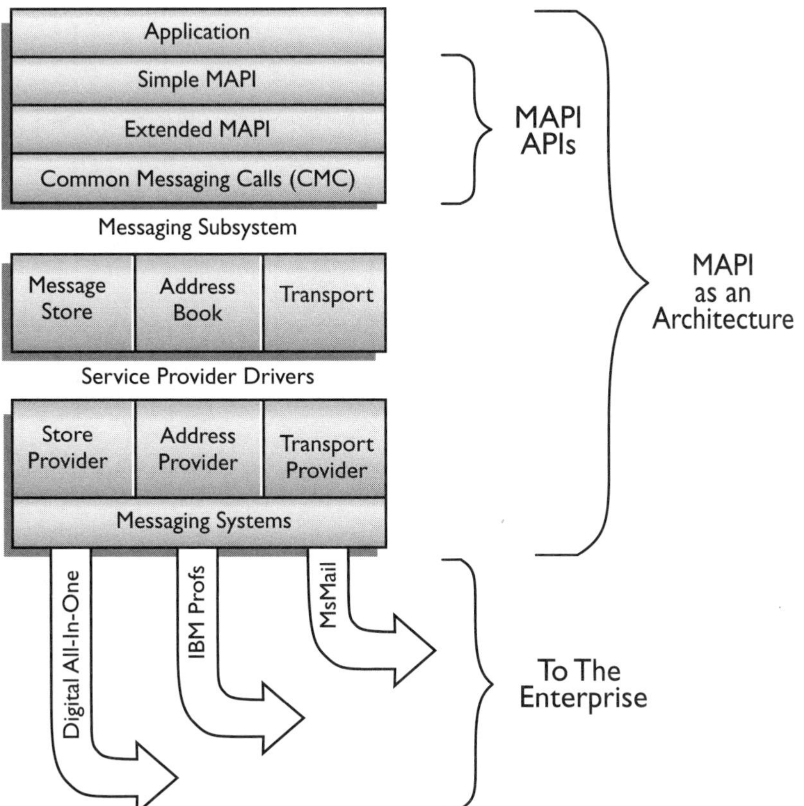

FIGURE 1-4 The COM-based MAPI architecture illustrating the relationship between an API and a SPI

The subsequent chapters in this book have a lot more in store. Figure 1-5 is a glimpse of that future where COM morphs into *Distributed COM* (DCOM), which was introduced with Windows NT 4.0. Microsoft Transaction Server (MTS) and Microsoft Message Queue (MSMQ) are more recent additions to the Microsoft architecture. MTS serves as a host for ActiveX, or what used to be known as OLE components. It'll take a bit to get there, but Figure 1-5 represents the application architecture of the future.

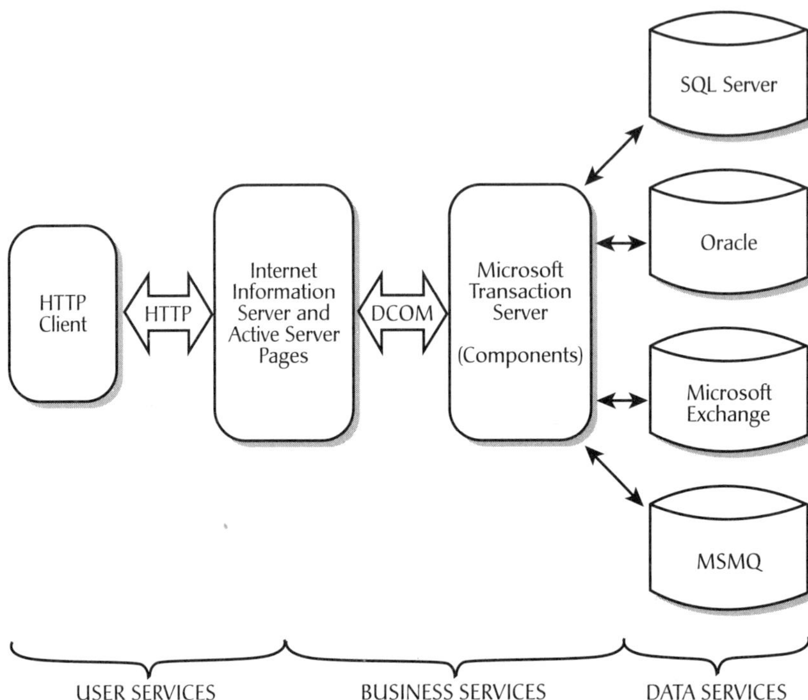

FIGURE 1-5 The COM-based four-tiered Web architecture

The Microsoft literature is replete with the terms *User Services, Business Services,* and *Data Services.* It is difficult to assign specific roles to all components of a tiered architecture. The term *Business Services* is confusing because it connotes business rules. Unfortunately, that is an oversimplification and I prefer the terms *Presentation Layer, Infrastructure Layer,* and *Data Services Layer.* The Presentation Layer and Data Services Layer are both clearly defined. What remains is the necessary application plumbing that may include business rules.

Basic COM

What is COM? In the simplest of terms it is a binary interface standard. Any appropriate programming language may be used, but certain guidelines must be followed. You already know that code is reused with Aggregation or Delegation. You also know that there are always two components, a client and a server, that function as service providers. How else can COM be described?

- COM uses the concept of an interface. It is quite unlike a traditional library with service interfaces. The client calls the COM object interface **IUnknown ::QueryInterface** to interrogate about rather than to use a service. Object interfaces support the infrastructure and are not client-service specific. Objects are implemented as a DLL for an in-process server within the client address space. Servers implemented on the same machine, but not in the client address space, are local servers. A local server and a remote server are implemented as an EXE.
- The COM architecture supports multiple interfaces. Emulation is a feature that supports obsolete object versions. An example is a client expecting version 1.0 support from a version 2.0 server object. Server version 1.0 will be emulated. Polymorphism is the ability to view different objects with the same interface. Emulation is an expression of polymorphism.
- COM objects are used in a multi-user environment. A reference count is maintained for logistical purposes. The object will be released when the reference count is zero.
- COM has a memory management mechanism. Data is passed between the client and server object and memory is allocated or deallocated as necessary.
- COM objects report error and status information.
- COM supports transparent communication across process boundaries. Communication to remote servers is with a RPC. Clients communicate with local servers via a *light-weight remote procedure call* (LRPC), which is an alias for an *interprocess communication* (IPC) call.
- COM supports a universal naming convention. The requested server is identified dynamically and placed in execution. This may occur across process or machine boundaries.

Those are COM's features, but what does COM look like? COM has grown up a bit in the last few years. Figure 1-4 represents the prior version of COM, which supported the OLE 2.0 architecture. (The newer features such as Connectable Objects are added later in this section when the current version of COM is discussed.) We layer software, why not layer the complexity issues presented in this book? Starting with COM as it exists today is unreasonably complex. This chapter starts with the introduction of the older OLE 2.0, which is the foundation for today's COM technology. OLE 1 was less than useful, but it did identify the problems solved by OLE 2.0 and COM. You should know it's older technology because I am using the older OLE term, which may not be as familiar as the current ActiveX naming convention. This book is about COM. It's a component world today and the Microsoft architecture is component-based.

And now back to basics with the traditional COM. Figure 1-6 represents the prior and traditional version of the COM architecture. It supports features and functions of the traditional Windows desktop environment and does not yet support remote objects. You may not be familiar with the terms, but you've used the features every day.

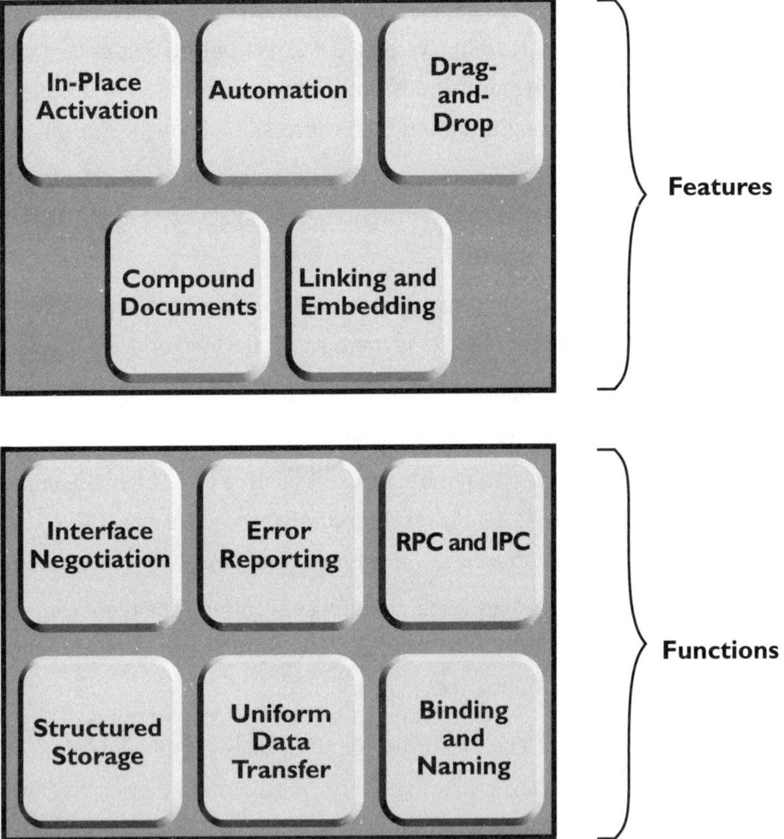

FIGURE 1-6 The traditional version of COM architecture showing COM as a foundation of object services

note **The traditional example of embedding is an Excel spreadsheet in a Word document. In-place activation or visual editing is the use of an older OCX or a newer ActiveX control. Activation of these controls is called *inside-out,* because the control is seamlessly integrated with the application and appears to be native to it. Inside-out activation occurs when the user moves the pointer over the object.**

Figure 1-6 mixes features and functionality, while Figure 1-7 is a simplified version of Figure 1-6 with features and functions separately identified. I believe the concepts are easier to understand if the material is introduced gradually. You may look at the next few sections as fundamental issues of COM. A discussion of the basic COM functions is followed by a discussion of how those features implement the functionality. COM's newer features are introduced after these discussions.

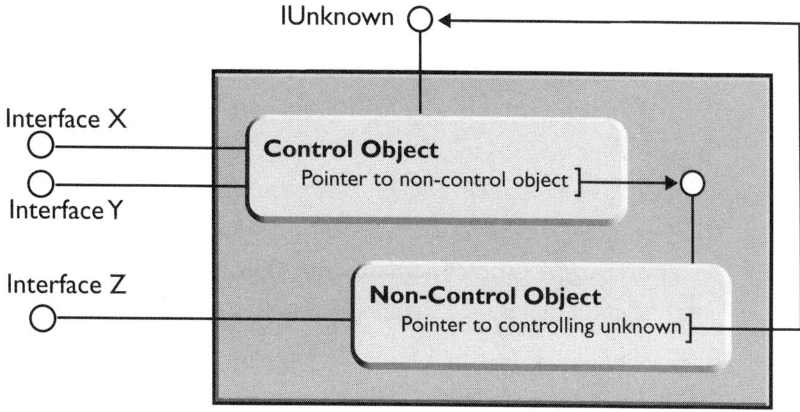

FIGURE 1-7 The features and functions of basic COM are illustrated in a simplified version of Figure 1-6.

Is COM an object model? Yes, it is within the context of the COM, but no, it isn't within the context of other *object-oriented* (OO) models. Do you compare apples with oranges? Hardly! COM supports the commonly accepted OO features of encapsulation, inheritance, and polymorphism.

Encapsulation

Encapsulation is the isolation of data from direct access by a client. The only client access to the data is with a server method, and direct access to server object data is not possible. The best example is a compound file or a structured file maintained by the server object for the client. There are multiple streams in the compound file representing different objects. A hypothetical example is a Word document with an embedded spreadsheet and an embedded *audio-visual interleave* (AVI) document describing specific features. With the proper permissions, you can read the binary image, but the context and content are unknown.

concept link

There is a programming example of encapsulation at the beginning of this chapter. By default, a C++ class begins with a private declaration as the default. This means that the declared data members are not directly accessible by the client.

COM supports encapsulation. Scripting (Automation or OLE Automation) uses the **IDispatch** interface to invoke methods encapsulated within a COM server object. Access to a method of a server object using this interface is with the related DISPID index. This makes a lot of sense when you consider that code space on a remote machine may be different. Windows NT supports the Intel, RISC, MIPS, and PowerPC platforms (at least it used to support MIPS and PowerPC). I am creating this epistle on an Intel toy, but I have Microsoft SQL Server on an Alpha-based machine that supports SQL-DMO (*distributed management objects*), a COM-based OLE technology. I can create VBA scripts on my Intel toy and manage my SQL server over my network. The hardware implementations are diametrically different. Encapsulation can be though of as asking the server object to perform a task versus the client performing the task. For data, the model is one of an abstraction, but for methods there are physical limitations.

Inheritance

It's apples and oranges time. COM is an interface model and not an implementation model. Implementation inheritance in the classic C++ sense is not supported. In fact, interface inheritance in COM is more robust than implementation inheritance in that it doesn't have the fragile base class problem. This is the problem with strict object-oriented inheritance, where changing the parent or root class forces the recompilation of all inherited classes.

Does COM support Inheritance? Yes, it does, with aggregation and delegation. At the infrastructure level, the **IUnknown** interface is required for all COM objects, and all other interfaces in a COM object inherit this interface. At the client level, aggregation or delegation within the object supports methods of older versions. The new server version contains only new methods that the client may have no knowledge of. The methods of the older version are aggregated with the new methods for a unified interface. The component has new features but the client doesn't use them because it is unaware of any changes.

How does COM interface inheritance work? Aggregation is the reuse of an object and requires support from the inner object. The aggregated object supports Interface Z and **IUnknown** of the control object, as shown in Figure 1-8. The client acquires a pointer to Interface Z through **IUnknown::QueryInterface** of the control object, which makes the services of Interface Z available to the client. It is a bit tricky to aggregate an object, because a pointer must be passed to the aggregated object at creation time. This will be a pointer to the controlling object **IUnknown** interface, and is done by either **CoCreateInstance** or **IClassFactory::CreateInstance**. When done, **IUnknown** of the control object reports all interfaces through the **QueryInterface** method. This means that the aggregated object must provide an **IUnknown** interface that is separate from all other interfaces. With such an interface, the parent object can call **IUnknown::QueryInterface** of the aggregated object and expose those interfaces as if they belonged to the parent object. This is the reporting of the Interface X and Interface Y along with the inherited Interface Z shown in Figure 1-8. The control object was delegated the responsibility of reporting Interface Z by the aggregated object. Aggregation can be likened to a shell or wrapper where the internal functioning does not change, but a unified interface of all services is presented to the client.

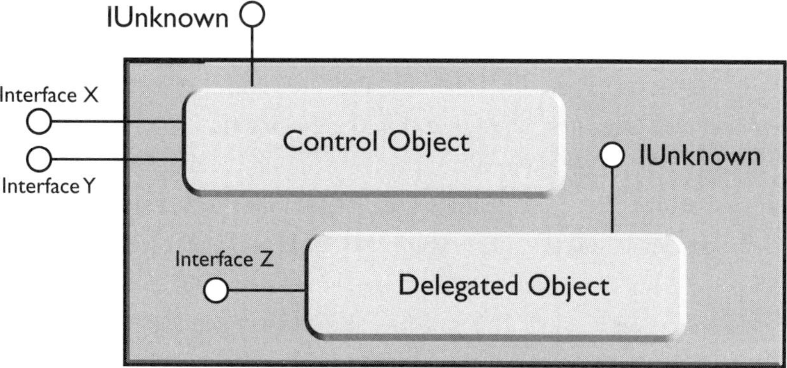

FIGURE 1-8 The internal structure of an aggregate illustrating the client's acquisition of a pointer from the controlling object

Delegation has two forms. The first form of delegation is *containment,* where the control object isolates the delegated object from client access. This is the most popular form of delegation. The second form of delegation is that of a *public object,* where client accesses is not restricted. Both of these forms of delegation are illustrated in Figure 1-9.

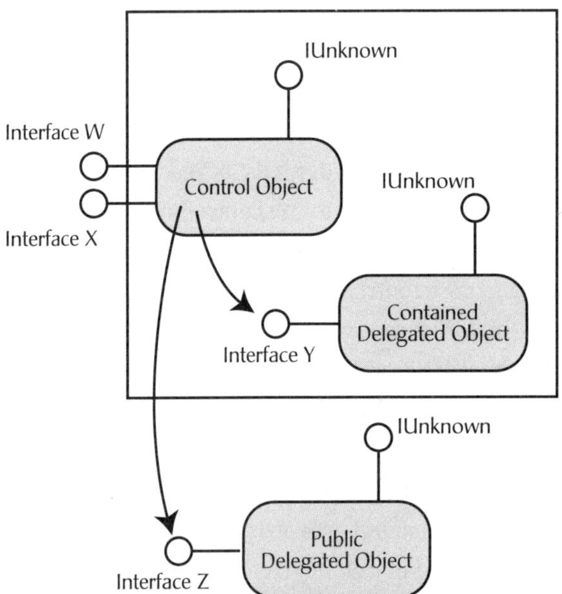

FIGURE 1-9 The delegated object is a client of the control object as a code reuse strategy.

Delegation is not too different from aggregation. The difference is that the control object may isolate the delegated object from client access. The significance of this is not readily apparent. Yes, the control object is a wrapper for the contained delegated object, but think of the practical application of this technology.

Suppose you have built a new COM object and you want to incorporate prior features. You could include the older features by hacking the code by cutting and pasting it, but eventually your new object will suffer from code bloat (fatware).

Another solution is to link the modules of the prior version with modules of the newer version. This solution also suffers from code bloat.

The third alternative is to treat the older version features as components, with the new object containing only new features and using the existing or prior features as necessary. This means that newer software versions can be installed without disturbing an existing version. The really profound issue here is that Microsoft has a logical model for reusing code. The original functionality remains intact, and no code hacking is necessary. There are many coding systems, but none of the others has a code-reuse model.

Figure 1-9 illustrates delegation of a contained object and a public accessible object. Interface Y, a contained and delegated object, is a client of the control object and direct user access is not possible. Interface Y cannot distinguish control between client access or access by the control object, and does not know that direct client access is impossible. Containment is the encapsulation of a delegated object. There is no specific requirement that a delegated object be encapsulated. The delegated object can be any publicly accessible COM component, as illustrated with Interface Z of Figure 1-9.

Both Interface Y and Interface Z of Figure 1-9 are delegated by the control object. The parent object in Figure 1-9 calls **CoCreateInstance** on CLSID_*<inner object>* asking for IID_InterfaceY of the contained object when the parent object is created. The parent object implements and maintains interfaces of delegated and contained objects. Interface Z is a public object and the interface is known or obtainable.

WHEN SOFTWARE IS THE ONLY REVENUE STREAM

Code bloat is defined as new and unwanted or unwarranted features that the software vendor adds in order to sell a new version of the software. Of course the vendor includes just enough bug fixes of the current version to entice a customer to purchase. A common expression is: "I'll try the new version. Maybe the problem is fixed there." This attitude encourages software vendors to not put forth their best efforts on any particular release level. It's the equivalent of rewarding an errant child.

Mainframe companies derived their primary revenue source from hardware sales and not from software sales. Software releases such as FORTRAN or COBOL occurred only when the ANSI specification was changed. This meant that software releases were relatively error-free, and code bloat or fatware was non-existent.

Summarizing Aggregation and Delegation or Containment

Containment or delegation and aggregation operate differently. With delegation, the outer object calls **CoCreateInstance** with the CLSID of the delegated inner interface when the outer object is created. Interface Y and Interface Z are delegated inner interfaces in Figure 1-9. The returned pointer is maintained by the outer object and released only when the outer object is released.

With aggregation, it's a bit different because the parent object passes its **IUnknown** pointer to the Interface Z **IClassFactory::CreateInstance** as a parameter (see Figure 1-8). The Interface Z object holds onto this pointer. This means that the aggregated object must provide an **IUnknown** that is separate from all other interfaces. With an interface on the aggregated object that supports **IUnknown**, the parent object can call **IUnknown** of the aggregated object and expose those interfaces as if they belonged to the parent object itself. This makes the parent object the controlling **IUnknown** because it exposes its own services and the services of the aggregated object. This is transparent to the requesting client. Reference counts are associated with the parent object and a pointer to the delegated object is acquired by the parent object for containment or delegation. For aggregation, the **IUknown** pointer of the parent object is passed to the aggregated object and the parent object remembers the **IUnknown** of the aggregated object from creation time.

Let's enumerate what we know:

- With aggregation, the parent object can use **IUnknown** to query the aggregated object and the aggregated object was passed the parent's **IUnknown** pointer at creation time. So both the parent and child objects are aware of the services offered by the other object. The aggregated object can access services of the parent, and the parent can access services of the aggregated object, hence aggregation.
- The parent object obtains the **IUnknown** interface pointer of the contained and delegated object when the contained object is created. But this is only a one-way street. The delegated object does not know the **IUnknown** of the delegating object. Figure 1-9 illustrates a contained and delegated object with Interface Y and a delegated object with Interface Z, which is a public object.

Microsoft Visual Basic only supports containment or delegation, not aggregation. There is a Visual Basic structural reason for this limitation. Microsoft Visual Basic only supports the export of pointers, not the import. An address may be passed with the **AddressOf** operator; however, the semantics of Visual Basic does not currently support pointers.

The Visual Basic **Implements** statement, when used with an **Interface** class, is used to delegate to the base class. The base class knows nothing about the delegating object. These concepts are difficult to understand, and at least one Visual Basic 5.0 book states that Microsoft Visual Basic supports aggregation. It does not. You'll find two labs on delegation and containment at the end of this chapter that should clarify the issue.

In summary, Microsoft Visual C++ supports both COM aggregation and containment or delegation. However Microsoft Visual Basic only supports COM delegation or containment. The Microsoft Visual Basic **Implements** statement is used to delegate to a base class or to delegate to a contained object, which I look at in detail in Chapter 2.

Polymorphism

So far you know that COM supports encapsulation and inheritance. The last question needing an answer is: Does COM support polymorphism? Yes, it does. *Polymorphism* is the ability to view different objects with the same interface. Interface inheritance, where an object can support the new features of the latest version while still supporting an older version, is polymorphic. COM methods such as a **Delete** method that deletes a record from a **RecordSet** object or that deletes an object from a collection are examples of polymorphism.

The question remains: Is COM an object-oriented paradigm? I say it is because it exhibits object-oriented properties at the conceptual level. It doesn't matter beyond that, because the ultimate goal of code reuse is realized, and that's what counts.

Key Point Summary

COM was originally designed as an interprocess or intraprocess communication mechanism; code reusability was a selling benefit. COM has evolved to the point of being a logical model for code reusability.

- COM supports interface inheritance but not implementation inheritance.
- COM is a binary specification. It is language-independent.
- A COM object differs from a traditional library that advertises services. All COM objects are required to have a minimal and standard interface. Services are not advertised. The client must query an interface for services.
- All COM objects are required to support the **IUnknown** interface. This interface is comprised of the **QueryInterface, AddRef,** and **Release** methods.
- COM interfaces are immutable. Once used, they cannot be changed. This is called a contract between the client and the server. New features are implemented with either delegation or aggregation and the original functionality is preserved.
- Containment is a form of delegation where the client is isolated from the object supporting the requested services.
- COM supports encapsulation, inheritance, and polymorphism, which are object-oriented principles.

Applying What You've Learned

The questions that follow measure your comprehension of this chapter. The issues addressed are the historical perspective, architecture, features, and benefits.

Instant Assessment

1. What is the unique difference between a traditional application library service call and that of a client accessing a COM server object interface?
2. What interface is required of all COM objects?
3. Name the three basic standards of interoperability for COM.
4. What feature does aggregation or delegation support?
5. What is another name for an application-programming interface (API)?
6. What is an SPI and who would use it?
7. Name four benefits of COM.
8. What is emulation?

9. What is a benefit of emulation?
10. What is aggregation?
11. Describe delegation.
12. Describe containment.
13. What characteristic of COM is not supported by Visual Basic?
14. Describe encapsulation.
15. What are the three commonly accepted criteria for object orientation?
16. Explain the differences between inheritance in C++ and inheritance in COM.
17. What is polymorphism?
18. What is the *fragile base class* problem?
19. How does COM avoid the *fragile base class* problem?

For answers to the Instant Assessment Questions, see Appendix B.

Lab Exercises

Microsoft Visual Basic is the common denominator for this book. These two labs illustrate two distinctly different issues of COM. The first lab is the implementation of an abstract base class, which uses the Visual Basic **Implements** keyword. The technique is a cornerstone of the new Distributed COM (DCOM), which is covered in Chapter 17. The second lab illustrates the COM issue of containment or delegation as implemented in Microsoft Visual Basic 5.0 and beyond.

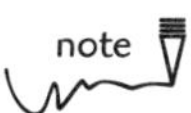

Microsoft Visual Basic does not support COM aggregation.

Lab 1.1 *Implementing Base Classes in Visual Basic*

This laboratory will implement a base class with a checkbook application using the **Implements** statement of Visual Basic. This laboratory is the construction of an interface class and the implementing of that interface class within a form module. An interface class may be used in another class or form module, but not within a standard module. The lab is composed of the following steps:

1. Start a new project in Visual Basic 5.0 or 6.0.

2. Add a class module to the project. Name the class module **ICheckBook**. This will be the interface class.

3. Enter the following code into the declaration section of the **ICheckBook** Interface class:

```
'(c) 1999 Bruce T. Prendergast
'    DBA Prendergast Consulting
'    DBA PCS
'    IDG Books WorldWide
'
' Interface Class Name: ICheckbook
'
Option Explicit
'
Public Property Get Balance() As Currency
'
End Property

Public Sub Withdrawal(Amount As Currency)
'
End Sub

Public Sub Deposit(Amount As Currency)
'
End Sub
```

4. Place the following code in the declarations section of the form.

```
Option Explicit
Implements ICheckbook
```

5. Attempt to start the project. An error will occur. The **Implements** statement requires that the **ICheckBook** interface definitions be created locally. This is delegation with containment. Another perspective is that the interface class is a document specifying the interface class requirements.

6. Place a command button on the form. Name the command button **cmdDeposit** with a caption of *Deposit*.

7. Place another command button on the form. Name this command button **cmdWithdrawal** with a caption of *Withdrawal*.
8. Place a text box on the form with the name **txtInput**.
9. Enter the following code in the declaration section of the form. Notice that the local implementations of the methods and properties of the **ICheckBook** interface class are declared as **Private**. This prevents the properties and methods of the interface class from being subsumed by the hosting form or class module. The project is now complete. Please feel free to experiment.

```
'(c) 1999 Bruce T. Prendergast
'    DBA Prendergast Consulting
'    DBA PCS
'    IDG Books WorldWide
'
Option Explicit
Implements ICheckbook

Private m_curBalance As Variant

Private Sub cmdDeposit_Click()
  ICheckbook_Deposit ([txtInput])
End Sub

Private Sub cmdWithdrawal_Click()
  ICheckbook_Withdrawal ([txtInput])
End Sub

Private Property Get ICheckBook_Balance() As Currency
  ICheckBook_Balance = m_curBalance
End Property

Private Sub ICheckbook_Withdrawal(Amount As Currency)
  m_curBalance = m_curBalance - Amount
  MsgBox "Balance is: " & m_curBalance
End Sub
```

```
Private Sub ICheckbook_Deposit(Amount As Currency)
  m_curBalance = m_curBalance + Amount
  MsgBox "Balance is: " & m_curBalance
End Sub
```

10. Every form or class module that implements an interface class must implement all methods and properties of the interface class. Note also that code, defined private variables, and events of the interface class are ignored. This explains why there is no code in the **ICheckbook** interface class. Congratulations. This completes the implementation of an abstract base class lab.

Lab 1.2 *Implementing Delegation in Visual Basic*

Microsoft Visual Basic does not support aggregation in the COM sense or implementation inheritance in the C++ sense. You can approximate implementation inheritance fairly well in Visual Basic with delegation to a base class, which is the goal of this lab. The delegating form module or class must be aware of the services and resources available in the base class. The steps below detail the construction of a form module that delegates to a base class.

1. Start a new project in Visual Basic 5.0 or 6.0.
2. Use the class wizard to create a base class with the name **CBank**. The class will have a **Balance** property, along with a **Deposit** and a **Withdrawal** method. The resulting code should be edited to correspond to the code below.

```
'(c) 1999 Bruce T. Prendergast
'    DBA Prendergast Consulting
'    DBA PCS
'    IDG Books WorldWide ISBN 0-7645-3314-2
'
'    CBank Class (Base class)
'
Option Explicit
Private mvarBalance As Variant
Public Sub Withdrawal(ByVal Amount As Currency)
  mvarBalance = mvarBalance - Amount
  MsgBox "New balance is: " & mvarBalance
End Sub
```

```
Public Sub Deposit(ByVal Amount As Currency)
  mvarBalance = mvarBalance + Amount
  MsgBox "New balance is: " & mvarBalance
End Sub

Public Property Let Balance(ByVal vData As Variant)
  mvarBalance = vData
End Property

Public Property Get Balance() As Variant
  Balance = mvarBalance
End Property
```

3. Place a command button on the form. Name the command button **cmdDeposit** with a caption of *Deposit*.
4. Place another command button on the form. Name this command button **cmdWithdrawal** with a caption of *Withdrawal*.
5. Place a text box on the form with the name *txtInput*.
6. Enter the following code in the declaration section of the form. Notice that the local implementations of the methods and properties of the **CBank** class are declared as **Private**. This prevents the properties and methods of the implemented class from being subsumed by the hosting form or class module. The project is now complete. Please feel free to experiment.

```
'(c) 1999 Bruce T. Prendergast
'    DBA Prendergast Consulting
'    DBA PCS
'    IDG Books WorldWide
'
Option Explicit
Implements CBank
Dim M_CBank As New CBank

Private Sub cmdDeposit_Click()
  CBank_Deposit [txtInput]
End Sub
```

```
Private Sub cmdWithdrawal_Click()
  CBank_Withdrawal [txtInput]
End Sub

Private Sub Form_Load()
  Set M_CBank = New CBank
End Sub

Private Sub CBank_Withdrawal(ByVal Amount As Currency)
  M_CBank.Withdrawal Amount
 End Sub

Private Sub CBank_Deposit(ByVal Amount As Currency)
  M_CBank.Deposit Amount
End Sub

Private Property Let CBank_Balance(ByVal vData As Variant)
  M_CBank.Balance = vData
End Property

Private Property Get CBank_Balance() As Variant
  CBank_Balance = M_CBank.Balance
End Property
```

7. The **CBank** base class is instantiated as the **M_CBank** object. The methods and properties of the base class are delegated from the locally implemented **CBank** base class through the **M_CBank** object instantiation. Congratulations. This completes the delegation to a base class from a form module.

CHAPTER

2

Object Interfacing

About Chapter 2

COM interfaces insulate the client from implementation details. This chapter deals with the concept of an interface and the infrastructure issues of COM.

Two types of interfaces are discussed: the *vtable,* or virtual table, which is a C/C++ pointer table, and *Idispatch,* which is a combination of the pointer table and an interpreted index known as a DISPID. The IDispatch interface is the key ingredient of Automation and is introduced here only as an interface. (Automation issues are discussed later in this book.)

Chapter 2 also introduces some common interfaces, followed by a map of the generic interfaces of basic COM. The chapter closes with the mechanics of instantiating COM servers.

Classes and Objects

The two labs at the conclusion of Chapter 1 indirectly introduced the concept of a class. Classes and objects are related to interfaces, so let's fill in the missing infrastructure.

A *class* is a template. A class is also a model of real-world phenomena or an abstraction of real-world entities. Classes have attributes and behavior. The *methods* of a class exhibit the class behavior, and exposed properties or encapsulated data represent the class attributes. But a class is only a template. An instantiation of a class is an *object*. Because more than one object may be instantiated from a class, an object has both a class name and an object name. The class identifier (CLSID) identifies the object. I discuss object name space in greater detail in Chapter 3.

A class and the resulting instantiated objects represent the first step of an object-oriented paradigm (OOP). The goal of OOP is the encapsulation of methods and properties within a class. As an example, a properly designed data access class that uses Data Access Objects (DAO) can readily be replaced with a new class that uses Remote Data Objects (RDO). This gives the software a "black box" appearance, which is a useful maintenance characteristic.

Even though a class represents encapsulation, the class implementation details are still exposed to the client. If you look at C++, you'll see that the language supports a syntactic encapsulation, whereas the C++ draft standard makes no mention of binary encapsulation. Isolating the implementation details is done with an interface, which also supplies the binary encapsulation. The language provides a syntactic encapsulation of the internal implementation details and the interface provides a binary encapsulation of the class properties and methods. The net result is a data type (interface) that is represented by one class, while the base class represents the data type's actual implementation. By always making the interface into a class, the binary encapsulation hides the internal details of the data type's implementation. The "lollipops" of Figures 1-8 and 1-9 in Chapter 1 each represent COM interfaces. Labs 1.1 and 1.2 of Chapter 1 illustrate declaring an interface as a class.

An interface is almost of mythical proportions, because there are many different interpretations of the word "interface." Let's take a look at the different perspectives of the word "interface."

- **What does a COM interface mean to a Microsoft marketer?** To a marketing organization, an interface is almost a silver bullet. It ranges from salvaging legacy COBOL code with wrapper functions, to the components of a tiered application architecture that always seems to include the Internet or an intranet.
- **What does a COM interface mean to a Microsoft Visual Basic developer?** The Visual Basic developer is not awestruck by the term *interfaces*. To the Visual Basic developer, an interface is a programming style. Lab 1.1 of Chapter 1 illustrates using an interface to enforce programming practices. The Visual Basic **Implements** statement requires an implementation of all methods and properties of the interface within local code. This is what provides the polymorphism. The developer supplies custom implementations in the local code.

  Laboratory 1-2 of Chapter 1 also used the Microsoft Visual Basic **Implements** statement to implement an interface. In this case the illustrated issue was not that of programming style, but that of accessing public methods and properties of a binary encapsulated object.
- **What does a COM interface mean to a Microsoft C/C++ developer?** A Visual C++ developer enjoys the same benefits of the Visual Basic developer with the enforcement of a programming style. But an interface is more than a programming style to a C++ developer. C++ is fraught with ambiguities and a COM interface represents a better C++.
- **What does a COM interface mean to a Microsoft C/C++ Compiler?** A COM interface is a C/C++ pointer table to the C/C++ compiler, which is our next topic.

Pointers and the Vtable

A *vtable* is an instance of an interface. A vtable consists of a pointer to an array of pointers, which in turn are pointers to property or method implementations. A pointer is a programming construct of C++, but the term *interface pointers* is an abstraction and an architectural issue. Pointers are manipulated directly as a programming construct in Microsoft C++; however, the COM contract with the client prohibits the changing or manipulation of interface pointers. Because interface pointers or vtable implementations cannot be edited or changed without violating the COM contract with the client, the context of interface pointers is an architectural issue and not a software implementation issue. The concept of a pointer is understood by C/C++ developers. The Microsoft Visual Basic (VB) language does not support the concept of a pointer; however, the **AddressOf** operator in VB, which provides a procedure address used for API callback functions, illustrates the concept of a pointer. Although it is not an interface pointer, it is nonetheless a pointer that illustrates the concept.

The client calls the COM library with a class identifier (CLSID) identifying the object and an interface identifier (IID) identifying the interface. COM loads the server if necessary, and starts it. A pointer is returned to the client if the object was loaded and started successfully. This is not a text on the obscure features of C/C++, even though I do discuss some C/C++ features very briefly. A *pointer* is a virtual address mapping to either a data structure or a method, and is a very necessary issue in the COM architecture.

You can probably guess the roots of COM object interfacing — the initial version of COM was constructed with C/C++. The natural implementation of an address for data, a structure, or a method in C/C++ is a pointer. C/C++ supports pointers, pointers to pointers, or, as in this case, a pointer to a pointer to a table of pointers. The object provides the implementation of each member function in the interface and creates an array of pointers to those functions called the vtable, which is a construct common to all C++ compilers. This is shared among all instances of the object class. To differentiate each instance, the object code allocates according to the object's internal implementation a second structure that contains its private data. The specifications for an OLE interface stipulate that the first four bytes in this data structure must be a 32-bit pointer to the vtable. An *interface pointer* is a pointer to the top of this instance structure; thus a pointer to a pointer to the vtable. It is through this interface pointer that a client accesses the object's implementation of the interface. The use of a pointer table is not new and has been with us since computers were first programmed. It was the common technique used to access operating system functionality before the advent of base-register addressing with memory protection.

An Interface Is a Contract

An interface is implemented as a vtable and is more than just a binary specification. A COM interface is a contract between the client and the interface. COM interfaces are immutable — the function order, function parameters, return values, and operations performed by a COM function never change. What is not specified is the implementation language or how to implement the function. New features are provided with a completely new interface inherited from the prior version. This accounts for interface names such as **IViewData** and **IViewData2**.

The fact that there are no restrictions on how a function is implemented, or what language is used, makes COM a binary specification that is platform-independent. The basic COM object interface context you are familiar with is the Visual C++ pointer, but COM objects are not limited to any one platform. Windows NT runs on the DEC Alpha, a RISC platform with 64-bit addressing, which is quite unlike the Intel CISC platform with 32-bit addressing. The physical implementation of an addressing scheme is interesting, but the important issue is that the logical COM implementations agree on both platforms.

You should recognize the vtable shown in Figure 2-1. **IUnknown** is the only required pointer, and the client must use **IUnknown::QueryInterface** to determine the other pointers. I'll expand the vtable concept shortly.

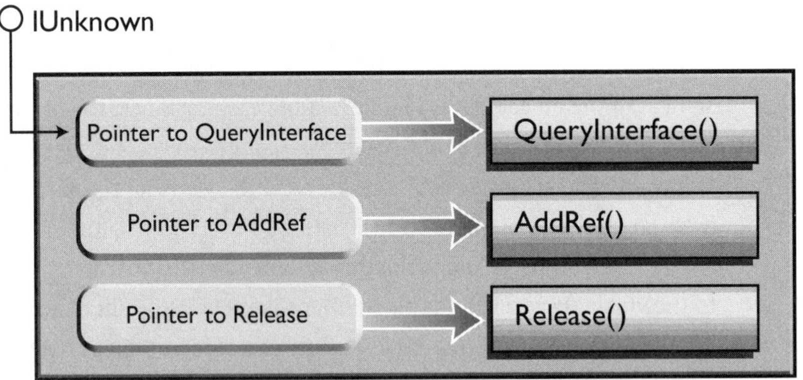

FIGURE 2-1 The IUnknown pointer is the only exposed pointer in this COM object.

Declaring a component object with the related pointers can be done in several ways, and of course they're all done with the C/C++ language. The stout of heart can use nested C structures, C++ nested classes, or C++ multiple inheritances to create the object classes.

Basic Object Interfaces

This section discusses the key functionality of an object. The **IUnknown** interface is a required interface for all objects and is the cornerstone of the COM architecture. **IClassFactory** is another key interface that is responsible for the creation of new objects. This is almost a historical issue because the **IUnknown** and **IClassFactory** interfaces are both required for COM; however, the new ActiveX reduces the object requirements to the **IUnknown** interface and the ability to self-register. Microsoft Visual Basic objects are self-registering and do not require the **IClassFactory** interface.

IUnknown

The discussion of the **IUnknown** interface begins with standard IDL definition. This example uses the interface definition language (IDL) syntax to illustrate the definition of the **IUnknown** interface along with the required **QueryInterface**, **AddRef**, and **Release** methods. The IDL syntax is self-explanatory as to content and is very similar to C/C++ syntax in that:

- IDL declares an object and associates that object with a universal unique identifier (UUID). The UUID is found in the IDL *attribute-reference list,* which is the section of the snippet below between the brackets.
- IDL names the interface as **IUnknown**. The *attribute-reference list* provides the interface name.
- IDL supports the **QueryInterface** method with an IID as input and a pointer as output.
- IDL supports the methods **AddRef** and **Release,** neither of which has an argument.

```
[
  uuid(00000000-0000-0000-C000-000000000046),
  pointer_default(unique)
]
interface IUnknown
{
  HRESULT QueryInterface([in] REFIID iid, [out] void **ppv) ;
```

```
  ULONG AddRef(void);
  ULONG Release(void);
}
```

The standard C++ implementation of **IUnknown** is shown below. The **Extern** keyword prevents symbolic name mangling by the C++ compiler and preserves the name.

```
Extern "C" const IID IID_IUnknown;
interface IUnknown
{
  virtual HRESULT STDMETHODCALLTYPE
  QueryInterface([in] REFIID iid, [out] void **ppv)= 0 ;
  virtual ULONG STDMETHODCALLTYPE AddRef(void)= 0 ;
  Virtual ULONG Release(void)= 0;
}
```

You can see some parallels between the C++ definition of the **IUnknown** interface and the functioning of the Visual Basic **Implements** statement. A *virtual* C++ function is one that is defined in a base class and that expects to be overridden by a function in a derived class with the same name and parameter types. This is the same circumstance you encountered in Labs 1.1 and 1.2 of Chapter 1, where the Visual Basic **Implements** statement forced a local implementation.

All COM interfaces are polymorphic with **IUnknown**. That is, the first three entries of every interface vtable contain pointers to **QueryInterface, AddRef,** and **Release.**

The **IUnknown** interface has two responsibilities. The first is locating and returning pointers to an interface based on the client-provided IID using the **QueryInterface** method. The second responsibility is reference counting. Reference counts control the life of an object. The creator of the object is responsible for establishing the initial value. If the object already exists, then the count is incremented. The **AddRef** method serves both situations. The **IUnknown::Release** decrements the object's reference count. Objects are released when the reference count is zero. Figure 2-2 illustrates the ubiquity of **IUnknown** within Microsoft Visual Basic.

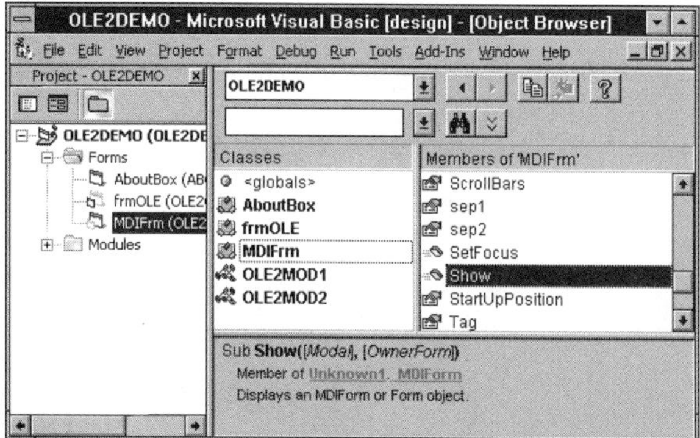

FIGURE 2-2 The IUnknown pointer in Microsoft Visual Basic

We shouldn't leave **IUnknown** without noting some special **QueryInterface** characteristics. The **QueryInterface** C++ call definition is defined as:

```
HRESULT QueryInterface(
  REFIID iid,          //Identifier of the requested interface
  void ** ppvObject    //Indirect pointer to the object
);
```

The **QueryInterface** method is analogous to C++'s **dynamic_cast** operator, which is best explained by giving an example.

```
Writer *writer = dynamic_cast<writer *>(Unemployed);
```

Dynamic_cast either returns a pointer of the requested type when an object of that class exists, or a NULL when the class object cannot be created. For our example above, a pointer of type **Writer** is returned when **Unemployed** is of type **Writer** and a factory object is available to create an object of type **Writer**.

The **QueryInterface** method is symmetric, reflexive, and transitive. The symmetric and transitive properties of the **QueryInterface** method are illustrated in Figure 2-3 and can be stated as follows:

- *Transitive:* If the IB interface is obtainable from the IA interface, and the IC interface is obtainable from the IB interface using the **QueryInterface** method, then the IC interface is obtainable from the IA interface using the **QueryInterface** method.
- *Symmetric:* If interface IB is obtainable from interface IA, then interface IA is obtainable from IB using the **QueryInterface** method.

- *Reflexive:* A pointer obtained from an interface must always succeed when the requested pointer type matches the interface type. (This property is not illustrated.)

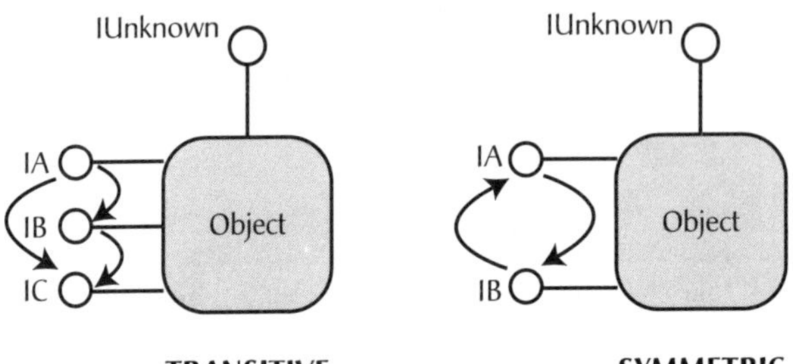

FIGURE 2-3 The transitive and symmetric properties of QueryInterface

IClassFactory

IClassFactory is one of several steps required for instantiation of a COM object. The **CreateMethod** of VB implies that creating an object is a one-step process. It is a one-step process when only one instance of an object is required. The client calls the COM API function **CoCreateInstance** with the CLSID of the object and IID of the required interface. When successful, a pointer to the requested interface is returned. Figure 2-4 illustrates the **IClassFactory** interface. **IClassFactory** is the server interface for instantiating all instances of an object.

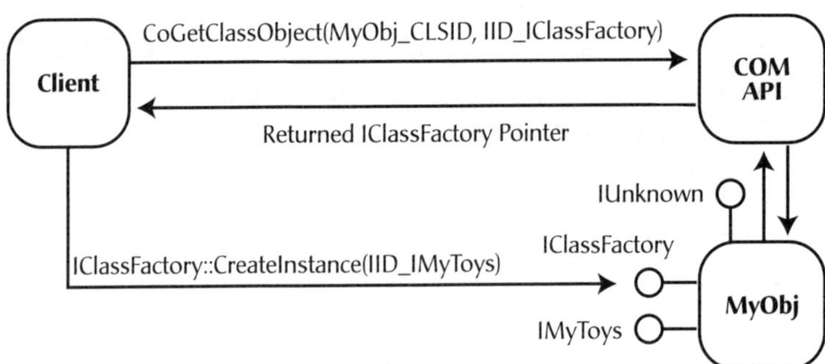

FIGURE 2-4 Using the IClassFactory interface to instantiate an object

When more than one object is required, the client calls **CoGetClassObject** with the object CLSID and IID_IClassFactory. The client then calls **IClassFactory::CreateInstance** with the returned **IClassFactory** pointer supplying the IID of the required interface. The **IClassFactory::CreateInstance** method creates an instance of the required object. **CoCreateInstance** is a wrapper for **CoGetClassObject** and **IClass:Factory::CreateInstance**. The object is later released with **IClassFactory::Release.** (See "Creating an In-Process Server" and "Creating a Local or Remote Server" later in this chapter.)

IClassFactory is a very necessary component of the COM architecture, and a minimal COM implementation requires only two interfaces: **IUnknown** and **IClass Factory**. This has been relaxed with ActiveX, which only requires the **IUnknown** interface and the capability to self register. Microsoft C++ objects must support the **IClassFactory** interface, whereas Microsoft Visual Basic objects are self-registering, and do not require the **IClassFactory** interface.

IClassFactory::LockServer is the only other method of **IClassFactory**. It keeps the OLE server locked in memory. A server must remain locked in memory during the life of an object.

IMalloc

The **IMalloc** interface is responsible for memory management. It inherits from **IUnknown** the methods **QueryInterface, AddRef**, and **Release,** and implements the methods **Alloc, Realloc, Free, GetSize,** and **DidAlloc**. The methods **Alloc, Realloc,** and **Free** are similar to the corresponding C library functions **alloc**, **realloc**, and **free**. These methods are mentioned only to illustrate of the **IMalloc** interface functionality available. The **IMalloc** interface should not be implemented directly, even though it is necessary to any COM implementation. The recommended procedure is to obtain a pointer to the **IMalloc** interface of the task allocator object with the COM library call **CoGetMalloc**. This technique guarantees a thread-safe implementation of **Imalloc.** A server implements a thread-safe object by serializing access to shared data within the object. This guarantees that a thread does not inadvertently replace the work of another thread. Here's how to implement a thread-safe environment:

- Use a critical section (Win32 Synchronization object) for each server method call. This provides every object with its own critical section by calling the Win32 **EnterCriticalSection** function at the beginning of every method call and the **LeaveCriticalSection** function at the end.

- Use a single critical section for all objects. The server calls **EnterCritical Section** when the server is initially loaded and **LeaveCriticalSection** when the server is unloaded. This option is the simplest, but performance suffers and the technique is not practical when used with multithreaded clients.
- Use critical sections for crucial shared data structures. This is the preferred technique. All data is isolated and access is handled through an internal interface.

The **IMalloc** interface supports allocation, release, size changes, size determinations, garbage collection, and block ownership. **IMalloc** is mentioned in the minimal implementation of a COM as an interface to use. It is not an interface of an object that requires implementation, but rather an interface of the task allocator object.

IMarshal

Marshaling is the packaging of interface data by a proxy before a remote procedure call (RPC) or local procedure call (LPC) sends the data to a local or remote site where a stub unpackages the data. Marshaling is done on an interface-by-interface basis, and not on an object-by-object basis, and is transparent to the application. The primary reason for marshaling is communicating with an object that uses apartment-model threading or with an out-of-process object. (Apartment-model threading only permits one active thread within a COM object, whereas free-threading does not limit the number of threads within a COM object.)

The proxy exists at the client site and is a surrogate for the requested object. It holds a pointer to the requested object and supplies the client with a pointer to itself. A client holding a pointer to a proxy believes that it is the actual object pointer. This is illustrated in Figure 2-5. The stub exists in the server process space. The proxy marshals arguments and unmarshals return values while the stub unmarshals arguments and marshals return values.

COM implements several internal interfaces in managing marshaling. **IRpc ProxyBuffer** is implemented at the client site and **IRpcStubBuffer** is implemented at the server site. **IRpcChannelBuffer::SendReceive** does the actual work of sending the marshaled data to the corresponding interface stub. When control is returned to **IRpcChannelBuffer::SendReceive**, the contents of the output buffer have been replaced with the returned values.

There are three levels of participation by the client in marshaling. The first level is accepting default marshaling. COM implements default marshaling automatically when the client object has not implemented the **IMarshal** interface. COM creates both the stub and the proxy using **ClassFactory::CreateInstance**.

The second level of participation is with the **IStdMarshalInfo** interface. An object that is using default marshaling can implement this interface and specify the handler to be loaded in the client process. COM starts by requesting the **IStdMarshalInfo** interface. When this interface is not exposed, COM inquires for an **IPersist** interface. If neither exists, a standard handler is used for marshaling.

The last, and obvious, level of participation is the implementation of custom marshaling. Considerations for custom marshaling include:

- Object states are stored in shared memory, and both the client and server processes exist on the same machine.
- The objects are immutable and their state does not change over time.
- Custom marshaling avoids creating a proxy to a proxy.
- Custom interfaces can cache data retrieved from a database, which enhances performance.

Marshaling support includes the **CoMarshalInterface** wrapper function, which writes proxy initialization data to a stream, whereas **CoUnMarshalInterface** is the COM library function that extracts the data and initializes the proxy. **CoMarshal Interface** will:

1. Query the object for the **IMarshal** interface. Marshaling is transparent to the client. The existence of the **IMarshal** interface on the client object indicates that the object is using custom marshaling. When none is available **CoMarshalInterface** acquires a pointer to the COM's default **IMarshal** implementation.
2. **IMarshal::GetUnmarshalClass** is called to get the CLSID of the object's proxy.
3. The returned CLSID is written to the stream.
4. The interface pointer is marshaled with **IMarshal::MarshalInterface**.

All other interfaces that may be implemented on an object are exposed in its object proxy through the aggregation of individual interface proxies.

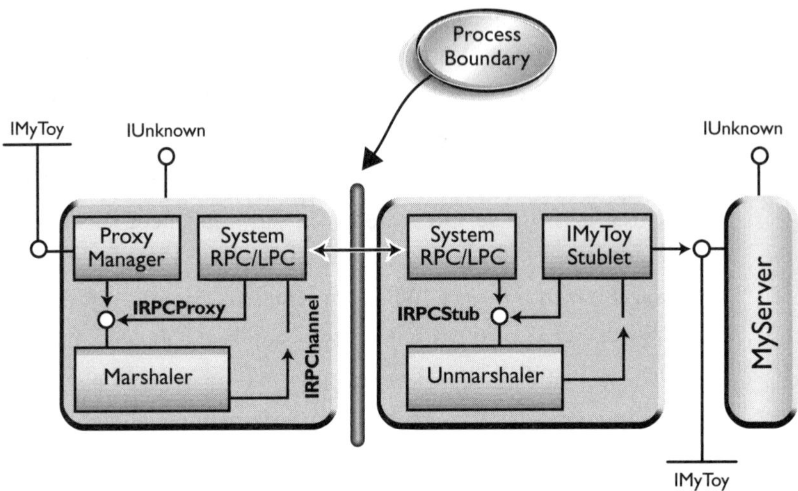

FIGURE 2-5 Marshaling is transparent to the client.

The last issue is the **IStdMarshaling** interface, which must be implemented for any object that supports class emulation. Emulation occurs as a result of selecting *activate-as* in the **Convert** dialog box. The **IStdMarshalInfo** interface determines the correct CLSID for the emulation.

The following is from a Windows NT Registry. It maps IIDs into proxy/stub CLSIDs. COM looks in the Registry for the proxy and stub under the name **ProxyStubClsid32** for 32-bit systems, and the name **ProxyStubClsid** for 16-bit systems, which is shown in Listing 2-1.

LISTING 2-1 Mapping IIDs on a 16-bit system using ProxyStubClsid in the Registry for default marshaling

```
// maps IIDs into proxy/stub class id
HKEY_CLASSES_ROOT\Interface\{00000000-0000-0000-C000-000000000046} = IUnknown
HKEY_CLASSES_ROOT\Interface\{00000000-0000-0000-C000-000000000046}\BaseInterface =
HKEY_CLASSES_ROOT\Interface\{00000000-0000-0000-C000-000000000046}\NumMethods = 3
HKEY_CLASSES_ROOT\Interface\{00000001-0000-0000-C000-000000000046} = IClassFactory
HKEY_CLASSES_ROOT\Interface\{00000001-0000-0000-C000-000000000046}\NumMethods = 5
HKEY_CLASSES_ROOT\Interface\{00000001-0000-0000-C000-000000000046}\ProxyStub Clsid
= {0000030E-0000-0000-C000-000000000046}
```

This has been an abbreviated tour of the minimal COM object. Let's move on to **IDispatch** and dispinterfaces.

IDispatch and Dispinterfaces

Our discussion of interfacing COM objects thus far has involved compiled code. What about the scripting supported by tools such as Microsoft Access, Word, Excel, or even the older Visual Basic? These tools are interpreters that use scripts, and the generalized use of address pointers is not possible with these tools. The natural interface for these type of tools is interpretive.

Interpreters need interfaces. Why an interpretive interface? You interface when you want to use one object to control another (Microsoft Access controlling Microsoft Excel is an example). This is OLE Automation, or, simply, Automation as it is known today. A server exposes its methods and properties with an **IDispatch** interface, thus enabling client programming.

An object implementing the **IDispatch** interface is by definition an Automation server. An Automation server exposes methods and properties that may be manipulated (programmed) by other objects. The **IDispatch** interface is generic, and an instance of an **IDispatch** interface by an Automation server is called a *dispinterface* and contains these methods:

- *Invoke:* Use a DISPID (index) to call a method or access a property of this dispinterface.
- *GetIDsOfNames:* Convert the text name of a property or a method to DISPID index.
- *GetTypeInfoCount:* Returns 0 if argument is not available, 1 if argument is available.
- *GetTypeInfo:* Retrieves the type information if **GetTypeInfoCount** is successful.

Figure 2-6 is the **IDispatch** vtable interface. The pointer to **IDispatch::Invoke** is an element of the vtable, and actual selection of the method or property doesn't occur until the function is entered.

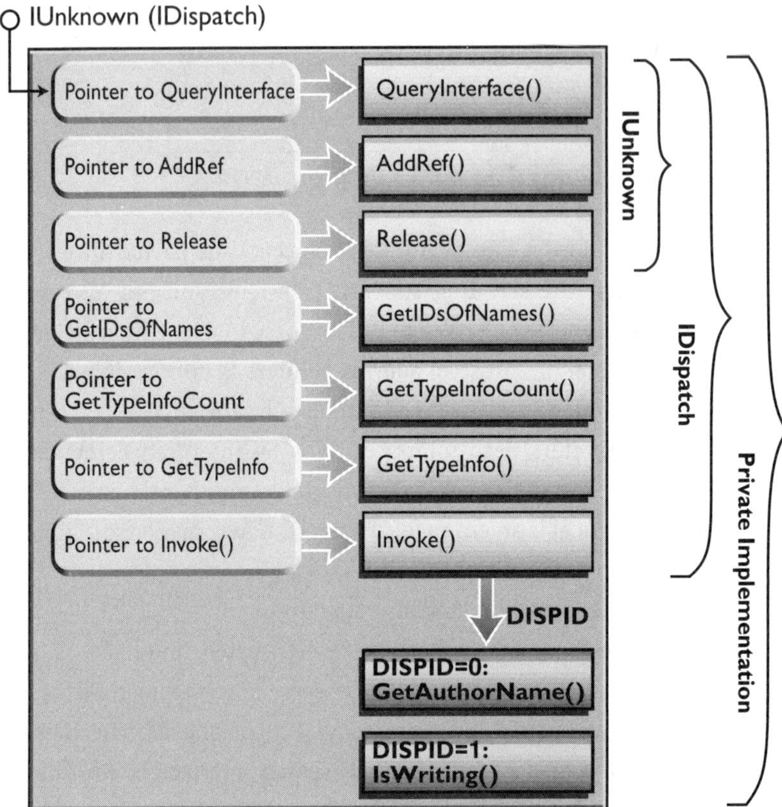

FIGURE 2-6 The IDispatch vtable interface used by Automation

The **IDispatch** interface illustrates many of the issues discussed previously:

- The **IDispatch** interface uses COM interface inheritance. This is illustrated by the inclusion of the three **IUnknown** methods: **QueryInterface, AddRef,** and **Release**.
- The **IDispatch** is certainly polymorphic in that the interface doesn't change when **IDispatch::Invoke** invokes a different method.
- Methods may be added for the pleasure of **IDispatch::Invoke** with no impact on the client. The client isn't aware of the new methods. Compare this to a vtable where any changes require a recompilation of related objects. **IDispatch** methods can be added at run time.
- The **IDispatch** interface gives a choice of either late or early binding.

- Passing data structures through an **IDispatch** interface is awkward and slow. The best that can be done is to wrap the values as properties and use **IDispatch::Invoke** on each property value. A better choice for transferring data is the **IDataObject** interface, which is discussed in Chapter 6.
- The **IDispatch** interface provides encapsulation. Access to values is by method invocation while a put is by reference.

Conceptually, the **IDispatch::Invoke** method can be thought of as a switch function, and the DISPID can be thought of as the switch variable. That is an oversimplification of the function, because **IDispatch::Invoke** has additional arguments, including these:

- *DISPID:* An index identifying the property or method.
- *Flags:* The type of call identifying a get, put, or dispatch.
- *Params:* A pointer to a data structure. This array may be new property values, indices for a property get, or variant method arguments.
- *LCID:* The locale identifier identifying the national language.
- *Results:* A pointer to a variant result structure.
- *Exception:* A pointer to a structure named EXCEPINFO for custom error codes.
- *ArgErr:* Contains the index of the first mismatched argument.

The Dual Interface of IDispatch

Automation is a complex process and a significant amount of overhead is involved. What's not readily apparent is the additional cost of converting the parameters that are stored as variants. Implicit type conversion brought about by sloppy client coding techniques contributes still more overhead.

It's possible to reduce this overhead by creating a dual interface. A dual interface retains all the vtable entries found in the **IDispatch** interface, but in addition, it has pointers to the methods and properties of the dispinterface. Shouldn't direct access to parameters or methods improve Automation performance? One would think so; however, what's apparent is not always true. Yes, a dual interface helps, but only with an in-process server, which is a server in your address space. A disproportionate amount of Automation overhead is spent in the stub and proxy marshaling code for both the local and remote servers. Figure 2-7 illustrates a dual **IDispatch** interface.

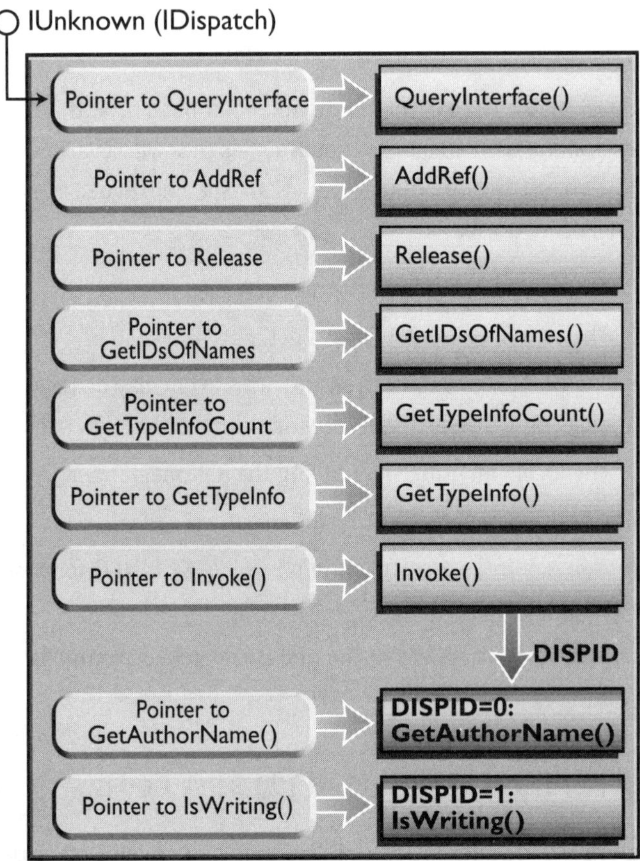

FIGURE 2-7 A dual **IDispatch** interface

Generic Interfaces

Time to catch our breath again. We know the general communication mechanisms between a client and the server. All COM interfaces use a vtable — a virtual pointer table for interfacing. The only exception is the **IDispatch** interface used by Automation. **IDispatch** uses the **IDispatch::Invoke** method as an interface for scripting clients.

I've barely touched on the generic interfaces available in COM. If I go back to original COM and indicate the typical generic COM interfaces, you'll have a better perspective of the interfaces available. I say *typical* because COM is always changing, and I am more interested in the architecture than in the machinations of any particular interface. Figure 2-8 is a roadmap to generic COM interfaces.

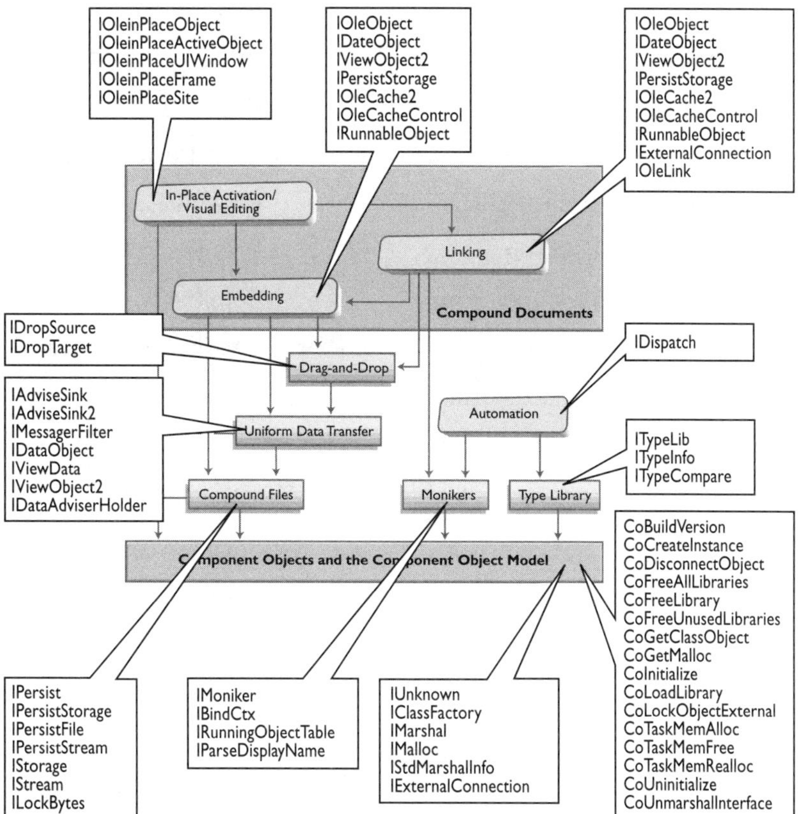

FIGURE 2-8 A roadmap to the generic interfaces of the COM architecture

note **The topology in Figure 2-8 is not quite correct. Figure 2-8 shows IadviseSink, IAdviseSink2, and IMessageFilter as *Uniform Data Transfer* (UDT) interfaces. That is not quite true. The scope of these three interfaces extends beyond UDT and placing them there only illustrates their universal functionality.**

COM implements the concept of a library. It is a collection of dynamic link libraries (DLLs) and EXEs whose names and attributes are mapped into the Registry. There is an example of that mapping below, but for now let's look in a little more detail at the COM library.

The pedestrian term for COM library is those system services that start with the letters *Co*. The following list enumerates a few of these system services without an explanation because the name is nearly always indicative of the function. The COM library **Co** functions are these:

CoCreateGuid	CoGetClassObject
CoCreateInstance	CoGetCurrentProcess
CoCreateStandardMalloc	CoGetMalloc
CoDisconnectObject	CoGetTreatAsClass
CoDosDateTimeToFileTime	CoInitialize
CoFileTimeNow	CoIsHandlerConnected
CoFileTimeToDosDateTime	CoLockExternal
CoFreeAllLibraries	CoMarshalResult
CoFreeLibraryCoFreeUnusedLibraries	CoMarshalInterface

These are not the only elements of the COM library. There are other support interfaces, many of which are listed in Figure 2-8. Figure 2-9 is my representation of the COM library, in which both the client and the object offer services. The COM library is the broker of these services and also offers these services. In this context, a container is also the client.

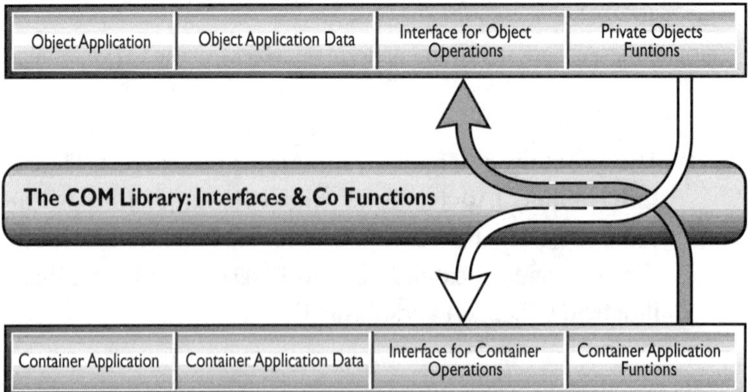

FIGURE 2-9 The COM library acting as a broker of services

There's a quite bit more here than meets the eye. Figure 2-8 associates COM interfaces with COM architectural functions, and Figure 2-9 shows the COM library used freely by both the client and the object. How are these interfaces managed? Well, if you haven't guessed by now, by the Registry. The Registry (REG) defines a complete topology of the interfaces and their relationships. Let's look at some of the characteristics for the .REG file protocol.

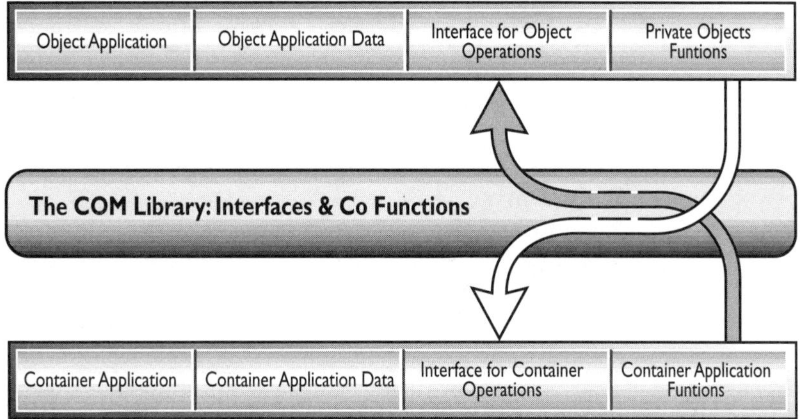

FIGURE 2-9 The COM library acting as a broker of services

Classes

The Windows NT COM information is located in the Registry hive HKEY_CLASSES_ROOT with information organized in a hierarchical manner. A class entry in the .REG file is formatted similar to the following:

```
HKEY_CLASSES_ROOT\CLSID\{class identifier}\Keyword = Value
```

Typical keywords for a class entry in the registry include:

```
LocalServer = <path to 16-bit or 32-bit exe>
LocalServer32 = <path to 32-bit exe >
InprocServer = <path to dll>
InprocServer32 = <path to 32-bit dll>
InprocHandler = <path to dll>
InprocHandler32 = <path to 32-bit dll>
Verb
    verb number = <name, menu flags, verb flags>
```

```
    {Examples:
        0 = &Edit, 0, 2
        1 = &Play, 0, 3
        -3 = Hide, 0, 1
        -2 = Open, 0, 1
        -1 = Show, 0, 1}
AuxUserType
    <form of type>
    {Examples:
        2 = <Short name>        Key 1 is not available!
        3 = <Application Name>}
MiscStatus = <default>
DataFormats = <formats>
    DefaultFile = <format>
    GetSet <n> = <format, aspect, medium, flag>
Insertable
ProgID = <ProgID>
TreatAs = <CLSID>
AutoTreatAs = <CLSID>
AutoConvertTo = <CLSID>
Conversion
   Readable
      Main = <format, format, format, . . .>
   Readwritable
      Main = <format, format, format, . . .>
DefaultIcon = <path to exe, index>
Interfaces = <IID, IID, IID, . . .>
VesionIndependentProgID = <Version Independent ProgID>
```

Interfaces

Interfaces entries in the Registry are much simpler than CLSID entries, and the format is essentially the same:

```
HKEY_CLASSES_ROOT\Interface\{interface identifier}\Keyword = Value
```

There are only three keywords of interest in a Registry interface entry:

- The first value is always the interface name. It's easily recognized because no assignment operator is associated.
- BaseInterface = < *CLSID of inherited interface*>
- NumMethods = <The number of methods this interface supports>
- ProxyStubClsid = <*The CLSID of the component providing marshaling*>

The following is a snippet from the OLE2.REG file with the interface registration information for **IPersist** and **IPersistFile**. This is a discussion of COM object interface information in the Registry and is not meant to be a discussion of either the **IPersistFile** or **IPersist** interfaces.

LISTING 2-2 COM object interface information found in the Registry

```
HKEY_CLASSES_ROOT\Interface\{0000010B-0000-0000-C000-000000000046} =
IPersistFile
HKEY_CLASSES_ROOT\Interface\{0000010B-0000-0000-C000-000000000046}\BaseInterface
= {0000010C-0000-0000-C000-000000000046}
HKEY_CLASSES_ROOT\Interface\{0000010B-0000-0000-C000-000000000046}\NumMethods =
9
HKEY_CLASSES_ROOT\Interface\{0000010B-0000-0000-
C000-000000000046}\ProxyStubClsid = {0000030C-0000-0000-C000-000000000046}
HKEY_CLASSES_ROOT\Interface\{0000010C-0000-0000-C000-000000000046} = IPersist
HKEY_CLASSES_ROOT\Interface\{0000010C-0000-0000-C000-000000000046}\NumMethods =
4
HKEY_CLASSES_ROOT\Interface\{0000010C-0000-0000-
C000-000000000046}\ProxyStubClsid = {0000030C-0000-0000-C000-000000000046}
```

The highlights are:

- The CLSID of **IPersistFile** is {0000010B-0000-0000-C000-0000000046}.
- The base interface for **IPersistfile** is {0000010C-0000-0000-C000-00000000046}. This is COM interface inheritance with the CLSID owned by **IPersist**. The **IPersistFile** interface inherits an interface from **IPersist**; **IPersist,** however, has no interface inheritance.

- **IPersistFile::NumMethods** = 9; there are nine methods available in the **IPersistFile** interface.
- **IPersistFile::ProxyStubClsid** is `{0000030C-0000-0000-C000-00000000046}`. This CLSID is the **PSGenObject** interface CLSID, which is an in-process server. The server is `OLE2PROX.DLL`, which does the proxy marshaling.

ProgIDs

I've discussed CLSIDs and interfaces so far. The topic of **ProgIDs** is also important because they are not unique. ProgIDs are a key component in resolving name conflicts.

Every OLE object class that is to appear in an insert object dialog box (hereafter referred to as an *insertable class*), must have a programmatic identifier or **ProgID**. A **ProgID** represents the most recently installed version of a class. The version-independent **ProgID** represents the application's class and does not change when a new version is installed.

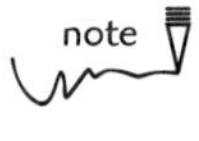

The ProgID is not guaranteed to be universally unique, which makes name collisions with older versions manageable. A ProgID is not more that 39 characters, contains no punctuation, and cannot start with a digit. The ProgID is the class name for an OLE class.

The two different versions of the ProgID enable the COM library to convert ProgID to CLSID using the construct `ROOT\<ProgID>\CLSID`. The reverse translation is done using the key `ROOT\CLSID\<ProgID>`, which is version-dependent. CLSID is a language-independent name in the form `<vendor>.<Component>.<Version>` such as Word.Document.6.

The structure of a generic Registry ProgID entry structure is illustrated in Listing 2-3. Not all detail is presented.

LISTING 2-3 **A generic Registry entry illustrating the structure of a ProgID entry**

```
CLSID < Main User Type Name> = <ProgID>
CLSID<ProgID> = < Main User Type Name >.version
Insertable    // class is insertable in OLE 2 containers
Protocol
   StdFileEditing
```

```
   Server = < full path to the OLE 2 object application >
   Verb
      0 = < verb 0 >
      1 = < verb 1>
      . . .
VersionIndependentProgID = <VersionIndependentProgID>
CLSID
Shell
    Print
    Open
    Command = < executable application name > %1
```

Not all the ProgID attributes are shown, but Listing 2-3 illustrates a generic structure of a ProgID entry.

The registry information presented thus far is from Windows NT, my choice of operating systems. Windows 95 has a Registry; however, the format and the support tools are different than in Windows NT. You can export Registry information in Windows 95 by selecting Export from the Registry menu. These files have the keyword *REGEDIT4* in the preamble while Windows NT files have the keyword *REGEDIT* in the header.

Service Control Manager

The *Service Control Manager* (SCM) is the host for all COM activation mechanisms. SCM is a component of the COM architecture, and it is different than the Service Control Manager of Windows NT that manages logons.

Each system has a SCM, and the services of the SCM are available through monikers, which are discussed in Chapter 5. For now, just assume that the SCM is readily accessible. Activation is considered the state in which methods of the object can be invoked, and COM has three activation models: binding to a class, creating new instances of a class, and activating an object based on the persistent state of the object. The various activation mechanisms hosted by the SCM are illustrated in Figure 2-10. **CoGetClassObject** is the lowest primitive and the other activation mechanisms represent additional wrappers. Let's peek briefly at each of these activation mechanisms.

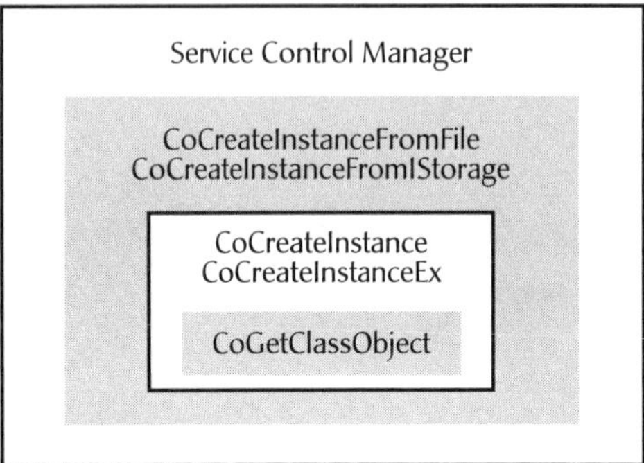

FIGURE 2-10 The Service Control Manager hosting activation mechanisms

- **CoGetClassObject:** A pointer is returned to a class object associated with a specific CLSID. **CoGetClassObject** is used when multiple objects are created from a class object. **CoGetClassObject** also supports class objects on a remote system.
- **CoCreateInstance:** Given a specific CLSID, **CoCreateInstance** creates a single uninitialized instance of an object on the local system.
- **CoCreateInstanceEx:** Given a specific CLSID, create a single uninitialized instance of an object on remote system.
- **CoCreateInstanceFromFile:** A new object is created on a local or remote machine using **IPersistFile::Load**. **IPersistFile** is an interface discussed in Chapter 4.
- **CoCreateInstanceFromIStorage:** A new object is created on a local or remote machine using **IPersistStorage::Load**. **IPersistStorage** is an interface discussed in Chapter 4.

Creating an In-Process Server

Well, we're making progress. We know how COM objects and interfaces are uniquely identified, and we know the architecture of a vtable. We also know that the SCM is responsible for the activation of all COM objects. How do we use all of this? The simplest explanation is to consider the situation in which a client application wishes to start a single instance of a COM server object. The application calls the COM library function **CoCreateInstance** with the *global unique identifier* (GUID) of the desired object and the IID of the desired interface. The COM library delegates the actual task of locating and instantiating an object to the SCM. The SCM searches the Registry and locates the server. The server is started and the SCM returns the requested pointer interface to the COM library, which in turn passes the pointer back to the client. (We're not discussing distributed COM [DCOM] yet; we're still dealing with pointers.)

An interesting issue is that COM cannot initialize the new object, and COM does not ask the server to initialize itself. The client does this. The client asks COM for the **IPersistFile** interface by calling **IUnknown::QueryInterface** with the IID of **IPersistFile**. Persistent data exists when this call is successful. The client calls **IPersistFile::Load** to load the persistent data. The object then initializes itself.

The issue of initializing a server introduces the concept of persistent data. This is just another term for *nonvolatile* data.

note **An IID is either the machine-readable portion of an interface, or 128 bits of chicken tracks. The human-readable interface name of the same interface always starts with an *I* and explains names such as IUnknown, IDispatch, and IPersistFile.**

An **IPersist** interface exists when the object exposes any of the **IPersist*** (any **IPersist** interface) interfaces. There are no specific rules of initialization, and an object is free to adopt any technique necessary to initialize. If a file is required for interfacing, the object will expose an **IPersistfile** interface. There is no requirement that a file actually exist. Simply exposing this interface gives the object a chance to initialize itself, even when a file is not used.

The object already knows how to initialize itself. There are no specific rules on initialization, and an object may not have a type library. The important fact is that an object must initialize itself. All objects must support a COM library in addition to the **IUnknown** interface. This ensures the object that the required support functionality is available.

Let's expand the detail of creating an in-process server that runs in your address space:

1. A client calls the COM library functions **CoGetClassObject** with the CLSID of the desired object and the IID of the desired interface. Because the object is being created, the IID of **IClassFactory** is the other input parameter to **CoGetClassObject**. What is eventually returned to the client is the pointer to **IClassFactory** of the desired object.

2. **CoGetClassObject** passes control to the SCM. The job of SCM is to locate the server.
3. The functions of the SCM include:
   - Looking up the class in the Registry.
   - Looking up the DLL in the Registry.
   - Calling the COM library function **CoLoadLibrary** to load the DLL.
   - Determining the DLL start address with **DLLGetClassObject**.
   - Starting the DLL.
4. The DLL creates the class factory.
5. The DLL returns the **IClassFactory** pointer to SCM.
6. SCM returns the **IClassFactory** pointer to the client.
7. The client now uses the returned **IClassFactory** pointer to call **IClassFactory::CreateInstance**. **IClassFactory::CreateInstance** creates the class object and returns a pointer to it. **IClassFactory** also increases the reference by calling **IUnknown::AddRef**.
8. The client can later invoke the method **IUnknown::Release** to decrement the reference count. The server will be destroyed when the count goes to zero.
9. The object can be used after initialization.

Because **IClassFactory::CreateInstance** creates a pointer to an object, it has the responsibility of incrementing the object reference count by calling **IUnknown ::AddRef**. **IUnknown::QueryInterface**, **IOleItemContainer::GetObject**, and **IOle Container::EnumObjects** are the other interfaces responsible for incrementing the reference count.

This sequence creates an uninitialized instance of an object class. The object can be initialized by one of these methods: **IPersistStorage::InitNew**, **IPersist Storage::Load**, **IPersistStream::Load**, or **IPersistFile::Load**. These methods are discussed in Chapter 4.

The interfaces **IUnknown** and **IClassFactory** are the minimum interfaces an OLE object must support, but an OLE object is not limited to just two interfaces.

Creating a Local or Remote Server

A local or remote server is an executable file, whereas an in-process server is a DLL. The sequence of events for creating a local server is almost identical to that of a remove server. The only difference is that the SCM provides a pointer to a local object proxy for local servers, or a pointer to a remote object proxy for remote servers. Either way, the process is transparent to the client.

Lets step through the process of creating a local Server. The client initiates the initial step and starts with:

1. A client calls the COM library functions **CoGetClassObject** with the CLSID of the desired object and the IID of the desired interface. The input IID is that of **IClassFactory** because a pointer to **IClassFactory** will be returned to the client.
2. **CoGetClassObject** passes control to the SCM. The job of the SCM is to locate the server.
3. The SCM does the following:
   - Looks up the class in the Registry.
   - Looks up EXE in the Registry.
   - The server may not be running, in which case the EXE starts with **WinExec.** If the server is already running, a new process is created with **CreateProcess**.
   - Control is passed to the EXE (**WinMain**).
4. EXE does the following:
   - Calls the COM library function **CoInitialize.**
   - Creates the class factory.
   - Calls the COM library **CoRegisterClassObject** with the **IClassFactory** pointer.
   - Control is returned to the SCM, which in turn passes control back to the client.

5. The client now has the **IClassFactory** pointer and initiates a the call to **IClassFactory::CreateInstance** with the CLSID of the object and the IID of the interface.
6. The client receives a pointer to the uninitialized object.
7. **IUnknown::AddRef** is used by the client to increase the reference count. This ensures that the server will not be destroyed. The client can later invoke the **IUnknown::Release** method to decrement the reference count. The server will be destroyed when the count goes to zero.
8. The object can be used after initialization.

This sequence is almost identical to that of an in-process server. The new object can be initialized in the same way with: **IPersistStorage::InitNew, IPersist Storage::Load, IPersistStream::Load**, or **IPersistFile::Load**. Now you have some insight into the mechanics of OLE servers.

Creating a server in Visual Basic is relatively simple and all the work is done under the hood. An example of creating Microsoft Access as a server is illustrated with:

```
Dim A As Object
Set A = CreateObject("Access.Application")
```

Microsoft Visual Basic does not support the **IClassFactory** interface, and the object's class interface is used to instantiate the new object. I'll look at this issue a bit more in Chapter 5, where I discuss monikers.

Key Point Summary

COM is a binary specification for process communication that is machine-independent. COM borrows terminology and constructs from C++, which is the Microsoft host implementation language. Key constructs are the concepts of a vtable, the **IUnknown** and the **IDispatch** interfaces, and the concept of marshaling.

- A vtable is the standard COM interface mechanism in the Microsoft implementation. It is a binary specification and language independent.
- The **IDispatch** interface used by Automation is a combination of a vtable and a dispinterface using **IDispatch::Invoke** with DISPIDs.

- COM objects must initialize themselves.
- **IClassFactory::CreateInstance** creates an instance of a server.
- Object life is managed with the **AddRef** and **Release** methods of **IUnknown**.
- **IUnknown::QueryInterface** is the COM universal interrogation mechanism.
- Transparent marshaling is supported for apartment-model threaded objects and remote objects.

Applying What You've Learned

A mastery of the mechanics of COM is required for all levels of developers. Visual Basic 5.0 now supports the creation of ActiveX controls and control creation is no longer limited to C++ developers. The questions that follow test your knowledge of the COM interfacing fundamentals.

Instant Assessment

1. What is a vtable?
2. What interface must all COM objects support?
3. What is the minimum number of interfaces for a COM object? Name the interfaces.
4. Name the three **IUnknown** methods.
5. Name two unique characteristics of the **IDispatch** interface.
6. What is a dual interface?
7. Under what condition might you use a dual interface?
8. What function is it that the COM library cannot do?
9. What is the role of the Service Control Manager?
10. What is the role of **IUnknown::AddRef** and **IUnknown::Release**?
11. Which component in the COM architecture is responsible for using **IUnknown::AddRef** and **IUnknown::Release**?
12. Identify the COM library component used to start a server.
13. Identify the information that must be supplied to the COM library component identified in Question 12 to successfully start a server.

For answers to the Instant Assessment Questions, see Appendix B.

Lab Exercise

This lab will expand your knowledge of the Registry. It deals with the version-independent ProgID. The basic problem is the latest version of software installed is always the version activated when an icon is double-clicked. The primary goal of this lab is to understand the version-independent ProgID mechanism. The secondary goal is to design a Registry protocol that preserves the original version-independent ProgID and which reverts to a version-dependent ProgID. A very crude workaround for this problem is to install a product such as Microsoft Office 97 and then immediately reinstall OfficePro 4.3. Both systems are available; however, double-clicking starts Word 6.0 and not Word 97.

Lab 2.3 *A Shortcoming of the version-independent ProgID*

Lab 2-3 investigates how to start a COM server. Assume the VBA statements below exist in a Visual Basic context. Statements of this nature are used to print reports from Microsoft Access rather than using the Crystal Reports that comes with Visual Basic.

```
Dim MyObj As Object
Set MyObj = CreateObject("Access.Application")
```

1. Go to your Windows NT Registry and the `HKEY_CLASSES_ROOT` hive.
2. Open the `HKEY_CLASSES_ROOT` hive and select Edit ➪ Find. For Windows NT 3.51 select View ➪ Find.
3. Search for Access.Application.

   I found three entries on my system:

   - `Access.Application`
   - `Access.Application.7`
   - `Access.Application.8`

   When I expanded these entries, I found that `Access.Application` has the same CLSID as `Access.Application.8`, which I expected.

   This system has Access 2.0, Access 95, and Access 97 installed. The problem is that when I double-click an icon, Access 97 automatically starts. This is because there is only one class registered for any version of Microsoft Access — .MDB. You can examine the class by searching the HKEY_CLASSES_ROOT hive for .MDB.

When I examined that entry I found `Access.Application.8`, which is not what I want. This is the version-independent ProgID discussed earlier. This is a general problem with the design of the Registry, which always uses the last installation version as the version-independent ProgID.

Design a Registry protocol that will provide a floating ProgID. In essence, what is wanted is a version-dependent and not a version-independent ProgID. A version-dependent ProgID will allow the installation of a new version; double-clicking an icon, however, will activate the dependent version and not the most recently installed version.

Do not change the Registry unless you are experienced and understand that a damaged Registry will make the system unbootable. However, do examine the Registry closely until this is understood. I champion a deprecated class whenever a new class is installed. This mechanism would not force unwanted and unneeded application upgrades, and both deprecated and new classes could exist on the same system.

CHAPTER

Interface Issues

3

About Chapter 3

This chapter deals with the fundamental issues of program communication. *Interprogram communication* had to be established before intraprogram communication was possible. The *name space* domain evolved slowly, primarily because there was no impetus for an international standard, and because name space was traditionally controlled by the application developer. COM requires a unique object identifier. This started the change towards a global name space. ActiveX (COM) objects evolved from a machine-oriented and process-oriented technology to the universal name space of the Internet. Intraprogram communication is now successful on a global basis. This process took nearly fifty years to complete.

The Global Name Space Problem

If you're with me so far, you know that my thesis is that COM is the natural order of software evolution. The name space domain in earlier programming languages was limited. If you wrote a subroutine using an earlier language, your only problem was to ensure that it didn't have the same name as a library subroutine. The result after compiling and linking the subroutine was a binary mass that probably required segmentation to execute properly. The only exposed names were the executable code segment and the FORTRAN Named Common Block names.

I recall a missile reentry program developed in the early 1960s at the Boeing Development Center in Seattle, Washington. The program was written in FORTRAN and used Named Common Blocks. Each common block was named after a brand of beer, a very limited name space, but adequate for the situation. In FORTRAN, Named Common Blocks are a fixed area of memory. Programs were not reentrant and each new overlay found the information from previous overlays through common blocks. A vexing problem was the reordering of common blocks, which occurred when one or more blocks were no longer in use.

The developer nearly always created the name space. I use the term *developer* to mean both individuals and software development companies. The individuals had complete freedom to create name spaces of their choice. Only internal standards and policies limited software companies. Users were forced to comply with the vendor-supplied naming conventions.

Here I am only discussing module or subroutine naming. Subroutine parameters were positional with no other context. The source code named parameters internally within the module and the process of compiling and linking the application masked the names, hence the application became an immutable *binary mass*. That has changed and today a Windows application is not immutable. Every time a Windows application is loaded, it is reconstituted from the current version of components that reside within the operating system.

The Open Systems Foundation (OSF) initially recognized the global naming problem in its distributed computing environment (DCE) specification. Digital Equipment Corporation, and Hewlett Packard Corporation, worked jointly on a solution to the problem, but the global solution was (and is) the Microsoft implementation of COM.

There may be better solutions to the name space problem than COM, but I believe that Microsoft was (and is) in a better position to implement global naming standards than were (are) other companies. Microsoft's size alone dictates a de facto standard.

What I find fascinating is that the software industry approached the fifty-year mark before a solution was proposed. I am certain that if we did not have a company the size of Microsoft, we would still be bickering. OSF recognized the problem with its release of the DCE specification in the early 1990s, and Microsoft implemented it in COM.

Solving the Global Name Space Problem with GUID

Microsoft borrowed the DCE *universal unique identifier* (UUID) concept in solving the name space problem, and in doing so, renamed it. The designated new name for a UUID is a *global unique identifier* (GUID). The implementation is 128 bits and comes in two versions: one version for object names and the second version for interface names. If you don't understand all the acronyms, here they are:

- Universal unique identifier (UUID) is an OSF DCE concept.
- A globally unique identifier (GUID) is the 128-bit Microsoft implementation of a UUID.
- A COM object class identifier (CLSID) is a GUID.
- A COM object interface identifier (IID) is a GUID.

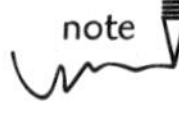

Please remember that I am discussing older technology. Today, this technology has all been replaced with new and exciting tools. Even though some of the techniques presented in this chapter are dated, it is important to understand the original concepts and the issues involved. It will make life in the trenches a little easier later on.

The GUID can be guaranteed unique on a global basis.It consists of the current date and time plus a clock sequence to deal with the retrograde motion of clocks, a forcibly incremented counter to deal with high-frequency allocations,

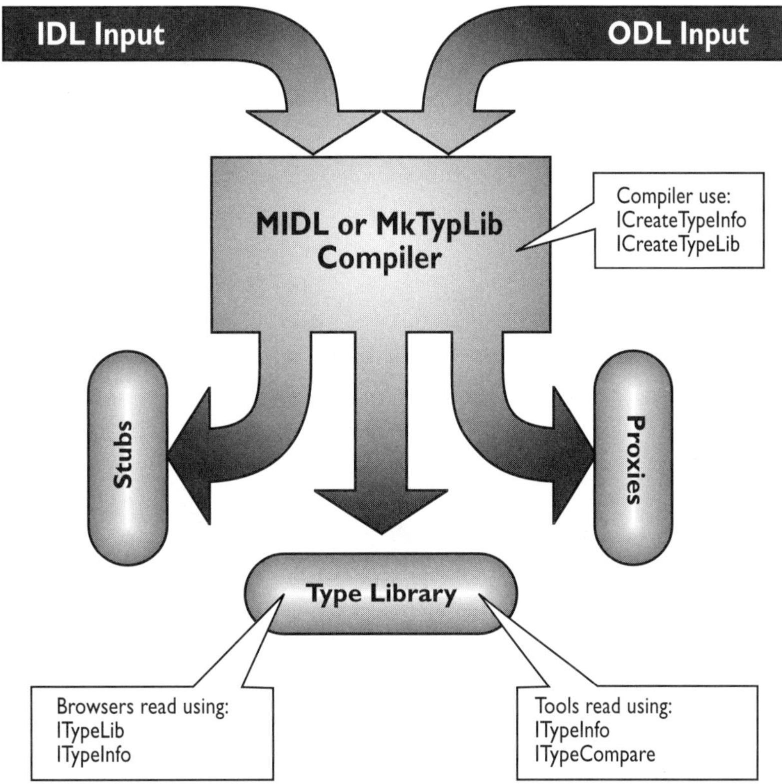

FIGURE 3-4 Creating a .TLB file

The compilers also generate C/C++ header files. The type library infrastructure can be summarized as:

- UUID, Properties, and methods of server objects are stored in a type library. Properties have data types, and methods return values or accept parameters.
- Type library is extended as a .TLB or as a .ODL.
- Object description language (ODL) files are plain-text files.
- MkTypLib creates a type library. Statements are based on the prototype ODL structure of Listing 3-1.

LISTING 3-1 A prototype .ODL file

```
[uuid<GUID>, <helpinfo>, <attributes>]
library <name>
  {
  importlib(<path to another type library>)
  typedef [<attributes>] <basename | struct | enum | union>
    {
    . . .
    } <type>;
    [attributes] module <name>
      {
      <element list>
      };
  [uuid(<GUID>), <helpinfo>, <attributes>]
  interface <name>
   {
   [<attributes>] <return type> [calling convention]
      <function name><arguments>);
      . . ..
   }
  [uuid(<GUID>), <helpinfo>, <attributes>]
  dispinterface <name>
    {
    properties:
      [<attributes>] <type> <name>;
      . . .
    methods:
      [<attributes>] <return type> <name> (<arguments>);
      . . .
    }
  [uuid(<GUID>), <helpinfo>, <attributes>]
  dispinterface <name>
    {
    interface <name>;
    }
```

```
[uuid(<GUID>), <helpinfo>, <attributes>]
coclass
  {
  [<attributes>] dispinterface < dispinterface name>;
  . . .
  [<attributes>] interface < interface name>;
  }
};
```

A type library is located through the Registry. The CLSID is used to locate the correct entry that identifies the .TLB file. A type library is used by browsers, by OLE Automation for runtime checking of interfaces, and by an EXE server for marshaling the dispinterface. Figure 3-5 shows the type library, which contains more than one hundred entries, on the machine I am using to type this.

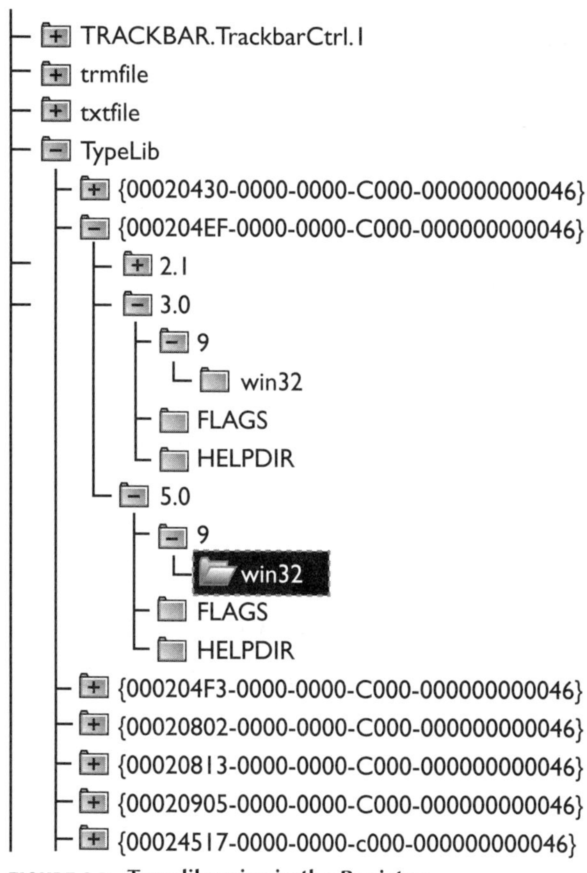

FIGURE 3-5 Type libraries in the Registry

Building a Type Library

Not all COM objects need a type library. If a type library is necessary, an ODL, or, preferably, an IDL, is created within the Visual C++ environment. The file is input to the MIDL or MKTYPLIB compiler and the result is a .TLB file. Let's have some fun and build an IDL file. Let's call the object **IAuthor** and the file will be IAUTHOR.IDL.

```
[
  object ,
  uuid(6c069860-88a5-11d0-928e-08002b2613ff),
  pointer_default(unique)
]
interface IAuthor : IUnknown
{
  import "unknwn.idl";
  HRESULT GetAuthorName([out], string, size_is(128) char *p);
  HRESULT IsWriting([out] BOOL *pBool);
}
```

The IDL file includes my two methods **GetAuthorName** and **IsWriting,** as well as the inherited methods, **QueryInterface, AddRef,** and **Release**. The C++ inheritance is from `<drive>:\VC40\INCLUDE\UNKNWN.H` and the `UNKNWN.IDL` file is from the same directory. This interface uses both implementation inheritance and interface inheritance. The implementation inheritance occurs on the Interface line in the IDL file and the interface inheritance occurs when I import another IDL file to my IDL file on the Import line. This is the equivalent of a cut and paste to the IDL file and gives me my interface inheritance. COM doesn't care if the underlying code uses implementation inheritance. All that's really important is that the concept of interface inheritance be adhered to.

Building a Type Library in Visual Basic

Life is simpler with Visual Basic 5.0/6.0. Type libraries are built automatically when the project is built. The type library is contained within the ActiveX component and direct access to an ActiveX component created by Visual Basic is not possible. We'll create a simple ActiveX EXE or DLL with the following dialog. You'll want to create an executable file (EXE) when the ActiveX server does not run in-process. Conversely, an ActiveX DLL will run in-process. Let's name our class

ICheckBook, which follows the naming conventions for object interfaces. Remember that the type library will be self-contained for this example.

To create **IcheckBook,** follow these steps:

1. Start Visual Basic 5.0/6.0
2. Select **New** and choose either an ActiveX EXE or an ActiveX DLL.
3. From the **View** menu select **Properties Window** and set the class name to **ICheckBook**. The default name should be **Class1**.
4. From the **View** menu, select **Project Explorer,** and double-click **ICheckbook**.
5. Enter the code shown in Listing 3-2 below.
6. From the File menu select **Make Project1.EXE** (or **Make Project1.DLL**).
7. Change the name to **ICheckbook.EXE** (or **ICheckbook.DLL**).
8. Select **OK.**
9. Congratulations! You have just built an ActiveX control. The type library information exists within your new control.

You can browse your new control. From the **View** menu select **Object Browser**.

The control is ready for use. The **Browse** button on the **References** dialog box can be used later to locate your new DLL or EXE file and set a reference to it. Checking your new control in the **References** dialog box will register it.

The VB **Implements** statement can be used with our new class. This is the equivalent of inheritance in C++. There is a restriction with the **Implements** statement not supporting outgoing interfaces (see Chapter 6). This means that any events declared in a class module are ignored.

LISTING 3-2 **The ICheckbook property in the Visual Basic ActiveX EXE or DLL**

```
Option Explicit
Private dblChkBookBal As Double
Property Get Balance() As Double
Balance = dblChkBookBal
End Property
Property Let Balance(ByVal dblNewChkBookBal As Double)
  If dblNewChkBookBal < 0 Then
    Err.Raise Number:=vbObjectError + 32112, _
```

```
    Description:="Overdraft"
  Else
    dblChkBookBal = dblNewChkBookBal
  End If
End Property
```

Registering a Type Library

Server registration can take several forms:

- Registering CLSIDs at object installation through a setup file.
- A self-registering object which is downloaded from the Internet.
- Dynamically registering objects at runtime with MFC.
- Compiling a Visual Basic Active component.
- Selecting **References ⇨ Browse** and selecting an ActiveX object from a VBA editor.

Registering a new server is necessary before a client can locate and use your new server. All server CLSIDs must be registered, which is normally done at installation time. The object setup file provides this information. Either system defaults are assumed at object installation, or, at the very minimum, the **CLSID** key and **AppID** key information is required. Important information is the designation of type, which can be in-process, out-of-process local, or out-of-process remote. **RemoteServerName** and **ActivateAtStorage** are also important because they let a client instantiate a server with no built-in server knowledge.

Help in creating a Visual Basic 5.0/6.0 setup file is found by selecting the **Help** menu and **Books on Line** from within VB. Enter **Setup** and you'll find displayed all the necessary information topics for using a Setup Wizard to create your new Visual Basic ActiveX control installation files. The setup kit is found in `...\VB\SetupKit`. Another choice is to use **Regsvr32** when the VB setup wizard isn't wanted.

The second registering technique can be done in C++ at runtime. An object may be registered at runtime with the MFC function **AfxOleRegisterTypeLib,** which is C++ specific.

```
VERIFY(AfxOleRegisterTypeLib(AfxGetInstanceHandle(), myTypeLibGuid,\
   "author.tlb"));
```

Of course, having the server register itself is a very special case. This occurs with Internet downloads where new objects register themselves.

The last example of registering an object is the example server constructed earlier. The **ICheckBook.EXE** file was registered automatically by Visual Basic when the project was compiled. Figure 3-6 shows the Registry for the **Project1.ICheckBook** project along with a CLSID.

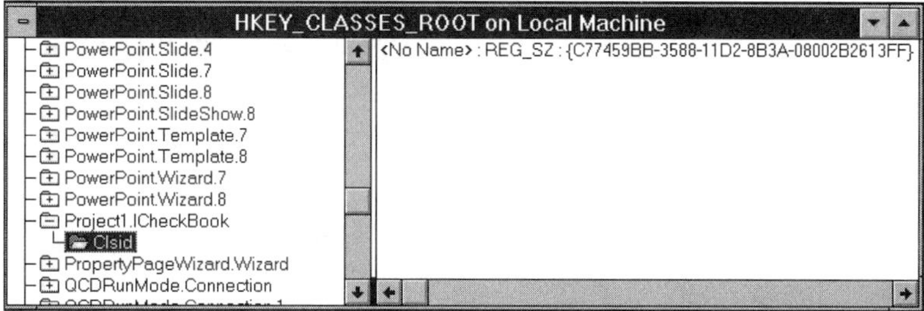

FIGURE 3-6 Windows NT Registry after compiling an ActiveX component

Before you rush to register information in the Registry, remember Windows NT's security issues. I always log on to Windows NT as Administrator and security is never an issue. I know that is not the way to do it, but my house, my rules. Your system may become inoperable if the Registry is edited incorrectly.

Listing 3-3 is an application registration file from the *Control Developers Kit* (CDK).

LISTING 3-3 The registration file for the Hello application

```
; Registration information for the hello application
;
; IDispatch*    Hello.Application {D3CE6D43-F1AF-1068-9FBB-08002B32372A}
; Type library: hello.tlb         {D3CE6D44-F1AF-1068-9FBB-08002B32372A}
; Interface:    IHello            {D3CE6D45-F1AF-1068-9FBB-08002B32372A}
;
;;;;;;;;;;;;;;;;;;;;;;;;;;;;;;;;;;;;;;;
; registration info Hello.Application (defaults to Hello.Application.1)
HKEY_CLASSES_ROOT\Hello.Application = OLE Automation Hello Application
HKEY_CLASSES_ROOT\Hello.Application\Clsid = {D3CE6D43-F1AF-1068-9FBB-
```

```
08002B32372A}
;;;;;;;;;;;;;;;;;;;;;;;;;;;;;;;;;;;;;;;;
; registration info Hello.Application.1
HKEY_CLASSES_ROOT\Hello.Application.1 = OLE Automation Hello 1.0 Application
HKEY_CLASSES_ROOT\Hello.Application.1\Clsid = {D3CE6D43-F1AF-1068-9FBB-
08002B32372A}
;;;;;;;;;;;;;;;;;;;;;;;;;;;;;;
; registration info Hello 1.0
HKEY_CLASSES_ROOT\CLSID\{D3CE6D43-F1AF-1068-9FBB-08002B32372A} = IDispatch Hello
Example
HKEY_CLASSES_ROOT\CLSID\{D3CE6D43-F1AF-1068-9FBB-08002B32372A}\ProgID =
Hello.Application.1
HKEY_CLASSES_ROOT\CLSID\{D3CE6D43-F1AF-1068-9FBB-
08002B32372A}\VersionIndependentProgID =
Hello.Application
HKEY_CLASSES_ROOT\CLSID\{D3CE6D43-F1AF-1068-9FBB-08002B32372A}\LocalServer32 =
hello.exe
/Automation
;;;;;;;;;;;;;;;;;;;;;;;;;;;;;;;;;;
; registration info Hello TypeLib
HKEY_CLASSES_ROOT\TypeLib\{D3CE6D44-F1AF-1068-9FBB-08002B32372A}
HKEY_CLASSES_ROOT\TypeLib\{D3CE6D44-F1AF-1068-9FBB-08002B32372A}\1.0 = OLE
Automation Hello 1.0
Type Library
HKEY_CLASSES_ROOT\TypeLib\{D3CE6D44-F1AF-1068-9FBB-08002B32372A}\1.0\HELPDIR =
;Localized language is US english
HKEY_CLASSES_ROOT\TypeLib\{D3CE6D44-F1AF-1068-9FBB-08002B32372A}\1.0\409\win32 =
hello.tlb
HKEY_CLASSES_ROOT\Interface\{D3CE6D46-F1AF-1068-9FBB-08002B32372A} = _DHello
HKEY_CLASSES_ROOT\Interface\{D3CE6D46-F1AF-1068-9FBB-
08002B32372A}\ProxyStubClsid32 = {00020420-0000-0000-C000-000000000046}
HKEY_CLASSES_ROOT\Interface\{D3CE6D46-F1AF-1068-9FBB-08002B32372A}\NumMethod = 7
HKEY_CLASSES_ROOT\Interface\{D3CE6D46-F1AF-1068-9FBB-08002B32372A}\BaseInterface
= {00020400-0000-0000-C000-000000000046}
```

We start the analysis of this .REG file by noting the first few comment lines. A different GUID is used to identify the object (this is an OLE Automation example), a type library, and an interface. Reading the file is self-explanatory until we encounter the line with the second CLSID of 00020420-0000-0000-C000-000000000046. I looked in OLE2.REG and found that OLEAUT32.DLL owned that CLSID. The name on the line is **ProxyStubClsid**. This means that OLEAUT32.DLL will do the marshaling for the server.

```
-- Registration info for OLE Automation private classes
HKEY_CLASSES_ROOT\CLSID\{00020420-0000-0000-C000-000000000046} = PSDispatch
HKEY_CLASSES_ROOT\CLSID\{00020420-0000-0000-C000-000000000046}\InprocServer =
ole2disp.dll
HKEY_CLASSES_ROOT\CLSID\{00020420-0000-0000-C000-000000000046}\InprocServer32 =
oleaut32.dll
```

The next unexplained issue is the line with the second CLSID of 00020400-0000-0000-C000-000000000046. This IID was also found in OLE2.REG. This is the OLE Automation interface IID that will also use OLEAUT32.DLL for marshaling.

```
-- IDispatch
HKEY_CLASSES_ROOT\Interface\{00020400-0000-0000-C000-000000000046} = IDispatch
HKEY_CLASSES_ROOT\Interface\{00020400-0000-0000-C000-000000000046}\NumMethods =
7
HKEY_CLASSES_ROOT\Interface\{00020400-0000-0000-
C000-000000000046}\ProxyStubClsid = {00020420-0000-0000-C000-000000000046}
HKEY_CLASSES_ROOT\Interface\{00020400-0000-0000-
C000-000000000046}\ProxyStubClsid32 = {00020420-0000-0000-C000-000000000046}
```

The concept of persistent data can be introduced by simply saying that the data is nonvolatile. This topic is discussed in much more detail in Chapter 4, but for now note that the file name of the EXE type library is stored in the Registry. There was a comment line at the top of this .REG file with the type library GUID. That GUID entry contains the EXE server type library file name. Anything stored in that file is by definition persistent and can be used by the EXE server for self-initialization and subsequent late binding. But more on this and other persistent types later.

A benefit of COM is locale sensitivity. UNICODE is a 2-byte character set with which any language can be represented. A global name space without sensitivity to a local language is of little value. UNICODE provides the capability of representing any language, a capability which is only a partial solution. The missing element of the global name problem solution is a *localized identifier* (LCID) that can be used with a GUID. Selecting the local language is done with the LCID. If you examine the type library definition line in the prior .REG example, you'll see the localization code for English.

Let's use French, whose locale identifier is 0x40c, as an example. Because I know its LCID, I can construct the header of a hypothetical IDL file with French as the language. The only other task is to convert the property names to French. I will store the generated IDL file as `MYCONTROLFR.IDL` so that I know it is the French version.

```
[
   uuid(xxxxxxxx-xxxx-xxxx-xxxx-xxxxxxxxxxxxxxxx),
   Version(1.0),
   lcid(0x040c)
]
library MyControl
{
   . . .
}
```

We really don't have to worry too much about ODL or IDL files that use our old friend the GUID. IDL files are simpler than the ODL files they replace because they deal only with interfaces. IDL files are constructed manually quite easily. The generation of the numerous other skeleton object files is reasonably automated with Visual C++ wizards, but the creation of an object does not remain a simple process.

The constructs for the MIDL compiler are C/C++ based and the new MIDL compiler supports all the essential ODL constructs. Complete MIDL compiler documentation can be found in the Microsoft Win 32 software developer's kit (SDK).

Life is now much sweeter with Microsoft Visual Basic 5.0/6.0 Enterprise Edition, which does all the under-the-hood type library work for us transparently.

Key Point Summary

We learned in Chapter 2 that COM requests an interface with **IUnknown::QueryInterface**. This isn't possible unless all objects and interfaces are named uniquely. Microsoft is the first software company to successfully solve the global name space problem and deliver products based on this solution.

- Name space is the limiting factor of intraprogram communication.
- The concept of a universal unique identifier (UUID) comes from the OSF DCE specification. Microsoft borrowed this concept and named it a globally unique identifier (GUID).
- A COM object class identifier (CLSID) is a GUID.
- A COM object interface identifier (IID) is a GUID.
- All COM objects have a GUID.
- Each COM object interface has an IID.
- Type libraries support objects, and objects cannot be browsed without a type library.
- An object is kept private without a type library.

Applying What You've Learned

The questions below will measure your understanding of the global name space and how it is managed. Some of the issues may appear to be artifacts of the past because modern tools such as Visual Basic have automated many of the issues.

Instant Assessment

1. What is the global name space problem?
2. How is the global name space problem solved?
3. Explain the differences between a UUID, a GUID, and an IID.
4. Name three methods of creating a UUID.
5. What is the unique requirement of an Insertable Object?
6. When doesn't an object require a GUID?
7. What is the difference between the ODL compiler `MKTYPLIB.EXE` and the IDL compiler MIDL?
8. Name four types of information created by an ODL or IDL compiler.
9. Name two instances where a GUID is necessary.
10. Name at least three ways a type library is registered.
11. Where is the type library for a Visual Basic ActiveX component located?

12. What is persistent data?

For answers to the Instant Assessment Questions, see Appendix C.

Lab Exercises

This set of labs will help you understand that all Microsoft products are component based. This means that each tool supports a type library and the VBA environment.

Lab 3.4 *Surveying your system*

Lab 3.4 helps you determine the type libraries in your system. Start by doing an inventory of each of your directories and noting the names and locations of all files with the .TLB extension.

1. How many .TLB files only exist in a product path such as `WINWORD`?
2. How many .TLB files exist only in the `SYSTEM` (`SYSTEM32` for Windows NT) directory?
3. List the .TLB files found in other directories that are not in the `SYSTEM` directory.

Lab 3.5 *Visual Basic 5.0/6.0 and type libraries*

Lab 3.5 begins with the Visual Basic 5.0/6.0 type library, which is accessed differently than other Microsoft products.

1. Start Visual Basic 5.0/6.0.
2. Click **References** from the **Project** menu. The available type libraries are now displayed. When an application doesn't work it is often because the proper type library is not selected. Also notice the **Browse** button. You use this for selecting a type library not found in the combo box on the **References** dialog form.

The next issue is to browse the existing type libraries of a Microsoft Visual Basic project.

1. Select **Object Browser** from the **View** menu. Here you will find the constants, methods, and properties of the type libraries on your system.
2. Browse the type libraries when you're stumped for a method. The method you want to use may be related to a different object.

Lab 3.6 *Word 97 and type libraries*

Each of the following tools supports the VBA environment. By supporting type libraries, each of these tools supports COM objects and illustrates the ubiquity of COM objects in the Microsoft architecture. The VBA code written in either Microsoft Access or VB can be used interchangeably with an occasional minor adjustment.

1. Start Word 97.
2. Select **Tools ⇨ Macro.**
3. Select Visual Basic Editor from the submenu.
4. In Visual Basic Editor, select **Tools ⇨ References**. The dialog box shown in Figure 3-7 is displayed.

Browsing a type library in Word 97 is quite similar to browsing a type library in Visual Basic 5.0/6.0. While in the editor, select **Object Browser** from the **View** menu.

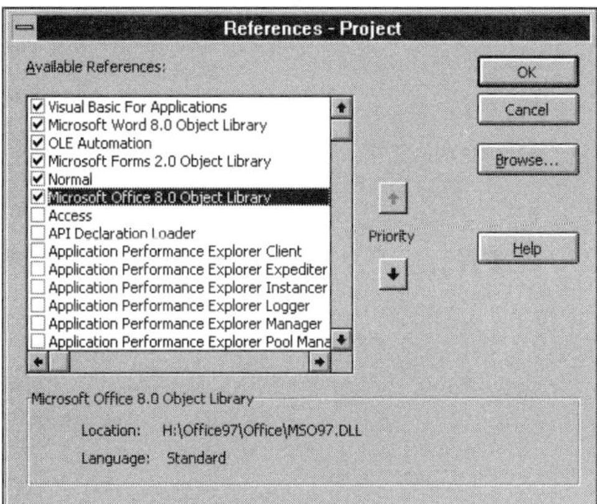

FIGURE 3-7 Word 97 type library references

Lab 3.7 *Access 97 and type libraries*

Referencing a type library in Access 97 takes the same amount of work as in Visual Basic 5.0/6.0. A control must be placed on a form before a type library can be referenced. To reference the libraries, follow these steps:

1. Start Access 97.
2. Create a new form.

3. Place a control on the form. Clicking a control in the toolbox and painting the control on the form does this.
4. With the control on the form selected, pick an event from the Properties dialog form. This places you in the VBA coding module.
5. Select **Tools ➪ References** to add or change a type library.
6. Select **View ➪ Object Browser** to browse properties, methods, or constants of an Access 97 type library.

Lab 3.8 *Excel 97 and type libraries*

Type library references in Excel 97 are accessed in the same manner as the Word 97 type library references. To reference the type libraries in Excel 97, follow these steps:

1. Select **Tools ➪ Macro**.
2. Select **Visual Basic Editor** from the submenu.
3. In the editor, select **Tools ➪ References**.

You'll see the now familiar References dialog box displayed. By selecting Object Browser from the View menu, the type libraries may be browsed.

Lab 3.9 *Outlook 97 and type libraries*

We're still in familiar territory with Outlook 97. The initial step to reference the type libraries is slightly different; however, once in the Visual Basic Editor, the steps are identical to that of Word 97 and Excel 97.

1. Start Outlook 97.
2. Once in Outlook 97, start a new message or double an existing e-mail message. This places you in editing mode.
3. Select **Tools ➪ Macro**.
4. Select **Visual Basic Editor** from the submenu.
5. In the editor, select **Tools ➪ References**.

You'll see the now familiar References dialog box displayed. By selecting Object Browser from the View menu, the type libraries may be browsed.

Lab 3.10 *PowerPoint 97 and type libraries*

This lab almost repeats Lab 3.9. The difference is that in PowerPoint there must be an active slide presentation, whereas Outlook 97 requires an active message. Either create a new presentation with a blank slide or access an existing presentation. Once this is accomplished, reference the type libraries in PowerPoint 97 with the following steps:

1. Start PowerPoint.
2. Select **Tools ➪ Macro**.
3. Select **Visual Basic Editor** from the submenu.
4. In the editor, select **Tools ➪ References**.

You'll see the now familiar References dialog box displayed. By selecting Object Browser from the View menu, the type libraries may be browsed.

Lab 3.11 *Microsoft Project 4.1 and type libraries*

This is Project 4.1 circa Windows 95, and it supports type libraries. Project is a task scheduling and planning tool and is not packaged with the standard Microsoft Office products such as Word, Excel, PowerPoint, and Access.

1. Start Microsoft Project.
2. Select **Tools ➪ Macros**.
3. Select **New** from the dialog box that appears. (Another alternative is to edit an existing project.)
4. Select **OK**.
5. In the editor, select **Tools ➪ References**.

You'll see the now familiar References dialog box displayed. By selecting Object Browser from the View menu, the type libraries may be browsed.

CHAPTER

Structured Storage

4

About Chapter 4

COM structured storage is a cornerstone of COM implementation. It supports the concept of a file system within a file system. OLE embedding might not exist without this supporting technology. This technology is also indispensable for supporting embedded objects. COM structured storage and its supporting interfaces are the focus of this chapter.

COM Structured Storage

We start our review of basic COM with structured storage. We'll add more features and the complexity will move upward until we finish with in-place activation of compound documents. Figure 4-1 illustrates the persistent interfaces for COM structured storage.

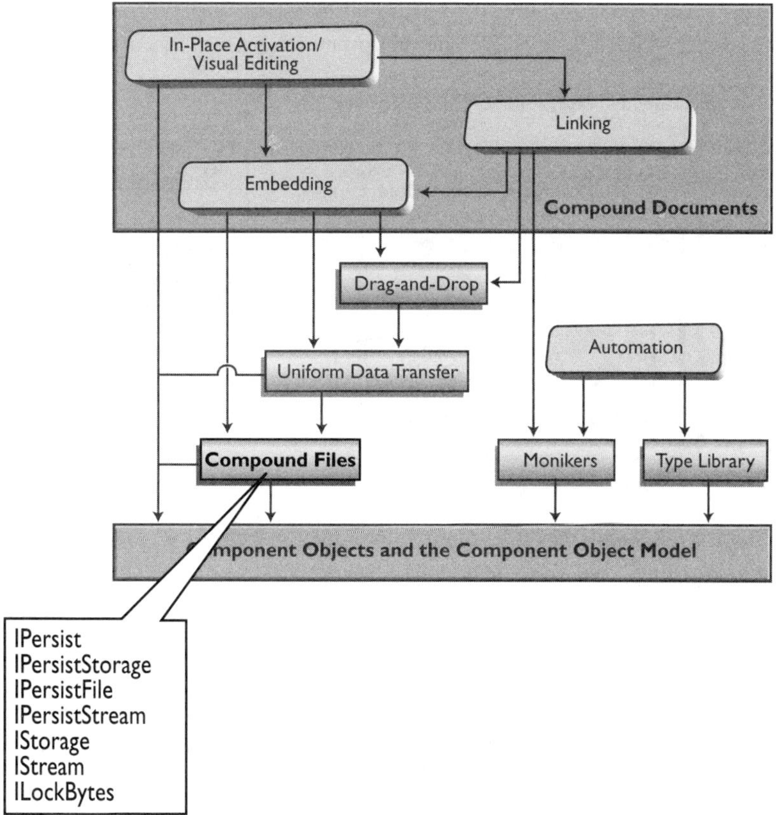

FIGURE 4-1 The COM structured storage stop on our COM technology roadmap

COM structured storage is the model for compound files in the COM architecture. It is also a technology that enables multiple COM objects to store persistent data within a single file. Compound files are necessary for a component architecture where there is persistent (nonvolatile) data. The data is either used by a component or it is used to initialize a component.

A container uses the COM structured storage model when it asks a server object to initialize itself. Complexity increases when the container has more than one server. The data of each of these servers must be maintained separately. A generalized approach to managing data from multiple sources is suggested, but is not required. The COM structured storage model simplifies data management, but it is not required. Figure 4-2 illustrates the complexity of managing nested data structures.

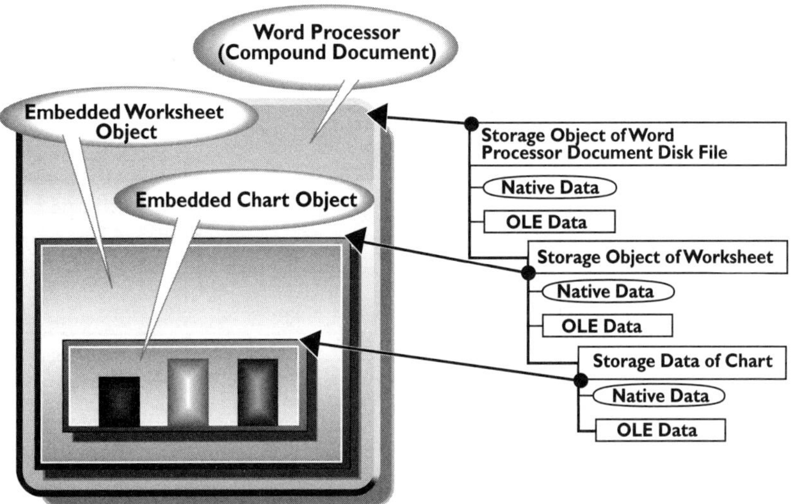

FIGURE 4-2 The complexity of nested data structures

Data comes in two categories. Data can be embedded at the container (client) site or a link may exist to the data source. Commingling data from the container site and the server can create very complex storage issues if the data is stored in flat files.

Managing different types of data is solved with a structured file that is many files in one. Each type of data is assigned to a separate stream within the COM structured storage model. The COM structured storage model isolates the developer from tracking each individual type of data from different sources. Figure 4-2 illustrates the diverse number of streams within a small compound file application.

The complexity of Figure 4-2 is managed with the model of Figure 4-3, which has only four objects. The **LockBytes** object sits between the **RootStorage** object and physical storage or global memory. A **RootStorage** object is the pinnacle object of a compound file structure and may have other storage objects (substorages) and files (streams). Other **Storage** objects and **Stream** objects may be subservient to a **Storage** object. *Streams* are the equivalent of files and *storages* are the equivalent of directories, hence the description, "a file system within a file system."

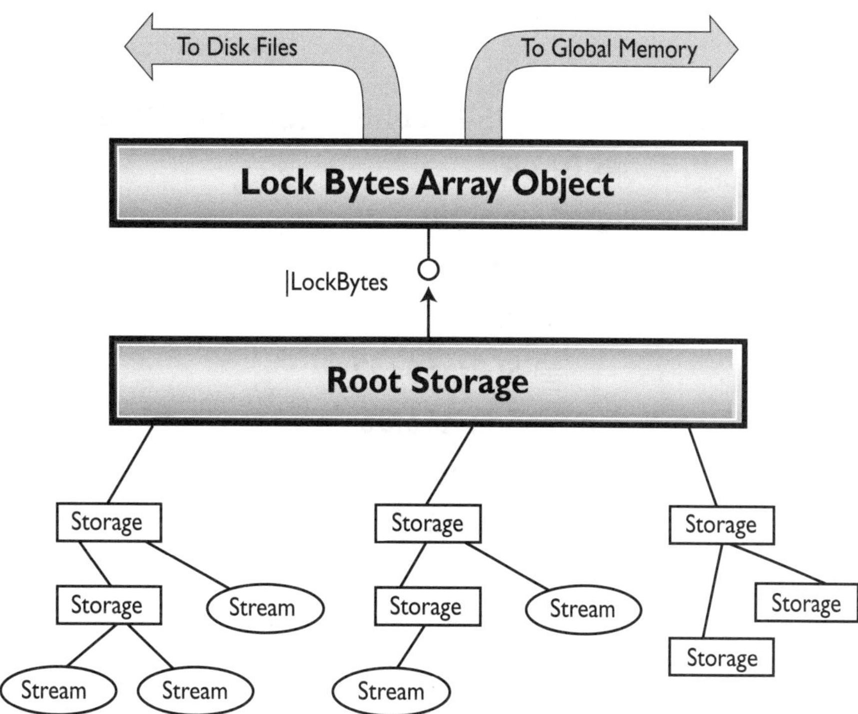

FIGURE 4-3 Managing storages and streams with the COM structured storage model

The **LockBytes** object manages structured storage transparently. It is passive and transparent to the user. The **LockBytes** object is managed by the **ILockBytes** interface, which does not alter data. The **ILockBytes** interface manages a byte array and insulates the developer from the underlying infrastructure issues. The **IStorage** and **IStream** interfaces automatically use this functionality for a compound document that can be disk file or global memory based.

For a more detailed look at ILockBytes, see Chapter 5. This is also where the interaction between the ILockBytes interface for synchronous storage and the IFillLockBytes wrapper for asynchronous storage is illustrated. Asynchronous storage is used by a URL moniker for downloading from the Internet where control is returned to the user before loading is complete.

Figure 4-4 is a peek at the internal structure of a compound document. You can readily identify some components of a compound file. The elements starting with 5 or 6 are streams and part of an OLE Document. The **Book** is the root storage and the **_VBA_Project** is a storage object. **ICompObj** is the CLSID of the object written with **IStorage::SetClass**.

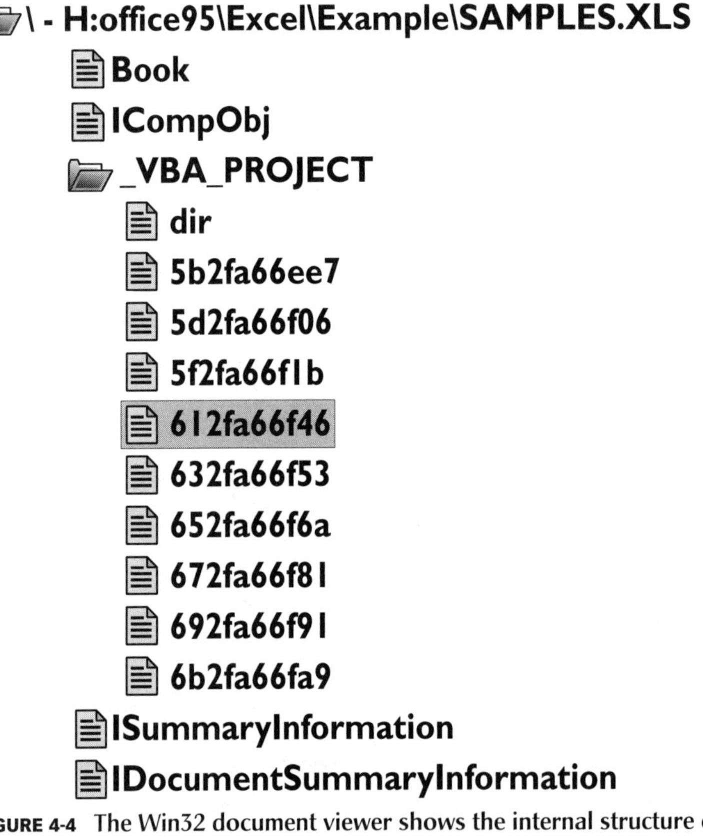

FIGURE 4-4 The Win32 document viewer shows the internal structure of a compound file

Benefits

Structured storage is designed to solve storage problems that do not have a solution in the flat-file models. Compound file benefits include:

- *File system and platform independence* — Compound file systems run on top of existing file systems, making them file-system and platform-independent.

- *Multiple files are encapsulated*—A compound file is externally represented as a single entity. However, within the compound file are many subfiles. This relationship is described as a "file system within a file system," which are discussed in Chapter 5.
- *Giving structure to data without structure*—The concept of streams permits the storing of files that are of arbitrary length. While it is true that other file systems do manage *binary large objects* (BLOBS), these other systems have no generalized tools for supporting BLOBS and the management is always ad hoc.
- *Incremental access*—Structures within a compound file may be loaded and saved individually. The complete compound file need not be loaded or saved.
- *Concurrency is supported*—Multiple users or applications can concurrently read or write information within the same compound file.
- *Transactions are supported*—Users of a compound file can read or write in transacted mode. Changes are buffered and are eventually committed or reverted.
- *Low memory save is supported*—A file save mechanism is supported which requires no additional memory. This allows the user to do a complete save in low memory situations. A traditional save fails because it requires additional overhead memory for the save process.

Features

Access modes, transactioning, element naming, incremental access, and shareability are features of structured storage. Some features have parallels with comparable technologies and function in the expected manner. Not all features have a parallel and the concept of sharing in COM is not based on access privileges, but on marshaling with a proxy.

Access Modes

The access modes for compound files are comparable to traditional file systems. The user specifies the access mode at file open time with one of the following flags. The flag name is descriptive.

STGM_READ, STGM_WRITE, STGM_READWRITE, STGM_SHARE_DENYNONE, STGM_SHARE_DENYREAD, STGM__SHARE_DENYWRITE, STGM_SHARE_EXCLUSIVE, and STGM_CREATE.

Transactioning

Compound files support the concept of transactions. An **IStorage::Commit** only changes data at the next level. This permits a local undo or revert operation. An example of this is **Undo** in Word, which reverts changes that have not yet been saved to a file.

All changes are lost when an object is released and the transaction has not been committed. The issue is to start at the bottom of the hierarchy and commit all transactions.

Doing a revert at the root level is the equivalent of undoing all lower level transactions in the hierarchy. Exiting from Word without a **Save** is such an example. The user is prompted to verify that this is the desired course of action. Once confirmed, all transactions are reverted.

Element naming

There are element-naming conventions for storages and streams. All element names are stored as Unicode on all platforms. The names are limited to thirty-one characters. The exception is the root storage associated with a disk file, which can have a name as long as the file system allows.

A file name can be any character above 32 (an ASCII space), except the characters <.>, <:>, <\>, </>, and <!>. A leading character with a value less than 32 is reserved for internal COM usage. The leading character is binary with the following rules:

- \000, \001, and \002 specify an OLE-managed element.
- Presentation data is marked as \002OlePres<xxx> when *xxx* is between 000 and 999.
- \001Ole contains object information such as linking status.
- \003 marks an element owned by the code that manages the parent storage.
- \004 is used exclusively by the COM structured storage implementation.
- \005 and \006 are used by COM for OLE Documents.
- \007 to \0x1f are reserved for the operating system.

Incremental access

Incremental access is the reading or editing of a single object within the compound file. Opening a Word document does not require the complete document to be loaded. There is the initial overhead of opening the root storage. This is followed by a sequence of **IStorage::OpenStorage** operations to locate the desired stream and a call to **IStorage::OpenStream** once the stream is located. The remainder of the compound file remains unopened.

A portion of a compound file is now open for editing. Editing a compound file leads to fragmentation of the compound file. A partial solution is to call **IStorage::CopyTo,** which will defragment the compound file but not the internal streams. All streams must be rewritten individually to completely defragment the compound file.

Shareable elements

Compound files are shareable across process boundaries. These are not Win32 shared files in global memory, but the use of custom marshaling to share files. The sharing may extend beyond the platform. A proxy and the object work together with entire state data stored on a shared medium such as disk. This improves performance because other components need not load the objects but instead acquire a copy of the current state information.

Storage Objects and IStorage

Storage objects support the concept of a file system within a file system. A storage object is a directory and the streams are individual files. A directory (storage object) can have other storage objects (directories) and files (streams).

StgCreateDocFile creates a root **IStorage** object while an existing compound file is opened with **StgOpenStorage**. The result of either operation is a root **IStorage** pointer. At this point **IStorage::OpenStorage** can be invoked to open an existing substorage. The alternative is to invoke **IStorage::CreateStorage** for a new substorage object. Invoking the **Release** method on a storage object releases memory.

A CLSID can be assigned to storages. This enables containers to find and load the object server that created the data.

The **IStorage** interface inherits **QueryInterface, AddRef,** and **Release** from the **IUnknown** interface. The **IStorage** interface supports the methods shown in Table 4-1.

TABLE 4-1 ISTORAGE METHODS

IStorage Method	*CommandLine*	*Description*
Commit	(None)	Ensures that all changes made to the storage are reflected in the parent storage.
CopyTo	Copy	Copies the entire contents of one storage to another. **CopyTo** is a defragmentation tool for compound files. The output streams are contiguous with no lost space between streams.
CreateStorage	Mkdir, Chdir	Creates and opens a new substorage nested within the existing storage object.
CreateStream	(None)	Creates and opens a stream. Transactions are not supported for stream objects.
DestroyElement	Del, Deltree	Deletes a specified storage or stream. If a substorage is deleted, all elements of the substorage are also destroyed.
EnumElements	Dir	Returns a STATSTG enumerator object, which implements **IEnumSTATSTG.**
MoveElementTo	Copy (+Del)	Copies or moves a substorage or a stream from one storage to another.
OpenStorage	Chdir	Opens an existing storage. Opening the same storage object for the same parent storage object is not permitted.
OpenStream	Copy	Opens an existing stream object. Two instances of the same open stream are not supported. Transactions are not supported for stream objects.
RenameElement	Rename	Renames the specified storage or stream.
Revert	(None)	Discards any transaction related changes to the storage since the last **IStorage::Commit**.
SetClass	(None)	Assigns the specified CLSID to this storage object.
SetElementTimes	(None)	The modification, access, and creation times are set if supported by the underlying file system.
SetStateBits	Attrib	Stores up to 32 bits of state information.
Stat	(Varies)	Returns the STATSTG structure for this storage object.

OleLoad is an API function that loads an object nested within a specified storage object. The advantage of using **OleLoad** is that it is a wrapper function and simplifies the object loading process. **OleLoad** has as call parameters:

- A pointer to a storage object, an **IStorage** instance.
- The IID of the requested interface that the client will use for communicating with this object.
- A pointer to the object's client site.
- A pointer to the newly loaded object.

OleLoad loads a linked or embedded object into memory. It invokes the **IPersistStorage::Load** method; however, the complete load task is somewhat complex and has six processing steps:

1. **OleLoad** calls **OleDoAutoConvert** to see if an auto conversion is necessary.
2. **OleLoad** gets the object CLSID by invoking **IStorage::Stat** on the object.
3. **OleLoad** calls **CoCreateInstance** to create an instance of a handler. The default handler is used when no handler is available. **OleCreateDefaultHandler** creates a default handler.
4. **OleLoad** invokes **IOleObject::SetClientSite** to inform the object of the client site.
5. **IUnknown::QueryInterface** is invoked asking for **IPersistStorage**. If this is successful, **IPersistStorage::Load** is invoked.
6. The client provides the IID of the object interface. **OleLoad** queries the object and returns the requested interface pointer.

OleSave is another helper API function that saves an open storage object in transacted mode. **OleSave** has as call parameters:

- A pointer to the object.
- A pointer to the destination storage object.
- TRUE if the destination storage is the same as the load storage; FALSE otherwise.

OleSave is a wrapper function for the standard COM interfaces. The internal **OleSave** steps include:

1. **OleSave** invokes **IPersistStorage::GetClassID** to get the CLSID.

2. The CLSID is written to the storage object with **WriteClassStg**.
3. **IPersistStorage::Save** is invoked to save the object.
4. **IPersistStorage::Commit** is invoked if there are no errors.

Stream Objects and IStream

The stream object is where the data is stored. Streams are analogous to traditional files and can be in compound documents that are disk- or global memory-based. A storage object may have any number of streams; for the sake of simplicity, however, in Figure 4-2 I've only indicated two streams. One is for native data and the other is for presentation data, which is the user's last view of the data before the object is deactivated. (Data within COM is managed with Uniform Data Transfer using the FORMATEC and STGMEDIUM structures. Data structures and transfer issues are discussed in Chapter 6.) Figure 4-3 illustrates additional structured storage complexity.

Streams do have restrictions. The OLE implementation of the **IStream** interface does not support stream transactions or region locking. The **IStream** methods **LockRegion, UnlockRegion, Commit,** and **Revert,** have no effect in an OLE compound file implementation.

Streams can be marshaled to another process without using global memory. This increases marshaling performance. The only problem is that both processes share the same storage object pointer. A desirable alternative is to clone the stream object and pass the cloned stream pointer to the other process. Both processes now have access to the same stream object with different pointers.

Memory resources are always an issue with large stream objects. Resource allocation problems occur when the stream size exceeds the system heap size, or the system has a memory size of 50MB or less. The system heap is a portion of Windows NT non-paged pool where look-aside lists (temporary buffers of varying sizes) and other temporary memory-resident data storage is maintained. Stream buffers are limited to 512 bytes. The solution is to use **SetSize** to preallocate memory in increments of 512 bytes. Use **VirtualAlloc,** which reserves or commits a region of pages in virtual memory, rather than **GlobalAlloc,** which allocates from the heap. The API call **CreateStreamOnHGlobal** creates an **IStream** object on global memory and returns a pointer to that object.

Creating an **IStream** object in a compound file requires a storage object pointer. **StgCreateDocFile** or **StgOpenStorage** returns a root storage object pointer. Either of these operations results in a root **IStorage** pointer. **IStorage::CreateStorage** can be used to create a new substorage, or an existing storage can be opened with **IStorage::OpenStorage**. The resulting substorage pointer is then used with either **CreateStream** or **OpenStream** to create an **IStream** object.

Invoking the **Release** method on a stream is equivalent to closing a file. The stream object is no longer available.

The **IStream** interface inherits **QueryInterface**, **AddRef**, and **Release** from the **IUnknown** interface and implements these methods:

- *Clone* — Creates a new stream object with its own seek pointer referencing the original data.
- *Commit* — Ensures that transacted mode changes are reflected in the parent object. If the stream is open in direct mode, **IStream::Commit** only flushes the buffers to the next storage level object. Transactions are not supported for streams in the OLE compound file implementation.
- *CopyTo* — Copies a specific number of bytes from one stream object to another stream object.
- *LockRegion* — Locks a specific range of bytes in a stream. Not all file system implementations may support this functionality. **IStream::UnlockRegion** must be invoked for further access. This method is not supported in an OLE compound file implementation
- *Read* — Reads a specific number of bytes from a stream object starting at the current seek pointer. This task is much more complex than it appears. This occurs when **IStream::Read** is invoked by an asynchronous moniker.Monikers are discussed in Chapter 5. For now, just understand that **IStream::Read** can be either synchronous or asynchronous. Synchronous operations return control to the client only after the operation is complete, which is quite unlike an Internet URL Moniker that returns control before the operation is complete.
- *Revert* — **IStream::Revert** discards all stream changes since the last **IStream::Commit**. **IStream::Revert** has no effect on streams opened in direct mode and streams using the OLE compound file implementation.
- *Seek* — Positions a pointer in the stream. This method is not available with an asynchronous moniker except to position back in the *data-push* model.
- *SetSize* — Specifies the new size of the stream in bytes.

- *Stat*—Retrieves the STATSTG structure for the stream.
- *UnlockRegion*—Unlocks a previously locked region in a stream. This method is not supported in an OLE compound file implementation.
- *Write*—Writes a specific number of bytes to a stream.

OleLoadFromStream is an API wrapper function for loading an object from a stream. Its call parameters are:

- A pointer to the source stream.
- The IID of the requested interface that the client will use for communication with this object.
- A storage location pointer.

OleLoadFromStream is a fairly simple interface, but it does have one unique requirement. The object CLSID must immediately precede the object's data in the stream or a NULL is returned as the object pointer. **OleLoadFromStream** encapsulates these steps:

- **ReadClassStm** is invoked to read the CLSID from the stream.
- **OleLoadFromStream** will call **CoCreateInstance** to create an instance of a handler. The default handler is used when no handler is available. **OleCreateDefaultHandler** creates a default handler.
- **IPersistStream::Load** is invoked to read the data.
- An **IStream** pointer is returned.

OleSaveToStream is an API wrapper function that saves an object to a stream. Its call parameters are:

- A pointer to the object that is to be saved in a stream. (A CLSID should precede the data. A NULL is written to the stream when a CLSID doesn't exist.)
- A pointer to the target stream.

OleSaveToStream encapsulates the following steps, simplifying the task of saving a stream object:

- **OleSaveToStream** obtains the CLSID by invoking **IPersistStream::GetClassID**.
- The CLSID is written to the stream with **WriteClassStm**.
- **OleSaveToStream** invokes **IPersistStream::Save** with the *dirty* flag set to TRUE.

LockBytes Object and ILockBytes

The LockBytes object provides a layer between the root storage object and the actual storage medium and is not exposed for default compound file implementations. Optionally, the user can allocate a byte array and then create and open a compound file over the byte array and the **LockBytes** object. Opening or creating a compound file with either a default or a custom implementation is enumerated with:

StgCreateDocFile	Opens a new compound file with a default file-based **LockBytes** object. An **IStorage** pointer is returned. The file may be transacted or direct. Options permit the overwriting of existing files.
StgOpenStorage	Opens an existing compound file and functions in the same manner as **StgCreateDocFile**.
StgCreateDocfileOnILockBytes	Creates a custom compound file implementation consisting of several steps: • Allocates the byte array with **GlobalAlloc**. Do this with care because the space comes from the heap. • Creates an **ILockBytes** object with **CreateILockBytesOnHGlobal** using the memory handle returned by **GlobalAlloc**. An **ILockBytes** interface pointer is returned. • Creates the compound file with **StgCreateDocfileOnILockBytes** using the returned **ILockBytes** interface. • Uses the returned **ILockBytes** pointer to open the file with **StgOpenDocfileOnILockBytes**. • StgOpenDocfileOnILockBytes Opens a compound file that does not reside on the disk with a provided ILockBytes pointer. An **IStorage** pointer is returned.

note **The LockBytes array object is one of three components that defines storage structures. The other two objects are Storage objects and Stream objects. Technically there is a RootObject; however, it could be considered an instance of a Storage object because Storage objects can have subservient Storage objects.**

A call to **StgCreateDocFile** creates an OLE compound-document file containing an **ILockBytes** implementation that associates a byte array with a disk file.

Now the nice part: The **IStream** and **IStorage** interfaces automatically call the **ILockBytes** methods for both types of compound-file storage objects. There is no need to access the **ILockBytes** methods directly.

You may choose to implement your own **ILockBytes** interface. If you do, you should consider custom marshaling by implementing the **IMarshal** interface. When the OLE implementations of the **IStorage** and **IStream** interfaces are marshaled to another process, the **ILockBytes** interface is also automatically marshaled. Implementing your own **IMarshal** interface prevents this automatic marshaling of the **ILockBytes** interface.

In summary, you do not need to call **ILockBytes** interfaces directly. This is done automatically by the OLE implementation of the **IStorage** and **IStream** interfaces. If you do implement your own version of **IlockBytes, StgCreatgeDocfileOnIlockBytes** can be used to create a compound file structure supported by your own **ILockBytes** interface.

The **ILockBytes** interface inherits **QueryInterface, AddRef,** and **Release** from the **IUnknown** interface and supports the following methods:

- *ReadAt* — Reads a fixed number of bytes from an offset in the byte array.
- *WriteAt* — Writes a fixed number of bytes to an offset in the byte array.
- *Flush* — Ensures the flushing of internal buffers to the storage device.
- *SetSize* — Changes the size of the byte array. Callers extending a byte array should not rely on `STG_E_MEDIUMFULL` being returned at the appropriate time because of cache buffering.
- *LockRegion* — Locks a range of bytes on the byte array for write or exclusive access. This function is not available for a global memory implementation.
- *UnlockRegion* — Reverses a previous **LockRegion** call. This function is not available for a global memory implementation.
- *Stat* — Returns a `STATSTG` structure detailing information about the object, which in turn reflects information about the device.

RootStorage Object and IRootStorage

The **RootStorage** object is optional and not required for implementations that are not file based. Obtaining the **IRootStorage** pointer is done with **IStorage::QueryInterface**(*IID_IRootStorage*), which uses the **IStorage** pointer that is returned when the compound file is opened or created.

The **IRootStorage** interface inherits **QueryInterface, AddRef,** and **Release** from the **IUnknown** interface. **IRootStorage::SwitchToFile** is the only method supported by this interface. This method is designed for use in low memory situations and is used as a full save operation on a compound file only after another operation on the compound file has failed because of low memory. It is possible to implement this interface to function as a **SaveAs** operation; however, Microsoft does not guarantee proper operation in future releases.

When a low memory situation occurs the **IStorage::CopyTo** method will probably fail because it requires additional memory. The following scenario will function in a zero-free memory environment:

- Obtain the **IRootStorage** interface with **IStorage::QueryInterface**(*IID_IRootStorage*).
- Create the new file with **IRootStorage::SwitchToFile**(*pszNewFile*). This uses no extra memory and uses the third handle obtained when the file was opened. (Haven't you ever wondered why it took three handles to open a compound file?)
- The last step is to call **IStorage::Commit,** which commits the data and uses no extra memory.

A root storage object is not required for compound document implementations that are not file based. This explains why there is no baseInterface entry in the Registry entry for the **IStorage** interface shown below.

```
HKEY_CLASSES_ROOT\Interface\{0000000B-0000-0000-C000-000000000046} = Istorage

HKEY_CLASSES_ROOT\Interface\{0000000B-0000-0000-C000-000000000046}\NumMethods =
18

HKEY_CLASSES_ROOT\Interface\{0000000B-0000-0000-
C000-000000000046}\ProxyStubClsid = {00000314-0000-0000-C000-000000000046}
```

IPersist

IPersist is the base interface for all **IPersist**-type interfaces. It supports the required **IUnknown** methods **QueryInterface, AddRef,** and **Release**. **GetClassID** is the only private method of this interface.

IPersistFile

The **IPersistFile** interface is usually implemented by the object application, but it can be implemented by container applications. It is the mechanism for loading or saving documents to or from disk files. The client application is responsible for opening or closing the file. Binding a linked object is the normal use of this interface. This is a link to an embedded object when the application is a container.

The **IPersistFile** interface inherits **QueryInterface, AddRef,** and **Release** from the **IUnknown** interface. It also inherits **GetClassID** from the **IPersist** interface. The **IPersistFile** interface also supports these methods:

- *IsDirty* — A flag is set. The client should call **Save** before releasing the object.
- *Load* — Loads an object into memory from an absolute path. **IMoniker::BindToObject** invokes this method (see Chapter 5).
- *Save* — Saves an object to storage. This includes all nested objects. The container must invoke **IPersistFile::SaveCompleted** after this operation is completed.
- *SaveCompleted* — The container has completed the file save with **IPersist::Save**.
- *GetCurFile* — Obtains the absolute path of the file associated with the document, or the default filename prompt if no file is available.
- *LoadFSP* — Loads a document but does not show it to the user.
- *SaveFSP* — Saves the document. If the file specification parameter (FSP) is null, then the operation is a file save. A non-NULL value for the FSP parameter is **FileSaveAS** or **FileSaveCopyAs**. The container must invoke the function **IPersistFile::SaveCompletedFSP** after the original save is complete.
- *SaveCompletedFSP* — The container has completed the file save with **IPersist::SaveFSP**.
- *GetCurFSP* — Returns the file specification name associated with the object or the default file name prompt.

IPersistMemory

An object implements the **IPersistMemory** interface to save itself in memory. The container invokes **IPersistMemory::Load** or **IPersistMemory::Save** to load or unload the object.

The **IPersistMemory** interface inherits **QueryInterface, AddRef,** and **Release** from the **IUnknown** interface. It also inherits **GetClassID** from the **IPersist** interface. **IPersistMemory** supports the following methods, which are functionally equivalent to the methods of the **IPersistStream** interface:

- *IsDirty* — A flag is set.
- *Load* — Initializes an object previously stored with **IPersistMemory::Save.**
- *Save* — Saves the current state of an object to a stream object. This call supports a dirty flag.
- *GetMaxSize* — Determines the maximum size for usage with **IPersistMemory::Save.**
- *InitNew* — Initializes the object to a default state.

IPersistMoniker

IPersistMoniker is designed for asynchronous-aware objects. Synchronous objects use the **IMoniker::BindToObject** interface for binding the **IpersistFile, IpersistStreamInit,** or **IPersistStorage** interfaces. The difference in techniques is that the **IPersistMoniker** implementation allows control to be given to the object being instantiated rather than binding its persistent data. This technique is used for binding URL monikers in the background after the application has regained control. The **IPersistMoniker** interface cannot be used for synchronous binding.

The **IPersistMoniker** interface does not include an **InitNew** method for initializing an object. The **IpersistStorageInit, IpersistMemory,** or **IPersistPropertybag** method **InitNew** must be used to initialize an object.

The **IPersistMoniker** interface inherits **QueryInterface, AddRef,** and **Release** from the **IUnknown** interface. It also inherits **GetClassID** from the **IPersist** interface. The **IPersistMoniker** interface supports these methods:

- *IsDirty* — A flag is set.
- *Load* — Loads an object using a specified moniker.
- *Save* — Saves the object specifying a destination moniker.

- *SaveCompleted*—Notifies the object that the save operation is complete.
- *GetCurMoniker*—Retrieves the moniker for the object's persistent state.

IPersistPropertyBag

The **IPersistPropertyBag** interface is used to save and load individual object properties. Implementers of the **IPersistPropertyBag** interface are free to store the information in any manner the application desires. It could be name/value pairs as text strings that a Visual Basic program stores. A natural implementation of this interface is a save-as-text operation. The object gives the container the format choice while retaining the decision as to which properties should be saved.

IErrorLog is a companion interface to the **IPropertyBag** interface, which does the actual storage and retrieval of property values, as shown in Figure 4-5. It is used for the logging of errors on a per property basis.

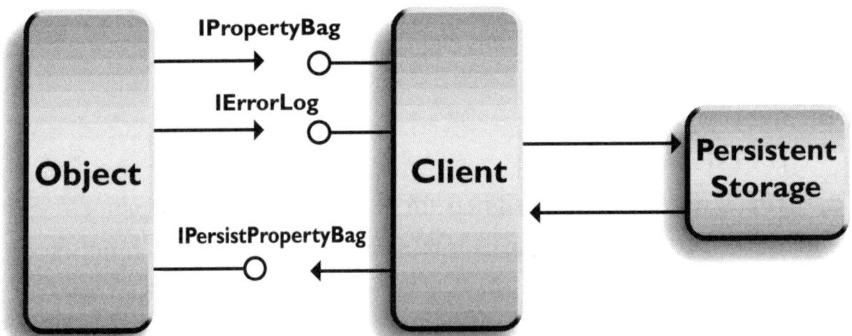

FIGURE 4-5 The IErrorLog is a companion interface to the IPropertyBag interface.

The **IPersistPropertyBag** interface inherits **QueryInterface, AddRef,** and **Release** from the **IUnknown** interface. It also inherits **GetClassID** from the **IPersist** interface. The **IPersistPropertyBag** interface supports these methods:

- *InitNew*—Initializes the property bag.
- *Load*—The container uses this method to load the control's properties.
- *Save*—Used by the container to save the object's properties.

IpersistStorage

Object handlers use the IPersistStorage interface or object applications to support container simple-stream objects such as monikers (see Chapter 5, Monikers).

The **IPersistStorage** interface inherits **QueryInterface, AddRef,** and **Release** from the **IUnknown** interface. It also inherits **GetClassI** from the **IPersist** interface. The **IPersistStorage** interface supports these methods:

- *IsDirty* —A flag is set.
- *InitNew*—Initializes the storage object
- *Load*—Loads an object into memory for the container or loads the object in running state for an object handler.
- *Save*—Saves an object to storage, including all nested objects.
- *SaveCompleted*—Terminates the *no scribble storage* mode or the *hands off* mode created by invoking **IPersistStorage::HandsOffStorage** You can think of this function as releasing a lock.
- *HandsOffStorage*—Sets the state for **IPersistStorage::Save**. Think of it as an interlock until the save function is completed.

IpersistStream

The**IPersistStream** interface is used to support simple stream objects such as monikers. The **IPersistStream** parameters are unique and are only valid during the call in which they are passed. The object does not retain them after the call is completed. An OLE container with embedded or linked objects will use the **IPersistStorage** interface instead of this interface.

The **IPersistSteam** interface inherits **QueryInterface, AddRef,** and **Release** from the **IUnknown** interface. It also inherits **GetClassID** from the **IPersist** interface. The **IPersistStream** stream supports these methods:

- *IsDirty*—A flag is set.
- *Load*—Initializes an object previously stored with **IPersistStream::Save**.
- *Save*—Saves the current state of an object to a stream object. This call supports a dirty flag.
- *GetMaxSize*—Determines the maximum size for usage with **IPersistStream::Save**.

IPersistStreamInit

The **IPersistStreamInit** interface replaces the **IPersistStream** interface. It is equivalent to the **IPersistStream** interface with the additional method **InitNew,** which initializes an object to a default state.

IOleCache2 (caching) cannot be supported when **IPersistStreamInit** is exposed because **IOleCache2** requires the **IPersistStorage** interface. The alternative is to render the object with **IDataObject::GetData,** which is discussed in Chapter 6.

The **IPersistSteamInit** interface inherits **QueryInterface, AddRef,** and **Release** from the **IUnknown** interface. It also inherits **GetClassID** from the **IPersist** interface. The **IPersistStream** stream supports these methods:

- *IsDirty* — A flag is set.
- *Load* — Initializes an object previously stored with **IPersistStream::Save**.
- *Save* — Saves the current state of an object to a stream object. This call supports a dirty flag.
- *GetMaxSize* — Determines the maximum size for usage with **IPersistStream::Save**.
- *InitNew* — Initializes an object to a default state.

Visual Basic and Structured Storage

Microsoft Visual Basic (VB) supports both the Win32 and Win16 APIs; however, this is not sufficient to support COM structured storage. COM is implemented with interfaces and pointers and not API calls. COM, as implemented within VB, is limited since VB cannot be the recipient of pointers even though VB supports pointer passing.

Desaware markets the StorageTools product, which is a VB control. The control manages the necessary pointer passing and control for compound file implementations from within VB. The product includes both a 16- and a 32-bit control that support the creation of compound files with storage objects and streams, as illustrated in Listing 4-1.

The product has several other key features that are of value to the VB developer. One example is an object browser written in VB. Compound file object browsers from a Microsoft System Development Kit (SDK) are now relics of the past. Another key feature of the StorageTools product is a Registry editor implemented within VB.

You'll find an evaluation copy of StorageTools 2.0 on the CD-ROM that accompanies this book. Please feel free to experiment with the product.

LISTING 4-1 Creating Streams and Storages with StorageTools from Desaware.

```
'(C) 1999 Bruce T. Prendergast
' DBA Prendergast Consulting
' DBA PCS
' IDG Books Worldwide ISBN 0-7645-3314-2
'
' The example is from the Desaware StorageTools 1.0
' product and is used with the permission of Desaware.
' An evaluation copy of StorageTools 2.0 is included
' on the CD-ROM that accompanies this book.
'
Option Explicit

' This will create a file with information stored in
' a non-trivial structure. The file will look like
' this:
'       test.stg
'             |
'             |- Section_Details
'             |           |
'             |           |- name
'             |           `- weight
'             |
'             `-Section_Other
'                         |
'                         |- zip
'                         `- phone
'
' This example does not include error checking.
' Error checking should always be provided in any
' application. The StorageTools product from Desaware
' includes examples of error checking.
'
```

```
' Declare the objects.  You could have objects for
' every single stream or storage, but that
' would waste memory (but not file handles).
'

Dim RootStorage As Object
Dim strg As Object
Dim strm As Object


Private Sub Command1_Click()
'
' Put and Get accept only variants.
'
  Dim varr As Variant ' Put and Get accept only variants.
'
' Create the compound file.
'
  Set RootStorage = DwStorage1.CreateStorageFile("c:\test.stg", _
    STG_CREATE Or STG_READWRITE Or STG_DIRECT Or STG_SHARE_EXCLUSIVE)
'
' Create one of the storages (the objects that act like directories)
'
  Set strg = RootStorage.CreateStorage("Section_Details", STG_CREATE _
    Or STG_DIRECT Or STG_SHARE_EXCLUSIVE Or STG_READWRITE)
'
' Create a stream (the objects that act like files)
'
  Set strm = strg.CreateStream("name", STG_CREATE Or STG_DIRECT Or _
    STG_SHARE_EXCLUSIVE Or STG_READWRITE)
'
' Put information into the stream. The information
' is split to illustrate writing multiple times into
' a stream.  VariantPut is used in order to save the
' data type, which means there is no guessing when
' later reading the data.
'
```

```
  varr = "John"
'
' "0" to start at the beginning of the stream.
'
  strm.VariantPut 0, varr
  varr = "Doe"
'
' "-1" : to write to current seek pointer location.
' The constant "STG_STREAM_SEEK_DONTMOVE" serves
' the same purpose.
'
  strm.VariantPut -1, varr
'
' Flush the stream buffer
'
  strm.Flush 0
'
' Create another stream in the first storage.
'
  Set strm = strg.CreateStream("weight", STG_CREATE Or STG_DIRECT _
    Or STG_SHARE_EXCLUSIVE Or STG_READWRITE)
  varr = 150
  strm.VariantPut 0, varr
  strm.Flush 0
'
' Permanently save the data in the storage buffer.
'
  strg.Commit 0
'
' Create another storage in the file.
'
  Set strg = RootStorage.CreateStorage("Section_Other", STG_CREATE _
    Or STG_DIRECT Or STG_SHARE_EXCLUSIVE Or STG_READWRITE)
'
' Create a stream for the second storage.
'
```

```
  Set strm = strg.CreateStream("zip", STG_CREATE Or STG_DIRECT Or _
    STG_SHARE_EXCLUSIVE Or STG_READWRITE)
  varr = 20910
  strm.VariantPut 0, varr
  strm.Flush 0
'
' Create the last stream.
'
  Set strm = strg.CreateStream("phone", STG_CREATE Or STG_DIRECT Or _
    STG_SHARE_EXCLUSIVE Or STG_READWRITE)
  varr = "(909) 555-1234"
  strm.VariantPut 0, varr
  strm.Flush 0

  strg.Commit 0
'
' Commit all changes to the file.
'
  RootStorage.Commit 0
'
' Release memory
'
  Set strm = Nothing
  Set strg = Nothing
  Set RootStorage = Nothing
End Sub
```

Key Point Summary

- The COM structured storage model is a file system within a file system. Storages are equivalent to directories and streams are equivalent to files.
- Compound files are the implementation of the COM structured storage model.

- Transactions are not supported for compound files. The Commit method exists; however, compound documents cannot be locked.
- The COM structured storage model supports the concept of persistence.
- Compound files and streams are suited for fragmented data collection or for real-time data collection.
- A compound file system based on the COM structured storage model can be implemented in either global memory or on disk.

Applying What You've Learned

Structured storage has roots in COM. It almost has blossomed into an independent technology. Structured storage supports the concept of a compound file, which is loosely termed a "file system within a file system."

Instant Assessment

1. What is the difference between structured storage and compound files?
2. Name the four objects of structured storage.
3. Which interface uses the **ILockBytes** interface?
4. Are there any restrictions on the **ILockBytes** Interface? If there are, what are they?
5. What is the purpose of the one **IRootStorage** method?
6. Name two issues when marshaling a stream object to another process.
7. What are the **IStream** interface limitations?
8. What is the role of **IPersistMoniker**?
9. Compare the role of **IPersistMoniker** and persistent data as compared to **IMoniker::BindToObject** and persistent data.
10. Describe using the **IPersistPropertyBag** interface
11. What is the primary use of **IpersistStream, IpersistStorage,** and **IPersistMemory**?
12. What valuable service does **IStorage::CopyTo** perform besides the utilitarian role of copying a storage object?

For answers to the Instant Assessment Questions, see Appendix B.

Lab Exercise

Developers are always faced with advances in technology. The issues raised by technological advances are to first understand the new technology and then to evaluate current applications for possible inclusion of the new technology. There also are ancillary issues such as whether the technology is stable and what is its impact on current production. The technology may be attractive, but the developers often overlook the issue of what are the benefits to the organization.

Lab 4.12 *Converting applications to the structured storage model*

New technology is directly related to Total Ownership Cost (TOC). These steps will facilitate evaluating new technology for possible inclusion in the enterprise. We'll use structured storage as a candidate technology for inclusion within the enterprise. These steps can serve as a guide for the evaluation of new technology.

1. *Understand the new technology*. There cannot be a comparative evaluation without a thorough understanding of the technology. Points to consider in the evaluation might be:

   Is this technology new? New technology is error prone and is not always a candidate worthy of including in the enterprise.

   Are other corporations using the technology? Is there a history? Being a technology pioneer is not desirable.

   Is this type of technology common in this type of business? What are the probabilities of a successful installation? Have other enterprises attempted to implement this technology and failed? What were the reasons for failure?

2. *Identify new technology candidates*. Since the candidate technology is structured storage, evaluate your current systems in terms of the storage structures used. Consider the feasibility and possibility of converting qualifying existing systems to the COM structured storage model. Remember that transactions are supported for compound documents, but not for streams within the compound document.

   Possible candidates to consider are applications with numerous small files. These files can be combined within a single compound file. Other candidates are data files that are shared. Microsoft Word, Excel, and Access are tools that currently share data and use compound files. Can your compound file candidate use a standard tool?

3. *Identify technology benefits*. What about special features such as a file save in a zero-free memory environment? Your organization may have thousands of desktop systems with limited memory. Can this feature be a benefit? Construct a list of all accrued benefits. Some may be intangible.
4. *Technology stability*. What is the vendor reputation for technology upgrades? It's not practical to upgrade ten thousand desktops every year.
5. *Organizational impact*. This issue is a major factor. Does the new technology require additional user training? Are users willing to accept a change? Do the users perceive a benefit in the technology?
6. *Implementation costs*. A simple rule of thumb is that an implementation or deployment will cost double the expected costs. Identify all direct costs. Indirect costs may include:

   The cost of running two systems in parallel during testing. These costs should include the cost of additional equipment plus the cost of temporary staff, since data is entered twice during parallel testing.

   Estimate lost productivity as the users learn to use the new technology.

   Estimate lost productivity when the new system fails.

   Estimate lost productivity during the design phase as users are queried about their needs and expectations for the new technology.
7. *Quantify the benefits*. The costs are known. Assign values to the benefits. It's simply a matter of subtracting the costs from the benefits. When there's a major benefit, do the implementation. A ten or twenty percent gain in productivity can be meaningless because the costs are only estimated and will be at least double the original expectations. Benefits and costs are amortized over a period and a payback must be realized before the next technology upgrade occurs. In other words, the amortized payback period cannot exceed the system upgrade cycle, which means that complete payback must occur before the next version of the technology is released.
8. *Probability of Success*. Assign a probability of success. What are the consequences of failure? If the project were to fail, are the consequences tolerable? Assuming that the project fails, will the cost of failure be significantly greater than the perceived benefits? Assuming that there is a twenty-five percent chance of failure, failing incurs the failure costs versus a seventy-five percent chance of success, which reaps the benefits.
9. *Cheat a bit*. Build the cost of failure in as an indirect cost. If the benefits far outweigh the direct costs, indirect costs, and the cost of failure, then the project is a go. The bottom line is that there must be a compelling need for the new technology.

Lab 4.13 *Visual Basic controls and the IPropertyBag interface*

We'll add the **IPropertyBag** interface to a Visual Basic control, which will provide the property persistence for an ActiveX control. The **WriteProperties** and **ReadProperties** methods of an ActiveX control use a property bag as parameter. The steps below detail the construction of a client and a control that illustrate implementing persistence for control properties.

1. Start a standard Visual Basic .EXE application.
2. Name the form module as *Teller*.
3. Place a text box on the form with the name *txtInput*.
4. Place another text box on the form with the name *txtBalance*. Set the **Enable** property of this control to FALSE.
5. Place a command button on the form with the name *cmdDeposit*. Change the caption of this control to the *Deposit*.
6. Place another command button on the form with the name *cmdWithdrawal*. Change the caption of this control to the *Withdrawal*.
7. From the **Project** menu, select *Add User Control*.
8. Click OK and change the control name to *Bank* in the **Properties** window.
9. Set the control **BorderStyle** to *1-Fixed Single*. Normally this isn't necessary; however, we want to set the **Balance** property to a specific value after the control is placed on the form.
10. Enter the following code in the Declarations section of the user control.

```
'(C) 1999 Bruce T. Prendergast
' DBA Prendergast Consulting
' DBA PCS
' IDG Books Worldwide ISBN 0-7645-3314-2
'
Option Explicit
Private m_Balance As Variant

Public Property Let Balance(ByVal varInput As Variant)
  m_Balance = varInput
  If CanPropertyChange("Balance") Then
    PropertyChanged "Balance"
    MsgBox "Notification occurred"
  Else
```

```
    MsgBox "Unable to change property"
  End If
End Property

Public Property Get Balance() As Variant
  Balance = m_Balance
End Property

Private Sub UserControl_InitProperties()
  MsgBox "InitProperties"
End Sub

Private Sub UserControl_ReadProperties(PropBag As PropertyBag)
  MsgBox "Attempting to Read Properties"
  With PropBag
    m_Balance = .ReadProperty("Balance")
    MsgBox "Reading Properties"
  End With
End Sub

Private Sub UserControl_WriteProperties(PropBag As PropertyBag)
  MsgBox "Writing Properties"
  With PropBag
    .WriteProperty "Balance", m_Balance
  End With
End Sub
```

11. Close out the code window of the user control designer.
12. When the user control form is visible select TOOLS ⇨ PROCEDURE ATTRIBUTES.
13. Verify that the name is *Balance*.
14. Enter a description if desired.
15. Select ADVANCED>.
16. Set the **Procedure ID** combo box to *(Default)*.
17. Set the **Procedure Category** combo box to *Data*.

18. Close out the user control designer. The user control will remain *greyed* on the toolbar until the user control designer is closed.
19. After the user control designer is closed, click the user control on the toolbar and paint the user control on the **Teller** form.
20. Select the user control on the form, go to the properties window for the user control, set **Balance** to *600* and change the control name to *Bank*. (Visual Basic changed the name to *Bank1* when the control was painted on the form.)
21. Enter the following code in the **Declarations** section of the *Teller* form.

```
'(C) 1999 Bruce T. Prendergast
' DBA Prendergast Consulting
' DBA PCS
' IDG Books Worldwide ISBN 0-7645-3314-2
'
Option Explicit
Private Sub cmdDeposit_Click()
  Bank.Balance = Val(Bank.Balance) + Val(txtInput)
  txtBalance = Bank.Balance
End Sub

Private Sub cmdWithdrawal_Click()
  Bank.Balance = Val(Bank.Balance) - Val(txtInput)
  txtBalance = Bank.Balance
End Sub

Private Sub Form_Load()
  txtBalance = Bank.Balance
End Sub
```

22. Start the application. *600* should initially appear in the **txtBalance** control. Enter *100* into the **txtInput** control and click the **cmdDeposit** command button. *700* should now appear in the **txtBalance** control. Congratulations. You've just implemented a control with a persistent property and updated that property.

CHAPTER

5

Monikers

About Chapter 5

The next stop on our tour of the COM architecture is binding components with *monikers*. As the COM roadmap in Figure 5-1 shows, we're gradually moving upward in functionality. It is hard to tell which portion of the COM technology represents the cornerstone, but binding with monikers wins the prize in my book. A component architecture requires a connection mechanism, which monikers provide.

Monikers are names that can describe the result of a query, a range of cells in a spreadsheet, or a paragraph in a document. They are persistent, intelligent names. Different moniker classes deal with different names, and they encapsulate a name and the intelligence to work with that name behind the polymorphic **IMoniker** interface. A moniker is an abstraction of the COM object connection mechanism.

A moniker has different representations. The physical representation of a moniker is that of a path, while the logical representation is that of an object with intelligence. Needless to say, there's quite a bit under the hood. This chapter provides the *why, when,* and *how* of binding components with monikers.

I've also tried to illuminate the operations of binding a URL moniker, as the Internet is almost everywhere. Monikers are commonplace in the Internet and every Web page is bound with a URL moniker.

Why a Moniker?

Tags are attached to entities in an object-oriented world. An action has a tag (*name* if you wish, or *method* if you purport to be programmer), and the data upon which the action operates also has a tag. The action may be anything you wish, and many actions do not have data on which to operate. Balancing your checkbook at the end of each month is an action that uses the data of your checkbook stubs and the bank statement.

A characteristic of COM is that instances of an object are not named. Yes, you use the class identifier (CLSID) to request instantiation of an object with **CoCreateInstance;** instantiation of the object, however, is not direct. A pointer to the object is returned, not a name. Technically, it is possible to instantiate an object directly, but this requires that every object requesting instantiation of another object must be aware of all the minutiae required to instantiate the requested object. The moniker solves two problems for the requesting object. It shields the requesting object from the details of instantiation and solves the additional problem of instantiating an object without actually knowing the object name.

Describing a moniker can be put in simpler terms by considering your car as a component object model. Components include such items as the battery, ignition coil, and starter motor, all of which are encapsulated within an assembly, euphemistically called a car. Individual operations are shielded from the vehicle operator. Starting your car means supplying electricity to the starter motor, timing a spark, and supplying gasoline.

These are all packaged behind a moniker called the ignition switch position. The vehicle operator requests an instantiation of the engine running by positioning the ignition switch to the starting position. The battery instantiates the starter motor. Spark is induced as the motor turns, gasoline ignites, and the engine starts. After the engine has started, the starter motor stops because it is no longer needed.

The same is true with a moniker. The moniker disappears after the object is instantiated. Both the ignition switch position and the starter motor are agents to start the engine. Once the gasoline ignites, the engine is started and there is no further need for either agent. A moniker is an agent that connects spreadsheet cells to your Word document. The moniker disappears after the connection is established.

A moniker uses persistent data to instantiate your spreadsheet rows. That data is no longer needed after the connection is established. In the same manner, the intelligence in your car is the connection of the battery, ignition switch, and starter motor to a specific switch position. That switch position is no longer needed after the car starts.

Naming and Binding with Monikers

A moniker is a conceptual connection mechanism to an object. It is often referred to as an *alias,* but this definition is too simple. A *moniker* is an object with a persistent name with intelligence that supports the **IMoniker** interface. I cheated a bit in Chapter 2 where I presented the dialog for activating servers without mentioning monikers. Monikers are essential to the COM object activation mechanism. We know so far that an interface is an object that isolates the client from implementation details. Monikers are also objects that isolate the client from object connection or activation details. Monikers complete the basic COM architecture with the client now isolated from both implementation and connection details.

Monikers have different sources: a method call may return a moniker, an API call may create a moniker, or the moniker may be represented by a string value. String values are the most flexible form of moniker with the user providing the *display name*. A case in point of a user-supplied display name is the Uniform Resource Locator (URL) that a user supplies to an Internet browser. Another example of a display name is a Microsoft Excel spreadsheet with an optional row and column parameter. **IMoniker::GetDisplayName** returns the display name of a moniker that can then be used to create a composite moniker. *Binding* is a process of locating and loading executable code. The **IMoniker** interface resolves a moniker to an object pointer that is returned to the client.

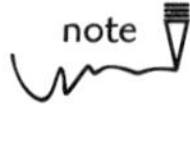

Because the IMoniker interface inherits from IPersistStream interface, which in turn inherits from Istream, IMoniker understands how to store and retrieve monikers that manage a stream.

Let's make a thumbnail sketch of the binding process. We'll take a closer look at **IMoniker::BindToObject** after we deal with several architectural issues of monikers.

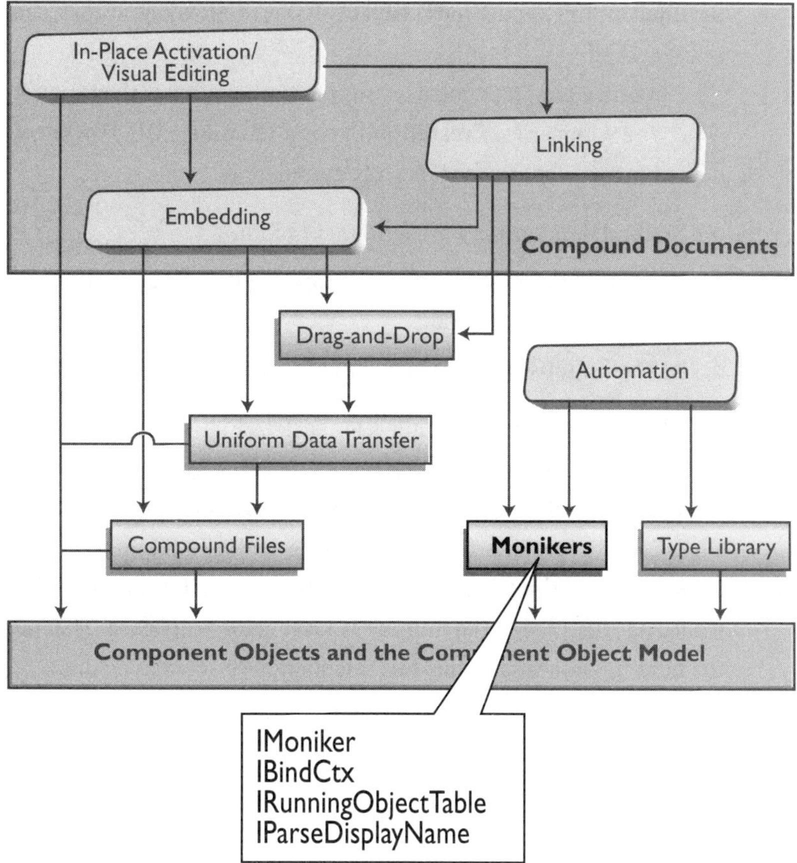

FIGURE 5-1 Visiting Monikers on our COM technology sojourn

The moniker-binding process starts with the requester establishing a binding context by calling **CreateBindCtx**. This creates a binding context and the interface **IBindCtx** becomes available. The next step is to declare the binding options with a call to **IBindCtx::SetBindOptions**. The third step is the client calling **MkParseDisplayName** with the supplied display name. The last step is passing the bind context parameters to **IMoniker::BindToObject** for binding. After the binding operation is complete, the bind context and the moniker are released by calling **IUnknown::Release,** which corresponds with our automobile ignition switch discussed previously. The moniker and binding context no longer exist; however, a new object is instantiated and available for client services.

Windows NT 4.0 introduced the new API function **CoGetObject** that simplifies the binding process by encapsulating **CreateBindCtx, MkParseDisplayName,**

SetBindOptions, and **BindToObject**. The **CoGetObject** architecture is illustrated in Figure 5-2.

Another binding choice for simple applications is the function **BindMoniker,** which is a wrapper for **CreateBindCtx** and **IMoniker::BindToObject**. The developer now has three choices for binding a moniker:

- Use **BindMoniker** for simple moniker binding.
- Call each of the required moniker binding interface functions individually for custom moniker binding.
- Use the **CoGetObject** API supplying the optional bind parameters.

Let's pause a moment and refer back to Figure 2-4 of Chapter 2, which illustrates control flow for instantiating an object. Figure 2-4 is early in the book and intentionally vague. Figure 5-2 shows the **CoGetObject** API apparently referencing the **IClassFactory** interface indirectly through the **IMoniker** interface. This is not a reference and the **IMoniker** interface is only binding the **IClassFactory** interface, while the client is referencing the **IClassFactory** interface. The individual steps in the binding process are numbered sequentially.

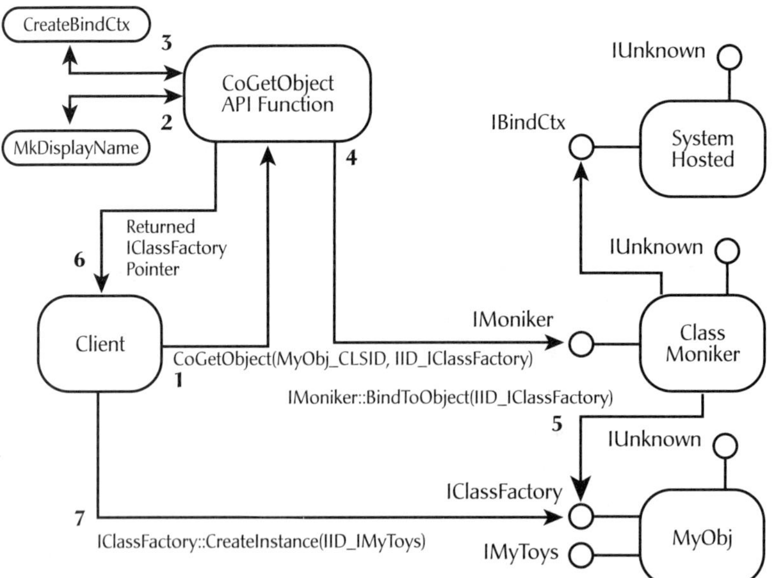

FIGURE 5-2 The CoGetObject binding process

Early and Late Binding

This is the *when* of binding. *Early binding* occurs during object compilation (object time), as opposed to binding at runtime, which is late binding. Early binding is done by a developer, while *late binding* is done by the user, and may depend upon the context of the application. In general, late binding fosters the Microsoft "docu-centric" approach to work, while early binding is often "application-centric." The user only deals with issues relating to the problem at hand with a "docu-centric" application. This is in contrast to "application-centric" applications where the user must address both problem-related issues and application infrastructure issues.

Binding types may be categorized as follows:

- A virtual table (vtable) is early binding.
- Dispinterface is late binding.
- A registered type library is required for early binding.
- Dynamic marshaling is required for late binding.

Vtables are addresses, and address pointers do not exist until objects are running. Thus, early binding on a vtable can only occur if the appropriate servers are already running along with the required proxy and stub software (assuming the object does not use the **IDispatch** interface).

Late binding is flexible and easy to use; early binding (compile time) is "type safe" and much faster. The compiler verifies data types during early binding, hence the term "type safe." Late binding depends upon client choices or client-supplied data and is not "type safe."

A dual interface simplifies early binding. Early binding is possible in Visual Basic (VB) by adding a reference to an object via the references dialog box and then declaring a variable as a specific object type instead of **As Object**.

The code fragments below illustrate the difference between early and late binding. The binding process doesn't commence in the first example until the **Set** statement is executed. The object in the second example is recognized at load time.

```
Private Sub Late_Binding()
  Dim MyWD As Object
  Set MyWD = CreateObject("word.basic")
  MyWD.Visible = True
```

```
  Exit Sub
End Sub
Private Sub Early_Binding()
  Dim MyWD As WordBasic
  Set MyWD = CreateObject("word.basic")
  MyWD.Visible = True
  Exit Sub
End Sub
```

Clients have four techniques for acquiring monikers and all involve late binding, or binding at execution time.

- *Enable Links from Insert Objects* — A moniker is created when an **Insert Dialog** box is used and *Enable Links* is checked on the **Insert Object** dialog box. An example is the *Object* of the Word **Insert** menu.
- *Enable Linking from Clipboard and Drag and Drop Operations* — This is more of a programming issue of enabling links in the FORMATETC structure.
- *Paste Link and PasteSpecial Commands* — These are common entries of an **Edit** menu with Word being a good example. A paste link function is performed.
- *Drag and Drop Linking Feedback* — Another programming issue where the **IDropTarget::Drop** function looks to see if both the Shift and Ctrl keys are pressed. If they are, a paste link action is performed.

Late binding is the preferred choice for a tiered component architecture. That is, client applications need not be recompiled for every design change.

Performance is also an issue. The sequence:

```
Dim myObj as Project1.Checkbook
. . .
Set myObj = New Project1.Checkbook
```

makes two server trips while the sequence:

```
Dim myObj as New Project1.Checkbook
. . .
Set myObj = Project1.Checkbook
```

makes only one trip to the server.

Moniker Types

Monikers come in many flavors. There are base types, decomposition types, and synthetic types (which are only used to resolve local syntax issues). Figure 5-3 illustrates a composite moniker. The following list describes the moniker types:

- *File Moniker* — A path in a file system. A file moniker is created with **CreateFileMoniker**. Only a file moniker and an item moniker can be persisted.
- *Class Moniker* — Represent an object class and bind the class object to the class for which it was created. Each class has a GUID as a class name and a class moniker is created with **CreateClassMoniker** from the class name. An example is:

```
"clsid:00020841-0000-0000-C000-000000000046:"
```

- *Item Moniker* — Identifies objects in a container. The object may be smaller than a file, such as a pseudo-object, which is only a portion of an object. Item monikers can be persisted and are created with **CreateItemMoniker**. Item monikers are illustrated in Figure 5-3.
- *Generic Composite Moniker* — Two or more monikers of an arbitrary type that are combined together. This class of monikers is created with **CreateGenericComposite**. A generic composite moniker is represented with a class moniker (GUID) concatenated with one or more item monikers. An example of a composite moniker using the item monikers of Figure 5-3 is represented by:

```
    "clsid:00020841-0000-0000-c000-
000000000046:!Sheet1!R1C1:R100C10"
```

- *Antimonikers* — The inverse of an item, file, or pointer moniker. Antimonikers are used in a relative path construction where the moniker to the left of the antimoniker must be annihilated. An antimoniker construct has a form similar to \..\. Antimonikers are created with **CreateAntiMoniker**. An antimoniker neutralizes the left context moniker.
- *Pointer Moniker* — A temporary moniker that functions as a pointer to a persistent moniker. The function of a pointer moniker varies depending upon the context. Pointer monikers are created with **CreatePointerMoniker**.

In essence, pointer monikers wrap real pointers and are not bindable. The client treats a pointer moniker as any other moniker and when the client calls **IMoniker::BindToObject,** no check is made on the Running Object Table (ROT, see the section below, "IRunningObjectTable"). Instead the moniker code calls **IUnknown::QueryInterface** directly using the **IUnknown** interface pointer stored within the ROT.

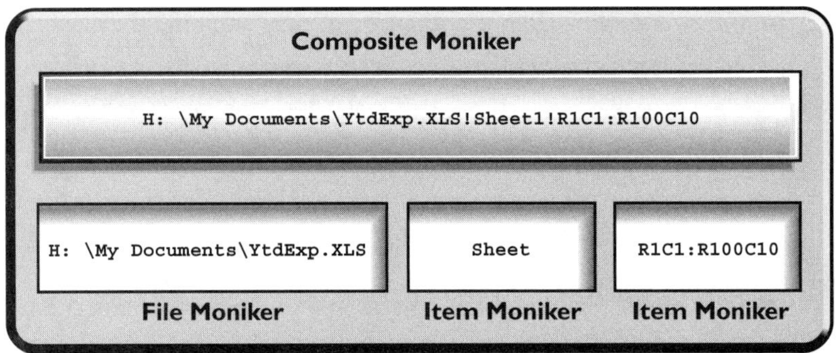

FIGURE 5-3 The file and item monikers combine to create a composite moniker.

The CLSID identifies monikers. The CLSID `{0000030x-0000-0000-C000-000000000046}` **is a CLSID with *x* identifying the moniker type. CLSID moniker codes are: 3 for file; 4 for item; 5 for anti; and 6 for pointer monikers.**

Under the Hood with IMoniker::BindToObject

A nontrivial moniker is represented by constituent monikers. The binding process starts from the right and the string is decomposed into the different moniker classes. A moniker will always have a left context. A moniker does not exist in isolation and will also have a right context. Normally the right context moniker isn't of immediate interest because it is already bound. This is illustrated in Figure 5-4 where *Item 1* is the current moniker of interest.

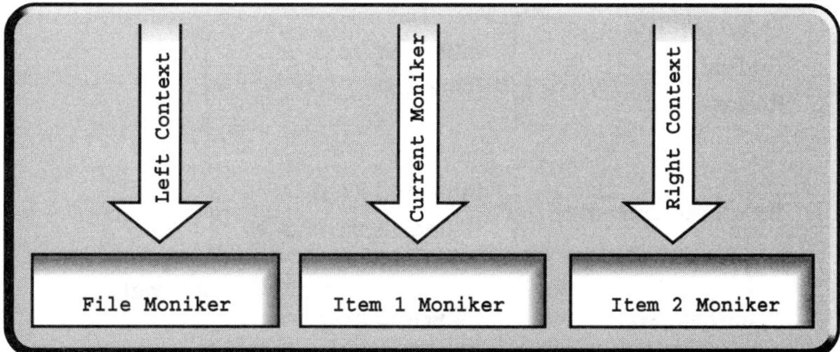

FIGURE 5-4 The right context moniker is already bound to the moniker of current interest (Item 1).

Decomposing a moniker into constituent components implies the existence of context between the individual components and presupposes a set of rules. Left context of a moniker is very important. Momentarily we'll find out why it is important, but first we must define two rules:

- *Rule 1*: During parsing of display names, every container must support **IParseDisplayName**. What better source of name parsing can there be than the container itself parsing the name? It knows what is expected.
- *Rule 2:* An item moniker requires the moniker in left context to support the **IOleItemContainer** interface. The reason is self-explanatory when you look at the **IOleItemContainer** interface in Figure 5-5, which is unique to the user context. The methods **GetObject, GetObjectStorage, and IsRunning** are methods that facilitate optimizing the binding process by locating running servers.

The missing keystone is that any **IMoniker** implementation must also implement the **IROTData** interface. This enables registering of an object in the Running Object Table. This puts in place the necessary tools to look at the Running Object Table and to know when the target server is already running. Binding is stopped at the point where the requested object exists in the Running Object Table. This places the importance of the moniker left context in the proper perspective.

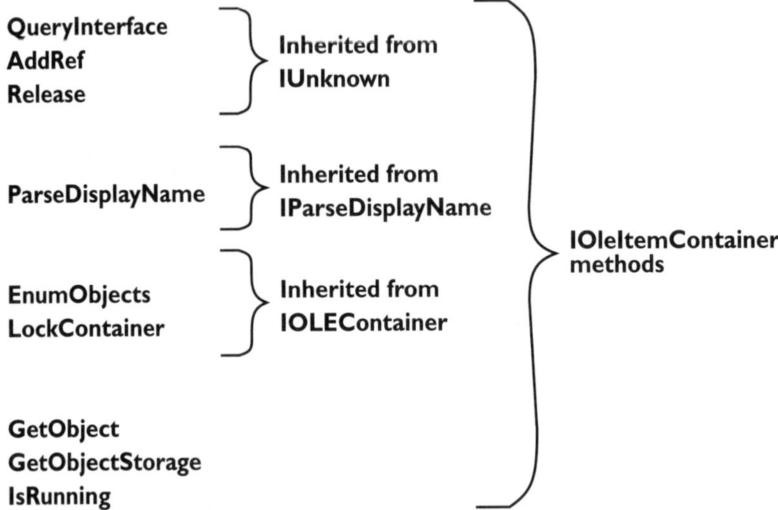

FIGURE 5-5 The methods used to create the IOleItemContainer interface

We're looking at pure elegance here. Remember that an object with the **IOleItemContainer** interface supports the moniker in left context. This means that as each **IMoniker::BindToObject** binding to the left is initiated, the **IMoniker** interface eventually returns a pointer to communicate either with the object through **IOleItemContainer::GetObject** or with the storage of that object through **IOleItemContainer::GetObjectStorage**. **IOleItemContainer** also parses names for its own objects.

We now have enough information to bind an object. But first, who uses the **IMoniker** interface? The two primary users of binding are file or object browsers that call the **IMoniker** interface and the **IOleLink** interface that supports embedded monikers of linked objects. Both interfaces share common features.

IOleUILinkContainer is another binding interface; however, it manages the functionality of the Links dialog box and uses the **IOleLink** interface.

I'll keep things simple for now and say that **MyServer** was browsed for **MyToys**. I'll make it still simpler and say that the composite moniker resolves down to just a file moniker. The simple binding example using a file moniker shown in Figure 5-6 assumes that the server is already running. The steps are numbered sequentially.

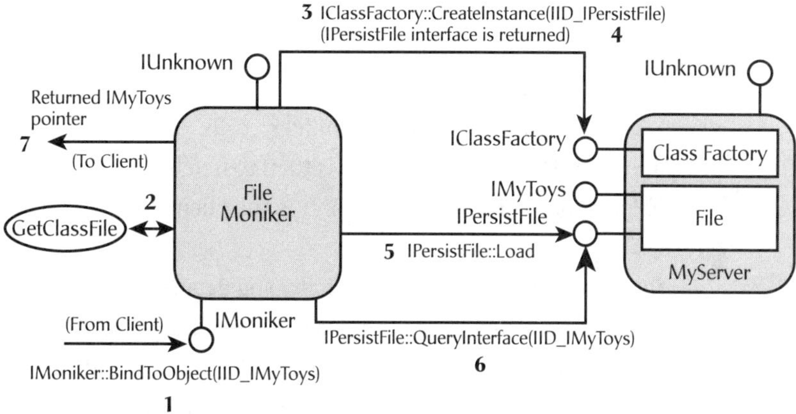

FIGURE 5-6 The details of binding a simple file moniker

The **IPersistFile::QueryInterface** is the correct syntax in both Figures 5-6 and 5-7 since the **IPersistFile** interface is aggregated. The **IUnknown::QueryInterface** idiom must be used when the interfaces are not aggregated.

Binding a simple moniker is illustrated in Figure 5-6 and starts with the client calling **IMoniker::BindToObject** with the interface identifier (IID); in this example, it is **IID_MyToys**. The moniker is resolved to a simple file moniker and the moniker calls **GetClassFile** to get the file CLSID. The moniker then calls **IClassFactory::CreateInstance** with the CLSID requesting **IPersistFile**. The file name is passed to **IPersistFile::Load,** which loads the file. The moniker then calls **IPersistFile::QueryInterface**(*IID_MyToys)* and the returned pointer is passed back to the client. The very last step, which is not shown, is the client connecting to and using the **IMyToys** interface.

This is all well and good, but I haven't used any of the contexts we've developed. So, let's bind a composite moniker, which has a file moniker and an item moniker. Once you see how the mechanism works for a single-item moniker, the additional steps needed for the multiple-item moniker are just recursions.

Just as we did above, the client calls **IMoniker::BindToObject** with the IID. In this example, it is **IID_MyToys**. The moniker is resolved to a file moniker and an item moniker. The item moniker then calls **LeftContext::BindToObject** (*IID_IOleItemContainer*). The file moniker knows that it has a filename and calls **GetClassFile** for the file CLSID. The file moniker then calls **IClassFactory::CreateInstance** with the CLSID requesting **IPersistFile**. The file name is passed to **IPersistFile::Load,** which loads the file.

Next, the item moniker calls **IPersistFile::QueryInterface** (*IID_IOleItem-Container)* and returns that pointer to the item moniker. (COM requires that **IPersistFile** and **IOleItemContainer** interfaces both be implemented on the same object.) In return, the item moniker calls **IOleItemContainer::GetObject** (*IID_IMyToys*). The returned pointer is then passed back to the client. The very last step, which is not shown in Figure 5-7, is the client connecting to and using the **IMyToys** interface.

The steps are numbered sequentially and details of constructing the composite moniker are omitted. No binding is necessary when the moniker item exists in the Running Object Table (ROT, see the section below, "IRunningObjectTable"). The item moniker extracts the **IUnknown** interface from the ROT and calls **IUnknown::QueryInterface**(*IID_IMyToys*) directly.

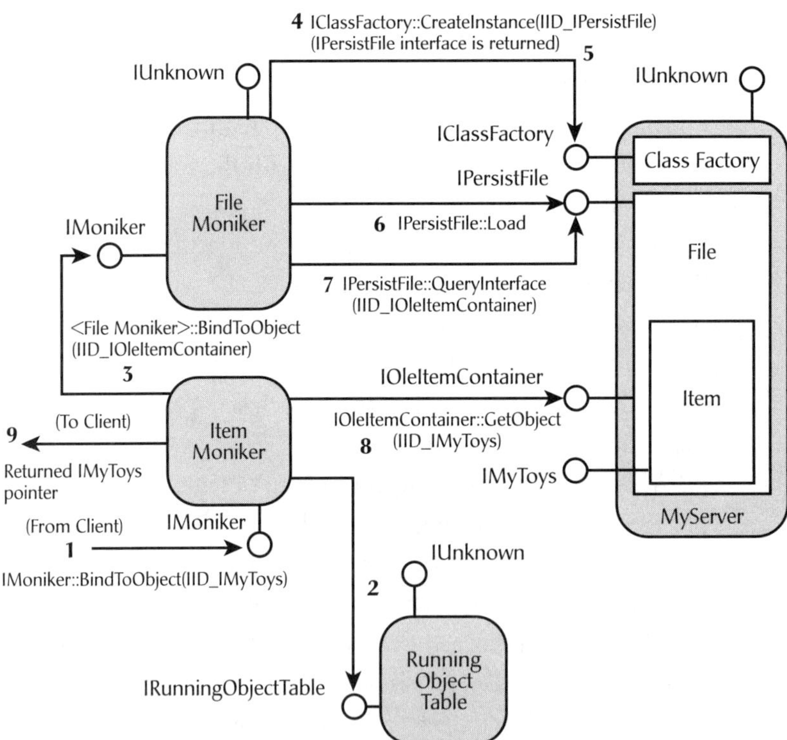

FIGURE 5-7 The details of binding a composite moniker

When there is more than one item moniker, the upward recursion is with each item moniker always calling **LeftContext::BindToObject** (*IID_IOleItem Container*). The downward recursion is that each item moniker must call

IOleItemContainer::GetObject and the last item moniker in the downward recursion has the additional responsibility of calling **IOleItemContainer::GetObject** (<*IID of requested interface*>). Remember that each nested item must support the **IOleItemContainer** interface. The rule is simple: The number of **IOleItemContainer** interfaces must equal the number of item monikers.

Synchronous Monikers

Synchronous monikers complete the binding process without client interaction. Figure 5-8 is the basic synchronous moniker binding architecture. This is contrasted with the asynchronous moniker binding architecture of Figure 5-10 where there is an ongoing dialog between the client and the asynchronous moniker through the **IBindStatusCallback** interface.

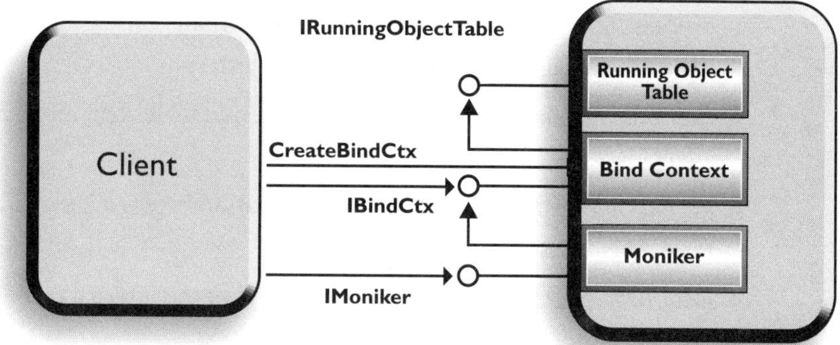

FIGURE 5-8 Synchronous monikers complete the binding process without client interaction

IBindCtx

The **IBindCtx** interface is for the management of options, bound objects, and object parameters related to binding. Methods of this interface are not called directly; however, pointers to different methods of this interface are found in many of the **IMoniker** interface calls. These methods are coroutines of the **IMoniker** interface.

The client calls **CreateBindCtx** with a pointer to the moniker for which it intends to request binding. This establishes an environment for the **IMoniker** interface and the client then calls **IMoniker::BindToObject** with the same pointer.

The **IBindCtx** interface inherits all methods of the **IUnknown** interface and **IBindCtx** supports the following methods:

- *RegisterObjectBound* — Remembers the passed object as being bound and that it must be released when overall binding is complete.
- *RevokeObjectBound* — The reverse operation of **IBindCtx::RegisterObjectBound**.
- *ReleaseBoundObjects* — Releases all currently bound objects.
- *SetBindOptions* — Remembers the parameters used by **IMoniker** functions.
- *GetBindOptions* — Returns the parameters set with **IBindCtx::SetBindOptions**.
- *GetRunningObjectTable* — Returns access to the Running Object Table. Moniker implementations should use this method rather than the global application programming interface (API) **GetRunningObjectTable**.
- *RegisterObjectParam* — Contextual information is passed to the binding process. String keys are case sensitive. The input consists of a name, under which the object is registered, and the object.
- *GetObjectParam* — Looks up a key in internal tables and returns the associated object.
- *RevokeObjectParam* — Revokes an association between a key in an internal table and an associated object.
- *EnumObjectParam* — Enumerates the keys of the internal contextual tables.

IMoniker

IMoniker::BindToObject is the workhorse of moniker binding. **IMoniker** is supported by a host of global API calls in addition to the **IBindCtx** interface. The **IBindCtx** methods are not called directly, but are supported coroutines that manage the moniker infrastructure.

A new moniker class requires the implementation of the **IMoniker** interface and the **IROTData** interface (see the section below, "IRunningObjectTable"). This allows your object to be registered in the Running Object Table.

IMoniker is well equipped for any moniker-binding task encountered. The interface inherits the required **IUnknown** interface. However, it also inherits

GetClassID from the **IPersist** interface and **IsDirty, Load, Save,** and **GetMaxSize** from the **IPersistStream** interface. **IMoniker** supports these methods:

- *BindToObject* — Locates and loads the object referenced by a given moniker. The bind process has both a right context and a left context. The left context requires **IOleItemContainer** support and the right context can involve binding to other objects. There isn't a need for this with the right context object support provided by the **IBindCtx** interface.
- *BindToStorage* — **IMoniker::BindToStorage** communicates with the object storage while **IMoniker::BindToObject** communicates with the object. This interface supports access to **IStorage, Istream, and ILockBytes**.
- *Reduce* — Compacts the moniker.
- *ComposeWith* — Returns a new moniker composed of the current, the left context, and the right context monikers.
- *Enum* — Enumerates the elements of a composite moniker.
- *IsEqual* — A moniker equality test.
- *Hash* — A moniker hash value. The hash value should rely on internal states and not memory addresses. Hashing is invariant under marshaling and a marshaled moniker returns the same hash value. Hashed values must be invariant for a global ROT.
- *IsRunning* — The moniker obtains the run status by calling **IBindCtx::GetRunningObjectTable** and interrogating the table.
- *GetTimeOfLastChange* — Provides time and date information for management purposes.
- *Inverse* — Returns an inverse moniker, which is needed for the implementations of **IMoniker::RelativePathTo**. An inverse moniker does not destroy a particular moniker. It destroys all monikers with a similar structure. Not all monikers can have inverse monikers. Objects embedded within other objects cannot have relative paths, and hence cannot have inverse monikers.
- *CommonPrefixWith* — Returns the longest common prefix shared by two monikers as a new moniker.
- *RelativePathTo* — Returns a moniker containing the relative path between the current and specified moniker when appended to the end of the current moniker.

- *GetDisplayName* — Returns the current moniker's display name.
- *ParseDisplayName* — Parses a composite moniker's remaining display name. **Moniker::ParseDisplayName** is called by **MkParseDisplayName**. It only parses as much as is appropriate from the tail of the moniker.
- *IsSystemMoniker* — Returns *S_OK* when the moniker is a member of the system-supplied moniker classes, otherwise *S_FALSE* is returned.

IParseDisplayName

The **IParseDisplayName** interface is inherited by several other interfaces and only has one method, **ParseDisplayName**. Objects invoking **MkParseDisplayName** or **MkParseDisplayNameEx** use **IParseDisplayName** indirectly.

Compound documents that support links to embedded objects or to pseudo-objects must support the **IOleItemContainer** interface, which is illustrated in Figure 5-5. The **IParseDisplayName** interface is inherited from **IOleItemContainer** and need not be implemented directly.

The alternative is to implement **IParseDisplayName** directly as part of a class object that has access to the interface available by invoking **CoGetClassObject**.

IRunningObjectTable

ROT optimizes binding by maintaining an active running object table. Passive objects are not included in this table; that is, all objects not in the table are by definition passive. **IMoniker::IsRunning** is invoked to see if the object in left context is running. Binding is not necessary if the object is already running and the moniker can call **IOleItemContainer::GetObject** rather than invoking **IMoniker::IBindToObject** on the left context.

Moniker providers use ROT. The moniker provider registers its own objects when it starts running and revokes their registration when they stop running.

The Win32 software developer's kit (SDK) includes a tool for viewing ROT, a sample of which is shown in Figure 5-9.

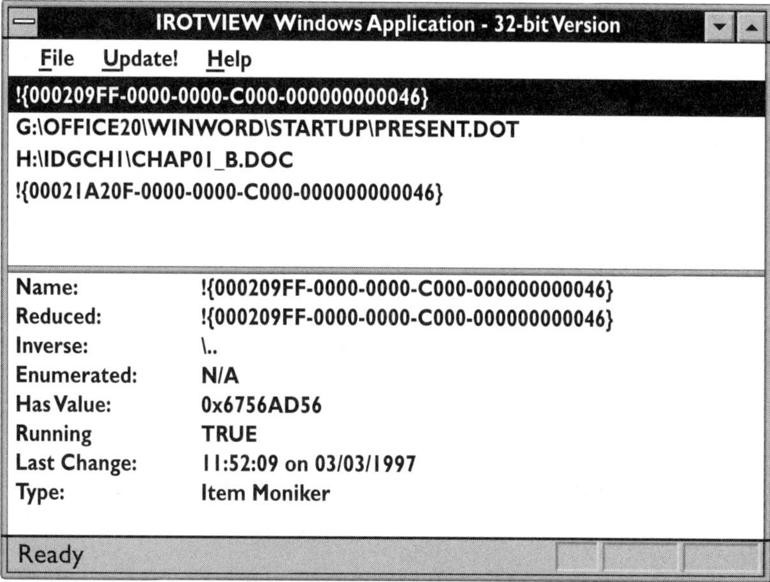

FIGURE 5-9 A Running Object Table viewed using the viewing tool from the Win32 SDK

Either clients or servers can access ROT by invoking the global API **GetRunningObjectTable**. Moniker implementations must access this table through the bind context that is passed to them and not through the global API. A moniker class accesses ROT by invoking **IBindCtx::GetRunningObjectTable** on the bind context for the current binding operation.

The **IRunningObjectTable** interface inherits all methods of **IUnknown.** **IRunningObjectTable** supports these methods:

- *Register* — Registers the designated object as having entered the running state.
- *Revoke* — Revokes the registered status of an object in ROT. It's assumed that the object is about to stop running. An error occurs if the object is not running.
- *IsRunning* — Tests to determine whether the object in question is running.
- *GetObject* — If the object is running, **GetObject** returns the object as it is actually registered.
- *NoteChangeTime* — Notes any changes in time for use by **IMoniker::Get TimeOfLastChange**.

- *GetTimeOfLastChange* — Reports the time of the last change. Moniker implementations should use their own implementation of **Moniker::Get TimeOfLastChange**.
- *EnumRunning* — Enumerates the objects of the type **IEnumMoniker**.

Moniker Support Functions

Moniker support functions are general utilities not supported by an interface. **CreateBindCtx** and **CreateFileMoniker** are good examples of utility supports.

The following are the supporting moniker global API calls:

- *BindMoniker* — A helper function that is a wrapper for **CreateBindCtx** and **IMoniker::BindToObject**. Calling **Moniker::BindToObject** directly is probably more efficient when there is more than one moniker.
- *CreateAntiMoniker* — An antimoniker that supports the **IMoniker::Inverse** method. An antimoniker removes the last component when appended to the end of a generic moniker.
- *CreateBindCtx* — Allocates and initializes an object linking and embedding (OLE) binding context before **IMoniker::BindToObject** is invoked.
- *CreateFileMoniker* — Creates a file moniker from a pathname.
- *CreateItemMoniker* — Returns a newly allocated item moniker.
- *CreatePointerMoniker* — A pointer moniker is a wrapper that, when used with different methods of the **IMoniker** interface, returns different values. The function of a pointer moniker varies with each of the **IMoniker** methods. A pointer moniker wraps an existing interface pointer in a moniker that can be passed to those interfaces that require monikers. Pointer monikers allow an object that has no persistent representation to participate in a moniker-binding operation. The results of using **IMoniker** methods with a pointer moniker are tabulated below.
  - **BindToObject** — Turns into a **QueryInterface** pointer.
  - **BindToStorage** — Returns a no storage status.
  - **Reduce** — Reduces the moniker to itself.
  - **ComposeWith** — Always does a generic composition.
  - **Enum** — Returns a Null.

  - **IsSystemMoniker** — Returns its own type.
  - **IsEqual** — Tests the other moniker, but only if it is the right type.
  - **Hash** — Returns a constant.
  - **GetTimeOfLastChange** — Returns a not available status.
  - **Inverse** — Returns an antimoniker.
  - **RelativePathTo** — Returns the other moniker.
  - **GetDisplayName** — Returns a NULL.
  - **ParseDisplayName** — Binds to the pointer using **IParseDisplayName**.
- *CreateGenericComposite* — Returns a newly allocated composite moniker.
- *GetRunningObjectTable* — Returns a pointer to the Running Object Table. Moniker implementations should not use this API call but should instead use the **IBindCtx::GetRunningObjectTable** method.
- *MkParseDisplayName* — Parses the input display name to a moniker. This is the inverse of **IMoniker::GetDisplayName**.
- *MonikerRelativePathTo* — Creates a moniker specifying a relative path.
- *MonikerCommonPrefixWith* — Returns the longest common path a moniker shares with another moniker.

Asynchronous Monikers

Asynchronous monikers return control to the client before binding is complete. Figure 5-10 shows the generic asynchronous moniker architecture where the moniker reports binding status back to the client with the **IBindStatusCallback** interface. This is an interim step to URL monikers, which are discussed in the next section.

The binding process uses a dialog between the client and the moniker. The client controls the binding process through the **IBinding** interface, while the asynchronous moniker uses the bind context object as a surrogate to return a status report, obtain binding priority, and notify the client of object or data availability. The client must register the **IBindStatusCallback** interface with the global API **RegisterBindStatusCallback**.

All methods within **IBindStatusCallback** may be called from within **IMoniker::BindToObject** and **IMoniker::BindToStorage**. The client receives a pointer to the **IBind** interface when the moniker calls **IBindStatusCallback::On StartBinding**.

The asynchronous moniker supports both a *data-pull* and a *data-push* model. The moniker provides data as it is available in the data-pull model, but is blocked from obtaining additional data until the client has read the current data. The client must read all available data before the moniker can return from **IBind StatusCallBack::OnDataAvailable**. Subsequent calls are made to **IBindStatusCall Back::OnDataAvailable** until the equivalent of a file EOF (end of file) is returned.

The data-push returns an OK status even if the client returns from **IBindStatusCallBack::OnDataAvailable** without reading all the data. The client can elect to skip the data; however, it is possible to use the seek method to position back in the stream and obtain the missing blocks. The backward seek is not available with the data-push model.

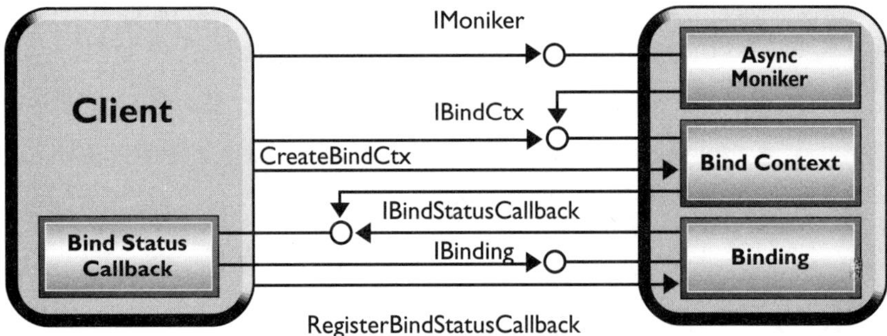

FIGURE 5-10 A generic asynchronous moniker architecture where the moniker reports binding status back to the client

IAsyncMoniker

The **IAsyncMoniker** is a small, but necessary interface. This interface contains only the **IUnknown** methods and its existence is simply a signal that an asynchronous moniker exists. Actual binding operations occur within the **IMoniker** interface.

IBindStatusCallback

IBindStatusCallback is the interface used by the methods of **IMoniker::Bind ToObject** and **IMoniker::BindToStorage**. This interface supports callbacks from binding operations that may be in any arbitrary order. Clients can register an **IBindStatusCallback** interface with the global API **RegisterBindStatusCallback**.

A **BindStatusCallback** object is required for each instance of an asynchronous binding operation. The **IBindStatusCallback** does not identify the type of bind operation associated with a notification.

The **IBindStatusCallback** interface inherits all methods of **IUnknown.** **IBindStatusCallback** implements these methods:

- *GetBindInfo* — This is called by an asynchronous moniker for binding information.
- *GetPriority* — The asynchronous moniker calls this method for the binding priority.
- *OnDataAvailable* — This is called by an asynchronous moniker when data is available. The moniker may be blocked for a data-pull model.
- *OnLowResource* — The client is notified by an asynchronous moniker that resources are low.
- *OnObjectAvailable* — The asynchronous moniker calls this method with a pointer to the new object.
- *OnProgress* — This is used by the asynchronous moniker to report load states.
- *OnStartBinding* — The asynchronous moniker notifies the client which callback methods are registered and available in the **IBind** interface.
- *OnStopBinding* — The client is notified that the binding operation is complete.
- *QueryInterface* — This is used by the asynchronous moniker to query for additional client services. **QueryInterface** is a method of the **IUnknown** interface and does not inherit from the **IUnknown** interface. The **Query Interface** method is available to the **IBindStatusCallBack** interface through aggregation.

IBinding

The IBinding interface is required for custom asynchronous moniker implementations. It provides client access to the binding process. A pointer to this interface is returned to the client when the moniker calls **IBindStatusCallBack:: OnStartBinding**.

The **IBinding** interface inherits all methods of **IUnknown**. **IBinding** implements these methods:

- *Abort* — The client aborts the bind operation.
- *GetBindResult* — The client queries a protocol-specific binding result.
- *GetPriority* — The client retrieves the bind priority.
- *Resume* — A suspended bind operation is resumed by the client.
- *SetPriority* — The binding priority is established by the client.
- *Suspend* — The binding is suspended by the client.

URL Monikers

A URL is associated with an Internet address such as `http://www.microsoft.com`. An *asynchronous URL moniker* adds additional complexity to our moniker architecture, but there really aren't too many changes. Figure 5-10 illustrates asynchronous monikers. Using this architecture, a new data format interface was added on the client side while I replaced the generic **Binding** object with the **Transport Protocol** object resulting in Figure 5-11. **BindStatusCallback, IBindCtx,** and **CreateBindCtx** are still there from the asynchronous monikers of Figure 5-10.

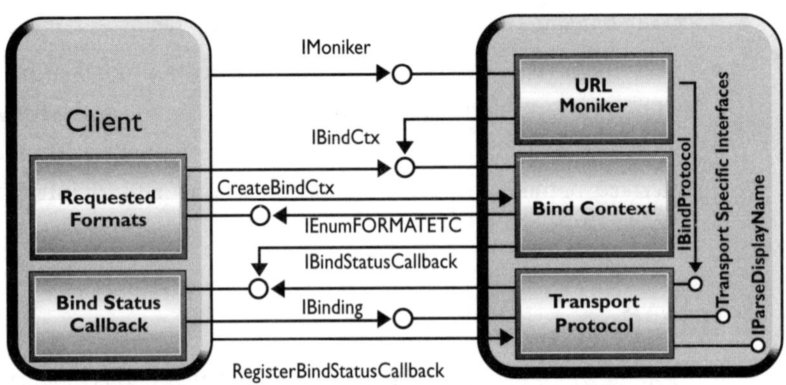

FIGURE 5-11 The details of URL monikers

How does this all work? It starts with a browser calling **MkParseDisplayName** with a URL. **MkParseDisplayName** returns a pointer to an asynchronous moniker. The browser doesn't know if the returned moniker is asynchronous, so it calls **IsAsyncMoniker**. If the moniker is asynchronous, the browser creates a bind context and registers the **IBindStatusCallback** with the newly acquired bind context.

The browser then calls **IMoniker::BindToObject**. The moniker binds to the object and queries the object for the **IPersistMoniker** interface.

Case 1: The moniker returns a pointer to **IPersistMoniker.**

1. The URL moniker calls **IPersistMoniker::Load** with its own **IMoniker** pointer to the object.
2. The object can choose between a push-data and a pull-data model (blocking versus nonblocking). The object modifies the bind context and registers its own **IBindStatusCallback**. The object then calls **IMoniker::BindToStorage** on the pointer it received through **IPersistMoniker::Load.**
3. The action now moves to the moniker, which creates an asynchronous storage and caches a reference to the wrapper object's **IFillLockBytes** interface. The **IProgressNotify** interface is registered on the root storage and **IPersistStorage::Load** is called with the asynchronous storage **IStorage** pointer. The moniker calls **IFillLockBytes** as the data arrives using **ILockBytes** on a temporary file.
4. Data is read from storage by the object and a control is returned to the object when it has sufficient data for self-initialization. The downloader receives a notification on **IProgressNotify** when the object attempts to access data not yet available. The **IProgressNotify::OnProgress** method does not block a data-push model.

Case 2: **IPersistMoniker** doesn't exist.

The moniker queries for **IPersistStorage,** which indicates a storage object. If a pointer to **IPersistStorage** is returned, these steps occur:

1. The moniker calls **IMoniker::BindToStorage** on itself requesting a blocking **IStorage** interface. Because **IPersistMoniker** doesn't exist, this is a synchronous moniker. Just like the first call to **IPersistMoniker** above, both **IMoniker::BindToStorage** and **IPersistMoniker::Load** bootstrap off the URL moniker.
2. Control returns to the moniker where a reference to the wrapper object's **IFillLockBytes** interface is cached. The **IProgressNotify** interface is regis-

tered on the root storage and **IPersistStorage::Load** is called with the asynchronous blocking storage **IStorage** pointer (see Figure 5-12). The moniker calls **IFillLockBytes** as the data arrives using **ILockBytes** on a temporary file.

Eventually the object returns from **IMoniker::BindToObject** and the browser has the desired object. The browser queries for **IOleObject** and hosts the object as a Document Object.

URL Monikers and Asynchronous Downloads

Figure 5-12 illustrates the asynchronous storage model. The unshaded areas of the figure represent the standard structured storage model of COM. The area of the figure labeled *DownLoader* induces a wrapper object for asynchronous storage downloads by URL monikers.

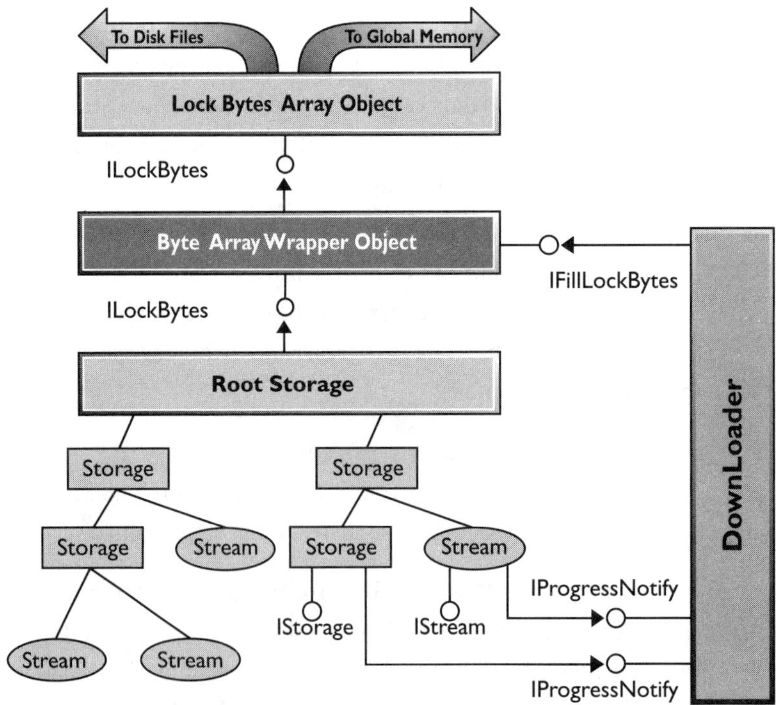

FIGURE 5-12 The asynchronous storage model

A URL moniker is an evolutionary step for an asynchronous moniker. Figure 5-12 shows a new URL moniker interface, **IProgressNotify,** which is not user callable. Another addition to the URL moniker is the hidden **IBindProtocol** interface of Figure 5-11. These interfaces are not discussed because they are not user callable and there is no immediate need to know their details.

The Object and Client Moniker Interface

These are the interfaces for the desktop. A client uses these interfaces indirectly when cutting, pasting, and linking objects from the desktop. As an example, the **IOleLinkContainer** interface discussed previously is a programmatic interface, while **IOleUILinkContainer** is the client-side equivalent.

IOleLink

Linked objects implement the **IOleLink** interface. The container queries the object for the **IOleLink** interface and assumes the object is not linked when the interface doesn't exist. The **IOleLink** interface must be implemented for linked objects. The container object uses this functionality for locating the link source and the cached presentation data, and to activate the link to the native data.

Not all **IOleLink** functions are called directly. A container invokes **IOleLink::BindToSource** indirectly by calling **IOleObject::DoVerb.**

IOleLink is implemented to support the **Links** dialog box. If the **Links** dialog box is displayed with **IOleUIEditLinks,** the equivalent **IOleLink** methods are implemented within the **IOleUILinkContainer** interface.

IOleLink inherits the **IUnknown** interface and implements these methods:

- *SetUpdateOptions* — Specifies cached data updating strategy.
- *GetUpdateOptions* — Returns cached data updating strategy.
- *SetSourceMoniker* — Sets the moniker of a newly linked source.
- *GetSourceMoniker* — Returns the moniker identifying the linked source.
- *SetSourceDisplayName* — Sets the display name for a newly linked source.
- *GetSourceDisplayName* — Returns the linked source display name.
- *BindToSource* — Activates the link source by binding the moniker found within the linked source.
- *BindIfRunning* — Activates the link between the source and link source, but only if the link source is already running.

- *GetBoundSource* — Returns the **IUnknown** pointer if the connection is currently active.
- *UnbindSource* — Closes the link between a linked object and a linked source.
- *Update* — Updates the cached data for a linked object (binding to the source may be necessary).

IOleUILinkContainer

The **IOleUILinkContainer** interface must be implemented by container objects using the global API **OleUIEditLinks** function to display a dialog box. This includes the **Links** dialog box, the **Change Source** dialog box, the **Update Links** dialog box, and the **Object Properties** dialog box.

The **Links** dialog box will call back to the container to manipulate container links indirectly. The links of a container and the types of link updating are enumerated with this interface. Updating can be manual or automatic.

This interface inherits all methods of **IUnknown**; no other interfaces are inherited. The implementation of this interface will use **IOleLink** interfaces. The methods of this interface include:

- *GetNextLink* — Enumerates the container links (the container link identifiers are returned in sequence).
- *SetLinkUpdateOptions* — Sets the update option to automatic or manual.
- *GetLinkUpdateOptions* — Returns the link update options.
- *SetLinkSource* — Calls from the **Change Source** dialog box.
- *GetLinkSource* — Calls during dialog box initialization or after returning from the Change Source dialog box.
- *OpenLinkSource* — Calls when the **OpenSource** button is selected from the **Links** dialog box (OLE links will call **IOleObject::DoVerb**).
- *UpdateLink* — Forces links to connect to their source and retrieve current information.
- *CancelLink* — Closes the link when the user selects the Break Link button from the **Links** dialog box.

Marshaling

The implementation of the **IMarshal** interface signals custom marshaling. Default marshaling occurs when the **IMarshal** interface does not exist. Late binding requires *dynamic marshaling*, which is a function of the COM library and is supported by the **IStdMarshalInfo** interface. The objects are bound at execution time, which requires the services of a local proxy and a remote stub. The **IStdMarshalInfo** interface uses default marshaling, however, COM queries the object for a special handler or a default proxy handler. When neither the **IStdMarshalInfo** interface nor an **IPersist** interface exist, default marshaling is accomplished with default handlers. (I call marshaling a loose end because it is not on our COM roadmap in Figure 5-1, although it is an essential issue of COM.) You'll find more about marshaling in Chapter 21 where we build an application using Distributed COM (DCOM).

The general concept of marshaling is illustrated in Figure 5-13, where an in-process server handles the *remote procedure call* (RPC) administration. As Figure 5-13 shows, this code is called the proxy. The proxy packages the data (marshals) before sending the data to a remote stub via an RPC channel. Figure 5-13 only shows one RPC channel; however, this is an oversimplification as an RPC channel is usually established with each remote object.

The corresponding code on the server is a stub that *unmarshals* the data before passing it to a server. This process is an example of standard marshaling in that no new objects are created. The dark, vertical bar denotes a process boundary: The target server may exist on the same machine or another machine.

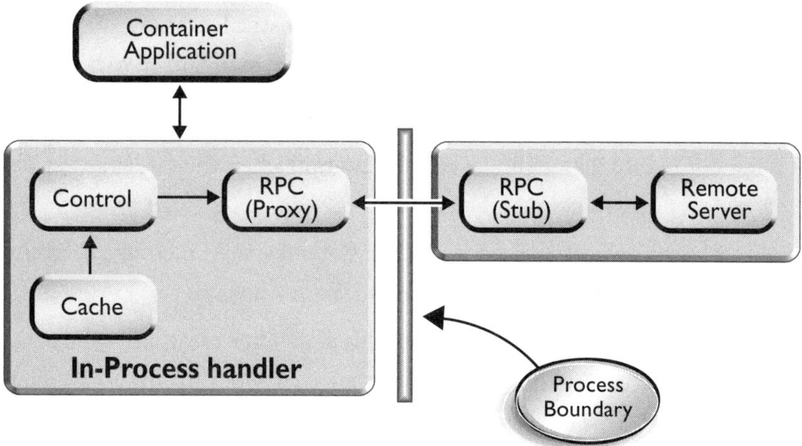

FIGURE 5-13 The RPC (proxy) marshals the data and the stub unmarshals it.

The code below is from an OLE 2.0 registration file, which supports the 16 bit OLE2.DLL implementation rather than the 32 bit OLE32.DLL . The code sample is presented for illustrative purposes only. It gives us some clues to the nature of such names as **ProxyStubClsid, IStdMarshalInfo, IRpcChannel, IMarshal,** and **IRpcStub,** which are the glue that makes marshaling work. (The **IMarshal** interface is only used for custom marshaling.)

LISTING 5-1 An example of Registry proxy stubs for marshaling from an OLE 2.0 registration file.

```
HKEY_CLASSES_ROOT\Interface\{0000000E-0000-0000-C000-000000000046} = IBindCtx
HKEY_CLASSES_ROOT\Interface\{0000000E-0000-0000-C000-000000000046}\NumMethods =
13
HKEY_CLASSES_ROOT\Interface\{0000000E-0000-0000-
C000-000000000046}\ProxyStubClsid = {00000312-0000-0000-C000-000000000046}

HKEY_CLASSES_ROOT\Interface\{0000000F-0000-0000-C000-000000000046} = IMoniker
HKEY_CLASSES_ROOT\Interface\{0000000F-0000-0000-C000-000000000046}\BaseInterface
= {00000109-0000-0000-C000-000000000046}

HKEY_CLASSES_ROOT\Interface\{0000000F-0000-0000-C000-000000000046}\NumMethods =
23
HKEY_CLASSES_ROOT\Interface\{0000000F-0000-0000-
C000-000000000046}\ProxyStubClsid = {0000030C-0000-0000-C000-000000000046}
```

Standard marshaling occurs automatically. There may be occasions where custom marshaling is a better choice than standard marshaling. Reasons to consider implementing custom marshaling include:

- Custom marshaling is a consideration when the target server object itself is a proxy for some other object.
- Some objects store their entire state in shared memory. Creating a custom proxy gives immediate access to the storage.
- Some objects have an immutable state after creation — the object cannot change. A custom proxy can create a copy of this immutable state without the overhead of an RPC channel.

- A custom proxy can be used to batch cached data until such time as a commit operation is performed.

Custom marshaling is a bit more complex than standard marshaling. The client starts by calling **IClassfactory::CreateInstance** on the remote server where the stub passes the request to the target object. The returned **IClassFactory** pointer is then passed to **CoGetClassObject** where this process occurs:

1. Within **CoGetClassObject,** COM attempts to acquire the proxy CLSID of the client proxy. The standard marshaling proxy CLSID is used when none is available.
2. COM asks the target object for a marshaling packet. When none is available COM creates a packet supporting standard marshaling.
3. The packet and the proxy CLSID are passed back to the client process.
4. The client creates an instance of the proxy using the CLSID that was just returned. The client then passes the packet to the new proxy.
5. The proxy connects with the target server. An interface pointer is returned to the original **CoGetClassObject** call, and the client can now communicate with the remote server with custom marshaling.

Steps 1 and 2 are wrapped in the COM API function **CoMarshalInterface,** while Steps 4 and 5 are wrapped in the **CoUnmarshalInterface**. Step 3 is specific to COM.

Key Point Summary

Monikers and moniker binding are under-the-hood technologies that make COM work. Late binding is always a choice, but late binding cannot work without the help and support of dynamic marshaling.

- Monikers can be synchronous or asynchronous.
- The **IPersistMoniker** interface signals an asynchronous moniker.
- The binding process starts by the client creating a binding context. This is done with the global API call **CreateBindCtx**. The next logical step is the client calling **IMoniker::BindToObject**.
- Active objects are maintained in the Running Object Table. The binding process takes advantage of this and increments the reference count for ob-

jects already instantiated. The presence of the Running Object Table realizes binding optimizations.

- The presence of the **IOleLink** interface indicates that an object is linked. It is also the linked object's interface to the linking and binding process with monikers.

Applying What You've Learned

Understanding what is under the hood always improves your design skills. Remember the car at the beginning of the chapter? Understanding the interplay between the components is essential when the architecture doesn't work. Is the battery dead? Are the cables in good condition? Is there a spark? All these questions are based on understanding the connection mechanism and relationship of the components to each other. The same strategy applies to COM components.

Instant Assessment: Monikers

1. Which interface must be supported for all item monikers?
2. In binding a composite moniker, which moniker is responsible for determining the pointer for the original IID passed in by the client?
3. When is the first action the client performs related to binding a moniker?
4. What is the second step?
5. Which important interface does **IMoniker** inherit besides **IUnknown**?
6. What is the Running Object Table?
7. What restrictions are there on the global API **GetRunningObjectTable** call?
8. What is the unique characteristic of the **IOleLink** interface?
9. What is the unique characteristic of the **IOleUILinkContainer** interface?
10. Explain the relationship between **MkParseDisplayName, IParseDisplayName,** and **IMoniker::GetDisplayName.**

Instant Assessment: Marshaling

1. What is the general meaning of *marshaling* within the COM context?
2. What are the generic names for the COM functions that perform marshaling?
3. What feature of COM requires marshaling?
4. The **IMarshal** interface defines custom marshaling. Default marshaling occurs when the **IMarshal** interface doesn't exist; however, the implemenation still has the opportunity to define a special handler with the **IStdMarshalInfo** interface. When neither the **IMarshal** interface nor the **IStdMarshalInfo** interfaces exist, default marshaling is done with a standard handler. Provide four reasons for custom marshaling.

For answers to the Instant Assessment questions, see Appendix B.

Lab Exercise

Lets poke under the hood and look at the Running Object table in action. The laboratory below requires Windows NT 3.51 or 4.0 and the platform Software Development Kit (SDK).

Lab 5.14 *The Running Object Table in Action*

This lab requires the platform SDK. Once you've loaded the SDK, you'll want to use the IROTVIEW.EXE application that accompanies the SDK. These steps are a peek at the Running Object Table.

1. Verify that no applications are running.
2. Start Microsoft Word 97, or your current version of Microsoft Word.
3. Open a known word document.
4. While Word 97 is running, start IROTVIEW.EXE from the platform SDK. This system is Windows NT 3.51 and Figure 5-14 is the Running Object Table for this system.

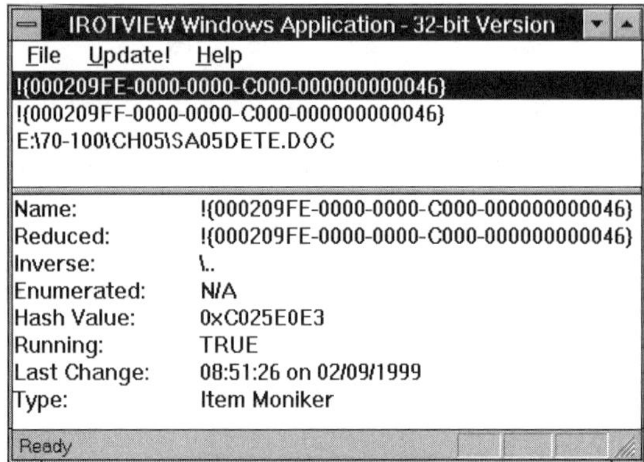

FIGURE 5-14 The Running Object Table displayed from the platform IROTVIEW application

5. Figure 5-14 includes an inverse moniker. To fully identify the objects displayed in the Running Object Table, start the Windows NT Registry editor REGEDT32.
6. Select the HKEY_CLASSES_ROOT hive.
7. From the Windows NT Registry editor, select the **View** menu then select the *Find Key* entry on either Windows NT 3.51 or Windows NT 4.0.
8. Enter either GUID; <209FE> or <209FF> in the search window and start the search. Make sure that *Match Whole Key* is not selected. Figure 5-15 is the result of the search. You'll find that the two GUIDs belong to VBA and Office 97 respectively.

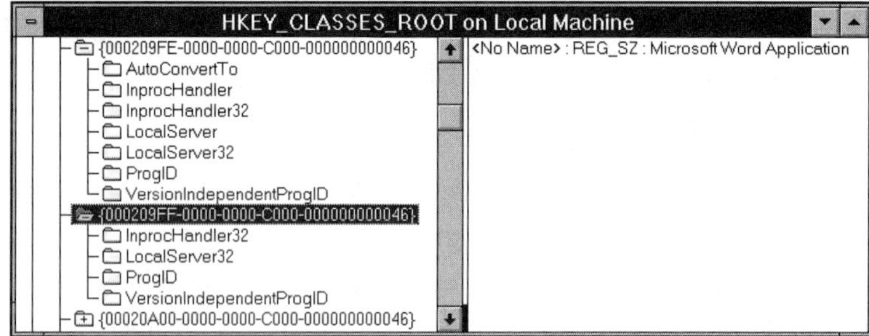

FIGURE 5-15 The results after locating the GUIDs in the Registry

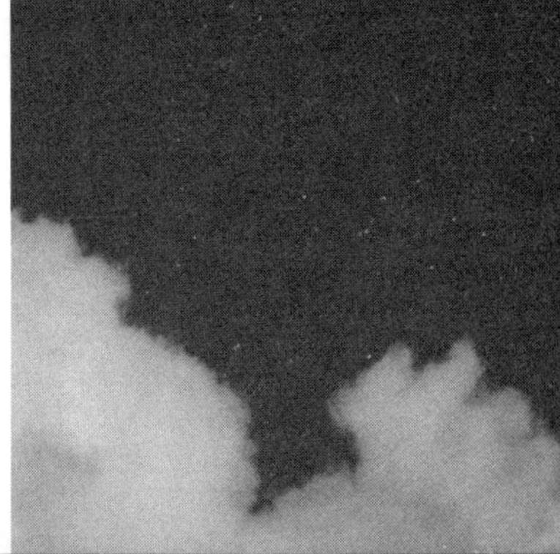

CHAPTER

Uniform Data Transfer

6

About Chapter 6

Uniform Data Transfer (UDT) is a key and necessary COM technology, but it is wrong to say UDT was specifically designed for COM. Earlier data transfer technology within the Windows operating system was overly complex with a specific API function for each type of data transfer. Managing API functions, parameters, handles, and buffers resulted in too much complexity with limited functionality. UDT is essential for COM and manages the complexity, however, it is also the garbage collection of prior technologies.

UDT is commonly characterized as the technology that removed the global memory bottleneck. *Dynamic Data Exchange* (DDE), the predecessor to COM, is a slow and early technology that only uses global memory. This use of global memory did not limit DDE's functionality, but did limit its application, and large data transfers in DDE are slow. It's also fair to say that OLE 1 suffered the same global memory malady.

UDT addresses both of these issues with two interfaces and two data structures. UDT is a generalized wrapper for device types and data formats. In UDT, formats are expanded beyond the clipboard-only format. UDT represents a single data object with the **IDataObject** interface, which can be used in any transfer protocol such as drag-and-drop, clipboard, or a compound document.

Supporting UDT with data change notifications is the **IAdviseSink** interface. This is a very important interface and is the first step on the path to connectable objects. Even though this is a chapter on UDT, we'll discuss notification mechanisms other than **IAdviseSink**. These topics are vaguely related to **IAdviseSink,** and we've included them here to provide closure on all notification issues. This chapter completes the thumbnail sketches of basic COM functionality and prepares us for the next two chapters of COM linking and embedding.

In the Beginning

UDT is our next stop on the COM roadmap (Figure 6-1) as we continue our visit to COM functionality. This section can be summarized in one sentence: Implementing the **IDataObject** interface is synonymous with Uniform Data Transfer. But it was not always this easy. DDE and the early version of OLE were resource hogs, and clipboard data transfers were unduly complex. UDT brought manageability and performance to an emerging and chaotic technology.

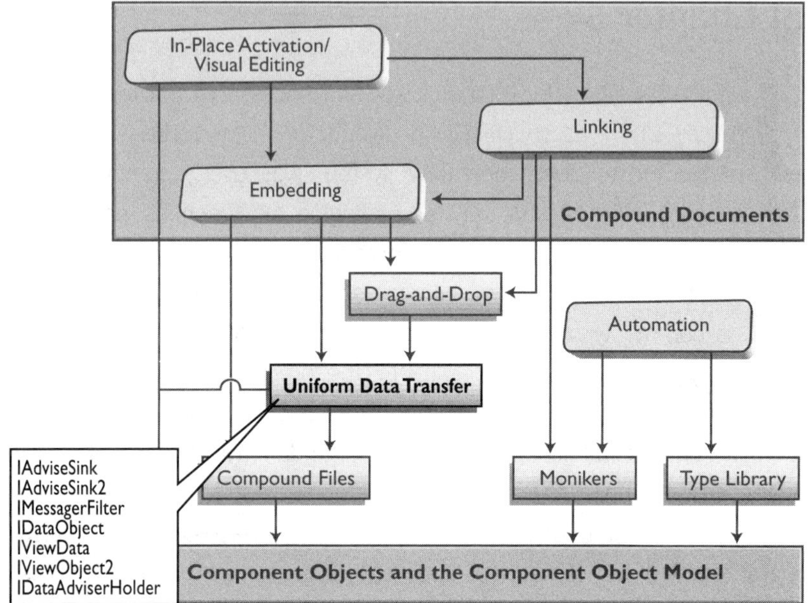

FIGURE 6-1 The Uniform Data Transfer stop on our COM technology roadmap

UDT is a wrapper that simplifies clipboard data transfer. A data object is created and used with data properties defined within two data structures. The data consumer deals only with obtaining a pointer to an **IDataObject** interface, rather than using a Windows API function, along with the infrastructure issues of managing buffers, handles, and data format specifications.

The first issue is to understand what existed before OLE 2:

- All transfers were done with API functions.
- Clipboard transfers were limited to a single type (UINT or a CF_* value, which are C/C++ data types).
- Structures existed only in memory.
- Transfers were only through global memory.

UDT generalizes data transfers with the **IDataObject** interface. It makes a paradigm shift by introducing the concept of transfer protocols. Rather than moving data to the consumer, the goal of UDT is to supply an **IDataObject** pointer to the consumer. **UDT** separates data from the transfer protocol. The transfer protocols for a compound document, clipboard, or a drag-and-drop operation each function differently. I'll review the four ways of obtaining a pointer to an object.

These are all general mechanisms, but I'll adapt them to acquiring an **IDataObject** pointer. The process of acquiring the pointer is known as a transfer protocol. * *Call an API function that creates an object of only one type.* The pointer returned is to one specific interface type or object type. This technique is illustrated by assuming that you have just installed a new proprietary board in your system. The board manufacturer also supplied a custom dynamic link library (DLL). Your application calls **CoCreateInstance** on the supplied class identifier (CLSID) and creates a specific instance of the proprietary DLL. Your application then uses **IDataObject** member functions to retrieve the data.

- There is a variation on this technique used by the clipboard protocol where an **IDataObject** pointer isn't actually created by an API function. An API function places an **IDataObject** pointer on the clipboard and another API function retrieves an **IDataObject** pointer from the clipboard.
- *Call an API function that can create an object based on class type.* Any interface pointer you request is returned. This is the most common object instantiation procedure and is the common technique used for compound documents, a discussion of which starts in Chapter 7. The general procedure is the client calling the COM library functions **CoGetClassObject** with the CLSID of the desired object and requested interface identifier (IID), which in this case is IID_IDataObject. Because the object is being created, the IID of **IClassFactory** is the other input parameter to **CoGetClassObject**. What eventually is returned to the client is the pointer to **IClassFactory** of the desired object. The client calls **IClassFactory::CreateInstance,** which instantiates the required object.
- *Call a member function of some interface that returns a specific interface pointer on another separate object.* The best example of this is calling **QueryInterface** on an object for an **IDataObject** interface pointer.
- *Implement interface functions on your own objects to which other object users pass their own interface pointers.* This technique is used by drag-and-drop, which is discussed later in this chapter. The process starts with an object registering itself as a drop target in a drag-and-drop operation. **DoDragDrop** is in a loop calling **WindowFromPoint.** When a valid window handle is returned from **WindowFromPoint,** it is checked for an **IDropTarget** pointer. If such a pointer exists, a call is marshaled to **IDropTarget::DragEnter** supplying the **IDataObject** pointer from the source object.

Comparing UDT with Prior Technologies

UDT generalizes and expands the prior technologies. Table 6-1 compares **IData Object** member functions with prior technology such as DDE, OLE 1, or the Clipboard protocol.

TABLE 6-1 COMPARING IDATAOBJECT MEMBER FUNCTIONS WITH PRIOR TECHNOLOGY

IDataObject Member Function	*Technology*	*Equivalent Windows function or message*
GetData	Clipboard	`GetClipboardData`
	DDE	`WM_DDE_REQUEST`, `WM_DDE_DATA`
	OLE 1	`OleGetData`
SetData	Clipboard	`SetClipboardData`
	DDE	`WM_DDE_POKE`
	OLE 1	`OleSetData`
QueryGetData	Clipboard	`IsClipboardFormatAvailable`
	DDE	None (`WM_DDE_CONNECT_ADVISE`, not quite the same)
	OLE 1	None
GetCanonicalFormatEtc	Clipboard	None
	DDE	None
	OLE 1	None
EnumFormatEtc	Clipboard	`EnumClipboardFormats` (direction only)
	DDE	None
	OLE 1	None
DAdvise	Clipboard	None
	DDE	`WM_DDE_ADVISE`
	OLE 1	None
DUnadvise	Clipboard	None
	DDE	`WM_DDE_UNADVISE`
	OLE 1	None

IDataObject Member Function	*Technology*	*Equivalent Windows function or message*
GetDataHere, QueryGetData, EnumDAdvise	Clipboard	None
	DDE	None
	OLE 1	None

Mapping IDataObject Functionality to DDE

Table 6-1 doesn't quite give us the complete picture. DDE appears to be mappable to UDT. Table 6-2 leads us to believe that conversion from DDE to UDT is a simple matter. Not so!

TABLE 6-2 Comparing IDataObject member functions with DDE messages

IDataObject Method	*DDE Message*
`IDataObject::SetData`	`WM_DDE_POKE`
`IDataObject::GetData`	`WM_DDE_RREQUEST`
`IDataObject::DAdvise`	`WM_DDE_ADVISE`
`IDataObject::DUnadvise`	`WM_DDE_UNADVISE`
IDataObject::SetData	WM_DDE_DATA

In spite of the apparent parallel functionality of the **IDataObject** interface and DDE, the mapping is not appropriate because DDE is inherently asynchronous and the **IDataObject** interface is synchronous. There is always an exception to any rule, and **IDataObject::DAdvise** is asynchronous under specific conditions.

That's the first problem. The second problem is the invocation process. An example DDE application starts a conversation with a service such as "Excel" and an example topic of "YearEnd.XLS." OLE 2 starts with a call on **CoCreateInstance** with a CLSID for Excel asking for the **IPersistFile** interface. The file is loaded with **IPersistFile::Load** ("YearEnd.XLS"). A **QueryInterface** call on **IPersistFile** for the **IDataObject** interface follows this.

The third problem area is the clipboard format. **IDataObject** does not support a standard field where a caller can specify a subset of data, whereas a DDE conversation allows a user to request data by specifying an item name and the clipboard format. In summary, converting a DDE application to UDT is not quite as simple as it appears.

Notifications

Notifications of data changes in prior technology were minimal and hand-tooled to specific applications. The developer could sandwich a custom dialog box between **MakeProcInstance** and **FreeProcInstance**. There are the DDE messages `WM_DDE_ADVISE` and `WM_DDE_UNADVISE`, but these only apply to DDE. This changes with the introduction of Uniform Data Transfer notifications that occur when data modeled by the **IDataObject** interface changes. The three COM transport protocols — drag-and-drop, clipboard, and compound document — each support the **IAdviseSink** interface for notifications, which is discussed in the next section. The **IAdviseSink** interface is a UDT component and is delegated the_responsibility of accepting the data changes generated by the data source.

The COM model has evolved and the general connection mechanism **IConnectionPointContainer** and **IConnectionPoint** is an outgrowth of the original **IAdviseSink** interface. (Several interfaces are included in this section that deal with COM object communications in general and not just **IDataObject** notifications.)

Uniform Data Transfer Components

This section discusses the core components of UDT. **IDataAdviseHolder** is included as a component of UDT; its role, however, is that of a helper function to **IDataObject**. **IDataAdviseHolder** is an optional interface that relieves the **IDataObject** interface of the mundane task of notifying consumers when data changes.

Describing Data with the FORMATETC Structure

UDT deals directly with the earlier performance issues of OLE, which transferred all data through global memory. It didn't take too much data to bring everything to a grinding halt. Data transfer formats are expanded beyond the clipboard-only format. The new FORMATETC (format et cetera), data structure supports both the internal OLE files, disk files, and global memory, whereas the earlier implementations only supported global memory.

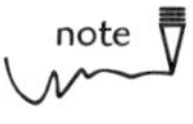

The FORMATETC data structure, the STGMEDIUM data structure, the IDataObject interface, and the IAdviseSink interface are the four key components of Uniform Data Transfer.

The FORMATETC structure, which is a generalized Clipboard format, is the first key element of three Uniform Data Transfer structures. Information stored in the FORMATETC structure includes the clipboard data type, a pointer to a target device type, the aspect, which can be the data itself, a thumbnail sketch of the data, an icon, or a preformatted printer image. The general FORMATETC format is:

- A word identifying the format. This is the improved version of the old clipboard format, although the term *clipboard* is used for historical reasons as the identified structures have nothing to do with the clipboard anymore.
- A pointer to a DVTARGETDEVICE structure which describes the device such as a screen or a printer, for which the data was rendered. This field is NULL when the specified data format is independent of the target data device, which is the case for most metafiles, or when the caller doesn't care which device is used.
- The aspect (view), which can be native data, an icon, a thumbnail sketch, or preformatted printer output. This represents the detail contained in the rendering.
- An identifier when the data must be split across boundaries. -1 indicates no data split. Otherwise useful only with `DVASPECT_CONTENT` or `DVASPECT_DOCPRINT` to identify the data segment.
- The storage type, which can be global memory, disk file, stream, storage, a bitmap, or a metafile.

The FORMATETC data structure is defined as follows. The notation is a C/C++ **typedef** structure.

```
typedef struct tagFORMATETC
{
  CLIPFORMAT      cfFormat;
  DVTARGETDEVICE  *ptd;
  DWORD           dwAspect;
```

```
  LONG            lindex;
  DWORD           tymed;
}FORMATETC, *LPFORMATETC;
```

Describing Storage with the DVTARGETDEVICE Structure

The DVTARGETDEVICE structure describes the target device with a driver name, a device name, a port name, and the device mode. A pointer to this structure is maintained within the FORMATETC data structure to the DVTARGETDEVICE structure. The DVTARGETDEVICE structure is illustrated below in C/C++ notation as a **typedef** structure.

```
typedef struct tagDVTARGETDEVICE
{
  DWORD tdSize;
  WORD  tdDriverNameOffset;
  WORD  tdDeviceNameOffset;
  WORD  tdPortNameOffset;
  WORD  tdExtDevmodeOffset;
  BYTE  tdData[1];
}DVTARGETDEVICE;
```

Describing Storage with the STGMEDIUM Structure

The STGMEDIUM structure is the most interesting of the three UDT data structures. The STGMEDIUM structure is a generalized global memory handle used by the **IAdviseSink, IDataObject,** and **IOleCache** interfaces for data transfer. The STGMEDIUM structure contains pointers to an **IStorage** interface and also an **IStream** interface. Some data in the STGMEDIUM structure overlaps a small amount of information found in the FORMATETC data structure. The STGMEDIUM format is:

- The storage type, which can be global memory, disk file, stream, storage, a bitmap, or a metafile. This describes the data location.
- A file handle.

- The file name.
- A pointer to a stream storage object.
- A pointer to a storage object.

The STGMEDIUM structure is illustrated below in C/C++ notation as a **typedef** structure.

```
typedef struct tagSTGMEDIUM
{
  DWORD tymed;
  [switch_type(DWORD), switch_is((DWORD) tymed)]
  union {
    [case(TYMED_GDI)]      HBITMAP        hBitmap;
    [case(TYMED_MFPICT)]   HMETAFILEPICT  hMetafilePict;
    [case(TYMED_ENHMF)]    HENHMETAFILE   hEnhMetaFile;
    [case(TYMED_HGLOBAL)]  HGLOBAL        hGlobal;
    [case(TYMED_FILE)]     LPWSTR         lpszFileName;
    [case(TYMED_ISTREAM)]  IStream        *pstm;
    [case(TYMED_ISTORAGE)] IStorage       *pstg;
    [default] ;
  };
  [unique] IUnknown *pUnkForRelease;
}STGMEDIUM;
typedef STGMEDIUM *LPSTGMEDIUM;
```

IDataObject

The **IDataObject** is implemented for any container or server application that is capable of transferring data. OLE compound document servers must implement **IDataObject** for both embedded and linked objects. The **IDataObject** interface is required for drag-and-drop operations. It is an optional but recommended interface for clipboard operations.

IDataObject uses the FORMATETC and STGMEDIUM data structures for transfer and rendering data. As shown in Figure 6-2, **IAdviseSink::OnDataChange** is the recipient of **IDataObject** notifications and is the only required method of **IAdviseSink** (see below) when used in the context of UDT.

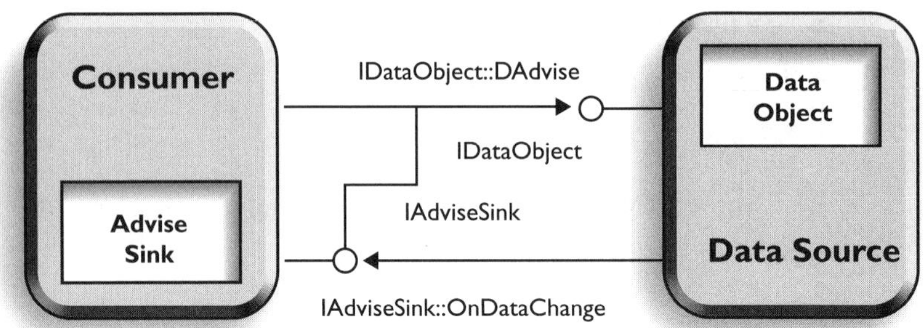

FIGURE 6-2 **The IDataObject and IAdviseSink interfaces, which illustrate IAdviseSink receiving notifications from IDataObject.**

The **IDataObject** interface inherits all methods of **IUnknown** and implements these methods:

- GetData — Transfers data through the STGMEDIUM structure and renders it to the FORMATETC specification. This can be native data, an icon, a thumbnail sketch, or preformatted printer output.
- *GetDataHere* — Transfers data through the STGMEDIUM structure to the client and renders it to the FORMATETC specification. This can be native data, an icon, a thumbnail sketch, or preformatted printer output.
- *QueryGetData* — Asks if the data object is capable of rendering data as described in the FORMATETC structure.
- *GetCanonicalFormatEtc* — Creates a logically equivalent FORMATETC structure.
- *SetData* — Sends data to the source as described by the FORMATETC and STGMEDIUM structures.
- *EnumFormatEtc* — Returns a newly created pointer for enumerating the FORMATETC supported by the object.
- *DAdvise* — Connects to **IAdviseSink** and establishes the notification connection.
- *DUnadvise* — Closes the notification link.
- *EnumDAdvise* — Returns a newly created pointer for enumerating the current advisory connections.

IAdviseSink

IAdviseSink occupies a rather unique place in COM. **IAdviseSink** was the first asynchronous COM interface. Until that time, all COM interfaces were synchronous. Almost all the other COM interfaces are still synchronous, except for asynchronous monikers or advisory notifications. (*Asynchronous* means that control is returned immediately to the caller.)

The **IAdviseSink** notification mechanism requires that the client implement **IDataObject::DAdvise** and **IOleObject::Advise**. In-process objects and handlers can optionally implement **IViewObject::SetAdvise**. Performance is an issue when **IAdviseSink::OnDataChange** must be marshaled. An example of this is data contained within an .EXE.

A document change has different contexts. There is the question of knowing when the document is saved, closed, or renamed. There is also the issue of knowing when the document's native data changes and when the document's presentation data changes. Requests for the different types of notifications are listed in Table 6-3.

TABLE 6-3 WHO TO CALL TO REQUEST A DOCUMENT CHANGE NOTIFICATION

Use This Method	*To Register a Request for Notification When:*
IOleObject::Advise	The document is saved, changed, or closed.
IDataObject::DAdvise	The document's native data changes.
IViewObject::SetAdvise	The document's presentation data changes.

IDataObject::ADdvise is the only UDT advisory request method in Table 6-3. **IOleObject::Advise** is an advisory request mechanism for compound documents, while **IViewObject::SetAdvise** is an advisory request mechanism for rendering objects.

Management of notification registration is simplified with the wrapper interfaces **IDataAdviseHolder** and **IOleAdviseHolder**. These interfaces track advisory connections and send the proper notifications using **IAdviseSink** interface pointers. **IDataAdviseHolder** simplifies life for **IDataObject** while **IOleAdviseHolder** performs the same task for **IOleObject**.

IAdviseSink is an asynchronous interface. This means that synchronous methods cannot be invoked in an **IAdviseSink** method. An example of this restriction is the method **IAdviseSink::OnViewChange** calling the method **IDataObject::GetData**. **IAdviseSink** inherits **IUnknown** and implements the following:

- *OnDataChange* - An advisory is issued when data changes. This is the only required method when the interface is used in a UDT context and the operation is asynchronous.
- *OnViewChange* - An advisory is issued when the object view changes. This method only applies to viewable objects and not data objects.
- *OnRename* - An advisory is issued when the object name changes.
- *OnSave* - An advisory is issued when the object is saved.
- *OnClose* - An advisory is issued when the object is closed.

IDataAdviseHolder

The OLE 2 specification states that any data object may receive multiple calls to **IDataObject::DAdvise**. This means that the data object is responsible for sending notifications to all interested advisory sinks. Delegating this task to the **IDataAdviseHolder** interface solves the logistical problem of managing multiple advisory sinks.

The methods of **IDataAdviseHolder** create and manage advisory connections between a data object and interested advisory sinks. **IDataAdviseHolder** is a custom implementation and is usually unnecessary. The standard OLE implementation can be used.

A custom **IDataAdviseHolder** interface implementation delegates the methods **IDataObject::DAdvise, IDataObject::DUnadvise, and IDataObject::Enum DAdvise** to the corresponding **IDataAdviseHolder** methods. **CreateDataAdvise Holder** creates a **DataAdviseHolder** object. This is done the first time a **IData Object::DAdvise** is received.

Multicasting occurs by **IDataObject** sending its own pointer and flags to **IDataAdviseHolder::SendOnDataChange** when data changes. **IDataAdviseHolder** enumerates the accumulated advisory list and calls **IAdviseSink::OnDataChange** for each member of the list. **IDataAdviseHolder** also calls **IDataObject::GetData** to obtain a rendering if the supplied flags do not include `ADVF_NODATA`. The acquired rendering is then sent to the sink.

IDataAdviseHolder inherits all methods of **IUnknown** and implements the following:

- *Advise* — Creates a data source and advisory sink connection.
- *Unadvise* — Destroys the connection.
- *EnumAdvise* — Returns a pointer to an enumeration object.
- *SendOnDataChange* — Notifies each waiting and managed advise sink of a data change. The standard advisory service is not the most optimal; better performance occurs with a custom implementation.

Table 6-4 summarizes the management role of the **IDataAdviseHolder** interface in managing advisory sinks for **IDataObject**.

TABLE 6-4 SUMMARIZING DELEGATED ADVISORY SINK RESPONSIBILITIES

Scenario	*Client - Data Source interaction*
Scenario 1, No delegation to **IDataAdviseHolder**	The client calls the data source represented by **IDataObject::DAdvise** supplying an **IAdviseSink** pointer for notifications when data changes. At a later time when the data changes, the data source notifies the client that the data has changed through the **IAdviseSink** interface. At a still later time the client dismisses data notifications by calling **IData Object::DUnadvise**.
Scenario 2, The data source has delegated all advisory sink management functions to the **IDataAdviseHolder** interface.	The client calls the data source represented by **IDataObject::DAdvise** supplying an **IAdviseSink** pointer for notifications when data changes. The data source delegates all advisory sink management to the **IData AdviseHolder** interface when the first **IDataObject::DAdvise** call is received. The data source delegates **IDataObject:: DUnadvise** to **IDataAdviseHolder:: Advise**. Correspondingly **IDataObject:: DUnadvise** is delegated to **IData AdviseHolder::Unadvise**

Continued

TABLE 6-4 *(Continued)*

SCENARIO	CLIENT - DATA SOURCE INTERACTION
	At a later time when the data changes, the data source calls **IDataAdviseHolder::SendOnDataChange**, which initiates the client notification mechanism from the **IDataAdviseHolder** interface.
	At a still later time the client dismisses further data notifications by calling **IDataObject::DUnadvise**, which has been delegated to **IDataAdvise Holder::Unadvise**.

Other Notifications

The COM notification mechanisms discussed in this section are not limited to notifications from the data object represented by the **IDataObject** interface to the **IAdviseSink** interface. **IAdviseSink** is the recipient of notifications from interfaces other than **IDataObject**.

This is indeed a chapter on Uniform Data Transfer, which uses the **IAdviseSink::OnDataChange** mechanism for data advisories. I elected to collect in the last portion of this chapter other advisory notification mechanisms. All of COM is related and by referencing all notification mechanisms that use the **IAdviseSink** interface, interfaces such as the **IOleObject** interface, which is not a data object interface but an embedded object interface, are drawn into the discussion. Be patient. There is a method to my madness and by the end of the chapter you'll know the minimum interfaces for an embedded object. This prepares you for the next two chapters, which deal with linked and embedded COM objects.

IAdviseSink2

IAdviseSink2 inherits all methods of **IAdviseSink** and adds the method **OnLinkSrcChange**. An advisory is issued when the link source changes. The link object should invoke **IAdviseSink::OnLinkSrcChange** when the link source is renamed. This is a notification mechanism for compound documents and not the **IDataObject** interface.

IAdviseSinkEx

IAdviseSinkEx inherits all methods of **IAdviseSink** and adds the method **OnViewStatusChange**. An advisory is issued when the view status changes. This is a notification mechanism for compound documents and not the **IDataObject** interface.

IOleAdviseHolder

IOleAdviseHolder does the same service for servers and compound documents that **IDataAdviseHolder** does for data sources and advisory sinks. The **IOleAdvise Holder** is a wrapper for the advisory methods of **IOleObject**.

The **IOleAdviseHolder** implementation is identical to that of **IDataAdvise Holder** in that the data object calls **CreateOleAdviseHolder** the first time **IOle Object::Advise** is invoked. When implementing **IOleObject** on the data object, the **IOleObject::Advise, IOleObject::Unadvise,** and **IOle::EnumAdvise** methods are delegated to the **IOleAdviseHolder** interface.

IOleAdvise inherits all methods of **IUnknown** and implements the following:

- Advise — Establishes an advisory sink and data object connection.
- *Unadvise* — Destroys the advisory connection.
- *EnumAdvise* — Returns a pointer to an enumeration object.
- *SendOnRename* — Notifies managed advisory sinks of a name change.
- *SendOnSave* — Notifies managed advisory sinks when the data object is saved.
- *SendOnClose* — Notifies managed advisory sinks when an object is closed.

IOleObject

IOleObject defines an embedded object. The **IOleObject** interface is used for managing embedded objects and for embedded objects communicating with the host container. **IOleObject** is to compound documents what **IDataObject** is to data objects. **IOleObject** is also a source of **IAdviseSink** notifications.

With **IOleObject,** things start to come together. In addition to **IDataObject** and **IPersistStorage**, **IOleObject** is an important building block. **IOleObject, IPersistStorage,** and **IDataObject** are the three required interfaces for each type of embedded object. They also represent three of the four necessary interfaces that constitute an embeddable but minimal compound document. Before the chapter ends, we'll have introduced all the required interfaces for a minimal compound document.

IOleObject has 21 methods; however, **DoVerb, SetHostNames,** and **Close** are the only nontrivial methods. Calls to all other methods are optional. **DoVerb** activates embedded objects, **SetHostNames** communicates container application and document names, and **Close** moves an embedded object from the running state to the loaded state. The **SetExtent, InitFromData, GetClipBoardData, SetColorScheme, SetMoniker, and GetMoniker** methods are optional and need not be implemented.

IOleObject inherits all methods of **IUnknown** and implements the following:

- *SetClientSite* — Informs the object of its container client site, which sets the **IOleClientSite** pointer.
- *GetClientSite* — Returns the object's client site.
- *SetHostNames* — Supplies an object with the names of its container application and the compound document in which it is embedded.
- *Close* — Changes a running object to the loaded state, optionally saving or discarding changes.
- *SetMoniker* — Notifies an object of its container's moniker, the object's own moniker relative to the container, or the object's full moniker.
- *GetMoniker* — Retrieves an embedded object's moniker.
- *InitFromData* — Initializes a newly created embedded object from selected data. This can be a paste from the clipboard or from data, which resides in the same container.
- *GetClipboardData* — Transfers a data object from the clipboard.
- *DoVerb* — Invokes an embedded object to perform a selected verb.
- *EnumVerbs* — Enumerates verbs (actions).
- *Update* — Updates the object.
- *IsUpToDate* — Checks the object for being up to date.
- *GetUserClassID* — Returns the object's CLSID. This might change with emulation.
- *GetUserType* — Returns the user-type name.
- *SetExtent* — Sets the object's display area extent.
- *GetExtent* — Retrieves the object's display area extent.

- *Advise* — Establishes an object and advisory sink connection.
- *Unadvise* — Destroys the advisory sink connection.
- *EnumAdvise* — Returns a pointer to an enumeration object.
- *GetMiscStatus* — Returns object status.
- *SetColorScheme* — Sets the color palette the object application should use when editing the specified object.

IViewObject

Object handlers and in-process servers that manage their own presentations implement the **IViewObject** interface. The **IViewObject** is functionally equivalent to **IDataObject,** however, **IViewObject** places a data representation on a device context (hDC), while a data representation is placed on a transfer medium by **IDataObject.**

Device contexts are valid only within a process. This means the **IViewObject** interface cannot be marshaled. This is logical as a bitmap on the screen is a local rendering dependent upon local attributes and characteristics.

The **IViewObject** interface inherits all methods of **IUnknown** and implements the following:

- *Draw* — Draws the object representation on the device context.
- *GetColorSet* — Returns the local object drawing palette.
- *Freeze* — Locks the drawn representation.
- *Unfreeze* — Unlocks the drawn representation.
- *SetAdvise* — Establishes a connection between the draw object and an advisory sink.
- *GetAdvise* — Returns the latest **SetAdvise** information.

The **IViewObject** is a major milestone for us. It is the last object we need to create an embedded object. We'll take a closer look at linked and embedded objects starting in Chapter 7.

The IPersistStorage, IDataObject, IOleObject, and IViewObject interfaces collectively represent a minimal and embeddable compound document object.

IViewObject2

The **IViewObject2** object extends the **IViewObject** object with one additional method. **GetExtent** returns the size of the view object from cache. **IViewObject2** inherits all methods of **IUnknown** and **IViewObject**.

IViewObjectEx

The **IViewObjectEx** interface inherits all methods on **IUnknown**, **IViewObject,** and **IViewObject2**. **IViewObjectEx** provides support for flicker-free drawings, hit testing on nonrectangular objects, and control sizing. The additional methods implemented are:

- *GetRect* — Returns a rectangle describing the requested drawing aspect.
- *GetViewStatus* — Identifies supported drawing aspects and returns opacity information.
- *QueryHitPoint* — Asks if a point is within a given object aspect.
- *QueryHitRect* — Asks if a point in a rectangle is within the object drawing aspect.
- *GetNaturalExtent* — Returns container-sizing hints for the object to use as the user resizes the object.

COM Messaging

That about covers object communication with advisory sinks; however, advisory sink messages are always asynchronous. Nearly all messaging in COM is synchronous; that is, the client loops until the message is complete. COM supports three messaging classes:

- *Synchronous* — The client loops until the response is received. This is the common COM communication mechanism.
- *Asynchronous* — Messages may be delivered at any time. COM supports five asynchronous methods:
  - **IAdviseSink::OnDataChange**
  - **IAdviseSink::OnViewChange**

  - **IAdviseSink::OnRename**
  - **IAdviseSink::OnSave**
  - **IAdviseSink::OnClose**
- *Input-Synchronized*— These are methods of compound documents that must complete to save user input before control is returned to the requester. I discuss these interfaces in Chapters 7 and 8 when I discuss linking and embedding of compound documents. These are the COM input-synchronized methods:
  - **IOleWindow::GetWindow**
  - **IOleInPlaceActiveObject::OnFrameWindowActivate**
  - **IOleInPlaceActiveObject::OnDocWindowActivate**
  - **IOleInPlaceActiveObject::ResizeBorder**
  - **IOleInPlaceUIWindow::GetBorder**
  - **IOleInPlaceUIWindow::RequestBorderSpace**
  - **IOleInPlaceUIWindow::SetBorderSpace**
  - **IOleInPlaceFrame::SetMenu**
  - **IOleInPlaceFrame::SetStatusText**
  - **IOleInPlaceObject::SetObjectRects**

IMessageFilter

Message filtering with **IMessageFilter** is used to resolve synchronous message deadlocks and is not directly related to advisory sinks. **IMessageFilter** is a recommended but optional interface. The interface provides OLE servers and applications with the ability to selectively handle incoming and outgoing OLE messages while waiting for responses from synchronous calls. Messages can be rejected or deferred and attempted at a later time. **IMessageFilter** presents a dialog box to resolve deadlocks giving the user an opportunity of dealing with the deadlock. An example of a blocking task is Excel computing formulas in the background at the behest of a Word document and ignoring incoming messages.

Another example of a deadlock is a client with a message loop inside **IRpcChannelBuffer::SendReceive**. The remote server is not responding and the application is deadlocked. COM notifies a message filter when a timeout condition or another blocking condition occurs. This allows the user to timeout and also handle any other incoming calls that occur. As you can see, **IMessageFilter** does more than just filter messages. It is a concurrency manager.

The **IMessageFilter** object is created with the COM library function **CoCreateMessageFilter**. Once registered, COM will call the message filter rather than the default messaging implementation.

IMessageFilter inherits all interfaces from **IUnknown** and implements:

- *HandleIncomingCall*—A single entry point for all incoming calls.
- *RetryRejectedCall*—A dialog box is presented to the user with retry, cancel, or task switch options.
- *MessagePending*—A Windows message arrived while OLE is waiting to respond to a remote call.

Connectable Objects

Connectable objects are a generalization of the advisory sink dialog. In fact, advisory sink messages are just a subset of the message functionality supported. When an object supports one or more outgoing interfaces it is said to be connectable. A source can have as many outgoing interfaces as it likes, where each interface is composed of a distinct set of member functions and each function represents a single event, notification, or request. Connectable objects are a feature of the COM model and are not limited to OLE controls even though connectable objects are often associated with OLE controls. The mechanics of a connectable object are illustrated in Figure 6-3.

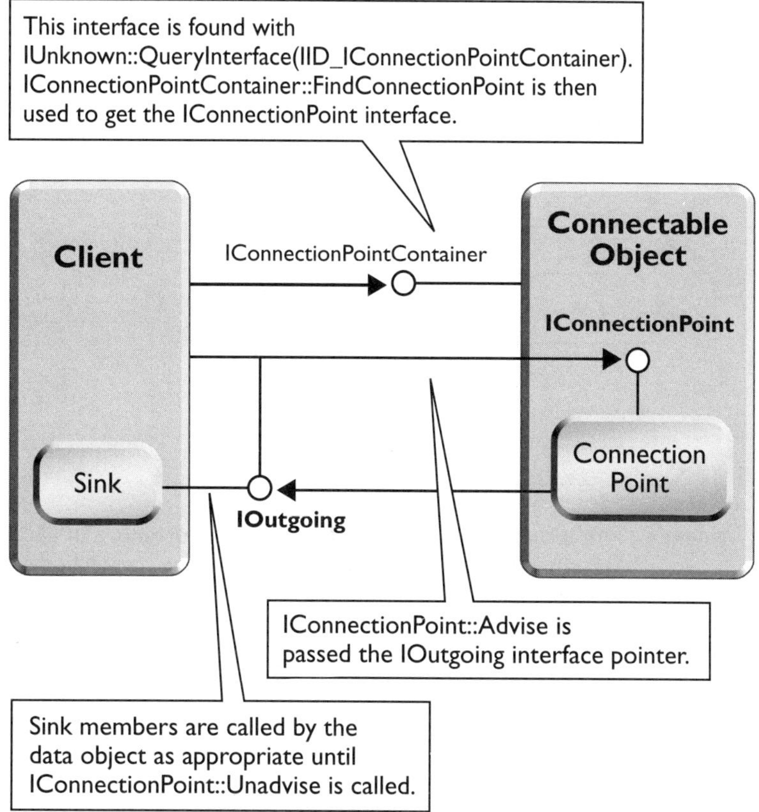

FIGURE 6-3 The details of connecting to a connectable object

The **IAdviseSink–IDataObject** advisory architecture is limited in that a client can only pass an **IAdvisorySink** interface pointer to **IDataObject**. Compare this with the **IConnectionPoint** interface, which can be passed the pointer of any interface. An **IConnectionPointContainer** may support more than one **IConnectionPoint** interface and more than one **IConnectionPoint** interface may use the same **IConnectionPointContainer** interface. Any sink can be connected to any number of data objects. Figure 6-4 shows more than one sink connected to an object while Figure 6-5 shows a sink connected to more than one object.

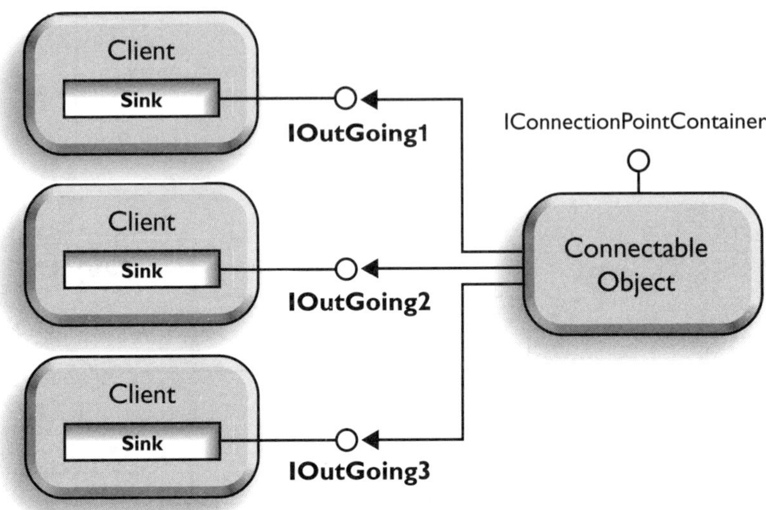

FIGURE 6-4 An IConnectionPointContainer can support more than one IConnectionPoint interface (a many-to-one connection).

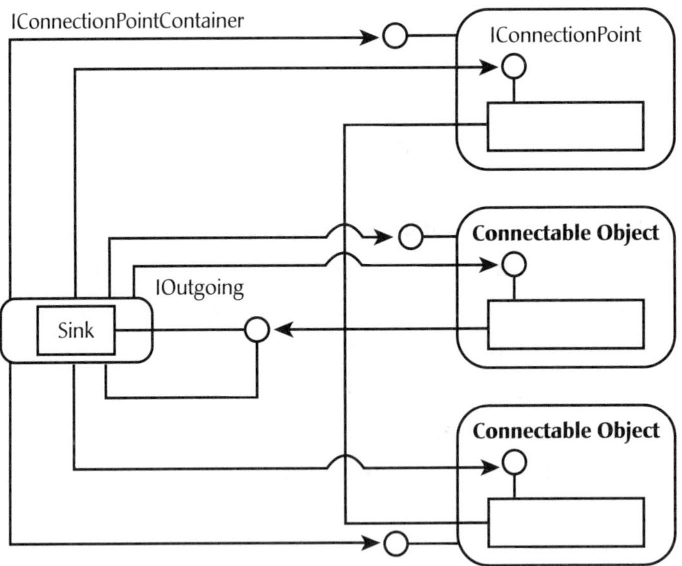

FIGURE 6-5 More than one IConnectionPoint interface may use the same client IOutgoing interface (a one-to-many connection).

IConnectionPointContainer

A connectable object has the **IConnectionPointContainer** interface implemented. It generalizes the object communication process and provides more than just advisory messages for sinks. A connectable object supports:

- The capability to connect and disconnect sinks to the objects for the outgoing IIDs. (This is the basic support offered the **IAdviseSink** interface by the **IDataObject**.) Connections are established with **IConnectionPoint::Advise** and the connection is broken with **IConnectionPoint::Unadvise**.
- Event sets from outgoing interfaces.
- The capability to enumerate the IIDs of outgoing interfaces.
- The capability to enumerate the existing connections to a particular interface.

IConnectionPointContainer supports all methods **of IUnknown**. **FindConnectionPoint** and **EnumConnectionPoints** are the two additional methods supported by **IConnectionPointContainer**.

Connecting to a connectable object starts by invoking **IUnknown::Query Interface** with **IID_IConnectionPointContainer**. A pointer is returned to the **I ConnectionPointContainer** if the object is connectable. The client then has two choices: either ask the **FindConnectionPoint** method for a particular connection or ask **EnumConnectionPoints** to return an enumeration object.

IConnectionPoint

The **IConnectionPoint** object is the client side of connectable objects. **IConnectionPoint** supports all methods of **IUnknown** and these methods:

- *GetConnectionInterface*—Returns the IID of the outgoing managed interface.
- *GetConnectionPointContainer*—Returns a pointer to the connectable object, which is the parent's **IConnectionPointContainer** interface.
- *Advise*—Creates a connection between the connectable object and a client's sink. (The sink implements the outgoing interface for the connectable object.)

- *Unadvise* — Destroys a sink connection previously created with **IConnectionPoint::Advise**.
- *EnumConnections* — Returns an enumeration object of the current connections for this connection point.

Drag and Drop: A Transfer Protocol

Drag and drop is a standard feature of the Microsoft Windows environment. It is a transfer protocol that requires the **IDataObject** interface, the primary topic of this chapter. Figure 6-6 shows the relationship of drag and drop to the linking and embedding features of compound documents.

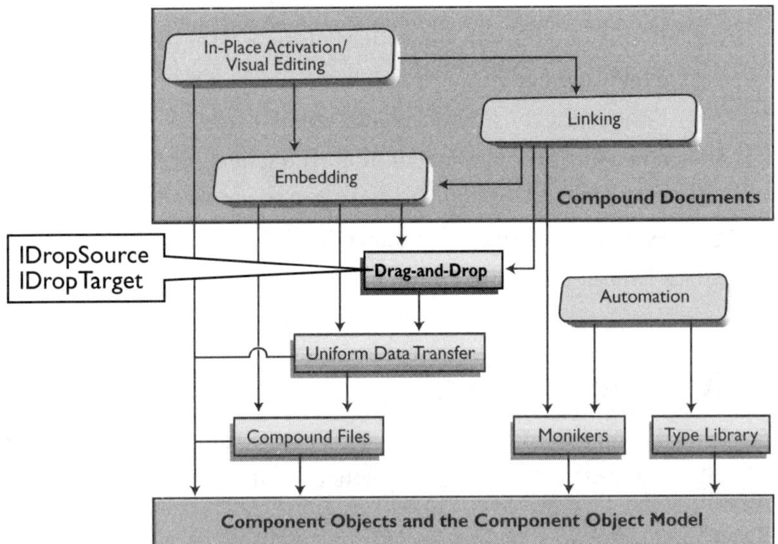

FIGURE 6-6 The various drag-and-drop interfaces

Drag and drop eliminates traditional application borders. Using *interwindow dragging,* objects can be copied or moved from one application window to another application window.

Drag and drop is an extension of clipboard. Quite often very little must be changed in the code to implement drag and drop. Rather than selecting an object, copying it to the clipboard, and then pasting it, drag and drop permits everything to be done in one operation.

Objects may be dragged from one container to another container using *interobject dragging*. Objects may also be dropped over icons such as printers or mailboxes that will process them.

Drag and drop is implemented with the two interfaces **IDropSource** and **IDropTarget**. Each interface has assigned responsibilities that enable smooth drag-and-drop operations. **DoDragDrop** is an API function that implements a loop used for tracking mouse and keyboard movement.

IDropSource

This is the first of two interfaces necessary to implement drag and drop. Any object containing data that can be dropped onto another interface implements **IDrop Source**. **IDropSource** is responsible for the following:

- Providing the drop target with the **IDataObject** and **IDropSource** interfaces.
- Generating pointer and source feedback.
- Determining when the drag has been canceled or a drop has occurred.
- Performing any action on the original data caused by the drop operation, such as deleting the data or creating a link to it.

IDropSource inherits all methods of **IUnknown** and implements the following methods:

- **QueryContinueDrag** — Returns the keyboard state and determines whether the escape key has been pressed.
- **GiveFeedback** — Provides feedback from the source application during a drag-and-drop operation as illustrated in Figure 6-8.

The architecture of drag and drop is shown in Figure 6-7 with both the **IDataObject** and **IDropSource** interfaces implemented at the source.

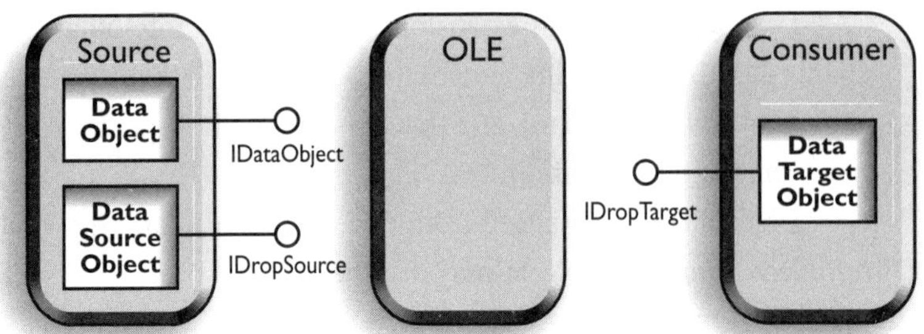

FIGURE 6-7 OLE as the intermediary between the data source and the data target

IDropTarget

The **IDropTarget** interface is implemented for all applications that can accept data. Any drag-and-drop application target must first be registered by calling **RegisterDragDrop** and passing the **IDropTarget** interface as an argument.

IDropTarget has the following responsibilities:

- Registering and revoking each drop target window.
- Determining the drag source effect at any given time.
- Drag scrolling.
- Target feedback.
- Integrating data when a drop occurs or if the drag is canceled.

IDropTarget supports all methods of **IUnknown** in addition to these methods:

- *DragEnter* — Determines the effect on the target window and whether the window can accept the data.
- *DragOver* — Provides feedback on the state of the drag operation to the user and to **DoDragDrop**.
- *DragLeave* — Causes the drop target to remove its feedback.
- *Drop* — Drops the data on the target application.

API functions that support drag and drop are:

- *RegisterDragDrop* — This API function must be called for each window able to accept dropped objects.

- *RevokeDragDrop* — This API function revokes the previous registration of an application window for drag-and-drop operations.
- *DoDragDrop* — This API function is used to initiate a drag-and-drop operation in a loop calling **WindowFromPoint** with the current mouse coordinates. Called by the drag source when a drag-and-drop operation starts. **DoDragDrop** calls **IDropTarget::DragEnter** when the mouse pointer passes over a window that is a registered drop target. The window is found by calling **WindowFromPoint** with the current mouse coordinates. When a valid window handle is returned from **WindowFromPoint,** it is checked for an **IDropTarget** pointer. If such a pointer exists, a call is marshaled to **IDropTarget::DragEnter** supplying the **IDataObject** pointer from the source object.

  DoDragDrop calls **IDropSource::QueryContinueDrag** during each loop iteration to determine whether the operation should continue. Consistent operation is assured with **IDropTarget::DragOver** and **IDropSource::Give Feedback** paired, giving the user the most up-to-date feedback information. Figure 6-8 identifies the relationships of a drag-and-drop operation.

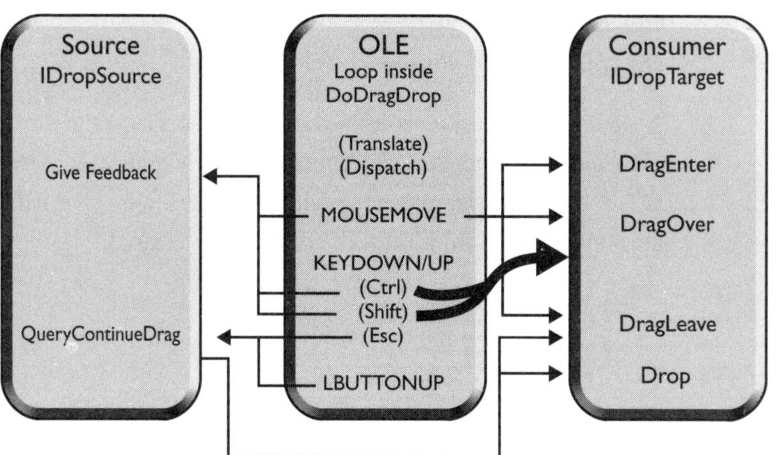

FIGURE 6-8 OLE managing keyboard functions for drag-and-drop operations

Clipboard: A Transfer Protocol

IDataObject supports the drag-and-drop, clipboard, and compound document transfer protocols. As with other transfer protocols, the clipboard transfer does not transfer actual data, but instead transfers an **IDataObject** pointer.

Setting up the FORMATETC data structure and the STGMEDIUM data structure can represent significant work. Using Uniform Data Transfer with the clipboard is optional. However, UDT must be used with compound documents.

There must be an anticipation of clipboard operations within the application. The object is started with **OleInitialize** rather than **CoInitialize.** This gives OLE a clipboard-handling window. Correspondingly, **OleUninitialize** is called rather than **CoUninitialize** when destroying the object. This ensures proper cleanup of OLE's clipboard window.

Managing clipboard operations is relatively simple once the FORMATETC and the STGMEDIUM data structures are initialized. Clipboard operations are supported by these three UDT operations:

- *OleSetClipboard*— Places an **IDataObject** pointer on the clipboard.
- *OleGetClipboard*— Retrieves an **IDataObject** pointer from the clipboard. The consumer must call **Release** when it is finished with the pointer.
- *OleFlushClipboard*— Flushes the clipboard.

Separating the protocols from the data creates an issue for clipboard operations. Recipients of clipboard data must be capable of delayed rendering when using UDT. The data source manages delayed rendering by capturing a snapshot of the data and holding onto it until the clipboard is cleared.

Key Point Summary

This completes a thumbnail sketch of basic COM functionality. We discussed the **IPersistStorage** interface in Chapter 4. The **IPersistStorage** interface and the **IDataObject, IOleObject,** and **IViewObject** interfaces, which were discussed in this chapter, constitute a minimal and embeddable compound document object. This sets the stage for Chapters 7 and 8, which discuss compound document linking and embedding. Of course, there are many frills missing, but the object is still a compound document. The functionality discussed so far includes:

- Structured storage with compound files
- Uniform Data Transfer
- Naming and binding with monikers
- Marshaling
- Drag-and-drop, clipboard, and compound document transfer protocols

We briefly discussed the **IDispatch** interface of Automation (formally OLE Automation) along with type libraries in a previous chapter. We pause now for a review before moving on to the next chapters, in which we look at compound documents that support linking, embedding, and in-place activation or visual editing.

- UDT is a wrapper and a generalization of what used to be clipboard-only data transfers. Formats and device types are now generalized.
- The basic UDT technology consists of the **IDataObject** and **IAdviseSink** interfaces and the STGMEDIUM and FORMATETC data structures.
- An object must implement the **IDataObject** interface to support UDT.
- Drag and drop requires the **IDataObject** interface.
- The **IDataObject–IAdviseSink** connection is the first COM asynchronous object link.
- Connectable objects communicate asynchronously and are a generalization of the **IDataObject–IAdviseSink** technology.

Applying What You've Learned

Objects are the present and the future for developers. A COM developer cannot be successful without understanding the functionality of each object. In this chapter, we looked at Uniform Data Transfer through the **IDataObject** interface. We also traced the evolution of notifications with COM. The questions and the lab will measure your understanding of UDT and notification issues.

There are several questions on the Microsoft Windows Architecture I examination pertaining to Uniform Data Transfer. The questions below address the issues raised by those questions.

Instant Assessment: Uniform Data Transfer

1. When is an application using Uniform Data Transfer?
2. Discuss the benefits of Uniform Data Transfer.
3. Identify the data structures associated with Uniform Data Transfer and describe the contents of each structure.
4. Describe the programming restriction that arises when implementing your own version of the **IAdviseSink** interface.
5. What interfaces are required to implement an advisory connection?
6. Explain the role of the interfaces **IDataAdviseHolder** and **IOleAdviseHolder**.
7. What interfaces define an embedded object?
8. You are building a container application. What are the three nontrivial methods of the **IOleObject** interface that must be implemented?
9. What method activates an embedded object?
10. Explain the difference between **IViewData** and **IDataObject**.
11. What is a limitation of the **IViewObject** interface?
12. What is the relationship between the **IAdviseSink** and **IConnectionPoint** interfaces?
13. What defines a connectable object?

Instant Assessment: Drag and Drop

1. What does drag and drop eliminate?
2. Drag and drop is an extension of what Microsoft operating system feature?
3. Name the two interfaces responsible for drag-and-drop operations and indicate when they should be implemented.
4. What is a requirement of the drag-and-drop target object?
5. What is the function of **DoDragDrop**?

For answers to the Instant Assessment Questions, see Appendix B.

Lab Exercises

Memory was a bottleneck for DDE and OLE 1.0. Both DDE and OLR 1.0 were originally implemented in an era when the memory of personal computers was limited to 16MB and 4-8MB was the norm. That has changed and the larger memory models of current systems mask the inefficiencies of older technologies such as dynamic data exchange. For example, my personal development system is 131MB and global memory is not an issue. DDE applications still exist and new DDE applications are still sold. It is difficult to benchmark DDE with the expanded memory models; Lab 6.15, however, should convince you of the cost effectiveness of using COM on the desktop.

The second laboratory illustrates implementing an advisory sink in Visual Basic. A class module creates an event that is sinked by a form module.

Lab 6.15 *When we take drag and drop for granted*

For one day, use your personal system normally—well, almost normally. Do not use any drag-and-drop operations, but copy everything to the clipboard. From the clipboard, copy the data to the target destination. You might function for a short period without drag and drop, but you will quickly appreciate the benefits of COM.

Lab 6.16 *Implementing advisory sinks in Visual Basic*

Microsoft Visual Basic uses the **Event** keyword to identify an advisory sink and the **RaiseEvent** keyword for creating an advisory sink event. We'll use our now familiar deposit and withdrawal model to illustrate user definable event sinking. The steps below detail the construction of a Visual Basic form module and a base class, which is roughly analogous to the **IDataObject-IAdviseSink** mechanism of COM.

1. Start a new project in Visual Basic 5.0 or 6.0.
2. Use the class wizard to create a base class with the name **CBank**. The class will have a **Balance** property, along with a **Deposit** and a **Withdrawal** method. The resulting code should be edited to correspond to the code below.

```
'(c) 1999 Bruce T. Prendergast
' DBA Prendergast Consulting
' DBA PCS
' IDG Books Worldwide ISBN 0-7645-3314-2
'
```

```
' CBank Class (Base class)
'
Option Explicit
Private mvarBalance As Variant

Public Sub Withdrawal(ByVal curAmount As Currency)
  mvarBalance = mvarBalance - curAmount
  RaiseEvent Form1.WithdrawalOccurred(curAmount)
End Sub

Public Sub Deposit(ByVal Amount As Currency)
  mvarBalance = mvarBalance + Amount
  MsgBox "New balance is: " & mvarBalance
End Sub
Public Property Let Balance(ByVal vData As Variant)
  mvarBalance = vData
End Property

Public Property Get Balance() As Variant
  Balance = mvarBalance
End Property
```

3. Place a command button on the form. Name the command button **cmdDeposit** with a caption of *Deposit*.
4. Place another command button on the form. Name this command button **cmdWithdrawal** with a caption of *Withdrawal*.
5. Place a text box on the form with the name *txtInput*.
6. Enter the following code in the declaration section of the form. Notice that the local implementations of the methods and properties of the **CBank** class are declared as **Private**. This prevents the properties and methods of the implemented class from being subsumed by the hosting form or class module. The project is now complete. Please feel free to experiment.

```
'(c) 1999 Bruce T. Prendergast
' DBA PCS
' IDG Books Worldwide ISBN 0-7645-3314-2
'
```

```
Option Explicit
Implements CBank
Dim m_CBank As New CBank

Public Event WithdrawalOccurred(ByVal curAmount As Currency)

Public Sub WithdrawalOccurred(ByVal curAmount As Currency)
  MsgBox "Withdrawal occurred for: " & curAmount
End Sub
Private Sub cmdDeposit_Click()
  CBank_Deposit [txtInput]
End Sub

Private Sub cmdWithdrawal_Click()
  CBank_Withdrawal [txtInput]
End Sub

Private Sub Form_Load()
  Set m_CBank = New CBank
End Sub

Private Sub CBank_Withdrawal(ByVal Amount As Currency)
  m_CBank.Withdrawal Amount
End Sub

Private Sub CBank_Deposit(ByVal Amount As Currency)
  m_CBank.Deposit Amount
End Sub

Private Property Let CBank_Balance(ByVal vData As Variant)
  m_CBank.Balance = vData
End Property

Private Property Get CBank_Balance() As Variant
  CBank_Balance = m_CBank.Balance
End Property
```

7. The **CBank** base class is instantiated as the m_**CBank** object. The methods and properties of the base class are delegated from the locally implemented **CBank** base class through the m_CBank instantiation. When a withdrawal occurs in the base class, an event is raised in the form module. This completes creating an advisory sink in Microsoft Visual Basic. Congratulations.

CHAPTER

7

Document Linking

About Chapter 7

The last few chapters built the necessary infrastructure that is the nuts and bolts under the COM hood. We've discussed a lot of the gritty details, such as **IDispatch** and **IUnknown,** and the higher level functionality, such as the **IDataObject** interface of Chapter 6. This is the first COM chapter where interfaces start to assume the semblance of an application. COM comes to life in this chapter with the linking of documents. We introduce the concepts of a document and of a container object. The prior chapters have been somewhat abstract and this chapter is a bit more practical. We take all the interfaces and assemble them into an application. (If you want to peek ahead, Figure 7-10 is where a linked OLE Document based on COM comes together.)

Before You're Confused

This chapter starts to put everything together with linked compound documents as the main topic. The problem is with the word *embedded.* I consider any compound document as being *embedded within a container*. Embedding a document in a container is independent of the type of data the document supports, which may be either embedded data or linked data. *Embedded data* or *linked data* classifies the type of compound document; as the chapter unfolds you'll find that there is very little difference between either type of compound document. Chapter 8 discusses compound documents with embedded data in more detail.

The word *document* is used in the context of modeled data. A spreadsheet represents data, yet when modeled with COM interfaces, it becomes an OLE Document; more precisely a COM compound document. *Linked data* is represented by a *linked document* and *embedded data* is referred to as an *embedded document,* which is not precisely correct. It is an embedded document independent of having embedded data. An embedded object with links to data is loosely referred to as a *linked object*. This definition isn't precise, but it suffices because we now understand the problem — the definition of *embedded*.

Compound Documents

OLE Documents represent an interaction model. A compound document refers to the embedding of one document within another document, or linking a document to an external document.

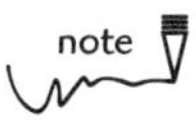

The use of the term *document* in this context does not just refer to word processing documents; it also includes spreadsheets, charts, drawings, and forms, as well as video or sound clips.

To understand the concept of compound documents requires defining two new concepts: a container and a server. Container and server functionality varies slightly for linked and embedded documents. The IOleLink interface is present for linked documents and is missing for embedded documents, which are discussed in Chapter 8.

OLE Documents support the compound document transfer protocol discussed in Chapter 6. It is the means of integrating data from any arbitrary compound document (a persistent file; see Chapter 4). The container is the host and manages compound document integration.

The unit of exchange for the OLE-document protocol is the compound document content object or simply the content object. The content object is unstructured and has no intrinsic identifier. Assigning a class identifier (CLSID) to the content object provides the necessary unique identification. The CLSID also marks the compound document type and identifies the server code that knows how to manipulate that data at the container's request. Container objects encapsulate their internal data formats and code behind a set of interfaces that define the prototype. These interfaces provide for persistence, structured data exchange, viewing, caching, and activation of the user interface in which the user can manipulate that data.

Data objects that retain their native full-featured editing and operating capabilities in their own container when moved or copied are called embedded objects. These objects are edited within the container using in-place or visual editing. This is different than a linked document, which is edited in a separate window.

OLE Document Definition, Features, and Benefits

Compound documents form half the keystone of component technology. The other half of the keystone is the OLE controls (now called ActiveX), which are discussed in Chapter 10. The features and benefits of linked and embedded documents and common characteristics are listed below. There is a very subtle distinction between an OLE component and an OLE document. Both use the Uniform Data Transfer (UDT) compound document transfer protocol; an OLE document, however, must support linking or embedding.

Common Characteristics of Compound Documents

The following are the common characteristics of compound documents:

- An OLE component object communicates with the compound document transfer protocol defined by Uniform Data Transfer.

- Business solutions can be built with prefabricated components.
- Rather than an Independent Software Vendor (ISV) building a complete application, a customized component can be used to add functionality to an existing application.
- An OLE Document object communicates with compound document transfer protocol defined by Uniform Data Transfer and supports at least one of the basic linking or embedding interfaces.
- OLE Documents may be used for word processing text, tabular data from a spreadsheet, a sound recording, or pictures created in another application.
- OLE Documents can seamlessly incorporate data from numerous sources including bitmaps, objects, and data of different formats.
- The sharing of general purpose interface mechanisms gives greater commonality between applications.
- Microsoft coined the word "document-centric." This means that applications are less "application-centric." Users can focus on the data needed to create the documents rather than the applications responsible for the data.
- OLE Documents allow applications to interoperate and end users need not be concerned with managing and switching between various object applications.

Characteristics of Linked Documents

The following are the common characteristics of linked documents:

- Object linking means that an image of the object is cached in the container document along with the moniker that refers to the location of the object's actual data. The persistent state (actual data) exists elsewhere and the moniker is stored in the document as a data link.
- Objects can be linked to or embedded in another object (or even part of an object) in the same OLE document. Changing a linked object changes the original and can affect the image that other users have of this object.
- Linked data may be read-only, meaning that it will only be displayed or played back.
- Data may be stored as a link to the original data with only a presentation copy available in the OLE Document.
- Documents can share data so that one copy of an object can serve many users.

- Linked objects are edited in a separate window. The target server is started and a new window opens for editing. Double-click an Excel-linked object and Excel will start with the object presented.

Characteristics of Embedded Documents

The following are the common characteristics of embedded documents:

- The entire object is embedded within the container. Restated, the object's persistent state is kept within the document itself.
- A copy of the data is stored in the OLE Document when the object is embedded. The data is not updated by the system and the user is responsible for updating the data. Updating locally embedded data does not affect the source data.
- Embedded objects are edited in-place, which is editing within the container. This is discussed in Chapter 8.

Figure 7-1 is illustrative of constructing an application with embedded objects. The application represents a collection of embedded objects, however most of the data is not embedded. The features of Figure 7-1 roughly parallel what I am currently using, Microsoft Word. The active document I am editing will be linked, however, other data such as a spelling dictionary will be embedded within the spell checker.

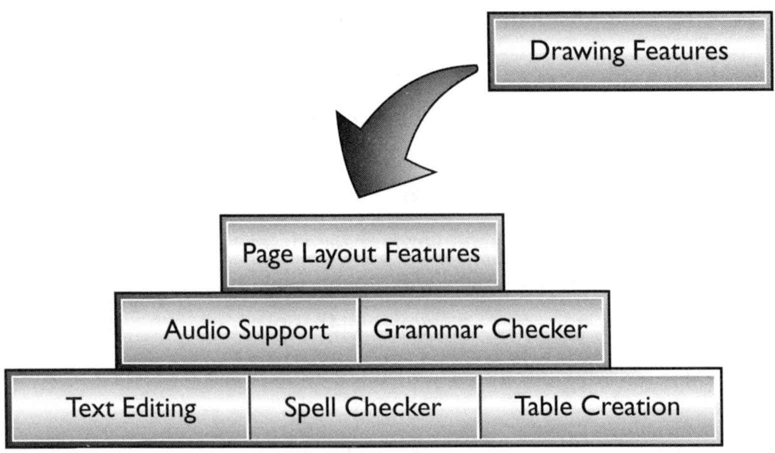

FIGURE 7-1 An application is built with components.

Displaying a Document

When displaying an OLE-embedded or OLE-linked object in its presentation or content form (as opposed to displaying the object as an icon), a cached metafile description is generally used. The object can be indistinguishable from native objects.

The **Show Objects** command is used to visually identify OLE-embedded or OLE-linked objects. Dashes should appear around the linked object and a thin line one pixel wide should appear around any embedded objects. If the link object is not current, then the dashed lines use the inactive text color. Lines are around the highest level only.

The mechanics of displaying a document depend upon **IDataObject** for rendering along with support from **IAdviseSink** or **IDataAdviseHolder** and at least one of the **IPersist*** interfaces. You'll see later in the chapter that rendering is accomplished with a handler, and is often accompanied by a caching mechanism.

A default label generally accompanies an embedded or linked object document stored as the icon. The icon's default label is one of the following for an OLE-embedded object:

- Name of the object (example: file name without the extension)
- The object's registered short-type name
- The object's registered full-type name
- "Document" if an object has no name, no short name type, and no registered name type

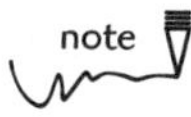

The icon label is the file name for an embedded object with linked data.

Linking Compound Documents

This is our first stop on our tour of compound documents. Figure 7-2 illustrates linking an Excel spreadsheet to a Word document. A linked OLE Document is always small. The native data is maintained at the source and the OLE Document only maintains presentation data. All attached users see the changes immediately when a linked document is edited. Links can be nested and combined with embedded objects.

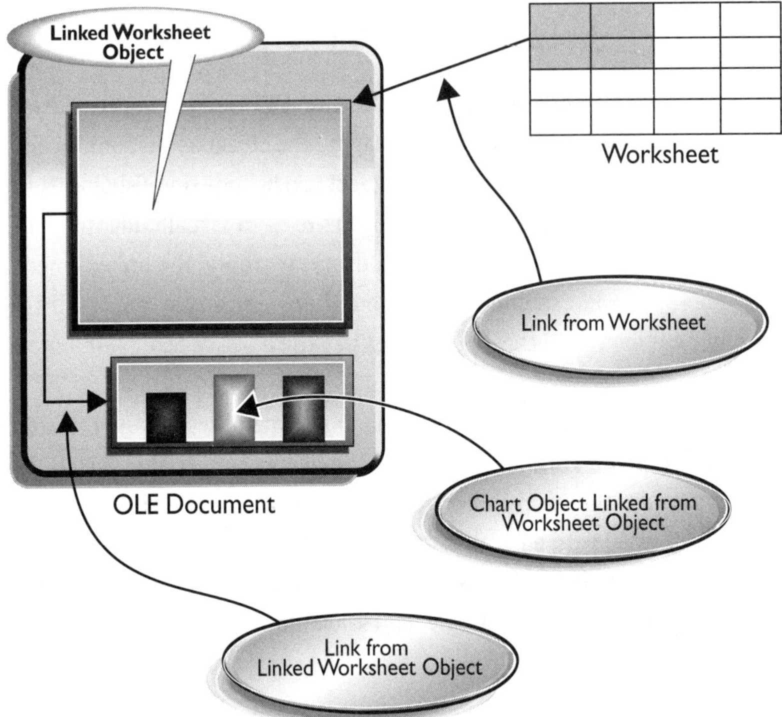

FIGURE 7-2 This example of a linked compound document links an Excel spreadsheet to a Word document.

A linked OLE object cannot be edited unless the source is active. Double-clicking the object activates the source. If original data is edited at the source, all other users who share the data have the reflected changes. Linked objects open in their own window for editing. A link may play in-place, but not be edited in-place.

tip

Updating from a link source is automatic by default. Manual updating can be accomplished by setting the linked object's Update property to *Manual*. When the user creates an OLE link, it is by default an automatic link.

An OLE-linked object includes a cached copy of the source's type at the time of the last update. When the type of a link's source changes, all links derived from that source object contain the old type and operations until either an update occurs or the link source is activated. In addition to the type (class), an OLE-linked object has two other properties: the name of the source and the updating basis.

What happens when the application is moved? Nothing happens if the path is still relative or the source wasn't moved, because the link is adaptable. Source location information is maintained in the Registry. This must be updated when the source is moved. An alternative is to use the linking-to application of the Links dialog box to reestablish the link.

An OLE-linked object includes a cached copy of its source's type at the time of the last update. When executing an operation on a link object, the link object compares the cached type with the current type of the link source. If they are the same, the linked object forwards the operation to the source. If they are different, the linked object informs the container. In response, the container can either:

- Execute the new type's operation, if the operation issued from the old link is syntactically identical to one of the operations registered for the source's new type; or
- Display a message box, if the operation is no longer supported by the link source's type.

A link is maintained with three properties: Type (or class), the name of the source data, and it's updating basis (automatic or manual). These properties are on a link page in the linked object's property sheet supplied by the container. A container application can supply a **Links** command that displays a dialog box for altering the properties. The dialog box has the commands: **Cancel, Update Now**, **Open Source**, **Change Source**, **Break Link,** and **Help**.

So by now you're probably wondering how this is managed. Like all other features in this chapter, linked OLE objects are managed with the interfaces, as shown in Figure 7-3. Figure 7-3 identifies our current position in the COM roadmap. As you can see from the roadmap, we are about to build our first COM application with a linked document.

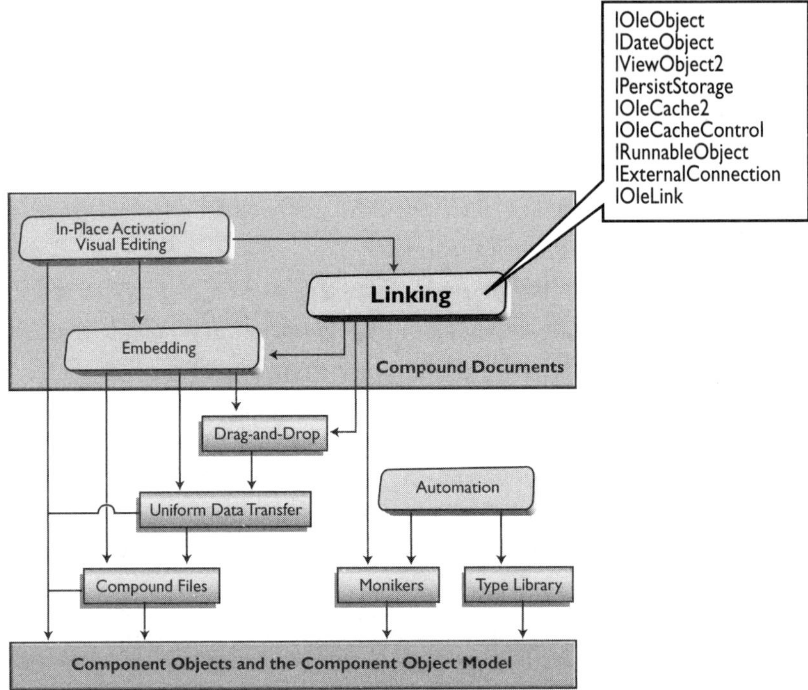

FIGURE 7-3 Interfaces for Linking Compound Documents

You should recognize some of the interfaces from earlier discussions. I'll discuss the new interfaces before delving into document linking.

CONTAINERS

Linking requires two components, a server and a container. Each has unique interfaces. I'll start with the simplest one — the container that is a host for compound documents provided by the server. This example presents a general case and not a container capable of supporting all the embedding or in-place activation features. I'll discuss this container type in Chapter 8.

Let's look at some container characteristics:

- A container can contain multiple nested, linked, or embedded OLE objects. Objects can be linked to or embedded in another object (or even as part of an object) in the same OLE Document. Changing a linked object will change the original and can affect the image that others have of this object. Only one object at a time may be active within a container.

- The container determines the selection behavior and appearance of embedded or linked objects. When a user selects an object, the object is displayed with an appropriate selection appearance for that type.
- Objects are blended with the features of the container. An object may display some adornments such as row or column headers; however, it may inherit from the container toolbars, menus, or supplemental palette windows. The operations available for an OLE-linked object are those supplied by its container and those supplied by the source. Toolbar negotiation is a good example.
- A container has adaptable links, which are maintained with monikers. COM maintains both an absolute moniker and a relative moniker as an aid in maintaining links when a file is moved. Windows NT tracks moved files, which is also an aid in maintaining links. An object may be linked to a complete or partial object (pseudo-object), with relative links. It is possible to move the destination, or both the source and destination may be moved together. The link is maintained as long as it is relative.
- OLE containers "export" properties to an object. This is done when the properties of the object do not match those of the container. The object inherits these properties and transforms its appearance to be more consistent with the object's container. To a user, the objects appear "smart" because they know how to transform themselves to match their container. This process saves the user time because the user does not need to adjust the object's properties before or after embedding it in the target container.
- When selecting access to an object, interaction with the object content is not provided. Select commands are made available to interact with the object as a whole. Only after activating the object is user access permitted to object content. The object is activated with **IOleObject::DoVerb**(*Verb*). **DoVerb** operations for a linked object are discussed in "Building an Application" below. The scenario for in-place activation of an object with embedded data is discussed in Chapter 8.
- The container can only retrieve those commands from the Registry that have been registered by the object's type.

- Outside-in or inside-out activation is permitted; the container, however, uses an activation style that is appropriate to the native style of activation. Even though an object has registered as inside-out activation, the container may not permit this.
- Outside-in activation requires an explicit user action. This is the typical case for containers that often embed large objects and treat them as whole units.
- Inside-out activation interaction with an object is direct. Inside-out objects are indistinguishable from native data. Inside-out activation requires close cooperation between the container and the object.

IOleContainer and IOleItemContainer

A container is a relatively simple stand-alone application that serves as a host for either linked or embedded data. The container requires an instance of the **IOleClientSite** and **IAdviseSink** interfaces for each contained object. When the content objects are linked, the **IOleItemContainer** interface is also supported for monikers. Both **IOleContainer** and **IOleItemContainer** were included in the discussion of monikers in Chapter 5. They are mentioned here because this is their proper place in the COM architecture.

A generic container is illustrated in Figure 7-4. The **IOleItemContainer** interfaces are not needed if the Documents are not linked. **IOleItemContainer** is required to resolve an item moniker.

Figure 7-4 illustrates container concepts and not server concepts. Hence, moniker resolution is not illustrated; for file moniker resolution, the **IPersistFile** interface would be paired at the outer content object level with **IOleItemContainer**. The same is true of **IPersistStorage**. The **IPersistStorage** interface is normally exposed on the inner content object for item moniker resolution. The **IOleItem Container** interface is not supported on the innermost content object. Figure 7-7 represents a reasonably complete application with link sourcing; however, it is a server and without any container interface. You might want to pause and compare Figure 7-7 with Figure 5-7 of Chapter 5. The structure of both Figure 7-7 and Figure 5-7 is quite similar and Figure 5-7 only shows the related moniker binding interfaces.

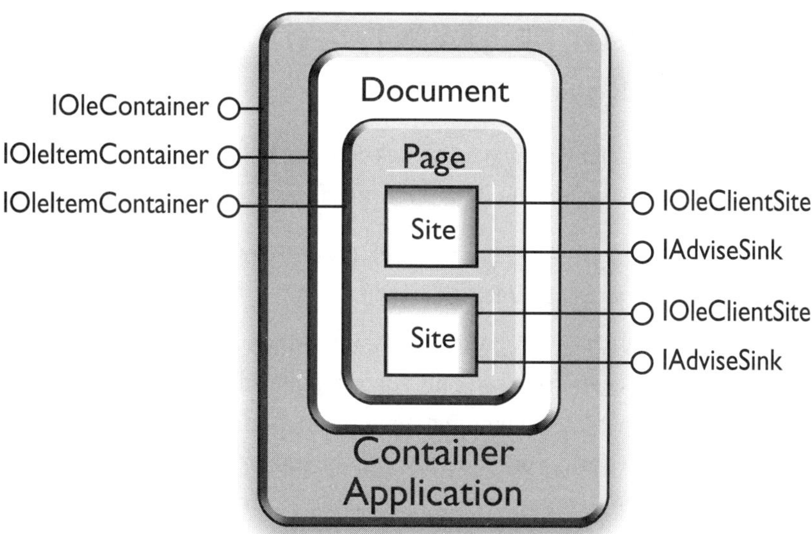

FIGURE 7-4 A generic container structure

IOleClientSite

We now have a new interface, **IOleClientSite**, which is the linked object's view of the local context. Think of this as an object that is wearing rose-colored glasses as it surveys its surrounding context. The interface supports all methods of **IUknown** and implements these:

- *GetContainer* — Returns a pointer to the embedding container's **IOleContainer** interface.
- *OnShowWindow* — Notifies a container when an object's window becomes visible or invisible.
- *GetMoniker* — Returns the container's moniker, the object's moniker relative to the container, or the object's full moniker.
- *RequestNewObjectLayout* — Called when a compound document asks for more or less room.
- *SaveObject* — Requests that the object attached to this client be saved.
- *ShowObject* — The container is asked to display the object.

The container uses **IOleObject::SetClientSite** to pass the content object the **IOleClientSite** interface pointer.

Object Handler, Mini, Local, and Full Servers

The container is only part of the equation. Let's look at the different types of server options before discussing server interfaces:

- *Full Server* — Similar to Excel, these are freestanding and support both linked and embedded objects.
- *Miniserver* — Similar to MS-Graph, which is shipped with Microsoft Word and Access, these can only support embedded objects and can only run in the context of a container application. A miniserver does not save its data to disk files and, consequently, cannot support linking. The data is usually saved to a container's compound file. Both full and miniservers are implemented as an EXE and are called local servers.
- *In-Process Server* — Similar to a miniserver but implemented as a dynamic link library (DLL) rather than as an EXE. No local procedure call (LPC) is required because it exists in the same address space as the application.
- *In-Process Object Handler* — Exists simply to display an object without the overhead of having to load a local server. It has minimal functionality.

Distinguishing between the different types of servers or handlers is important. For example, a data cache object must write directly to the container's window. The container owns the presentation window. This means that object rendering must be implemented as either an in-process server or as an in-process handler. It cannot be implemented as part of a local server such as Excel. COM provides default handlers. Figure 7-10 illustrates both a default object handler and a default cache handler.

Let's start with the minimal compound document we discovered in Chapter 6, which consists of the **IPersistStorage, IDataObject, IOleObject,** and **IViewObject** interfaces . It is a simple example that sources a whole object and not a partial (pseudo) object. I've added the **IOleCache2** interface (added below) and the **IViewObject2** interface for a realistic compound document model. Let's look at the role of each interface.

- **IOleObject** does all the work. **IOleObject::DoVerb** starts the object and **IOleObject::Close** stops the object.

- **IDataObject** (Chapter 6) manages the data extent and is used by containers when requesting a copy of specific data. It is also the interface through which the default handler (see Figure 7-10) asks for presentation data such as a bitmap or a metafile.
- The **IPersistStorage** (Chapter 4) interface manages the native data.

It ensures that the document is presented incrementally.

- **IOleCache2** manages the presentation data that is available to the container of the object even when the server application is not running or is unavailable. This interface is discussed below. **IOleCache** is the base class and **IOleCache2** is the desired implementation.
- **IViewObject2** (Chapter 6) manages object renderings onto a device context. **IViewObject2** is normally used by the default handler (see Figure 7-10).
- **IClassFactory** (Chapter 2) is responsible for object instantiation.

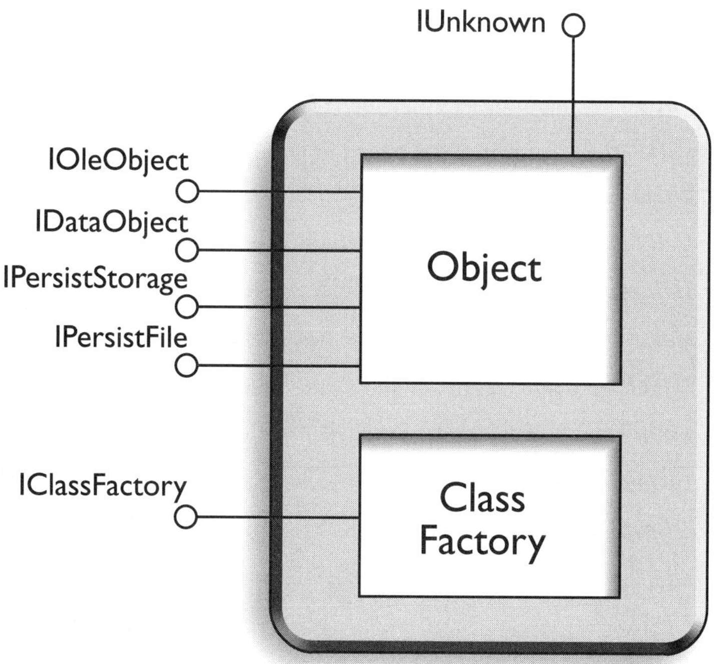

Link Source Server

FIGURE 7-5 A compound document embedded in a local server

IOleObject

You should be familiar with most of the interfaces mentioned above. The **IPersist*** interfaces control persistence, while the **IDataObject** interface controls Uniform Data Transfer. The new interface is **IOleObject,** which is the primary interface through which a linked or embedded object provides functionality to the container. It's not really new; we discussed this interface in Chapter 6. The **IOleObject** interface defines the content object. The object application must implement **IOle Object, IDataObject,** and **IPersistStorage** for each type of embedded object it supports.

IOleObject supports all methods of **IUnknown** and implements:

- *SetClientSite* — Informs a newly created or loaded embedded object of its client site in the container.
- *GetClientSite* — Queries an object for the pointer to its current client site in the container.
- *SetHostNames* — Specifies window title information to display when an object is open for editing.
- *Close* — Transitions an embedded object back to the loaded state.
- *SetMoniker* — Notifies the object of either its own moniker or its container's moniker.
- *GetMoniker* — Returns a connectable moniker to the object.
- *InitFromData* — Initializes an object with the supplied data.
- *GetClipBoardData* — Returns an exact copy of clipboard data.
- *DoVerb* — Requests that an object perform one of its verbs.
- *EnumVerbs* — Enumerates available verbs for an object in verb number order.
- *Update* — Ensures object data or view caches are current.
- *IsUpToDate* — Recursively checks to see if an object is up-to-date.
- *GetUserClassID* — Returns the CLSID corresponding to **IOleObject::Get UserType**.
- **GetUserType** — Determines the human-readable identification.
- **SetExtent** — Sets the logical rectangular limits.
- *GetExtent* — **IOleObject::GetExtent** returns the current extent, while **IViewObject2::GetExtent** allocates an extent from cache.

- *Advise* — Sets an advisory connection for the notification of close, save, rename, and link source changes to the object.
- *Unadvise* — Deletes an advisory connection.
- *EnumAdvise* — Enumerates the advisory connection for an object.
- *GetMiscStatus* — Returns miscellaneous status information.
- *SetColorScheme* — Specifies the color palette to use when editing the object.

Figures 7-5, 7-6, and 7-7 each represent different complexity levels of a compound document. The figures also represent the assembling of the technologies of the prior chapters. **IClassFactory** was discussed in Chapter 2, the **IPersist*** interfaces were discussed in Chapter 4, and **IDataObject** was discussed in Chapter 6. **IOleObject** was introduced in Chapter 6 only because it sources notifications to **IAdviseSink.** Its proper place is in this chapter. Binding with a moniker cannot be discussed meaningfully without the **IOleItemContainer** interface so it was discussed in Chapter 5; however, its proper place is in this chapter.

Figure 7-5 is too simple and only represents a compound document. Figure 7-6 represents an application with a portion of a linked object known as a pseudo-object. **IPersistFile** and **IOleItemContainer** are exposed on the document, while **IPersistStorage** is exposed on the embedded object. This is the expected architecture for moniker binding.

Identifying a pseudo-object was a question on the original Windows Open Services Architecture (WOSA) core examination; I don't recall, however, encountering this question on the new Windows Architecture I and II core examinations.

We can actually do something useful with the server illustrated in Figure 7-6. Let's not stop here as we peel back layers of complexity. We'll go one level deeper to illustrate the necessary connections.

Figure 7-7 provides us with a clue as to the purpose of **IOleItemContainer**. You may think of **IOleItemContainer** as the rental office for local sites. The container provides both services and resources to the client objects and Figure 7-7 shows the interfaces used for each interior object. **IOleItemContainer** is an extension of **IOleContainer**. Containers that use item monikers must implement **IOleItemContainer**. This interface is discussed extensively in Chapter 5; thus, this material should only be a review. Refer to Chapter 5 for **IOleItemContainer**'s participation in the moniker binding process.

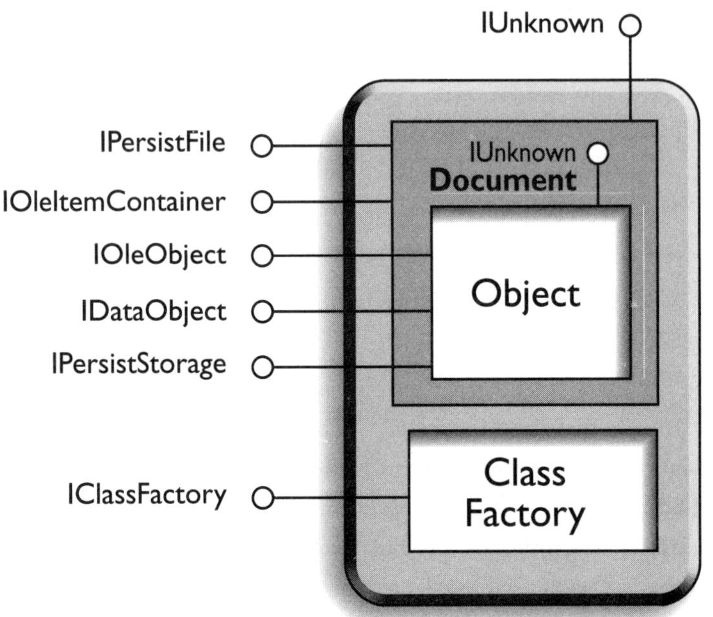

Link Source Server

FIGURE 7-6 An application with a portion of a linked object known as a pseudo-object

IOleItemContainer inherits all methods of **IUnknown**. It aggregates the method **IParseDisplayName** and inherits the methods of **IOleContainer. IOleItem Container** supports these methods:

- *GetObject* — Returns an item moniker as part of the binding process.
- *GetObjectSource* — Returns a storage pointer for the named object.
- *IsRunning* — Returns the object's running status.

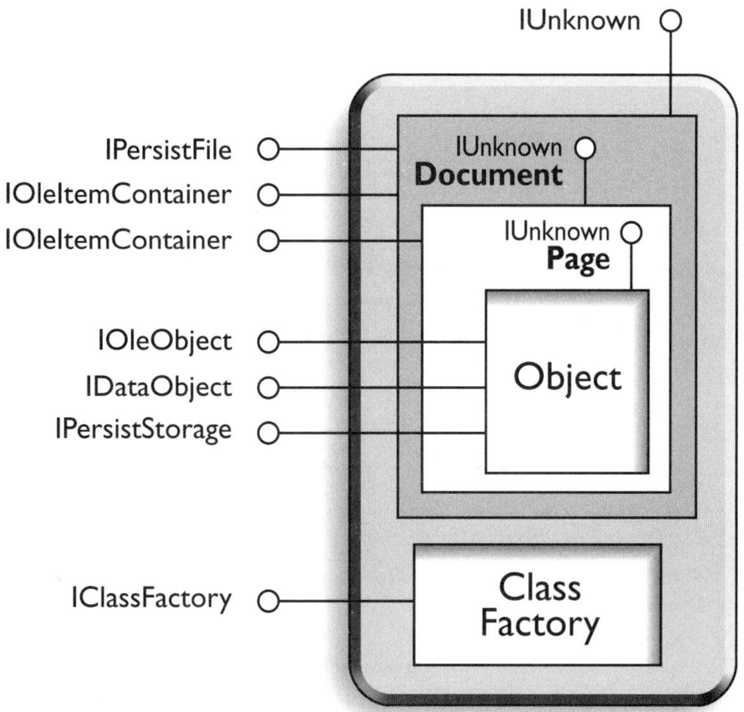

FIGURE 7-7 A link source for an embedded object

Building an Application

So far we've assembled a container with embedded content objects and the supporting interfaces. We also presented different levels of server complexity. The application is not complete and is not "runnable" without additional help from either an in-process server or an in-process handler. A handler that looks like an in-process server is the final element of the object linking equation. The basic data flow of an in-process handler is shown in Figure 7-8. This is a default handler with generic interfaces; implementing a custom handler, however, is always an option for the developer. Figure 7-9 expands Figure 7-8 to show the complete in-process handler supporting data flow for a linked object. The container owns the presentation window. Rendering is done by the in-process handler, which must run in the address space of the container. Marshaling is used to communicate with the object application.

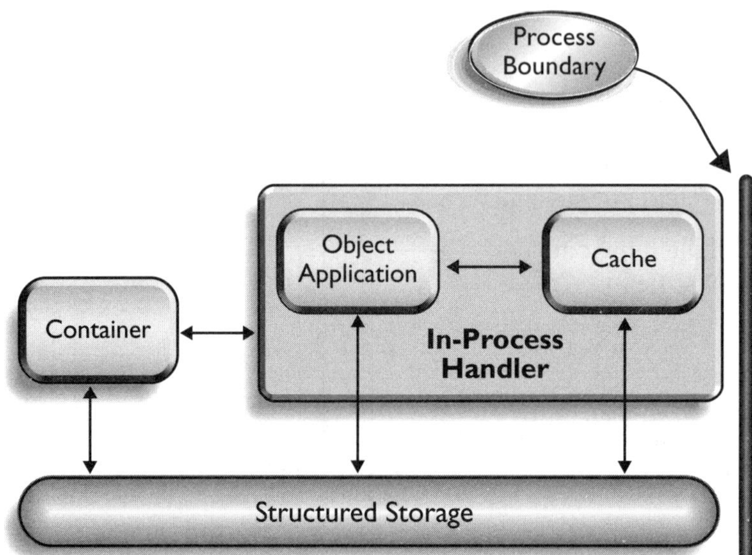

FIGURE 7-8 The basic data flow of an in-process handler

We know the functionality of the default handler. Let's consider the COM interfaces necessary for the default handler to connect the container site and server object and build our application. We start with the rule that a DLL object application must implement **IExternalConnection, IRunnableObject,** and the **IOleObject** interfaces. It generally implements at least **IDataObject** and **IPersistStorage**. **IPersistStorage::Save** and **IOleObject::Update** must call **IOleCache2::Update Cache** to update the cache nodes.

Even though some of the common interfaces are not shown, everything is put together in Figure 7-10, which represents the complete application. The in-process handlers have been merged with the content object, a container, and a cache handler. The linked object architecture of Figure 7-10 shouldn't be intimidating; we've discussed most of the interfaces previously. Note that the default object handler is aggregated with the default cache handler.

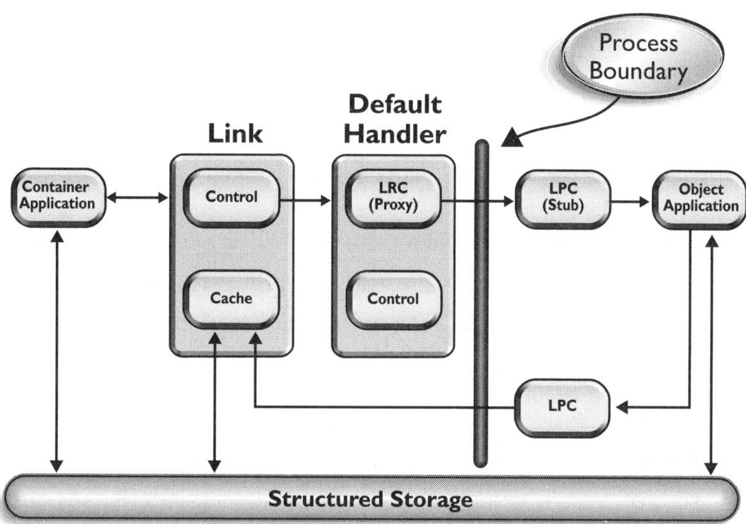

FIGURE 7-9 The complete in-process handler supporting a linked object's data flow

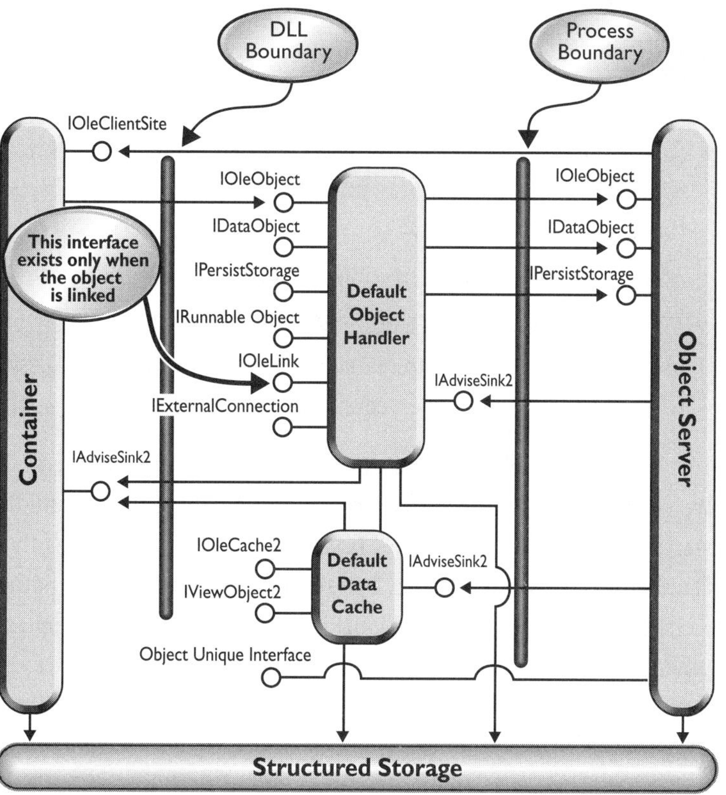

FIGURE 7-10 A complete application with interfaces for a linked object

Interfaces such as **IOleItemContainer** are not exposed in Figure 7-10. Detail is missing from both the Default Object Handler and the Object Server. Even without all the detail, Figure 7-10 does illustrate the general interface interactions.

Let's review the function of each interface and then fill in the missing pieces for those interfaces we have yet to discuss. (Not all interfaces are illustrated.)

- *IOleClientSite*—Provides the object's view of the context and is implemented by a container site. (Do not confuse this with a container document, which is managed with the **IOleItemContainer** interface.)
- *IAdviseSink2*—Receives asynchronous notifications. Equivalent to **IAdviseSink** with the added function **LinkSrcChanged**.
- *IOleObject*—The primary interface through which a linked or embedded object supplies functionality to the container. **IOleObject** represents a content object.
- *IDataObject*—Implements Uniform Data Transfer.
- *IPersistStorage*—Manages the **IStorage** interface.
- *IRunnableObject*—Manages transition to and from the running state.
- *IOleLink*—Signals that the item is linked.
- *IOleCache2*—An extension of **IOleCache** that enables an object to control what data is cached. It is very important because it saves a cached picture of the last image the user saw.
- *IViewObject2*—Renders the object using cache data.
- *IExternalConnection*—Required for silent updates of linked data. A link used by external objects to manage the lock count. Guarantees that data will not be lost on a broken connection.

Figure 7-10 is due some explanation beyond the enumeration of interfaces. We've built the application piecemeal, but its complexity is still formidable. Let's start first with the dual exposed **IOleObject** interfaces on both the Default Object Handler and the Object Server. The simple explanation is that both are content objects, but that doesn't suffice. Consider the scenario of a user opening a Word document. This makes Word the container in Figure 7-10. During the compound document loading process, structured storage items (streams) are encountered for Excel. Word loads a default in-process handler over the default cache object, which forces a delegation of the cache object. Word then passes the Excel data storage pointer to the **IPersistStorage** interface on the newly constructed in-process default handler. **IViewObject2** is used by Word to display the cached Excel data. Word finishes initialization and everything is displayed; however Excel hasn't started. There is no reason to start Excel until the user asks for activation.

At some later time, the user selects *Open* from the pop-up menu displayed on a mouse right-click. Word passes the verb to **IOleObject::DoVerb** to open the spreadsheet. (The OLE specifications state that the *Open* verb will open a presentation in a new window, which it eventually does.)

IOleObject::DoVerb is invoked on the in-process handler and not the local server, which in this case is Excel. This puts in motion a server instantiation mechanism with moniker binding (see Chapter 2 and Chapter 5), roughly described by these steps:

- OLE (from **DoVerb** on the default in-process handler implementation) calls **IMoniker::BindToObject(***IID_IOleObject***)**. This starts the retrieval process for the moniker stored within the in-process default handler object. (I've skipped some detail here such as **IBindCtx.** See Chapter 5 for additional detail.)
- **GetClassFile** is called. It calls **StgOpenStorage** and **ReadClassStg** and tries to retrieve the CLSID. (Recall that the CLSID immediately precedes the stream data and was placed there by **OleSaveToStream**. See Chapter 4.)
- When no CLSID is found, **GetClassFile** searches the Registry for the ProgID representing that file extension. The ProgID is then used to locate a CLSID stored in the Registry. If this fails, **BindToObject** fails.
- Assuming that nothing has failed, **BindToObject** calls **CoCreateInstance** for Excel with the supplied CLSID.
- The file moniker calls **IClassFactory::CreateInstance. IUnknown::QueryInterface** is called on the returned pointer asking for the **IPersistFile** interface.
- The file moniker next loads the file with a call to **IPersistFile::Load.**
- The **IPersistFile** interface is released by the file moniker by first calling **IPersistFile::QueryInterface**(*IID_IOleObject),* which retrieves the **IOleObject** pointer on the Excel object. This is followed by a call to **IPersistFile::Release**. This chicanery works since the OLE 2 design specification states that **IOleObject, IDataObject,** and **IPersistStorage** must be on the same interface as the source server's **IPersistFile** interface.

- The file moniker's last act is to return the just acquired Excel **IOleObject** pointer to the in-process default handler implementation of **IOleObject::DoVerb**.
- The **IOleObject::DoVerb** in-process handler implementation uses the returned **IOleObject** pointer and delegates the original *Open* verb to the local Excel server that is now running.
- Excel data changes are communicated back to the cache and the in-process handler interfaces with the two **IAdviseSink2** interfaces.

I said Figure 7-10 represented a linked object. Yes, it does. But it is also an embedded object. Remove the **IOleLink** interface and it becomes an embedded object. So, technically speaking, a linked object is an extension of an embedded object. I've established my introduction to Chapter 8. A linked object and an embedded object share common features. Each maintains a cache, each uses container functionality, and each requires its own storage object.

A container cannot tell the difference between a linked and an embedded object. The presence of the **IOleLink** interface signals a linked object. COM supplies default **IOleLink** implementation; the developer, however, always has the choice of providing a custom installation. **IOleLink** supplies the tools for managing the serialized moniker found in the object's storage and the moniker supplies the external data location.

Supporting Cast Members in Our Application

There are four new interfaces that haven't been mentioned yet: **IExternal Connection, IRunnableObject, IOleLink,** and **IOleCache2**. I'll throw in **IOleCache** because **IOleCache2** inherits from it. I'll also throw in **IOleCacheControl** to complete the picture. You're familiar with many of the supporting characters in our application. Here are some cast members from Figure 7-10 I've not discussed before and an update on some with which you have a passing acquaintance.

IExternalConnection

The IExternalConnection interface is not required for linking, but a developer is probably foolish for not implementing this interface. **IExternalConnection** is one of the three required interfaces for a DLL implementation. The other two required interfaces are **IRunnableObject** and **IOleObject**.

The **IExternalConnection** interface is a tool used for managing silent updates of linked data. The interface is a mechanism to track external locks on an embedded object, which ensures an orderly shutdown of the object. This prevents possible data loss during shutdown that occurs with unsaved changes when a connection is broken.

This interface supports all methods of **IUnknown** and implements these methods:

- *AddConnection* — Creates a strong external connection, which precludes the object from being prematurely released. A strong connection is created with locks or a moniker binding.
- *ReleaseConnection* — Releases an external connection.

This interface should be implemented with all embeddable compound-document objects that support links to themselves. (Rows in a spreadsheet are an example.) An in-place container uses the **OleLockRunning** API function to manage the lock states of an object. The stub manager has the responsibility of calling **IExternalConnection** whenever the connection status changes.

IRunnableObject

Object handlers and DLL object applications can determine when to transition into the running state and when to become a contained state. Silent (automatic) updates are supported. The default object handler supports **IOleContainer::Lock-Container,** as must any other DLL object implementation. **IRunnableObject** inherits all methods of **IUnknown** and implements:

- *GetRunningClass* — Returns CLSID of the running object.
- *Run* — Places an object in run state.
- *IsRunning* — Determines whether an object is running.
- *LockRunning* — Locks a running object into run state or unlocks a running object. (The object is closed on the last unlock.)

- *SetContainedObject* — Indicates the object is embedded in an OLE container.

IOleLink

We introduced the **IOleLink** interface in Chapter 5 as the bridge between a document and binding. It is repeated here, as this is its proper location in the architecture. The mere presence of the **IOleLink** interface means the document is linked. Without this interface the document is not linked. Linking requires monikers and the **IOleItem Container,** an interface introduced in Chapter 5, supports moniker binding.

The **IOleLink** interface supplies the necessary functionality to manage the object's moniker and update the linked object. An object is considered embedded in the absence of this interface. **IOleLink** inherits all methods of **IUnknown** and implements these methods:

- *SetUpdateOptions* — Sets the linked object's update options.
- *GetUpdateOptions* — Retrieves an object's update options.
- *SetSourceMoniker* — Stores the source moniker inside the object.
- *GetSourceMoniker* — Retrieves the source moniker from the object.
- *SetSourceDisplayName* — Parses a linked object's display name and stores that name within the object.
- *GetSourceDisplayName* — Retrieves the display name from the object.
- *BindToSource* — Binds the moniker contained within the linked object.
- *BindIfRunning* — Binds to the source if it is running with **IOleLink::Bind ToSource**.
- *GetBoundSource* — Retrieves the object connected to the link source.
- *UnbindSource* — Unbinds an object from a linked source.
- *Update* — Updates a linked object with the latest link source data.

IOleCache

This interface supports caching and wasn't used directly in Figure 7-10; however, **IOleCache** inherits all methods of **IUnknown** and supports these methods:

- *Cache* — Specifies the data format and other data to be cached within an embedded object.

- *Uncache* — Deletes a cache connection.
- *EnumCache* — Enumerates present cache connections.
- *InitCache* — Fills cache with either clipboard or drag-and-drop data.
- *SetData* — Fills cache from the indicated storage medium.

IOleCache2

IOleCache2 is an extension of **IOleCache,** which enables cache updating by a client object. **IOleCache2** inherits all methods of **IOleCache** and **IUnknown,** and, in addition, supports these methods:

- *UpdateCache* — Updates cache using supplied parameters.
- *DiscardCache* — Flushes memory caches. (**IDataObject::GetData** will revert to disk files.)

IOleCacheControl

This is the last tidbit on linking minutiae. **IOleCacheControl** is a specialized interface that a container does not need. It is used exclusively by object handlers and DLL object applications as the cache connection to the **IDataObject** implementation. This interface supports all methods of **IUnknown** and these methods:

- *OnRun* — Notifies the cache that the compound document has entered run state. (This creates a data advisory sink between the running object and cache.)
- *OnStop* — Notifies the cache that it should terminate any existing connections previously established by **IOleCacheControlOnRun**.

Key Point Summary

A compound document is an interaction model, which comes in two styles — embedded or linked. A linked document is almost a trivial extension of an embedded document. Except for the **IOleLink** interface, a container cannot distinguish between an embedded and a linked document. The major difference is that linked documents have a link to the data source embedded in the content object (serialized moniker), while an embedded object has a copy of the data.

- An OLE Document is an object that supports either the basic linking or embedding.
- Linked documents can be text, tabular data, a sound recording, a video recording, or pictures created by an application. This is not an inclusive list, only illustrative.
- All copies of a linked document reflect changes made by other users. This differs from embedded documents, which have a copy of the data. Editing of embedded documents does not affect other users.
- Linked documents may play in-place but cannot be edited in-place. They will open in their own windows for editing.
- Linked documents always use the least resources. Native data remains at the source.
- A container can support multiple levels of linking.
- Linked objects blend with the properties of the container. The container exports ambient properties to the object. These are display properties, and not properties of the linked source.

Applying What You've Learned

Here are a few review questions before we move on to embedding documents in the next chapter.

Instant Assessment

1. What is an OLE Documents representation?
2. What is the definition of an OLE component?
3. What is the definition of an OLE Document?
4. Explain compound document embedding.
5. Explain compound document linking.
6. What is the compelling reason to use linked OLE Documents instead of embedded documents?
7. What is an adaptable link?

8. An object is selected. When can object editing start?
9. What is outside-in activation?
10. What is inside-out activation?
11. Name an example of a full server.
12. When is a miniserver used?
13. What is an in-process server?
14. What is an in-process object handler?
15. The presence of what interface indicates a linked object?
16. What are the three nontrivial interfaces required for an object handler implementation?

For answers to the Instant Assessment Questions, see Appendix B.

Lab Exercise

Lab 7.17 measures the cost of linking versus embedding. Any object may be used, but one classic example is embedding a spreadsheet into a Word document. For this lab, let's assume you are using a Word document for the container.

There are two ways to measure the resources involved. The first is save the document on a periodic basis and monitor the size. You can monitor global memory from Microsoft Word 97. To view global memory from Microsoft Word 97 select: HELP ⇨ About Microsoft Word ⇨ System Info.

Lab 7.17 *Linking Objects Conserves Resources*

1. Create a Word document and save it. Note the file size. You should save two copies of this blank document. We'll use the second copy later for measuring the cost of embedding documents.
2. Create an Excel spread sheet with data. An easier choice is to locate a .jpg file and link it to the Word document. But don't stop there. Link in three more copies. This gives a total of four linked images. If your container is Word, go to the **Insert** menu and select **Object**. A dialog box is presented. Always **Create from File**. The object will be linked or embedded depending upon your position in this scenario.
3. Save the Word document and look at the file size. Subtract the original size and divide the extra space by four and you have a rough approximation of the cost of linking.

4. Repeat the above sequence, but this time embed the object. Be sure you start with a new blank Word document.
5. Compare the results.

CHAPTER

8

Document Embedding

About Chapter 8

You now know that document linking is just an extension of document embedding. This chapter and the previous chapter are collectively a discussion of OLE Documents, with this chapter focusing on the mechanics of in-place activation of an embedded document, which is a feature of OLE Documents.

Our old friend **IOleLink** is not found in this architecture. All of the interfaces supporting an embedded document are the same as those supporting a linked document. The differences are the interfaces that are necessary to support in-place activation and the absence of the **IOleLink** interface. Even though this chapter is titled "Document Embedding," the topic is in-place activation of embedded documents and the supporting interfaces.

We closed Chapter 7 after building an application and taking a close look at activating a linked object. We do the same in this chapter. As you've probably guessed, some new characters are added to our supporting cast. Because the topic is embedded document activation, it seems natural that most of the new characters are container-related OLE Document features. The new container interfaces include **IOleInPlaceSite, IOleInPlaceFrame,** and **IOleInplaceUIWindow; IOleInplaceObject** and **IOleInplaceActiveObject** are the new server interfaces. (You can see how this all fits together by peeking ahead at Figure 8-8, which is our application from Chapter 7 that is now capable of in-place activation.)

Before We Begin

This chapter is about only one issue: the in-place activation of a single Excel spreadsheet. There are a few general issues about embedded objects at the start of the chapter; however, use the illustrations as your guides to the chapter:

- *Figure 8-1* — The multiple levels of an Excel spreadsheet are identified.
- *Figure 8-2* — An embedded object with exposed sizing handles is activated.
- *Figure 8-3* — The structured storage for the Excel spreadsheet is represented. Note that the class identifier (CLSID) is stored in the data object, not in the container data stream (Word in our example) as it is with linked documents.
- *Figure 8-4* — Data flow for an embedded object. This is also the data flow for Figures 8-1, 8-2, and 8-8, which is the completed application.
- *Figure 8-5* — Our roadmap to the COM architecture, which identifies the interfaces required for in-place activation.
- *Figure 8-6* — An in-place capable container with the interfaces necessary for in-place activation exposed. This container is the same container as in Figures 8-4 and 8-8. Its presence is implied in Figures 8-1 and 8-2.
- *Figure 8-7* — An in-place capable server with the necessary in-place activation interfaces. This server is the same server as in Figures 8-4 and 8-8. Its presence is implied in Figures 8-1 and 8-2.
- *Figure 8-8* — The server of Figure 8-7 is merged with the container of Figure 8-6 along with our new interfaces and an in-process default handler to form our application. Figures 8-1, 8-2, 8-3, 8-4, and 8-8 are all different representations of the same embedded spreadsheet application.

Figure 8-8 is a bit complex. I will ease you into the more arcane issues of COM with a bit less frustration. This is one of the more difficult chapters in this book. If you comprehend this chapter, then Chapter 10, which is about OLE Controls or ActiveX components, will be a piece of cake because it is an extension of this material. Good Eating!

Compound Document Embedding and In-Place Activation

OLE linking uses the least memory resources because the data is kept at the source. Each embedded object is a copy of the original data. Consequently, embedded objects require significantly more resources than OLE linked objects that only store a link to the source.

Editing will affect all shared users of linked documents, but editing of embedded documents will not affect other users. For this reason in-place activation of linked documents is possible, but is not recommended. Data is stored locally in the container with an embedded document. OLE embedded documents retain their native, full-featured editing and operating capabilities in the container, and are edited in-place within the container and not in a separate window. Edits made to the data become a part of the document immediately and automatically, just like edits to native data. The user's last view of the data is cached and is known as presentation data. Both the presentation data and native date are changed with in-place editing. The presentation data does not change until the user edits the data with another in-place activation.

OLE embedded objects participate in the undo stack of the window in which they are activated. Changes can be abandoned if the topmost container includes an explicit command that prompts the user to save or discard changes to the container's file.

The user places a copy of the data in the container. The container can be another object or an OLE Document. Documents may be embedded within documents, as illustrated in Figure 8-1. Any of the traditional document embedding mechanisms can be used, an example being the Word **Insert** menu and the *Object* entry. When the **Link to Data** checkbox is not checked, the data is embedded in the container, which in this case is Word. The only difference between a linked document and an embedded document is the **IOleLink** interface. Object handlers play the same role for embedded documents that is played for linked documents.

Recognize in Figure 8-1 that the worksheet is the chart container while the OLE Document is said to be the spreadsheet's container.

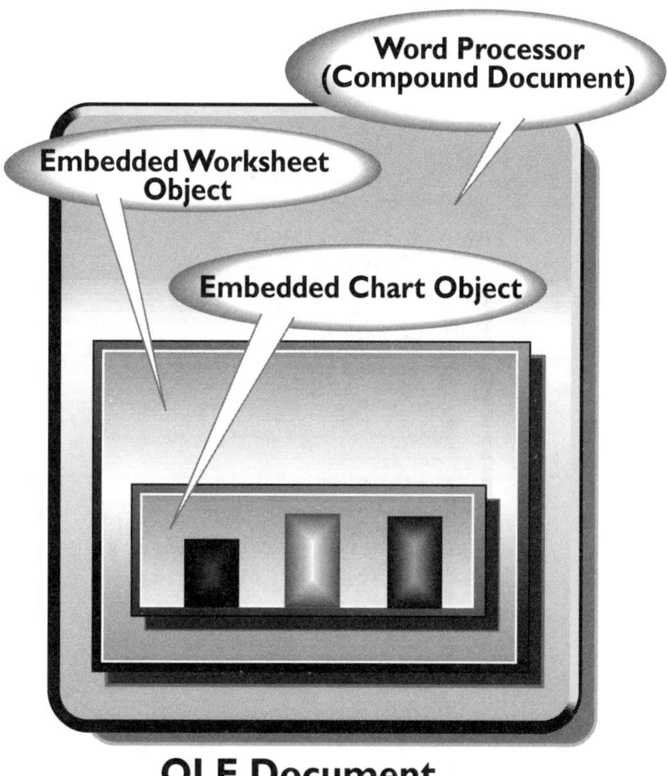

FIGURE 8-1 The multiple levels of an embedded Excel spreadsheet

The user can open OLE embedded objects in the active window. The object will have a 45-degree angle "hatched" pattern when the object is opened in its own window. This pattern is only displayed when the active object's menus appear in the topmost container's menu bar. Figure 8-1 is opened in its own window by double-clicking the object. This is a VISIO object, and the double-clicking results are shown in Figure 8-2.

OLE embedded documents support both outside-in and inside-out activation. Outside-in activation is the normal double-click sequence where the user "drills-down" on an object. A double-click from the mouse is required for each nested layer of the object. An object may be marked as `OLEMISC_ACTIVATEWHENVISIBLE`. This is still outside-in activation even though the top layer is activated automatically when visible. An object marked as OLEMISC_INSIDEOUT only requires one mouse click. When the mouse is clicked over a nested embedding, all layers are activated. This is inside-out activation where the object appears as native container data.

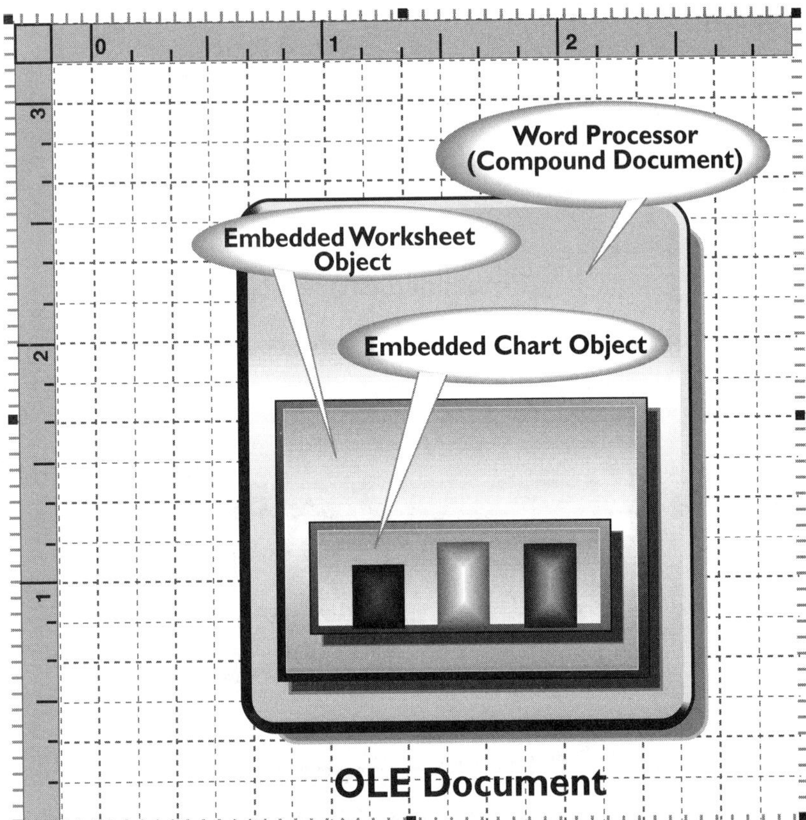

FIGURE 8-2 An embedded and activated object with exposed sizing handles

Let's interrupt our chain of thought for a moment and look at what the compound file might be for this object. I have often referred to compound files as a multi-headed hydra, in that there can be numerous streams opened simultaneously. Figure 8-3 shows the native data, the presentation data (the last user view), and the CLSID stored within a data object. Moniker binding is not required with an embedded object because the CLSID is known directly.

Figure 8-4 is the data flow for an embedded object and it is also the data flow for Figures 8-1, 8-2, and 8-3. Note that the object application, the container application, and the default object handler all have access to structured storage.

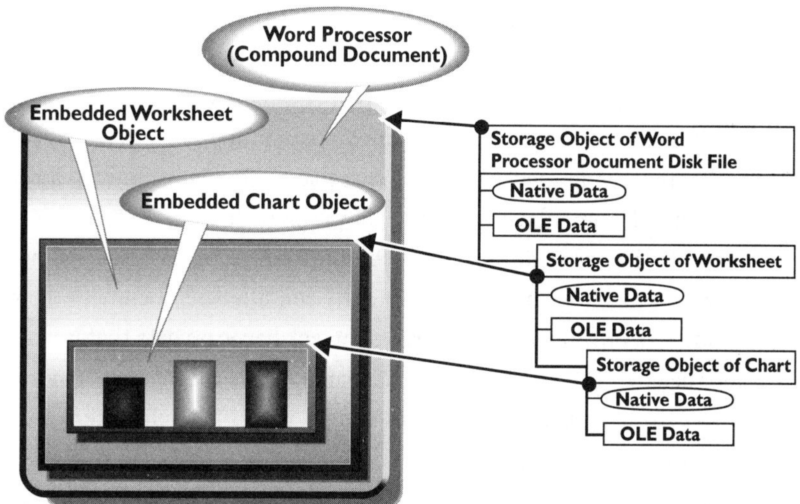

FIGURE 8-3 Compound storage structure for an embedded document

FIGURE 8-4 The data flow of an embedded object

We're now back on track with in-place activation. *Visual editing* is sometimes referred to as *in-place activation,* where a user double-clicks the object to edit the object in-place. This is different than editing a linked object that opens in its own window. Visual editing is a document-centric approach that insulates the user from the underlying mechanisms. In-place activation is commonly associated with embedded documents; it is possible, however, to do in-place activation on linked documents. The procedure is not recommended because of the surprise that the other users will get when you inadvertently edit a linked document. Poor planning, distraction, or simply carelessness can wreck havoc on data that is inadvertently edited or deleted. The accompanying sidebar sketches a few personal horror stories.

In-place activation merges menus, places a hatch pattern around the object's border, and changes the menu bar to reflect the new controls. The degree of change to the container's interface is determined solely by the container. This determination is made independent of the embedded object's capability. It is common to merge toolbars and menu bars, but this is not a requirement.

The following is a list of the characteristics of visual editing:

- ALT+ENTER is now the recommended shortcut key for the Properties command.
- OLE embedded objects can be supported by a pop-up menu using the SHIFT + F10 key.
- When an embedded OLE object is activated, it may display "adornments" and change menu bars. The title remains unchanged.
- Only a single level may be active at one time.
- If the object's menus appear in the menu bar, then a hatched pattern is shown around the border of the object.

Building an Embedded Document Application

You already know that the **IOleLink** interface distinguishes a linked object from an embedded object, so I'll move on to the finer details of in-place activation. The absence of key interfaces signals when an embedded document cannot be in-place activated. Figure 8-5 identifies the new interfaces needed to give our embedded document in-place activation or visual editing.

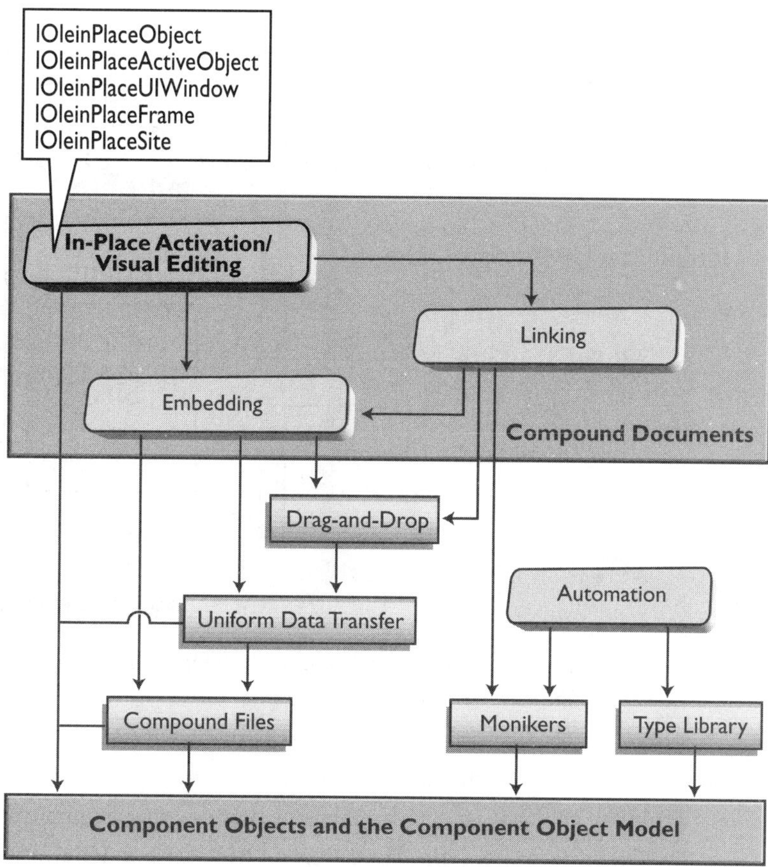

FIGURE 8-5 Our roadmap to the COM architecture, which identifies the interfaces required for in-place activation.

Let's see how these interfaces are used for in-place activation.

The container in Figure 8-6 has three new supporting interfaces for embedded document activation (visual editing):

- *IOleInPlaceFrame*—A new container-level interface that defines the concept of a frame and controls the container's top-level frame window. Only one of these interfaces is permitted per container. The interface manages merging the top-level user interface such as menu items and toolbars.
- *IOleInPlaceUIWindow*—This interface is used by object applications to negotiate border space on the document or frame window. It establishes a communication channel between the object and each frame and document window.

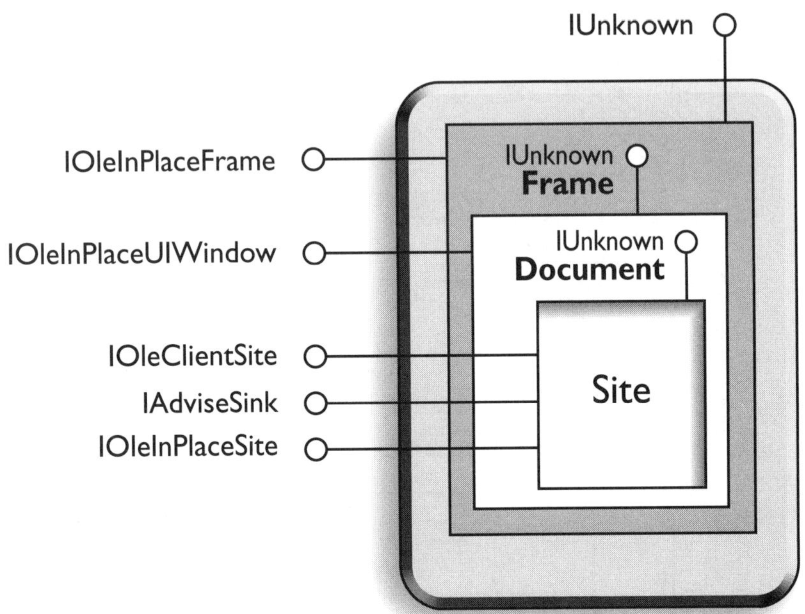

FIGURE 8-6 An in-place capable container with the interfaces necessary for in-place activation exposed

- *IOleInPlaceSite* — The duo is now a trio. The site representation object within the container is increased by one new member and now consists of the **IOleInPlaceSite, IOleClientSite,** and **IAdviseSink. IOleInPlaceSite** marks a site as in-place capable. Each embeddable site will expose these three interfaces.

The server illustrated in Figure 8-7 supports two new interfaces for in-place activation. One manages activation and deactivation while the other is quite elusive, existing only during activation.

- The interface **IOleInPlaceObject** marks objects as in-place capable. This interface can always be found with **QueryInterface** on any other interface of the object.
- The active object presents the **IOleInPlaceActiveObject,** which isn't found by the other interfaces. Consequently, **IOleInPlaceActiveObject** supplies its own **QueryInterface** definition. You can think of **IOleInPlaceActiveObject** as only a temporary interface. The **IOleInPlaceActiveObject** pointer is supplied by the object to the document with a call to **IOleInPlaceUIWindow::**

SetActiveObject and then to the container with a call to **IOleInPlaceFrame ::SetActiveObject**.

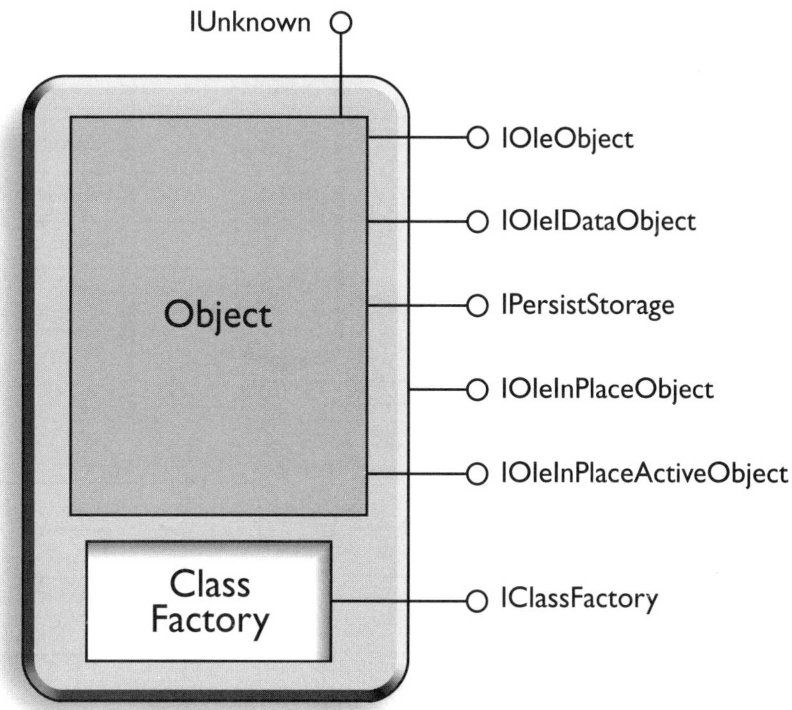

FIGURE 8-7 An in-place capable server with the necessary in-place activation interfaces

Figure 8-8 is built from three major pieces. The container of Figure 8-6 represents the container of Figure 8-8. The object server of Figure 8-8 was derived from Figure 8-7. The default handler is the same one we encountered in Chapter 7. Figure 8-8 is greatly simplified and detail is omitted. However, it should be very obvious that there is significant overhead with in-place activation. Why? Because all the server interfaces must be marshaled to the container.

Figure 8-4 is the equivalent of Figure 8-8. It represents the data flow for Figure 8-8. The local procedure calls (LPC) of Figure 8-4 are synonymous with a marshaling proxy and stub. The notation is just simplified. Remember that the server exists in a different address space than the container and in-process default handler. Now you should have an idea of why COM is so complex and servers don't always start immediately.

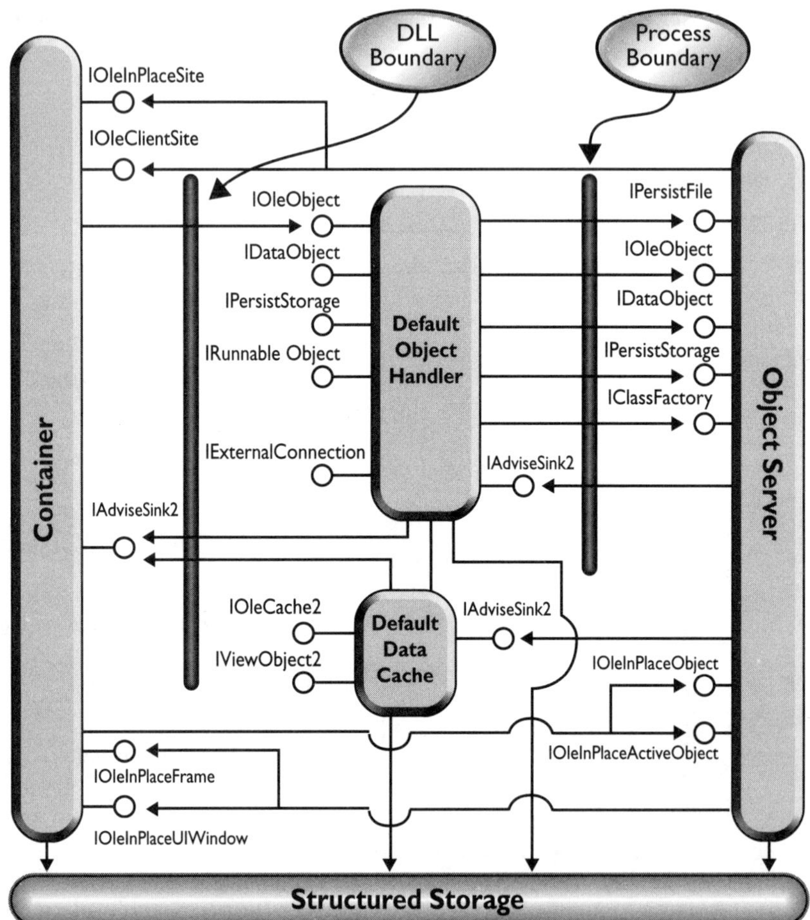

FIGURE 8-8 This embedded document is capable of in-place activation.

What are the missing links? In-place activation starts with **IOleObject::DoVerb**. The object then calls the container with **IOleClientSite::QueryInterface** looking for **IOleInPlaceSite**. The container returns a pointer to **IOleInPlaceSite** if it exists. The object opens as a regular embedded object when this interface doesn't exist. The in-place activation site exists, but can it be used? The next call is to the site itself asking for in-place activation support. This is done with the pointer just returned and the object calls **IOleInPlaceSite::CanInPlaceActivate** asking permission to in-place activate. (COM is quite polite. Later we learn where it warns the container of its intentions.) We now have the missing interface rules for both linked and embedded objects:

- An object is linked when the **IOleLink** interface is supported.
- An object server must expose the **IOleInPlaceObject** interface and the container must expose the **IOleInPlaceSite** interface to enable in-place activation. That doesn't always guarantee in-place activation, as you will discover in the next section.

Activating an Embedded Document

These are the necessary steps to activate an embedded document. The invocation mechanism is different than the linked document activation discussed in Chapter 7. That mechanism uses a moniker encountered in the Word stream to instantiate the Excel server. Binding is not necessary with server instantiation of an embedded document because the server CLSID, server data, and cache presentation are all stored together in the embedded data object as shown in Figure 8-2. Let's assume this is an Excel activation from Word similar to the activation example in Chapter 7.

Things start very easily for embedded documents during the loading process. As before, Word encounters the cache data object during the load process and loads a default in-process handler over the default cache object. This forces a delegation of the cache object. Word then passes the Excel cache data storage pointer to the **IPersistStorage** interface on the newly constructed in-process default handler. **IViewObject2** is used by Word to display the cached Excel data. Word finishes initialization and everything is displayed; Excel, however, hasn't started. There is no reason to start Excel until the user asks for activation.

At some later time the user double-clicks an embedded document and Word passes the *Edit* verb to the in-process default handler implementation of **IOleObject::DoVerb**. (The OLE specifications state that the *Edit* verb will open a presentation in a window of the host container.)

IOleObject::DoVerb is invoked on the in-process handler and not the local server, which in this case is Excel. This puts in motion a standard server instantiation mechanism (Chapter 2), roughly described by these steps:

1. OLE (from **DoVerb** on the default in-process handler implementation) calls **CoGetClassObject** with the Excel CLSID obtained from the embedded storage object and requests the **IClassFactory** interface. The **IOleLink** interface is missing and **DoVerb** knows this is an embedded document object.

2. **DoVerb** calls **IClassFactory::CreateInstance**. The returned object pointer is used to call **IUnknown::QueryInterface** and locates the **IPersistStorage** interface.
3. The object is initialized with a call to **IPersistStorage::Load**.
4. The **IPersistStorage** interface is released by the in-process default handler implementation of **DoVerb** by first calling **IPersistStorage::Query Interface**(*IID_IOleObject),* which retrieves the **IOleObject** pointer on the Excel object. The **IPersistStorage::Release** follows this. This chicanery works because the OLE 2 design specification states that **IOleObject, IDataObject, IPersistStorage,** and **IPersistFile** must all be on the same interface.
5. The in-process default handler implementation of **IOleObject::DoVerb** uses the returned **IOleObject** pointer and now delegates the original *Edit* verb to the local Excel server, which is now running. Up to this point, everything is classical COM object instantiation.
6. The object, Excel in our case, knows it has work to do because it was passed an *Edit* verb. An **IOleClientSite** pointer was passed to Excel along with the *Edit* verb and Excel calls **IOleClientSite::QueryInterface** asking for the **IOleInPlaceSite** interface. The container supports embedding when this interface exists. If it doesn't exist, the object will be opened in a separate window.
7. The container site exists, but can it be used? The server now calls **IOleInPlaceSite::CanInPlaceActive**. A negative reply will always be received if the container is displayed in an aspect other than `DVASPECT_CONTENT`. As in the last step, the alternative is always a separate window.
8. In-place activation needs the document and frame context. The interfaces **IOleInPlaceFrame** and **IOleInPlaceUIWindow** are each in different interfaces (see Figure 8-6), and are not available through **IOleInPlaceSite::QueryInterface**. An alternate mechanism is to call **IOleInPlaceSite::GetWindowContext** that returns the **IOleInPlaceFrame** and **IOleInPlaceUIWindow** interfaces.
9. The server declares its intention of in-place activation by calling **IOleInPlaceSite::OnInPlaceActivate**. This tells the container to allocate the necessary structures. The object's editing window is moved to the container, merging container and server menus and creating toolbars.

10. The document is now in the in-place active state. Nothing further is done when the requested state is `OLEIVERB_INPLACEACTIVE`.
11. When we want to proceed further to full activation, the container is warned of our intentions by calling **IOleInPlaceSite::OnUIActivate**. The **IOleInPlaceActiveObject** pointer is supplied by the object to the document with a call to **IOleInPlaceUIWindow::SetActiveObject** and then to the container with a call to **IOleInPlaceFrame::SetActiveObject**.
12. Several housekeeping steps remain, which I'll skip. Menus must be merged, toolbars displayed, and accelerator keys managed. The interfaces are now established and the embedded object looks quite like a custom control. Housekeeping is done and the object is activated.
13. Excel data changes are communicated back to the cache and the in-process handler interfaces with the two **IAdviseSink2** interfaces.

I'm nearly through with my discussion of compound documents, so I'll quickly move through the supporting interfaces I've just illustrated for in-place activation.

Supporting Cast Members in Our Application

It's not a "cast of thousands," so how about a cast of the "valuable few"? These are the definitions of the new interfaces introduced in this chapter to support in-place activation of embedded documents.

IOleWindow

This interface is the fountainhead of all **IOleInPlace*** interfaces; yet it hides in the background. This interface isn't shown in Figure 8-5, but all **IOleInPlace*** interfaces inherit all methods of this interface. Interfaces, which inherit from **IOleWindow** include **IOleInPlaceObject, IOleInPlaceActiveObject, IOleInPlace UIWindow, IOleInPlaceFrame, IOleInPlaceSite, IOleInPlaceSiteEx, IOleIn PlaceSiteWindowless,** and **IOleInPlaceObjectWindowless**. This interface inherits all methods of **IUnknown** and implements these methods:

- *GetWindow* — Returns the window handle of the window participating in the in-place activation. This can be a frame, document, parent, or in-place object window.
- *ContextSensitiveHelp* — Determines when help mode should be entered during in-place activation.

IOleInPlaceObject

The immediate container manages the activation and deactivation of an in-place object through the **IOleInPlaceObject** interface. This interface also determines how much of the in-place object should be visible.

IOleInPlaceObject inherits all methods of **IOleWindow** and **IUnknown**. **IOleInPlaceObject** implements these methods:

- *InPlaceDeactivate* — Deactivates an in-place object and discards the object's undo state.
- *UIDeactivate* — Deactivates and removes the user interface supporting in-place activation.
- *SetObjectRects* — Determines how much of the in-place object is visible.
- *ReactivateAndUndo* — Reactivates an object.

IOleInPlaceActiveObject

This interface is the communication channel between the document window containing the in-place object and the outermost window frame. The communications include message translation, window state (active or deactivated), and the document state (active or deactivated). The interface also notifies the object when to resize its borders and manages modeless dialog boxes.

This interface is not available through any **QueryInterface**. It is supplied by the object to the document with a call to **IOleInPlaceUIWindow::SetActiveObject** and then to the container with a call to **IOleInPlaceFrame::SetActiveObject**. These methods must be called in this order. The container uses this pointer in processing **IOleInPlaceFrame::SetMenu**.

This interface inherits all methods of **IOleWindow** and **IUnknown**. **IOleIn PlaceActiveObject** implements these methods:

- *TranslateAccelerator* — Translates messages from the active object's message queue.
- *OnFrameWindowActivate* — Notifies the active object when the container's top-level frame is activated or deactivated.
- *OnDocWindowsActivate* — Notifies the active in-place object when the container's document window is activated or deactivated.
- *ResizeBorder* — Notifies the object when to resize its border space with supplied parameters.
- *EnableModeless* — Enables or disables a modeless dialog box.

IOleInPlaceUIWindow

This is a container interface, which is used to negotiate border space on the document or frame window. This interface inherits all methods of **IOleWindow** and **IUnknown**. **IOleInPlaceUIWindow** implements these methods:

- *GetBorder* — Returns a RECT (see Win32 application programming procedure (API(documentation) structure for active use of toolbars and similar controls.
- *RequestBorderSpace* — Requests border space around the active in-place object's frame window.
- *SetBorderSpace* — Allocates border space requested in the **IOleInPlaceUIWindow::GetBorder** call.
- *SetActiveObject* — Establishes a direct channel between the active in-place object and the frame and document windows.

IOleInPlaceFrame

Container applications use this interface to control the display and placement of the composite menu, keystroke accelerator translation, context-sensitive help mode, and modeless dialog boxes. This interface inherits all methods of **IOleWindow, IOleUIWindow,** and **IUnknown**. **IOleInPlaceFrame** implements these methods:

- *InsertMenus*—Called by the object application to allow the container to insert its menu groups in the composite menu.
- *SetMenu*—The composite menu is installed into the window frame containing the object being activated.
- *RemoveMenus*—A request from the object application to the container application. The container is asked to remove its menu elements from the composite menu.
- *SetStatusText*—Text is set and displayed in the container's frame window status line.
- *EnableModeless*—A frame's modeless dialog box is enabled or disabled.
- *TranslateAccelerator*—Accelerator keystrokes that are targeted for the container's frame are translated.

IOleInPlaceSite

This interface is implemented by container applications and is used to interact with the object's in-place client site. This interface inherits all methods of **IOleWindow** and **IUnknown**. **IOleInPlaceSite** implements these methods:

- *CanInPlaceActivate*—Determines if the object can be activated in-place.
- *OnInPlaceActivate*—Notifies the container when one of its objects is being activated in-place.
- *OnUIActivate*—Notifies the container that in-place activation is about to occur and the container's menu will be replaced with the in-place composite menu.
- *GetWindowContext*—The in-place object retrieves the window interfaces that form the window object hierarchy. Also returns the position in the parent window.
- *Scroll*—The in-place object requests to the container to scroll the in-place object by the supplied pixel count.
- *OnUIDeactivate*—Notifies the container that it should reinstall its user interface and take focus.
- *OnInPlaceDeactivate*—Sends a notification to the container that the object is no longer active.

- *DiscardUndoState* — The active object sends a request for the container to discard its Undo State.
- *DeactivateAndUndo* — The active object sends this to the container when a user invokes Undo immediately after activating an object.
- *OnPosRectChange* — The in-place object calls this when the active object's extents have changed.

Compound Document Optimizations

The following interfaces are not part of the original OLE implementation using COM; they came about as a result of ActiveX Controls 96 and the need to improve the functionality of OLE/ActiveX controls on the Internet. They are included in this chapter strictly for closure because they all inherit from **IOleWindow**.

IOleInPlaceSiteEx

This is an add-on interface to **IOleInPlaceSite.** It avoids unnecessary screen flashing when an object is activated or deactivated. This interface inherits all methods of **IOleWindow, IOleInPlaceSite,** and **IUnknown**. **IOleInPlaceSiteEx** implements these methods:

- *OnInPlaceActivateEx* — The embedded object calls this interface at acti vation to determine if it needs redrawing.
- *OnInPlaceDeactivateEx* — The container is notified whether the object needs to be redrawn at deactivation.
- *RequestUIActivate* — The container is notified that the object is about to enter the UI-active state.

IOleInPlaceSiteWindowless

IOleInPlaceSiteWindowless works with **IOleInPlaceObjectWindowless** to implement an environment where an in-place object can be activated without requiring a window or the associated window resources.

Small controls do not need a window. The **IOleInPlaceSiteWindowless** interface addresses these matters:

- It is an extra burden on a control to have a window that isn't needed or wanted.
- The **IOleInPlaceSiteWindowless** interface supports nonrectangular controls, a feature not previously available.
- Requiring a window prevents the control from being transparent.

Windowless objects are an extension of normal compound documents. The windowed and windowless objects both use the same definitions for OLE states. The only difference is that windowless objects do not consume window resources. The container provides the services to the object, which are normally associated with a window.

A windowless object in a client server application should query its site for the **IOleInPlaceSiteWindowless** interface. The object calls the container with **IOleInPlaceSiteWindowless::CanWindowlessActivate** when the interface exists. The object should behave like a standard compound document and create a window environment when the **IOleInPlaceSiteWindowless** interface does not exist.

Windowless objects must be in-place active to receive mouse or keyboard messages. Windowless objects obtain services from the container for capturing the mouse, setting focus, obtaining a device context, or deciding to paint.

The **IOleInPlaceSiteWindowless** interface is derived from the **IOleIn PlaceSiteEx** interface and inherits all methods of **IOleWindow, IOleInPlaceSite, IOleInPlaceSiteEx,** and **IUnknown. IOleInPlaceSiteWindowless** implements these methods:

- *AdjustRect* — Adjusts a rectangle when it is partially or entirely covered by opaque objects.
- *CanWindowlessActivate* — Informs an object when its container can support a windowless in-place activation.
- *GetCapture* — Determines whether mouse capture is available to the active in-place windowless object.
- *GetDC* — Returns a handle to the device context (see Win32 API documentation).

- *GetFocus* — Determines whether an active in-place windowless object has keyboard focus.
- *InvalidateRect* — Enables an object to invalidate a specified rectangle of its in-place image on the screen.
- *InvalidateRgn* — Enables an object to invalidate a specified rectangle of its in-place image on the screen.
- *OnDefWindowMessage* — Invokes default-message handling for the object.
- *ReleaseDC* — Releases the device context obtained with **IOleInPlaceSite Windowless::GetDC**.
- *ScrollRect* — Scrolls through an area with the in-place object's image on the screen.
- *SetCapture* — Enables the capturing of all mouse messages for an in-place windowless object.
- *SetFocus* — Sets the keyboard focus to an in-place windowless object.

IOleInPlaceObjectWindowless

IOleInPlaceObjectWindowless is the other half of the windowless object equation. This interface enables a windowless object to process window messages and participate in drag-and-drop operations.

Small controls do not need windows. The container is expected to implement the **IOleInPlaceSiteWindowless** interface. The object must act as a normal compound document when the **IOleInPlaceSiteWindowless** interface does not exist.

IOleInPlaceObjectWindowless is derived from **IUnknown, IOleWindow, and IOleInPlaceObject**. **IOleInPlaceObjectWindowless** implements these methods:

- *OnWindowMessage* — Dispatches a message from the container to a windowless object.
- *GetDropTarget* — Supplies the **IDropTarget** interface for a windowless object.

Key Point Summary

In-place activation of embedded objects is quite powerful and eases the user's burden. This comes at a significant cost:

- In-place activation of embedded documents promotes management problems where there may be multiple copies of the data, each of which is different.
- Applications supporting embedded documents are complex to develop. It's fair to say that any application that supports OLE Documents is complex to develop and this includes both linked and embedded documents. The easiest-to-use applications are always the most difficult to implement.
- Embedded documents are resource intensive. A private copy of the native data is stored in the container object.
- Editing an embedded document changes both the presentation and native data immediately.
- Editing an embedded document does not affect other users.
- Embedded documents are edited in their own window.
- An embedded document merges menus and toolbars.

Applying What You've Learned

Embedding an object is almost a cliché when Excel is embedded in Word. Many other Microsoft tools, however, support embedded objects. The questions that follow will test your understanding of the embedded document architecture, while the laboratories will show you that a container is not always a container. That is, the containers respond differently to an embedding of the same object. Your goal as a developer is to always have your tools respond in the same manner. Unconventional software is very error-prone even though the implementation is very clever. Function should always come before form and form should not be unique.

Instant Assessment

1. What is another name for in-place activation?
2. Explain the difference between an embedded document and a linked document.
3. What interface does the object request of the container when in-place activation starts?
4. Assume that the interface **IOleInPlaceSite** exists. What is the next logical step for in-process activation?
5. You have implemented an embedded application. The user complains that the screen flashes too much. Which interface is faulty (or which did you forget to implement)?
6. Explain a windowless object implementation.
7. What type of object is a candidate for a windowless object implementation?
8. Which container interface must exist before an object can do a windowless activation?
9. When will a windowless control be activated as a normal object?
10. When will the edited data of an embedded object be saved?

For answers to the Instant Assessment Questions, see Appendix B.

Lab Exercises

These labs are designed to acquaint the new Microsoft user with embedding objects. There are two methods for doing this. For these exercises, we'll use the mouse and embed our object using menus. The other method is to drag and drop, which is found in an earlier section.

I've created a small object with VISIO, which you can use for testing object embedding. The file `BLOB.jpg` is located on the CD-ROM in the <unit>\EXAMPLES\CHAPTER8 folder that accompanies this book.

Lab 8.18 *Visual Basic and object embedding*

1. Start Visual Basic 5.0 or Visual Basic 6.0.

2. Select **Toolbox** from the **View** menu if no toolbox is present.
3. Click an **Image** control and paint it on the form.
4. Click a **Picture** control and paint it on the form.
5. Click an **OLE** control and paint it on the form. The **OLE** control responds with a dialog box.
6. Select **Create Form File** and browse the path of `BLOB.jpg`
7. Set the **Picture** property of both the **Image** control and the **Picture** control to the path for `BLOB.jpg`.
8. Run the form.
9. Double-click all controls.

In-place activation occurs for only the **OLE** control. Neither the **Image** control nor the **Picture** control, which is an extended version of the **Image** control, will activate.

Lab 8.19 *Access 97 and object embedding*

Access 97 reacts quite differently to embedding an object. Access 97 is an automation controller and has the capability of managing embedded objects.

1. Open Access 97.
2. Create a blank form.
3. Select **Object** from the **Insert** menu.
4. Browse your system until you find `BLOB.jpg` or any other .jpg file.
5. Click **OK**.

After a few seconds the object will appear on the form. Look at it very carefully. Access 97 has packaged the object within an OLE container. It is in an unbound object frame, which you can inspect using the property window of Access 97.

Access 97 and Visual Basic are each different in subtle ways. Both can support embedded objects; Access 97, however, has an **Insert** menu while Visual Basic 5.0 and 6.0 do not.

1. Select an **Image** control and paint it on the form.
2. Answer the **Insert Picture** dialog box by browsing for `BLOB.jpg`.
3. Select an **Unbound Object Frame** and paint it on the form.
4. Select **Create From File** and browse for `BLOB.jpg`.

You should have three copies of `BLOB.jpg` on the form. Two copies are in an **Unbound Object Frame** and one copy is in an **Image** control.

5. Set the **Enabled** property of the **Unbound Object Frames** to *Yes* and set the **Locked** property of those it controls to *No*. Note that the **Image** control does not have an **Enabled** or **Locked** property.
6. Start Access 97. The **Unbound Object Frames** will activate in place while the **Image** control cannot be activated.

In-place activation also works for **Bound Object Frame**.

Lab 8.20 *Excel 97 and object embedding*

Objects may be embedded in Microsoft Excel 97.

1. Start Excel.
2. Select a cell in the center of the screen.
3. Select **Object** from the **Insert** menu.
4. Select **Create From File** and browse for `BLOB.jpg`
5. After the image is displayed, click on another cell and then double-click the image. Paintbrush will start.
6. Return to Excel.

Note that you can drag the image. The image was not embedded in the cell, but was placed on top of the worksheet.

Lab 8.21 *Outlook 97 and object embedding*

Objects may also be embedded in Microsoft Outlook 97. Start Outlook 97.

1. Double-click an existing e-mail message or create a new message.
2. Tap the space bar to move the cursor in slightly and then select **Object** from the **Insert** menu.
3. Select **Create From File** and browse for `BLOB.jpg`.
4. After the image is displayed, double-click it. Paintbrush will open.

Lab 8.22 *Power Point 97 and object embedding*

Microsoft Power Point 97 can have embedded objects. In-place activation, however, cannot be done when in **Slide Show** mode. An object may be embedded on an individual slide or it may be embedded in the master slide, which makes it visible on all other slides.

1. Start Power Point 97.
2. Create a new presentation or open an existing presentation.
3. For an object that should be visible on all slides, such as a logo, select **Master ⇨ Slide Master** from the **View** menu.
4. Embed the object by selecting **Object** from the **Insert** menu.
5. Select **Create From File** and browse for `BLOB.jpg`.
6. After the image is displayed, double-click it. Paintbrush will open.

Lab 8.23 *Microsoft Project 4.1 and object embedding*

An object may be embedded in Microsoft Project 4.1. Like Excel 97, Project 4.1 opens with a default working document and an object can be embedded directly.

1. Start Project 4.1.
2. Embed the object by selecting **Object** from the **Insert** menu.
3. Select **Create From File** and browse for `BLOB.jpg`.
4. After the image is displayed, double-click it. Paintbrush will open.

CHAPTER

9

Automation

About Chapter 9

This chapter is about a different technology based on COM. *Automation* or what used to be known as *OLE Automation* is the exposing of properties and methods for manipulation by a client application. This technology is separate from OLE technology, which is also based on COM. The confusion comes about because both OLE Documents (linking and embedding), and Automation may be used by an object, but each are separate technologies based on COM. Unfortunately, the term OLE has been loosely applied to any technology based on COM, which is not correct. OLE Automation does not support linking and embedding of documents. It only supports the exposing of properties and methods for manipulation by a client application, which is now known as Automation.

Automation is the **IDispatch** interface discussed in Chapter 2. We briefly discuss some Automation issues in this chapter, and then step into examples of Automation.

Automation: A Different COM Technology

Welcome to Automation. It's been a long trip getting here, but the difficulty was worth it. This section is where we start to tie everything together. You'll shortly discover that COM interfaces are everywhere and the **IUnknown** interface is ubiquitous in the Microsoft architecture. Figure 9-1 represents an OLE Automation object that uses the classic COM **IUnknown** interface, first introduced in Chapter 2. Automation uses COM but it is not OLE linking or embedding. (Embedding and linking are not features of Automation.) *OLE Automation* is the capability of an application object (application server) to define a set of properties and commands and make them accessible to other applications to enable programming. The public exposure of these properties and commands allows one application to contain code that manipulates another application.

An Automation object contains the **IUnknown** interface (see Figure 9-2), which has become a ubiquitous component of the Microsoft architecture. I said earlier in this book that component technology is now. **IUnknown** is an element of every ActiveX component, which is illustrated by the C++ OLEVIEW tool and a very simple COM component.

What's in a Name?

Apparently Microsoft marketing names technology. Such is the case with technologies based on COM. Neither OLE Automation nor OLE Database (OLEDB) support linking or embedding; however, both use the acronym OLE. OLE Automation was eventually renamed *Automation*.

Microsoft marketing also renames technology to create an aura of innovation. OLE Messaging, Messaging API (MAPI), and Collaborative Data Objects (CDO) are each the same basic technology, however, anyone unaware of the Microsoft marketing machinations will believe that each of these technologies is new and wonderful.

Sometimes Microsoft warns us that technology is being renamed. Such is the case with the renaming of OLE Controls to ActiveX. Nothing changed except the name. ActiveX controls evolved, not because of the renaming, but because of Internet performance requirements.

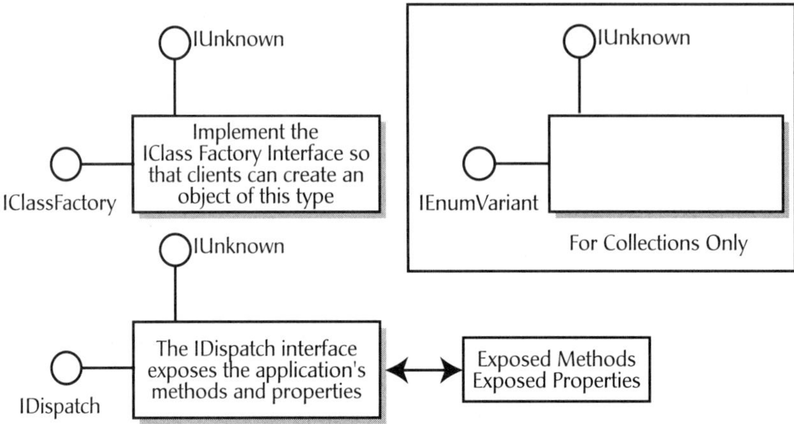

FIGURE 9-1 An OLE Automation (Automation) Object

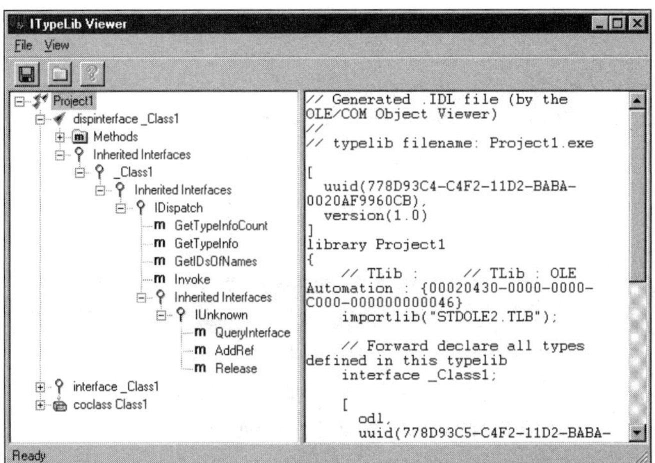

FIGURE 9-2 IUnknown is a ubiquitous feature of Microsoft architecture

Automation uses COM and the supporting infrastructure. You should recognize the interfaces from Figure 9-1. The key difference is that Automation does not support the linking or embedding that are features of OLE compound documents. The key infrastructure issues of Automation include:

- A storage mechanism that can support transactions and incremental loading and storing which promotes efficient use of memory. This is the structured storage of COM, which is available to all COM participants. There is no requirement to use structured storage with Automation files because the files are generally not compound files.

- The ability to associate a logical name with an object is required for unique object identification. This requirement exists for both OLE Documents and Automation objects. The global unique identifier (GUID) and interface identifier (IID) are used in both technologies.
- A mechanism for interprocess communications that combines data in a package before sending it. The mechanism can service all applications regardless of whether they support OLE Documents. (This is an example of marshaling, which was discussed in Chapter 5.)
- The application that creates an object need not support OLE; however, the accepting application must support OLE.
- Both OLE Documents and Automation use the Registry to locate servers. Server and parameter attributes are stored in type libraries.

OLE Automation refers to the ability of an application to define a set of properties and commands and make them accessible to other applications to enable programmability. Two components participate in Automation: a client and an Automation object or server:

- An *OLE Automation controller* or client is an application that can manipulate exposed components belonging to another application.
- The application that exposes the components is called the *OLE Automation server.*

The role of an Automation controller is to use the inherent features of the application to manipulate the exposed methods and properties of an OLE Automation server. *Being a good OLE client is a requirement for being an OLE Automation application controller*. An OLE client is a program that can store and display OLE objects, which may be either linked or embedded. A good OLE client provides support for both visual editing and drag and drop.

Programmability is a key issue in being a good OLE Automation controller, as this is the primary tool used to manipulate the OLE Automation server. This is different than an OLE server, which is a program that can edit and create OLE objects for other programs to display and store. OLE servers provide objects (either linked or embedded) that OLE clients can display.

Choosing an application controller is a function of the type of data. The first question to ask is, "What type of data will the integrated solution present or be allowed access to?" Microsoft Access supports OLE Automation and has visual editing. Access is the tool of choice for storing and manipulating data. It can be tightly integrated with Microsoft Excel, which is a good OLE Automation server. Microsoft Excel, however, is a better choice when your data is worksheet-related.

Microsoft Visual Basic is not designed for any particular type of data, but it is an excellent container for OLE objects. Visual Basic also supports OLE Automation and has visual editing support.

I suspect there is some confusion about now because nearly all Microsoft products support Visual Basic for Applications (VBA). The supporting of VBA does not make a tool an Automation controller. In the weakest sense, it is performing remote Automation using VBA.

Another way to look at Automation is to note that only Microsoft Access and Microsoft Visual Basic support the embedding of OLE objects in controls. This provides the container through which methods and properties are exposed.

I repeat the statement *being a good OLE client is a requirement for being an OLE Automation application controller* in Table 9-1. The rules are not hard and fast, as VBA is ubiquitous in Microsoft Office 97, but in the strictest sense, Table 9-1 represents practical and reasonable choices. Microsoft Word is not a good Automation controller since it does not support drag –and drop. Yes, I suppose Excel could be an Automation controller in some circumstances, but there are limitations, such as the lack of drag-and-drop control.

TABLE 9-1 FACTORS IN CHOOSING AN AUTOMATION CONTROLLER

GOOD OLE CLIENT	*GOOD OLE AUTOMATION CLIENT*	*OLE AUTOMATION SERVER*	*VISUAL EDITING*	*CONTROLLER*
Word	X		X	X
Project	X		X	X
Access	X	X	X	X
Excel	X	X	X	X
Visual Basic	X	X	X	X
Visio			X	X

Table 9-1 shows that Visual Basic and Access are not OLE servers because they cannot be controlled.

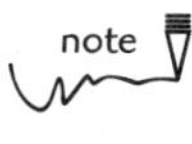

Visual Basic is probably the best choice for the centralized control model because it is not designed to handle any particular type of data.

Figure 9-3 illustrates a very simple application consisting of numerous components. This is obviously a standalone application and a reasonably realistic architecture is tiered. I'm sure most of you have dealt with a two-tier architecture where the client is linked to the server.

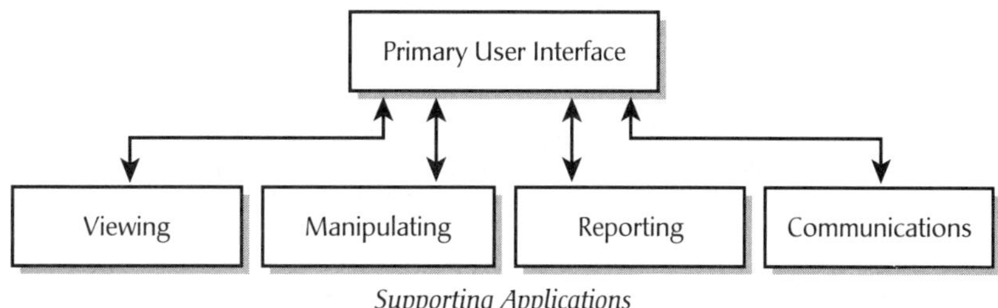

FIGURE 9-3 A centralized control model composed of several applications

Automation as a Portal to Newer Technology

Automation will remain with us but it is just the first of many steps to newer and more advanced technologies. The first logical step after Automation is *Remote Automation*. Technology has advanced beyond Remote Automation and Microsoft delivered Distributed COM (DCOM, see Chapter 21) with Windows NT 4.0. Still another technology step is the Distributed Transaction Coordinator (DTC) of Microsoft SQL Server 6.5. This technology is now encapsulated within Microsoft Transaction Server (MTS). Another recent technology is Microsoft Message Queue (MSMQ), which is one more component architecture building block. Both MTS and MSMQ depend upon DCOM as the enabling technology.

Figure 9-4 represents a component application, whose architecture is one of assembling building-block components. The unique feature of Figure 9-4 is that all the components are in a near proximity, which means the same address space.

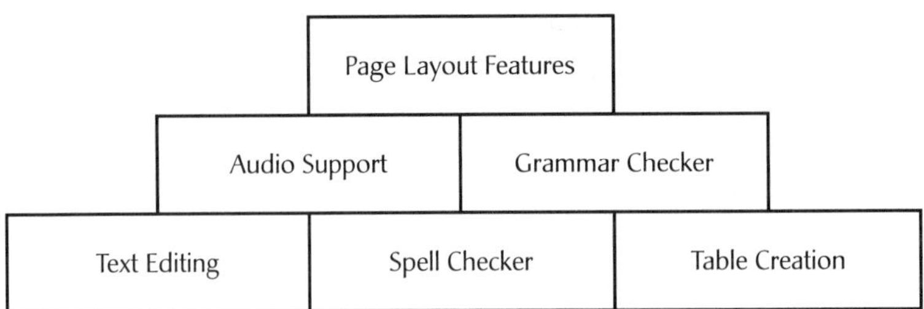

FIGURE 9-4 **A conventional component application with all the components sharing the same address space**

Take Figure 9-4 and provide both lateral and longitudinal separation. Rename the functions and you have the tiered architecture of Figure 9-5.

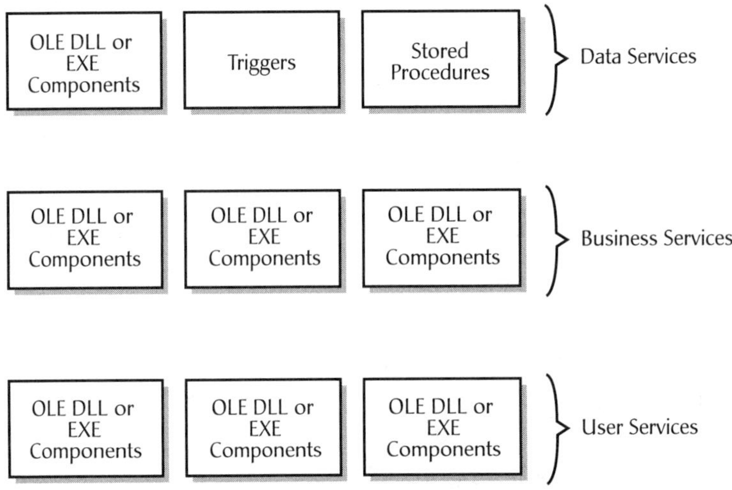

FIGURE 9-5 **A generic three-tier business application**

There is no upper limit to the number of tiers in an architecture; Figure 1-5 of Chapter 1 represents a four-tier architecture. It is always a matter of the problem at hand. The smallest nontrivial tiered architecture has three tiers. These tiers can be reasonably divided into user services, business services, and data services. Figure 9-5 illustrates such an architecture. The objects in this architecture communicate with DCOM, but that is not a requirement. User services and business services may exist on the same host. Remote business rules are not a requirement for a tiered architecture and Figure 9-5 is a logical model and not a physical model. The transparency is in the stub and proxy mechanism that supports marshaling (see Chapter 5, and Chapter 21,). Substituting a stub and a proxy on the client system changes a *local procedure call* (LPC) to a *remote procedure call* (RPC). Microsoft promised that the implementation of DCOM would be transparent and it was.

note **The layers in an architecture can increase very quickly. A departmental roll-up application can have three tiers. That may feed into a regional roll-up application, which in turn may feed into a corporate roll-up.**

Figure 9-5 will have business rules as the second tier. Both the second and third tier will be shared applications; hence, the need for an object-oriented architecture.

Figure 9-5 is history in the making. Automation is the first step in separating business rules from the coding process. Business rules are still embedded in code today, but the separation of processing functions has started an evolutionary process. The earlier COBOL programs were very primitive. They had both data definitions and business rules embedded in the code. That has changed and today data definitions have evolved into the modern relational database where data definitions are no longer embedded in the code, but are embedded within the data. This is a true separation of function and data. This same type of paradigm shift must also occur for business rules, which shift is currently in the very early and formative stages of doing. A tiered architecture isolates functionality; the business rules, however, are still embedded in code. To put this in perspective, this is the current frontier of computing technology. I fully expect to see business rule engines on the market within the next five years. These engines will bring business rules to a par with data definitions, which are managed by database engines.

Let's step back in time and look at an old COBOL program. COBOL has a File Definition section known as a FD. The shortcoming of this is that file specifications are embedded in the program. It took the programming community thirty years to evolve out of the primordial ooze of computing to the point where data definitions are now defined within the data and not within the process. This is the power of the relational database. It separated data from the process.

Guess what! We're still primitive. Business rules can evolve only *after* data evolves, and business rules haven't evolved yet. When a developer writes a trigger, that's a business rule. It's embedded in code (the process). The evolution of business rules starts with a change to a multitier architecture that is fueled by Automation. Creating a tiered architecture moves the business rules from the process to an intermediate level; however, the business rules are still embedded in code.

Business rules are managed today reactively. They should be managed proactively with an officer of the corporation adjusting rules dynamically to changing business conditions. This can't happen until business rules are separated from the code (process).

You can liken the business rule issue of today to that of the COBOL FD. File definitions are buried in the COBOL FD and a programmer must modify the program to change the data definition. The same issue is true of business rules today. A programmer must modify a trigger or stored procedure to effect a business rule change. Like the data definition buried in the program, a business rule is buried in still another program, in this case a trigger, a stored procedure, or a component of a tiered architecture. The evolutionary path is always slow. Business rules are still embedded in the process, but a component architecture isolates the business rules, which is a step in the right direction.

Automation Examples

This is not a section on integrated applications, but rather a sampling of Automation examples from various Microsoft products. With these examples I've tried to illustrate that everything today is component technology. Tools such as Microsoft Access and Microsoft Visual Basic are not monolithic products; rather they are the integration of numerous Automation components.

The examples use Microsoft Office 97, Microsoft Access 97, Microsoft Visual Basic Enterprise Edition, and Microsoft SQL Server 6.5, which are all current technologies. A few examples only work with Office 95 and do not work with Office 97. This is intentional since code for Object Word 97 is not interchangeable with Word 6.0/95 WordBasic code.

The examples using Microsoft SQL Server will require that the server names and data paths be changed to correspond to the local environment. The SQL Server examples will not run unless you have access to a SQL Server database.

Office 95 was reinstalled after Office 97 was installed, making Office 95 the default for creating Automation objects. This is my personal choice and I prefer Word 6.0/95 over Word 97. I do use Word 97 for spelling and grammar checking, but the smaller footprint and reliability of Word 6.0 (OfficePro 4.3) make it my preferred word processor.

note **I wish to thank Pat Birch of the MCSDChat forum for coining the phrase "little birdhouses." This chapter is replete with many little birdhouses.**

Another issue is the order of tool installation. I installed OfficePro 4.3 in a directory named OFFICE93. Office 95 is installed in a directory named OFFICE95, and Office 97 is installed in the OFFICE97 directory. The order of installation is important and this relates to the default **ProgID** in the Registry. When installing Office 97 last, double-clicking a .DOC file will start Word 97. Note that Word 95 and Word 6 are still available through an icon. As stated previously, Office 95 was installed last on the development system.

All examples for the book are in the `EXAMPLES` folder of the CD-ROM that accompanies this book. For example, the Automation examples for this chapter are found in the folder `<unit>\EXAMPLES\CHAPTER9`. In this folder, you will find `AUTO.VBP`, which is a Visual Basic (VB) project for all the VB examples in this chapter. You will also find `AUTO.MDB`, which is an Access 97 database that contains Automation examples. The MDB database is a copy of the examples in the `AUTO.VBP` project. I did this because it begs the question a little too much to show an Access example from Access. There is a `README.TXT` file in the folder, which indicates the file dependencies. Although the `Option Explicit` statement is not visibly displayed in any of the code fragments, it exists in the module declaration section for all examples. The examples in this book are all complete code fragments that will execute; well, they executed at least twice for me. Once when I developed them, and once during my review of this book.

The code in Listing 9-1 registers the drive where you have placed the `EXAMPLES` folder. You may leave the CD-ROM mounted at all times, and when prompted, enter the CD-ROM unit. The alternative is to drag the folder to any other unit on your system. Listing 9-1 expects the `EXAMPLES` directory to be in the root of the designated drive. When requested, the routine will place the unit in the Registry. You will be prompted for the unit until it is registered; however, there is no requirement that the unit containing the `EXAMPLES` folder be registered. You can find this example on the CD-ROM that accompanies the book in the Visual Basic `AUTO.BAS` module of the `AUTO.VBP` project located in the `EXAMPLES\CHAPTER09` folder.

LISTING 9-1 Registering the unit for the EXAMPLES folder

```
Function GetUnit() As String
' (C) 1999 Bruce T. Prendergast
' DBA Prendergast Consulting
' DBA PCS
'
' IDG Books Worldwide ISBN 0-7645-3314-2
'
' Listing 9-1 Registering the examples
' Places the EXAMPLES folder unit in the registry
' under with the key:
' HKEY_CURRENT_USER
'   \SOFTWARE
'     \VB and VBA Program Settings
'       \SolutionArchitectures
'         \Examples
'           \Unit
'
Dim Saved_Unit As String ' Unit in Registry
Dim Input_Unit As String ' User supplied unit
Dim Msg, Style, Title, Help, Ctxt, Response, MyString
Dim LoopCount As Integer ' Loop Limiter
Dim Unit_Path As String ' Resulting unit path
Dim Answer As String ' User answer for registering
Msg = "Solution Architectures location is not Registered" & vbCrLf & _
  "What is the unit where the EXAMPLES directory is stored?"
'
' get the registered unit from the registry
'
  GetSetting "SolutionArchitectures", "Examples", "Unit", Saved_Unit
  If Len(Saved_Unit) = 0 Then
    Unit_Path = ""
    LoopCount = 3
    On Error GoTo GarbageIn
ResumeInput:
    While Unit_Path = "" And LoopCount > 0
```

```
        Input_Unit = InputBox(Msg, _
          "Please enter the unit of the Examples folder.")
        Saved_Unit = UCase$(Input_Unit)
        LoopCount = LoopCount - 1
        Unit_Path = CurDir(Saved_Unit & ":\Examples")
      Wend
      If Unit_Path = "" Then
        MsgBox "Invalid Unit designation. Program Terminating"
        Exit Sub
      End If
    End If

    Msg = "Do you wish to register the EXAMPLES directory"
    Style = vbYesNo
    Title = "Examples Not Registered"
    Response = MsgBox(Msg, Style, Title)
    If Response = vbYes Then
      SaveSetting "SolutionArchitectures", "Examples", "Unit", Saved_Unit
      MsgBox "Examples registered with key: SolutionArchitectures\Examples\Unit"
    End If
    GetUnit = Saved_Unit
    Exit Function
  GarbageIn:
    Resume ResumeInput
  End Function
```

DAO from Visual Basic

We start with *Data Access Objects* (DAO), a component of Microsoft Access, which has been with us for a very long time. DAO is commonly used from Visual Basic and offers these advantages:

- Visual Basic can use DAO to query either an Access or a SQL Server database.
- DAO is a component of Microsoft Access and has a smaller memory footprint than Microsoft Access.
- Microsoft Access requires a runtime license while DAO does not.

Accessing DAO is illustrated with:

```
Set MyWS = DBEngine.Workspaces(0)
```

This statement is the common shorthand notation and the **DAO** declaration is assumed because it is the parent object of **DBEngine**. The formal statement is shown below, where a user-defined variable is instantiated with an instance of an Access **Workspace** object. This is the form we'll use in this example because we explicitly want **DAO** and want to avoid loading Access.

```
Set MyWS = DAO.DBEngine.Workspaces(0)
```

The reference is created in the code module by selecting **Tools ➪ References ➪ Microsoft DAO 3.5 Object Library**.

It must create a workspace and a database before creating a pass-through query to a SQL Server. This example will not work unless Microsoft SQL Server is installed. You can find this example on the CD-ROM that accompanies this book in the `AUTO.VBP` project of the `EXAMPLES\CHAPTER09` folder. Listing 9-3 is the Access 97 version of Listing 9-2. Listing 9-2 has a smaller memory footprint because only DAO is loaded, while Listing 9-3 accesses DAO from within Access and all of Microsoft Access is loaded.

LISTING 9-2 Using DAO from Visual Basic

```
Private Sub DAO_from_VisualBasic_Click()
'(C) 1999 Bruce T. Prendergast
' DBA Prendergast Consulting
' DBA PCS
' IDG Books Worldwide ISBN 0-7645-3314-2
'
' Listing 9-2 Visual Basic version of DAO 3.5
'
Dim MyDAO As DBEngine
Dim MyWS As Workspace
Dim MyDB As Database
Dim MyFld As Field
Dim MyQry As QueryDef, MyRS As Recordset
'
' Note that the line below only loads DAO.
```

```
' the line: Set MyDAO = New Access.DBEngine
' loads all of Access which is a large footprint
'
Set MyDAO = New DAO.DBEngine
'
' get a workspace
'
Set MyWS = CreateWorkspace("", "admin", "")
If Dir("MyDB.mdb") <> "" Then Kill "MyDB.mdb"
'
' create a new database
'
Set MyDB = MyWS.CreateDatabase("MyDB.mdb", dbLangGeneral, dbEncrypt)
'
'   The zero-length string creates a temporary query
'
Set MyQry = MyDB.CreateQueryDef("")
Dim SourceConnectStr As String
SourceConnectStr = "ODBC;DATABASE=Pubs;UID=sa;PWD=;DSN=Thor;"
'
'   This is a pass-through query so the connect
'   string is set first which stops Jet from
'   parsing the SQL placed in the SQL property
'   of the QueryDef.
'
MyQry.Connect = SourceConnectStr
MyQry.ReturnsRecords = True
MyQry.SQL = "sp_who" ' an SQL Server stored procedure
'
'   Now create the snapshot and print the returned data
'
Set MyRS = MyQry.OpenRecordset()
'
' enumerate fields
'
Debug.Print "Fields:  Name,  Type,  Value"
For Each MyFld In MyRS.Fields
```

```
  Debug.Print " "; MyFld.Name; " "; MyFld.Type; " "; MyFld.Value
Next MyFld
MsgBox "SQL Pass-Through query completed successfully"
Exit Sub
End Sub
```

DAO from Microsoft Access

Let's redo Listing 9-2 again from Microsoft Access 97. This example is located in the Microsoft Access 97 AUTO.MDB database in the EXAMPLES\CHAPTER9 folder on the CD-ROM, or the unit where you have relocated the EXAMPLES folder.

LISTING 9-3 Using DAO from Microsoft Access

```
Private Sub DAO_from_Access_Click()
' (C) 1999 Bruce T. Prendergast
' DBA Prendergast Consulting
' DBA PCS
'
' IDG Books Worldwide ISBN 0-7645-3314-2
'
' Listing 9-3 DAO from Access 97
'
Dim MyWS As Workspace, MyDB As Database
Dim MyFld As Field
Dim MyQry As QueryDef, MyRS As Recordset
Set MyWS = DBEngine.Workspaces(0)
Set MyDB = MyWS.Databases(0)
'
'   The zero-length string creates a temporary query
'
Set MyQry = MyDB.CreateQueryDef("")
Dim SourceConnectStr As String
SourceConnectStr = "ODBC;DATABASE=Pubs;UID=sa;PWD=;DSN=Thor;"
'
'   This is a pass-through query so the connect
```

```
'   string is set first which stops Jet from
'   parsing the SQL placed in the SQL property
'   of the QueryDef.
'
MyQry.Connect = SourceConnectStr
MyQry.ReturnsRecords = True
MyQry.SQL = "sp_who" ' an SQL Server stored procedure
'
' Now create the snapshot and print the returned data
'
Set MyRS = MyQry.OpenRecordset()
'
' enumerate fields
'
Debug.Print "Fields:  Name,  Type,  Value"
For Each MyFld In MyRS.Fields
    Debug.Print " "; MyFld.Name; " "; MyFld.Type; " "; MyFld.Value
Next MyFld
MsgBox "SQL Pass-Through query completed successfully"
Exit Sub
End Sub
```

ADO from Visual Basic

Listing 9-4 is our third and final version of the SQL Server **sp_who** stored procedure example. The example uses Active Data Objects (ADO) and requires that a reference be created in the code module by selecting **Tools ➪ References ➪ Microsoft OLE DB ActiveX Data Objects 1.0 Library**. This reference conflicts with the DAO 3.5 Object Library. Because of the conflict, this example is located in the Visual Basic `ADO-VB.VBP` project located in the `EXAMPLES\CHAPTER9` folder on the CD-ROM, or the unit where you have relocated the `EXAMPLES` folder.

LISTING 9-4 Using ADO from Visual Basic

```
Private Sub ADO_From_VB_Click()
'(C)1999 Bruce T. Prendergast
' DBA Prendergast Consulting
```

```
' DBA PCS
' IDG Books Worldwide ISBN 0-7645-3314-2
'
' Listing 9-4 Using ADO from Visual Basic
'
Dim MyCon As Connection
Dim MyCmd As Command
Dim MyPar As Parameter
Dim MyRS As Recordset
Dim MyFld As Field
Dim MyErr As Error
Dim RecordsAffected As Long
'
' declare and create a connection
'
  On Error GoTo ADO_Error
  Set MyCon = New ADODB.Connection
  MyCon.ConnectionString = "DATABASE=pubs;UID=sa;PWD=;DSN=THOR"
'
' switch to no error handling
'
  On Error Resume Next
  MyCon.Open
  Set MyCmd = New ADODB.Command
'
' link command to connection
'
MyCmd.ActiveConnection = MyCon
'
' get the data
'
  MyCmd.CommandText = "sp_who"
  Set MyRS = MyCmd.Execute(RecordsAffected, , adCmdText)
'
' the recordset
'
  Debug.Print "Fields:  Name,  Type,  Value"
```

```
    For Each MyFld In MyRS.Fields
       Debug.Print " "; MyFld.Name; " "; MyFld.Type; " "; MyFld.Value
    Next MyFld
    MsgBox "SQL Pass-Through query completed successfully"

  normal_exit:
    Set MyRS = Nothing
    Set MyCmd = Nothing
    Set MyCon = Nothing
    Exit Sub
  ADO_Error:
    If MyRS.ActiveConnection.Errors.Count = 0 Then
      MsgBox "Error is: " & Err.Number
      MsgBox Err.Description
    Else
      For Each MyErr In MyRS.ActiveConnection.Errors
        MsgBox "Error: " & MyErr.Number & " " & MyErr.Description
      Next MyErr
    End If
    Resume normal_exit
    Exit Sub
  End Sub
```

Microsoft Access from Microsoft Visual Basic

Microsoft Visual Basic does not have a native report writer. Crystal Reports ships with Visual Basic, but it is a third-party product. Listing 9-5 creates an instance of Access 95 to print a report. The object variable is defined within the event routine and goes out of scope when the event ends. A practical application should declare the variable at the form level, which preserves it over events. As stated previously, this application will have a very large memory footprint. Note that a specific version of Microsoft Access is instantiated.

The example does not require a reference to an object library. You'll find the example in the `AUTO.VBP` project located in the `EXAMPLES\CHAPTER9` folder on the CD-ROM, or the unit where you have relocated the `EXAMPLES` folder.

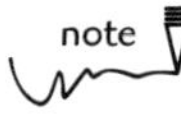

This is not a recommended solution for a distributed application because Microsoft Access requires a runtime license for each client unless the Access Developers Toolkit (ADT) is used. Crystal Reports should be your choice for a distributed application.

LISTING 9-5 Creating Access reports from Visual Basic

```
Private Sub Access_Automation_Click()
'(C) 1999 Bruce T. Prendergast
' DBA Prendergast Consulting
' DBA PCS
'
' IDG Books Worldwide ISBN 0-7645-3314-2
'
' Listing 9-5 Microsoft Access from Visual Basic
'
Dim MyObj As Object
  Set MyObj = CreateObject("Access.Application.7")
  With MyObj
    .OpenCurrentDatabase _
      "H:\Office95\Access\Samples\Northwind.mdb"
    .Visible = True
    .DoCmd.OpenReport "Products by Category", acPreview
  End With
  Set MyObj = Nothing
End Sub
```

Microsoft Excel from Visual Basic

This is an example of calling Microsoft Excel 97 from Microsoft Access 97. Listing 9-6 is the VBA fragment that creates the Excel example, and Listing 9-7 is a very simple interaction mechanism for rotating the spreadsheet. A reference must be created to the Excel type library before compiling the VBA script. The reference is created in the code module by selecting **Tools ➪ References ➪ Microsoft Excel 8.0 Object Library**.

This example is located in the Microsoft Access 97 AUTO.MDB database in the EXAMPLES\CHAPTER9 folder on the CD-ROM, or the unit where you have relocated the EXAMPLES folder.

LISTING 9-6 Controlling Excel 97 from Access 97

```
Private Sub Excel_from_Access_Click()
' (C) 1999 Bruce T. Prendergast
' DBA Prendergast Consulting
' DBA PCS
'
' IDG Books Worldwide ISBN 0-7645-3314-2
'
' Listing 9-6 Excel 97 from Access 97
'
'   these are the preserved form level variables
'
'Dim MyXL As Object
'Dim MyChrt As Object
'Dim xl3DColumn As Integer
'
'   This is late binding
'
Dim i As Integer
  xl3DColumn = -4100 'xl constant for 3D Column chart
  Set MyXL = CreateObject("Excel.Application.8")
  With MyXL
    .Visible = True
    .Workbooks.Add
    .Range("a1").Value = 4
    .Range("a2").Value = 1
    .Range("a3").Value = 3
    .Range("a4").Value = 2
    .Range("a1:a4").Select

  End With
  Set MyChrt = MyXL.Charts.Add()
  MyChrt.Type = xl3DColumn
```

```
  For i = 30 To 180 Step 10
    MyChrt.Rotation = i
  Next
End Sub
```

A command button exists on the form that rotates the Excel spreadsheet. The code in Listing 9-7 rotates the spreadsheet with small incremental steps.

LISTING 9-7 Interacting with Excel by rotating the spreadsheet

```
Private Sub Rotate_Excel_Click()
  If MyChrt Is Nothing Then Exit Sub
  IRotate = (IRotate + 15) Mod 180
  MyChrt.Rotation = IRotate
'
' activate Excel, I assume it is the next sibling window
'
  SendKeys "%{TAB}"
  DoEvents
End Sub
```

These are the form level variables used in Listing 9-6 and 9-7:

```
Option Compare Database
Option Explicit
Dim MyXL As Object
Dim MyChrt As Object
Dim xl3DColumn As Integer
Dim IRotate As Integer
```

As you can see from the main code, the spreadsheet constants are wired into the VBA code. The application works by starting the Access 97 MDB `AUTO.MDB`. There is only one form in this MDB. Click the command button **Excel 95 from Access 97**. The application starts Excel with Automation. The chart is then rotated 180 degrees with Automation. Reduce the screen size by clicking the **Min** button of Excel and drag the Excel window down until you can see the **Rotate Excel Chart** command button on the Access 97 form. Click that button and it will rotate in 15-degree increments. Turn to the labs at the end of this chapter for more examples of adding features to this application.

OLE Messaging

This is an example of e-mail using OLE Messaging. The implementation uses late binding to send a message to Microsoft Outlook 97. Microsoft Outlook 97 is the default e-mail provider on a Windows NT workstation. (Microsoft Exchange server is an alternate e-mail provider choice.) The example requires references to the OLE/Messaging Object Library, which are created in the code module by selecting **Tools ➪ References ➪ OLE/Messaging 1.0 Object Library**.

The message in Listing 9-8 was sent to an e-mail recipient with the name Dudley Doright. I am reasonably sure that Dudley Doright is not a valid mailbox on your system. Create a new mailbox with the name Dudley Doright or modify the example code in Listing 9-8 to reflect an existing e-mail recipient on your system. This example is located in the Microsoft Access 97 AUTO.MDB database in the EXAMPLES\CHAPTER9 folder on the CD-ROM, or the unit where you have relocated the EXAMPLES folder.

LISTING 9-8 **Sending e-mail with OLE messaging**

```
Private Sub OLE_Messaging_Click()
' (C) 1999 Bruce T. Prendergast
' DBA Prendergast Consulting
' DBA PCS
'
' IDG Books Worldwide ISBN 0-7645-3314-2
'
' Listing 9-8 OLE Messaging from Access 97
'
Dim MAPISession As Object
Dim MapiMessage As Object
Dim MapiRecipient As Object
Dim MyMsg As Object
Dim ErrObj As Long
Dim Errmsg As Variant
On Error GoTo MapiError
  Set MAPISession = CreateObject("MAPI.Session")
  MAPISession.Logon ProfileName:="Bruce T. Prendergast"
  Set MapiMessage = MAPISession.Outbox.Messages.Add
```

```
    'Const MapiTo As Integer = 1
    With MapiMessage
      .Subject = "Snidely Whiplash"
      .Text = "I've caught Snidely Whiplash"
    End With
    Set MapiRecipient = MapiMessage.Recipients.Add
    MapiRecipient.Name = "Dudley Doright"
    MapiRecipient.Type = MapiTo
    MapiRecipient.Resolve
    MapiMessage.Send ShowDialog:=False
    MsgBox "message sent"
    MAPISession.Logoff
  MapiExit:
    Exit Sub
  MapiError:
    ErrObj = Err - vbObjectError    ' strip OLE Automation error
    Select Case ErrObj
      Case 275
        Resume MapiExit
      Case Else
        Errmsg = MsgBox("Error " & ErrObj & " was returned.")
        Resume MapiExit
    End Select
    Exit Sub
  End Sub
```

Microsoft Office Binder

This example is slightly more complicated. Microsoft Access 97 directs Word 97 to build a Binder 97 binder. This takes two object library references and both are selected while in the code module. The first library is selected with **Tools ➪ References ➪ Microsoft Word 8.0 Object Library**. The second library is selected with **Tools ➪ References ➪ Microsoft Binder 8.0 Object Library**. This example is located in the Microsoft Access 97 `AUTO.MDB` database in the `EXAMPLES\CHAPTER9` folder on the CD-ROM, or the unit where you have relocated the `EXAMPLES` folder.

This example will not work as constituted because the files referenced are local to the development system. Use the example as a prototype skeleton to place your files within the bindery. The application is unique with respect to other examples in this chapter. The example in Listing 9-9 uses Automation on two different objects. This example must use Word 97 (Word 8.0) and not Word 6 or Word 95 (Word 7.0).

LISTING 9-9 The Access 97 VBA code that creates Figure 9-6

```
Private Sub Access97_Word97_Binder97_Click()
'(C) 1999 Bruce T. Prendergast
' DBA Prendergast Consulting
' DBA PCS
'
' IDG Books Worldwide ISBN 0-7645-3314-2
'
' Listing 9-9 a binder with Word 97 from Access 97
'
Dim MyBnd As OfficeBinder.Binder
Dim MyWrd As Word.Application
Dim MyDoc As Document
Dim MyFont As Font

  Set MyBnd = CreateObject("Office.Binder.8")
  MyBnd.Visible = True
  Set MyWrd = CreateObject("Word.Application.8")
  Documents.Add
  Set MyFont = New Font
  MyFont.Bold = True
  MyFont.Italic = True
  MyFont.Size = 22
  MyFont.Name = "Arial"
  ActiveDocument.Paragraphs(1).Range.Font = MyFont
  With ActiveDocument.Content
    .InsertBefore "Component Technology"
  End With

  ActiveDocument.SaveAs FileName:= "E:\70-100\CH09\Examples\BindSum.DOC"
```

```
    MyWrd.Quit
    Set MyWrd = Nothing

    MyBnd.Sections.Add FileName:= "E:\70-100\CH01\SA_01.doc"
    MyBnd.Sections.Add FileName:= "E:\70-100\CH02\SA_02.doc"
    MyBnd.Sections.Add FileName:= "E:\70-100\CH03\SA_03.doc"
    MyBnd.Sections.Add FileName:= "E:\70-100\CH04\SA_04.doc"
    MyBnd.Sections.Add FileName:= "E:\70-100\CH05\SA_05.doc"
    MyBnd.Sections.Add FileName:= "E:\70-100\CH06\SA_06.doc"
    MyBnd.Sections.Add FileName:= "E:\70-100\CH07\SA_07.doc"
    MyBnd.Sections.Add FileName:= "E:\70-100\CH08\SA_08.doc"
    MyBnd.Sections.Add FileName:= "E:\70-100\CH09\SA_09.doc"

    MyBnd.Sections(1).Name = "IDG Chapters 1-9 Component Technology"
    MyBnd.SaveAs FileName:= "E:\70-100\CH09\Examples\MyIDGbinder.obd", _
      saveOption:=bindDisplayDialog
    Exit Sub
  End Sub
```

Figure 9-6 illustrates the results of the Microsoft Binder 97 example in Listing 9-9.

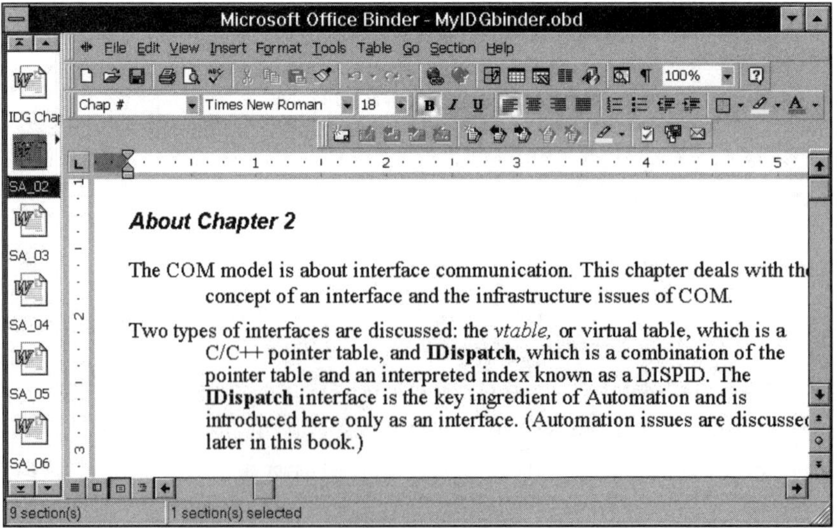

FIGURE 9-6 The results of Listing 9-9

Microsoft PowerPoint

PowerPoint raises some interesting issues. You may be accustomed to using PowerPoint for slide show presentations. You clicked the mouse when you wanted and everything progressed nicely. But what if your slide presentation is in a kiosk? Automation is the natural choice.

Figure 9-7 illustrates that PowerPoint 97 supports component technology. The page is nothing special. I picked *Corporate Home Page* while in the setup wizard. I dropped the VBA toolboxes on the form to illustrate the issue that PowerPoint is far from being a static presentation medium.

You can also embed ActiveX controls on a PowerPoint page. This is another alternative to using either Microsoft Front Page or Microsoft Visual InterDev to create Web pages, which we discuss later in the book.

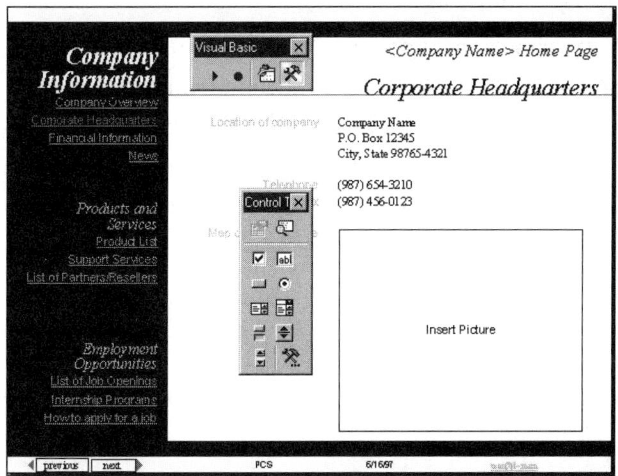

FIGURE 9-7 A Web page created in PowerPoint 97 showing that PowerPoint supports component technology

This is a standard PowerPoint presentation. A text box and a command button are embedded on the master slide. Anything on the master slide is always visible to all slides of the presentation. The purpose of the example is to illustrate that interaction with a PowerPoint slide is possible. You'll find a lab at the end of this chapter that builds a PowerPoint Internet kiosk presentation.

This example is located in the Microsoft PowerPoint 97 `AUTO.PPT` presentation in the `EXAMPLES\CHAPTER9` folder on the CD-ROM, or the unit where you have relocated the `EXAMPLES` folder.

The code below is in the click event of the command button. Start the presentation in PowerPoint 97. Clicking the command button will toggle the text box.

```
Private Sub CommandButton1_Click()
  Static Icount
  Icount = (Icount + 1) Mod 2
  If Icount = 0 Then
    TextBox1 = ""
  Else
    TextBox1 = "Ouch, you clicked me!"
  End If
End Sub
```

Microsoft Project

This is a small example that sets up a schedule for turning in chapters of a book to your publisher. (Don't believe it — it is much too simplistic when all of the edit cycles are considered!) A fictitious chapter-writing schedule is created with Listing 9-10 and Figure 9-8 shows the bogus results of the example. The example is located in the Microsoft Access 97 `AUTO.MDB` database in the `EXAMPLES\CHAPTER9` folder on the CD-ROM, or the unit where you have relocated the `EXAMPLES` folder.

LISTING 9-10 A fictitious chapter-writing schedule

```
Private Sub MSProject4p1_Click()
' (C) 1999 Bruce T. Prendergast
' DBA Prendergast Consulting
' DBA PCS
'
' IDG Books Worldwide ISBN 0-7645-3314-2
'
' Listing 9-10 A fictious chapter-writing schedule
'
```

```
Dim MyProj As Object, MyDoc As Object
Dim MyTask As Object
Dim MySuccessor As Object
Dim i As Integer
  Set MyProj = CreateObject("MSProject.Application")
  MyProj.Visible = True
  MyProj.FileNew SummaryInfo:=False
  Set MyDoc = MyProj.ActiveProject
'
'   create the tasks
'
  For i = 1 To 9
    MyDoc.Tasks.Add Name:="Chapter " & i
  Next i
  For i = 1 To 9
    If i = 1 Then Set MyTask = MyDoc.Tasks("Chapter " & i)
    MyTask.ActualDuration = 1440
    If i < 9 Then
      Set MySuccessor = MyDoc.Tasks("Chapter " & i + 1)
      MyTask.LinkSuccessors MySuccessor
      Set MyTask = MySuccessor
      Set MySuccessor = Nothing
    End If
  Next i
  Set MyTask = Nothing
  MyProj.FileSave
  MyProj.Quit
End Sub
```

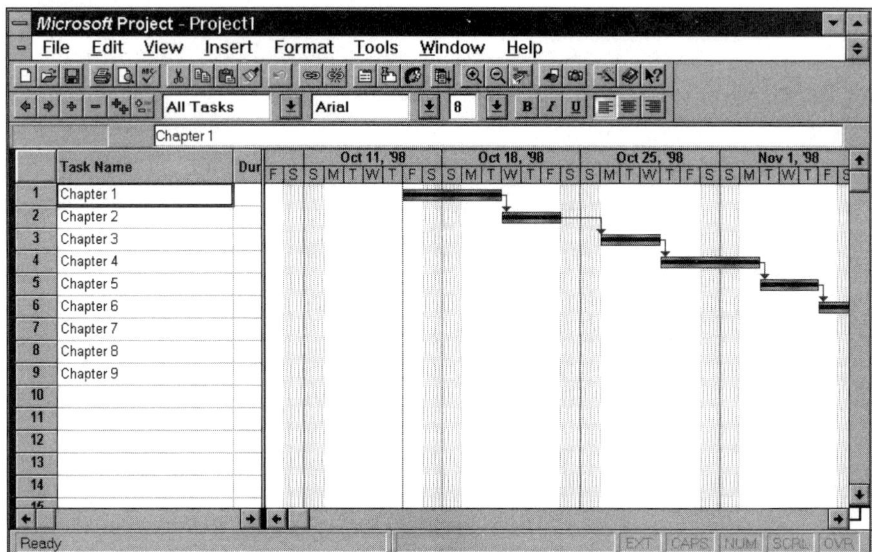

FIGURE 9-8 The result in Microsoft Project of creating the schedule of Listing 9-10

Microsoft Word

Book editors do not want graphics embedded within a chapter sent to them in Microsoft Word. As an author, I need the graphics to maintain a perspective. The example in Listing 9-11 keeps us both happy. I insert the graphics I need to maintain my perspective, and then use this example to strip the graphics from my chapter before I e-mail it. Listing 9-11 is the VBA code that strips the graphics from my Word document.

The source document for this example is from Word 6.0, which requires the use of the Microsoft WordBasic 95 Type Library. (This library cannot be used with Word 97.) This code fragment uses WordBasic to strip embedded graphics from a .DOC file. The output file is then given the prefix of "NG" before being e-mailed to my editor. This example is located in the Microsoft Access 97 `AUTO.MDB` database in the `EXAMPLES\CHAPTER9` folder on the CD-ROM, or the unit where you have relocated the `EXAMPLES` folder.

LISTING 9-11 **I keep my editor happy by stripping inserted objects from my chapter manuscript**

```
Private Sub File_Strip_Click()
'(C) 1999 Bruce T. Prendergast
' DBA Prendergast Consulting
```

```
' DBA PCS
'
' IDG Books Worldwide ISBN 0-7645-3314-2
'
' Listing 9-11 Strip object from .DOC file
'
'   The routine strips graphics from a Word
'   document. Editors don't like to work on
'   documents with embedded graphics.
'
'   New files have the prefix "NG".
          ' that indicates "No Graphics"
'
'   Uses: Microsoft Word Basic 95 Type Library
'
'   The input document type is Word 6.0
'
Dim iGraphPos As Long
Dim iDeleted As Integer
Dim objWord As Object
Dim iPos As Integer
Dim iNewSlash As Integer
Dim strFile As String
Dim strPath As String
Dim strFullPath As String
Dim strResp As Variant
'
  While UCase(strResp) <> "Y" And UCase(strResp) <> "N"
    strResp = InputBox("Do You wish to continue (Y/N)?", _
      "Strip Graphics")
    If strResp = "" Then Exit Sub
    If UCase$(strResp) = "N" Then Exit Sub
  Wend
'*************************************
'** step 1 - get full path         **
'*************************************
```

```
  strFullPath = ""
  strFullPath = InputBox(".DOC File Name with full path")
  If strFullPath = "" Then Exit Sub
'
'**************************************
'** step 2 - build path             **
'**************************************
'
  DoCmd.Hourglass True
  iPos = 1
  While InStr(iPos, strFullPath, "\", vbBinaryCompare) > 0
     iNewSlash = InStr(iPos, strFullPath, "\", vbBinaryCompare)
     iPos = iPos + iNewSlash
  Wend
  strPath = Mid$(strFullPath, 1, iNewSlash - 1)
  strFile = Mid$(strFullPath, iNewSlash + 1)
'
'**************************************
'** step 3 - strip the graphics      **
'**************************************
'
  Set objWord = CreateObject("Word.basic")
  With objWord
    .FileOpen Name:=strPath & "\" & strFile
    .StartOfDocument
    iGraphPos = .GetSelStartPos()
    .EditGoTo "g"
    While iGraphPos <> .GetSelStartPos()
      iGraphPos = .GetSelStartPos()
      .EditClear
      iDeleted = iDeleted + 1
      .EditGoTo "g"
    Wend
    .FileSaveAs strPath & "\NG" & strFile
    .FileClose 1
    Set objWord = Nothing
```

```
  End With
  DoCmd.Hourglass False
  Exit Sub
End Sub
```

Microsoft SQL Server

This example is located in the Microsoft Visual Basic AUTO.VBP project in the EXAMPLES\CHAPTER9 folder on the CD-ROM that accompanies this book, or the unit where you have relocated the EXAMPLES folder. SQL Distributed Management Objects (SQL-DMO) is a very rich Automation tool that is used for managing Microsoft SQL Server. Listing 9-12 uses SQL-DMO to enumerate the databases supported by a SQL Server known as *Thor*.

LISTING 9-12 Using SQL-DMO to report SQL Server supported databases

```
Private Sub SQLDMO_VB_Click()
'(C) 1999 Bruce T. Prendergast
' DBA Prendergast Consulting
' DBA PCS
'
' IDG Books Worldwide ISBN 0-7645-3314-2
'
' Listing 9-12 SQL-DMO from Visual Basic
'
Dim MySQL As Object
Dim MyDB As Object
Dim MyStr As String
Dim SourceConnect As String

  On Error GoTo SQLDMOError
  Set MySQL = CreateObject("SQLOLE.SQLServer")
  MySQL.Connect "Thor", "sa", ""
  Debug.Print "Databases on Thor"
  For Each MyDB In MySQL.Databases
    Debug.Print "Database: " & MyDB.Name
  Next
```

```
  MySQL.Disconnect
  Exit Sub
SQLDMOExit:
  Exit Sub
SQLDMOError:
  MsgBox Err.Description
  Resume SQLDMOExit
End Sub
```

WebBrowser Control

Browsing the Internet/Intranet is done from Visual Basic using the Microsoft Internet Controls (`SHDOCVW.OCA`) or the WebBrowser control. The control is inserted into a Visual Basic application by selecting *Components* from the **Project** menu and then checking *Microsoft Internet Controls* and selecting *OK*. Drag the control from the toolbox onto a form and expand it. The one line of code below created Figure 9-9 when the application was started. The Web site is functional within the WebBrowser control, but there are no back links on the page. Because the site is hosted in the WebBrowser control and not the Internet Explorer, there is no method for returning to the home page once you leave it. The developer must supply the missing functionality of Internet Explorer when using the WebBrowser control. You'll find this example on your CD-ROM in the `EXAMPLES\CHAPTER9` folder as Visual Basic Enterprise Edition `BROWSER.VBP` project.

```
Private Sub Form_Load()
  Me!WebBrowser1.Navigate "HTTP://Zeus/Myweb"
End Sub
```

FIGURE 9-9 The WebBrowser control in a Visual Basic application

Internet Explorer

The WebBrowser control is not the only choice of a browser for the Visual Basic developer. Microsoft Internet Explorer is available through Automation as illustrated by the code fragment below which instantiates Internet Explorer. The WebBrowser control and the Internet Explorer share properties as indicated by the **Navigate** method. The object variable is declared as public variable in a module. You'll find this example in the CD-ROM `EXAMPLES\CHAPTER9` folder as Visual Basic Enterprise Edition `OLETEST.VBP` project.

```
Private Sub InternetExplorer_Click()
Set IEObj = CreateObject("InternetExplorer.Application")
  IEObj.Visible = True
  IEObj.navigate "HTTP://Zeus/MyWeb"
End Sub
```

WinInet

A Visual Basic application initiates FTP and HTTP file transfers between Web sites with the Microsoft Internet Transfer Control (`MSINET.OCA`) or the WinInet control. The control is inserted into a Visual Basic 5.0/6.0 application by selecting *Components* from the **Project** menu and then checking *Microsoft Internet Transfer Control 5.0*. Select *OK* and drop the control onto a form and provide the supporting Visual Basic for Applications (VBA) code. The code in Listing 9-12 responds to the different states of the WinInet control during a transfer operation. Clicking the single command button starts the FTP transfer. You'll find this example in the CD-ROM `EXAMPLES\CHAPTER9` folder as Visual Basic Enterprise Edition `FTP.VBP` project.

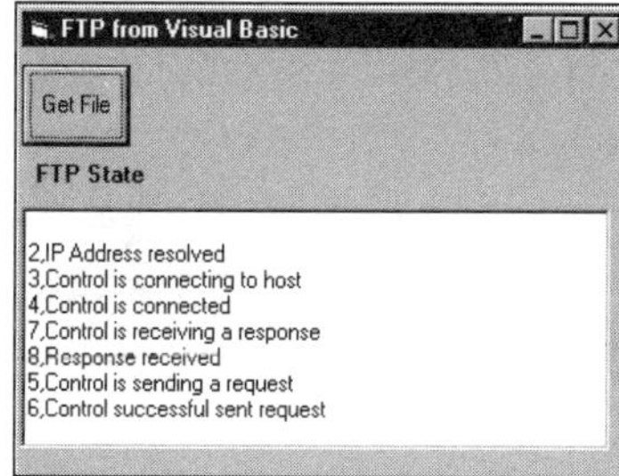

FIGURE 9-10 The WinInet control in a Visual Basic Application

LISTING 9-12 The VBA code of Figure 9-10

```
Private Sub cmdSendFile_Click()
Inet1.Execute "FTP://ZEUS", "GET myFTP/ftpTest.txt" & _
  " e:\70-100\CH09\Examples\ftptest.txt"
End Sub

Private Sub Inet1_StateChanged(ByVal State As Integer)
'(C) 1999 Bruce T. Prendergast
'   DBA Prendergast Consulting
'   DBA PCS
'   IDG Books Worldwide ISBN 0-7645-3314-2
'
'   Listing 9-12 The WinInet Control
'
 Select Case State
  Case icNone
    FTPState.Text = FTPState.Text & vbCrLf & "0,None"
  Case icHostResolvingHost
    FTPState.Text = FTPState.Text & vbCrLf & "1,Find the IP address"
  Case icHostResolved
    FTPState.Text = FTPState.Text & vbCrLf & "2,IP Address resolved"
  Case icConnecting
    FTPState.Text = FTPState.Text & vbCrLf & "3,Connecting to host"
  Case icConnected
    FTPState.Text = FTPState.Text & vbCrLf & "4,Control is connected"
  Case icRequesting
    FTPState.Text = FTPState.Text & vbCrLf & "5,Sending a request"
  Case icRequestSent
    FTPState.Text = FTPState.Text & vbCrLf & "6,Successful send request"
  Case icReceivingResponse
    FTPState.Text = FTPState.Text & vbCrLf & "7,Receiving a response"
  Case icResponseReceived
    FTPState.Text = FTPState.Text & vbCrLf & "8,Response received"
  Case icDisconnecting
    FTPState.Text = FTPState.Text & vbCrLf & "9,Disconnecting"
```

```
    Case icDisconnected
      FTPState.Text = FTPState.Text & vbCrLf & "10,Disconnected"
    Case icError
      FTPState.Text = FTPState.Text & vbCrLf & _
  "11,Error:Inetl.ResponseCode:" & Inetl.ResponseInfo
    Case icResponseCompleted
      FTPState.Text = FTPState.Text & vbCrLf & "12,Response Completed"
  End Select
End Sub
```

Listing 9-12 is the code for both the **command** button and the **WinInet** control of Figure 9-10.

Key Point Summary

Using a Microsoft tool is quite deceiving. It is only after enumerating Automation examples that you realize the significance and importance of the role Automation plays in application development. Understanding Automation in the Microsoft architecture is necessary to become a successful developer. Rather than writing a custom application, the successful and smart developer uses Automation on the available components and delivers a timely solution. The solution is probably more robust than a custom application because it includes proven and existing components that are already in use. That is not to say there won't be bugs, but they should certainly be fewer.

- Automation is the new name for OLE Automation
- Automation uses COM, but the technology does not support linking or embedding. An OLE Document supports either linking or embedding.
- Automation is the exposing of methods and properties for manipulation by a client object.
- OLE and Automation may be combined within an object. There is no restriction on an object only supporting one technology.
- The **IDispatch** interface signals an Automation server.
- Automation is a ubiquitous feature of the Microsoft component technology.

Applying What You've Learned

The following questions will test your understanding of Automation. The laboratories illustrate Automation with either Visual Basic 5.0/6.0 or Access 97 controlling the editing of Word 97, Word 95, or Word 6 .DOC files.

Instant Assessment

1. What is the definition of Automation?
2. What distinguishes Automation from an OLE Document?
3. Explain what a dual interface is.
4. Explain the statement, *being a good OLE client is a requirement for being an OLE Automation application controller.*
5. Explain why Microsoft Visual Basic cannot be an OLE Automation server.
6. Name the three nontrivial tiers of an architecture. Which are candidates for Automation?
7. In what way are business rules primitive?

For answers to the Instant Assessment Questions, see Appendix B.

Lab Exercises

This is where we use Automation to supply intelligence to our objects. The project we pursue in the next series of labs is Automation using a VBA code fragment to edit a Word 6, Word 95, or Word 97 document.

WordBasic is used for editing the Word 6 or Word 95 document, and Object Word is used for the Word 97 document. The required libraries are shown below. Don't mix and match libraries. It does work but there are always complications.

- Word 6.0 Microsoft WordBasic Object Library
- Word 95 Microsoft WordBasic 95 Object Library
- Word 97 Microsoft Word 8.0 Object Library

There are two versions of the VBA for this example. The first uses the WordBasic model which is 900+ references with no object model. The second example uses the new object model of Word 97. Remember that you can't mix and match Word 97 with either Word 6 or Word 95. Feel free to use the editor of your choice.

The first task is to create the following text in the editor of your choice. I prefer Word 95 for this demonstration. You might save the file under various names such as TEST1.DOC, TEST2.DOC, and TEST3.DOC. This will keep you from having to restore the original files after every Automation example.

This is the text to use in the example and it is also the file AUTO.DOC in the EXAMPLES\CHAPTER9 folder on your CD-ROM:

Dear Reader,

Thank you for buying this book.

$Author$

I put the text in italics only to separate it from this text. You need not do the same.

The Automation example consists of a small VBA fragment, which modifies the text of the .DOC file. I hope you can see the import of this. VBA may be used to create custom letters that can be tuned to the unique attributes of the target recipient.

The VBA code for Word 6 or Word 95 is shown below. If you have problems, this example can be found in the AUTO.MDB Access 97 database in the EXAMPLES\CHAPTER9 folder on the CD-ROM or the unit where you have relocated the EXAMPLES folder.

```
Private Sub VBA_Test_Click()     ' This line need not be entered
'
'Automation example
'
  Dim objWord As Object
  DoCmd.Hourglass True
  Set objWord = CreateObject("Word.Basic")
  With objWord
    .FileOpen Name:= "E:\70-100\CH09\Examples\AUTO.DOC" 'Edit this
    .StartOfDocument
    .EditReplace Find:="$Author$", _
    Replace:="Bruce T. Prendergast", _
```

```
    WholeWord:=1, ReplaceOne:=1
    .FilePrint ' this may be replaced with a .FileClose 1
  End With
  Set objWord = Nothing
  DoCmd.Hourglass False
  Exit Sub
End Sub' This Line need not be entered.
```

The VBA code for Word 97 using the new object model is:

```
Private Sub Command1_Click()      ' This line need not be entered
'
' Word 97 example for search replace
'
Dim MyRange As Object
Dim objWord As Object
Dim MyDoc As Document
  Set objWord = CreateObject("Word.application")
  objWord.Documents.Add "E:\70-100\CH09\Examples\AUTO.DOC" 'Edit this
  Set MyRange = ActiveDocument.Content
  With MyRange.Find
    .ClearFormatting
    .Text = "$Author$"
    With .Replacement
      .ClearFormatting
      .Text = "Bruce T. Prendergast"
    End With
    .Execute Replace:=wdReplaceAll, _
    Format:=True, MatchCase:=True, MatchWholeWord:=True
  End With
  ActiveDocument.SaveAs "E:\idgch1ex\test1.doc" 'Edit this
  ActiveDocument.Close
  Set MyRange = Nothing
  Set objWord = Nothing
  Exit Sub
End Sub      ' This line need not be entered
```

Lab 9.24 *Visual Basic 5.0/6.0 and Automation with WordBasic*

Our first victim is either Visual Basic 5.0 or 6.0.

1. Open Visual Basic and place a command button on a form. If the toolbox isn't present then select **Toolbox** from the **View** menu.
2. Select a command button in the toolbox and paint it on the form.
3. Double-click the command button that displays the VBA editing environment.
4. Enter the code illustrated above for Word 6 or Word 95.You'll have to adjust the location of the .DOC file. The original `AUTO.DOC` file is in your `EXAMPLES\CHAPTER9` folder.
5. Before running the application, select **Project**⇨**References** and verify that either the Microsoft WordBasic Object Library for Word 6 or the Microsoft WordBasic 95 Object Library is selected.
6. After the text is entered in the command button click **Event** and select **Start With Full Compile** from the **Run** menu. **Option Explicit** was not used because this is a very small application. Every nontrivial form and every module should have the **Option Explicit** statement, which catches spelling errors.
7. Go to either Word 6 or Word 95 and verify your results.

```
Private Sub Command1_Click()
  Dim objWord As Object
  DoCmd.Hourglass True
  Set objWord = CreateObject("Word.Basic")
  With objWord
    .FileOpen Name:="E:\IDGEXAMP\AUTO.DOC" 'Edit this
    .StartOfDocument
    .EditReplace Find:="$Author$", _
    Replace:="Bruce T. Prendergast", _
    WholeWord:=1, ReplaceOne:=1
    .FileClose 1 'This may be replaced with a .FilePrint
  End With
  Set objWord = Nothing
  DoCmd.Hourglass False
  Exit Sub
End Sub
```

Lab 9.25 *Visual Basic 5.0/6.0 and Automation with Object Word 97*

1. Open Visual Basic and place a command button on the form. If the toolbox isn't present then select **Toolbox** from the **View** menu.
2. Select a command button in the toolbox and paint it on the form.
3. Double-click the command button that displays the VBA editing environment.
4. Enter the code illustrated for Word 97 above. (It is not necessary to enter the first and last lines of the sample VBA text.)
5. Adjust the path of the .DOC file located in the **.FileOpen** statement. The `AUTO.DOC` file is located in the `EXAMPLES\CHAPTER9` folder of the CD-ROM that accompanies this book.
6. Before running the application select **Project ⇨ References** and verify that the Microsoft Word 8.0 Object Library is selected. This is a different library than the one we used for the WordBasic model.
7. After the text is entered in the command button click **Event**, select **Start With Full Compile** from the **Run** menu. **Option Explicit** was not used because this is a very small application. Every form and every module should have the **Option Explicit** statement, which catches spelling errors.
8. Go to Word 97 and verify your results.

Lab 9.26 *Access 97 and Automation with WordBasic or Object Word*

Repeat the same exercise as in Lab 9.25 for Access 97 (remember to use the right library), then follow these steps:

1. Start Access 97 and create a blank form. (Ascertain that the Toolbox Wizard is *Off* on the toolbox.)
2. Select a command button and paint it on the form.
3. Select the click **Event ⇨ Code Builder** from the properties window.
4. Enter the appropriate WordBasic or Object Word VBA code and test it.
5. While in the VBA editor, verify the proper libraries by selecting **References** from the **Tools** menu.
6. Run the code and test it.

Lab 9.27 *Animating a Web Page with PowerPoint and a Marquee control*

Lab 9.27 is a fun lab in which we illustrate adding animation to a Web page. We do it by hyper-linking to a PowerPoint Internet kiosk presentation. You'll find the example easy to create and very intriguing.

1. Create a new Web site in FrontPage 98. A single home page is all this is necessary to illustrate the issue.
2. Place FrontPage 98 on the task bar and start PowerPoint 97.
3. Select **Cancel** for the first dialog box.
4. Select **New** from the File menu.
5. Select the **Web Pages** tab.
6. Select **Banner2**.
7. Select **OK**.
8. Choose **Save As**.
9. Save the presentation in your new Web site directory.
10. Exit PowerPoint.
11. Restart FrontPage 98.
12. While in FrontPage 98 Explorer, Navigator view, double-click the page where the animation is to appear.
13. When the selected page is displayed in FrontPage 98 Editor, place the cursor at the position where the hyperlink is to be inserted.
14. Select **Hyperlink** from the Insert menu.
15. Double-click your new PowerPoint file.
16. Select **Active Elements** from the Insert menu to add a marquee.
17. Enter a text message and select **OK**.
18. Select **Preview in Browser** from the File menu. The marquee will start immediately when the page is displayed.
19. Click the hyperlink. The PowerPoint animation is played back. (You might want to go back to PowerPoint and examine the animation techniques in the original presentation.)

CHAPTER

10

OLE Controls: Using It All (Well, Almost)

About Chapter 10

This chapter is the culmination of our discussion of component technology. We started in Chapter 1 with intertask/intratask communications issues. Subsequent chapters introduced basic COM technology, while building on the technology of previous chapters. Chapter 2 addressed object interfaces while Chapter 3 completed the discussion of interfaces by discussing type libraries. Chapter 4 introduced COM structured storage. The orderly march through COM basics continued with monikers in Chapter 5. The two cornerstones of COM are the concepts of an interface and a moniker. An interface insulates the client from implementation details, while a moniker insulates the client from connection details. The COM fundamentals were completed with Chapter 6 discussing Uniform Data Transfer (UDT) and connectable objects. No discussion of connectable objects is complete without some mention of **IAdviseSink**, which is the first asynchronous COM object. Chapter 7 saw us use the COM infrastructure for linking OLE Documents. Remember that an OLE Document is a COM object that supports linking or embedding. Additional pieces came together in Chapter 8 with embedded documents and in-place activation. A somewhat disjoint technology named Automation appeared in Chapter 9. Automation technology is based on COM but does not support linking or embedding.

This chapter is about OLE Controls, which represent all the technologies we've discussed so far, including Automation, except for linking. Controls do not support linking. This chapter adds the two missing OLE Control features: properties and events.

The chapter starts with a general discussion of OLE Controls as an extension of COM. OLE Controls are a general replacement for the Visual Basic 3.0 Custom Control (VBX). With the implementation of OLE Controls came the concept of an *event* and *properties* in a *property bag*. COM supports properties through the **IDispatch** interface; however, the mechanism is inadequate for general use. Both of these new features assured the success of OLE Controls.

Enter the Internet! Microsoft renamed OLE Controls to ActiveX and with a fury seldom seen in software development, made massive performance enhancement to OLE Controls (ActiveX). This was in the time frame that Microsoft decided that the Internet was a viable concept and is euphemistically called the period where *the 800-pound gorilla learned how to run.*

OLE Controls

OLE Controls are the next logical extension of COM. Microsoft introduced the first *OLE Custom Control* (OCX) in 1994 when the Windows architecture was undergoing an upgrade to the 32-bit model. Microsoft Visual Basic 3.0 was quite successful with the *Visual Basic custom control* (VBX); however, it was only 16 bits and conversion to 32 bits was not simple. An additional requirement for the Windows architecture upgrade was that any replacement for a VBX must not be limited to Visual Basic. These factors spawned the OLE Control, which is 32 bits, not specific to any Microsoft tool, and Unicode-compliant.

Up to this point, COM supported OLE Documents with linking and embedding and OLE Automation or Automation. A COM component did not yet support its own interface. Automation was a one-way dialog. An application controller manipulates exposed methods of a server. This is adequate for simple problems. What was needed is functionality that exposes both incoming and outgoing interfaces. The roots of this functionality begin with **IAdviseSink,** which is a one-way dialog. A successor to this interface is connectable objects that use the **IConnectionPoint** interface. This interface goes beyond a two-way dialog by supporting event sets, the enumeration of interface identifiers (IIDs) (available functionality), the ability to connect and disconnect advisory sinks, and the ability to enumerate connections to a particular outgoing interface. (By the way, this interface is the workhorse of Microsoft Visual InterDev, which is the new Internet development tool.)

The COM model used for OLE Documents and OLE Automation did not have a model for properties. Properties were exposed by an Automation virtual table (vtable), but there was no logical model. OLE Controls needed a standard for specifying their own interface. They also needed a generalized way of handling properties. Up to this point, properties were accessed with a **DISPID,** which is implementation specific. Figure 10-1 is a dual **IDispatch** interface with the property **IsWriting**. **IDispatch::Invoke** recognizes the entry as a property when a flag is set. The **IDispatch::Invoke** method supports these flags:

- *DISPATCH_METHOD* — The referenced element is a method. Both this flag and the **DISPATCH_PROPERTYGET** flag may be set when a property has the same name.

- *DISPATCH_PROPERTYGET* — The referenced element is retrieved as a property or data member.
- *DISPATCH_PROPERTYPUT* — The referenced element is changed as a property or data member.
- *DISPATCH_PROPERTYPUTREF* — Changes to the referenced element are by reference rather than value assignment. Only valid when the property accepts a reference to an object.

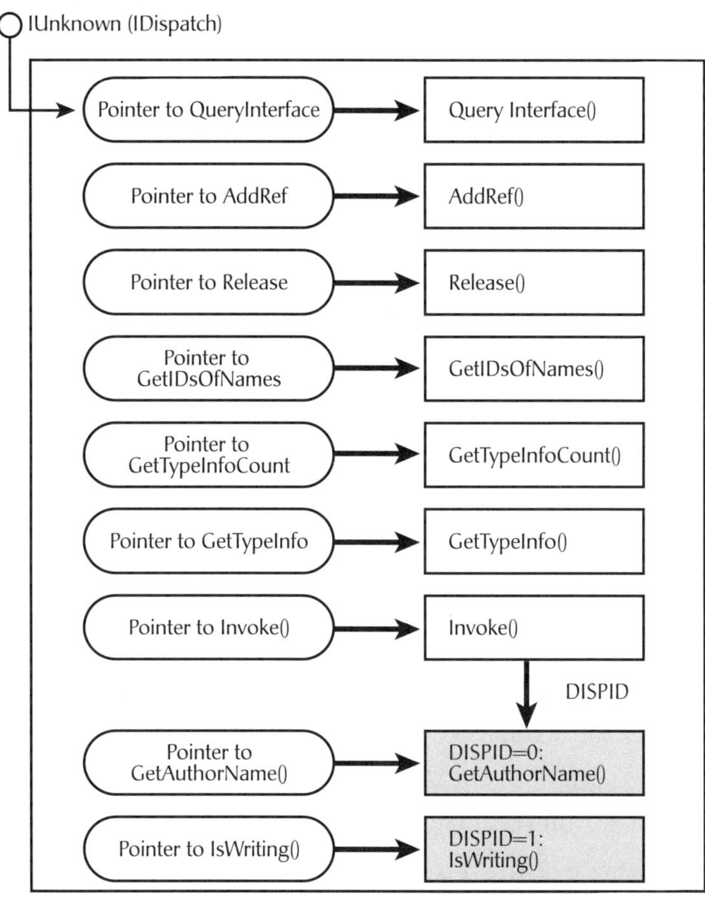

FIGURE 10-1 A dual IDispatch interface with a property

The other missing element is events. An event is a notification of a state change in a property. Common events in the Visual tools are **On_Click, On_LostFocus,** and **On_Change**. The solution here is definitional; define an event as a method of an interface that is called when a property changes state. Methods exist and objects have both incoming and outgoing interfaces. An event is an invoked method that creates an outgoing message to a waiting advisory sink.

Rename a few objects, use the technology we've developed so far, and add a model for property pages and you have an OLE Control. OLE Controls are considered a significant milestone in the evolution of COM technology. OLE Controls don't quite use all the technology we've developed—they support embedding but not linking.

OLE Features

The original OLE Control specification permitted a control to maintain its own interface, send events to a control container, let a container set properties, and negotiate interfaces. An OLE Control adds many new interfaces to COM, which are in addition to the COM interfaces discussed thus far. This means that an OLE Control can also be used as an Automation object or as a data source for compound document control.

OLE Controls can be created by all the popular Microsoft tools, which include Microsoft C++, Visual Foxpro, Visual J++, and Microsoft Visual Basic starting with version 4.0. Microsoft Access, Microsoft Visual Basic, and Microsoft Internet Explorer are the popular COM containers for OLE Controls. The nominal OLE Control implementation is as an in-process server.

Features of the OLE Control using the COM model include:

- Events that are fired by the control. This is the control accessing a method of the control container.
- OLE Controls that are 32-bit Unicode-based. (Note that Unicode is memory intensive with 16-bit rather than the traditional 8-bit characters.)
- Ambient Properties. These are environmental properties of the container, and the control adapts to these properties to interface seamlessly. An example is the default background color.

- Extended Properties. The control may support extended properties such as position, size, layout, or automatic headers and footers for displayed pages. There is no limit on these properties and they are specific to the implementation.
- An OCX supports object embedding and Automation, but not linking.

OLE Benefits

The benefits of OLE Controls (OCX) include the following:

- OLE Controls are not limited to Visual Basic as are VBXs.
- OLE Controls are easier to develop than a VBX. This is certainly demonstrated in Visual Basic 5.0 where even the beginning developer can create an ActiveX control in just a few minutes with a few mouse clicks. Before Visual Basic 5.0, creating an ActiveX control was a task more suited to the C^{++} developer.
- An OLE Control (OCX) is based on COM. This means that emulation or conversion is supported. A control can emulate an earlier version, or an older version can be upgraded.
- An OLE Control promotes reusable software in that it is a component and may be "plugged-in." The component can be off-the-shelf or custom developed.

OLE Controls are transparent to the user. An OLE Control starts with inside-out activation, while an OLE Document always starts with outside-in activation. Inside-out activation means the control is integrated seamlessly with the container and is activated by only one click of the mouse button. This means that the control is always active. Outside-in activation requires an overt action by the user, with a double-click to activate the control.

OLE Controls Interface Architecture

This is a book on Microsoft architecture and, as such, it is not my intent to make you conversant with every COM interface. You should recognize most of the interfaces illustrated in Figure 10-2, but here we'll only look at the interfaces for properties.

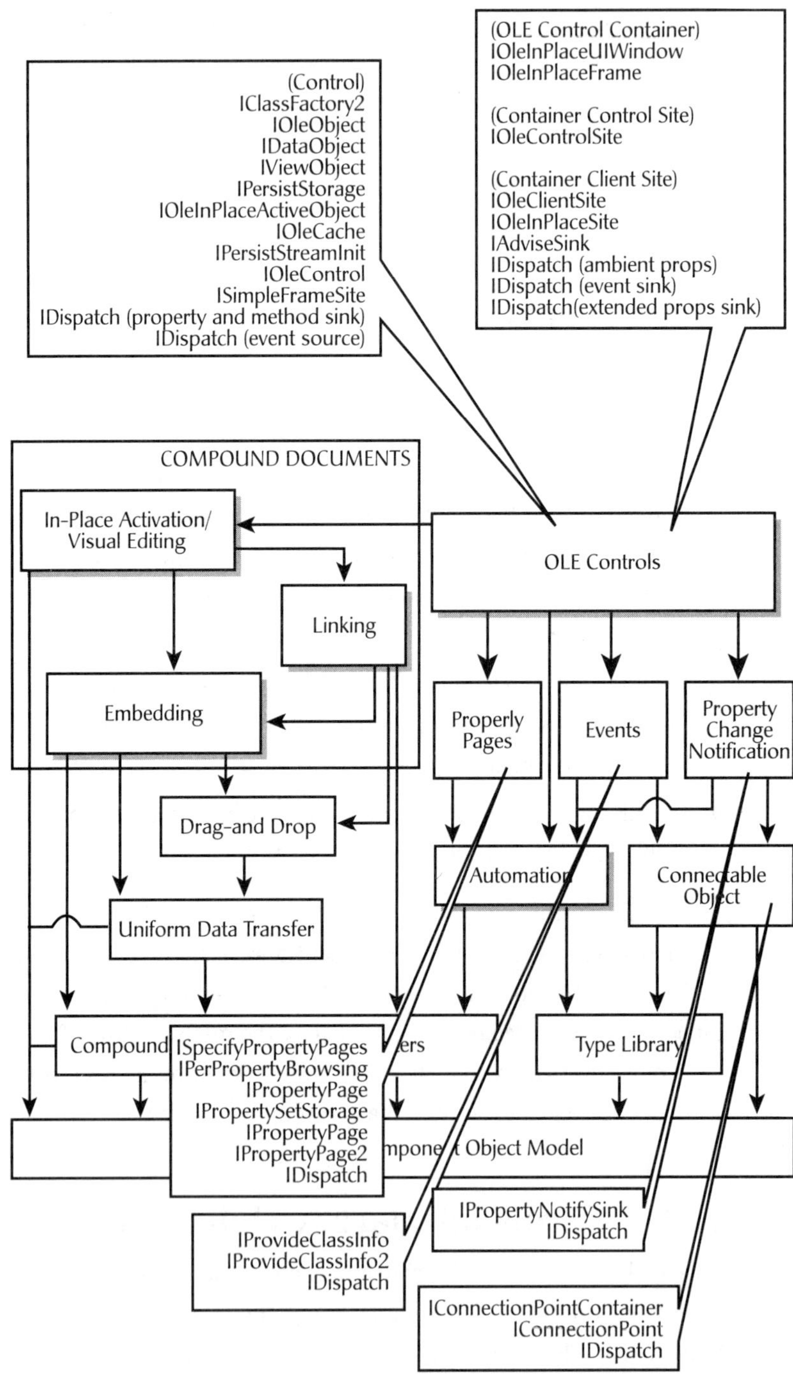

FIGURE 10-2 OLE Control interface architecture

Figure 10-2 is the road map for this chapter. As you can see, OLE Controls use nearly all of COM. There are a few new ones that we'll discuss shortly. The interfaces indicated by the captions at the top of Figure 10-2 represent the cumulative technology discussed through and including Chapter 8.

At the bottom of Figure 10-2 are the **IConnectionPointContainer** and **IConnectionPoint** interfaces that were both discussed previously in this chapter. Connectable objects are used extensively with OLE Controls. Properties and events are the remaining OLE Control technologies not discussed thus far. We start now with properties.

OLE Control Properties

Properties are a feature new to OLE Controls, although all controls may not have properties. The majority of the new interfaces shown in Figure 10-2 concern properties. Properties existed in COM before OLE Controls, but the design was not formalized. COM updated for OLE Controls provides a complete protocol for managing properties and property pages of an OLE Control. Figure 10-3 is a closer look at the details of property page communication. (You might want to review the **IPersistPropertyBag** interface covered in Chapter 4.)

There is a missing link in Figure 10-3. The missing interface is the persistent storage implementation — and the developer of an OLE Control has several persistent storage options. The following list outlines the persistent storage choices for the developer, which are also the persistent storage choices indicated in Figure 10-3:

- Implement the **IPropertyStorage** interface for a single property to a file implementation.
- Implement the **IPropertySetStorage** interface for a group of properties to a file implementation.
- Create or use a compound file implementation with **StgCreateDocFile** or **StgOpenStorage** (see Chapter 4). **IStorage::QueryInterface** is interrogated for **IID_IPropertySetStorage** once this is accomplished.
- Implement the **IPropertyBag** interface (see Chapter 4). The container implements this interface.

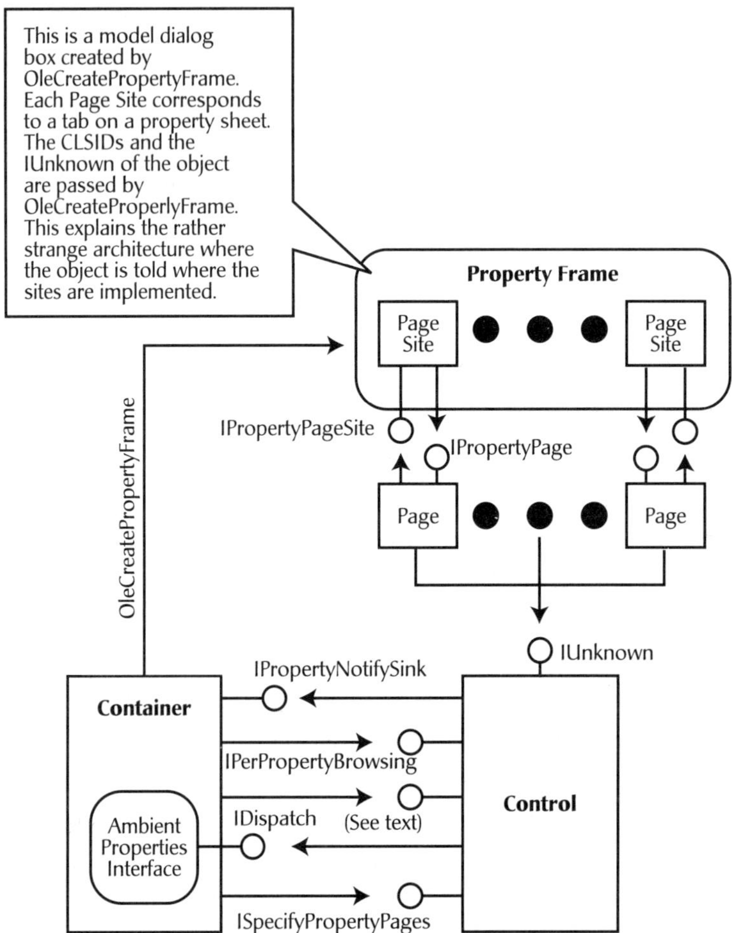

FIGURE 10-3 Control property pages with a displayed property page

ISpecifyPropertyPages

ISpecifyPropertyPages is the elementary property interface. Its existence signals that the control supports properties. This interface implements all methods of **IUnknown** and implements the method **GetPages**. This method returns all CLSIDs that this object wants displayed.

An object signals its ability to interact with one or more property pages by implementing this interface. **ISpecifyPropertyPages::GetPages** returns a counted array of CLSIDs to the client that collectively describes the property pages that the object wants displayed. This interface and the **IPropertyPage, IPropertyPageSite,** and **ISpecifyPropertyPages** interfaces collectively manage property pages as shown in Figure 10-3. All of the functionality described here enables properties to be worked within a page on an object-by-object basis along with property frames.

IPerPropertyBrowsing

Property pages of an object can be accessed with the **IPerPropertyBrowsing** interface. This interface is required for all objects that a client can browse. This interface supports all methods of **IUnknown** and implements the following:

- *GetDisplayString* — Returns a text description of the specified property.
- *MapPropertyToPage* — Returns the CLSID of the property page for property manipulation.
- *GetPredefinedStrings* — Returns a pointer array that can be used by **IPerPropertyBrowsing::GetPredefinedValue**.
- *GetPredefinedValue* — Returns a value based on a pointer returned by **IPerPropertyBrowsing::GetPredefinedString.**

IPropertyNotifySink

The **IPropertyNotifySink** interface is implemented on the control container and accepts property change notifications from the OLE Control. The **IPropertyNotifySink** interface is equivalent to an "outgoing" interface of a connectable object (see Chapter 6). The object is required to call **IPropertyNotifySink** for only those properties marked with the **Bindable** or **RequestEdit** attributes in the object's type information. When properties are so marked the control will call **IPropertyNotifySink::OnChanged** whenever a change occurs or will call **IPropertyNotifySink::OnRequest Edit** whenever an edit request occurs. The exception to these rules is object initialization and object loading time. This interface inherits all methods of **IUnknown** and these are the only two methods of **IPropertyNotifySink**.

IPropertyPage

The in-process object implements this interface to the actual property page. A different property page object is required for each unique property page within a property sheet. It is through this interface that the property frame supplies the necessary commands and information to each property page in the sheet. The sequence of events for Figure 10-3 starts with **OleCreatePropertyFrame** creating a modal dialog, and then attempting to instantiate and initialize the property page using the supplied CLSIDs. (**IOleCreatePropertyFrameIndirect** performs the same type of function and is not illustrated.) A properly managed dialog box (modal) should only display controls for those properties defined within the property sheet. The page should have the Windows style **WS_CHILD**; it should not have a style related to a frame, caption, system menus, or controls.

IPropertyPage implements all methods of **IUnknown** and implements the following:

- *SetPageSite* — Initializes a property page and provides the page with a pointer to the **IPropertyPageSite** interface. The interface is used for property frame communication.
- *Activate* — Creates the dialog box window for the property page.
- *Deactivate* — Destroys the window created with Activate.
- *GetPageInfo* — Returns a PROPPAGEINFO structure with property information.
- *SetObjects* — Provides an array of the **IUnknown** pointers of the objects affected by the property sheet in which this property page must be displayed.
- *Show* — Makes the property dialog box visible or invisible.
- *Move* — Resizes and repositions the property page dialog box with the frame.
- *IsPageDirty* — Indicates whether the page has changed since the last activation.
- *Apply* — Applies current property page values to underlying objects specified through **SetObjects**.
- *Help* — Invokes help in response to a user request.
- *TranslateAccelerator* — Provides a pointer to a MSG structure for keystroke translation.

IPropertyPage2

IPropertyPage2 is an extension of **IPropertyPage** that tells the page which property to highlight or to receive focus when the page is activated. The interface implements all methods of **IUnknown, IPropertyPage,** and the method, **EditProperty,** which identifies the property to receive focus when the page is activated.

IPropertyPageSite

IPropertyPageSite is the last of the property page interfaces. It is the interface that provides the main features for a property site object. A property page site is created for each property page within the property frame. The property page site stores some state global data and this interface provides access to that data for all property pages. The interface receives notifications when changes occur from the page through **IPropertyPageSite::OnStatusChange**. The frame in turn initiates a call to **IPropertyPage::IsPageDirty** when a change occurs. The return value is then used to either enable or disable the frame's apply button. Initially, the button is disabled.

IPropertyPageSite supports all methods of **IUnknown** and implements:

- *OnStatusChange* — Called when the user has changed property values on the property page.
- *GetLocaleID* — Returns the locale identifier. The property pages are then adjusted to the country-specific setting.
- *GetPageContainer* — The IUnknown pointer for the object representing the entire property frame dialog box is returned. This object contains all the property pages.
- *TranslateAccelerator* — Passes a keystroke to the property frame.

ActiveX

Microsoft renames technologies on a regular basis. Maybe this is because the technologies were not well-named in the first place. Microsoft did attach the name OLE to almost all technologies that used the earlier COM model. Microsoft marketing, however, in going through one of their rites of passage, concluded that they must have a new name for COM technology used with an Internet or Intranet. Hence, the new name *ActiveX*. Microsoft Messaging API (MAPI) is a COM-based technology that went through similar name machinations. The MAPI lineage started with MAPI, was followed consecutively by OLE Messaging, and Active Messaging, and now is called Collaborative Data Objects (CDO). CDO supports scripting, however, the three previous versions were only name changes.

ActiveX is not new. ActiveX consists of all the COM technology discussed thus far. Yes, ActiveX contains additional technology that I haven't discussed, and other technology that evolved after the renaming from OLE Controls to ActiveX. The technology was evolving independent of the name change. I reason that we would still have the same technology today, even without a name change. Microsoft did, however, compartmentalize COM technology a bit better with ActiveX. Linking and embedding, or what was known as OLE Documents, is now known as OLE technology. So an OLE Control is really an ActiveX control. Most of you should be familiar with the aliasing of an API function. Microsoft marketing is just aliasing a technology.

ActiveX Performance Enhancements

The Internet has helped us all, even indirectly when we don't use it. Before the Internet, component technology consisted of OLE with OLE Automation, OLE Controls, and OLE Compound Documents. Each of these technologies suffered from the same affliction, code bloat. The advent of the Internet forced Microsoft to rethink COM, which resulted in a reduced footprint and performance enhancements. Microsoft, however may be going too far. Now I think they are afflicted with *hammeritis,* which is to give someone a hammer and everything becomes a nail. If Microsoft has it their way, everything will be a COM object. On second thought, maybe they're afflicted by *COMitis*. It's not COM and it's not Microsoft; however, new technology has a habit of throwing out older technology even when some aspects of the older technology still have merit. Every application need not be component based.

Let's take a look at what I consider the neat stuff: all the enhancements to COM that came about as a result of trying to use an OLE Control on the Web. Those issues discussed previously will just be mentioned. The performance enhancements discussed here are outlined in the Microsoft document, *ActiveX Controls 96*. This white paper is found in the OC96 directory of the Microsoft ActiveX Development Kit published by the Microsoft Developer Network (MSDN).

Many of the interfaces mentioned below were discussed previously within the context of a COM Document. I'll review them briefly here, since they are also used in an OLE Control. You'll find references to earlier material for each of the previously introduced interfaces.

IPointerInactive

The Internet forced some rather nice performance improvements and this is one of them. The **IPointerInactive** interface is new and permits drag-and-drop operations for inactive objects. Minimizing the active object count results in an obvious performance boost. The interface is implemented by giving intelligence to the activation process. OLE 2.0 has only two states: active and inactive, and that isn't enough for drag-and-drop operations over inactive objects.

The **IPointerInactive** interface removes the need for controls to be activated when visible. It is now the responsibility of the container to forward all mouse movements to controls, which must conform to the OCX96/ActiveX Controls 96 specification. This reduces the considerable overhead of activating all of the visible controls when loading forms. Inactive controls still need some way of interacting with the user. For example, a control might want to act as the drop target, or respond to the mouse, but being inactive prevents it from doing this, as it has no window. **IPointerInactive** provides this capability.

This interface uses the COM library definition:

```
#define OLEMISC_IGNOREACTIVATEWHENVISIBLE . . .
```

The importance of this definition is that an object with this flag set, assuming, of course, that the container understands the flag and uses **IPointerInactive, should** ignore the flag OLEMISC_ACTIVEWHENVISIBLE and not do in-place activation when the object becomes visible. The object itself determines when in-place activation should occur.

IPointerInactive inherits all methods of **IUnknown** and implements the following:

- *GetActivationPolicy* — Returns the present activation policy for the object. Occurs when the mouse is over the object. The object may or may not request activation.
- *OnInactiveSetCursor* — Called by the container for the inactive object under the mouse pointer. This occurs with the receipt of a WM_SETCURSOR message.
- *OnInactiveMouseMove* — Indicates to an inactive object that the mouse pointer is over the object.

IViewObject::Draw

The **IViewObject** interface was presented in Chapter 6, as the companion to **IDataObject**. **IViewObject** renders the data presentation, while **IDataObject** manages the data. These comments here are specific to only one method of the **IViewObject** interface. This is not to imply that **Draw** is the only method of **IViewObject,** but that the *ActiveX Controls 96* specification optimizes the **Draw** method. The net result of the enhancement is to reduce the unnecessary selecting and deselecting of the font, brush, and pen when rendering an object. OLE 2 has the restriction that all GDI objects selected into the hDC passed to **IViewObject::Draw** be deselected before returning. The problem is solved with the **DVASPECTINFO** structure passed as a parameter to **IViewObject::Draw**.

IViewObjectEx and IOleInPlaceSiteEx

The **IViewObjectEx** and **IOleInPlaceSiteEx** interfaces were discussed previously. **IViewObjectEx** was discussed in Chapter 6, while **IOIleInPlaceSiteEx** was discussed in Chapter 8. The changes promote a flicker-free environment. Changes were also made to **IViewObjectEx** to support non-rectangular objects.

IOleInPlaceSiteWindowless and IOleInPlaceObjectWindowless

These interfaces were discussed in Chapter 8. Both of these interfaces are derived from **IOleInPlaceSiteEx**. They enable an object to be windowless and use the services of the container. The net result is small irregular objects that can be transparent and irregular. It also enables an object to draw itself when active.

IQuickActivate

This is a new interface for minimizing the overhead of loading a control into a container. The net result is the combining of the load-time and initialization-time handshaking into one call. Reducing the handshaking process down to one call is accomplished with the **QACONTAINER** structure with default parameters based on other controls.

Before the **IQuickActivate** interface, the process of activating a control was a serialized process involving calls to **QueryInterface** and the container's **IDispatch** interface. Activating a control can be reduced to one call when the control supports the **IQuickActivate** interface. A container that supports quick activation queries a control for the **IQuickActivate** interface. When this interface exists, the container fills up a QACONTAINER structure with pointers to the key interfaces needed by the control and calls **IQuickActivate::QuickActivate.**

IQuickActivate inherits all methods of **IUnknown** and implements:

- *QuickActivate* — The QACONTAINER structure is passed to the method. In return, the control supplies required parameters in QACONTROL.
- *SetContentExtent* — Called by the container to set the control extent.
- *GetContentExtent* — Called by the container to get the control extent.

IOleUndoManager

The **IOleUndoManager** interface is not necessarily a performance issue, however Microsoft enhanced the COM model to implement multilevel undo and redo. These actions also incorporate undo actions performed on contained controls. These changes incorporate three new interfaces and an undo manager is required because of the complexity.

Undo information is saved on a stack. Not everything can be restored when the stack is not large enough. The only objects contributing to the undo stack are the active objects with a user interface. Windowless objects and inactive objects do not participate in the undo process.

IOleUndoManager inherits all methods of **IUnknown** and implements:

- *Open* — This is equivalent to **IOleParentUndoUnit::Open**. The undo manager is opened.
- *Close* — This is equivalent to **IOleParentUndoUnit::Close**. The undo manager is closed.
- *Add* — This is equivalent to **IOleParentUndoUnit::Add**. The undo manager places the unit on the undo stack and discards the entire redo stack when it is the base state. The undo manager places new items in the undo stack when in the undo mode and new units on the redo stack when in redo mode.

- *GetOpenParentState* — Returns false on no open parent, otherwise it delegates the open unit's **GetParentMethod.**
- *DiscardFrom* — Discards the specified undo item and all other undo items below in the undo stack. The undo manager must first search the undo stack for the item with **IOleParentUndoUnit::FindUnit**.
- *UndoTo* — The undo manager is instructed to perform undo actions down to and including a specified undo unit.
- *RedoTo* — The undo manager is instructed to perform redo actions down to and including a specified redo unit.
- *EnumUndoable* — Enumerates the top-level units in the undo stack.
- *EnumRedoable* — Enumerates the top-level units in the redo stack.
- *GetLastUndoDescription* — Fetches the description from the top of the undo stack.
- *GetLastRedoDescription* — Fetches the description from the top of the redo stack.
- *Enable* — Used by the container to enable or disable the undo manager. Useful for objects that do not support multilevel undo operations.

IOleUndoUnit

The undo unit is responsible for undo or redo operations. When there is no undo manager, the **IOleUndoUnit** performs the undo or redo directly and nothing is placed on either stack. The converse is true when the undo manager exists and the undo or redo unit is placed on the appropriate stack.

IOleUndoUnit inherits all methods of **IUnknown** and implements:

- *Do* — The undo unit has the responsibility of placing itself on the property stack. This occurs by calling **IOleUndoManager::Open** or **IOleUndoManager::Add**. The state of the undo unit determines the stack that will be used. Parent units should place themselves on the appropriate undo or redo stack before calling this method for their children.
- *GetDescription* — Fetches the description of the undo unit. The caller must release this string and all units are required to provide a user-readable description.

- *GetUnitType*—Determines whether special handling is required. The CLSID and the type ID must uniquely identify the unit.
- *OnNextAdd*—A parent notifies the last undo unit that a new undo unit has been added.

IOleParentUndoUnit

The **IOleParentUndoUnit** interface is supported by units that are capable of containing other units. It inherits all methods of **IUknown** and **IOleUndoUnit** and implements:

- *Open*—Creates a new parent undo unit. The stack is left open and new units are passed to the stack until it is closed.
- *Close*—The most recent undo unit is closed. An optional parameter is provided for closing the stack.
- *Add*—The undo manager or the parent undo unit must accept any undo unit passed. Blocking is the only exception to this rule.
- *GetParentState*—Returns state information on the innermost open parent undo unit.
- *FindUnit*—Normally called by the undo manager to locate an undo unit. The parent looks in its own list first. When the unit isn't found a delegation is done to each child that is a parent. A child is designated as a parent if the interface **IOleParentUndoUnit** is found with **QueryInterface**.

Microsoft has added a little too much complexity here. If I change the foreground color and some other attributes of a control, I would expect to reset them myself. Common implementations of software typically provide a reset to installation defaults. This is probably not possible when the control you'll use fifteen minutes from now hasn't been downloaded from the Web yet. I am sure they'll provide a good rationale for this feature; however, it adds to the overall application complexity and I'm not convinced it is needed.

ActiveX and the Internet/Intranet

We can thank the Internet/intranet for many COM improvements, however, some of the additional COM functionality is Internet/intranet specific, which means that Microsoft's focus is the Internet/intranet and COM enhancements are mostly Internet/intranet related. In this section we'll peek at the issues of downloading ActiveX components from an Internet/intranet.

We're getting a bit ahead of ourselves here, so consider this section bridge material to later chapters in this book. Listings 10-1, 10-2, and 10-3 are Visual Basic scripts from a hypothetical Active Server Page (ASP) of Microsoft Internet Information Server (IIS).

CoGetClassObjectFromURL

This COM library function, while not a performance enhancement, is the workhorse of Internet downloads. The Internet Download Component architecture is illustrated in Figure 10-4. A Uniform Resource Locator (URL) is a Web address and http://www.microsoft.com is a commonly recognized URL.

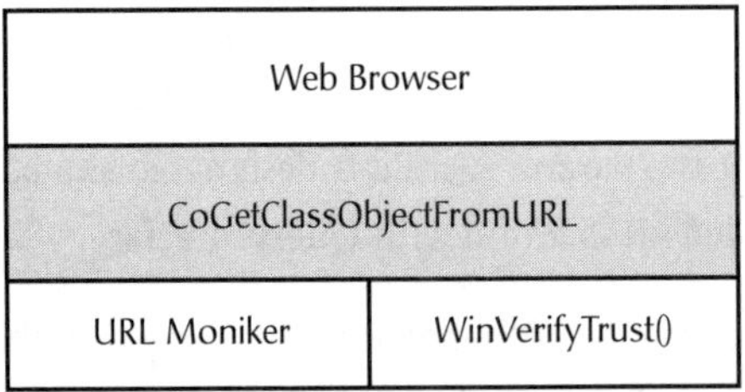

FIGURE 10-4 Internet download component architecture

URL Moniker in Figure 10-4 is the URL implementation of IMoniker, which was discussed in Chapter 5.

CoGetClassObjectFromURL does everything necessary to download and install a new component. Microsoft Internet Explorer uses this code when it encounters a CODEBASE attribute inside a HyperText Markup Language (HTML) OBJECT tag. **CoGetClassObjectFromURL** uses the **IBindStatusCallBack** interface for communication with the client. **CoGetClassObjectFromURL** returns an **IClassFactory**

object for a CLSID. When no CLSID is given it interprets the Internet MIME type stored in *szContentType,* an argument to **CoGetClassObjectFromURL.**

An existing object is instantiated by **CoGetClassObjectFromURL.** New objects are downloaded from *szCodeURL,* an argument to **CoGetClassObjectFromURL,** or from an Object Store on the Internet Search Path.

CoGetClassObjectFromURL performs the following functions:

- Downloads the appropriate files which may be .CAB, .INF, or .EXE using URL Monikers.
- Calls **WinVerifyTrust** to verify that all downloaded components are safe to install. **WinVerifyTrust** searches the downloaded file for a signature block, which contains information about the file author, a public key, and an encrypted digest of the file's contents. The certificate is validated when a signature exists. The validation process uses the concept of a trust hierarchy with each parent certificate inspected until the root certificate is located.
- Ascertains the self-registration of all COM components.
- Adds Registry entries to track downloaded code.
- Calls **CoGetClassObject** for the desired CLSID.

Internet Downloads

Internet downloads are tools that support content. The server must know the client capabilities before a download is possible. Even if one is possible, is it useful? I'll try to integrate the discussion of the Internet Download Component with a practical application. We'll start with Listing 10-1 that looks at the browser type. The second example in Listing 10-2 asks if the browser can support ActiveX controls and the Internet Download Component is invoked only when the browser supports ActiveX controls. This is almost like Active Data Objects (ADO) where the developer uses the **Supports** method to verify that the functionality is supported.

LISTING 10-1 Using the Marquee Control for Internet Explorer

```
<%
    '
    '     Use HTML Marquee if Internet Explorer
    '
```

```
   Set MyObj = Server.CreateObject("MSWC.BrowserType")
   if (MyObj.browser = "IE") Then
%>
     <marquee bgcolor="#00005B" direction="LEFT" behavior="SCROLL" >
       Thank you for buying Solution Architectures MCSD Study Guide
     </marquee>
<%
   Else
%>
     <center>
       Thank you for buying Solution Architectures MCSD Study Guide
     </center>
<%
   End If
%>
```

We're adding some intelligence to our active server page. Listing 10-1 uses the browser capabilities component to determine the type of browser. When Internet Explorer is the client browser, the browser uses the HTML Marquee element, otherwise a text message is displayed. Most browsers probably support the HTML Marquee element, so this example is merely illustrative.

The type of browser is not the only issue. Does the browser support ActiveX controls? The script shown in Listing 10-2 raises the functionality a notch by deciding between downloading an ActiveX control and displaying a message of the Billboard Rotator Component of Microsoft Internet Information Server (IIS). The Billboard Rotator Component rotates advertising images on a Web page and can be configured so the browser gets a new message each time the Active Server Page (ASP) is requested. (If that's not clear, then remember that the MWSC Adrotator control is an Internet Information Server component, and only an image can be downloaded.)

LISTING 10-2 Deciding between the Adrotator control and a custom control

```
<%
   '
   '   Use HTML Marquee if Internet Explorer
   '
```

```
    Set MyObj = Server.CreateObject("MSWC.BrowserType")
    if MyObj.ActiveXControls =TRUE Then
%>
      <OBJECT CODEBASE="/MyWeb/MyBillBoard.CAB#version=8,0,0,8"
        WIDTH=570 HEIGHT=70 DATA="/MyWeb/Controls/MyBillBoard.ods"
        CLSID=clsid:11111111-2222-3333-4444-555555555555">
      </OBJECT>
<%
    Else
      Set MyAD=Server.CreateObject(MWSC.Adrotator")
      Response.Write(MyAD.GetAdvertisement("/MyWeb/ad.txt"))
    End If
%>
```

The script is busy making download decisions. When the script encounters the CODEBASE attribute of the HTML OBJECT tag, **CoGetClassObjectFromURL,** is invoked directly. All the URL Moniker machinations we previously discussed now come into play.

`#version=8,0,0,8` is a URL fragment of Listing 10-2 that represents the version number. This portion of the URL is pivotal in the load process because it determines if the component will be downloaded. When this value is `-1,-1,-1,-1` a new version of the component is always downloaded. When no version is present, the currently loaded version is considered acceptable, otherwise the Internet Download Component will download a new version only when the requested version is more recent than the existing version. When no component is loaded, and no version is present, the URL path is searched for the component.

The Internet Download Component processes three file categories:

- *PE*—A portable executable such as a `.OCX`, `.DLL`, or `.EXE`. A single executable is downloaded, installed, and registered in one operation. The file category may be code-signed. The Internet Download Component will try to start self-registration for those components marked as such. The Internet Download Component ignores the `OleSelfRegister` flag if the main URL code points directly to an `.EXE` file. This type of file is not platform independent except with HTTP.

- *CAB*—A `.CAB` file has the advantage of compression and can be code-signed. A `.CAB` file-required component is an `.INF` file which contains the packaging instructions. A `.CAB` file is not platform independent without HTTP format negotiation.
- *INF*—An `.INF` file that cannot be code-signed, but it is platform independent. The `.INF` file is a map of all required files. This file download category is useful in an intranet environment but is unsafe on the Internet.

Developers should always use a `.CAB` file because it uses compression, reduces component download time, and increases client satisfaction. The `CAB-SDK.EXE`, `CABVIEW.EXE` tool, and the code-signing tool `AUTH2SDK.EXE` are all downloadable from Microsoft. Rather than publishing a URL in this book that will change, go to the Microsoft home page at `http://www. microsoft.com`. and search for the text *authenticode*. Numerous download site hyperlinks will be displayed.

Code Signing

Code Signing is used with either a *PE* or a *CAB* file when used with the Internet Download Component. Microsoft supports code signing for .exe, .cab, .ocx, and .vbd files. Code signing is a digital signature that is transmitted with the document to guarantee authenticity. The authenticity is guaranteed by holding either an individual or a corporation accountable for any destruction caused by a digitally signed and downloaded file. The signature accompanying the downloaded file identifies the legal entity that created the software, which may be an individual or a corporation.

Microsoft calls digital signing Authenticode. Authenticode consists of a public key and a private key. The software publisher applies for a certificate to a Certification Authority (CA), a trusted entity. Before applying, the software publisher generates a key pair that uses either hardware or software. One key will become the public key and the other key will be the private key of the requesting publisher. The CA verifies the credentials of the individual or corporation and a certificate is issued when the credentials are verified. The credentials are a positive identification of the individual or firm along with a pledge not to distribute malicious software. The certificate contains the public key and will always be sent with the signed document.

A Local Registering Agency (LRA) assumes some of the responsibilities of a CA, but does not issue certificates. Approved applications are passed on by the LRA to a CA. The CA organization structure is hierarchical with many roots. A root is a CA. Beneath the root CA may be local CAs. A root CA will hold certificates signed by all CAs immediately below the root. Moving down the tree a bit further, the next level of CA will hold certificates for all those CAs immediately below it, and so on. Beneath each CA is one or more LRAs. Based on this hierarchical structure, certificates can be verified for all individuals or entities.

The document itself is not signed. What is signed is a one-way hash of the document. Both the signed hash and the document are transmitted to the recipient. The recipient generates a one-way hash. When the generated one-way hash matches the transmitted hash, the document is valid.

AUTH2SDK.EXE, the code signing toolkit, is a self-extracting file that is downloadable from Microsoft. Within the SDK the developer will find the following:

- *MakeCert* — Creates a text X.509 certificate. It creates a public/private key pair for digital signatures and associates this key pair with a chosen name.
- *Cert2SPC* — Creates a test Software Publisher Certificate (SPC). This is a test only program since the valid SPC is obtained from a CA.
- *SignCode* — Signs the code using a SPC.
- *PeSigMgr* — A utility to see if the file was signed.
- *ChkTrust* — Tests the validity of the signed file.

Licensing and the Internet

Licensing with the Internet is very similar to licensing with standard controls. The **IClassFactory2** interface (see Chapter 2) is used at design time. This is the same licensing mechanism currently used for implementing the licensing of existing controls. A developer acquires a license, and the authoring tools or utilities call **IClassFactory2::RequestLicKey** to store the runtime licenses for all the controls used on the page as an array of (CLSID, license) pairs. The array is stored in a .LPK file. The HTML page points to the license package via a *relative* URL reference inside the HTML. A relative URL makes pirating inconvenient, but does not stop it.

IClassFactory2::CreateInstanceLic is used at runtime by the web browser to extract the necessary runtime licenses from the license package. The licensed objects are instantiated after the licenses are extracted. Listing 10-2 is updated in Listing 10-3 with a .LPK file illustrating a licensed custom control.

LISTING 10-3 Licensing the custom BillBoard control

```
<%
  '
  ' Use HTML Marquee if Internet Explorer
  '
  Set MyObj = Server.CreateObject("MSWC.BrowserType")
  if MyObj.ActiveXControls =TRUE  Then
%>
    <OBJECT CODEBASE="/MyWeb/MyBillBoard.CAB#version=8,0,0,8
       WIDTH=570 HEIGHT=70 DATA="/MyWeb/Controls/MyBillBoard.ods"
       CLSID="clsid:11111111-2222-3333-4444-555555555555">
       <PARAM NAME="LPKPath" VALUE= {relative URL path} >
         <EMBED SRC = "BRUCE.LPK">
    </OBJECT>
<%
  Else
    Set MyAD=Server.CreateObject(MWSC.Adrotator")
    Response.Write(MyAD.GetAdvertisement("/MyWeb/ad.txt"))
  End If
%>
```

Active Documents

COM continues to evolve and Active Documents (Document Objects or Doc Objects) are a recent extension of COM. A Doc Object is a full-scale (complete) document that is embedded in a container. Traditional embedded COM objects do not have complete control over their content while an embedded Doc Object maintains complete control and exploits the native functionality of the server. Microsoft

Word and Microsoft Excel are both Active Document servers. Microsoft Binder and Microsoft Internet Explorer are both examples of Active Document containers. An Active Document is illustrated by dropping a Word Document onto Internet Explorer. The interface created should be very familiar to a Word user. Internet Explorer provides the basic menus, status bars, and tool bars and Word merges all of its menus, status bars, and tool bars with those of Internet Explorer.

There is a significant intrinsic benefit with an Active Document application, which is reducing the Total Cost of Ownership (TOC). A runtime engine need not be distributed with an Active Document since Microsoft Internet Explorer can be the runtime engine.

Another Active Document issue is software control and licensing. It is difficult to enforce licensing over the Internet; however, an alternative is to provide a freely downloadable Active Document server and to license the Active Document container. Of course this involves constructing a proprietary Active Document container.

Figure 10-5 is from Enterprise Edition of Microsoft Visual Basic. The ActiveX Document EXE in Figure 10-5 represents an Active Document container, whereas an ActiveX Document server is represented by either an ActiveX Document DLL or an ActiveX Document EXE. When an active document project is compiled, Visual Basic creates either the DLL or EXE along with a file that has a Visual Basic Document (VBD) extension. (A VBD extension was mentioned above as a supported file type for code-signing.) Microsoft Word and a DOC file are roughly equivalent to a VBD file and the supporting ActiveX DLL or EXE file.

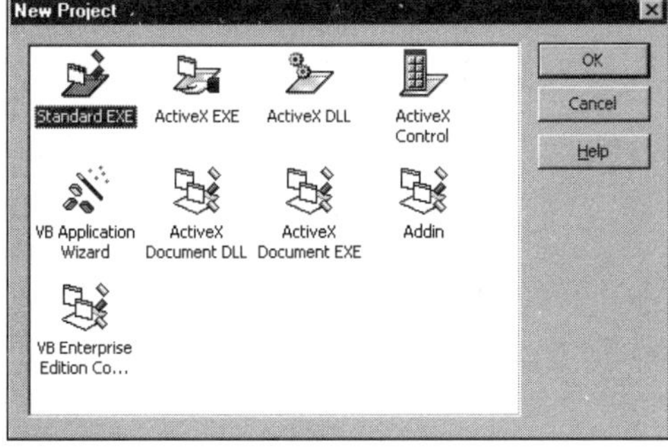

FIGURE 10-5 Visual Basic and Active Document components

Active Document Server

An Active Document server is an OLE local server that functions in a manner similar to an OLE in-place server. An Active Document server uses many of the COM interfaces we've discussed so far. Table 10-1 identifies the required and optional interfaces of an Active Document server.

TABLE 10-1 REQUIRED INTERFACES FOR AN ACTIVE DOCUMENT SERVER

Interface	*Description*
IOleDocument	An interface that enables a document object to communicate to prospective containers the supported viewing capability and other functionality.
IOleDocumentView	The interface used by a container to communicate with a specific document view.
IPersistStorage	An interface used by object handlers to support container simple-stream objects, such as monikers.
IOleObject	An interface used by the container to execute verbs, communicate information, or to close a view (see Chapter 6).
IDataObject	A required interface for the rendering of data (see Chapter 6).
IOleInPlaceObject	Used by the container to either activate or deactivate the object (see Chapters 6 and 8).
IOleInPlaceActiveObject	Effectively a channel used by the container for communication with the document. Issues include state information, message translation, management of modeless dialog boxes, and resizing requests (see Chapters 6 and 8).
IEnumFORMATETC	An optional interface that is used by the container to enumerate the supported data structures.
IEnumOleDocumentViews	An optional interface that is used by the container to enumerate the document views available.

INTERFACE	DESCRIPTION
IOleCommandTarget	An optional interface that defines a channel used by the container and document to communicate commands such as Print, Page Setup, and Properties to an in-place active object. The **IOleCommandTarget** interface replaces the **IDispatch** functionality, but with reduced overhead. Both an Active Document server and an Active Document container may implement this interface.
IPrint	An optional interface used by the container to instruct a document to print itself specifying control flags, the target device, the pages of interest, and other options.

There are many old acquaintances in Table 10-1, so let's take a quick peek at the new interfaces.

IOleDocument

The **IOleDocument** interface is defined by the Active Document server for enumerating views and miscellaneous document information. **IOleDocument** inherits all methods of the **IUnknown** interface and supports these methods.

- CreateView — Creates a new document view.
- *GetDocMiscStatus* — Returns document object status bits.
- *EnumViews* — Enumerates the views supported by the Active Document.

IOleDocumentView

Container communication with each supported document view is accomplished with the **IOleDocumentView** interface. In addition, each document view object is expected to implement the **IOleInPlaceObject, IoleInPlaceActiveObject** interfaces and optional interfaces such as **IOleCommandTarget** and **IPrint**. The **IOle DocumentView** interface inherits all methods of the **IUnknown** interface and supports these methods:

- *SetInPlaceSite* — Associates a view with a container site.
- *GetInPlaceSite* — Retrieves the last site passed to **SetInPlaceSite**.

- *GetDocument* — Returns the **IUnknown** pointer of the document object that owns the view.
- *SetRect* — Sets the view port coordinates.
- *GetRect* — Retrieves the last **SetRect** view port coordinates.
- *SetRectComplex* — Sets the size box, scroll bars, and view port coordinates.
- *Show* — Either activates or deactivates a view.
- *UIActivate* — Either in-place activates or in-place deactivates user-interface elements.
- *Open* — Displays a view in a separate pop-up window.
- *Close* — The container instructs the view to close.
- *SaveViewState* — The view state is saved into a stream.
- *ApplyViewState* — Initializes a document view with that previously stored by **SaveViewState**.
- *Clone* — Creates a duplicate view object.

IEnumOleDocumentViews

The **IEnumOleDocumentViews** interface is used by the container to enumerate the views of an Active Document and is implemented on enumerator objects associated with document objects that support more than one view of their data. The common enumerator methods of **Next, Skip, Reset,** and **Clone** are supported by this interface.

IOleCommandTarget

The **IOleCommandTarget** interface is a bi-directional command channel that the Active Document uses to sends commands to the container and the container can in turn send commands to the **Document** Object. Common document commands from tool bars include **Print, Print Preview, Save, New,** and **Zoom,** while containers must send such commands as **Print, Page Setup, and Properties** to an in-place active object. These commands are supported with existing OLE Automation standards and the **IDispatch** interface, however the overhead is excessive. The **IOleCommandTarget** interface inherits all methods of the **IUnknown** interface and supports these methods:

- *QueryStatus* — Queries the object for status.
- *Exec* — Executes a command.

IPrint

The **IPrint** interface enables programmatic printing of an Active Document. Active Documents that support the **IPrint** interface must self-register with the **Printable** keyword stored under the object's CLSID. A generic example of such a key is:

```
HKEY_CLASSES_ROOT\CLSID\{. . .}\Printable
```

IPrint is an optional interface and is typically implemented on an object that supports either the **IPersistFile** or **IPersistStorage** interface. The **IOleCommand Target** interface inherits all methods of the **IUnknown** interface and supports these methods.

- *SetInitialPageNum* — Sets first page number.
- *GetPageInfo* — Returns page count and first page number.
- *Print* — Print object's persistent state.

Active Document Container

An Active Document container is the other half of the Active Document equation. An Active Document container supplies the Active Document view. Instead of providing a document in which an in-place object resides, the Active Document container provides the basic user interface features specific to the container. The container also allows the server to merge its menus and toolbars and any other user interface components in the container view area. The Active Document container requires a minimum of four interfaces, all of which are enumerated in Table 10-2.

TABLE 10-2 REQUIRED INTERFACES FOR AN ACTIVE DOCUMENT SERVER

INTERFACE	*DESCRIPTION*
IOleDocumentSite	Used by the Active Document to ask the container to activate the document object.
IOleClientSite	Supplies container site information and services to the embedded document object (see Chapter 7).
IOleInPlaceSite	Manages the interaction between in-place objects (see Chapter 8).

Continued

TABLE 10-2 *(continued)*

Interface	*Description*
IAdviseSink	Used by the Active Document to notify the Active Document container of state, value, or name changes (see Chapter 6).
IOleCommandTarget	An optional interface that defines a channel used by the container and document to communicate commands such as **Print**, **Page Setup**, and **Properties** to an in-place active object. The **IOleCommandTarget** interface replaces the **IDispatch** functionality, but with reduced overhead. Both an Active Document server and an Active Document container may implement this interface (see previous section, Active Document server).
IContinueCallback	Optional generic callback mechanism for interrupted processes.

IOleDocumentSite and **IContinueCallback** are the only interfaces not previously mentioned.

IOleDocumentSite

A container must provide a document site for each Active Document to be hosted by the container. The **IOleDocumentSite** interface allows a document implemented as an Active Document to bypass the normal activation sequence for in-place active objects and to direct its client site to activate it as a Document Object. The Document Object calls **IOleDocumentSite::ActiveMe** to ask its document site to activate it. The request is usually in response to the container's calling **IOleObject::DoVerb**. The **IOleDocument** inherits all methods of **IUnknown** and **ActiveMe** is the only supported method.

IContinueCallback

The **IContinueCallback** interface is a generic callback mechanism for interruptible processes. The interface should periodically interrogate the object associated with this interface to continue the process. The IContinueCallback interface inherits all methods of the **IUnknown** interface and supports these two methods.

- *FContinue* — Determines if an operation should continue.
- *FContinuePrinting* — Determines if a printing operation should continue.

Component Technology in Review

In theory, COM is a dream come true for developers. In reality, the promises are held at bay by uneven implementation problems, created by the increase in application volume and interface complexity. It is true that the COM model reduces interface complexity with a standard interface; however, this reduction in complexity is offset by an increase in the number of interfaces. Microsoft appears to have overlooked some very important software engineering factors. COM increases two programming metrics: application volume and application complexity. Bugs increase as either of these metrics increases, and the increase is not linear! I see a definite deterioration in service levels between Microsoft OfficePro 4.3, Microsoft Office 95, and Microsoft Office 97.

The COM model will *never* be reliable because the client is always exposed to new code even if the new features are not used directly. Compare this to a legacy library. The closest a production application comes to new library features is that they may coexist on the same disk. Legacy applications such as FORTRAN and COBOL have a feature that is often overlooked. This is the immutability of the application. The application is a binary mass. (I have clients who have legacy programs that haven't been compiled in years.) COM has an immutable interface and that's all. Microsoft touts this interface as a contract with the client. Indeed, it is a contract, but you don't know who owns the contract today and you can be sure the contract will be sold tomorrow (which is done though the coding mechanism of aggregation or delegation). The selling of the interface contract appears to be itself a Machiavellian contract with Mephistopheles, because the interface contract is promised to be resold forever. The poor unsuspecting COM client does not know whether the new contract owner is malevolent or benevolent, hence the continuing unreliability of COM.

The COM Contract Doesn't Benefit the Enterprise

Yes, COM version control works, but it is a developer feature and the user reaps no tangible benefits. It is a version control that forces users to upgrade software even if the current version is functional and without errors. The application model espoused by the Microsoft marketing spin-makers yields no benefits other than new features that are not wanted or needed. The result is bloated software that is maintained in a constant state of flux, which creates an environment of continual errors. Microsoft dictates the version you should use, and you have no choice but to upgrade! When the client doesn't upgrade, the software is *orphaned*. An example of orphaned software is that no Windows 3.1 user can use 32-bit tools. That does not help the bottom line of an enterprise. The small gains made with the reusability of software at the interface level do not even begin to offset the expense of implementing the next Microsoft release of a product. Microsoft's theme of software reusability with COM is quite hollow where users get no reusability at all at the application level. The reusability of COM is useful to Microsoft developers only, and not to consumers.

Immutability of Applications

There's much more to a system than writing methods behind an interface. It is an issue of strategic planning with software upgrades controlled by the enterprise and not the software vendor. It is deciding when and how to upgrade; not the Microsoft-forced upgrades. A component application, at least in theory, could use a new DLL every day. Of course, it's absurd that such an environment should exist anywhere except at Microsoft where systems are referenced by build numbers. Your application task changes when a new DLL is installed from a service pack. The component application does not possess the immutability of legacy software where a legacy application changes only when recompiled and relinked by the developer. You install a service pack to repair a problem with your modems and your accounting applications develop a problem. It's Microsoft's policy that a service release is not just a collection of bug fixes, but is a vehicle to implement new features. As long as this is a policy, there can be no software stability. The unfortunate client, who needs the service pack to correct a problem, will inevitably host new problems in the *green* code representing the new features.

I believe the maelstrom of software change must slow down and software must become reliable. My thesis is very simple: Production applications and the operating system itself should be a binary mass, at least to the point that it is immutable over time. I discussed this point earlier in the book with a deprecated class. Preserve existing production applications by either deprecating their class or providing each new version release of a product as a new class. That's the way COM works. Each new interface, even if it inherits from another interface, gets a new

CLSID. New product versions should have new classes. Why can't Microsoft product releases function in the same manner as COM?

The second issue is that a user should have a choice in protecting an existing technology from *versionitis* and declare it as immutable. I've done that, but my personal system is 131MB with 8GB and many boots where I hide technology from other boots. It shouldn't be this way. I can't continue to keep all prior versions online forever. We'll be measuring blips in the sales of disk drives with each new release of a Microsoft product.

Making the operating system immutable to change may not be possible because the basic Microsoft Windows architecture consists of numerable DLLs, many of which are dependent on other DLLs. I believe the DLL concept is flawed since the concept of a DLL sponsors volatility. I have 20/20 hindsight like everyone else, and it is easy to take issue with concepts. That is an apology, because I am sure a great deal of work went into the DLL concept. Along with the volatility is the fact that DLL use is not controlled. DLLs are used by both the system and applications, and updates to system DLLs are an implied update to an application. At this late date there is really not much that can be done. Commonality of code may have gone too far. A DLL library for the exclusive use of the operating system is the first step in controlling DLL use and insulates the application from operating system upgrades. The concept of a DLL library is good to a point. However, the level at which Microsoft creates new software has made the concept of a DLL library very questionable. There are simply too many changes with no stability and everything is co-dependent.

In spite of the apparent high sales volume, I have no long-term expectations for the success of the Windows architecture, even though Microsoft has an apparent monopoly. It is too volatile. Users will switch to the first viable alternative, which may be Linux. Mainframes are known to be reliable. The relief may be mainframe servers for thin Java clients, and UNIX still remains a viable alternative. If the UNIX camp loses too many sales, they'll retrench and provide a prettier interface, as that is one of the few features that Microsoft offers. Yes, Microsoft has lots of clever software, but none of it is useful unless it is stable, and it is not. I give Microsoft an *A+* for user interface design and a *C-* for system engineering.

This brings us to the end of component technology. I hope I've enlightened you to some of the inner workings of COM. Many of the chapters to follow utilize COM. You'll see COM used in Microsoft Transaction Server (MTS), Microsoft

Message Queue (MSMQ), Distributed COM (DCOM), Collaborative Data Objects (CDO), Active Data Objects (ADO), and Remote Data Objects (RDO). The Open Database Connectivity (ODBC) journey is next. ODBC is the root technology for database access and we'll explore the current variations of this outstanding technology. Persevere.

Key Point Summary

COM technology is not mature. We can't do without it, so we'll have to learn to live with it. Maybe my small voice and the voice of you, my reader, can convince Microsoft that reliability is more important than features. But then, what is life without an occasional fantasy? The key points below address the theme of this chapter, that OLE Controls are a key milestone of COM.

- An ActiveX is an alias for an OLE Control. Microsoft marketing decreed that, henceforth, OLE Controls shall be know as ActiveX controls.
- OLE Controls are the pinnacle of COM technology. They incorporate all prior COM technology except linking. This includes Automation.
- OLE Controls added support for properties and property pages to the COM model.
- Events are a new feature of OLE Controls.
- OLE Controls are 32-bit and support Unicode.
- OLE Controls use inside-out activation because they integrate seamlessly with the container object. This is compared to outside-in activation of an OLE embedded document.

Applying What You've Learned

OLE Controls are a turning point for COM. This chapter builds on previously presented COM technology. A key feature missing with COM was a formal model for properties. The extensions to COM include new objects that model properties.

The missing ingredient for an OLE Control is the concept of an *event*. An event is a method that is called when state changes, which is definitional because COM already supports methods. Rename specific methods and you have events.

Use events with the connectable objects (see Chapter 5), and the picture of an OLE Control is complete. The questions below will test your general understanding of these issues.

Instant Assessment

1. Name a new feature of OLE Controls.
2. OLE Controls are considered the pinnacle of COM technology in that they use nearly all COM features. What key COM feature is missing with OLE Controls?
3. What new feature did OLE Controls bring to the COM model?
4. How are events implemented within OLE Controls?
5. What activation method is used for OLE Controls?
6. What is the purpose of the **IPointerInactive** interface?
7. What is an Active Document and what are the advantages of using one?

For answers to the Instant Assessment Questions, see Appendix B.

Lab Exercise

This chapter has two interesting labs. The first lab builds an ActiveX control with both a property bag and a property page, while the second lab illustrates callbacks from the Visual Basic environment.

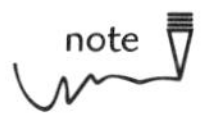

The name of the default interface is the name of the class prefixed with an underscore. _Bank is the default interface to the Bank class and the underscore hides the name from the type browser. Don't confuse the default interface with the VB continuation character, which is also an underscore.

Lab 10.28 *Visual Basic Property Bags and Property Pages*

We'll add both a property page and the **IPropertyBag** interface to a Visual Basic control, which will provide the property persistence for an ActiveX control. The **WriteProperties** and **ReadProperties** methods of an ActiveX control use a property bag as parameter. The steps below detail the construction of a client and a control that illustrate implementing persistence for control properties.

1. Start a standard Visual Basic .EXE application.
2. Name the form module as *Teller*.
3. Place a text box on the form with the name *txtInput*.
4. Place another text box on the form with the name *txtBalance*. Set the **Enable** property of this control to FALSE.
5. Place a command button on the form with the name *cmdDeposit*. Change the caption of this control to the *Deposit*.
6. Place another command button on the form with the name *cmdWithdrawal*. Change the caption of this control to the *Withdrawal*.
7. From the **Project** menu, select *Add User Control*.
8. Click **OK** and change the control name to *Bank* in the **Properties** window.
9. Set the control **BorderStyle** to *1-Fixed Single*. Normally this isn't necessary, however, we want to set the **Balance** property to a specific value after the control is placed on the form.
10. Enter the following code in the Declarations section of the user control:

```
'(C) 1999 Bruce T. Prendergast
' DBA Prendergast Consulting
' DBA PCS
' IDG Books Worldwide ISBN 0-7645-3314-2
'
Option Explicit
Private m_Balance As Variant

Public Property Let Balance(ByVal varInput As Variant)
  m_Balance = varInput
  If CanPropertyChange("Balance") Then
    PropertyChanged "Balance"
    MsgBox "Notification occurred"
  Else
    MsgBox "Unable to change property"
  End If
End Property

Public Property Get Balance() As Variant
  Balance = m_Balance
End Property
```

```
Private Sub UserControl_InitProperties()
  MsgBox "InitProperties"
End Sub

Private Sub UserControl_ReadProperties(PropBag As PropertyBag)
  MsgBox "Attempting to Read Properties"
  With PropBag
    m_Balance = .ReadProperty("Balance")
    MsgBox "Reading Properties"
  End With
End Sub

Private Sub UserControl_WriteProperties(PropBag As PropertyBag)
  MsgBox "Writing Properties"
  With PropBag
    .WriteProperty "Balance", m_Balance
  End With
End Sub
```

11. Close the user control code window.
12. Choose **Project ➪ Add Property page** and accept the defaults.
13. Set the property page **Name** property to *MyPropertyPage*.
14. Place a text box on the property page form and set the **Name** property to *txtBalance*.
15. Place a label on the property page form and set the **Caption** value to *Initial Balance*.
16. Open the property page code window and add the following code:

```
Option Explicit
Private Sub PropertyPage_ApplyChanges()
  SelectedControls(0).Balance = txtBalance
  MsgBox "Changes applied"
End Sub

Private Sub PropertyPage_SelectionChanged()
  txtBalance = SelectedControls(0).Balance
  MsgBox "Selection has changed"
End Sub
```

```
Private Sub txtBalance_Change()
  Changed = True
End Sub
```

17. Open the code window for the **Bank** control.
18. Select **Tools** ➪ **Procedure Attributes.**
19. Verify that the **Name** box contains **Balance**.
20. Click **Advanced.**
21. Set **Use This Page in Property Browser Box** to *MyPropertyPage* and click **OK.**
22. Close the **Bank** control code window.
23. Open the **Bank** control window.
24. Double click the **PropertyPages** property.
25. Select all property pages and click **OK.**
26. Close out the user control designer. The user control will remain *grayed* on the toolbar until the user control designer is closed.
27. After the user control designer is closed, open the **Teller** form.
28. Click the user control on the toolbar and paint it on the **Teller** form.
29. Select the **Bank** control on the **Teller** form and go to the properties window and set the control **Name** property to *Bank*.
30. Click the ellipses of the **Balance** property and the property page will be displayed.
31. Congratulations. The property page is now displayed. Set the **txtBalance** text box on the property page to 499. Close the property page.
32. Open the **Teller** form code window and enter the following code in the **Declarations** section of the **Teller** form:

```
'(C) 1999 Bruce T. Prendergast
' DBA Prendergast Consulting
' DBA PCS
' IDG Books Worldwide ISBN 0-7645-3314-2
'
Option Explicit
Private Sub cmdDeposit_Click()
  Bank.Balance = Bank.Balance + Val(txtInput)
  txtBalance = Bank.Balance
End Sub
```

```
Private Sub cmdWithdrawal_Click()
  Bank.Balance = Bank.Balance - Val(txtInput)
  txtBalance = Bank.Balance
End Sub

Private Sub Form_Load()
  txtBalance = Bank.Balance
End Sub
```

33. Start the application. *499* should initially appear in the **txtBalance** control. Enter *100* into the **txtInput** control and click the **cmdDeposit** command button. *599* should now appear in the **txtBalance** control. Congratulations. You've just implemented a control with a property bag and a property page.

Lab 10.29 *Callbacks in Visual Basic*

The **AddressOf** keyword is used for callbacks from Win32 API functions. The callback we'll build in this laboratory is between components in a tiered architecture. A callback is one of two component asynchronous communication mechanisms. The first asynchronous component communication mechanism is with the **WithEvents** keyword, which is illustrated by a laboratory at the conclusion of Chapter 6. The steps below detail the construction of a callback application, which is the second type of asynchronous communication. The form module interrogates the **Author** component, and the **Author** component returns a reply to the supplied recipient, which in this example is the **Editor** component. The steps below construct this example of a callback application.

1. Start a standard Visual Basic .EXE 5.0 or 6.0 application.
2. Place a command button on the form and label it as **cmdAsk**. In the **Caption** property set the value *Ask the Author*.
3. Enter the following code in the **Declarations** section of the form:

```
'(C) 1999 Bruce T. Prendergast
' DBA Prendergast Consulting
' DBA PCS
'
' IDG Books Worldwide ISBN 0-7645-3314-2
'
Option Explicit
Public m_Author As Author
```

```
Public m_Editor As Editor

Private Sub cmdAsk_Click()
  Set m_Editor = New Editor
  Set m_Author = New Author
  Call m_Author.TellMeWhenReady(m_Editor)
End Sub
```

4. Add a class module using the Class Wizard. Name the class as **INotifyMe** with the **Public** method **ChapterIsReady**. This class will becomes our interface to the callback recipient component. The code for this class should appear as:

```
Option Explicit
Public Sub ChapterIsReady()
End Sub
```

5. Use the Class Builder Utility to create another class and name the class as **Editor**. This is the component accepting the callback from another component. Add the **ChapterIsReady** method without arguments to this class. Close the Class Builder Utility and open the Editor class code window. Edit the code to appear as follows:

```
Option Explicit
Implements INotifyMe
Private Sub INotifyMe_ChapterIsReady()
  MsgBox "Chapter is ready"
End Sub
```

6. Use the Class Builder Utility to create the **Author** class with the method **TellMeWhenReady**, which has the **ByVal** argument of the **INotifyMe** interface. After editing, the class code should appear as follows:

```
Option Explicit
Public m_en As INotifyMe
Public Sub TellMeWhenReady(ByVal en As INotifyMe)
  Set m_en = en
  '
  ' assume logic of some sort when chapter is ready
  '
  Const ChapterIsWritten = True
  Const ChapterExamplesWork = True
```

```
    If ChapterIsWritten And ChapterExamplesWork Then
      m_en.ChapterIsReady
    End If
  End Sub
```

7. Congratulations. You've just completed a component callback application. Run the application and click the command button. You should see a message box display the message *Chapter is ready.*

PART

Tiered Architecture Building Blocks

II

This is the database access technology section. Included in this section are chapters on Open Database Connectivity (ODBC), Remote Data Objects (RDO), and Active Data Objects (ADO).

Chapter 11: ODBC - ODBC 3.0 is sketched and the chapter closes with an ODBC API quick reference.

Chapter 12: ODBC Applications - Examples highlight each ODBC function group.

Chapter 13: RDO - The essentials of RDO are introduced.

Chapter 14: RDO Queries - RDO continues with a focus on query operations.

Chapter 15: ADO - The chapter starts with the ADO architecture and closes with ADO properties.

Chapter 16: ADO Queries - Examples illustrate ADO methods.

CHAPTER

11

ODBC

About Chapter 11

The chapter begins with a description and a brief history of *Open Database Connectivity* (ODBC). ODBC is a data access technology. ODBC uses existing network protocols and stands between the client and a remote relational database. Although originally developed by Microsoft, ODBC is no longer proprietary and conforms to international standards. ODBC's intrinsic value is the ability to supply connections to hetrogeneous databases, which does not mean *heterogeneous joins* in the SQL language sense. In my opinion, ODBC is the most important software ever written by Microsoft. It's the glue that connects the enterprise to diverse internal and external databases. An application that incorporates ODBC can connect to diverse databases such as Microsoft's SQL Server or IBM's DB2. The brief history survey is followed by a discussion of the ODBC architecture and the different roles played by the ODBC application, data source, driver manager, network software, and driver.

The last half of the chapter is dedicated to ODBC driver issues. Drivers are written to conformance levels, and it is up to the vendor as to which level a driver is written. A conformance level is a specified level of functionality. To say that a driver conforms to a specific conformance level means that the driver supports at *least that level offunctionality.* Next in the chapter is an ODBC API quick reference, associating the API function with the conformance level. The reference contains a description of each API function. By comparing application requirements against the quick reference, you can quickly determine the API conformance level that is necessary for a driver.

ODBC: A Database Connectivity Standard

ODBC came about in an era when Microsoft's primary focus was connectivity between the desktop and the enterprise. The focus has now changed to the Internet. Spin-off technologies for the enterprise, such as corporate intranets, are useful to the enterprise, but Microsoft is likely to ignore corporate needs that do not fit the Internet model. The Internet paradigm has an "e-mail" flavor with data encapsulated and sent in small packets. This paradigm is acceptable for the Internet, but is far from acceptable when connecting to a DB2 database on an IBM AS/400.

ODBC is the first heterogeneous database access technology. It is not the last one. The core ODBC technology evolves through various other database access technologies, and eventually evolves into OLE-DB, which is also a heterogeneous database access technology. Using ODBC as the base data access technology, the evolution starts with DAO as the first ODBC wrapper followed shortly thereafter with RDO as another ODBC wrapper. The next step in the evolution is ODBCDirect, which is a DAO specific version of an ODBC wrapper. The evolution takes a very large step with the announcement of OLE-DB, which will replace all existing data access technologies. The deprecation includes DAO, RDO, ODBCDirect, and surprisingly ODBC. ODBC will still exist, but only as a standard. Microsoft's goal is a native OLE-DB driver for all data access. An example of this is that OLE-DB is the native driver for Microsoft SQL Server 7.0 and not ODBC. ODBC is an open technology while OLE-DB (see Chapters 15–16), the new pretender to the throne of database connectivity, is not. ODBC is a charter member of the Windows Open Services Architecture (WOSA), while OLE-DB is the latest member of the new Windows Digital Network Architecture (DNA). ODBC 3.0 is certainly an open technology with X/Open and ISO compliance, but OLE-DB is not an open technology; it is a proprietary Microsoft architecture with no published standards. OLE-DB appears to be a useful technology for the Internet; however, to impose that technology on enterprise database connectivity is too self-serving of Microsoft.

Relational databases use Structured Query Language (SQL), which is defined with the ANSI SQL-92 standard, but not all relational databases are SQL-92 compliant. ODBC also conforms to the SQL-92 standard and solves the incompatibility problem by translating the application supplied SQL to the native SQL of the target platform. The ODBC driver expects SQL-92 compliant statements. These will be translated; however, if the SQL statement is not recognized as SQL-92 compliant, it is passed directly to the target relational database. An example of this is the **Use** statement of Microsoft SQL Server, which is not SQL-92 compliant. It is a developer error to supply ODBC with SQL of the native platform and not ODBC SQL (SQL-92). When the developer uses ODBC SQL, the application can communicate with a different database by simply changing ODBC drivers. When the application is developed with native SQL of the initial target platform, the application must be rewritten before communication with a different database is possible

ODBC is a specification for a database application programming interface (API). This specification is independent of any one particular *database management system* (DBMS). The natural consequence of this is that ODBC is a tool for heterogeneous connection of different databases.

The ODBC specification is language-independent, even though the Microsoft ODBC implementation is a C/C++ version. Chapter 12 has examples based on Visual Basic for Applications (VBA), which improves the readability of the examples. Dependency on the implementation language does present issues, however.

The first issue is that the SQL data type `SQL_VARCHAR` does not map into a C/C++ data type. The compromise is to declare a variable length string in VBA, preinitialize the string to binary zero, and then declare the data type as `SQL_C_CHAR`. This is a relatively minor compromise if the maximum string lengths are known. But the fact remains that SQL data types should all map to the underlying data types of the implementation language for ODBC even if it is language-independent.

The second issue is using the ODBC API from VBA. Microsoft says you can do it and publishes examples. The issue is the binding of columns to be used with **SQLExtendedFetch** where the columns are character arrays. The C/C++ implementation is to increment the array address. It is a bit more difficult with VBA, but it can be done. This probably explains why ODBC articles always provide unbound column examples using **SQLGetData**. (See the **SQLExtendedFetch** example in Chapter 12.)

Unicode, which has a 16-bit character mapping, is the third issue. Microsoft publishes techniques for Unicode mapping, but the real problem is that Unicode is not an integrated data type. It is an ad hoc add-on technology that is not needed for communication with legacy databases, which is why ODBC was implemented. Microsoft's zeal in providing Internet technology ignores the fact that corporate America's bread-and-butter computer systems are still COBOL-based. Unicode is a hindrance in communicating with legacy databases. You'll find the definition of both Unicode and the double-byte character set (DBCS, which isn't always two bytes), in Chapter 12.

This chapter reflects the recently released ODBC 3.0 specification. ODBC 3.0 currently meets all X/Open and ISO/IEC Call-Level Interface (CLI) specifications using SQL as its database access language. Prior releases of ODBC were based on preliminary specifications and did not fully implement all features. ODBC 3.0 specifications are a superset of the X/Open CAE Specification, Data Management: SQL Call-Level Interface (CLI) and ISO/IEC 9075-3:1995 (E) Call-Level Interface (SQL/CLI). ODBC 3.0 fully implements this specification, and prior versions were based on the preliminary version of this specification but didn't fully implement it.

An ODBC driver written to the X/Open and ISO CLI specifications will work with any ODBC 3.0 application. All ODBC 3.0 drivers are required to support the Core Interface conformance level specification (see "ODBC Driver API Conformance Levels" later in this chapter). This means that an ODBC driver will support all features used by a standards-compliant application.

Microsoft ODBC contains features beyond the call-level specifications of ISO/IEC and X/Open CLI standards. The following is an *inclusive* list and includes accumulated features from prior versions. Connection pooling and bulk operations are two of the new and important features of ODBC 3.0.

Microsoft ODBC has these features:

- Multirow fetches by a single function call
- Binding to an array of parameters
- Bookmark support, including fetching by bookmark, variable-length bookmarks, and bulk update and delete by bookmark operations on discontiguous rows
- Row-wise binding
- Binding offsets
- Support for batches of SQL statements, either in a stored procedure or as a sequence of SQL statements executed through **SQLExecute** or **SQLExecDirect**
- Positioned updates and delete operations, and batched updates and delete operations by function call (**SQLSetPos**)
- Exact or approximate cursor row counts
- Catalog functions that extract information from the information schema without the need for supporting information schema views
- Escape sequences for outer joins, scalar functions, date-time literals, interval literals, and stored procedures
- Code-page translation libraries
- Reporting of a driver's ANSI-conformance level and SQL support
- On-demand automatic population of implementation parameter descriptor
- Enhanced diagnostics with row and parameter status arrays
- Date-time, interval, numeric/decimal, and 64-bit integer application buffer types

- Asynchronous execution
- Stored procedure support, including escape sequences, output parameter binding mechanisms, and catalog functions
- Connection enhancements including support for connection attributes and attribute browsing

ODBC History

Dr. E. F. Codd created *Structured Query Language* (SQL) at IBM in the 1970s. SQL became an American National Standards Institute (ANSI) standard in 1986 and is the standard used in relational database implementations today. Microsoft conforms to current standards and supports SQL-92 in SQL Server 6.5, while other desktop products, such as Microsoft Access support specialized dialects of SQL including fragments of SQL-92, SQL-89, and proprietary Microsoft SQL implementations. Microsoft Access does not have a standardized SQL implementation. Embedded SQL, a nonstandard form of SQL that can be compiled into a C++ program, is available in the MSDN library.

SQL implementation typically occurred in three forms:

- **Embedded SQL,** where the SQL statements are compiled directly into the program.
- **SQL modules,** where an application program invokes system resident modules.
- **Call-level interface (CLI),** which consists of functions to pass SQL statements to the DBMS and receive results from the DBMS.

As the definition of an enterprise changed, corporate data needs extended beyond departmental or even corporate level computing to external data sources. SQL is used as the standard for this database connectivity, and of the three types of SQL interfacing, the CLI interface is the only possible choice for a heterogeneous DBMS interface. Both embedded SQL and SQL modules are dependent upon local operating system implementation features. Hence, ODBC, a heterogeneous relational database interface specification, was born.

ODBC is a call-level interface, but it is also much more. To understand why, some knowledge of the computing industry before ODBC is necessary. Before

Microsoft arrived, the computing community consisted of mainframes, which were being encroached upon by minicomputers. Minicomputers were introduced around 1969. These were large, single-board systems that had no immediate impact on mainframes. Databases started with mainframes and were traditionally supplied by the mainframe manufacturer; hence there was no urgency to provide common interfaces or conversion tools. It would be heresy for a hardware manufacturer to provide a common interface, or conversion tools. Why would a manufacturer want to make it easy to convert to another manufacturer's hardware?

There were a number of third-party databases, but these were mostly in the IBM market. Burroughs, National Cash Register (NCR), Univac, and Control Data (CDC) all had their own unique database management systems. They were not necessarily relational in the true sense because Dr. Codd's relational theory was new and still being developed. Databases evolved over time, but it was not quite as bad as the Tower of Babel. There was one common unifying thread — Structured Query Language (SQL). Nothing was shared and even SQL was fractured into varying dialects. Standards eventually evolved for SQL, but that didn't stop vendors from adding proprietary extensions. The stage was now set for Microsoft with ODBC and a common SQL. ODBC unified heterogeneous databases with a single architecture, a common interface, and a common SQL for all applications. (The author considers ODBC Microsoft's most profound software contribution.)

ODBC solves the problem of heterogeneous database access by standardizing an interface. ODBC does all of the following:

- Defines a call-level interface that meets internationally recognized standards.
- Defines a common SQL grammar. (Application programs write to the ODBC SQL grammar and the driver translates the SQL to the SQL of the target data source. SQL statements that are not recognized are passed directly to the data source. The Microsoft SQL Server USE <database name> is an example.)
- Manages multiple databases simultaneously. (This permits the heterogeneous interconnection of different databases; ODBC, however, is not a heterogeneous database join engine, nor is it a distributed transaction processor. Applications that use ODBC are responsible for any cross-database functionality.)
- Exposes numerous database features; however, the driver is not required to expose all features to the application. (A database driver need not support all database features.)

ODBC Benefits

The byproduct of standards is nearly always reduced costs. Code reuse occurs, application complexity is reduced, and client satisfaction increases. These are only local benefits, however. There are other benefits as well, such as the creating of new software markets and the solution to problems that were, heretofore, too expensive to solve.

ODBC should be thought of in a global context where companies merge on almost a daily basis. ODBC is an ideal solution for the corporation with a newly acquired division that has an incompatible DBMS. Connecting the disparate databases with ODBC is relatively inexpensive compared to converting the database. Data warehouses are an example in which economics dictates a connectivity solution rather than a conversion solution.

ODBC exposes database capabilities, making heterogeneous database connections possible. ODBC does not supplant database capabilities. An ODBC connection to a simple database will not transform it into a full-featured relational database engine. Nor are ODBC driver writers expected to implement functionality not already found in the underlying database.

ODBC should also be recognized as a major advancement in DBMS technology. Before ODBC, all connectivity solutions were proprietary. Microsoft has turned database connectivity into a commodity we can all afford. Microsoft has given us a positive example of their leadership capability with ODBC.

These are ODBC's benefits:

- ODBC is vendor-neutral. ODBC drivers from different vendors can be used interchangeably by an application when the drivers support the application's required conformance levels.
- ODBC is open. Microsoft has obtained a broad consensus from many vendors. In addition to the SQL Access Group (SAG), ODBC is the connectivity tool of choice for many Web tools.
- ODBC is powerful. It supports both on-line transaction processing (OLTP) and decision support systems (DSS). Many features are available including transactions, scrollable cursors, system table transparency, array fetch and update, catalog functions, a flexible connection model, and stored procedures.
- ODBC permits DBMS access from more than one location. More than one server may be accessed from the same application.

- ODBC allows users to access more than one DBMS from within a single application. Varied data sources are available and third-party drivers for ODBC 3.0 are now shipping. The Intersolve ODBC 3.0 driver supports: ALLBASE; dBase; INFORMIX; SQL/400; Btrieve; Digital Alpha Workstations; INGRESS; SQL/DS; Centura SQLBase; Digital AlphaServer ES; Microsoft SQL Server; Sybase SQL Server 4; Clipper; Microsoft .XLS files; NetWare SQL; Sybase System 10; DB2; Foxbase; Oracle; Teradata; DB2/2; FoxPro; Paradox; Text files; DB2/6000; IMAGE/SQL; PROGRESS; and XDB.
- ODBC simplifies application development. The developer creates a single application and only changes the ODBC drivers to communicate with another DBMS.
- ODBC is a portable API. The same interface and access technology may be used on different platforms. ODBC conforms to the Windows Open Services Architecture.
- ODBC insulates applications from changes to the underlying network and DBMS. Any modifications made to the supporting network infrastructure or the target DBMS will not affect current ODBC applications.
- ODBC promotes the use of SQL. ODBC 3.0 is X/Open ISO compliant.
- ODBC helps corporations protect their DBMS investments and the acquired DBMS developer skills. At the same time, “downsizing” or “rightsizing” can still be used to contain costs.

ODBC Architecture

This section discusses the ODBC architecture, which is simple and consists of only five components: the application, the driver manager, the ODBC driver, the network software, and the data source. I start with a discussion of the problems solved by the ODBC architecture. The relationship of WOSA to ODBC is next, and the section closes with a sketch of each ODBC architecture component.

The Database Access Problem

ODBC is the Windows architecture solution for connecting to different databases in a heterogeneous environment. ODBC is not always the optimal solution for communicating with a single database; it is, however, the optimal solution for communicating with more than one database in a heterogeneous environment.

The native API of the data source is always the optimal database connectivity solution when communicating with a single database, which is certainly not a heterogeneous environment. It exposes the application program to data source version changes. An example of this is that the Microsoft SQL Server DB-LIB, the native SQL Server API, only communicates with Microsoft SQL Server. Changes to DB-LIB or the DB-LIB interface can impact the application program. The application is not isolated from underlying system changes. This doesn't happen with ODBC, which insulates the application from data and source version changes. ODBC provides the additional benefit of heterogeneous database communication.

ODBC is just one component of WOSA. The WOSA solution provides a single API to interface various enterprise computing networks. A single interface hides the complexities of communicating in a heterogeneous environment from the developer and from the user. The high-cost labor-intensive task of communication in a heterogeneous environment is reduced to only one interface. A single WOSA interface enables seamless integration of applications with multiple services across multiple computing environments. Costs are significantly reduced because developers only need to learn one API for all implementations. This makes it possible to build long-term stable enterprise solutions.

Service Provider Interface Model

The Microsoft Windows Open Services Architecture model of a *service provider interface* (SPI) and an API insulates the application from implementation details. Figure 11-1 illustrates how ODBC conforms to this model with both an application interface and an enterprise interface.

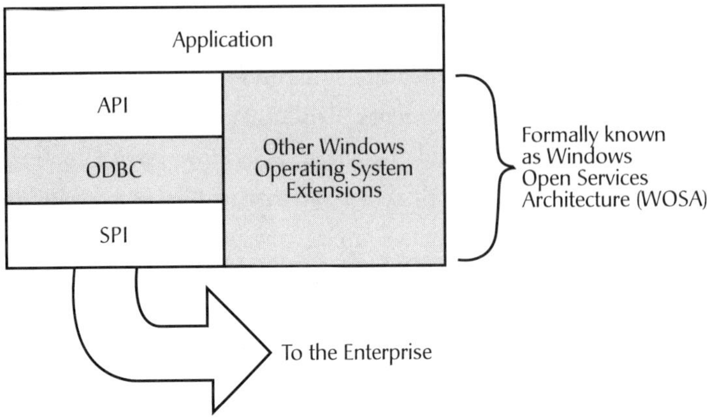

FIGURE 11-1 Windows Open Services Architecture

Figure 11-2 illustrates additional details of the ODBC model and helps explain how the ODBC model works.

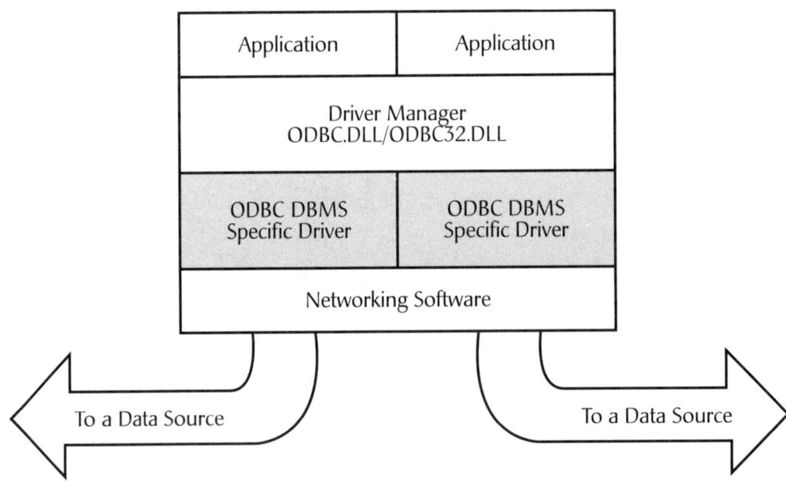

FIGURE 11-2 ODBC in the Windows Open Services Architecture

The ODBC API provides a common interface for all applications. Figure 11-2 illustrates more than one application interfacing the same DBMS and the possibility of an application communicating with more than one DBMS. The vendor-provided ODBC drivers have the role of service providers in this model. Each component of Figure 11-2 has a unique role to play. The identifiable components are the application, the data source, the driver manager, the driver, and network software, all of which are discussed in the sections that follow.

The Role of the Application

The *application* is the user interface to the system. It uses the ODBC API to submit SQL statements and retrieve results, and does not directly interface the ODBC driver. All application requests are directed to the ODBC driver manager, which interfaces with the driver. This insulates the application from data source and network implementation issues. The role of the application is best understood by enumerating the data retrieval tasks. The application:

- Creates a data structure before connecting to a data source with user supplied connection information.
- Optionally declares the start of a transaction. Transactions are only necessary for updates, and are optional but recommended.
- Creates one or more SQL statements and supplies any needed parameters.
- Assigns a cursor name to a possible result set, or optionally allows the ODBC driver to assign a cursor name. Not all statements will create a result set.
- Submits the query for immediate execution or as a prepared statement.
- Assigns and initializes column storage and retrieves the result set if necessary.
- Retrieves and manages any error information returned from the ODBC driver.
- Completes each transaction by either rolling it back or committing it.
- Terminates the connection when processing is complete, and releases all allocated structures.

The Role of the ODBC Data Source

A *data source* is a collection of objects. These objects are the platform where the DBMS resides, the DBMS that resides on that platform, and the data the user wants to access. This aggregation of objects is technically not classified as a data source until the data source is registered. Microsoft SQL Server is a relational database, but it is not an ODBC data source until it is registered.

Registering a data source can be done from the Control Panel or, as illustrated below in Figure 11-3, from the ODBC panel of the ODBC software developer's kit (SDK). The ODBC SDK is a component of the Microsoft SQL Server Programmers Toolkit and is found in the Microsoft SQL Server workstation version.

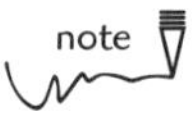

No, I didn't make a mistake. Figure 11-3 is indeed the ODBC 2.5 interface. This SDK still supports 16-bit drivers while the ODBC 3.0 SDK is without the 16-bit ODBC Administrator icons. Both SDKs are installed on this system.

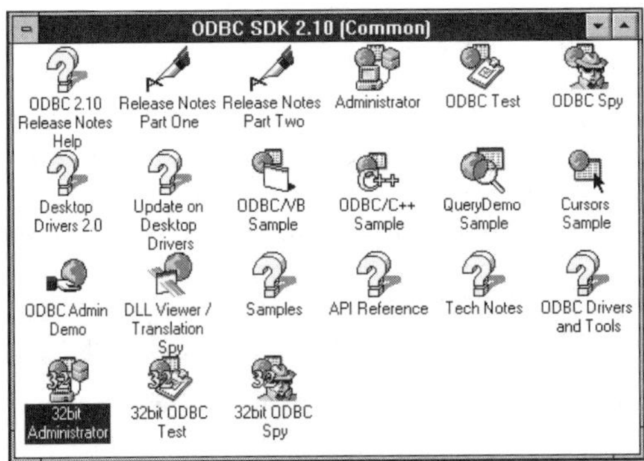

FIGURE 11-3 ODBC SDK

Registering your data source is just a matter of double-clicking the 16-bit or 32-bit icons. If you do that, you'll see a display similar to Figure 11-4, which was created by double-clicking the 32-bit ODBC Administrator icon.

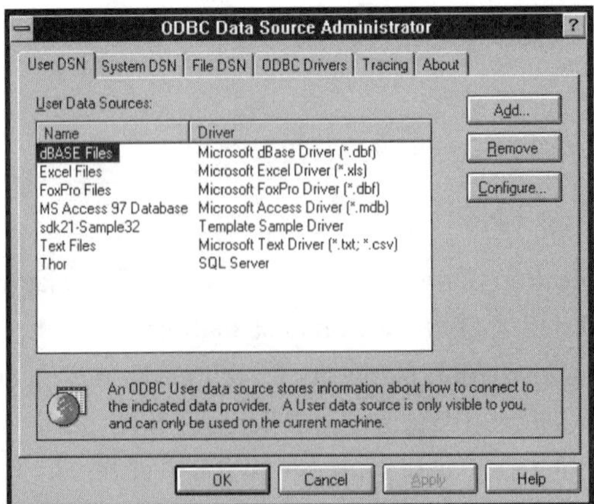

FIGURE 11-4 ODBC 3.0 Administrator

note **The ODBC 3.5 SDK is available from Microsoft home page at www.microsoft.com and can only be installed on Windows NT 4.0 or Windows 95 and later systems. The ODBC 3.0 SDK is available from Microsoft Press as ISBN 1-57231-516-4.**

The Role of the ODBC Driver Manager

The *ODBC driver manager* is the gateway to the data source. The driver manager:

- Forwards application calls to the ODBC driver.
- Satisfies some information and initialization requests without invoking the ODBC driver.
- Is responsible for loading and starting the ODBC driver. (Earlier ODBC drivers were not cached, which resulted in prohibitive connection time. This is the primary reason that earlier applications that used ODBC maintained the connection to the data source. Recent ODBC driver managers cache the ODBC driver, eliminating the need to maintain the connection. The ODBC 3.0 Driver Manager advances the technology with connection pooling. Connections are drawn from the pool when the application calls **SQLConnect** or **SQLDriverConnect**, and are returned to the pool when the application calls **SQLDisconnect**.)
- Optionally logs application calls.
- Manages error and state checking.

The Role of the ODBC Driver

The *ODBC driver* has the responsibility of converting the ODBC SQL to the SQL of the proprietary database. If the ODBC doesn't recognize the SQL command (such as the Microsoft SQL Server `USE` command), the ODBC driver forwards the SQL statement directly to the data source in what is called pass-through mode.

A developer who writes an ODBC driver to access file data is required to supply a database engine that supports at least the minimal SQL functionality. This is not true with OLE-DB, our goal for the future. An OLE-DB *provider* is a wrapper around file data and *provider* is not required to support an SQL engine. This explains why the OLE-DB memory footprint is quite small for file access; there's no SQL engine.

The ODBC driver also has the responsibility of creating and maintaining a connection with the data source. A SQL query is forwarded to the data source and a result set is returned to the application task. The driver:

- Connects to and disconnects from the data source requested by the application.
- Submits application requests to the data source. The application requests may be modified by the driver before submission to the data source.
- Translates to or from other formats when requested by the application. This is limited to escape sequences or to a conversion function on a specific column, such as converting from `SQL_SMALLINT` to `SQL_CHAR`.
- Returns result sets to the client application.
- Captures and formats errors for client analysis.
- Creates and manages cursors if necessary. This operation is transparent to the application.
- Initiates a required data source transaction when necessary. This action is invisible to the application.

The Role of Network Software

The *network software,* as defined in the ODBC architecture and illustrated in Figure 11-2, is only a logical definition. It is not ODBC software, but is all the software that comprises the supporting infrastructure. This consists of transport protocols and operating system support at both the ODBC client application site and at the data source site. Another view is that network software in the ODBC context, is all the software between the client ODBC driver and the target data source, which is usually SQL Server.

ODBC Drivers

The remainder of the chapter addresses ODBC driver issues. First discussed is the ODBC Driver API conformance levels, followed by the ODBC Driver SQL conformance levels. The chapter closes with an ODBC 3.0 API quick reference.

ODBC Driver API Conformance Levels

The vendor-neutral environment of ODBC is created by defining three levels of APIs and three levels of SQL grammar conformance. A unique benefit of this approach is that the application can communicate with diverse databases, each having varying dialects of SQL. A single application program is written using ODBC SQL. Different drivers translate the SQL for different databases. Changing the database driver is the only necessary change to communicate with a different data source. Communicating to diverse databases without application reprogramming is a significant ODBC benefit.

The SQL driver is responsible for converting the ODBC SQL to the SQL of the proprietary database. If the ODBC driver doesn't recognize the SQL command, (such as the SQL Server `USE` statement), the ODBC driver forwards the SQL directly to the data source in what is called pass-through mode.

This database independence is possible only with compliance to the API and SQL grammar conformance levels. Driver writers are encouraged to support the Level 1 API (at a minimum); however, not all ODBC drivers support the same level of interoperability. This problem can be eased with still another layer of software, a leveling library (see Figure 11-5).

You may wonder, "Why must I use ODBC SQL in my application? If I provide Transact-SQL (Microsoft SQL Server T-SQL), it will be passed through directly to SQL Server without translation." The answer is that if you're using data source SQL statements, the application is not functioning in a heterogeneous environment and ODBC is the wrong choice. The optimal interface is always the native API of the data source. A heterogeneous interface will always have more overhead than the native API. A skilled manager of a client-server project will not allow unnecessary dependencies to be built into the application and a native language is a dependency.

ODBC is a standard, but that is where it ends. Developers see ODBC as a means to an end and use the DBMS-specific (syntactically) SQL. They'll write an application using Transact-SQL of Microsoft SQL Server. The developer knows that Transact-SQL-specific statements will be passed directly to SQL Server when the ODBC driver doesn't recognize it. This is precisely what ODBC is not. ODBC is a standard for heterogeneous interconnection of databases. If you are writing an application in Transact-SQL using ODBC, then this is a major programming error. The developer should always use the native API when writing an application to a vendor-specific application. Developers use ODBC because it is relatively easy and convenient to use. They probably don't even know that a native API exists.

A different perspective is that desktop software is often an adjunct to an enterprise. The Information Systems (IS) manager is responsible for what is euphemistically called legacy systems and for desktop systems. The IS manager may be conversant with desktop software issues at other than a superficial level, but it may not be the level necessary for strategic planning.

On the other hand, the new crop of IS managers, who were weaned on a Commodore or a Tandy from Radio Shack, will not have an appreciation for conformance to standards. By standards, I don't mean program layout, and how a screen looks, but the use of software that conforms to standards. In my opinion, traditional IS managers have abrogated their management responsibilities with respect to Microsoft-related software. Developers are able to use whatever Microsoft specific implementation they choose. I chuckle when I read about companies that let Microsoft come in and implement their enterprise applications. Those companies are in for a big surprise, because they are no longer in control of their destiny. It won't happen today or tomorrow, but eventually, application conversion will be necessary. The corporation no longer has a vendor choice. In my opinion, the new crop of managers doesn't understand the issue of conformance to standards. They'll use anything that appears clever and useful, and when they do, it demonstrates a wanton disregard for enterprise strategic planning.

Some rules of the road for considering an ODBC implementation are:

- When only one database must be accessed, the best performance is always from the native API. Don't use ODBC just because it is convenient. Whatever the usage is today, it will be double next year, and double the year after. Starting with less than the best is not a good strategy in software development.
- As a developer, you are probably not aware of all strategic planning issues within your enterprise. Arbitrarily using vendor-specific SQL constructs, limits the application portability and may hinder strategic deployment.
- Use only American National Standards Institute (ANSI)-standard SQL constructs. Avoid using vendor-specific SQL implementations. Vendor-specific SQL implementations will lock you into the current vendor. Vendor-specific

features have a *creep* factor. You're seduced, and the feature is gradually enhanced. Your conversion costs escalate to the point where conversion to another DBMS system becomes prohibitive. In other words, you're hooked!

- Always write to ODBC SQL specifications. This maintains software portability.

Microsoft always ships a level of ODBC that is compatible with the current release of Microsoft SQL Server. This is all well and good. Microsoft, however, still doesn't understand the enterprise. The SQL-92 upgrade wasn't a singular update. Pieces of SQL-92 shipped with different upgrades to SQL Server. The syntax of some SQL statements changed between SQL Server releases 6.0 and 6.5 and application performance was negatively impacted. This places the enterprise at risk.

The solution to this problem of whipsawing is quite simple: always code application SQL to the ODBC standard, and never implement a version of Microsoft SQL Server that is incomplete at the standards implementation level. This may be a difficult rule to enforce because the application only uses ODBC and Microsoft SQL Server. Your application developers will want to write statements directly in Transact-SQL. They do not understand the problem of dependency. These problems can be avoided with proper application program management.

We're all stubborn and don't seem able to learn from history. Software manufacturers from the legacy era shipped a COBOL compiler with full current compliance to industry standards. There were no partial shipments. If COBOL-66 shipped, it included all ANSI specifications. Another compiler wasn't shipped until the standards changed. Microsoft fails to recognize that an incremental upgrade to the enterprise is no different than a complete upgrade. A new release is quite often ready to ship before the enterprise has completely evaluated the last incremental release.

What is important about SQL Server, for example, is that all development energy should focus on compliance with industry standards, and neither time nor money should be spent on items such as the SQL Server 6.5 Web Wizard until a robust and standards-compliant version is shipped. The Web Wizard is fine, but it should be an optional add-on only after standards implementations are complete. Microsoft software does not have a reputation for being robust, and additional and unsolicited software features simply increase the probability of a software failure. What makes a thin client appealing is that it involves less software and is by definition more reliable.

Different levels of conformance are found at the tool level. Microsoft Visual Basic supports the Level 1 API and the Core SQL Grammar, while Microsoft Access supports the Level 1 API and the Minimum SQL Grammar.

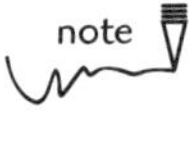

ODBC specifications are currently changing. ODBC 2.5 represents the 32-bit release, ODBC 3.0 is the X/Open standards-compliant release, and ODBC 3.5 is the latest release, which supports UNICODE compliant applications.

The conformance levels are valuable from the perspective of knowing which driver is appropriate and when additional functionality must be added by the application. The bottom line is that the application program must provide missing functionality, and this can significantly increase development costs.

Core API

The following list outlines the minimal functionality an ODBC driver must support to qualify for CORE API support designation. (Functionality, however, is not limited to this list.)

- Allocate and free environment, connection, and statement handles.
- Connect to data sources. Use multiple statements on a connection.
- Prepare and execute SQL statements. Execute SQL statements immediately.
- Assign storage for parameters in SQL statement and result columns.
- Retrieve data from a result set. Retrieve information about a result set.
- Commit or roll back transactions.
- Retrieve error information.

Level 1 API

This list outlines the minimal functionality an ODBC driver must support to qualify for Level 1 support designation. (Functionality, however, is not limited to this list.)

- Core API functionality.
- Connect to data sources with driver-specific dialog boxes.
- Set and inquire values of statement and connection options.

- Send part or all of a parameter value (useful for long data).
- Retrieve part or all of a result column value (useful for long data).
- Retrieve catalog information (columns, special columns, statistics, and tables).
- Retrieve information about driver and data source capabilities, such as supported data types, scalar functions, and ODBC functions.

Level 2 API

The following list outlines the minimal functionality an ODBC driver must support to qualify for Level 2 API support designation. (Functionality, however, is not limited to this list.)

- Core and Level 1 functionality.
- Browse connection information and list available data sources.
- Send arrays of parameter values. Retrieve arrays of result column values.
- Retrieve the number of parameters and describe individual parameters.
- Use a scrollable cursor.
- Retrieve the native form of a SQL statement.
- Retrieve catalog information (privileges, keys, and procedures).
- Call a translation DLL.

ODBC Driver SQL Grammar Conformance Levels

The ODBC SQL conformance levels correspond roughly to the SQL Access Group SQL CAE specification (1992).

Minimum SQL Grammar

This list outlines the minimal functionality an ODBC driver must support to qualify for minimum SQL grammar support designation. (Functionality, however, is not limited to this list.)

- Data Definition Language (DDL): `CREATE TABLE` and `DROP TABLE`.
- Data Manipulation Language (DML): simple `SELECT`, `INSERT`, `UPDATE SEARCHED`, and `DELETE SEARCHED`.
- Expressions: Simple (such as A > B + C).
- Data types: `CHAR`, `VARCHAR`, or `LONG VARCHAR`.

Core SQL Grammar

The following list outlines the minimal functionality an ODBC driver must support to qualify for Core SQL grammar support designation. (Functionality, however, is not limited to this list.)

- Minimum SQL grammar and data types.
- `ALTER TABLE`, `CREATE INDEX`, `DROP INDEX`, `CREATE VIEW`, `DROP VIEW`, `GRANT`, and `REVOKE`.
- Full `SELECT`.
- Expressions: subquery, set functions such as `SUM` and `MIN`.
- Data types: `DECIMAL`, `NUMERIC`, `SMALLINT`, `INTEGER`, `REAL`, `FLOAT`, `DOUBLE PRECISION`.

Extended SQL Grammar

The following list outlines the minimal functionality an ODBC driver must support to qualify for extended SQL grammar support designation. (Functionality, however, is not limited to this list.)

- Minimum and Core SQL grammar and data types.
- Outer joins, positioned `UPDATE`, positioned `DELETE`, `SELECT FOR UPDATE`, and unions.
- Expressions: scalar functions such as `SUBSTRING` and `ABS`, date, time, and time stamp literals.
- Data types: `BIT`, `TINYINT`, `BIGINT`, `BINARY`, `VARBINARY`, `LONG VARBINARY`, `DATE`, `TIME`, `TIMESTAMP`.
- Batch SQL statements.
- Procedure calls.

ODBC API Quick Reference

The following tables list the client-side ODBC API functions by category with the standards compliance level, conformance level, function name, description, and ODBC version when introduced. Deprecated functions are noted. Use this quick reference when designing your ODBC application and identify the basic functionality needed. Correlate this with ODBC functionality and identify the conformance level necessary for your application.

TABLE 11-1 Managing the Data Source Connection

Compliance	*Conformance*	*ODBC Function*	*Description*
Deprecated ODBC 1.0	Core	**SQLAllocConnect**	Allocates memory for a connection handle. An environment handle is required. See **SQLAllocHandle**.
ISO 92 ODBC 3.0	Core	**SQLAllocHandle**	Allocates an environment, connection, statement, or descriptor handle.
ODBC ODBC 1.0	Level 2	**SQLBrowseConnect**	Iterative enumeration of data source attributes and attribute values.
ISO 92 ODBC 1.0	Core	**SQLConnect**	Connects to a registered data source.
ISO 92 ODBC 1.0	Core	**SQLDisconnect**	Closes a connection associated with a connection handle.
ODBC ODBC 1.0	Level 1	**SQLDriverConnect**	An alternative to **SQLConnect** with extended connection parameters.
Deprecated ODBC 1.0	Core	**SQLFreeConnect**	Releases a connection handle and free the associated memory. See **SQLFreeHandle**.
ISO 92 ODBC 3.0	Core	**SQLFreeHandle**	Frees an environment, connection, statement, or description handle.

TABLE 11-2 MANAGING THE ENVIRONMENT

COMPLIANCE	CONFORMANCE	ODBC FUNCTION	DESCRIPTION
Deprecated ODBC 1.0	Core	**SQLAllocEnv**	Allocates memory for an environment handle. See **SQLAllocHandle**.
Deprecated ODBC 1.0	Core	**SQLFreeEnv**	Releases the environment handle and frees the associated memory. See **SQLFreeHandle**.
ISO 92 ODBC 3.0	Core	**SQLGetEnvAttr**	Returns the setting of an environment attribute.
ISO 92 ODBC 3.0	Core	**SQLSetEnvAttr**	Sets an environment attribute.

TABLE 11-3 OBTAINING INFORMATION ABOUT A DRIVER AND DATA SOURCE

COMPLIANCE	CONFORMANCE	ODBC FUNCTION	DESCRIPTION
ISO 92 ODBC 1.0	Level 2	**SQLDataSources**	Lists data source names.
ODBC ODBC 2.0	Level 2	**SQLDrivers**	List drivers. A function of the driver manager.
ISO 92 ODBC 1.0	Level 1	**SQLGetFunctions**	Returns supported ODBC function information. May be driver or driver manager implemented.
ISO 92 ODBC 1.0	Level 1	**SQLGetInfo**	Returns general driver and data source information specific to a connection handle.
ISO 92 ODBC 1.0	Level 1	**SQLGetTypeInfo**	Returns data source information about the data types that are supported.

TABLE 11-4 Setting and Retrieving Driver Options

Compliance	Conformance	ODBC Function	Description
ODBC ODBC 3.0	Level 1	**SQLBulkOperations**	Performs bulk inserts or updates.
ISO 92 ODBC 3.0	Core	**SQLGetConnectAttr**	Returns the current setting of a connection attribute.
Deprecated ODBC 1.0	Level 1	**SQLGetConnectOption**	Gets the value of a connection option.
ISO 92 ODBC 3.0	Level 1	**SQLGetStmtAttr**	Returns the value of a statement attribute.
Deprecated ODBC 1.0	Level 1	**SQLGetStmtOption**	Returns the current value of a statement option. See **SQLGetStmtAttr**.
ISO 92 ODBC 3.0	Level 1	**SQLSetConnectAttr**	Returns the setting of a connect attribute.
Deprecated ODBC 1.0	Level 1	**SQLSetConnectOption**	Sets the setting of a connect option. See **SQLGetConnectAttr**.
ISO 92 ODBC 3.0	Level 1	**SQLSetStmtAttr**	Sets the value of a statement attribute.
Deprecated ODBC 1.0	Level 1	**SQLSetStmtOption**	Sets the value of statement option. See **SQLSetStmtAttr**

TABLE 11-5 Preparing SQL Statements

Compliance	Conformance	ODBC Function	Description
Deprecated ODBC 1.0	Core	**SQLAllocStmt**	Allocates memory for a statement handle. See **SQLAllocHandle**.
ISO 92 ODBC 1.0	Core	**SQLPrepare**	Prepares a SQL statement for execution. Use this statement whenever statement execution is repeated.

Continued

TABLE 11-5 *(continued)*

Compliance	Conformance	ODBC Function	Description
ODBC ODBC 2.0	Level 1	**SQLBindParameter**	Binds a buffer to a parameter marker in a SQL statement.
ISO 92 ODBC 3.0	Core	**SQLCloseCursor**	Closes a cursor opened on a statement.
Deprecated ODBC 1.0	Level 2	**SQLParamOptions**	Permits bulk updates. An application can specify multiple values for a set of parameters assigned by **SQLBindParameter**. See **SQLSetStmtAttr**.
ISO 92 ODBC 1.0	Core	**SQLGetCursorName**	Returns the cursor name associated with a statement handle.
ISO 92 ODBC 1.0	Core	**SQLSetCursorName**	Associates a cursor name with a statement handle.
Deprecated ODBC 1.0	Core	**SQLSetParam**	Binds data to a parameter. See **SQLBindParameter**.
Deprecated ODBC 1.0	Level 2	**SQLSetScrollOptions**	Sets result set scrolling options. See **SQLSetStmtAttr**

TABLE 11-6 Submitting Requests

Compliance	Conformance	ODBC Function	Description
ISO 92 ODBC 1.0	Core	**SQLExecDirect**	The fastest way to submit a SQL statement for a one-time execution. The statement may be preparable but need not be prepared.
ISO 92 ODBC 1.0	Core	**SQLExecute**	Executes a prepared statement.
ODBC ODBC 1.0	Level 2	**SQLNativeSQL**	Returns the driver-translated SQL string.

COMPLIANCE	CONFORMANCE	ODBC FUNCTION	DESCRIPTION
ODBC ODBC 1.0	Level 2	**SQLDescribeParam**	Returns the description of a parameter marker associated with a prepared SQL statement.
ISO 92 ODBC 1.0	Level 2	**SQLNumParams**	Returns the parameter count of a SQL statement.
ISO 92 ODBC 1.0	Level 1	**SQLParamData**	Used with **SQLPutData** to supply parameter data at execution time.
ISO 92 ODBC 1.0	Level 1	**SQLPutData**	Sends characters or binary data to the driver at execution time.

TABLE 11-7 RETRIEVING RESULTS AND INFORMATION ABOUT RESULTS

COMPLIANCE	CONFORMANCE	ODBC FUNCTION	DESCRIPTION
ISO 92 ODBC 1.0	Core	**SQLBindCol**	Assigns the storage and data type for a result set column.
ISO 92 ODBC 3.0	Core	**SQLColAttribute**	A generalized version of **SQLDescribeCol**.
Deprecated ODBC 1.0	Core	**SQLColAttributes**	A generalized version of **SQLDescribeCol**.
ISO 92 ODBC 1.0	Core	**SQLDescribeCol**	Returns the result descriptor, which contains the column name, type, precision, scale, and nullability. This function cannot be used for bookmarks.
Deprecated ODBC 1.0	Core	**SQLError**	Returns error or status information. See **SQLGetDiagRec**.
Deprecated ODBC 1.0	Level 2	**SQLExtendedFetch**	An extended version of **SQLFetch**. An array is returned for each bound column. See **SQLFetchScroll**.

Continued

TABLE 11-7 *(continued)*

Compliance	Conformance	ODBC Function	Description
ISO 92 ODBC 1.0	Core	**SQLFetch**	Retrieves a row from a result set. Only the driver returns data for columns bound to storage locations with **SQLBindCol**.
ISO 92 ODBC 3.0	Core	**SQLFetchScroll**	Retrieves the specified row set from a result set. Retrieval is absolute or relative.
ISO 92 ODBC 1.0	Level 1	**SQLGetData**	Retrieves data for a single unbound column.
ODBC ODBC 1.0	Level 2	**SQLMoreResults**	Determines if additional results are available for a statement handle.
ISO 92 ODBC 1.0	Core	**SQLNumResultCols**	Returns the number of columns in a result set.
ISO 92 ODBC 1.0	Core	**SQLRowCount**	Returns the row count of a SQL `UPDATE INSERT`, or `DELETE`statement.
ODBC ODBC 1.0	Level 2	**SQLSetPos**	Sets the cursor position in a row set.

TABLE 11-8 Obtaining Data Source System Table Information (Catalog Functions)

Compliance	Conformance	ODBC Function	Description
ODBC ODBC 1.0	Level 2	**SQLColumnPrivileges**	Returns as a result set the column names and privileges for a table associated with a statement handle.
X/Open ODBC 1.0	Level 1	**SQLColumns**	Returns as a result set the table column names associated with a statement handle.

COMPLIANCE	CONFORMANCE	ODBC FUNCTION	DESCRIPTION
ODBC ODBC 1.0	Level 2	**SQLForeignKeys**	Returns as a result set the list of foreign keys in a table and a list of foreign keys in other tables that refer to the primary key in the referenced table.
ODBC ODBC 1.0	Level 2	**SQLPrimaryKeys**	Returns as a result set the primary key column names.
ODBC ODBC 1.0	Level 2	**SQLProcedureColumns**	Returns as a result set the list of input and output parameters and column names that make up a result set for a specific procedure.
ODBC ODBC 1.0	Level 2	**SQLProcedures**	Returns as a result set a list of procedure names at the data source.
X/Open ODBC 1.0	Level 1	**SQLSpecialColumns**	Returns as a result set the optimal set of columns that uniquely identify a row and the columns that are automatically updated when any value in a row is changed.
ISO 92 ODBC 1.0	Level 1	**SQLStatistics**	Returns the statistics and indexes for a table.
ODBC ODBC 1.0	Level 2	**SQLTablePrivileges**	Returns a list of tables and the associated privileges for each table. The information is returned as a result set.
X/Open ODBC 1.0	Level 1	**SQLTables**	Returns a list of data source tables.

TABLE 11-9 MANAGING DESCRIPTORS

COMPLIANCE	CONFORMANCE	ODBC FUNCTION	DESCRIPTION
ISO 92 ODBC 3.0	Core	**SQLCopyDesc**	Copies descriptor information from one handle to another.
ISO 92 ODBC 3.0	Core	**SQLGetDescField**	Returns the current setting of a single field within a descriptor record.
ISO 92 ODBC 3.0	Core	**SQLGetDescRec**	Returns multiple fields from a descriptor record.
ISO 92 ODBC 3.0	Core	**SQLGetDiagField**	Returns the current value of a field in a diagnostic record.
ISO 92 ODBC 3.0	Core	**SQLGetDiagRec**	Returns multiple fields from a diagnostic record.
ISO 92 ODBC 3.0	Core	**SQLSetDescField**	Sets the value of a single field in a descriptor record.
ISO 92 ODBC 3.0	Core	**SQLSetDescRec**	Sets multiple fields in a descriptor record.

TABLE 11-10 TERMINATING A STATEMENT

COMPLIANCE	CONFORMANCE	ODBC FUNCTION	DESCRIPTION
ISO 92 ODBC 1.0	Core	**SQLCancel**	Cancels the processing associated with a statement handle.
ISO 92 ODBC 3.0	Core	**SQLEndTran**	Requests a commit or rollback for all active operations on all operations associated with a connection.
ISO 92 ODBC 1.0	Core	**SQLFreeStmt**	Stops processing, closes all cursors, pending results are discarded, and all resources are released (an option), for a specific statement handle.
Deprecated ODBC 1.0	Core	**SQLTransact**	Requests a commit or a rollback on all active statement handles associated with a connection. See **SQLEndTran**.

ODBC Driver Leveling

Not all ODBC drivers are created equally. ODBC drivers conform to vendor-specified conformance levels; consequently all drivers may not be equal. The problem occurs in a heterogeneous environment where an application must communicate with two different databases and the conformance level between the drivers does not agree. The problem and the solution are illustrated in Figure 11-5.

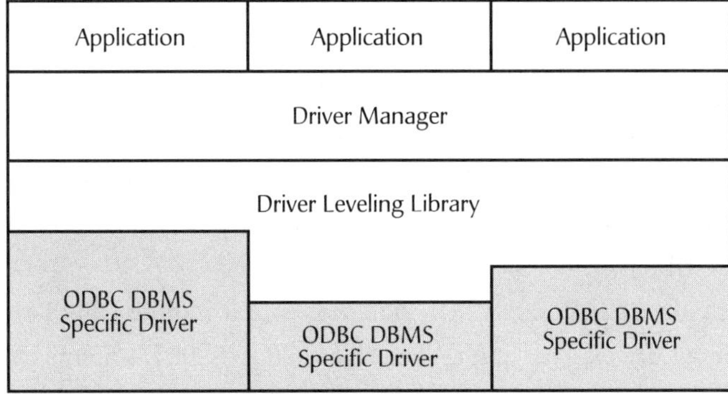

FIGURE 11-5 A driver leveling library

A library developed by Q+E, (recently merged with Intersolve), provides a uniform ODBC interface that gives the same level of functionality to the application interface, even though each driver might support a different level of conformance. Q+E (Intersolve) developed and marketed a driver leveling library. Explorer is the current Intersolve name for this product. Intersolve may be found at `http://www.intersolve.com`.

A second use of a leveling library is when user requirements exceed driver capability. The general problem is that the applications program must provide missing driver functionality. An ODBC leveling library can reduce the application-programming task.

ODBC Driver Architecture

The simplest classification scheme for driver architecture is to note where the SQL statements are processed. The single-tier driver will process the SQL statements, whereas themulti-tier driver passes the SQL statements to the data source.

Single-Tier Drivers

Single-tier drivers are commonly used for flat-file access. A single-tier driver processes SQL statements locally. In the case of a flat file, the driver writer provides a minimal SQL implementation. A driver that accesses an xBase file is an example of a single-tier driver implementation. Single-tier drivers have a file-based engine rather than a DBMS-based engine. Microsoft Access is an example of a single-tier driver in that the SQL statements are processed locally and not sent to a DBMS.

Any driver that sends SQL statements to a remote DBMS is classified as a multitiered driver. The single-tier driver converts SQL statements locally to file access commands and issues the input-output (I/O) commands to retrieve the data. A single-tier driver is associated with non-SQL-based databases. The definitions are not clear-cut and Microsoft Access can be used with either a file-based single-tier driver or with a DBMS-based multitiered driver. When used with Microsoft Access, the single-tiered file driver accesses the .MDB file of Access directly. Figure 11-6 illustrates both a single-tier local file-based data source and a single-tier remote file-based data source.

Two-Tier Drivers

There are two variations of a two-tier driver. The first variation is with SQL statements passed to a data source. The data source can be local as we observed in single-tier drivers, but this is not the norm. Figure 11-7 illustrates the first variation of a two-tier driver: the driver does not process the SQL statement but passes the statement to a SQL engine at the data source.

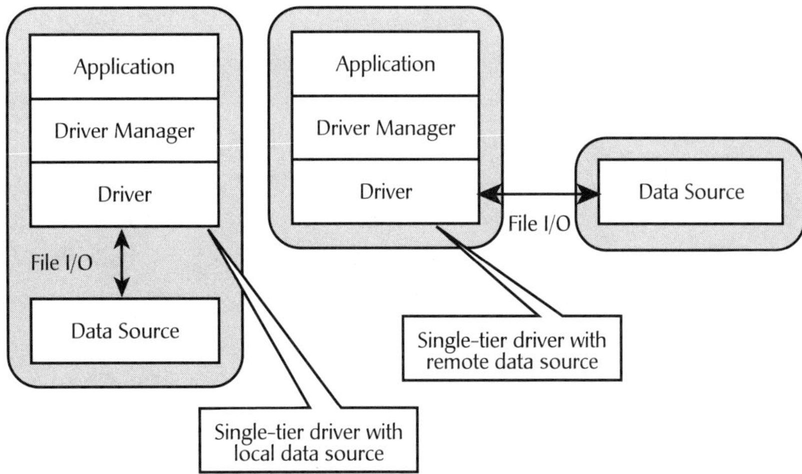

FIGURE 11-6 Two single-tier ODBC driver architectures

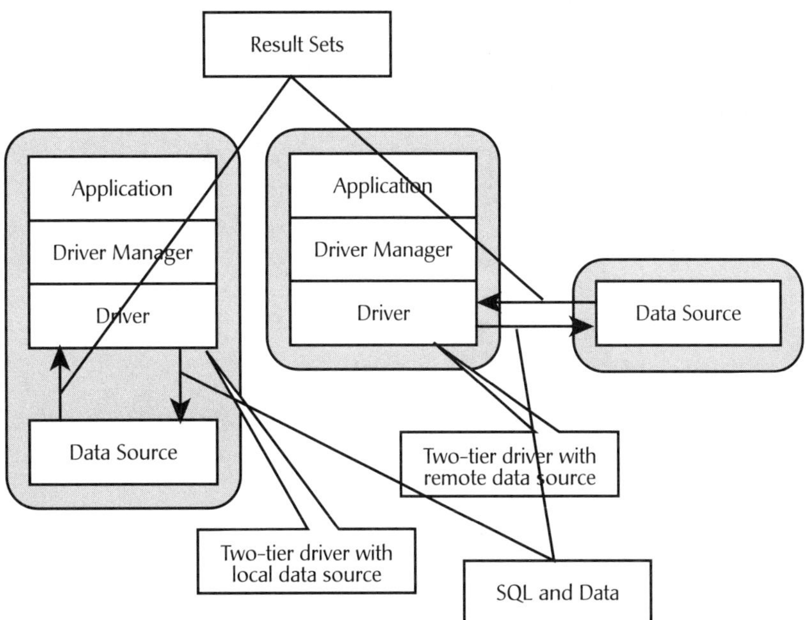

FIGURE 11-7 A variation of a two-tier ODBC driver architecture

The second variation of a two-tier driver is used by proprietary databases that are not SQL based. A two-tier driver may pass SQL statements that are partially parsed or it may pass basic file I/O operations to the data source. In either case, the data source uses an ODBC Gateway to the proprietary database.

Another interesting feature is that the non-SQL data source can have a SQL engine that resides on either the data source or at the client site. Each version has an ODBC Gateway at the data source; the SQL engine, however, can reside on either the client or at the data source. The ODBC Gateway software can support SQL-based and non-SQL-based data sources. Figure 11-8 illustrates a two-tier driver with a remote SQL engine. The variation with a client-based SQL engine is not illustrated.

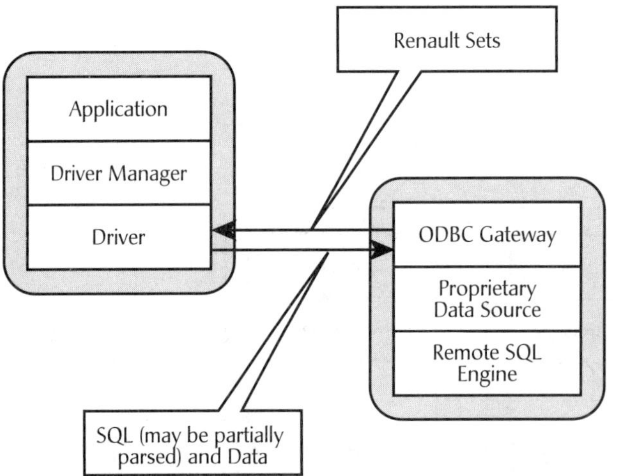

FIGURE 11-8 A two-tier ODBC driver with a remote SQL Engine

Three-Tier Drivers

Only one aspect distinguishes a three-tier driver from a two-tier driver. The two-tier driver has gateway software residing at the data source, whereas the three-tier driver has gateway software residing on an intermediary system. Other than the location of the gateway software, the configuration variations between a two- and a three-tier driver are the same. Figure 11-9 illustrates a three-tier driver.

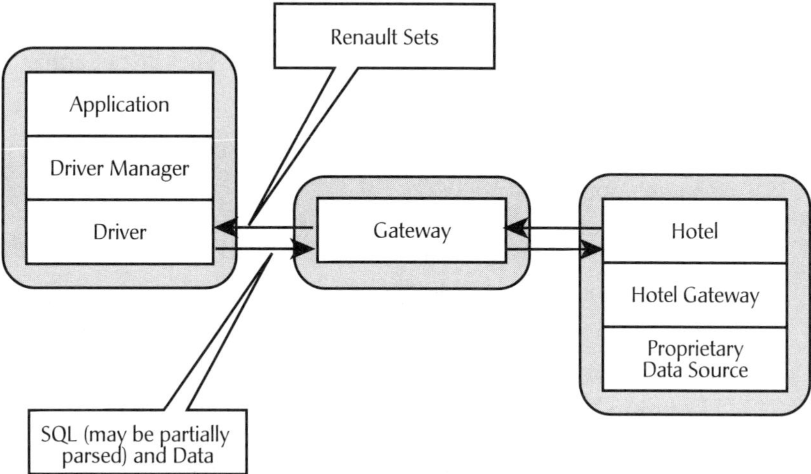

FIGURE 11-9 A three-tier ODBC driver architecture as a gateway

Key Point Summary

ODBC presents a uniform interface with a standardized SQL for heterogeneous interconnection of different databases. ODBC is not a heterogeneous database join engine, nor is it a distributed transaction processor. Applications that use ODBC are responsible for any cross-database functionality.

- ODBC is a standard.
- ODBC defines a common SQL. Applications are written to the ODBC SQL standard, and not the SQL of specific databases. This approach allows an application to be moved to another database by changing ODBC drivers.
- ODBC is language-independent.
- ODBC is vendor-neutral.
- ODBC is portable.
- ODBC insulates an application from the flux of the underlying network infrastructure and DBMS.
- ODBC uses a CLI.
- ODBC is a connectivity mechanism for registered ODBC data sources.
- There are only four components in the ODBC architecture: the application, the driver manager, the driver, and the data source.

- The application only interfaces the driver manager.
- ODBC drivers expose database functionality. They do not enhance it.
- An ODBC data source must provide a minimal SQL engine. This means the developers writing ODBC file drivers must supply a SQL engine with minimum functionality.

API and SQL Grammar conformance levels define the ODBC driver. This makes software interchangeable and any driver can be used that meets a standard. The conformance levels normalize database access. Conformance levels make ODBC drivers vendor-neutral. Each driver's required functionality should work identically; however, this does not prevent a vendor from adding extra functionality.

- ODBC drivers have an API and a SQL conformance level.
- The ODBC vendor chooses the level of conformance for its driver product.
- Missing functionality must be added by the application. As an example, an application requiring a scrollable cursor needs an ODBC driver with a Level 2 API conformance level.
- A single-tier ODBC driver is used for file systems.
- A three-tier ODBC architecture is commonly used as a bridge.
- An ODBC driver must support a local or a remote SQL engine. The remote SQL engine may be SQL Server, but the ODBC driver developer is required to supply a minimal SQL engine for a file access. Providing a minimal SQL engine is not a burden to the new OLE-DB. An OLE-DB driver (*provider*) does not require a minimal SQL engine for mailbox access. Compare that with an ODBC mailbox driver, which does require a minimal SQL engine.

Applying What You've Learned

A keen understanding of API and SQL Grammar conformance levels is required for a successful ODBC application. The developer analyzes the client requirements and selects an ODBC driver that meets these minimum requirements. When an ODBC driver does not meet the requirements, the developer then either provides the additional functionality in the application or removes the requirement from the specification. The following questions test your understanding of conformance levels with respect to application requirements.

Instant Assessment

1. Name the major components of the ODBC architecture.
2. Name five benefits of the ODBC architecture.
3. What role does the ODBC driver play in the Microsoft Windows Architecture?
4. Explain the role of each component in the ODBC architecture.
5. Explain the purpose of conformance levels.
6. Discuss ODBC driver functionality versus client application requirements.
7. The application design requires a time stamp for transactions. Which conformance level is required?
8. The client wishes to do a browse connect. Which conformance level is required?
9. The client wants optimal performance with prepared SQL statements. Which API conformance level is required?
10. Which ODBC API conformance level supports a scrollable cursor?
11. Explain a single-tier driver.
12. What is the difference between a single-tier and a two-tier ODBC driver?
13. What is the basic difference between a two-tier and a three-tier ODBC driver?
14. What is a driver-leveling library?

Lab Exercises

Lab 11.31 *Preparing for an ODBC application*

We'll be building ODBC applications in the next chapter, so let's look under the ODBC hood before we delve into some applications. Acquire the ODBC 3.0 software developer's kit (SDK) if you don't have it. Sources for this include the Microsoft home page at `www.microsoft.com` or the Microsoft FTP site at `ftp://ftp.microsoft.com`. The ODBC 3.0 SDK with documentation is also available from Microsoft Press as ISBN1-57231-516-4. Microsoft SQL Server always ships with a level of ODBC drivers that are appropriate for SQL Server. Independent of the ODBC SDK level, ascertain that the appropriate SQL Server provided ODBC drivers are installed.

Do not use the ODBC 3.0 SDK with Windows 3.1 and 16-bit applications. ODBC 3.0 is 32 bits. The ODBC 3.5 SDK can only be installed on Windows 95 or Windows NT 4.0 and later systems.

Our goal is to use ODBC Test to survey your ODBC environment. When you have the ODBC 3.0 SDK, you'll start by using **SQLAllocEnv**. After you have an environment, use **SQLAllocConnect**. Now use **SQLGetConnectOption** and browse the connection options. Continue until you are comfortable using ODBC Test.

The exercise assumes you are using ODBC SDK 3.0.

1. Select the ODBC SDK icon and double-click **ODBC Test**.
2. Click the **Connection** menu and select *Full Connect.* This assumes that SQL Server is already started. If it isn't, go to the SQL Server Service Manager and start SQL Server.
3. Let's look at ODBC functions supported by this driver. Start by again clicking the **Connection** menu and select *SQLGetFunctions.* You will be presented with a result set that enumerates all supported functions. The value `SQL_TRUE` indicates the function is supported.
4. We could look at each attribute individually, but instead let's look at the complete connection functionality. The quantity of information provided will surprise you; it scrolls for several seconds. Start by again clicking the **Connection** menu and select *Get Info All.*
5. We'll move over to statements. From the **Statement** menu select *Show Cursor Settings*. A dialog box is presented with the default cursor settings. Although we won't show further functionality, the value of the ODBC SDK cannot be overstated.

CHAPTER

12

ODBC Applications

About Chapter 12

The last chapter *discussed* ODBC; this chapter is where we *do* it. Chapter 12 is about programming an ODBC application, which may appear complex when compared to Remote Data Objects (RDO) of Visual Basic Enterprise Edition. It isn't, and programming an ODBC application is a matter of understanding the issues and using an organized approach. ODBC will always have higher performance since all other database access technologies (except special versions of OLE-DB providers), are ODBC wrappers. RDO represents an ODBC wrapper and will have an apparent ease of use until an unsolvable issue is encountered.

All the key ODBC programming issues are discussed in this chapter. The chapter starts with the ODBC application guidelines, followed by a series of ODBC functionality topics, including cursors, transactions, concurrency, transaction isolation levels, and the ACID properties. The ACID properties are characteristics of a database transaction: atomicity, consistency, integrity, and durability. These are defined later in the chapter, but for now a database is not a true database unless it exhibits these properties for transactions.

The ODBC programming protocol is discussed next. ODBC statements must be in the correct order or an ODBC state transition error occurs. Included with the programming protocol are a few notes on debugging with ODBC Test.

Next in the order of business for this chapter are six ODBC code fragments (little birdhouses) that are Unicode compliant. Each birdhouse represents a category of ODBC functionality and not all ODBC functions are illustrated. Programming an ODBC application in Visual Basic for Applications (VBA) requires an understanding of two languages. The ODBC specifications and examples are defined in C++ and the VBA developer must translate the C++ definitions for use in a VBA scripting tool. The ODBC examples are written in Visual Basic, and you'll find these examples in the Microsoft Visual Basic `ODBC.VBP` project of the `EXAMPLES\ CHAPTER12` folder located on the CD-ROM that accompanies this book.

An ODBC "Tarpits" section concludes this chapter, since poorly written SQL statements account for many ODBC performance problems.

The examples in this chapter may be found in the `CHAPTER12.VBP` Visual Basic Enterprise Edition project located in the `EXAMPLES\ CHAPTER12` folder of the CD-ROM located at the back of this book. The ODBC examples in this chapter require ODBC 3.0.

ODBC Application Guidelines before Programming

ODBC applications are special. As you learned in Chapter 11, there are API and SQL conformance levels. There are two choices when your client application requirements cannot be satisfied with the ODBC drivers available. You can:

- Reduce the application functionality and inform the client, or
- Provide the required functionality in the application.

A good example is backward-scrolling cursors. Although backward-scrolling cursors are not recommended, the application must provide the missing functionality.

Another example is **SQLBrowseConnect**. You have a hard choice to make if your driver does not support Level 2 API conformance and your client wishes to do a browse connect. When user requirements specify a level of functionality that is not supported by the ODBC driver, the application program must supply the missing functionality. The choice is to supply the missing functionality in the ODBC application or inform the user that the required functionality is not forthcoming.

ODBC application development can be a very easy or a very difficult task. To properly address all of the development issues, follow these guidelines:

- Completely understand the client's requirements. There is no substitute for thinking or hard work. Don't be tempted to start programming with the modern *rapid access development* (RAD) tools until all aspects of the requirements are understood. The power of the new modern programming tools is such that it tempts us to do a bottom-up design, which is always a sure path to a disaster. It is excruciatingly hard to resist programming until each detail is completely understood.
- Survey the ODBC drivers available and compare driver functionality with your requirements. If the application requirements are clear, then this is the time for hard choices. Decide whether the application will supply any missing functionality. Select your third-party driver.
- Ensure you have a programming specification and have selected an ODBC driver. This step is critical. You must test your newly acquired driver before you start programming. This is a precautionary measure to verify that your driver supports your required functionality. The ODBC driver can be tested as illustrated in Figure 12-1 with ODBC Test from the ODBC SDK.

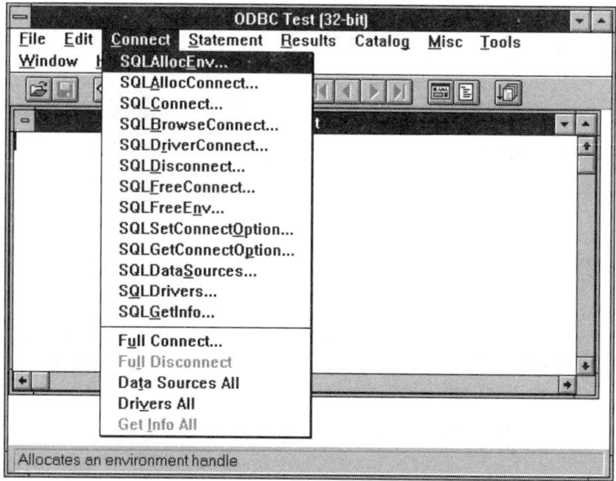

FIGURE 12-1 Starting the allocation of a connection with 32-bit ODBC Test

- Test the ODBC drivers against your specifications. One of the greatest mistakes in ODBC programming is to consider the application as monolithic. Now is the time to consider the ODBC architecture with a division of labor. This can be the writing of stored procedures for SQL Server, or it can be a slightly more elegant solution with a tiered architecture.

  Acquire an intimate understanding of the ODBC driver. This is done by reading the supplied ODBC driver documentation and by testing all the ODBC driver features required for the ODBC application. The ODBC driver may support features that are not necessary, but it is critical that all required ODBC driver features be tested before application development starts. Use this knowledge to compare supported data source functionality with client requirements. An intimate knowledge of the data source is necessary to write a good ODBC application. The developer determines missing data source functionality by calling **SQLGetInfo,** or by using ODBC Test. Questions can be answered as to transaction support, cursor behavior on commit or rollback, the support of multiple active statements per connections, scalar functions supported, and the data types supported. A successful ODBC programmer must have an intimate understanding of the data source's characteristics.

Programming Your ODBC Application

Programming an ODBC application involves managing the handles that represent data structures and the calling of ODBC API functions.

Handles

The ODBC environment requires four different classes of handles. Their allocation sequence is ordered and an error occurs if handles are not allocated in the proper order.

An ODBC application starts with these steps:

- The first step is to allocate an environment handle to determine the data access context. This is an opportunity to collect and cache driver information before the application commences any data operations. The most important issue of the environment is the registering of the ODBC version. This is done with **SQLSetEnvAttr** and setting the `SQL_ATTR_APP_ODBC_VER` attribute. This establishes the deprecation level for ODBC 3.0, which automatically maps older API functions to the new ODBC 3.0 functions.
- The second step is to allocate a connection handle, or at least to go through the motions of doing such. The application issues a connection allocation request to the driver manager. The driver manager recognizes the request but doesn't perform the task immediately. The driver manager allocates the connection handle only after the application has selected a data source driver. An environment handle may have one or more connection handles.

Connections have been a traditional problem with ODBC. Earlier versions of ODBC did not cache the driver, hence the additional time necessary to load the driver. There is also the issue of limited connections to SQL Server. ODBC 3.0 pools connections, and this factor alone is a strong impetus to upgrade existing ODBC applications (see the Orphans sidebar below).

- The third step is to allocate and use a statement handle. Not all ODBC API calls require a statement handle. It is associated with a SQL statement and common usage is the binding of parameters along with both direct and prepared statement executions. Overlooked by many ODBC programmers is the fact that a statement handle may be reused. The statement context may dictate otherwise, but the release of just the column or parameter buffers is certainly more efficient than the complete deallocation of all statement handle resources.

Error reporting in ODBC is slightly more complex then in the average application. There are the typical error messages for such items as invalid argument types, invalid data, and the like, but there is also something additional. ODBC reports state transition errors when a handle is not in the proper state. The three handles — environment, connection, and statement — each have three states: unallocated, allocated, and connected. State transition errors occur when the programming protocol is not adhered to and ODBC API functions are referenced in the wrong order. A discussion of the programming protocol is just ahead, so let's finish this discussion of handles by introducing the new handles of ODBC 3.0.

There are two divisions of labor — the application and the driver — and two classes of data — rows and parameters. The new handles are identified when the word *driver* is replaced with the word *implementation,* and all combinations of labor and metadata are enumerated.

The new descriptor types for ODBC 3.0 are listed next along with a description of the information maintained by each descriptor.

- **Application Parameter Descriptor (APD):** application buffers bound to parameters in a SQL statement. Information includes addresses, lengths, and C data types.
- **Implementation (Driver) Parameter Descriptor (IPD):** parameter information as to SQL data types, lengths, and nullability.
- **Application Row Descriptor (ARD):** application buffers bound to columns in a result set. Information includes addresses, lengths, and C data types.
- **Implementation (Driver) Row Descriptor (IRD):** column information as to SQL data types, lengths, and nullability.

Microsoft helps us out with these new descriptors. They are allocated automatically when a statement is allocated.

Transactions

Transactions are required in SQL 92, which ODBC 3.0 supports. The default Transaction State for ODBC is AUTOCOMMIT. This means that a statement is committed automatically when it completes.

The ODBC 3.0 API function **SQLEndTran** supports a commit or rollback option. This statement is only used in manual-commit mode.

ODBC transactions are not explicitly initiated. An implicit default transaction begins when the application initiates database operations.

The cursor behavior of a transaction, which is either committed or rolled back, is data source-dependent and is dictated by one of these actions occurring:

- The commit or rollback closes the cursor and deletes all query plans for prepared statements.
- The commit or rollback closes the cursor and preserves the query plan for prepared statements.
- The commit or rollback closes the cursor and deletes all query plans for prepared statements.

Determining the cursor behavior is an important step in application initialization. The cursor behavior for a COMMIT and a ROLLBACK operation should be determined with **SQLGetInfo** after connecting to the data source. The attributes to interrogate are `SQL_CURSOR_COMMIT_BEHAVIOR` and `SQL_CURSOR_ROLLBACK_BEHAVIOR`. Possible return values include:

- `SQL_CB_DELETE`—Close cursor and delete prepared statement along with query plan.
- `SQL_CB_CLOSE`—Close cursor. (Prepared statements and query plans are preserved.)
- `SQL_CB_PRESERVE`—Cursor and query plans are preserved. (**SQLCloseCursor** is used to close the cursor.)

SQLExecute, SQLExecDirect, SQLBulkOperations, SQLSetPos, or **SQL CloseCursor** automatically commit a transaction when in AUTOCOMMIT mode.

Transaction Isolation Levels

Transaction isolation is the degree of interaction between multiple concurrent transactions. There is, however, a simple rule that describes the issue. Maximum consistency (highest transaction isolation level) is also the lowest concurrency level. Conversely, the highest concurrency level yields the lowest consistency level. Maximum performance (I'll call it apparent performance) yields the lowest consistency level. No specific recommendation can be made as to the appropriateness of a transaction isolation level other than to use the lowest possible transaction isolation level consistent with the ODBC application design.

There are four transaction isolation levels, which are read uncommitted, read committed, repeatable read, and serializable. The transaction isolation levels manage dirty reads, nonrepeatable reads, and phantom reads, which are undesirable read phenomena. The undesirable read phenomena are described as follows:

- **Dirty Read,** which is the reading of transaction data of another application before the data is rolled back. The data read is considered dirty if there is a possibility that the transaction can be rolled back. The data may or may not exist within the database even though it was read by an application.
- **Nonrepeatable Read,** which occurs when the application reads a row and gets a different result each time. Another application updated the row before the second read occurred.
- **Phantom Read,** which is a row that matches a search criteria but isn't seen by the application. A second application has added a new row that meets the search criteria after the initial rows were read.

The read phenomena is managed with a lock protocol. How the individual transaction levels manage locks can be described as follows:

- **Read uncommitted** — No transaction isolation occurs. Transactions running at this level are typically read-only. Locks are ignored.
- **Read committed** — The transaction is forced to wait until write-locked applications release data locks.
- **Repeatable read** — The transaction waits until write-locks on rows are released by other applications. The transaction holds a read-lock on all rows it returns to the application and write-locks on all rows it changes, deletes, or inserts.

- **Serializable** — The application holds read-locks on all rows affected by a read. A write-lock is placed on all rows affected by a change, delete, or insertion.

The different transaction isolation levels can now be enumerated. For example, assume there are two independent applications. Application A has an open transaction with *repeatable read* as the transaction isolation level. It is possible for application B to experience a *phantom read* while the transaction for application A remains open. Table 12-1 relates read phenomena to the different transaction isolation levels.

READ PHENOMENA AND TRANSACTION ISOLATION LEVELS

TRANSACTION ISOLATION LEVEL	DIRTY READS	NONREPEATABLE READS	PHANTOM READS
Read uncommitted	X	X	X
Read committed		X	X
Repeatable read			X
Serializable			

Concurrency

Increasing the level of transaction isolation reduces the level of *concurrency*. ODBC offers these four methods of concurrency control by a cursor:

- **Read-only** — The data is read-only and the cursor cannot update or delete data.
- **Locking** — The cursor establishes the lowest locking level consistent with application design. Very low concurrency levels occur when the locking design choice is repeatable read or serialize.
- **Optimistic concurrency using row versions** — Row versioning is a feature of an Oracle database, and not all database management systems support row versioning. Optimistic concurrency adopts the strategy of not locking the row until the update occurs. The row version is compared with the prior row version to see if the data has changed. Conversely, pessimistic locking locks the row immediately. A developer uses this approach when collisions are commonplace and expected.

- **Optimistic concurrency using values** — Row versioning with values is a feature of both Sybase and Microsoft SQL Server. The lock strategy for optimistic concurrency using a time stamp is identical to that of row versioning. The only difference is that comparisons are made between time stamp values and not row versions.

ACID, Consistency, and Measuring Database Transactions

An important feature of any database is transactions. The ACID properties declare the requirements necessary for consistent transactions:

- **Atomicity** — Either all or none of the transaction's changes are present when the transaction completes.
- **Consistency** — The transaction respects all business rules and referential integrity. Inconsistent updates can be done, but will violate system integrity.
- **Isolation** — Transactions are isolated. SQL Server uses the `SET` statement

```
SET TRANSACTION ISOLATION LEVEL
READ COMMITTED | READ UNCOMMITTED |
REPEATABLE READ | SERIALIZABLE
```

  The SQL Server transaction isolation levels are maintained for the all Recordsets of the transaction. On the other hand, Microsoft Access does not have a unified approach. Various RecordSet options can be used, such as **dbSeeChanges,** however, the options must be set for every RecordSet, which is an error-prone mechanism. Microsoft Access does have the **IsolateODBCTrans** for the **Workspace** object, but that just isolates one transaction from another and does not manage transaction isolation levels.

- **Durability** — Once the commit occurs, the transactions must be present even if the system fails. SQL Server supports this property with write-ahead into a log; Microsoft Access, however, does not. SQL Server will recover all closed transactions during recovery and will purge all open transactions. Microsoft Access does not have a log, and a system failure can mean loss of the database and the logical loss of the related disk. Microsoft Access is commonly used as a server, which is a serious architectural error. A solution is to back up the Access database before posting transactions. Another solution is to replicate the Access database on other sites. Either of these solutions for the **Durability** property issue is ad hoc and is not integrated into the Microsoft Access architecture. They each require operator intervention, whereas the log file and recovery mechanism of SQL Server is ingrained in the SQL Server architecture. Failure to support the **Durability** property is a good reason to not use Microsoft Access as a Server.

Cursors

A cursor is a mechanism for managing a returned rowset of a result set. ODBC supports the concept of a block cursor and a scrollable cursor. Block cursors (also known as *fat cursors*) are the default for an application using ODBC 3.0. A block cursor is a returned rowset that cannot be scrolled; that is, the user cannot scroll back and forth between rows. An ODBC 3.0 application uses block cursors by setting the rowset size, binds the rowset buffers with **SQLColBind,** and calls either **SQLFetch** or **SQLFetchScroll.**

Cursor management in ODBC 3.0 is enhanced with the addition of cursor offsets. Column bindings are changed without an additional reference to **SQLColBind.** (This feature is not available for ODBC 2.0.)

Block Cursors

Block cursors return multiple rows. Support for block cursors is an inherent feature of ODBC 3.0. **SQLFetch** always returns a rowset from a result set in ODBC 3.0, while **SQLFetch** in ODBC 2.0/2.5 returns only a single row from a result set to the application. The situation changes slightly when an ODBC 3.0 application calls **SQLFetch** using an ODBC 2.0 driver. The ODBC driver will only return one row unless the driver supports **SQLExtendedFetch.**

Block cursors are efficient and include many rows while **SQLGetData** operates on a single column of a single row, and is not efficient. It is not designed for fetching data from multiple rows. Its intended use is the retrieval of long data, data that occurs in segments and cannot be retrieved in a single **SQLGetData** call. Long data can be either character or binary data.

Scrollable Cursors

Scrollable cursors enable the user, through the client application, to scroll the returned rows of a result set. The scrollable cursor models are related to transaction isolation levels discussed above. The transaction isolation level determines the change detection threshold for scrollable cursors. Scrollable cursors come in these four flavors:

- **Static** — No data changes are detected by the client application. The snapshot type **RecordSet** of the Microsoft Jet engine uses a static cursor.
- **Dynamic** — This cursor detects all changes, but is difficult to implement; and, of course, difficult software is always error prone. The change detection threshold is managed by setting the `SQL_ATTR_TXN_ISOLATION` connection attribute.
- **Keyset-driven** — A keyset-driven cursor is almost a hybrid of static and dynamic cursors. The change detection threshold is managed by setting the `SQL_ATTR_TXN_ISOLATION` connection attribute. This cursor can detect deleted rows but not the addition of new rows.

  The complete keyset for the result set is saved when the cursor is opened. Rows deleted by another application are detectable; newly added rows, however, are not detectable. Looking at `SQL_STATIC_SENSITIVITY` with **SQLGetInfo** will determine if keyset-driven cursors can detect their own deletes.
- **Mixed** — A combination of a keyset-driven and a dynamic cursor. Rowset size should be less than the keyset size for a mixed cursor. A mixed cursor is equivalent to a dynamic cursor when the keyset size is set to 1. It is equivalent to a keyset-driven cursor when the keyset size is equal to the result set size.

  The cursor will always detect deletions when scrolling within the keyset established when the cursor opened. The cursor assumes dynamic cursor behavior when the client application scrolls beyond the keyset size initially established and is unable to determine deleted rows. A rowset refresh will establish a new keyset and will return the cursor behavior to that of a keyset-driven cursor so long as the client application does not scroll beyond the established keyset limits.

Cursor Library Support

ODBC supports a block scrollable cursor for any driver that is Level 1 API compliant. The supported cursors are static and forward only. The cursor library also supports positioned update and delete statements for result sets created by SELECT statements.

Programming Protocol

The ODBC API is a series of single API functions that must be called in a prescribed order. An ODBC application follows an organized flow, or protocol, with ODBC API calls performing specific functions. Figure 12-2 illustrates the overall control flow of connecting to a data source and processing SQL statements.

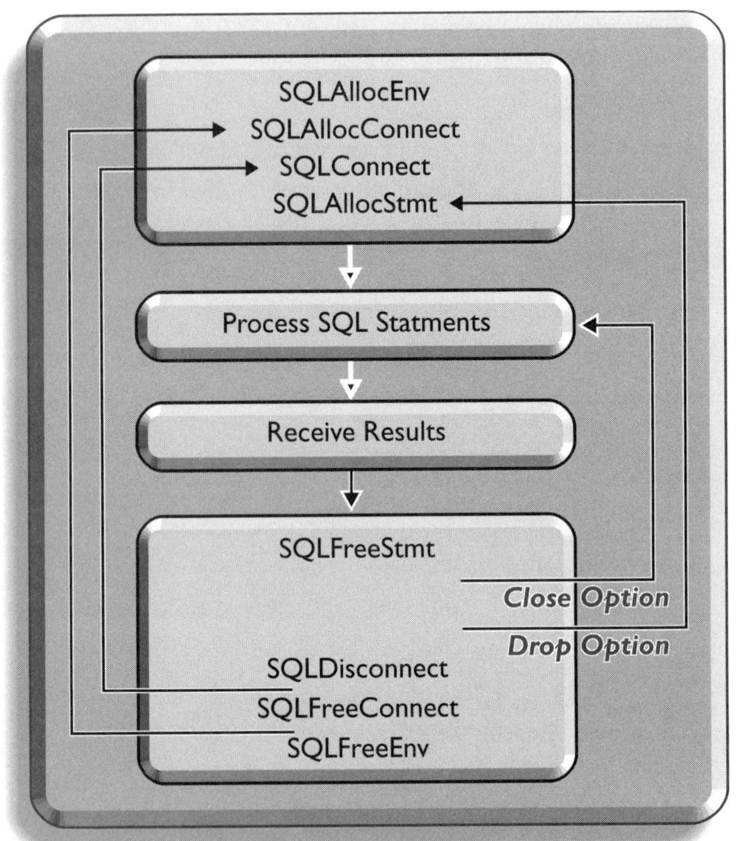

FIGURE 12-2 Basic ODBC programming protocol

SQL processing detail is expanded in Figure 12-3; however, not all of the API functionality is shown. The example illustrated in Figure 12-3 is not an optimal solution, but it serves the purpose of illustrating additional API call sequence detail. You'll note that **SQLDescribeCol** is used in Figure 12-3. This is an arbitrary choice and **SQLColAttributes** is a generalized alternative to using **SQLDescribeCol.**

Optimal performance is obtained by calling **SQLColAttributes, SQLDescribeCol,** and **SQLNumResultCols** after a statement execution. These functions may execute slower for data sources that emulate statement preparation, or may not be supported by the target data source.

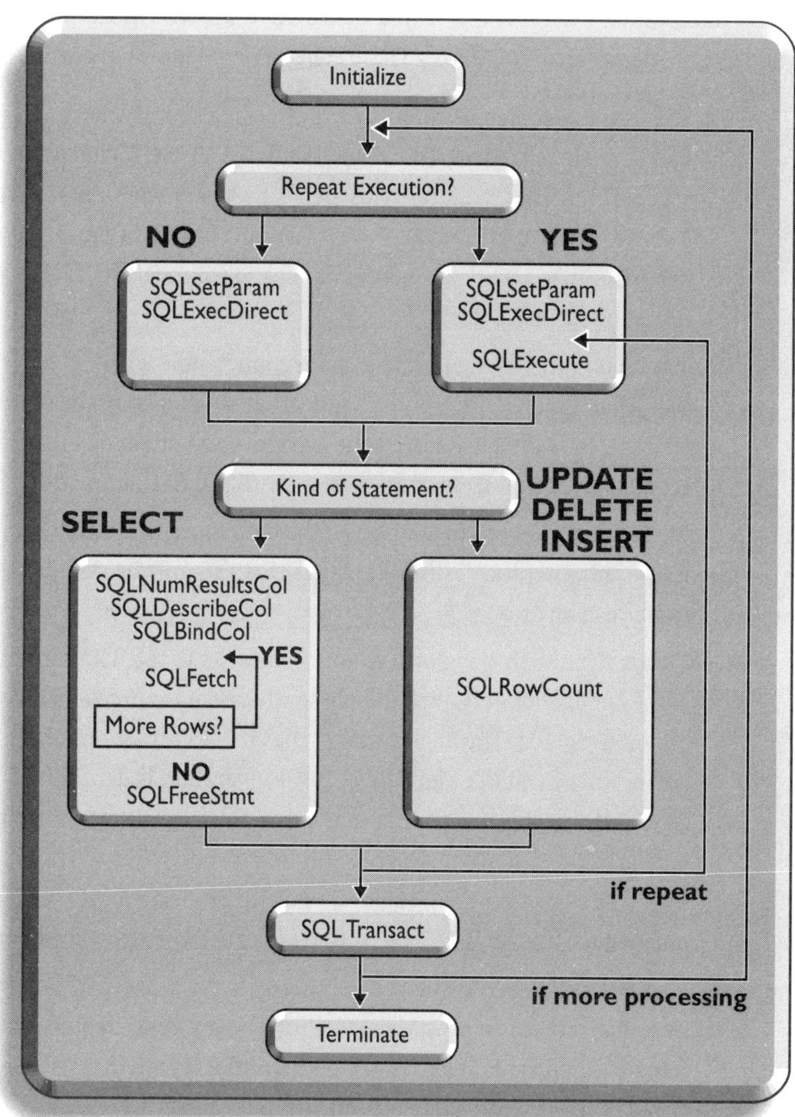

FIGURE 12-3 Advanced ODBC programming protocol

Figures 12-2 and 12-3 represent logical flow of an ODBC application. Figure 12-2 represents ODBC functions used in resource allocation and control flow of an ODBC application. Figure 12-3 represents the ODBC functions used for building a query and processing query results. The programming steps using ODBC 3.0 functions are outlined below. As an example, the function **SQLAllocHandle**(STMT) is used rather than the deprecated ODBC 2.0 **SQLAllocStmt**. (See Chapter 11, for a list of deprecated functions.) These steps are procedural in nature:

1. This is the first step in connecting to the data source where an environment handle is allocated with **SQLAllocHandle**(ENV). **SQLSetEnvAttr** is used to set environment attributes. This step is the point where **SQLSetEnvAttr** is called to set `SQL_ATTR_ODBC_VER` before using **SQLConnect**. It is the only opportunity to institute a behavioral change with ODBC 3.0 behavior changing to ODBC 2.*x*.
2. The second step is to allocate a connection handle with **SQLAllocHandle**(DBC). Some connection attributes can be set after the connection is established. Set those connection attributes that cannot be set after the connection is established with**SQLSetConnectAttr**.
3. **SQLConnect** is used to connect to the data source. **SQLSetConnectAttr** is now used to set the desired attributes that can only be set after the connection is established.
4. This is the fourth step and a connection exists to the data source. This step is the application initialization phase where data source and driver behavior are interrogated. The application caches this information. The cursor behavior for a COMMIT and a ROLLBACK operation is determined with **SQLGetInfo** after connecting to the data source. The attributes to interrogate are `SQL_CURSOR_COMMIT_BEHAVIOR` and `SQL_CURSOR_ROLLBACK_BEHAVIOR`. (See "Transactions," earlier in this chapter, for further detail.) **SQLGetInfo** is used when needed to acquire necessary information.
5. The application is now initialized. Processing a query requires a statement handle which is obtained by calling **SQLAllocHandle**(STM). Statement attributes are set with **SQLSetStmtAttr**.

6. Execution starts with any of the catalog functions such as **SQLColumns**, **SQLProcedures**, **SQLStatistics**, or it may be the binding of parameters with **SQLBindParameter** followed by **SQLExecDirect**. **SQLPrepare** and **SQLExecute** are other options.
7. Result sets are now returned. **SQLNumResultCols** counts the number of result set columns. Using **SQLDescribeCol** is optional if the column data types are already known. The application loops on **SQLDescribeCol** followed by **SQLBindCol** for each bound column in the result set. **SQLFetch** retrieves the data directly into the bound variables. Use **SQLGetData** when the columns are unbound or for long data. **SQLSetPos** moves the cursor.
8. The ODBC application uses **SQLRowCount** to verify that the expected number of rows is correct for the update or delete. When in manual transaction mode, theapplication rolls back the transaction when the expected row count is incorrect.
9. **SQLEndTran** is the logical step that follows an update or delete operation in the ODBC programming protocol. It is used to commit or rollback a transaction, but only when transaction processing is in manual mode. **SQLEndTran** is not applicable to query or catalog operations.
10. Finally, the connection is closed using the API functions **SQLFreeHandle** (STMT), **SQLDisconnect, SQLFreeHandle**(DBC), and **SQLFree Handle**(ENV).

Debugging an ODBC Application

No discussion of programming is complete without a mention of debugging tools. ODBC has a trace mechanism for debugging an ODBC application. The trace output that follows is generated from the first example in the Examples section below. It was created by selecting Options ⇨ ODBC Trace from the ODBC 2.0/2.5 Administrator. ODBC Test is an invaluable tool in debugging an ODBC application. Listing 12-1 is the trace output from ODBC Test of the ODBC 2.1 SDK for the Access 2.0 query using ODBC 2.0/2.5:

```
USE Pubs
SELECT au_fname, au_lname FROM authors;
```

LISTING 12-1 Trace output from an OBDC Test for Microsoft Access 2.0 query using ODBC 2.0/2.5

```
SQLAllocEnv(phenv1DEF0000);
SQLAllocConnect(henv1DEF0000, phdbc32D70000);
SQLConnect(hdbc32D70000, "Thor", 4, "sa", 2, "", 0);
SQLAllocStmt(hdbc32D70000, phstmt32A70000);
SQLExecDirect(hstmt32A70000, "USE Pubs", 127);
SQLExecDirect(hstmt32A70000, "SELECT au_fname, au_lname FROM authors;", 128);
SQLFetch(hstmt32A70000);
SQLNumResultCols(hstmt32A70000, pccol);
SQLGetData(hstmt32A70000, 1, 1, rgbValue, 33, pcbValue);
SQLGetData(hstmt32A70000, 2, 1, rgbValue, 33, pcbValue);
SQLFreeStmt(hstmt32A70000, 1);
SQLDisconnect(hdbc32D70000);
SQLFreeConnect(hdbc32D70000);
SQLFreeEnv(henv1DEF0000);
```

The same query was run in Listing 12-2 with the ODBC 3.0 SDK using Microsoft Access. Note the richness of content. The trace was started with the ODBC 3.0 dialog shown in Figure 12-4.

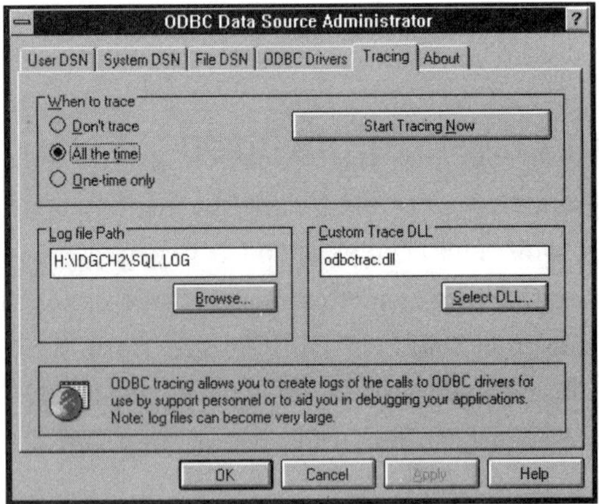

FIGURE 12-4 ODBC 3.0 Administrator dialog box

Listing 12-2 is the trace output from ODBC Test of the ODBC 3.0 SDK for the ODBC 3.0 query:

```
USE Pubs
SELECT au_fname, au_lname FROM authors;
```

Note the differences in output. The ODBC Test from the ODBC 3.0 SDK provides finer detail of the operations associated with an ODBC query. All of the output for the simple query of the PUBS database is shown in Listing 12-2. Use ODBC Test of the ODBC 3.0 SDK with caution. You may fill your disk with trace output!

LISTING 12-2 Tracing a query which uses ODBC 3.0

```
MSACCESS 7b:76     ENTER SQLAllocConnect
      HENV     0x092a18e0
      HDBC *   0x001761d0
MSACCESS 7b:76      EXIT SQLAllocConnect with return code 0 (SQL_SUCCESS)
      HENV     0x092a18e0
      HDBC *   0x001761d0 ( 0x092a2d28)
MSACCESS 7b:76     ENTER SQLConnect
      HDBC  0x092a2d28
      UCHAR *     0x0018555c [ 4] "Thor"
      SWORD 4
      UCHAR *     0x001854dc [ 2] "sa"
      SWORD 2
      UCHAR *     0x001c53a4
      SWORD 0
MSACCESS 7b:76   ENTER SQLConnectW
      HDBC       0x092a2d28
      WCHAR *    0x092a0cc0 [ 8] "Thor"
      SWORD 8
      WCHAR *    0x092a2de8 [ 4] "sa"
      SWORD 4
      WCHAR *    0x092a2df8
      SWORD 0
```

Output omitted for brevity

ODBC and Unicode

There are obvious language differences between the United States versions of software and the versions for other countries. The problems extend far beyond mechanical translation of languages and can involve religious and cultural issues. Unicode is a tool for the internationalizing of an application, which is not a simple task for the fainthearted. It is a complex, very costly, time consuming, and iterative process. This chapter and this section are not about internationalization of an application per se, but the use of Unicode by ODBC. The paragraphs below provide a brief sketch of the character set issues of internationalization.

Character translation starts with an *input method editor* (IME) that translates text entered on a 101-key keyboard to the target character set. When you don't know Japanese, and if you have access to an IME, names like "Toyota" or "Suzuki" can be typed. The appropriate double-byte character is created and the results are displayed immediately. To understand what's involved in the translation, let's start with the definition of the character sets used today. Table 12-2 maps the support for the different character sets and Table 12-3 illustrates the various implementations of the character A, each of which is unique.

The Unicode standard is defined in two volumes: *Worldwide Character Encoding* Version 1.0, Volume 1 (ISBN 0-201-56788-1) and Volume 2 (ISBN 0-201-60845-6). Additional Unicode information may be found at `ftp://unicode.org`.

ANSI, DBCS, and Unicode Implementations

Environment	Character set(s)
Visual basic	Unicode
32-bit object libraries	Unicode
16-bit object libraries	ANSI and DBCS
Windows NT API	Unicode
Automation in Windows NT	Unicode
Windows 95 API	ANSI and DBCS
Automation in Windows 95	Unicode

Character codes for "A" in ANSI, Unicode, and DBCS	
The character <A>	*Hexadecimal Equivalent*
ANSI character "A"	&H41
Unicode character "A"	&H41 &H00
DBCS character that represents a Japanese wide-width "A"	&H82 &H60
Unicode wide-width "A"	&H21 &HFF

Let's mention a few kind words about each of the character sets:

- ***ANSI*** — ANSI represents the traditional American Standard Code for Information Interchange (ASCII) character set. It is the most popular and is the legacy character set. The implementation is eight bits.
- ***Unicode*** — Unicode is a standard and not an invention of Microsoft.

  The Unicode standard is defined in two volumes: *Worldwide Character Encoding* Version 1.0, Volume 1 and Volume 2. Additional Unicode information may be found at `ftp://unicode.org`.

  Unicode is a character-encoding scheme that uses two bytes to represent every character. This scheme is capable of encoding all known characters and is used as a worldwide character-encoding standard. Unicode is supported by all 32-bit versions of Microsoft Windows and by 32-bit OLE technology. All versions of Microsoft Access after Version 2.0 are component-based (OLE) and by definition support Unicode. The same is true for Visual Basic 4.0 and later. Unicode is relatively new even though it is a standard. Legacy applications do not use Unicode.
- ***DBCS*** — The double-byte character set is used with Windows operating systems that are distributed in most regions of Asia. For example, Japanese has four alphabets, each of which are encoded in DBCS:
  - ***Kanji*** — Ideograms or meaning not related to pronunciation.
  - ***Hiragana*** — Phoenetic alphabet that is used for Japanese words.
  - ***Katakana*** — Phoenetic alphabet used for foreign words.
  - ***Romanji*** — Latin letter alphabet.

The name *double-byte character set* is a misnomer. It is possible to combine a *single-byte character set* (SBCS) with a DBCS. The result is a character string that is relatively complex to scan. Figure 12-5 illustrates the different character combinations. The current cursor position in each string is noted. Position a cursor at the wrong position in a DBCS string and chaos ensues. The SBCS range is limited to the inclusive values of 20 hexadecimal (hex) to 7F hex. The lead DBCS character is always an extended character that is always greater than 7F hex. The trailing character is not limited in value and may be either a SBCS or a DBCS character.

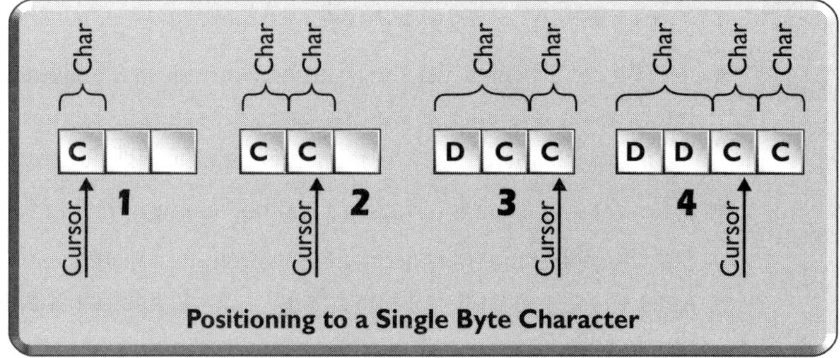

Legend: D > 7F, C >= 20 and <= 7F

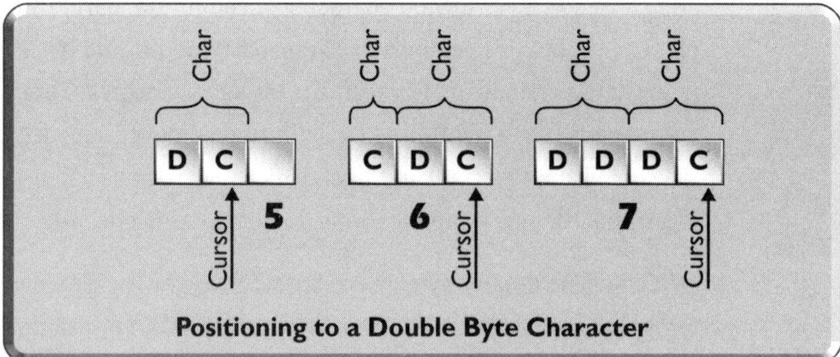

FIGURE 12-5 Double-byte and single-byte character combinations

Character strings 3 and 4 for Figure 12-5 illustrate that the trailing byte may assume any value. This makes DBCS string parsing difficult. Microsoft supplies the function **IsDBCSLeadByte,** which returns a `TRUE` only when the lead byte is a candidate lead byte. Lead-byte determination is also based on the context of the character. An example is the second character of String 4, which is a candidate lead byte and is a trailing byte. **IsDBCSLeadByte** will return TRUE for this character but the context is that of a trailing byte. The Visual C++ operators ++ and -- are no longer safe with DBCS character strings. **CharNext** and **CharPrev** are the 32-bit implementations of character positioning, while **AnsiNext** and **AnsiPrev** are the 16-bit implementations.

A DBCS is not case sensitive.

ODBC Unicode Examples

The examples use Visual Basic 5.0/6.0 and ODBC 3.0 and the 32-bit ODBC32.DLL, which means that result sets are returned in Unicode, at least on Windows NT, which is my system of choice. Unicode engenders additional complexity that is significant. This is unfortunate, because Microsoft needs Unicode to sell software on a worldwide basis, whereas a legacy database does not need Unicode. What's really unfortunate is that ODBC was specifically designed for heterogeneous access to legacy databases. To understand this complexity issue, let's first look at a code fragment from a 16-bit tool such as Microsoft Access 2.0 or Microsoft Visual Basic 4.0, 16-bit edition, both of which use ODBC.DLL. The data in question is the *Pubs* database, *Authors* table, and the *au_id* column. The code fragment below binds the column and returns the data.

```
RetCode = BTPSQLBindCol(hstmt, 1, SQL_C_CHAR, au_id, _
   MAX_DATA, cbau_id)
RetCode = BTPSQLFetch(hstmt)
```

That's relatively simple, now let's repeat the same functional code, but with Unicode. The first issue is that Unicode characters must be read into a byte array. This means that a User Defined Type (UDT) must be declared for each Unicode field. We do that by placing the code fragment below in the **Declarations** section of the Visual Basic form.

```
Private Type udtAu_ID
  uniAu_ID(MAX_DATA) As Byte
  cbAu_ID As Long
End Type
```

The code fragment above is not the only overhead issue of Unicode. The data must also be converted from Unicode to string format, which is done with the following code fragment.

```
Function BytesToStr(MyByteArray() As Byte) As String
  Dim v As Variant
  Dim s As String
  v = MyByteArray()
  #If Win32 Then
     s = StrConv(v, vbUnicode)
  #Else
     s = v
  #End If
  BytesToStr = s
End Function
```

Now that we've declared our overhead issues, the Unicode code fragment doesn't look too much different than the non-Unicode version, the real problem is managing the numerous UDT structures, and the character conversion, which is illustrated by the code fragment below.

```
RetCode = BTPSQLBindCol(hstmt, 1, SQL_C_CHAR, _
  uAU_ID.uniAU_ID(0), MAX_DATA, uAU_ID.cbAU_ID)
RetCode = BTPSQLFetch(hstmt)
au_id = BytesToStr(uAU_ID.uniAU_ID())
```

UNICODE HELPS MICROSOFT MARKET WORLDWIDE

Unicode is a solution to a problem that Microsoft needs to sell software worldwide. I can certainly see the configuration issues for Microsoft without Unicode; however, you and I do not need Unicode. It is more of a question of Microsoft being able to sell products worldwide. This software solution to the problem of internationalization will probably cost the software community tens or even hundreds of millions of dollars. It's a great marketing model for Microsoft. Normally the features of a product are of value to the purchaser, but not this time.

Now that we've covered the preliminaries, let's return to the issue at hand: the ODBC examples. The ODBC API examples start with two common subroutines: The first subroutine creates a host environment; the second subroutine releases the environment. The two common subroutines are found in a standard module of the Microsoft Visual Basic `ODBC.VBP` project of Chapter 12. The module also contains the ODBC API function declarations for the ODBC API functions used in the examples. All ODBC API declarations are aliased with <BTP> to prevent conflicts with other API declarations. The Visual Basic `ODBC.BAS` standard module is located on the CD-ROM in the `<unit>\EXAMPLES\CHAPTER12` folder that accompanies this book. The `ODBC.BAS` contains a common error routine and the Visual Basic aliased API declarations. Executing the `ODBC.VBP` project and the `ODBC.FRM` results in Figure 12-6, which contains all the sample applications discussed in this chapter.

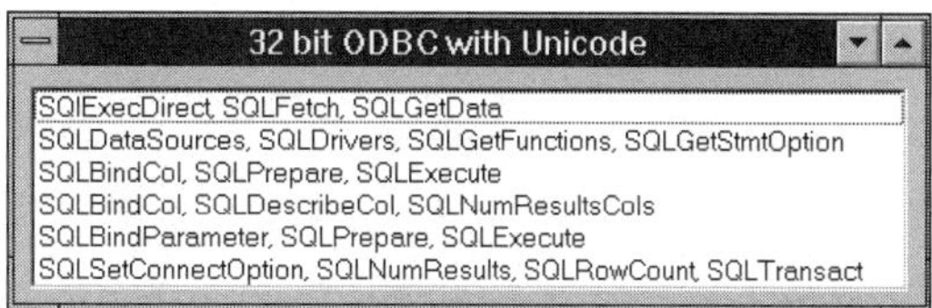

FIGURE 12-6 The ODBC.FRM of the ODBC.VBP project

SQLAllocEnv, SQLAllocConnect, SQLAllocStmt, and SQLConnect

Both the ODBC 2.0 SDK and the ODBC 3.0 SDK espouse naming conventions. I will not follow those conventions, but use literals directly in the interest of brevity and succinctness. As an example of a naming convention, *szSqlStr* is a null-terminated string where the SQL statement is stored. *SqlStr* represents the contextual functionality. The string size is represented by the parameter *cbSqlStr*, which is the count in bytes of a string with a contextual functionality of *SqlStr*. Another example is *pcbColDef*, which is defined as a pointer to a byte count for the *ColDef* parameter. I won't follow these naming conventions; however, the reader is encouraged to follow the espoused naming conventions, since I do not wish to be known as a "killer of large trees."

The **Create_Connection** function of Listing 12-3 is common to all the subsequent examples of this chapter. The function allocates two statement handles because the last example is a positioned update that requires two statement handles. The extra statement handle is not used by the other examples. Technically, it is not a good coding technique, so don't be confused by the extra statement handle. It will eventually be used in the last example. The program steps below are a model for creating a connection. The prescribed order of the table should be followed. The connection handle cannot be established until the environment handle is established. The last step is to allocate a statement handle, which requires a connection handle. The code is linear and the error handler, which is not shown, does not return control. The create connection function is illustrated in Listing 12-3, while the termination function is shown in Listing 12-4. The reader must edit this function for the name user id and password of the local SQL Server installation.

To create a **Create_Connection** function, follow these steps:

1. Allocate an environment handle for the variable *henv*.
2. Allocate a connection handle for the variable *hdbc* using the environment handle *henv*.
3. Connect to a Microsoft SQL Server named *Thor* as *sa* with a zero-length password. The server name and password must be changed to agree with the local SQL server.
4. Use **SQLExecDirect** to connect to the *Pubs* database of Microsoft SQL Server. A prepared statement isn't used because there are no parameters and this statement is not repeated.
5. Allocate a statement handle for the variable *hstmt* using the connection handle *hdbc*.
6. Allocate a statement handle for the variable *hstmtU* using the connection handle *hdbc*. This statement handle isn't used until the last example with the positioned update.

LISTING 12-3 **A common Create_Connection function**

```
Function Create_Connection() As Integer
'(C) 1999 Bruce T. Prendergast
' DBA Prendergast Consulting
' DBA PCS
' IDG Books Worldwide ISBN 0-7645-3314-2
```

```
 '
 Dim RetCode As Integer
 Dim szSqlStr As String * 128

   RetCode = BTPSQLAllocEnv(henv)
   If RetCode <> SQL_SUCCESS Then Log_Error err_Env, RetCode

   RetCode = BTPSQLAllocConnect(henv, hdbc)
   If RetCode <> SQL_SUCCESS Then Log_Error err_All, RetCode
   '
   ' Edit the line below for the
   '   local SQL Server logon parameters
   '
   RetCode = BTPSQLConnect(hdbc, "Thor", 4, "sa", 2, "", 0)
   If (RetCode <> SQL_SUCCESS) And (RetCode <> _
     SQL_SUCCESS_WITH_INFO) Then Log_Error err_Con, RetCode

   RetCode = BTPSQLAllocStmt(hdbc, hstmt)
   If RetCode <> SQL_SUCCESS Then Log_Error err_Ash, RetCode
   szSqlStr = "USE Pubs" & Chr$(0)    ' on SQL Server
   RetCode = BTPSQLExecDirect(hstmt, szSqlStr, Len(szSqlStr))
   If (RetCode <> SQL_SUCCESS) And (RetCode <> _
     SQL_SUCCESS_WITH_INFO) Then Log_Error err_Pna, RetCode
   RetCode = BTPSQLFreeStmt(hstmt, SQL_UNBIND)
   Create_Connection = True
   Exit Function
End Function
```

SQLDisconnect, SQLFreeConnect, SQLFreeStmt, and SQLFreeEnv

The **Release_Connection** function of Listing 12-4 is common to all examples in this chapter. The function is representative of the steps necessary to close a connection. The function releases all allocated resources and the connection. Note that **SQLFreeEnv** and **SQLFreeConnect** are deprecated in ODBC 3.0. The program steps below are a model for closing a connection. The prescribed order of the table should be followed. This is because a statement handle depends on a connection handle, and a connection handle depends on an environment handle. The last step is to release the environment handle. Error logging is not done in this function since this function is called by the error logger when an error occurs. Logging an error in the **Release_Connection** function may cause an endless loop.

To create a **Release_Connection** program, follow these steps:

1. Free the statement handle for the variable *hstmt*.
2. Free the statement handle for the variable *hstmtU*.
3. Disconnect from Microsoft SQL Server using the handle *hdbc*.
4. Free the connection for handle *hdbc*.
5. Free the environment for the handle *henv*.

LISTING 12-4 **A common Release_Connection function**

```
Function Release_Connection() As Integer
'(C) 1999 Bruce T. Prendergast
' DBA Prendergast Consulting
' DBA PCS
' IDG Books Worldwide ISBN 0-7645-3314-2
'
Dim RetCode As Integer
  If hstmt <> 0 Then
    RetCode = BTPSQLFreeStmt(hstmt, SQL_DROP)
    If RetCode <> SQL_SUCCESS Then
      MsgBox "Unable to free statement handle"
      End
    End If
  End If
  If hdbc <> 0 Then
    RetCode = BTPSQLDisconnect(hdbc)
    If RetCode <> SQL_SUCCESS Then
      MsgBox "Unable to disconnect"
      End
    End If
    RetCode = BTPSQLFreeConnect(hdbc)
    If RetCode <> SQL_SUCCESS Then
```

```
      MsgBox "Unable to free connection"
      End
    End If
  End If

  If henv <> 0 Then
    RetCode = BTPSQLFreeEnv(henv)
    If RetCode <> SQL_SUCCESS Then
      MsgBox "Unable to release environment"
      End
    End If
  End If
  Release_Connection = True
  Exit Function
End Function
```

SQLExecDirect, SQLFetch, and SQLGetData

These ODBC statements are typically used with unbound columns, or with a query that is not repeated. **SQLGetData** is easy to use, but the function is not efficient. The examples in this chapter gradually grow in complexity, and **SQLGetData** can soon be relegated to your newbie ODBC experiences.

This example issues a query against the `authors` table in the *Pubs* database on Microsoft SQL Server. It is represented by the code in the **ODBC1** function of Listing 12-5. The data is moved from unbound columns to local program variables. Since the data is unbound, Unicode plays no part of data conversion and the example is relatively simple. The code is elementary in that it only retrieves data from a single column of a single row. Using the **SQLGetData** function is a favorite of computer magazine articles that purport to show the reader how to use ODBC. The function is relatively easy to use, and serves only as a good teaching tool. It is not representative of how an ODBC application should be coded. This code is defective in two contexts:

- **SQLGetData** is quite inefficient and only operates on a single row. The primary use for **SQLGetData** is repeated calls on a column to retrieve segmented data. **SQLGetData** is called after the data is fetched, which results in late binding and the late binding only lasts for the duration of the call.

- The attributes of the database columns are explicitly declared in the program. Changing database column attributes adversely impacts an application program; that is, change the database and the program crashes. Using **SQLDescribeCol** and **SQLColAttributes** precludes declaring attribute properties in local application code. (See Listing 12-8)

  The issue is of historical import because a relational database gave us freedom from the program construct with the definition of the data stored within the data. This is quite unlike a COBOL File Definition (FD) that contains embedded data definitions. When we embed database attribute definitions in an application, we're stepping backward on the computing evolutionary scale and reverting to primordial computing issues of the past.

The **ODBC1** function is described with these steps:

1. Call the function **Create_Connection** to establish all handles.
2. Construct and issue a query using **SQLExecDirect** against the *authors* table of the *Pubs* database asking for the columns *au_fname* and *au_lname*.
4. Retrieve a row with **SQLFetch**
3. Use **SQLGetData** for the two columns of data using the statement handle *hstmt*. Display the results.
4. Use the function **Release_Connection** to release all handles and the connection.

LISTING 12-5 **An ODBC example using SQLExecDirect, SQLFetch, And SQLGetData**

```
Private Sub ODBC1()
'(C) 1999 Bruce T. Prendergast
' DBA Prendergast Consulting
' DBA PCS
' IDG Books Worldwide ISBN 0-7645-3314-2
'
' SQLExecDirect, SQLFetch, SQLGetData
'
Dim cblname As Long, cbfname As Long
Dim au_lname As String * 32, au_fname As String * 32
Dim RetCode As Integer
Dim szSqlStr As String * 128  ' SQL query storage
```

```
    If Not Create_Connection() Then Exit Sub
    szSqlStr = "SELECT au_fname, au_lname FROM authors;" & Chr$(0)
    RetCode = BTPSQLExecDirect(hstmt, szSqlStr, Len(szSqlStr))
    If RetCode <> SQL_SUCCESS Then Log_Error err_Eop, RetCode
    RetCode = BTPSQLFetch(hstmt)
    RetCode = BTPSQLGetData(hstmt, 1, SQL_C_CHAR, au_fname, _
      Len(au_fname), cbfname)
    RetCode = BTPSQLGetData(hstmt, 2, SQL_C_CHAR, au_lname, _
      Len(au_lname), cblname)
    MsgBox Mid$(au_fname, 1, cbfname) & " " & Mid$(au_lname, 1, cblname)
    RetCode = Release_Connection()
    Exit Sub
  End Sub
```

SQLDataSources, SQLDrivers, SQLFunctions, and SQLGetStmtOption

The **ODBC2** function of Listing 12-6 is representative of the application program caching data source information at application startup. These functions are infrequently used for an ODBC application with a single data source. The developer already knows the supported functionality and codes it directly. General use of these functions is with an application that supports more than one data source since resources from different data sources may vary. The developer must query each data source for the supported functionality to determine when application support is necessary. As an example, the ODBC application may be generalized and may support browsing for those data sources that do not support browsing. **SQLGetStmtOption** is deprecated in ODBC 3.0 and the corresponding ODBC 3.0 function is **SQLGetStmtAttr.**

The **ODBC2** function is described with these steps:

1. Call the function **Create_Connection** to establish all handles.
2. Use **SQLDataSources** to construct a result set of the data sources available. The parameter *fDirection* is set to `SQL_FETCH_FIRST` for the first row.
3. Scroll the remainder of the result set with the *fDirection* set to `SQL_FETCH_NEXT` for the remaining rows. The point of this example is to illustrate giving the client the ability to select a data source at execution time.

4. Use **SQLDrivers** to construct a result set of the drivers available. The parameter *fDirection* is set to SQL_FETCH_FIRST for the first row.
5. Scroll the remainder of the result set with the *fDirection* set to SQL_FETCH_NEXT for the remaining drivers.
6. Use **SQLGetFunctions** with the handle *hdbc* and ask if the driver for this connection supports foreign keys. The parameter *fFunction* is set to SQL_API_FOREIGNKEYS.
7. Use **SQLGetStmtOption** to obtain the rowset size for the statement identified by handle *hstmt*. The rowset size is returned in the parameter *pvParaml* and the input parameter *fOption* is set to SQL_ROWSET_SIZE.
8. Use **SQLGetStmtOption** to obtain the cursor type for the statement identified by handle *hstmt*. The cursor type is returned in the parameter *pvParaml* and the input parameter *fOption* is set to SQL_CURSOR_TYPE.
9. Use the function **Release_Connection** to release all handles and the connection.

LISTING 12-6 An ODBC example using SQLDataSources, SQLDrivers, SQLGetFunctions, and SQLGetStmtOption

```
Private Sub ODBC2()
'(C) 1999 Bruce T. Prendergast
' DBA Prendergast Consulting
' DBA PCS
' IDG Books Worldwide ISBN 0-7645-3314-2
'
' SQLDataSources, SQLDrivers, SQLGetFunctions,
' SQLGetStmtOption
'
Const MAX_LENGTH = 128
Dim RetCode As Integer
Dim szDSN As String * 128          ' Data Source Name
Dim cbDSN As Integer               ' DSN byte count
Dim szDescription As String * 128  ' DSN description
Dim cbDescription As Integer       ' Description byte count
Dim szDriverDesc As String * 128   ' Driver description
Dim cbDriverDesc As Integer        ' Returned byte count
Dim szDriverAttr As String * 128   ' Driver attributes
```

```
Dim cbDriverAttr As Integer       ' Attribute byte count
Dim fExists As Integer            ' Query result
Dim pvParaml As Long              ' 32 bit status
Dim pvParams As String * 128      ' Returned string value

  If Not Create_Connection() Then Exit Sub
  RetCode = BTPSQLDataSources(henv, SQL_FETCH_FIRST, _
    szDSN, MAX_LENGTH, cbDSN, szDescription, MAX_LENGTH, cbDescription)
  If RetCode <> SQL_SUCCESS Then Log_Error err_Dsr, RetCode
  While RetCode = SQL_SUCCESS
    MsgBox "Data source: " & szDSN & "known as " & szDescription
    RetCode = BTPSQLDataSources(henv, SQL_FETCH_NEXT, _
      szDSN, MAX_LENGTH, cbDSN, szDescription, MAX_LENGTH, cbDescription)
  Wend
  RetCode = BTPSQLDrivers(henv, SQL_FETCH_FIRST, szDriverDesc, MAX_LENGTH, _
    cbDriverDesc, szDriverAttr, MAX_LENGTH, cbDriverAttr)
  If RetCode <> SQL_SUCCESS Then Log_Error err_Gdr, RetCode
  While RetCode = SQL_SUCCESS
    MsgBox "Driver: " & szDriverDesc & " with attributes " & szDriverAttr
    RetCode = BTPSQLDrivers(henv, SQL_FETCH_NEXT, szDriverDesc, MAX_LENGTH, _
      cbDriverDesc, szDriverAttr, MAX_LENGTH, cbDriverAttr)
  Wend
  RetCode = BTPSQLGetFunctions(hdbc, SQL_API_FOREIGNKEYS, fExists)
  If RetCode <> SQL_SUCCESS Then Log_Error err_Gfn, RetCode
  If fExists Then
    MsgBox "Driver supports foreign keys"
  Else
    MsgBox "Driver does not support foreign keys"
  End If
  RetCode = BTPSQLGetStmtOption(hstmt, SQL_ROWSET_SIZE, pvParaml)
  If RetCode <> SQL_SUCCESS Then Log_Error err_Gso, RetCode
  RetCode = BTPSQLGetStmtOption(hstmt, SQL_CURSOR_TYPE, pvParaml)
  If RetCode <> SQL_SUCCESS Then Log_Error err_Gso, RetCode
  If pvParaml = 0 Then _
    MsgBox "SQL_Cursor_Type is: SQL_CURSOR_FORWARD_ONLY"
  RetCode = Release_Connection()
```

```
    MsgBox "All operations completed successfully"
    Exit Sub
  End Sub
```

SQLBindCol, SQLPrepare, and SQLExecute

Our first useful query is the code in the **ODBC3_Click** event represented by Listing 12-7. This example issues a query against the *authors* table in the *Pubs* database on Microsoft SQL Server. When compared to this query, the earlier example of using **SQLGetData** in Listing 12-5 is trivial. This query has two bound columns and uses a prepared SQL statement. Unfortunately this is our first example with Unicode, which increases the query complexity.

This example illustrates a preferred technique when compared to using **SQLGetData,** however, using a prepared SQL statement and bound parameters is not always the proper technique. Let's start by recalling that ODBC uses a call-level interface (CLI). The developer falls into the trap of using **SQLBindCol, SQLPrepare,** and **SQLExecute** in a procedural loop, retrieving a row for each pass through the loop. The developer converting from a legacy environment such as COBOL or FORTRAN will always have a difficult time with this issue. Their programming history is with procedural languages and writing a procedural loop is second nature to a legacy developer. SQL is not record oriented; it is set oriented. Data is returned as a result set, although you can scroll between rows. The ability to scroll between rows gives the appearance of record-oriented data, but it is not. Simply understanding ODBC commands and having a mechanical facility with ODBC, development tools, and the operating system will not make an individual an ODBC developer. The individual must also be able to visualize data as sets and not as records.

This is our first Unicode example. Listing 12-5, which uses the **SQLGetData** function does not require Unicode support, while the **SQLBindCol** function supports Unicode. The line:

```
fname = BytesToStr(uFname.uniAu_Fname()) ' Unicode
```

converts a **Byte** array that contains the Unicode characters to a string value. The **Byte** array is defined in the **Declarations** section of the VBA application as a User Defined Type (UDT).

ORPHANS

Microsoft has created a new class of orphans with Internet Information Server (IIS) 4.0 and ODBC 3.5. These two technologies, when combined, provide connection pooling for Microsoft SQL Server, which is supposed to be a scalability benefit. The reverse is true and Microsoft SQL Server is unstable with connection pooling and the preparation of SQL Server queries.

To understand this issue, developers are encouraged to always prepare (compile) any query that will be used more than once. This improves performance and is intuitively desirable for enterprise applications. With Web applications it is not intuitive that the compilation of queries is necessary for a Web page, because the user expects at least some waiting time and the same query will not always be used repeatedly.

The preparation of a query creates a temporary stored procedure in an internal Microsoft SQL Server database, namely TembDB. When a connection is returned to the pool, the temporary stored procedure remains in TempDB. Eventually TempDB fills up and Microsoft SQL Server crashes. The original SQL Server ODBC 2.65 driver by default automatically released all temporary stored procedures when the connection was broken. The new SQL Server ODBC 3.5 driver does not release temporary stored procedures when a connection is returned to the pool, hence the orphaned stored procedures. The solution to this problem is a Microsoft specific ODBC API connection option. The option is illustrated in Listing 12-7, which is the `SQL_USE_PROCEDURE_FOR_PREPARE` option.

In case you've forgotten, a SQL statement is prepared by compiling a query plan and saving that plan for later use. Three issues should be noted in this example:

- ODBC is implemented in C/C++ and the SQL data type `SQL_VARCHAR` is not supported by C/C++. I set the column type to `SQL_C_CHAR`, which is, as I understand it, close enough for government work.
- The two bound variables in the example are `fname` and `lname`. Both must be initialized to zero using the **String$** statement of VBA.
- The returned strings are null terminated. The returned length is used to examine the columns.

The **ODBC3** function is described with these steps:

1. Call the function **Create_Connection** to establish all handles.
2. Construct and query against the *authors* table of the *Pubs* database and ask for the columns *au_fname* and *au_lname*.
3. Use **SQLPrepare** to prepare the query identified by the statement handle *hstmt* of the statement *szSqlStr* with length *cbSqlStr*.
4. Use **SQLExecute** to execute a prepared statement using the *hstmt* handle.

5. Bind the first column of the SQL statement identified by the handle *hstmt*. The bind type is `SQL_C_CHAR` and the parameter *lname* is where the data is returned.
6. Bind the second column to the local variable *fname*.
7. Use **SQLFetch** to retrieve the data. Display the data using the returned character count since the data is NULL terminated.
8. Use the function **Release_Connection** to release all handles and the connection.

LISTING 12-7 **An ODBC example using SQLBindCol, SQLPrepare, and SQLExecute**

```
Private Sub ODBC3()
'(C) 1999 Bruce T. Prendergast
' DBA Prendergast Consulting
' DBA PCS
' IDG Books Worldwide ISBN 0-7645-3314-2
'
' SQLBindCol, SQLPrepare, SQLExecute
'
Dim RetCode As Integer
Dim szSqlStr As String * 128
Dim lname As String * MAX_DATA
Dim fname As String * MAX_DATA
Dim i As Integer
Dim uLname As udtAu_Lname        ' UDT for Unicode
Dim uFname As udtAu_Fname
  For i = 1 To MAX_DATA
    uLname.uniAu_Lname(i) = 0
    uFname.uniAu_Fname(i) = 0
  Next i
  If Not Create_Connection() Then End
  szSqlStr = "SELECT au_fname, au_lname FROM authors " & _
     "WHERE au_id= '172-32-1176';" & Chr$(0)
'
' A little magic here. We'll define a Microsoft SQL
' Server specific ODBC connection option that will drop
```

```
' temporary stored procedures on the next SQLPrepare
' API reference or will drop all stored procedures
' when the statement is released.
'
Const SQL_USE_PROCEDURE_FOR_PREPARE = 1202
Const SQL_UP_ON_DROP = 2
  RetCode = BTPSQLSetConnectOption(hdbc, _
    SQL_USE_PROCEDURE_FOR_PREPARE, SQL_UP_ON_DROP)
  If RetCode <> SQL_SUCCESS Then Log_Error err_Pre, RetCode
  RetCode = BTPSQLPrepare(hstmt, szSqlStr, Len(szSqlStr))
  If RetCode <> SQL_SUCCESS Then Log_Error err_Pre, RetCode
  RetCode = BTPSQLExecute(hstmt)
  If RetCode <> SQL_SUCCESS Then Log_Error err_Eop, RetCode
  RetCode = BTPSQLBindCol(hstmt, 1, SQL_C_CHAR, _
     uFname.uniAu_Fname(0), MAX_DATA, uFname.cbAu_Fname)
  RetCode = BTPSQLBindCol(hstmt, 2, SQL_C_CHAR, _
    uLname.uniAu_Lname(0), MAX_DATA, uLname.cbAu_Lname)
  RetCode = BTPSQLFetch(hstmt)
  fname = BytesToStr(uFname.uniAu_Fname()) ' Unicode
  lname = BytesToStr(uLname.uniAu_Lname())
  MsgBox Mid$(fname, 1, uFname.cbAu_Fname) & " " & _
    Mid$(lname, 1, uLname.cbAu_Lname)
  RetCode = Release_Connection()
End Sub
```

SQLBindCol, SQLDescribeCol, and SQLNumResultCols

With this example we begin to see the power of ODBC. Listing 12-9 (**ODBC4** function) is a repeat of Listing 12-7 with additional complexity. This example issues a prepared SQL statement as a query against the *authors* table in the *Pubs* database on Microsoft SQL Server. The additional complexity is that the **ODBC4** function knows nothing about the incoming result set in terms of column names or column attributes. The issue is that the column attributes are determined at execution time; they are not embedded in the code. Everything is unknown to the application. **SQLNumResultCols** determines the number of columns in the result set. A loop is then executed, which calls the functions **SQLColAttributes, SQLDescribeCol,** and **SQLBindCol**. The code of this example is a model of an ODBC query. Rather than hard-coding column names, column sizes, and attributes, the application obtains the attributes from the incoming query and acts accordingly. This technique eases application maintenance. This approach doesn't necessarily make the application portable, but it doesn't prevent an application from being portable.

The code works fine, but there is a problem. The attributes should be cached at the start of the ODBC application. This example illustrates the technique of binding unknown columns. To do that, three User Data Type (UDT) arrays are required. The control array is aptly named name *UnicodeControl* while the other two structures are named *UnicodeFields* and *NonUnicodeFields* respectively. The only shortcoming of this approach is that every Unicode field is allocated the character storage space of the largest field. This is a Visual Basic limitation and a C++ implementation will be very clean. Listing 12-8 illustrates the control structures for managing Unicode when the field types are unknown. The example in Listing 12-9 is considerably more complex than the previous Unicode example in Listing 12-7. The techniques used in Listing 12-9 form the basis for the ODBC class example at the end of this chapter.

LISTING 12-8 Unicode control structures for unknown query fields

```
Private Type UnicodeControl
  FieldType As String * 1     ' "U" or "N"
  FieldIndex As Integer       ' relative index to either
                            ' UnicodeFields or NonUnicodeFields
End Type
Private Type UnicodeFields
  ByteArray(MAX_DATA) As Byte
  cbField As Long
  Result As String * MAX_DATA
  Name As String * MAX_DATA
  cbName As Integer
End Type
Private Type NonUnicodeFields
  cbField As Long
  Result As Variant
```

```
  Name As String * MAX_DATA
  cbName As Integer
End Type
```

The **ODBC4** function is described with these steps:

1. Call the function **Create_Connection** to establish all handles.
2. Construct a query against the *authors* table of the *Pubs* database asking for the columns *au_fname* and *au_lname*.
3. Use **SQLPrepare** to prepare the query identified by statement handle *hstmt* of the statement *szSqlStr* with length *cbSqlStr*.
4. Use **SQLExecute** to execute a prepared statement using the *hstmt* handle.
5. Use **SQLNumResultCols** to determine the number of result columns for the statement handle *hstmt*.
6. Loop on each column to determine the column type with **SQLDescribeCol** for statement handle *hstmt*.
7. Bind the column determined by the loop variable *iCol*.
8. Loop on all columns. There are only two in this simplified example.
9. Use **SQLFetch** to retrieve the data and display it.
10. Use the function **Release_Connection** to release all handles and the connection.

LISTING 12-9 Processing a Unicode SQL query with unknown query fields

```
Private Sub ODBC4()
'(C) 1999 Bruce T. Prendergast
' DBA Prendergast Consulting
' DBA PCS
' IDG Books Worldwide ISBN 0-7645-3314-2
'
' SQLBindCol, SQLDescribeCol, SQLNumResultsCol
'
Dim lUnicodeControl() As UnicodeControl
Dim lUnicodeFields() As UnicodeFields
Dim lNonUnicodeFields() As NonUnicodeFields
```

```
Dim UnicodeCount As Integer
Dim NonUnicodeCount As Integer
Dim cCol As Integer, s As String, i As Integer

Dim szColName As String * MAX_DATA
Dim pcbColName As Integer       ' Return name size
Dim pfSQLType As Integer        ' attribute of interest
Dim pcbColDef As Long           ' Data column precision
Dim pibScale As Integer         ' Output scale
Dim pfNullable As Integer       ' SQL_NO_NULLS, SQL_NULLABLE,
                                ' SQL_NULLABLE_UNKNOWN
Dim icol As Integer             ' Results column
Dim RetCode As Integer
Dim szSqlStr As String * 128    ' SQL query storage

  If Not Create_Connection() Then End
  szSqlStr = "SELECT au_fname, au_lname FROM authors;"
  RetCode = BTPSQLPrepare(hstmt, szSqlStr, Len(szSqlStr))
  If RetCode <> SQL_SUCCESS Then Log_Error err_Pre, RetCode
  RetCode = BTPSQLExecute(hstmt)
  If RetCode <> SQL_SUCCESS Then Log_Error err_Eop, RetCode
  RetCode = BTPSQLNumResultCols(hstmt, cCol)
  If RetCode <> SQL_SUCCESS Then Log_Error err_Nrc, RetCode
  ReDim lUnicodeControl(cCol)
'
' the next two lines are because REDIM  PRESERVE
' doesn't work in a loop
'
  ReDim Preserve lUnicodeFields(cCol)
  ReDim Preserve lNonUnicodeFields(cCol)
  For icol = 1 To cCol
  RetCode = BTPSQLDescribeCol(hstmt, icol, szColName, _
    MAX_DATA, pcbColName, pfSQLType, pcbColDef, pibScale, pfNullable)
  If pfSQLType = SQL_VARCHAR Then
    '
    '  Unicode binding
```

```
    '
    UnicodeCount = UnicodeCount + 1
    lUnicodeControl(icol).FieldIndex = UnicodeCount
    lUnicodeControl(icol).FieldType = "U"
' Bug Here!
'   ReDim Preserve lUnicodeFields(UnicodeCount)
    lUnicodeFields(UnicodeCount).Name = Mid$(szColName, 1, pcbColName)
    If pcbColName > MAX_DATA Then pcbColName = MAX_DATA
    If pcbColDef > MAX_DATA Then pcbColDef = MAX_DATA
    lUnicodeFields(UnicodeCount).cbName = pcbColName
    RetCode = BTPSQLBindCol(hstmt, icol, SQL_C_CHAR, _
     lUnicodeFields(UnicodeCount).ByteArray(0), _
     pcbColDef, lUnicodeFields(UnicodeCount).cbField)
  Else
    NonUnicodeCount = NonUnicodeCount + 1
    lUnicodeControl(icol).FieldIndex = NonUnicodeCount
    lUnicodeControl(icol).FieldType = "N"
' Bug Here!
'   ReDim Preserve lNonUnicodeFields(NonUnicodeCount)
    lNonUnicodeFields(NonUnicodeCount).Name = Mid$(szColName, 1, pcbColName)
    If pcbColName > MAX_DATA Then pcbColName = MAX_DATA
    lNonUnicodeFields(NonUnicodeCount).cbName = pcbColName
    RetCode = BTPSQLBindCol(hstmt, icol, pfSQLType, _
    lNonUnicodeFields(NonUnicodeCount).Result, pcbColDef, _
      lNonUnicodeFields(NonUnicodeCount).cbField)
  End If
  Next icol
  RetCode = BTPSQLFetch(hstmt)
  For icol = 1 To cCol
   If lUnicodeControl(icol).FieldType = "U" Then
     i = lUnicodeControl(icol).FieldIndex
     lUnicodeFields(i).Result = BytesToStr(lUnicodeFields(i).ByteArray())
    End If
  Next icol
  s = Mid$(lUnicodeFields(1).Result, 1, lUnicodeFields(1).cbField)
  s = s & " " & Mid$(lUnicodeFields(2).Result, 1, lUnicodeFields(2).cbField)
```

```
    MsgBox s
    RetCode = Release_Connection()
    Exit Sub
End Sub
```

SQLBindParameter, SQLPrepare, and SQLExecute

We've been binding output columns. The Listing 12-10 example (**ODBC5** function) is a change of pace where an input parameter is bound. I don't have an example of **SQLPutData**, nor do I want to publish one. The worst possible programming example is using the system interactively with **SQLPutData** and unbound input parameters. Numerous other users are locked out until the transaction completes, hence the need for bound parameters. The **SQLPutData** function has limited application, but like **SQLGetData**, it is useful for teaching ODBC concepts.

The **ODBC5** function is described with these steps:

1. Call the function **Create_Connection** to establish all handles.
2. Construct query against the *authors* table of the *Pubs* database asking for the columns *au_fname* and *au_lname*.
3. Use **SQLPrepare** to prepare the query identified by statement handle *hstmt* of the statement *szSqlStr* with length *cbSqlStr*.
4. Use **SQLBindParameter** to bind a parameter with *iPar* identifying the parameter number and setting *fParamType* to `SQL_PARAM_INPUT`.
5. Use **SQLExecute** to execute a prepared statement using the *hstmt* handle.
6. Use **SQLBindCol** to bind the first column of the statement identified by the handle *hstmt*.
7. Use **SQLFetch** to retrieve the data. Display the data after converting it to Unicode.
8. Use the function **Release_Connection** to release all handles and the connection.

LISTING 12-10 **Binding a parameter and returning a Unicode result set**

```
 Private Sub ODBC5()
'(C) 1999 Bruce T. Prendergast
' DBA Prendergast Consulting
' DBA PCS
' IDG BooksWorldwide ISBN 0-7645-3314-2
'
'   Listing 12-10 SQLBindParameter, SQLPrepare, SQLExecute
'
Dim uLname As udtAu_Lname         ' UDT for Unicode
Dim uFname As udtAu_Fname
Dim lname As String               ' storage for last name
Dim fname As String               ' storage for first name
Dim RetCode As Integer
Dim szSqlStr As String * 128      ' SQL query storage

  If Not Create_Connection() Then End
  szSqlStr = "SELECT au_fname, au_lname FROM authors WHERE au_id = ?;"
  RetCode = BTPSQLPrepare(hstmt, szSqlStr, Len(szSqlStr))
  If RetCode <> SQL_SUCCESS Then Log_Error err_Pre, RetCode
  RetCode = BTPSQLBindParameter(hstmt, 1, SQL_PARAM_INPUT, _
    SQL_C_CHAR, SQL_VARCHAR, MAX_DATA, 0, "172-32-1176", _
    MAX_DATA, Len("172-32-1176"))
  If RetCode <> SQL_SUCCESS Then Log_Error err_Par, RetCode
  RetCode = BTPSQLExecute(hstmt)
  If RetCode <> SQL_SUCCESS Then Log_Error err_Eop, RetCode
  RetCode = BTPSQLBindCol(hstmt, 1, SQL_C_CHAR, _
    uFname.uniAu_Fname(0), MAX_DATA, uFname.cbAu_Fname)
  RetCode = BTPSQLBindCol(hstmt, 2, SQL_C_CHAR, _
    uLname.uniAu_Lname(0), MAX_DATA, uLname.cbAu_Lname)
  RetCode = BTPSQLFetch(hstmt)
  fname = BytesToStr(uFname.uniAu_Fname()) ' Unicode
  lname = BytesToStr(uLname.uniAu_Lname())
  MsgBox Mid$(fname, 1, uFname.cbAu_Fname) & " " & _
    Mid$(lname, 1, uLname.cbAu_Lname)
  RetCode = Release_Connection()
  Exit Sub
End Sub
```

SQLSetConnectOption, SQLRowCount, and SQLTransact

The complexity goes up a bit more with Listing 12-11 (**ODBC6** function) where a transaction is managed. **SQLSetConnectOption** changes the `AUTOCOMMIT` option. This function is deprecated in ODBC 3.0 and the equivalent ODBC 3.0 function is **SQLSetConnectAttr**.

The example demonstrates a searched update. The `UPDATE` and `WHERE` keywords in the SQL statement identify a positioned update statement. I did the initial testing with a search value I knew existed and then changed it to an unknown value after the code fragment worked. This is artificial, but I'm only creating an example.

Note that there are both input and output parameters in the SQL statement. This is really not a good design, and care must be taken not to mix processing of the different parameter types. It is not a good programming practice to combine input and output parameter binding in the same module. The probability of an error is very high. It's a terrible design, but let's move on and just remember to keep input parameter-binding separate from output parameter-binding. They can be confused very easily.

The **ODBC6** function is described with these steps:

1. Call the function **Create_Connection** to establish all handles.
2. Use **SQLSetConnectOption** to set the transaction to `AUTOCOMMIT`. The connection parameter is identified by *fOption,* which is set to `SQL_AUTOMMIT`. The value to set this connection option, `SQL_AUTOCOMMIT_ON`, is in parameter *vParam*.
3. Construct an action query to change the column *au_lname* against the *authors* table of the *Pubs* database.
4. Use **SQLPrepare** to prepare the query identified by statement handle *hstmt* of the statement *szSqlStr* with length *cbSqlStr*. This statement has two input parameters.
5. Use **SQLNumParams** to verify the number of parameters for statement handle *hstmt*.
6. Bind both input parameters using **SQLBindParameter** for the statement handle *hstmt*. Note that the second input parameter has bogus data and the WHERE selection will fail.

7. Use **SQLExecute** to execute a prepared statement the *hstmt* handle.
8. This is an action query, so use **SQLRowCount** to determine the row count for statement handle *hstmt*.
9. The query will fail, as we know it should. Set the transaction parameter *fType* to the value `SQL_ROLLBACK` and use **SQLTransact** to rollback the transaction.
10. Use the function **Release_Connection** to release all handles and the connection.

LISTING 12-11 An ODBC transaction with erroneous data

```
Private Sub ODBC6()
'(C) 1999 Bruce T. Prendergast
' DBA Prendergast Consulting
' DBA PCS
' IDG BooksWorldwide ISBN 0-7645-3314-2
'
' Listing 12-11 SQLSetConnectOption, SQLRowCount,
' SQLNumParams, SQLTransact, SQLPrepare, SQLExecute
'
Dim pcPar As Integer          ' returned parameter count
Dim pcRow As Long             ' returned row count
Dim RetCode As Integer
Dim szSqlStr As String * 128  ' SQL query storage

  If Not Create_Connection() Then End
  RetCode = BTPSQLSetConnectOption(hdbc, SQL_AUTOCOMMIT, SQL_AUTOCOMMIT_ON)
  If RetCode <> SQL_SUCCESS Then Log_Error err_Sco, RetCode
  szSqlStr = "UPDATE authors SET au_fname = ? WHERE au_lname = ?;"
  RetCode = BTPSQLPrepare(hstmt, szSqlStr, Len(szSqlStr))
  If RetCode <> SQL_SUCCESS Then Log_Error err_Pre, RetCode
  RetCode = BTPSQLNumParams(hstmt, pcPar)
  If (RetCode <> SQL_SUCCESS) Or (pcPar <> 2) Then Log_Error err_Npr, RetCode
  RetCode = BTPSQLBindParameter(hstmt, 1, SQL_PARAM_INPUT, _
    SQL_C_CHAR, SQL_VARCHAR, MAX_DATA, 0, "John", MAX_DATA, Len("John"))
  If RetCode <> SQL_SUCCESS Then Log_Error err_Par, RetCode
```

```
    RetCode = BTPSQLBindParameter(hstmt, 2, SQL_PARAM_INPUT, _
      SQL_C_CHAR, SQL_VARCHAR, MAX_DATA, 0, "Whitey", MAX_DATA, Len("Whitey"))
    If RetCode <> SQL_SUCCESS Then Log_Error err_Par, RetCode
    RetCode = BTPSQLExecute(hstmt)
    If RetCode <> SQL_SUCCESS Then Log_Error err_Eop, RetCode
    RetCode = BTPSQLRowCount(hstmt, pcRow)
    If pcRow <> 1 Then
    RetCode = BTPSQLTransact(henv, hdbc, SQL_ROLLBACK)
      MsgBox "Transaction rolled back. " & _
        "Row count was: " & Str$(pcRow)
    Else
      RetCode = BTPSQLTransact(henv, hdbc, SQL_COMMIT)
      MsgBox "Transaction committed"
    End If
    RetCode = Release_Connection()
    Exit Sub
  End Sub
```

Let's catch our breath and review our examples:

- **Listing 12-3:** A model for establishing an ODBC connection.
- **Listing 12-4:** A model for releasing all resources and the connection.
- **Listing 12-5:** A very simple query on unbound columns using **SQLExecDirect, SQLFetch,** and **SQLGetData**. The code is too simplistic to be useful.
- **Listing 12-6:** This example determines the data source parameters and ODBC driver parameters at execution time. Very useful for a heterogeneous application, but quite often not needed for ODBC application written for a specific data source.
- **Listing 12-7:** Using a prepared SQL statement (this assumes the statement will be used more than once), and bind output columns. This is an escalation step and this example knows a priori what values are in what column. For example, the column *au_fname* is in the first field position in the query (the query is built locally), and the binding process takes advantage of this fact.
- **Listing 12-8:** User defined types used for Unicode processing.

- **Listing 12-9:** Column counts, column names, and attributes are unknown to the application. **SQLBindCol, SQLDescribeCol,** and **SQLNumResultsCols** retrieve the necessary information from the incoming result set. This doesn't guarantee that an application will be portable, but using the programming technique doesn't stop the application from being portable. It should be a model for all ODBC developers so that dependencies are not built into the code.
- **Listing 12-10:** This example illustrates the concept of binding input parameters. The reader is cautioned against using **SQLPutData** with unbound data, because the data source will stop with a lock on a table until the user answers the prompt and supplies the data. At best, you slow the system down; at worst, you stop the system until you have supplied the data.
- **Listing 12-11:** The last example illustrates an ODBC transaction. Incorrect data is presented in the transaction and when **SQLRowCount** returns the incorrect row count, the transaction is rolled back.

ODBC Tarpits

In the discussion that follows, I assume you, the reader, have some SQL knowledge, because a requirement for successful ODBC programming is a working knowledge of SQL. (See Chapter 18 for a more complete discussion of SQL.)

Performance is always an issue when data is shipped over the wire. This section is an enumeration of ODBC performance issues where some of the issues are common sense. A mechanical facility with ODBC API functions is not necessarily a guarantee of successful ODBC application. The successful ODBC programmer understands the characteristics and idiosyncrasies of the target data source, has a keen understanding of the problem at hand, and has the ability to recognize when programming tasks should be delegated.

A Division of Labor

You should always conduct a careful assessment of the architecture before you begin ODBC coding. Even though all tasks may be performed at the client site, there are certainly some intermediate steps that should be performed at the server. Stored procedures at the server always improve the performance of a client server application. A well-crafted ODBC application solution is not always a monolithic application program. It is architecture with the sharing of responsibilities.

A Procedural Solution

The greatest risk is in believing a good ODBC solution exists when in fact one doesn't. As stated previously, writing ODBC calls is a very straightforward process. The problem is that ODBC is only the messenger and the real issue is the use of ODBC, not the ODBC code itself. The specific problem is writing procedural code in a loop.

Procedural code that processes individual rows is not efficient. SQL deals with sets. If the client requires a browse capability, an optional solution is to download result sets to the client and browse the data locally. Replace code loops with SQL statements. **SQLGetData** in a loop is an example of a procedural solution. The proper solution is either column-wise binding or row-wise binding and using **SQLFetchScroll** to retrieve a complete rowset result set rather than a single-row result set.

Bookmarks

Bookmarks are off by default. Turn unneeded bookmarks off in ODBC 2.0 with **SQLSetStmtOption** and in ODBC 3.0 with **SQLSetStmtAttr**.

Buffers

Always allocate a large enough *buffer*. A diagnostic record is created every time a record is truncated. This can be a major performance issue. An error message is created for each truncated row. Always allocate enough buffer space and avoid truncation.

Comparing Columns

The goal of any SQL query is to retrieve data. The goal of the developer is to construct a query that is search-limited. A search-limited query always compares a column value to a constant and will not scan the complete table. The constant allows the SQL engine to use index tables and limit the query. A query that is not search-limited, by definition performs a complete table scan. This is a major performance issue when the table has millions of rows. Comparing different columns in the same table is never search-limited, and is always a table scan. The query breaks the search-limited rule of not comparing a column with a constant. The problem is easily understood when you understand that each row must be read *before* it can be considered for inclusion in the result set.

Data Source Catalog

The ODBC application is probably not the only client of Microsoft SQL Server. The SQL server system control tables must be queried for catalog information. This operation is expensive, involves complex queries on the server with many joins, and may impact other users. The data comes from dynamic catalog functions such as **SQLTables, SQLColumns,** and **SQLPrimaryKeys**. A wise choice is to cache the information when the application starts. The same caching rule also applies to the static catalog functions such as **SQLGetTypeInfo**.

Expressions in a SQL Query

The expression `sales * 12 > 48000` is not search-limited because the column must be retrieved and the calculation performed before the comparison is made. Combining constants results in the expression `sales > 4000`, which is search-limited.

Limiting A Result Set

Common sense says don't pull any more data down the wire than is absolutely necessary. This applies to both unneeded rows and columns. This issue is also one of addressing scalability. Large result sets can be inappropriate for a list box. Data limiting doesn't apply only to query requests. It also applies to information functions such as **SQLTables,** which can return thousands of rows.

List Boxes

Care must be exercised when designing the application form. A query is required for each list box and this can make the form startup time prohibitive. Limit the number of list boxes on the application form.

Managing a BLOB

A BLOB is a binary large object that can be either binary or character data. The data isn't returned in a result set for a BLOB when the bound control for the BLOB is hidden. A BLOB should only be loaded when requested by the user.

Mixed Mode Expressions

Search limiting cannot be done with *Nulls*. A column that allows Nulls is changed from the CHAR type to the VARCHAR type by Microsoft SQL Server at column-definition time. Consequently, any query looking at that column results in a mixed mode expression (CHAR compared with VARCHAR) and the resulting query is not search-limited. A mixed mode expression is a form of expression calculation, which by definition is not search-limited.

An integer column with nulls and an integer column without nulls are not considered different data types. A column that the developer declares as CHAR and allows Nulls is changed by SQL Server to VARCHAR. SQL Server does not change the data type of an integer column when nulls are allowed. This means that an expression that involves columns of integer data that allow nulls is not considered a mixed mode expression.

Output Data Binding

Data from an unbound column can be obtained directly by calling **SQLGetData**. The preferable alternative is to use **SQLBindCol,** which binds a program variable to the column. The same choices exist here that exist for preparing a SQL statement. **SQLGetData** is an acceptable approach for a single value of data retrieved once. **SQLBindCol** is only done once for each output column of the query.

These are nice words, but it is somewhat idealistic to say that all columns should be bound. The Microsoft implementation of ODBC is C/C++ based. This means that column binding must be a mapping from a SQL data type to a C data type. C does not have an equivalent data type for the SQL data type VARCHAR, which means you cannot bind a VARCHAR column. The compromise is to create a variable length string and initialize it to a zero value and then declare it as a `SQL_C_CHAR` data type.

The other binding issue is Unicode, which has no C data type mapping. Characters are no longer 8-bit, but are now 16-bits. Characters and bytes are no longer synonymous. Any Microsoft-based application that uses Visual Basic for Applications is at risk when using character input/output (I/O).

Preparing a SQL Statement

SQL statements can be executed directly with the **SQLExecDirect** statement or the query can be prepared (compiled) with **SQLPrepare** and executed with **SQLExecute**. A query plan is created when a SQL statement is prepared. The **SQLExecute** statement lets the same statement be reused without compiling a new query plan. **SQLExecDirect** can be used for single statement execution; however, the use of **SQLPrepare** and **SQLExecute** is preferred when statement execution is repeated.

Primary Keys

Always bind the primary key column. This keeps rows in a result set unique when using a cursor.

Recombining Strings

Data that is returned to the application, as null-terminated strings must have the termination character stripped before the strings are recombined. The application program using string operators or functions normally performs this task.

Record Length

Buffer length is different than record length. The record length reflects the original record size even if truncation has occurred. Don't blindly use the record length. Compare the record length against the buffer length before using it. The problem is that although no data is lost because the query can be reissued, each truncated record does result in an error message. This can dramatically affect network bandwidth.

Search Limited

Microsoft SQL Server uses a cost based optimizer for query optimization. Within this context there are only two types of queries: those that are search-limited and those that are not. A query which is not search-limited will always do a table scan, which is usually the least desirable scenario. This is not always true because a table scan may be more efficient when the query selectivity is low. A table scan will occur when an index doesn't exist on the column of interest or the index on the column is not useful. A search-limited query uses an inclusion operator to compare a column in a table with a constant. The general syntax for such an expression is:

```
<column> <inclusion operator> <constant> [ AND ... ]
```

Some examples are:

```
fname = 'Bruce'
lname= 'Prendergast'
title='wannabe author'
fname = 'Bruce' AND lname = 'Prendergast'
salary < 10000
```

<, >, =, `BETWEEN`, and `LIKE` are the inclusion operators. All columns of a search-limited expression must be in the same table. `BETWEEN` is really not an inclusion operator for a search argument. It is converted in the optimizer parsing phase to two search arguments using the operators > and < joined by the `AND`.

`LIKE` is a qualified inclusion operator in that `LIKE <character string>%` is search-limited while `LIKE %<character string>` is not search-limited.

Nonsearch arguments are those operators that force more than one scan of the target table. The operators `NOT`, `NOT IN ()`, `!=`, and `<>` are not search-limited arguments. To find members that are not in a result set, the SQL engine must first find those elements that are members of the original set. The `NOT IN` members are those members not contained in the original set. This process requires two table scans.

It is possible to convert some nonsearch argument operators. The expression `<column> <> 0` can be converted to `<column> > 0` if the number is positive.

Expressions with the `OR` operator are not search-limited because the `OR` operator is the union of two distinct queries. By definition the operator <> is not search-limited. Converting the original expression to an expression of the form `column > 0 OR column < 0` is still not search-limited because the expression uses the `OR` operator.

SQLFetchScroll

There are always two ways to perform a task — a wrong way and a right way and the issue is the choice of cursors. Block cursors are the ultimate in performance when rows and columns are bound directly into arrays. This is closely approximated by the **GetRows** method of Remote Data Objects (RDO), which is a thin ODBC wrapper. The secondary issue of cursors is the user requirements. The ODBC driver must support the Level 2 API conformance level for scrollable cursors. When the ODBC driver does not support the Level 2 API conformance level, the developer must either supply the missing cursor functionality or deprecate the user requirements.

Key Point Summary

Several key issues were discussed in this chapter. The first was that the order in which the ODBC functions are used must be understood for a successful ODBC application. Recall that ODBC uses a call-level interface (CLI) and does not use object models.

The second major issue was to understand that a client-server application using ODBC forms an interaction model. Without other users, there are no problems. The ODBC interaction model is controlled by the transaction isolation levels set by other applications with open transactions. Of course, this is not an issue when there is no common table or row. Let's imagine a fun scenario:

The Vice President of Finance is scrolling the yearly profit and loss statement while another task is posting year-end information. The data includes a detail line item where XYZ Corporation made a $1,000,000 sale. This gives the company a small profit for the year. The Vice President captures this information because the transaction is open and the transaction isolation level is set to **read uncommitted** (dirty read).

The transaction is rolled back because the XYZ Corporation $1,000,000 entry is an error. The transaction is rerun with corrected input and the company now has a loss for the year. The Vice President of Finance still has the report showing the small company profit. He presents it to the CEO and....

Microsoft Access is not a DBMS because it does not support the **durability** property of a transaction. Microsoft Access does not fully support transaction isolation levels, another reason for never using Access as a server.

The other key issue for the developer is to understand which ACID properties of a transaction are supported by the target DBMS. Without proper ACID property support for transactions, the developer must provide a scenario for contingencies. The ACID properties of Microsoft Access can be managed by using replication to more that one site. Another plan of action is to backup the Access database before applying the transactions, and then applying the transaction in single-user mode.

These are the important points of this chapter. ODBC 3.0 includes new performance enhancements and many of the ODBC 2.0/2.5 functions are deprecated. Some functions are not deprecated, but function differently. **SQLFetch** is such an example and now returns a rowset from the results set, while **SQLFetch** in ODBC 2.0/2.5 only returned a single row from a results set. You'll want to carefully review your ODBC 2.0/2.5 application before upgrading to ODBC 3.0. Important ODBC 3.0 features are listed below.

- ODBC function statements must be issued in the proper order. A state transition error occurs when statements are issued in the wrong order.
- Three handles control ODBC: the environment handle, the connection handle, and the statement handle.
- Each handle has three states: unallocated, allocated, and connected.
- Block cursors are the default in ODBC 3.0
- ODBC 3.0 is enhanced with cursor offsets. This means that every row need not be bound. This feature is not available in ODBC 2.0
- ODBC 3.0 supports SQL 92. Autocommit transactions are the default.
- ODBC 3.0 has four new descriptors that are allocated automatically by ODBC 3.0. They are the Application Parameter Descriptor (APD), Implementation (Driver) Parameter Descriptor (IPD), Application Row Descriptor (ARD), and Implementation (Driver) Row Descriptor (IRD).
- ODBC supports a cursor library for those drivers that are Level 1 compliant.
- A transaction rolls back all open transactions for the particular environment.

Applying What You've Learned

The questions below are quite comprehensive. If you know the answers and understand the issues, then you are well on your way to becoming a competent and proficient ODBC developer. The answers to these questions are useful for the Windows Architecture I examination.

Instant Assessment

1. Explain the concept of a search-limited expression. Give several examples of search limited expressions.
2. What is the fastest processing technique for a single SQL statement? What is the fastest processing technique for repeated statements?
3. Explain why a SQL query with the `NOT IN` operator is not search-limited.
4. What is the problem with calculations in a query expression?
5. What is unique about a SQL expression containing an `OR` clause?
6. What advantage does preparing a SQL statement offer?
7. What is a state transition error?
8. What is a fat cursor?
9. What is the unique characteristic of a static cursor?
10. Explain the operating principles of a dynamic cursor.
11. What are the limitations of a keyset-driven cursor?
12. Name a limitation of the Microsoft implementation of ODBC in C/C++.
13. What important function must be performed after an environment handle is allocated?
14. Describe the differences between the ODBC 2.*x* **SQLFetch** and the ODBC 3.0 **SQLFetch**.
15. Name a new and very useful connection attribute that enhances performance.
16. Describe long data and how to process it.
17. **SQLGetData** has a unique property. What is it?
18. What new binding feature is not supported in ODBC 2.0? Is it a performance issue?

19. What is a catalog function?
20. Name the catalog functions.
21. When is **SQLDescribeCols** used?
22. When is the ODBC API function **SQLEndTran** used?
23. What happens to a SQL statement that the ODBC driver cannot translate?
24. What is the scope of a transaction?
25. Describe using the API function **SQLExecute**.
26. What is the default transaction mode for ODBC?
27. What determines cursor behavior for commit or rollback operations?
28. When is a cursor closed automatically?
29. Describe a performance issue with manual commit transactions.
30. Compare optimistic concurrency with pessimistic concurrency.
31. Describe ODBC cursor library support.

Lab Exercise

Lab 12.32 is our first example of a tiered architecture. We'll use the techniques developed in Listing 12-9 of this chapter to create an ODBC class and this ODBC class will be used later in the book when we meet Microsoft Transaction Server (MTS).

This lab will draw on software concepts used in legacy software, which is the concept of a *driver class*. A driver class is not a Microsoft invention, but a code implementation technique used in operating systems. Digital Equipment Corporation introduced the concept of a class driver in the mid-1980s, with the purpose of creating software layers for hardware device management. This example uses the same basic structure. The **frmODBC** form starts by instantiating the **ClassDriver** class. The **ClassDriver** class in turn instantiates the **ODBCClass** to retrieve the data from the **Pubs** database of Microsoft SQL Server. The **ClassDriver** class then instantiates both the **DataClass** class and the **DataClassCollection** class. The **ClassDriver** class builds the returned data as a **DataClassCollection** class, which is a private collection of the **DataClass** class. Control returns to the main form and the **Fill** method of the **DriverClass** class fills the combo box. The **GetOne** method of the **DriverClass** retrieves data based on the combo box selection.

Lab 12.32 *Creating an ODBC class*

I apologize that this lab is not simpler, however, this is a minimal working tiered architecture. Technically speaking, there are four tiers. The form occupies the top tier, the **ClassDriver** class is the second tier and so on. Brevity dictates minimal error handling, that is, the errors are checked but the errors are not processed. We'll recreate this lab later in the book in the Remote Data Objects (RDO) and Active Data Objects (ADO) chapters where we'll replace the **ODBCClass** class with either the **RDOClass** or the **ADOClass** class. The other classes will remain unchanged except for one source line in the **ClassDriver** class. Normally, I ask the reader to construct a lab, however, this lab is an exception because of the size. To run this application, open the `ODBC.VBP` project in the Chapter 12 [12?]folder of the CD-ROM that accompanies this book. You'll need Microsoft Visual Basic 5.0 or 6.0 and Microsoft SQL Server 6.5. Once the project is open in the Visual Basic Integrated Development Environment (IDE), you'll want to select: PROJECT ➪ ODBC Properties and change the startup form to *frmLab*. You'll also want to change the Microsoft SQL Server 6.5 connection parameters in the **Class_ Initialize** event of the **ODBCClass** class. Let's start with the code for the main form, which is illustrated in Listing 12-12. The application consists of a combo box and two text boxes. The combo box is filled with the *au_id* column of the Pubs database of Microsoft SQL server. The form code is a model of simplicity.

LISTING 12-12 The VBA code of the Visual Basic frmLab form

```
'(C) 1999 Bruce T. Prendergast
' DBA Prendergast Consulting
' DBA PCS
' IDG Books Worldwide ISBN 0-7645-3314-2
'
' ODBC form for data class, class driver, collection
'
Option Explicit

Private lClassDriver As New ClassDriver
Private lDataClass As DataClass
Private lDataClassCollection As DataClassCollection

Private Sub cmbAU_ID_Click()
```

```
  lClassDriver.GetOne [cmbAU_ID], txtAu_fname, txtAu_lname
End Sub
Private Sub Form_Load()
  lClassDriver.RunQuery _
    "SELECT au_id, au_fname, au_lname FROM authors;" & Chr$(0)
  If lClassDriver.Status Then
    lClassDriver.Fill cmbAU_ID
  Else
    MsgBox "SQL Server is not available"
  End If
  Exit Sub
End Sub
```

Let's move on to the **ClassDriver** class, which is illustrated in Listing 12-13. The **RunQuery** method of this class has some interesting code. The data is returned as a long string from the **ODBCClass** class with each field separated by a pipe character. This is done so that the **ODBCClass** class appears to have a generic interface. You'll learn more about this technique in Chapter 21 where we discuss Distributed COM (DCOM). The **ODBCClass** class consists of these properties and one method:

- **ODBCQuery** — The only method which submits the supplied query string to Microsoft SQL Server.
- **Response** — The piped results property. Rows are separated by two pipe characters.
- **Preamble** — Field type specifications are returned in this piped string.
- **Status** — A simple status return.

LISTING 12-13 The ClassDriver class of the frmLab application

```
'(C) 1999 Bruce T. Prendergast
' DBA Prendergast Consulting
' DBA PCS
' IDG Books Worldwide ISBN 0-7645-3314-2
'
' ClassDriver
'
```

```
Option Explicit
Dim lODBCClass As ODBCClass
Dim lDataClass As New DataClass
Private mvarStatus As Variant
Private Sub Class_Terminate()
  Set lODBCClass = Nothing
End Sub
Public Sub Fill(obj As ComboBox)
Dim id As DataClass
  For Each id In lDataClass.DataClassCollection
    obj.AddItem id.au_id
  Next id
  obj.ListIndex = -1
End Sub
Public Sub GetOne(ByVal inp As String, txt1 As TextBox, txt2 As TextBox)
Dim id As DataClass
  Set id = lDataClass.DataClassCollection(inp)
  txt1 = id.au_fname
  txt2 = id.au_lname
  Exit Sub
End Sub
Public Sub RunQuery(ByVal QueryString As String)
Dim i As Integer, j As Integer
Dim auid As String, aufname As String, aulname As String
Dim Results As Variant
Dim ColumnCount As Integer
  Set lODBCClass = New ODBCClass
  lODBCClass.ODBCQuery QueryString
  mvarStatus = lODBCClass.Status
  If lODBCClass.Status Then
    Results = lODBCClass.Response
    j = UBound(Results)
    ColumnCount = Results(1)
    If Results(2) > 2 Then
      For i = 3 To j Step ColumnCount
        auid = Results(i)
```

```
        aufname = Results(i + 1)
        aulname = Results(i + 2)
        lDataClass.DataClassCollection.Add auid, aufname, aulname, auid
      Next i
    End If
  End If
  Exit Sub
End Sub
Public Property Get Status() As Variant
  Status = mvarStatus
End Property
```

The next element of our tiered application is the **DataClass** class, which is a very lazy class since it delegates its work to the **DataCollectionClass** class. Listing 12-14 illustrates the **DataClass** class that was created with the Class Wizard and then tailored.

LISTING 12-14 **The DataClass class of the frmLab application**

```
'(C) 1999 Bruce T. Prendergast
' DBA Prendergast Consulting
' DBA PCS
' IDG Books Worldwide ISBN 0-7645-3314-2
'
' DataClass
'
Option Explicit
Private mvarau_fname As Variant
Private mvarau_lname As Variant
Private mvarau_id As Variant
Private mvarDataClassCollection As DataClassCollection
Public Property Get DataClassCollection() As DataClassCollection
  If mvarDataClassCollection Is Nothing Then
    Set mvarDataClassCollection = New DataClassCollection
  End If
  Set DataClassCollection = mvarDataClassCollection
End Property
Public Property Set DataClassCollection(vData As DataClassCollection)
```

```
  Set mvarDataClassCollection = vData
End Property
Private Sub Class_Terminate()
  Set mvarDataClassCollection = Nothing
End Sub
Public Property Let au_lname(ByVal vData As Variant)
  mvarau_lname = vData
End Property
Public Property Set au_lname(ByVal vData As Object)
  Set mvarau_lname = vData
End Property
Public Property Get au_lname() As Variant
  au_lname = mvarau_lname
End Property
Public Property Let au_id(ByVal vData As Variant)
  mvarau_id = vData
End Property
Public Property Set au_id(ByVal vData As Object)
  Set mvarau_id = vData
End Property
Public Property Get au_id() As Variant
  au_id = mvarau_id
End Property
Public Property Let au_fname(ByVal vData As Variant)
  mvarau_fname = vData
End Property
Public Property Set au_fname(ByVal vData As Object)
  Set mvarau_fname = vData
End Property
Public Property Get au_fname() As Variant
  au_fname = mvarau_fname
End Property
```

We've still got two more classes. The next class in our tiered component application is the **DataCollectionClass** class, which is illustrated in Listing 12-15. This class is a private collection of the **DataClass** class. Note the use of the **IUnknown** interface in the **NewEnum** method of this class. Those chapters on

COM were not in vain. The **DataCollectionClass** class was built with the Visual Basic Class Wizard and the resulting edited code is illustrated in Listing 12-15.

LISTING 12-15 The DataCollection Class class of the frmLab application

```
'(C) 1999 Bruce T. Prendergast
' DBA Prendergast Consulting
' DBA PCS
' IDG Books Worldwide ISBN 0-7645-3314-2
'
' DataClassCollection
'
Option Explicit
Private mCol As Collection
Public Function Add(auid As Variant, aufname As Variant, _
  aulname As Variant, sKey As String) As DataClass
Dim objNewMember As DataClass
  Set objNewMember = New DataClass
  objNewMember.au_fname = aufname
  objNewMember.au_lname = aulname
  objNewMember.au_id = auid
  mCol.Add objNewMember, sKey
  Set Add = objNewMember
  Set objNewMember = Nothing
End Function
Public Property Get Item(vntIndexKey As Variant) As DataClass
  Set Item = mCol(vntIndexKey)
End Property
Public Property Get Count() As Long
  Count = mCol.Count
End Property
Public Sub Remove(vntIndexKey As Variant)
  mCol.Remove vntIndexKey
End Sub
Public Property Get NewEnum() As IUnknown
  Set NewEnum = mCol.[_NewEnum]
End Property
```

```
Private Sub Class_Initialize()
  Set mCol = New Collection
End Sub
Private Sub Class_Terminate()
  Set mCol = Nothing
End Sub
```

The last component in our tiered application is the **ODBCClass** class. Note that a connection is established in the **Initialize_Class** event and the connection is dropped in the **Terminate_Class** event. This design is in anticipation of this class being eventually used within Microsoft Transaction Server (MTS), which pools connections. When MTS will not be an element of the solution, an alternative architecture is to create the handles in the class driver and pass them to the **ODBCClass** class. The **Initialize_Class** and **Terminate_Class** of the **ClassDriver** class now have the responsibility of maintaining the connection.

A nice feature of the **ODBCClass** class is the ability to process an arbitrary number of columns. The basic design is to use the **Redim Preserve** statement in a loop on the columns and acquire the UDT structures as necessary. Unfortunately Visual Basic apparently has a bug with **Redim Preserve** and UDT structures, which is noted in the comments of Listing 12-16.

LISTING 12-16 **The ODBCClass class of the frmLab application**

```
'(C) 1999 Bruce T. Prendergast
' DBA Prendergast Consulting
' DBA PCS
' IDG Books Worldwide ISBN 0-7645-3314-2
'
' ODBC Class method example
'
' Declaration section
'
Option Explicit
Dim hdbc As Long              ' connection handle
Dim henv As Long              ' environment handle
Dim hstmt As Long             ' statement handle
```

```
Private mvarResponse As Variant
Private mvarStatus As Variant
Private mvarPreamble As Variant
Private Type UnicodeControl
  FieldType As String * 1 ' "U" or "N"
  FieldIndex As Integer   ' relative index to either
                          ' UnicodeFields or NonUnicodeFields
End Type
Private Type UnicodeFields
  ByteArray(MAX_DATA) As Byte
  cbField As Long
  Result As String * MAX_DATA
  Name As String * MAX_DATA
  cbName As Integer
End Type
Private Type NonUnicodeFields
  cbField As Long
  Result As Variant
  Name As String * MAX_DATA
  cbName As Integer
End Type
Public Property Get Preamble() As Variant
  Preamble = mvarPreamble
End Property

Public Sub ODBCQuery(ByVal QueryString As String)
'(C) 1999 Bruce T. Prendergast
' DBA Prendergast Consulting
' DBA PCS
' IDG Books Worldwide ISBN 0-7645-3314-2
'
' ODBC Class method example
'
Dim lUnicodeControl() As UnicodeControl
Dim lUnicodeFields() As UnicodeFields
Dim lNonUnicodeFields() As NonUnicodeFields
```

```
Dim UnicodeCount As Integer
Dim NonUnicodeCount As Integer
Dim cCol As Integer, s As String, i As Integer
Dim Results() As Variant      ' Result set
Dim ResultCount As Integer     ' aggregate column count
Dim szColName As String * MAX_DATA
Dim pcbColName As Integer      ' Return name size
Dim pfSQLType As Integer       ' attribute of interest
Dim pcbColDef As Long          ' Data column precision
Dim pibScale As Integer        ' Output scale
Dim pfNullable As Integer      ' SQL_NO_NULLS, SQL_NULLABLE,
                               ' SQL_NULLABLE_UNKNOWN
Dim icol As Integer            ' Results column
Dim RetCode As Integer
Dim szSqlStr As String * 128
'
' set default status and NULL response
'
  mvarStatus = False
  mvarResponse = ""
  szSqlStr = QueryString & Chr$(0)
  If QueryString = "" Then Stop
  RetCode = BTPSQLPrepare(hstmt, szSqlStr, Len(szSqlStr))
  If RetCode <> SQL_SUCCESS Then Stop
  RetCode = BTPSQLExecute(hstmt)
  If RetCode <> SQL_SUCCESS Then Stop
  RetCode = BTPSQLNumResultCols(hstmt, cCol)
  If RetCode <> SQL_SUCCESS Then Stop
  ReDim lUnicodeControl(cCol)
'
' the next two lines are because REDIM PRESERVE
' doesn't work in a loop
'
  ReDim Preserve lUnicodeFields(cCol)
  ReDim Preserve lNonUnicodeFields(cCol)
  For icol = 1 To cCol
```

```
  RetCode = BTPSQLDescribeCol(hstmt, icol, szColName, _
    MAX_DATA, pcbColName, pfSQLType, pcbColDef, pibScale, pfNullable)
  mvarPreamble = mvarPreamble & Mid$(szColName, 1, pcbColName) & "|"
  If pfSQLType = SQL_VARCHAR Then
  '
  '  Unicode binding
  '
    UnicodeCount = UnicodeCount + 1
    lUnicodeControl(icol).FieldIndex = UnicodeCount
    lUnicodeControl(icol).FieldType = "U"
  ' Bug Here!
  ' ReDim Preserve lUnicodeFields(UnicodeCount)
    lUnicodeFields(UnicodeCount).Name = Mid$(szColName, 1, pcbColName)
    If pcbColName > MAX_DATA Then pcbColName = MAX_DATA
    If pcbColDef + 1 > MAX_DATA Then pcbColDef = MAX_DATA - 1
    lUnicodeFields(UnicodeCount).cbName = pcbColName
    RetCode = BTPSQLBindCol(hstmt, icol, SQL_C_CHAR, _
    lUnicodeFields(UnicodeCount).ByteArray(0), _
    pcbColDef + 1, lUnicodeFields(UnicodeCount).cbField)
  Else
    NonUnicodeCount = NonUnicodeCount + 1
    lUnicodeControl(icol).FieldIndex = NonUnicodeCount
    lUnicodeControl(icol).FieldType = "N"
  ' Bug Here!
  ' ReDim Preserve lNonUnicodeFields(NonUnicodeCount)
    lNonUnicodeFields(NonUnicodeCount).Name = _
      Mid$(szColName, 1, pcbColName)
    If pcbColName > MAX_DATA Then pcbColName = MAX_DATA
    lNonUnicodeFields(NonUnicodeCount).cbName = pcbColName
    RetCode = BTPSQLBindCol(hstmt, icol, pfSQLType, _
      lNonUnicodeFields(NonUnicodeCount).Result, _
      pcbColDef, lNonUnicodeFields( _
      NonUnicodeCount).cbField)
  End If
Next icol
'
```

```
  ' convert the stack from Unicode and output
  '
  RetCode = BTPSQLFetch(hstmt)
  ReDim Results(2)
  ResultCount = 2
  Results(1) = cCol   ' Column count
  Results(2) = 2      ' aggregate result count
  While RetCode = SQL_SUCCESS_WITH_INFO Or RetCode = SQL_SUCCESS
    For icol = 1 To cCol
      i = lUnicodeControl(icol).FieldIndex
      If lUnicodeControl(icol).FieldType = "U" Then
        lUnicodeFields(i).Result = BytesToStr(lUnicodeFields(i).ByteArray())
        ResultCount = ResultCount + 1
        ReDim Preserve Results(ResultCount)
        Results(ResultCount) = Trim$(Mid$(lUnicodeFields(i).Result, _
          1, lUnicodeFields(i).cbField))
      Else
        ResultCount = ResultCount + 1
        ReDim Preserve Results(ResultCount)
        Results(ResultCount) = lNonUnicodeFields(i).Result
      End If
    Next icol
    RetCode = BTPSQLFetch(hstmt)
  Wend
  Results(2) = ResultCount
  mvarResponse = Results()
  mvarStatus = True
Exit Sub
End Sub

Public Property Get Status() As Variant
  If IsObject(mvarStatus) Then
    Set Status = mvarStatus
  Else
    Status = mvarStatus
  End If
```

```
End Property

Public Property Get Response() As Variant
  If IsObject(mvarResponse) Then
    Set Response = mvarResponse
  Else
    Response = mvarResponse
  End If
End Property

Private Sub Class_Initialize()
'(C) 1999 Bruce T. Prendergast
' DBA Prendergast Consulting
' DBA PCS
' IDG Books Worldwide ISBN 0-7645-3314-2
'
Dim RetCode As Integer
Dim szSqlStr As String * 128
'
' set default connection status
'
  mvarStatus = False
  RetCode = BTPSQLAllocEnv(henv)
  If RetCode <> SQL_SUCCESS Then Stop

  RetCode = BTPSQLAllocConnect(henv, hdbc)
  If RetCode <> SQL_SUCCESS Then Stop
'
' change the line below to match your local server
'
  RetCode = BTPSQLConnect(hdbc, "Thor", 4, "sa", 2, "", 0)
  If (RetCode <> SQL_SUCCESS) And _
    (RetCode <> SQL_SUCCESS_WITH_INFO) Then Stop

  RetCode = BTPSQLAllocStmt(hdbc, hstmt)
  If RetCode <> SQL_SUCCESS Then Stop
```

```
  szSqlStr = "USE Pubs" & Chr$(0)
  RetCode = BTPSQLExecDirect(hstmt, szSqlStr, Len(szSqlStr))
  If (RetCode <> SQL_SUCCESS) And _
    (RetCode <> SQL_SUCCESS_WITH_INFO) Then Stop
  RetCode = BTPSQLFreeStmt(hstmt, SQL_UNBIND)
'
' return good connection status
'
  mvarStatus = True
  Exit Sub
End Sub

Private Sub Class_Terminate()
'(C) 1999 Bruce T. Prendergast
' DBA Prendergast Consulting
' DBA PCS
' IDG Books Worldwide ISBN 0-7645-3314-2
'
Dim RetCode As Integer
  If hstmt <> 0 Then RetCode = BTPSQLFreeStmt(hstmt, SQL_DROP)
  If hdbc <> 0 Then
    RetCode = BTPSQLDisconnect(hdbc)
    RetCode = BTPSQLFreeConnect(hdbc)
  End If
  If henv <> 0 Then RetCode = BTPSQLFreeEnv(henv)
  mvarStatus = False
  Exit Sub
End Sub
```

CHAPTER

13

RDO

About Chapter 13

This chapter is about Remote Data Objects (RDO). RDO is a thin ODBC wrapper that is used to access ODBC compliant databases. RDO first saw the light of day with Visual Basic 4.0 Enterprise Edition, and version 2.0 of RDO was delivered with Visual Basic 5.0 Enterprise Edition. Microsoft Access developers cannot use RDO but have their own version with ODBCDirect of Data Access Objects (DAO) 3.5.

ODBCDirect is the DAO equivalent of RDO. Microsoft Access developers clamoring for a lean and mean version of DAO will believe that ODBCDirect was developed just for them. I don't believe that to be true, and to understand why we must look at the grand plan of component technology that Microsoft espouses.

The examples in this chapter may be found in the `CHAPTER13.VBP` **Visual Basic Enterprise Edition project located in the** `EXAMPLES\CHAPTER13` **folder of the CD-ROM located at the back of this book. The RDO examples in this chapter require Microsoft Visual Basic Enterprise Edition and the Microsoft Remote Data Object Library 2.0**

RDO as a Transition Technology

What is the position of RDO in this ever-changing flux of database access technology software? RDO was the first OCX data control. The concept of an OCX data control was further polished with RDO version 2.0. ODBCDirect is a feature of DAO 3.5 and not a control in its own right, although it maintains the characteristics of RDO. There are advantages to both RDO and ODBCDirect. Neither has an SQL engine and ODBCDirect does not need the Jet engine. Microsoft Access developers will believe that ODBCDirect was developed just for them, as will Microsoft Visual Basic developers believe that RDO was developed just for them. Neither group is correct. It is all part of a grand plan by Microsoft to migrate everything—and I do mean everything—to component technology.

Is this the end of the road? Certainly not. Microsoft has already disavowed each of these technologies. Microsoft's publicly stated goal is to replace DAO and RDO with OLE-DB, a technology that is discussed in Chapters 15 and 16. The import of this is that there is no foreseeable stability in database access software. So, in addition to the bug rate of Microsoft software, adopting these technologies is a dead-end path, unless of course you're an Internet maven. The only hope for a corporation in this maelstrom of change is to adopt the ODBC standard and avoid other database access technologies until Microsoft realizes its goal and stabilizes the software. But don't look for this to happen soon.

RDO and DAO

RDO has the look and feel of DAO. It is simpler to program than DAO because there are fewer objects. There are some minor changes you must make because a DAO **Workspace** object is the equivalent of a **rdoEnvironment** object. There is a lot of parallelism, but there is not a one-to-one mapping of RDO objects to DAO objects. Table 13-1 enumerates the basic differences between RDO and DAO. DAO items marked with an asterisk are new with ODBCDirect.

TABLE 13-1 Mapping DAO to RDO

DAO Item	*Equivalent RDO Item*
DBEngine	rdoEngine
User	N/A
Workspace	rdoEnvironment
Database	N/A
Connection*	rdoConnection
TableDef	rdoTable
Index	N/A
Recordset	rdoResultset
Table	rdoTable
Dynaset	Keyset
Snapshot	Static
Dynamic*	Dynamic
Forward-Only*	Forward-Only
Field	rdoColumn
QueryDef	rdoQuery
Parameter	rdoParameter

Binding in DAO is with the **Data** control and the equivalent binding in RDO is with the Remote Data Control (RDC). Many of the RDO methods have the same name as the corresponding DAO method. Converting from DAO to RDO is not difficult.

Both RDO and DAO **RecordSet** object (rowset if you're speaking RDOese) types are discussed below. They are nearly the same except RDO doesn't support a table-type cursor.

- **Table:** One of the original RecordSet definitions of Microsoft Access and the earlier version of Jet and DAO. RDO does not support this cursor type.
- **Snapshot:** Another original Access DAO **RecordSet** definition. The data is captured at a point in time and updates or deletions are not visible to the client. This **RecordSet** type is equivalent to an ODBC Static cursor. This is the RDO static-type rowset.
- **Dynaset:** A Keyset type **RecordSet** that may have either pessimistic or optimistic locking. Deleted rows can be detected but newly added rows go undetected. This rowset type is a **Keyset** cursor in the ODBC API, the DAO ODBCDirect, and in RDO.
- **Forward only:** This is a new **RecordSet** that uses a minimum of resources. If you recall from the last chapter, the ODBC default cursor is forward only with a snapshot-type record. This **RecordSet** is equivalent to a **Snapshot** without a cursor. A forward-only cursor is available in the ODBCDirect of DAO or in RDO. Only one row is visible.
- **Dynamic:** This is a new **RecordSet** type and it is reserved for access to ODBC-registered data sources. The dynamic-type cursor is limited to ODBCDirect in DAO and RDO. It is not available to Jet. A **Dynamic** cursor is equivalent to a **Dynaset** or **Keyset** cursor except that new rows are added to the keyset. A simpler way of saying this is that the keyset membership is not fixed. Bookmarks are not available with a **Dynamic** cursor.

RDO does not support updateable joins, heterogeneous joins, or data definition language (DDL) statements, all of which are supported in Microsoft Access. RDO uses the DDL statements of the host server.

Neither ODBCDirect of DAO nor RDO requires a query processor. Microsoft touts this as reducing the footprint, which is a specious argument in a virtual memory system. With respect to ODBCDirect, the DAO reincarnation of RDO, it is an issue of automation objects not requiring a Microsoft Access license.

The greatest difference between RDO and DAO is that DAO does not support the ACID properties of a transaction (see Chapter 11) and only supports read-committed for the default transaction isolation level. RDO doesn't support a transaction isolation level directly, but since RDO is a thin ODBC wrapper, supporting transaction isolation levels is done through ODBC (see Listing 13-3). RDO supports read-committed as the default transaction isolation level.

Microsoft Access has always had asynchronous queries. Data was available from queries while population of the result set occurred in the background. Microsoft states that ODBCDirect and RDO both support asynchronous queries. That is true: the application can continue execution and the **StillExecuting** property of RDO can be interrogated. The data, however, is not available until the query terminates. The problem with this implementation is that the **rdoResultset** object is not valid until the query completes. Microsoft may have created a problem for itself with this design approach. *I believe that it is a very basic design error to encapsulate result sets.* Encapsulation of process components is a very well understood technology, but the encapsulation of result sets is contrary to enterprise data processing; on the other hand, it is what you might expect if the orientation is from an e-mail perspective that a Web application requires. Bandwidth is reduced when data is encapsulated into neat little packages, which means that not everything should be encapsulated into a COM object.

RDO and ODBC

ODBC is a core technology. It is a standard and the technology is not burdened with esoteric programming constructs. I don't mean to say that object-oriented programming isn't useful or valid, but there is a time and a place for everything. The very rich ODBC API function library supports every conceivable database access need.

RDO is an ODBC wrapper. The touted features of RDO are really ODBC API features. RDO exposes the ODBC environment handle **hEnv,** the connection handle **hDbc,** and the statement handle **hStmt**. These handles expose all facets of ODBC to the developer. Objects do not enhance ODBC. Objects simply make it easy for someone not skilled in using the ODBC API to access a relational database. Remember that Microsoft is intent on de-skilling and automating tasks. This makes its products usable by a larger community, which, in turn, increases its sales. RDO is another version of refried beans, which is ODBC wrapped in a control.

What Is RDO?

RDO is an independent database access technology designed for and used by Microsoft Visual Basic Enterprise Edition. RDO is designed specifically for the client-server environment and 32-bit systems. It is not a good technology choice for a Microsoft Access database.

RDO cannot be redistributed except as a technology within an OLE Automation server. RDO is only available in Microsoft Visual Basic Enterprise Edition. RDO may be used in a VBA environment of another tool only when Microsoft Visual Basic Enterprise Edition is installed on the same machine.

RDO objects support the concept of a **rdoEnvironment** object enabling access to remote-registered ODBC databases. This environment is similar to the **Workspace** object of Microsoft Access.

RDO is relational database oriented. To impress on us that this is a relational database connectivity technology Microsoft has changed the RDO vernacular to agree with the terminology used in relational databases. Records are now called rows and fields are now called columns. What's amusing is that Microsoft changes the vernacular back to *records* and *fields* with OLE-Database (OLE-DB) and Active Data Objects (ADO).

RDO is a very thin ODBC wrapper and is quite similar to ODBCDirect in that it does not support data definition language (DDL) operations, updateable joins, or heterogeneous joins. Neither RDO nor ODBCDirect support bound forms, although a data control is available for each. Both DAO and RDO have a remote data control for binding purposes. These controls are not the same as the RDO control in Visual Basic Enterprise Edition named **MSRDC20.OCX** or Access 97's RDC named **MSRDC32.OCX.**

RDO is implemented as a series of objects. These objects have a strict hierarchical relationship and the objects must all be instantiated in a specific order. Of course, the order is also logical because a result set must have a query, a query must have a connection, a connection must have an environment, and an environment must have an engine. The objects are not object-oriented in the programming sense, but hierarchical in the classical sense. Object collections are defined, and both properties and methods of collections or objects are accessible to a Visual Basic Enterprise Edition application program.

RDO uses the ODBC API implicitly with RDO objects calling the ODBC driver manager. This is quite unlike the call-level interface of ODBC. RDO is an ODBC

API wrapper for ODBC functions along with other methods and properties. The use of ODBC functions is implicit — not explicit — in that ODBC functions are not directly called when executing a RDO method.

RDO lacks some of Microsoft Access's flexibility in creating a result set. RDO can create a result set from a table, a SQL string, or from a **rdoQuery**. A result set cannot be created from another result set or from another query, both of which are features of Microsoft Access.

RDO Architecture

The RDO architecture is illustrated in Figure 13-1. The details of Figure 13-1, which are the properties, methods, and objects of the RDO architecture are listed immediately after Figure 13-1 in object hierarchical order. The level of indentation implies ownership by the previous level in the hierarchy and all objects are listed in their hierarchical order. We'll have an example of each object from this hierarchy along with examples of many of the methods and properties of this architecture in this and the next chapter.

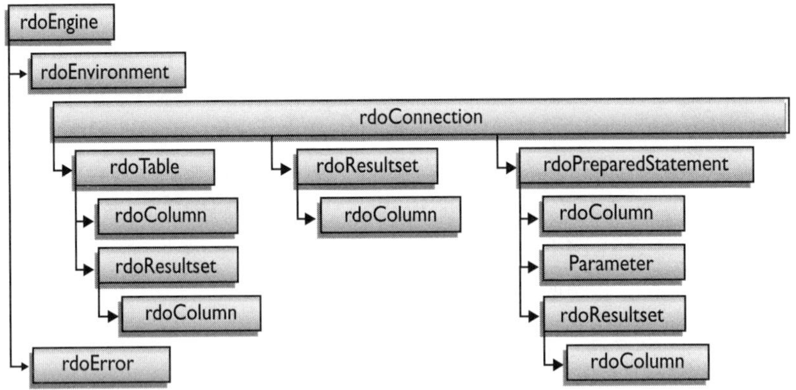

FIGURE 13-1 The RDO Object Hierarchy

```
rdoEngine
  Event : InfoMessage
  Methods : rdoCreateEnvironment, rdoRegisterDataSource
  Properties : rdoDefaultCursorDriver, rdoDefaultErrorThreshold,
```

```
  rdoDefaultLoginTimeout, rdoDefaultPassword, rdoDefaultUser, rdoLocaleID,
  rdoVersion
rdoErrors Collection
  Methods : Clear
  Properties : Count, Item
  Error Object
    Properties: Description, HelpContext, HelpFile, Number, Source,
      SQLRetCode, SQLState
rdoEnvironments Collection
  Methods : Add, Remove
  Properties : Count, Item
    Environment Object
      Events : BeginTrans, CommitTrans, RollbackTrans
      Methods : BeginTrans, Close, CommitTrans, OpenConnection, RollbackTrans
      Properties : CursorDriver, hEnv, LoginTimeout, Name, Password, UserName
      rdoConnections Collection
        Methods : Add, Remove
        Properties : Count, Item
        rdoConnection Object
          Events : BeforeConnect, Connect, Disconnect, QueryComplete,
            QueryTimeout, WillExecute
          Methods : BeginTrans, Cancel, Close, CommitTrans, CreateQuery,
            EstablishConnection, Execute, OpenResultSet, RollbackTrans
          Properties : AsyncCheckInterval, Connect, CursorDriver, hDbc,
            LastQueryResults, LoginTimeout, LogMessages, Name,QueryTimeout,
            RowsAffected, StillConnecting, StillExecting, Transactions,
            Updatable, Version
          rdoQueries Collection
            Properties : Count, Item
              rdoQuery Object
                Methods : Cancel, Close, Execute,
                  OpenResultset
                Properties : ActiveConnection, BindThreshold, CursorType,
                  hStmt, KeysetSize, LockType, MaxRows, Name, Prepared,
                  QueryTimeout, RowsAffected, RowsetSize, SQL,
                  StillExecuting, Type
```

```
          rdoColumns Collection
            Methods : Refresh
            Properties : Count, Item
            rdoColumn Object
              Events : DataChanged, WillChangeData
              Methods : AppendChunk, ColumnSize, GetChunk
              Properties : AllowZeroLength, Attributes,
                BatchConflictValue, ChunkRequired, KeyColumn, Name,
                OrdinalPosition, OriginalValue, Required, Size,
                SourceColumn, SourceTable, Status, Type, Updatable,
                Value
          rdoParameters Collection
            Properties : Count, Item
            rdoParameter Object
              Method : AppendChunk
              Properties : Direction, Name, Type, Value
    rdoResultSets Collection
      Properties : Count, Item
      rdoResultset Object
        Events : Associate, Dissociate, ResultsChanged,
          RowCurrencyChanged, RowStatusChanged, WillAssociate,
          WillDissociate, WillUpdateRows
        Methods : AddNew, BatchUpdate, Cancel, CancelBatch,
          CancelUpdate, Close, Delete, Edit, GetClipString, GetRows,
          MoreResults, Move, MoveFirst, MoveLast, MoveNext,
          MovePrevious, Requery, Resync, Update
        Properties : AbsolutePosition,
          ActiveConnection, BatchCollisionCount, BatchSize, BOF,
          Bookmark, Bookmarkable, EditMode, EOF, hStmt, LastModified,
          LockEdits, LockType, Name, PercentPosition, Restartable,
          RowCount, Status, StillExecuting, Transactions, Type,
          Updatable,  UpdateCriteria, UpdateOperation
        rdoColumns Collection (see rdoQuery Object)
    rdoTables Collection
      Methods : Refresh
      Properties : Count, Item
      rdoTable Object
```

```
Methods : OpenResultset, Refresh
Properties : Name, RowCount, Type, Updatable
rdoColumns Collection (see rdoQuery Object)
```

rdoEngine Object

This is dirty fingernails time. Let's track the RDO collections and objects in the default hierarchical order: **rdoEngine, rdoError, rdoEnvironment, rdoConnection,** and **rdoTable**. **rdoQuery, rdoResultset, rdoColumn,** and **rdoParameter** are reserved for the next chapter.

The **rdoEngine** is the first object used in the RDO hierarchy to obtain access to other objects. It is not a member of a collection and **rdoEngine** objects cannot be created since the **rdoEngine** is predefined; however the **rdoEngine** can be initialized. A **rdoEngine** represents a remote Open Database Connectivity (ODBC) data source and is the first stop in the RDO architecture.

***rdoEngine** Object Definition*

Event: InfoMessage

Methods: **rdoCreateEnvironment, rdoRegisterDataSource**

Properties: **rdoDefaultCursorDriver, rdoDefaultErrorThreshold, rdoDefaultLoginTimeout, rdoDefaultPassword, rdoDefaultUser, rdoVersion, rdoLocaleID**

Collections: **rdoEnvironments, rdoErrors**

Before creating the **rdoEngine** object, a reference must be set to *the Microsoft Remote Data Object 2.0 library* of Visual Basic Enterprise Edition. The ODBC data source must be registered before accessing it with the **rdoEngine**.

RDO 2.0 includes the concept of events. The **rdoEngine** object supports the **InfoMessage** event and other RDO objects such as **rdoConnection** object, and the **rdoResultset** object also support events.

rdoEngine events

The RDO model is further enriched by the **InfoMessage** event of the **rdoEngine**. This event occurs when RDO or the data source reports an error. The **InfoMessage** event is raised after the last message of a group is appended to the **rdoErrors** collection.

RDO error processing has changed since RDO 1.0, which used the traditional construct:

```
  Dim myErr as rdoError
  On Error GoTo Found_Error
  . . .

FoundError:
  For Each myErr In rdoErrors
    Debug.Print MyErr.Description, myErr.Number
  Next myErr
  Resume Next
```

The traditional construct of RDO 1.0 is now replaced with the event construct of RDO 2.0:

```
  Option Explicit
  Private WithEvents FoundAnError as rdoEngine
  Dim myErr as rdoError
  . . .

Private Sub FoundAnError_InfoMessage()
  For Each myErr In rdoErrors
    Debug.Print MyErr.Description, myErr.Number
  Next myErr
  Exit Sub
```

The new event construct simplifies error processing with RDO and data source specific errors managed with RDO event processing, while traditional processing manages the other errors.

rdoEngine methods

The **rdoEngine** has only two methods; **rdoCreateEnvironment** and **rdoRegisterDataSource**, both of which are illustrated in listings 13-1 and 13-2 respectively.

rdoCreateEnvironment

This method creates the equivalent of a session. More than one session can be created and each session can have many connections. The newly created **rdoEnvironment** object is automatically appended to the **rdoEnvironments** collection.

Syntax:

> **Set** *rdoEnviron* = **rdoEngine.rdoCreateEnvironment**(*Name, User, Password*)

Where:

> *rdoEnviron:* An object variable of type **rdoEnvironment**
>
> *Name:* A **String** variable representing the user name
>
> *User:* A **String** variable identifying the owner of the **rdoEnvironment** object
>
> *Password:* A **String** variable representing the user password

An alternative method of creating the initial session is to use the default **rdoEnvironments**(0), which is created when the **rdoEngine** object is initialized. When this is done the **Name** parameter is initialized from **rdoDefaultUser** and the **Password** parameter is initialized from **rdoDefaultPassword**. An example of this technique is shown in Listing 13-1. Included with Listing 13-1 is the **InfoMessage** event, which handles RDO and data source errors. Note that the **Starting_rdo Engine_Click** event processes non-RDO errors at the **Non_RDO_Error** label.

A **rdoEnvironment** object is removed from the **rdoEnvironments** collection when it is closed. The **rdoEnvironment**(0), which is the default session object, cannot be closed.

Only the **UserName** and **Timeout** properties can be modified after a **rdoEnvironment** object is created.

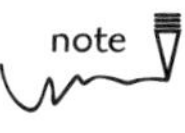

Transactions are global to an environment or local to a connection. When a CommitTrans operation is performed with a rdoEnvironment object, all of the open transactions of all connections of the rdoEnvironment object are committed.

LISTING13-1 Starting the rdoEngine

```
'(C) 1999 Bruce T. Prendergast
' DBA Prendergast Consulting
' DBA PCS
```

```
' IDG Books Worldwide ISBN 0-7645-3314-2
'
' Listing 13-1 error event processing
'
Option Explicit
Private Declare Function BTPSQLSetConnectOption Lib "odbc32.dll" ( _
  ByVal hdbc&, _
  ByVal fOption%, _
  ByVal vParam As Any) As Integer
Private WithEvents UnableToConnect As rdoEngine

Private Sub UnableToConnect_InfoMessage()
  Dim myErr As rdoError
  For Each myErr In rdoEngine.rdoErrors
    '
    ' I expect warning messages.
    ' Ignore the With_Info messages such as
    ' "connecting to pubs", etc.,
    '
    If (myErr.SQLRetcode <> rdSQLSuccessWithInfo) Then
      MsgBox myErr.Description & " State:" & myErr.SQLState & _
        " SQLRetCode:" & myErr.SQLRetcode & " NativeErrorCode:" & myErr.Number
    End If
  Next myErr
  Stop
End Sub
Private Sub Starting_rdoEngine_Click()
'(C) 1999 Bruce T. Prendergast
' DBA Prendergast Consulting
' DBA PCS
' IDG Books Worldwide ISBN 0-7645-3314-2
'
' Listing 13-1 starting the rdoEngine
'
    Dim RdoEnv As rdoEnvironment
    Dim RdoCon As rdoConnection
```

```
    Dim myErr As rdoError
    Dim c As rdoConnection
    On Error GoTo Non_RDO_Error
    '
    '   create an RDO environment
    '
    Set RdoEnv = rdoEngine.rdoEnvironments(0)
    '
    '   connect with RDO connect string
    '
    Set RdoCon = RdoEnv.OpenConnection("", rdDriverNoPrompt, True, _
      "DATABASE=Pubs;UID=sa;PWD=;DSN=Thor;")
    '
    '   verify that the connection exists
    '
    For Each c In RdoEnv.rdoConnections
        MsgBox "Connection: " & c.Name
    Next c
    '
    ' this is an experiment
    '
    rdoEngine.rdoEnvironments(0).Close
    MsgBox "RDO connection completed successfully"
    Exit Sub
Non_RDO_Error:
    '
    ' RDO or data source errors are handled in the
    ' UnableToConnect event
    '
    For Each myErr In rdoEngine.rdoErrors
      MsgBox myErr.Description & myErr.Number
    Next myErr
    Stop
End Sub
```

rdoRegisterDataSource

RDO only communicates with registered ODBC data sources. The **rdoRegister DataSource** method registers a new data source or updates existing registered data sources.

Syntax:

rdoEngine.**rdoRegisterDataSource** *DSName, Driver, Silent, Attributes*

Where:

DSName: The name of the data source. Typically the Windows NT Server name, although this isn't a requirement.

Driver: A string variable identifying the ODBC driver name. This is not a dynamic link library (DLL) name but the registered ODBC name, which is typically SQL Server. The *Driver* name must be registered before the data source can be registered.

Silent: No dialog box is shown when this value is TRUE. An error occurs for missing information. Set the parameter to FALSE and note the parameters in the dialog box. Once they are recorded correctly, permanently set this parameter to TRUE.

Attributes: These are the parameter values of the dialog box entered in carriage return-delimited string format.

Listing 13-2 illustrates registering an ODBC data source.

LISTING 13-2 Registering an ODBC data source

```
Private Sub Register_DataSource_Click()
'(C) 1999 Bruce T. Prendergast
' DBA Prendergast Consulting
' DBA PCS
' IDG Books Worldwide ISBN 0-7645-3314-2
'
' Listing 13-2 Registering a data source and
' enumerating the errors collection.
'
    Dim RdoEnv As rdoEnvironment
    Dim RdoCon As rdoConnection
```

```
Dim myErr As rdoError
Dim c As rdoConnection
On Error GoTo Non_RDO_Error

Dim Attr As String
'
' Build keywords string.
'
Attr = "Description=SQL Server on server" & "Thor" & Chr$(13)
Attr = Attr & "OemToAnsi=No" & Chr$(13)
Attr = Attr & "Server=Thor" & Chr$(13)
Attr = Attr & "Network=DBNMPNTW" & Chr$(13)
Attr = Attr & "Address= \\Thor\PIPE\SQL\QUERY" & Chr$(13)
Attr = Attr & "Database=Pubs"
'
'   create an RDO environment
'
Set RdoEnv = rdoEngine.rdoEnvironments(0)
'
' Update the Registry
'
rdoEngine.rdoRegisterDataSource "Thor", "SQL Server", True, Attr
'
'   connect with RDO connect string
'
Set RdoCon = RdoEnv.OpenConnection("", rdDriverNoPrompt, True, _
  "DATABASE=Pubs;UID=sa;PWD=;DSN=Thor;")
'
'  verify that the connection exists
'
For Each c In RdoEnv.rdoConnections
  MsgBox "Connection: " & c.Name
Next c

MsgBox "RDO data source registration was successfull"
Exit Sub
```

```
Non_RDO_Error:
    '
    ' RDO or data source errors are handled in the
    ' UnableToConnect event
    '
    For Each myErr In rdoEngine.rdoErrors
      MsgBox myErr.Description & myErr.Number
    Next myErr
    Stop
End Sub
```

rdoEngine properties

The **rdoEngine** object is the repository of default properties, which are assigned in the absence of user assigned values. Table 13-2 enumerates the properties of the **rdoEngine** object.

TABLE 13-2 RDOENGINE OBJECT PROPERTIES

Property	*Description*
rdoDefaultCursorDriver	Returns or sets the type of cursor:
rdUseIfNeeded <0>	ODBC drive will choose the appropriate cursors. Server-side cursors are used when available.
rdUseOdbc <1>	RDO uses the IDBC cursor library.
rdUseServer <2>	Use server-side cursors.
rdUseClientBatch <3>	RDO uses the optimistic batch cursor library. Required for disconnected Recordsets.
rdUseNone <4>	Result set is not returned as a cursor.
rdoDefaultErrorThreshold	Sets or returns the default value for the **rdoErrorThreshold** property. This feature is backward compatible with RDO 1.0, however, error threshold logic should be replaced with the RDO **InfoMessage** event.
rdoDefaultLoginTimeout	Sets or returns the number of seconds that the ODBC driver will wait before returning a connection error.
rdoDefaultPassword	Sets or returns the default password used by any new **rdoEnvironment** object.

Property	*Description*
rdoDefaultUser	Sets or returns the default user name used by any new **rdoEnvironment** object.
rdoLocaleID	Returns or sets the RDO library locale. Used for internationalization. Values are:
	rdLocaleSystem <0>: System
	rdLocaleEnglish <0>: English
	rdLocaleFrench <0>: French
	rdLocaleGerman <0>: German
	rdLocaleItalian <0>: Italian
	rdLocaleJapanese <0>: Japanese
	rdLocaleSpanish <0>: Spanish
	rdLocaleChinese <0>: Chinese
	rdLocaleSimplifiedChinese <0>: Simplified Chinese
	rdLocaleKorean <0>: Korean
rdoVersion	Returns the major and minor version as #.#.####.

Working with Default Collections

The **rdoEngine** is the only object without a collection even though it has a default collection. Another way of saying this is that no new **rdoEngine** objects can be created. There is only one RDO engine.

Result sets may be created from a connection directly. This means the SQL statement is neither prepared nor compiled when issued from a connection object. Tables and prepared statements also create result sets, or more precisely, a **rdoResultset** may be created from both a **rdoTable** object and a **rdoResultset** object. This is a hierarchical relationship and not an object-oriented relationship even though objects have collections. Table 13-3 enumerates the RDO default collections.

TABLE 13-3 DEFAULT COLLECTIONS OF RDO OBJECTS

OBJECT	DEFAULT COLLECTION
rdoResultset	**rdoColumns**
rdoConnection	**rdoTables**
rdoQuery	**rdoParameters**
rdoTable	**rdoColumns**

Default collection provides a shortcut mechanism for addressing lower level methods and properties. The **rdoResultset** collection has the **rdoColumns** collection, which is the default collection. Assume for the moment that the **Fields** collection contains two fields named *au_fname* and *au_lname* with ordinals of zero and one, respectively. Assume also that the collection belongs to the **rdoResultset** object **MyRS**. The default collection is illustrated below where all four lines are equivalent and the first two lines use the default collection; that is, the **rdoColumns** collection is not referenced. Note that the default property of a **rdoColumn** object is the **Value** property.

```
Debug.Print MyRS!au_fname
Debug.Print MyRS("au_fname")
Debug.Print MyRS.rdoColumns("au_fname").Value
Debug.Print MyRS.rdoColumns(0).Value
```

Working with Collections

All collections have a **Count** property and an **Item** property. The **Clear** method is the only method of the **rdoErrors** collection. **Add** and **Remove** are the only methods of the **rdoEnvironments** and **rdoConnections** collections while Refresh is the only method of the **rdoTable** and **rdoColumns** collections. There are no other methods or properties of RDO collections. There are, however, many properties and methods of objects within these collections, many of which have parallels in DAO.

Unlike DAO objects, RDO 1.0 objects could not be saved. That has changed with RDO 2.0 and objects are persisted by being automatically appended to their respective collection. When appropriate, a **Close** operation deletes an object from a collection, or the **Remove** method will remove specific objects from limited collections.

Collection Methods

Add, Remove

Add and **Remove** are the only methods of the **rdoEnvironments** and **rdoConnections** collections. The **Add** method is illustrated with:

```
RdoEngine.rdoEnviroments.Add <new rdoEnvironment object>
```

Normally a new **rdoEnvironment** object is appended automatically to the **rdoEnviroments** collection, except when a name is not entered.

A **rdoConnection** object is automatically appended to the **rdoConnections** collection when the **OpenConnection** method or the **RemoteData** control is used. Standalone **rdoConnection** objects are not automatically appended to the **rdoConnection** collection. Automatically appending a **rdoConnection** object to the **rdoConnections** collection is illustrated with:

```
Set RdoEnv = rdoEngine.rdoEnvironments(0)
Set RdoCon = RdoEnv.OpenConnection(<connection string> ...)
```

The Data Source Name (DSN) from the connection string becomes the **rdoConnection** object name, which is automatically appended to the **rdoConnections** collection.

Clear

Clear is a method of only the **rdoErrors** collection, which is illustrated with:

```
rdoErrors.Clear
```

Refresh

Refresh is defined as a method is defined in only the **rdoColumns** and **rdoTables** collections. Refreshing a collection is done after a new element is appended.

```
RdoCon.rdoTables.Refresh
```

Collection Properties

Collections have very few properties, and collections within RDO are no different.

Count

Count is the only property of all collections. The **Count** property of the **rdoErrors** collection is illustrated with:

```
For I = 0 to rdoErrors.Count - 1
```

Item

Item is not a property even though I've listed it as such. It isn't a method either, but it functions in a manner similar to a method. The **Item** method is used to extract elements from a collection The following two lines are equivalent.

```
Debug.print rdoCon(1)
Debug.Print rdoCon.Item(1)
```

The rdoErrors Collection

The **rdoErrors** collection is the accumulation of errors that occur during execution. It is an accumulation because an error at a lower level quite often precipitates other errors.

***rdoErrors** Collection Definition*

Methods: **Clear**

Properties: **Count, Item**

***rdoError** object*

Methods: none

Properties: **Description, HelpContext, HelpFile, Number, Source, SQLRetCode, SQLState**

The **rdoEngine** supports the **Errors** collection. The **rdoDefaultError Threshold** property of the **rdoEngine** contains the default value for the **rdoErrorThreshold** property of the **RemoteData** object and the **rdoQuery** object. The **rdoDefaultErrorThreshold** does not limit errors unrelated to either the **RemoteData** object or the **rdoQuery** object. Setting the error threshold is a deprecated feature of RDO 1.0, which is replaced by the **InfoMessage** event construct of RDO 2.0.

The secondary issue is that error logging significantly impacts performance, even though the errors are of a warning nature. Identify all errors and take corrective measures to prevent their occurrence. It is not always the unreported fatal error that is a problem, but the numerous *With_Info* messages that subtract from the overall performance of a system.

This is not a course on programming; simply exposing the error and crashing the application is not sufficient. Visual Basic for Applications (VBA) has the feature that an error handler cannot handle an error that occurs within the error handler. This can be used to our advantage. When an error occurs, do the necessary bookkeeping and then execute the **RAISE** statement. The parameter values for this command will have been filled in and the next error handler in the stack will process the error message. This is called *unwinding the stack*.

The primary cause of an error is the first object in the stack or **rdoErrors**(0). The errors in the stack always represent only one error. The multitude of error objects is each of the different software layers reporting their disenchantment with the miscreant service.

The **rdoError** object has no methods while the **rdoErrors** collection has only the **Clear** method, which clears the collection. You'll find that all the RDO program examples have simple error reporting. Listing13-1 illustrates starting the **rdoEngine** and the enumeration of the **rdoErrors** collection from the **InfoMessage** event.

The rdoEnvironments Collection

A session is an environment, which is a host for connection objects, open database objects, and transaction processing. Transactions are global to an environment and operate within a security context. New environments are automatically appended to the **rdoEnvironments** collections and **rdoEnvironment** objects are removed from the collection when the object is closed. The default environment cannot be closed and has the name *Default_Environment,* which is the object **rdoEnvironments**(0). The **rdoCreateEnvironment** method is not used to create the default **rdoEnvironments**(0). **rdoEnvironments**(0) is created automatically at the first reference.

rdoEnvironments *Collection Definition*

Methods: **Add, Remove**

Properties: **Count, Item**

rdoEnvironment *object*

Methods: **BeginTrans, Close, CommitTrans, OpenConnection, RollbackTrans**

Properties: **CursorDriver, hEnv, LoginTimeout, Name, Password, UserName**

Collections: **rdoConnections**

Events: **BeginTrans, CommitTrans, RollbackTrans**

rdoEnvironment Properties

The **rdoEnvironment** is similar to the **Workspace** object of DAO. A **rdoEnvironment** object hosts one or more **rdoConnection** objects. Table 13-4 enumerates the properties of the **rdoEnvironment** object.

TABLE 13-4 RDOENVIRONMENT OBJECT PROPERTIES

Property	*Description*
rdoDefaultCursorDriver	Returns or sets the type of cursor: **rdUseIfNeeded** <0>: ODBC drive will choose the appropriate cursors. Server-side cursors are used when available. **rdUseOdbc** <1>: RDO uses the IDBC cursor library. **rdUseServer** <2>: Use server-side cursors. **rdUseClientBatch** <3>: RDO uses the optimistic batch cursor library. Required for disconnected Recordsets. **rdUseNone** <4>: Result set is not returned as a cursor.
hEnv	A **Long** that contains the ODBC environment handle.
LoginTimeout	The number is seconds the driver manager waits before timing out.

Property	*Description*
Name	A string value that is the object name. **rdoEnvironments**(0) defaults to the name "Default_Environment."
Password	A write-only property with the initial value "". The **rdoDefaultPassword** property of the **rdoEngine** is used when none is defined.
UserName	A string value representing the user name that is set automatically when the **rdoEnvironment** object is created or at the first reference to the remote data control.
Item	When supplied with an index, the **Item** property returns an element of a collection.

rdoEnvironment Methods

BeginTrans, CommitTrans, And RollbackTrans

These methods are used to manage transactions from the RDO environment. Nested transactions are only supported if your data source supports them. ODBC does not support nested transactions and RDO is a thin ODBC wrapper.

Syntax:

Object.**BeginTrans | CommitTrans | RollbackTrans**

Where:

Object: Either a **rdoEnvironment** object or a **rdoConnection** object.

A transaction example is shown in Listing 13-3. An update is made to the *Authors* table of the *Pubs* database on Microsoft SQL Server. The transaction is immediately rolled back, the target column is interrogated for the current value, and the appropriate message is issued.

The transaction example illustrated in Listing 13-3 was tested with both a **rdoConnection** object and a **rdoEnvironment** object. I encourage you to always use a **rdoEnvironment** object so you'll not forget that transactions are global to the environment.

The example in Listing 13-3 has two distinct error-handling routines. The first captures any errors during a connection. The second routine performs a **Roll-**

backTrans on an error and reports all messages. The last error-handling routine is actuated after the rollback is complete.

LISTING 13-3 **A RDO transaction**

```
Private Sub Transaction_Click()
'(C) 1999 Bruce T. Prendergast
' DBA Prendergast Consulting
' DBA PCS
' IDG Books Worldwide ISBN 0-7645-3314-2
'
' Listing 13-3 an RDO transaction with
' transaction isolation
'
    Dim RdoEnv As rdoEnvironment
    Dim RdoCon As rdoConnection
    Dim RdoQry As rdoQuery
    Dim MyRS As rdoResultset
    Dim Response As Integer
    Dim myErr As rdoError
    Dim c As rdoConnection
    On Error GoTo Normal_Error
    '
    '   create an RDO environment
    '
    Set RdoEnv = rdoEngine.rdoEnvironments(0)
    '
    '   connect with RDO connect string
    '
    Set RdoCon = RdoEnv.OpenConnection("" rdDriverNoPrompt, False, _
      "DATABASE=Pubs;UID=sa;PWD=;DSN=Thor;")
    '
    ' set transaction isolation level
    ' Transaction isolation option masks
    '
    Const SQL_TXN_ISOLATION As Long = 108
    Const SQL_TXN_READ_UNCOMMITTED As Long = &H1&
```

```
Const SQL_TXN_READ_COMMITTED As Long = &H2&
Const SQL_TXN_REPEATABLE_READ As Long = &H4&
Const SQL_TXN_SERIALIZABLE As Long = &H8&
Const SQL_TXN_VERSIONING As Long = &H10&
'
' We're calling ODBC from RDO here
'
Response = BTPSQLSetConnectOption(RdoCon.hdbc, _
  SQL_TXN_ISOLATION, SQL_TXN_READ_UNCOMMITTED)
'
' ODBC and not RDO error handling is required
' here, which is omitted for brevity. See
' Chapter 12 for ODBC error handling.
'
If Response <> 0 Then Stop

Set RdoQry = RdoCon.CreateQuery("MyPS", _
  "UPDATE authors " & _
  "SET au_fname='John' " & _
  "WHERE au_id = '172-32-1176'")
RdoQry.Prepared = False
'
' Do the action query
'
On Error GoTo Transaction_Error
RdoEnv.BeginTrans
RdoQry.Execute
RdoEnv.RollbackTrans
On Error GoTo Normal_Error
'

' now let's see that we didn't change anything
'
RdoQry.Close
Set RdoQry = Nothing
Set RdoQry = RdoCon.CreateQuery("MyPS", _
```

```
      "SELECT au_fname " & _
      "FROM authors " & _
      "WHERE au_id = '172-32-1176'")
    Set MyRS = RdoQry.OpenResultset(rdOpenForwardOnly, rdConcurReadOnly)
    If MyRS(0) <> "Johnson" Then
      MsgBox "Rollback failed"
      Exit Sub
    Else
      MsgBox "RDO Transaction statement completed successfully"
    End If
    Exit Sub

Transaction_Error:
    RdoEnv.RollbackTrans
    MsgBox "Transaction failure, Transaction rolled back"
Normal_Error:
  For Each myErr In rdoEngine.rdoErrors
    MsgBox myErr.Description & " State:" & _myErr.SQLState & _
      " SQLRetCode:" & myErr.SQLRetcode & " NativeErrorCode:" & myErr.Number
  Next myErr
  Resume Error_Exit
Error_Exit:
    Exit Sub
End Sub
```

Close

The **Close** method may be used for any **rdoEnvironment** object other than the default environment object. Open transactions in an environment are rolled back on a close. Action queries that are not wrapped in a transaction may be terminated with unpredictable results.

Syntax:

Object.**Close**

Where:

Object: An object of type **rdoEnvironment, rdoConnection, rdoQuery, rdoResultset**.

RDO objects are closed when the object variable goes out of scope or the **Close** method is explicitly applied to the object. Implicit closing of an RDO object occurs when the **Set** statement changes the object reference. RDO objects are not persistent and closing a RDO object removes it from the respective collection.

OpenConnection

The **rdoConnection** object is used for managing data source connections. Browsing typically takes two connections. One connection is used for updating and the other is used for queries. RDO 2.0 supports the *Options* parameter of the **OpenConnection** method, which permits opening a connection asynchronously.

Syntax:

Set *rdoCon* = *rdoEnv*.**OpenConnection**(*DSName*, *Prompt*, *ReadOnly*, *Connect*, *Options*)

Where:

rdoCon: A variable of type **rdoConnection**

RdoEnv: A Variable of type **rdoEnvironment**

DSName: A **String** containing the data source name. The name must be a registered ODBC data source. If no name is provided, the user is prompted unless *Prompt* is set to **rdDriverNoPrompt**. In this situation, an error occurs.

Prompt: One of: **rdDriverNoPrompt, rdDriverPrompt, rdDriverComplete**, or **rdDriverCompleteRequired**

ReadOnly: The database is opened read-only when this field is TRUE.

Connect: A **String** representing the connection parameters to the database. It should be the same as the data access objects (DAO) connect string except the clause *"ODBC;"* is not used. See Listing 13-3 for an example of parameters used in a RDO connection string.

Option: Establishes an asynchronous connection with the intrinsic constant **rdAsyncEnable**.

All RDO examples of this chapter contain code for opening a connection and additional examples are unwarranted.

The rdoConnections Collection

The **rdoConnection** object is required for manipulating a database. Queries may be issued directly from a connection.

rdoConnections *Collection Definition*

Methods: Add, Remove

Properties: **Count, Item**

rdoConnection *object*

Events: **BeforeConnect, Connect, Disconnect, QueryComplete, QueryTimeout, WillExecute**

Methods : **BeginTrans, Cancel, Close, CommitTrans, CreateQuery, EstablishConnection, Execute, OpenResultSet, RollbackTrans**

Properties: **AsyncCheckInterval, Connect, CursorDriver, hDbc, LastQueryResults, LoginTimeout, LogMessages, Name, QueryTimeout, RowsAffected, StillConnecting, StillExecuting, Transactions, UpdateOperation, Version**

Collections: **rdoQueries, rdoResultsets, rdoTables**

rdoConnection events

Events in RDO are starting to approach the rich event architecture of Microsoft Access and the Jet engine. Table13-5 enumerates the events available with the **rdoConnection** object.

TABLE 13-5 RDOCONNECTION EVENTS

Event	*When fired*
BeforeConnect	Before ODBC is called to establish the connection.
Connect	After a connection is established.
Disconnect	After a connection is closed.
QueryComplete	After a query of this connection completes.
QueryTimeout	After the **QueryTimeout** period is exhausted.
WillExecute	Before the Query executes.

Numerous tasks can be performed from a connection including:

- An action query may be run or an SQL statement passed to a database.
- A result set may be opened with **rdoOpenResultset**.
- A prepared (compiled) SQL statement can be created by setting the **Prepared** property of a **rdoQuery** object to TRUE.
- The **rdoConnection** object supports transactions and the number of affected rows can be tested. For example, a transaction can be rolled back with **RollbackTrans** if the number of rows is incorrect. The **RowsAffected** property applies to both the **rdoConnection** object and the **rdoQuery** object.
- A **rdoConnection** object exposes the ODBC connection handle **hDbc,** the **rdoConnection** object.
- RDO 2.0 introduces the concept of managing the **rdoConnection** object with events. Table 13-5 enumerates the new **rdoConnection** object events of RDO 2.0.

rdoConnection methods

What's new with RDO 2.0 is the transaction support for an individual connection. Traditional transaction support is from the **rdoEnvironment** object, which encompasses all connections.

BeginTrans, CommitTrans, and RollbackTrans

The methods **BeginTrans, CommitTrans,** and **RollBackTrans** only apply to objects of a **rdoConnection** when used as methods of the **rdoConnection** object. Transactions span all **rdoConnection** objects when the methods **BeginTrans, CommitTrans,** and **RollBackTrans** are used as methods of a **rdoEnvironment** object. Please see the **rdoEnvironment** object for comments on using these methods.

Cancel

The **Cancel** method cancels pending results or instructs the remote data source to stop work on the query.

Syntax:

*Object.***Cancel**

Where:

Object: An object variable of type **rdoConnection, rdoQuery,** or **rdoResultset**

The **Cancel** method may be used on an asynchronous result set. All remaining rows of the current result set are flushed. These result sets are created with the **rdAsyncEnable** parameter from either the **Execute** or **OpenResultset** method.

The **MoreResults** method of the **rdoResultset** object flushes the current result set. The next pending result is current, if there is one. Listing 13-4 illustrates an asynchronous query and the **Cancel** method.

LISTING 13-4 An Asynchronous Query using StillExecuting and Cancel

```
Private Sub Asynchronous_Click()
'(C) 1999 Bruce T. Prendergast
' DBA Prendergast Consulting
' DBA PCS
' IDG Books Worldwide ISBN 0-7645-3314-2
'
' Listing 13-4 A prepared and asynchronous RDO query
'
    Dim RdoEnv As rdoEnvironment
    Dim RdoCon As rdoConnection
    Dim RdoQry As rdoQuery
    Dim MyRS As rdoResultset
    Dim WaitTime As Long

    Dim myErr As rdoError
    Dim c As rdoConnection
    Dim RetCode As Integer
    On Error GoTo Non_RDO_Error
    '
    '   create an RDO environment
    '
    Set RdoEnv = rdoEngine.rdoEnvironments(0)
    '
    '   connect with RDO connect string
    '
```

```
Set RdoCon = RdoEnv.OpenConnection("", _
  rdDriverNoPrompt, False, "DATABASE=Pubs;UID=sa;PWD=;DSN=Thor;")
Set RdoQry = RdoCon.CreateQuery("MyPS", _
  "SELECT au_lname, au_fname " & _
  "FROM authors " & _
  "WHERE au_lname LIKE 'G%' ")
'
' A little magic here. We'll define a Microsoft SQL
' Server specific ODBC connection option that drops
' temporary stored procedures on the next SQLPrepare
' API reference or will drop all stored procedures
' when the statement is released. See the sidebar in
' Chapter 12.
'
' We're using the ODBC API here
'
Const SQL_USE_PROCEDURE_FOR_PREPARE = 1202
Const SQL_UP_ON_DROP As Long = 2
Const SQL_SUCCESS As Integer = 0
'
' Use ODBC error processing
'
On Error GoTo ODBC_Error_Processing
'
RetCode = BTPSQLSetConnectOption(RdoCon.hdbc, _
  SQL_USE_PROCEDURE_FOR_PREPARE,  SQL_UP_ON_DROP)
If RetCode <> SQL_SUCCESS Then Stop
On Error GoTo Non_RDO_Error
RdoQry.Prepared = True
'
' start an asynchronous query
'
Set MyRS = RdoQry.OpenResultset(rdOpenForwardOnly, rdConcurReadOnly, _
  rdAsyncEnable)
WaitTime = Timer
While (Timer - WaitTime) < 5
```

```
    Wend
    Do While RdoQry.StillExecuting
      If MsgBox("No query yet--keep waiting?", _
          vbYesNo) = vbNo Then
        RdoQry.Cancel
        Exit Sub
      Else
        WaitTime = Timer
        While (Timer - WaitTime) < 5
        Wend
      End If
    Loop
    While Not MyRS.EOF
      Debug.Print MyRS(0), MyRS(1)
      MyRS.MoveNext
    Wend
    MsgBox "Successful asynchronous prepared statement"
    Exit Sub
ODBC_Error_Processing:
    For Each myErr In rdoEngine.rdoErrors
      '
      ' I expect warning messages.
      ' Ignore just the With_Info messages such as
      ' "connecting to pubs", etc.,
      '
      If ((myErr.SQLRetcode <> rdSQLSuccessWithInfo)) Then
        MsgBox myErr.Description & " State:" & myErr.SQLState & _
        " SQLRetCode:" & myErr.SQLRetcode & " NativeErrorCode:" & myErr.Number
      End If
    Next myErr
    Resume Next
Non_RDO_Error:
    '
    ' RDO or data source errors are handled in the
    ' UnableToConnect event
    '
```

```
    For Each myErr In rdoEngine.rdoErrors
      MsgBox myErr.Description & myErr.Number
    Next myErr
    Stop
End Sub
```

Close

Implicit closing of an object occurs when the **Set** statement changes the RDO object reference. A closed object is automatically removed from a collection. Objects that cannot be closed include **rdoEngine, rdoError, rdoParameter, rdoColumn, rdoTable,** and **rdoEnvironments**(0). Objects that can be closed include **rdoEnvironment, rdoConnection, rdoQuery, rdoResultset,** and **rdoConnection.**

Syntax:

*Object.***Close**

Where:

Object: An object variable of type **rdoConnection, rdoQuery, rdoResultset,** or **rdoEnvironment**

CreateQuery

A **rdoQuery** object is temporary and is deleted when the connection is closed. A query that is to be used repeatedly should be prepared (compiled), which is done by setting the **Prepared** property of the **rdoQuery** to TRUE. A query cannot be prepared when there is an unpopulated resultset pending on the data source that only supports single operations.

Syntax:

Set rdoQry = rdoCon.**CreateQuery**(*Name, SQLString*)

Where:

rdoPre: A variable of type **rdoQuery**

rdoCon: A variable of type **rdoConnection**

Name: A required field even though it may be a zero-length string. An error occurs if *Name* exists in the **rdoQueries** collection. This also includes a zero-length string.

SQLString: A **String** variable containing a valid SQL statement.

See Listing 13-4 for an example of a prepared asynchronous query.

EstablishConnection

This method establishes a connection to an ODBC data source.

Syntax:

rdoCon.**EstablishConnection** *Prompt, ReadOnly, Options*

Where:

rdoCon: A variable of type **rdoConnection.**

Prompt: One of: **rdDriverNoPrompt, rdDriverPrompt, rdDriverComplete,** or **rdDriverCompleteRequired.**

ReadOnly: The database is opened read-only when this field is TRUE.

Option: Establish an asynchronous connection with the intrinsic constant **rdAsyncEnable.**

Execute

This is a method of both the **rdoConnection** object and the **rdoQuery** object. The method executes an action query or a query that does not return rows.

Syntax:

rdoCon.**Execute** *Source* [,*Options*]

rdoPre.**Execute** [*Options*]

Where:

rdoCon: A variable of type **rdoConnection.**

rdoPre: A variable of type **rdoQuery.**

Source: A **String** variable containing a valid SQL statement or the name of an existing **rdoQuery** object.

Options: The optional intrinsic constant **rdAsyncEnable** declares an asynchronous query.

See Listing 13-4 for an example of using the **Execute** method with an asynchronous query.

OpenResultset

This method creates a new **rdoResultset** object. A **rdoResultset** object can be created from the **rdoConnection** object by supplying a **rdoTable** name, a valid SQL statement, or the name of an existing **rdoQuery**. A **rdoResultset** object can also be created from a **rdoTable** object or a **rdoQuery** object.

Syntax:

> **Set** *rdoRes* = *rdoCon*.**OpenResultset**(*Source* [, *Type [, LockType* [, *Options*]]])
>
> **Set** *rdoRes* = *Object*.**OpenResultset***(Type* [, *LockType* [, *Options*]])

Where:

> *rdoRes:* A variable of type **rdoResultset**
>
> *Object:* Either a **rdoTable** object or a **rdoQuery** object. The **rdoTable** object must be refreshed before creating a resultset.
>
> *Source:* A **rdoTable** name, a **rdoQuery** name, or a valid SQL statement that may return rows.
>
> *Type:* One of these intrinsic constants: **rdOpenForwardOnly, rdOpenStatic, rdOpenKeyset,** or **rdOpenDynamic**.
>
> *LockType:* One of these intrinsic constants: **rdConcurLock** (pessimistic), **rdConcurReadOnly** (default), **rdConcorRowver** (optimistic on row ID), or **rdConcurValues** (optimistic on row values).
>
> *Options:* The optional intrinsic constant **rdAsyncEnable** declares an asynchronous query.

Listing 13-4 illustrates opening an asynchronous resultset from a **rdoQuery** object.

rdoConnection properties

The DAO **Database** object is equivalent to the **rdoConnection** object, and a query may be created from either object. The major difference between the two objects is the enhancing of asynchronous query operations within RDO.

RDO also represents a thin ODBC wrapper and the **rdoConnection** object exposes the ODBC handle **hDbc,** which is used to access ODBC API directly when RDO does not support the required functionality. Table 13-6 enumerates the properties of the **rdoConnection** object.

TABLE 13-6 RDOCONNECTION OBJECT PROPERTIES

Property	*Description*
AsyncCheckInterval	Returns or sets the interval size in milliseconds that RDO will wait before checking query completion. Defaults to 1000 milliseconds, which is one second.
Connect	Returns or sets the connection string to an ODBC data source.
CursorDriver	Returns or sets the type of cursor: **rdUseIfNeeded** <0>**:** ODBC drive will choose the appropriate cursors. Server-side cursors are used when available. **rdUseODBC** <1>**:** RDO uses the ODBC cursor library. **rdUseServer <2>:** Use server-side cursors. **rdUseClientBatch** <3>: RDO uses the optimistic batch cursor library. Required for disconnected recordsets. **rdUseNone** <4>: Result set is not returned as a cursor.
hDbc	A **Long**, the ODBC handle exposed by the **rdoConnection** object.
LastQueryResults	Returns the last **rdoResultset** object created by the last query. None may be available. This property is for supporting developer supplied queries and stored procedures, which can called as methods of the parent connection object.
LoginTimeout	Sets or returns the number of minutes the ODBC driver manager will wait before returning a timeout error. When the initial value is zero no timeout will occur and no error will be reported.
LogMessages	Sets or returns the ODBC trace file path.
Name	Connection DSN source name.
QueryTimeout	Time in seconds before the ODBC manager issues a timeout error.
RowsAffected	A **Long**, which is the number of rows deleted, updated, or inserted by an action query.
StillConnecting	TRUE when the query is still connecting. Until the connection is established, using any functionality of the **rdoConnection** object other than the **Cancel** method and the **StillExecuting** property will result in a trappable error.

PROPERTY	*DESCRIPTION*
StillExecuting	TRUEwhen the query is still executing. This property is also set TRUE on a move operation. Use the **Cancel** method to terminate the query if necessary.
Transactions	TRUE when transactions are supported.
UpdateOperation	Set to **rdOperationUpdate** (default, value = 0) when an UPDATE statement is used to modify each row. Set to **rdOperationDelIns**, which has a value of <1> when a pair of DELETE and INSERT statements is used for updating each row. This property is described in the MSDN that ships with Microsoft Visual Basic 6.0 Professional Edition. The property is not visible in Microsoft Visual Basic 6.0 of Visual Studio Enterprise Edition. The property appears useful and apparently MSDN and Visual Basic are not synchronized.
Version	Returns the data source identification as ##.##.####, which are the major and minor version numbers followed by the build number.

The rdoTables Collection

The **rdoTables** collection represents the database definitions. The tables in the database can be enumerated, the columns in a table can be enumerated, and the column attributes can be listed. No schema definitions such as foreign keys are available.

rdoTables Collection Definition

Methods: **Refresh**

Properties: **Count, Item**

rdoTable Object

Methods: OpenResultset

Properties: **Name, RowCount, Type, Updatable**

Collections: **rdoColumns**

The **OpenResultset** method is the only method of the **rdoTable** object, which can create performance problems when used in a production environment (see the

rdoConnection object for a discussion of this method). Data definition language (DDL) commands are not supported by RDO and the developer must use DDL of the data source.

A result set from a **rdoTable** object is not recommended. It is the equivalent of a SQL SELECT * and all rows of all tables will be in the result set. The best choice is where table names are enumerated in a list box as outlined in Listing 13-5. Clicking a table name, clicking a column name, and displaying the properties in a tabular control such as a grid accomplish drill-down.

The **Refresh** method of the **rdoTables** collection must be used to populate the **rdoTables** collection before use. Listing 13-5 is an example of this method. Frequent use of this method is not recommended if your SQL Server has numerous users.

rdoTable properties

RDO does not support data definition language (DDL) statements; hence there are no useful methods or any extensive properties of the **rdoTable** object.

TABLE 13-7 RDOTABLE OBJECT PROPERTIES

Property	*Description*
Name	The database table name after the **rdoTables** collection is populated.
RowCount	A **Long**, the number of table rows.
Type	A generic string name such as "VIEW", "ALIAS", or "LOCAL TEMPORARY".
Updatable	When TRUE the table can be updated by a query.

LISTING 13-5 **Enumerating the rdoTable Object**

```
Private Sub rdoTables_Click()
'(C) 1999 Bruce T. Prendergast
' DBA Prendergast Consulting
' DBA PCS
```

```
' IDG Books Worldwide ISBN 0-7645-3314-2
'
' Listing 13-5 enumerating the rdoTables collection.
'
    Dim RdoEnv As rdoEnvironment
    Dim RdoCon As rdoConnection
    Dim RdoPre As rdoPreparedStatement
    Dim rdoTbl As rdoTable
    Dim rdoCol As rdoColumn
    Dim MyRS As rdoResultset
    Dim i As Integer
    Dim myErr As rdoError
    Dim c As rdoConnection
    On Error GoTo Non_RDO_Error
    '
    '   create an RDO environment
    '
    Set RdoEnv = rdoEngine.rdoEnvironments(0)
    '
    '   connect with RDO connect string
    '
    Set RdoCon = RdoEnv.OpenConnection("", rdDriverNoPrompt, False, _
      "DATABASE=Pubs;UID=sa;PWD=;DSN=Thor;")
    RdoCon.rdoTables.Refresh
    '
    ' enumerate all tables in this database
    '
    For Each rdoTbl In RdoCon.rdoTables
      Debug.Print "Table name is :" & rdoTbl.Name
    Next rdoTbl

    MsgBox "rdoTables enumeration is complete"
    '
    ' assume that the loop above placed the table names
    ' in a combo or list box. Pick a table and enumerate
    ' the columns. I am assuming that the name was picked
```

```
' from a list box in the fragment below.
'
'
' enumerate all columns of a selected table
'
Set rdoTbl = RdoCon.rdoTables("authors")
For Each rdoCol In rdoTbl.rdoColumns
  Debug.Print "Column name is: " & rdoCol.Name
Next rdoCol
MsgBox "Column names of " & rdoTbl.Name & " enumerated successfully"
'
' carrying your imagination a little further,
' you have just clicked a column name in a list
' box. This enumerates those properties.
'
'
' we'll leave it at the "authors" table and assume
' that the "au_fname" column was clicked
'
Set rdoCol = rdoTbl.rdoColumns("au_fname")
'
' these are the rdoColumn properties. They are not
' in a collection and are enumerated directly
'
Debug.Print "AllowZeroLength: " & rdoCol.AllowZeroLength
Debug.Print "Attributes: " & rdoCol.Attributes
Debug.Print "ChunkRequired: " & _rdoCol.ChunkRequired
Debug.Print "Name: " & rdoCol.Name
Debug.Print "OrdinalPosition: " & rdoCol.OrdinalPosition
Debug.Print "Required: " & rdoCol.Required
Debug.Print "Size: " & rdoCol.Size
Debug.Print "SourceColumn: " & rdoCol.SourceColumn
Debug.Print "SourceTable: " & rdoCol.SourceTable
Debug.Print "Type: " & rdoCol.Type
Debug.Print "Updatable: " & rdoCol.Updatable
'
' the next line can't be enumerated since this is
' a rdoTables collection and not a result set.
```

```
    '
    'debug.print "Value: " & rdoCol.Value

    MsgBox "Property Enumeration is complete"
    Exit Sub
Non_RDO_Error:
    '
    ' RDO or data source errors are handled in the
    ' UnableToConnect event
    '
    For Each myErr In rdoEngine.rdoErrors
      MsgBox myErr.Description & myErr.Number
    Next myErr
    Stop
End Sub
```

Key Point Summary

This chapter presented a thumbnail sketch of the **rdoEngine, rdoErrors** collection, **rdoEnvironments** collection, **rdoConnection** collection, and the **rdoTables** collection. These are objects at the top of the RDO hierarchy and do not represent all RDO objects. The remaining RDO objects are discussed in Chapter 14.

RDO is a feature of Microsoft Visual Basic Enterprise. RDO can only be used when Microsoft Visual Basic Enterprise is installed on the same system, which limits the usability of the technology. Granted, the software occupies a smaller footprint than Access; a better choice for the developer is ODBCDirect of DAO 3.5, which needs neither an Access license nor Visual Basic Enterprise. RDO may only be redistributed when embedded in an Automation server. Your understanding of this technology may be moot because Microsoft has already announced that both DAO and RDO will be replaced by the new OLE-DB database access technology (see Chapters 15 and 16).

RDO and ODBCDirect of DAO 3.5 are closely related. RDO 1.0 predates ODBCDirect and the difference between ODBCDirect and RDO 1.0 is evolutionary. The evolution continues with events added to the **rdoConnection** object of RDO 2.0. How far the evolution will proceed is unknown because Microsoft has stated that both RDO and DAO are to be replaced with OLE-DB.

Key issues of this chapter include:

- RDO is a very thin ODBC wrapper.
- The ODBCDirect technology is a direct descendant of RDO; however, Microsoft changed the nomenclature when creating ODBCDirect.
- RDO is a component of Visual Basic Enterprise Edition.
- RDO is designed as a client-server tool to access ODBC data sources.
- RDO is a 32-bit only tool.
- RDO cannot be redistributed except as an embedded technology in an Automation server.
- RDO does not support bound forms, DDL statements, updateable joins, or heterogeneous joins. However, a RDC control is available.
- ODBCDirect of DAO and RDO have a lot of similarities at both the functional and the execution levels.
- Data definition language (DDL) statements are not available in RDO. The application must use the remote server's DDL statements.

Applying What You've Learned

An understanding of each of the database access technologies is one of the keys for selecting the proper database access technology. These questions assess your understanding of the RDO issues discussed in this chapter. The laboratory continues our concept of component construction with a RDO class that returns a disconnected **RecordSet.** The laboratory builds upon the technology developed in the ODBC class example of Chapter 12.

Instant Assessment

1. Name the first object in the RDO hierarchy.
2. Name a property of all collections.
3. Which RDO object does not have a default collection?
4. Give an example of a default collection.
5. Name an object that is automatically appended to a collection.

6. When does RDO ignore the **Close** method?
7. Name a collection where objects cannot be removed with the **Close** method.
8. Name three objects that share the same collection.
9. Name two DAO and Jet features not available in RDO.
10. What is the default collection of the **rdoEngine** object?
11. Explain the difference in optimistic concurrency in RDO as compared to DAO.
12. You have two **rdoConnection** objects, each with a result set. The **rdoEnvironment** object is not the default environment. What happens when it is closed?
13. You are attempting to register a data source using RDO. It fails and you can find nothing wrong with your VBA code. What is the likely problem?
14. What is a unique characteristic of the **rdoEnvironments**(0) object?
15. You have an error. There are many error messages and it is quite confusing because every layer of the system has its own interpretation of the problem. Where is the primary RDO error message located?
16. What must be done before accessing the **rdoTables** collection?
17. What is the scope of a transaction?
18. Why is RDO not a good choice for heterogeneous connection of the enterprise?
19. You have developed this killer application that uses RDO. What must be done to license the software?

For answers to the Instant Assessment questions, see Appendix B.

Lab Exercise

Lab 13.33 *Implementing an RDO class*

We'll take the ODBC laboratory of Chapter 12 and convert it to a RDO laboratory. The **ODBCClass** class of Chapter 12 will be replaced by a **RDOClass** class. The steps below will create the **RDOClass** class.

1. Copy the Chapter 12 laboratory into a new and empty folder.
2. Start Visual Basic and open the `ODBC.VBP` project in the new folder.
3. Remove the `ODBC.BAS` module from the project.
4. Remove the **ODBCClass** class from the project.
5. Remove the **ODBC.frm** form from the project.
6. Change the project name to **RDODemo** and the default startup form to the **frmLab** form.
7. Save the project as `RDO.VBP`.
8. Use the Visual Basic Class Wizard to create the **RDOClass** class module listed below in Listing 13-6. Select PROJECT ➪ Add Class Module ➪ New ➪ Open. Enter the code found in Listing 13-6 in the class **Declaration** section. Change the class name to *RDOClass*. The SQL Server connection string in Listing 13-6 must be modified to reflect the local SQL Server name, login, and password. The **RDOClass** class module is rather succinct when compared to the **ODBCClass** class module.

LISTING 13-6 **The RDOClass module code.**

```
'(C) 1999 Bruce T. Prendergast
' DBA Prendergast Consulting
' DBA PCS
' IDG Books Worldwide ISBN 0-7645-3314-2
'
' RDO class
'
Option Explicit
Private rdoEnv As rdoEnvironment
Private rdoCon As rdoConnection
Private rdoQry As RDOQuery
Private rdoRes As rdoResultset

Private mvarResponse As Variant
Private mvarStatus As Variant

Public Property Get Status() As Variant
  Status = mvarStatus
End Property
```

```
Public Property Get Response() As Variant
  Response = mvarResponse
End Property

Public Sub RDOQuery(ByVal QueryString As String)
  Dim MyRS As rdoResultset
  Dim RetRows As Variant                ' returned row array
  Dim RetCount As Long                  ' returned row count
  Dim i As Integer                      ' scratch integer
  Dim Results() As Variant
  Dim ResultCount As Integer
  '
  '  exit if unable to connect
  '
  If mvarStatus = False Then Exit Sub
  Set MyRS = rdoCon.OpenResultset(QueryString, rdOpenForwardOnly, _
    rdConcurReadOnly)
    '
    ' Pipe the data back. Get the rows 10 at a time
    '
    ReDim Results(2)

    Results(1) = MyRS.rdoColumns.Count
    Results(2) = 0
    ResultCount = 2
    Do Until MyRS.EOF
      RetRows = MyRS.GetRows(10)
      '
      ' Loop through the records. I am not using the
      ' resultset row count but am depending on the
      ' actual returned rows from a keyset
      '
      RetCount = UBound(RetRows, 2) + 1
      For i = 0 To RetCount - 1
        ResultCount = ResultCount + 3
        ReDim Preserve Results(ResultCount)
```

```
        Results(ResultCount - 2) = RetRows(0, i)
        Results(ResultCount - 1) = RetRows(1, i)
        Results(ResultCount) = RetRows(2, i)
      Next i
    Loop
    Results(2) = ResultCount
  mvarResponse = Results()
  Exit Sub
End Sub

Private Sub Class_Initialize()
  mvarStatus = False
  On Error GoTo Initialize_Error:
  Set rdoEnv = rdoEngine.rdoEnvironments(0)
  Set rdoCon = rdoEnv.OpenConnection("", rdDriverNoPrompt, False, _
    "DATABASE=pubs;UID=sa;PWD=;DSN=Thor;")
  mvarStatus = True
  mvarResponse = ""
Initialize_Error:
  Exit Sub
End Sub

Private Sub Class_Terminate()
  If mvarStatus Then rdoCon.Close
End Sub
```

9. Edit the **ClassDriver** class module and replace each occurrence of <ODBC> with <RDO>.
10. From **References,** select the *Microsoft Remote Data Object 2.0* library.
11. Ascertain that your local copy of Microsoft SQL Server 6.5 is running.
12. Start the project. Congratulations. You've just completed the RDO class laboratory.

CHAPTER

RDO Queries

14

About Chapter 14

Chapter 13 discussed Remote Data Objects (RDO) infrastructure issues. In Chapter 13 we discussed the RDO database connection and infrastructure in terms of the **rdoEngine, rdoEnvironment,** and **rdoConnection** object. Chapter 14 is the nuts and bolts of database management, covering the **rdoQueries, rdoResultsets, rdoColumns,** and **rdoParameters** collections.

Several methods are shared between collections. (Methods of different RDO objects overlay and I won't repeat any discussion of Chapter 13 methods in this chapter, but I will refer you to the appropriate collection in Chapter 13.) There are no surprises here. Many methods of RDO retain the name of the equivalent DAO method. There are a few new methods and properties such as the statement handle property **hStmt**. RDO is a Spartan technology that supplies the basic functionality for most ODBC data source access requirements. The developer can optionally use the **hStmt** handle to access additional features of the ODBC API directly. (We used the hDbc ODBC connection handle with a **rdoConnection** object in Listing 13-5.) The ODBC API is an alternate source for required functionality that is missing in RDO.

The examples in this chapter may be found in the CHAPTER14.VBP Visual Basic Enterprise Edition project located in the `EXAMPLES\CHAPTER14` **folder of the CD-ROM located at the back of this book.**

The rdoQueries Collection

The **rdoQueries** collection is a collection of **rdoQuery** objects, each of which represents a query. Query types include: action queries that insert, update or delete; select queries that return result sets; or procedure queries that run stored procedures. **rdoQuery** is one of two RDO objects that expose **hStmt,** the statement handle of ODBC API. (The **rdoResultset** object also exposes **hStmt,** the ODBC API statement handle.)

With DAO Microsoft always admonished developers to, "Be sure and prepare your query." There was even a question or so on the old Windows Open Services Architecture (WOSA) certification test about query preparation. With RDO 1.0 there was no choice and each RDO query was prepared. RDO 2.0 surfaces the

Prepared property of the **rdoQuery** object making a prepared (compiled) query a developer option. See the sidebar in Chapter 12 concerning Microsoft SQL Server tempDB database and prepared queries.

The **rdoQueries** collection is defined as:

rdoQueries *Collection Definition*

Properties: **Count, Item**

rdoQuery Object

Events: **QueryComplete**, **QueryTimeout, WillExecute**

Methods: **Cancel, Close, Execute, OpenResultset**

Properties: **ActiveConnection, BindThreshold, CursorType, hStmt, KeySetSize, LockType, MaxRows, Name, Prepared, QueryTimeout, RowsAffected, RowsetSize, SQL, StillExecuting, Type**

Collections: **rdoColumns, rdoParameters**

See the *rdoEngine Events* section of Chapter 13 for an example of creating an RDO event.

rdoQuery events

Events are a new feature of RDO 2.0. Chapter 13 illustrated the **InfoMessage** event of the **rdoEngine** object. Table 14-1 enumerates the events of the **rdoQuery** object.

TABLE 14-1 RDOQUERY EVENTS

Event	*When fired*
QueryComplete	Occurs when a query completes.
QueryTimeout	Occurs when the **QueryTimeout** period has elapsed and no rows have been returned.
WillExecute	Occurs immediately before query execution allowing last minute SQL changes, or to cancel the query.

rdoQuery methods

There's not much available in terms of **rdoQuery** object methods. The query can be run, closed, cancelled, or a result set can be created from a **rdoQuery** object.

Cancel

See the **rdoConnection** object (Chapter 13) for a discussion of this method.

Close

See the **rdoConnection** object (Chapter 13) for a discussion of this method.

Execute

See the **rdoConnection** object (Chapter 13) for a discussion of this method.

OpenResultset

See the **rdoConnection** object (Chapter 13) for a discussion of this method. I'm not going to repeat the **OpenResultset** discussion, but Listing 14-1 provides an interesting example where I've stripped off some of the RDO veneer and used the ODBC API directly. The example uses the **hStmt** of the **rdoResultset** object and not the **hStmt** of the **rdoQuery** object. This example uses ODBC 3.0, which is the ODBC32.DLL.

The **SQLError** and the **SQLNumResultCols** API functions are both declared in the declaration section of the form as **Private.** A few constants are hard-coded precluding the need to bring in whole libraries for just two API references.

The ODBC API error code follows ODBC conventions and not RDO code conventions. No error event occurs with an ODBC API call and the return code must be tested for a legitimate value. Listing 14-1 goes under the thin ODBC wrapper of RDO and calls ODBC API functions directly.

LISTING 14-1 **An rdoResultset Object and the ODBC API**

```
Private Sub ODBC_API_Click()
'(C) 1999 Bruce T. Prendergast
' DBA Prendergast Consulting
' DBA PCS
' IDG Books Worldwide ISBN 0-7645-3314-2
'
```

```
' Listing 14-1 A prepared query and the ODBC API from RDO
'
    Dim RdoEnv As rdoEnvironment
    Dim RdoCon As rdoConnection
    Dim RdoQry As rdoQuery
    Dim MyRS As rdoResultset
    Dim RetCode As Integer   ' Return code from ODBC API
    Dim ipCol As Integer     ' Returned row count
    '
    '   SQLError parameters
    '
    Const MAX_STRING_LENGTH = 128
    Dim ErrCode As Integer
    Dim ErrorMsg As String * MAX_STRING_LENGTH
    Dim cbErrorMsg As Integer
    Dim NativeError As Long
    Dim SqlState As String * MAX_STRING_LENGTH
    Const SQL_SUCCESS = 0
    '/* SQLError defines */
    Const SQL_NULL_HENV = 0
    Const SQL_NULL_HDBC = 0
    Const SQL_NULL_HSTMT = 0
    Dim myErr As rdoError
    Dim c As rdoConnection
    On Error GoTo Non_RDO_Error
    '
    '   create an RDO environment
    '
    Set RdoEnv = rdoEngine.rdoEnvironments(0)
    '
    '   connect with RDO connect string
    '
    Set RdoCon = RdoEnv.OpenConnection("", rdDriverNoPrompt, False, _
      "DATABASE=Pubs;UID=sa;PWD=;DSN=Thor;")
    Set RdoQry = RdoCon.CreateQuery("MyPS", _
      "SELECT au_lname, au_fname " & _
```

```
  "FROM authors " & _
  "WHERE au_lname LIKE 'G%' ")
'
' A little magic here. We'll define a Microsoft SQL
' Server specific ODBC connection option that drops
' temporary stored procedures on the next SQLPrepare
' API reference or will drop all stored procedures
' when the statement is released. See the sidebar in
' Chapter 12 that discusses SQL Server tembDB tables.

'
' We're using the ODBC API here
'
Const SQL_USE_PROCEDURE_FOR_PREPARE = 1202
Const SQL_UP_ON_DROP As Long = 2
'
' Switch to ODBC error processing
'
On Error GoTo ODBC_Error_Processing
RetCode = BTPSQLSetConnectOption(RdoCon.hdbc, _
  SQL_USE_PROCEDURE_FOR_PREPARE, SQL_UP_ON_DROP)
If RetCode <> SQL_SUCCESS Then Stop
RdoQry.Prepared = True
Set MyRS = RdoQry.OpenResultset(rdOpenForwardOnly, rdConcurReadOnly)
'
' get the result set row count
'
RetCode = BTPSQLNumResultCols(MyRS.hstmt, ipCol)
  '
' this error code analysis follows ODBC conventions
' and not RDO conventions
'
  If RetCode <> SQL_SUCCESS Then
    MsgBox "ODBC API call failed with return code:" & Str$(RetCode)
    ErrCode = BTPSQLError(RdoEnv.henv, RdoCon.hdbc, RdoQry.hstmt, _
      SqlState, NativeError, ErrorMsg, MAX_STRING_LENGTH, cbErrorMsg)
```

```
      MsgBox "RetCode is: " & Str$(RetCode)
      MsgBox "Error message: " & Mid$(ErrorMsg, 1, cbErrorMsg)
      MsgBox "SQL State: " & SqlState
      MsgBox "Native error code: " & Str$(NativeError)
      Exit Sub
    End If
    If ipCol <> 2 Then
      MsgBox "ipcol is: " & Str$(ipCol)
      MsgBox "SQLNumResultCols returned wrong value"
      Exit Sub
    End If
    While Not MyRS.EOF
      Debug.Print MyRS(0), MyRS(1)
      MyRS.MoveNext
    Wend
    MsgBox "ODBC API statement was successful"
    Exit Sub
ODBC_Error_Processing:
    For Each myErr In rdoEngine.rdoErrors
      '
      ' I expect warning messages.
      ' Ignore just the With_Info messages such as
      ' "connecting to pubs", etc.,
      '
      If (myErr.SQLRetcode <> rdSQLSuccessWithInfo) Then
        MsgBox myErr.Description & " State:" & myErr.SqlState & _
          " SQLRetCode:" & myErr.SQLRetcode & "NativeErrorCode:" & myErr.Number
      End If
    Next myErr
    Resume Next
Non_RDO_Error:
    '
    ' RDO or data source errors are handled in the
    ' UnableToConnect event
    '
    For Each myErr In rdoEngine.rdoErrors
```

```
      MsgBox myErr.Description & myErr.Number
    Next myErr
    Stop
End Sub
```

rdoQuery properties

rdoResultset objects are created using the **OpenResultset** method of the **rdoQuery, rdoTable,** or **rdoConnection** object, or by using the **RemoteData** control. Table 14-2 enumerates the properties of the **rdoQuery** object, some of which overlap other RDO objects.

TABLE 14-2 RDOQUERY PROPERTIES

Property	*Description*
ActiveConnection	The **ActiveConnection** property, when paired with the **CursorDriver** property with a value of **rdUseClientBatch**, manages disconnected recordsets. The **ActiveConnection** property is set to **Nothing**, effectively disconnecting the recordset.
BindThreshold	Binary large objects (BLOBS) are managed with the **BindThreshold**, **GetChunk**, and **AppendChunk** methods. The **BindThreshold** property sets the column size in bytes. Data larger than this threshold must use the **AppendChunk** and **GetChunk** methods of the **rdoColumn** object.
CursorType	Returns or sets the type of cursor. These intrinsic constants, (**ResultsetTypeConstants**) define the possible values of the **CursorType** property. **rdUseIfNeeded** <0>: ODBC drive will choose the appropriate cursors. Server-side cursors are used when available. **rdUseODBC** <1>: RDO uses the ODBC cursor library. **rdUseServer** <2>: Use server-side cursors. **rdUseClientBatch** <3>: RDO uses the optimistic batch cursor library. Required for disconnected recordsets. **rdUseNone** <4>: Result set is not returned as a cursor.

continued

TABLE 14-2 RDOQUERY PROPERTIES *(CONTINUED)*

Property	*Description*
hStmt	The **rdoQuery** object exposes the ODBC statement handle **hStmt**, which is also exposed by the **rdoResultset** object.
KeysetSize	Set or returns the number of rows in the keyset buffer. A zero value results in a *keyset driven* cursor. A value other than zero results in a *mixed* cursor where keys in the keyset are keyset driven and keys not in the keyset are dynamic driven. The driver buffers extra rows when **KeysetSize** is greater than **RowsetSize**.
LockType	Manages the concurrency with these intrinsic constants: **rdConcurReadOnly** <1>: Default read-only cursor with no updates permitted. **rdConcurLock** <2>: Pessimistic concurrency. **rdConcurRowVer** <3>: Use Row ID for optimistic concurrency. **rdConcurValues** <4>: Use row values for optimistic concurrency. **rdConcurBatch** <5>: Batch mode optimistic concurrency. A status is returned for each row updated.
MaxRows	The **MaxRows** property defines the maximum number of rows returned by a query or the maximum number of rows processed in an action query.
Name	A string value that represents the object name.
Prepared	A query is compiled (prepared) by setting the **Prepare** property to TRUE, which is also the default value. The query is executed using the ODBC **SQLExecDirect** API when the **Prepare** property is False; the ODBC **SQLPrepare** API is used when the **Prepare** property is TRUE. Temporary stored procedures (compiled queries) are stored in tempDB of Microsoft SQL Server. When not managed properly, preparing a query may crash SQL Server (See sidebar Chapter 12).
QueryTimeout	The query time out period in seconds can be set with the **QueryTimeout** property.
RowsAffected	Returns the number of rows as a result of the last **Execute** method. This property can be tested against an expected value of an action query and if the value is wrong, the transaction can be aborted.

PROPERTY	*DESCRIPTION*
RowsetSize	Sets the maximum row count of a subsequent **rdoResultset** cursor. Set the number or rows (and associated data pages) locked when pessimistic concurrency is in effect. At least **RowsetSize** rows (and associated data pages) remain locked until the cursor is closed.
SQL	The SQL source is stored in this property.
StillExecuting	Returns TRUE while the query is executing and FALSE otherwise. Also set to TRUE when a move method is invoked.
Type	Type of query determined with these intrinsic constants: **rdQSelect** <0>: Select query, data is returned. **rdQAction** <1>: Action query, which can be an insert, delete, or update. **rdQProcedure** <2>: A query that runs a stored procedure. **rdQCompound** <3>: A query that contains SELECT statements and an action query.

THE RDORESULTSETS COLLECTION

The **rdoResultsets** collection represents the currently open **rdoResultset** objects created using the Remote Data Control, or using the **OpenResultset** method of the **rdoQuery, rdoTable,** or **rdoConnection** object. In RDO 1.0, setting a **rdoResultset** object to another **rdoResultset** object did not close the previous result set. In RDO 2.0, the previous **rdoResultset** object is automatically closed when the object is set to a new **rdoResultset** value.

The **rdoResultsets** collection is defined as:

***rdoResultsets** Collection Definition*

Properties: **Count, Item**

***rdoResultset** Object*

Events: **Associate, Dissociate, ResultsChanged, RowStatusChanged, RowCurrencyChange, WillAssociate, WillDissociate, WillUpdateRows**

Methods: **AddNew, BatchUpdate, Cancel, CancelBatch, CancelUpdate, CancelBatch, Close, Delete, Edit, GetClipString, GetRows, MoreResults, Move, MoveFirst, MoveLast, MoveNext, MovePrevious, Requery, Resync, Update**

Properties: **AbsolutePosition, ActiveConnection, BatchCollisionCount, BatchCollisionRows, BatchSize, BOF, Bookmark, Bookmarkable, EditMode, EOF, hStmt, LastModified, LockEdits, LockType, Name, PercentPosition, Restartable, RowCount, Status, StillExecuting, Transactions, Type, Updatable, UpdateCriteria, UpdateOperation**

Both the rdoResultset object and the rdoQuery object expose the ODBC statement handle hStmt.

A **rdoResultset** is an object that represents rows returned from a query. A result set is created by (see **rdoConnection::OpenResultset** in Chapter 13 for the precise syntax):

- Opening a **rdoResultset** object from a **rdoConnection** using the name of an existing **rdoTable** object, the name of a **rdoQuery** object, or a SQL statement.
- Opening a **rdoResultset** object from an existing **rdoTable** object or an existing **rdoQuery** object.

The **rdoResultset** object has most of the properties of the DAO **Recordset** object. The only property that is obviously missing is the **RecordsetClone** property, which is useful in synchronizing a bound Microsoft Access form. However, this property isn't needed because RDO supports data-aware controls and not bound forms.

rdoResultset Events

Events in RDO offer a dimension not available in the cousin of RDO, ODBCDirect of DAO. Table 14-3 enumerates the events available with the **rdoResultset** object.

rdoResultset Methods

This is where the work is done. The **rdoResultset** methods are very rich and parallel many of those available in DAO. There are obvious parallels with DAO such as the generic move methods and the **GetRows** method.

TABLE 14-3 RDORESULTSET EVENTS

EVENT	*DESCRIPTION*
Associate	Event occurs when a new connection is associated with the **rdoResultset** object.
Dissociate	Event occurs when the **ActiveConnection** property of the **rdoResultset** object is set to **Nothing**.
ResultsChanged	Event occurs when the current row set is changed and multiple result sets exist.
RowCurrencyChange	Event occurs when the current row pointer is repositioned.
RowStatusChanged	Event occurs when the row status changes as a result of an edit, delete, or insert.
WillAssociate	Event occurs before a new connection is associated with the **rdoResultset** object.
WillDissociate	Event occurs before the **ActiveConnection** property is set to **Nothing**.
WillUpdateRows	Event occurs before a server update.

AddNew

AddNew adds a new row to a row set. The newly added row may or may not be visible to other applications. This is a function of the cursor type.

The row that was current before the new row was added remains the current row. Setting the **Bookmark** property to the **LastModified** property can set the new row current.

A pending **AddNew** operation can be canceled with the **CancelUpdate** method but only before the row is updated with the **Update** method. Figure 14-1 illustrates the general sequence of operations.

Syntax:

*rdoRes.**AddNew***

Where:

rdoRes: An object of type **rdoResultset**

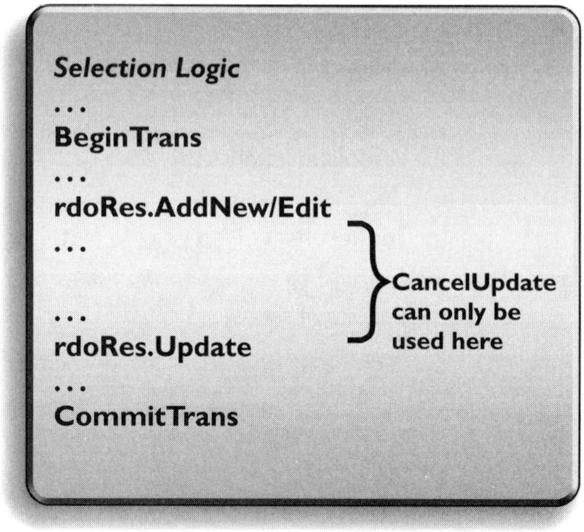

FIGURE 14-1 Using AddNew, Edit, CancelUpdate, and Update

The record (row) editing facilities of RDO appear to be identical to those of DAO. The **CancelUpdate** method is supported in both DAO and RDO and has the advantage of canceling an update without manipulation of the cursor. The editing and updating techniques of RDO are illustrated in Listing 14-2. Listing 14-2 also illustrates the **CancelUpdate** method and the rolling back of a transaction. The successful transaction rollback is verified.

LISTING 14-2 Canceling an update with CancelUpdate and rolling back a transaction with RollbackTrans

```
Private Sub Updating_Rowsets_Click()
'(C)1999 Bruce T. Prendergast
' DBA Prendergast Consulting
' DBA PCS
' IDG Books Worldwide ISBN 0-7645-3314-2
'
' Listing 14-2 Canceling an update and rolling
' back a transaction
'
    Dim RdoEnv As rdoEnvironment
    Dim RdoCon As rdoConnection
    Dim RdoQry As rdoQuery
```

```
Dim MyRS As rdoResultset

Dim myErr As rdoError
Dim c As rdoConnection
On Error GoTo Non_RDO_Error
'
'   create an RDO environment
'
Set RdoEnv = rdoEngine.rdoEnvironments(0)
'
'   connect with RDO connect string
'
Set RdoCon = RdoEnv.OpenConnection("", rdDriverNoPrompt, False, _
  "DATABASE=Pubs;UID=sa;PWD=;DSN=Thor;")
Set RdoQry = RdoCon.CreateQuery("MyPS", _
  "SELECT au_fname, au_lname, au_id " & _
  "FROM authors " & _
  "WHERE au_id = '172-32-1176'")
Set MyRS = RdoQry.OpenResultset(rdOpenDynamic, _
     rdConcurLock)
'
' Do the action query
'
On Error GoTo Transaction_Error
RdoEnv.BeginTrans
With MyRS
  .MoveFirst
  Do While Not .EOF
    If !au_id <> "172-32-1176" Then
      .MoveNext
    Else
      '
      ' found it, edit it, and change our mind
      '
      .Edit
      !au_fname = "John"
      .CancelUpdate
```

```
                Exit Do
            End If
        Loop
    End With
    '
    ' a null transaction rollback, but it should work
    '
    RdoEnv.RollbackTrans
    MyRS.Close
    Set MyRS = Nothing
    On Error GoTo Non_RDO_Error
    '
    ' now let's see that we didn't change anything
    '
    Set RdoQry = Nothing
    Set RdoQry = RdoCon.CreateQuery("MyPS", _
      "SELECT au_fname " & _
      "FROM authors " & _
      "WHERE au_id = '172-32-1176'")
    Set MyRS = RdoQry.OpenResultset(rdOpenDynamic, _
      rdConcurLock)
    If MyRS(0) <> "Johnson" Then
      MsgBox "CancelUpdate failed"
    Else
      MsgBox "RDO CancelUpdate statement was successful"
    End If
    Set MyRS = Nothing
    Set RdoQry = Nothing
    Exit Sub
Transaction_Error:
    RdoEnv.RollbackTrans
    MsgBox "Transaction failed and rolled back"
Non_RDO_Error:
    '
    ' RDO or data source errors are handled in the
    ' UnableToConnect event
    '
```

```
    For Each myErr In rdoEngine.rdoErrors
      MsgBox myErr.Description & myErr.Number
    Next myErr
    Stop
End Sub
```

BatchUpdate

BatchUpdate performs a batched optimistic update. This update mechanism is used when the Client Batch cursor library is in use. This occurs when the **CursorDriver** property of the **rdoQuery** object or **rdoConnection** object is set to the intrinsic value **rdUseClientBatch**. The **BatchUpdate** method updates both the **BatchCollisionRows** and **BatchCollisionCount** properties.

Syntax:

rdoRes.**BatchUpdate**(*SingleRow, Force*)

Where:

rdoRes: A variable of type **rdoResultset.**

SingleRow: A variable of type **Boolean** value that is TRUE for a single row update.

Force: A variable of type **Boolean** value that is TRUE when a row or rows will overwrite an existing row or rows independent of batch collisions.

Table 14-4 enumerates the different combinations of the *SingleRow* and *Force* parameters.

TABLE 14-4 SINGLEROW AND FORCE COMBINATIONS

State Combinations	*Actions*
SingleRow = TRUE	
Force = TRUE	Overwrite a single row with the current **rdoResultset** row.
SingleRow = FALSE	
Force = TRUE	Force all row updates ignoring optimistic concurrency.
SingleRow = TRUE	
Force = FALSE	Batch update a single row with optimistic concurrency.

Cancel

See the **rdoConnection** object (Chapter 13) for discussion of this method.

CancelBatch

CancelBatch cancels all uncommitted changes in the local cursor. Data reverts back to the original database fetch state, which is the equivalent to the **OriginalValue** property of the **rdoColumn** object.

Syntax:

*rdoRes.*CancelBatch

Where:

rdoRes: A variable of type **rdoResultset**.

CancelUpdate

CancelUpdate flushes the copy buffer. It has the same effect as moving to another row. All changes are lost. Listing 14-3 illustrates the **CancelUpdate** method.

Syntax:

*rdoRes.*CancelUpdate

Where:

rdoRes: A variable of type rdoResultset.

Close

See the **rdoConnection** object (Chapter 13) for discussion of this method.

Delete

This method deletes the current row of an updatable row set. A current row must exist when using this method or an error will occur.

The cursor must be positioned to another row after the deletion even though the deleted row is no longer accessible. The **CancelUpdate** method is not applicable to a deletion. A deleted row can only be restored with the **RollbackTrans** method on a **rdoEnvironment** object.

A delete may fail for numerous reasons. Factors to consider on a delete failure include:

- There is no current row.
- The **rdoConnection** object or the **rdoResultset** object is read-only.
- Columns in the row are not updateable.
- The row doesn't exist, it has already been deleted.
- The row or data page is locked by another user.
- The user permissions do not allow a delete operation.

Syntax:

*rdoRes.***Delete**

Where:

rdoRes: A variable of type **rdoResultset**.

Edit

This method updates a row in a row set. Changes are placed in the copy buffer until removed with the **CancelUpdate** method, the cursor is moved to another row, or the **Update** method is used to update the row.

The **LockEdits** field manages concurrency. Concurrency is the ability of other users to access the system while an update is in process. This requires an understanding of pessimistic and optimistic locking:

- ***Pessimistic Locking*** — The ODBC data source determines when row or page locking is used. Row or table locking occurs when the editing starts. This point is identified by the execution of the **Edit** method. The lock is released after the **Update** method completes.
- ***Optimistic Locking*** — The row or page is not locked until an attempt is made to update the row with the **Update** method. This is called optimistic locking because the developer believes that there will be few lock collisions. This is an intuitive judgment call on the part of the developer and performance from optimistic locking may be less than when using pessimistic locking. The **Update** method manages the concurrency and reads the current version of the newly locked row. An error is returned when either the

row values or the row ID (see Table 14-5, **Locktype** property) don't match the row in the row set at the start of the edit as marked by the **Edit** method.

The **LockEdits** property is set TRUE for pessimistic locking which can be either row or page locking An error occurs when the row or page is locked and pessimistic concurrency is in use. The **LockEdits** field is set false for optimistic concurrency. With optimistic concurrency the new row is compared with the previous version and an error occurs if another user has changed the row. The **LockEdits** property is set when the resultset is opened and is an integer that specifies the type of concurrency control. A default concurrency of **rdConcurReadOnly** is assumed. The **Edit** method fails when:

- A current row doesn't exist.
- The **rdoConnection** or **rdoResultset** object is read-only.
- Columns in the row are not updateable.
- The **EditMode** property indicates an edit is already in process.
- Another user locks the row or data page.

Syntax:

rdoRes.**Edit**

Where:

rdoRes: A variable of type **rdoResultset**.

See Listing 14-2 for an example that uses this method.

GetClipString

The **GetClipString** method is the string equivalent of the **GetRows** method. Rather than returning the data as a 2-dimensional array, the data is returned as a delimited string. The **GetClipString** method is useful in formatting data for grid controls.

Syntax:

ResultSetString=rdoRes.**GetClipString**(NumRows, [ColumnDelimiter], [RowDelimiter], [NullExpr])

Where:

ResultSetString: A variable used to reference the entire result set as a delimited string.

rdoRes: A variable of type **rdoResultset.**

NumRows: A variable of type **Long,** the number of rows in the clip string.

ColumnDelimiter: A **Variant** of type **String**. An expression describing the column delimiter. Default is **vbTab.**

RowDelimiter: A **Variant** of type **String.** An expression describing the row delimiter. Default is **vbCr.**

NullExpr: A **Variant** of type **String** that is used when **Null** values are encountered.

GetRows

This method retrieves one or more rows into a **Variant** variable and should be considered when performance is an issue with a remote server. This method further partitions the concept of a resultset with multiple keysets. A logical approach is to have a keyset size, which is an integral number of **GetRows** block sizes. **GetRows** will not retrieve data for any column where the **ChunkRequired** property is true.

Syntax:

varArray = *rdoRes*.**GetRows**(Rows)

Where:

varArray: A variable of type **Variant.**

rdoRes: An object of type **rdoResultset.**

Rows: A number of type **Long.**

Listing 14-3 uses the RDO **GetRows** method to return values into a variant array that is indexed by row and column. The number of rows returned is unpredictable and the code in Listing 14-3 calculates the returned row count with the **Ubound** function of VBA.

LISTING 14-3 Improving RDO performance with GetRows

```
Private Sub GetRows_Click()
'(C) 1999 Bruce T. Prendergast
' DBA Prendergast Consulting
```

```
' DBA PCS
' IDG Books Worldwide ISBN 0-7645-3314-2
'
' Listing 14-3 Using GetRows in RDO
'
  Dim RdoEnv As rdoEnvironment
  Dim RdoCon As rdoConnection
  Dim RdoPre As rdoPreparedStatement
  Dim MyRS As rdoResultset

  Dim RetRows As Variant          ' returned row array
  Dim RetCount As Long            ' returned row count
  Dim i As Integer                ' scratch integer

  Dim myErr As rdoError
  Dim c As rdoConnection
  On Error GoTo Non_RDO_Error
  '
  '   create an RDO environment
  '
  Set RdoEnv = rdoEngine.rdoEnvironments(0)
  '
  '   connect with RDO connect string
  '
  Set RdoCon = RdoEnv.OpenConnection("", rdDriverNoPrompt, False, _
    "DATABASE=Pubs;UID=sa;PWD=;DSN=Thor;")
  Set MyRS = RdoCon.OpenResultset( _
    "SELECT au_lname, au_fname, au_id " & _
    "FROM authors ", _
    rdOpenForwardOnly, rdConcurReadOnly)
  '
  ' get the rows 10 at a time
  '
  Do Until MyRS.EOF
    RetRows = MyRS.GetRows(10)
    '
```

```
            ' Loop through the records. I am not using the
            ' resultset row count but am depending on the
            ' actual returned rows from a keyset
            '
            RetCount = UBound(RetRows, 2) + 1
            For i = 0 To RetCount - 1
              Debug.Print RetRows(0, i);
              Debug.Print RetRows(1, i);
              Debug.Print RetRows(2, i)
            Next i
          Loop
          MsgBox "GetRows example completed successfully"
          Exit Sub
      Non_RDO_Error:
          '
          ' RDO or data source errors are handled in the
          ' UnableToConnect event
          '
          For Each myErr In rdoEngine.rdoErrors
            MsgBox myErr.Description & myErr.Number
          Next myErr
          Stop
      End Sub
```

MoreResults

The current result set is cleared and a value of TRUE is returned when additional result sets are pending. The **BOF** and **EOF** properties are both set to TRUE when there are no further result sets.

The **Cancel method** flushes the current result set; however, it also flushes all pending result sets.

Syntax:

varBool = *rdoRes*.**MoreResults**

Where:

varBool: A variable of type **Boolean**.

rdoRes: An object of type **rdoResultset**.

The **MoreResults** implementation manages multiple select queries, which is useful when loading a Visual Basic form that has many combo or list boxes that must be populated. Listing 14-4 illustrates using the **MoreResults** method.

LISTING 14-4 Processing Multiple Queries with MoreResults

```
Private Sub MoreResults_Click()
'(C) 1999 Bruce T. Prendergast
' DBA Prendergast Consulting
' DBA PCS
' IDG Books Worldwide ISBN 0-7645-3314-2
'
' Listing 14-4 Using the MoreResults method in RDO
'
    Dim RdoEnv As rdoEnvironment
    Dim RdoCon As rdoConnection
    Dim MyRS As rdoResultset
    Dim myErr As rdoError
    Dim c As rdoConnection
    Dim MySQL As String
    On Error GoTo Non_RDO_Error
    '
    '   create an RDO environment
    '
    Set RdoEnv = rdoEngine.rdoEnvironments(0)
    '
    ' I must use ODBC for multiple queries
    '
    RdoEnv.CursorDriver = rdUseOdbc
    '
    '   connect with RDO connect string
    '
    Set RdoCon = RdoEnv.OpenConnection("", rdDriverNoPrompt, False, _
      "DATABASE=Pubs;UID=sa;PWD=;DSN=Thor;")
    '
    ' Build two statements
    '
```

```
    Set MyRS = RdoCon.OpenResultset( _
      " SELECT au_lname, au_fname, au_id " & _
      " FROM authors " & _
      " WHERE au_id = '172-32-1176'" & _
      " SELECT title_id, title FROM titles", _
      rdOpenForwardOnly, rdConcurReadOnly)
    Debug.Print MyRS!au_fname; " "; MyRS!au_lname; " "; MyRS!au_id
    Do While MyRS.MoreResults
      Do Until MyRS.EOF
        Debug.Print MyRS!title_id; " "; MyRS!Title
        MyRS.MoveNext
      Loop
    Loop
    MsgBox "Multiple Query statement was successful"
    Exit Sub
Non_RDO_Error:
    '
    ' RDO or data source errors are handled
    ' in the UnableToConnect event
    '
    For Each myErr In rdoEngine.rdoErrors
      MsgBox myErr.Description & myErr.Number
    Next myErr
    Stop
End Sub
```

Move, MoveFirst, MoveLast, MoveNext, And MovePrevious

These are standard methods for navigating within a result set. Movement is relative to the current position of a bookmark. Movement is always relative to the current row unless a bookmark is specified.

An error occurs when using the **Move** method and there are no rows.

The **BOF** property is set when positioning before the first row and the **EOF** property is set when positioning beyond the last row.

Syntax:

rdoRes.**Move** *Rows* [, *Start*]

rdoRes.**{MoveFirst | MoveLast | MoveNext | MovePrevious}**

Where:

rdoRes: An object of type **rdoResultset**

Rows: a signed **Long** that specifies the number of rows to position

Start: A variable of type **Variant** identifying a bookmark

Most examples use one of these methods.

Requery

The data in a **rdoResultset** is updated with this method. Previous bookmarks are lost after performing a **Requery**. A new result set is created when **rdoParameter** objects have changed. Objects with their **Restartable** property set to **False** cannot use this method.

Syntax:

rdoRes.**Requery**

Where:

rdoRes: An object of type **rdoResultset.**

An example usage of the **Requery** method is a click event of a combo box where parameters are updated from text boxes.

```
myRes.Parameters(0) = txtf_name
myRes.Parameters(1) = txtl_name
MyRes.Requery
```

Update

This is the last of the **rdoResultset** object methods. The row set is updated from the data placed in the copy buffer by either **Edit** or **AddNew**. **CancelUpdate** can be used until the **Update** method is applied. After that, only the **RollbackTrans** method can reverse the changes.

Syntax:

rdoRes.**Update**

Where:

rdoRes: An object of type **rdoResultset.**

rdoResultset properties

What follows is a discussion of **rdoResultset** properties. It is not a formal presentation, but an enumeration of the salient facts and issues. So let's begin our sketch of the properties of the **rdoResultset** object in Table 14-5.

TABLE 14-5 RDORESULTSET OBJECT PROPERTIES

Property	*Description*
AbsolutePosition	Returns or sets the absolute row number. The **AbsolutePosition** property is used to position the current row pointer to a specific row, but only if the **rdoResultset** object is a *keyset* cursor or a *static-type* cursor. Setting an absolute position is not supported for either *dynamic* or *forward-only* type **rdoResultset** objects. The **BookMarkable** property of the **rdoResultset** object must be TRUE before the **AbsolutePosition** property can be used.
ActiveConnection	Sets or returns an object representing the connection. The **ActiveConnection** property, when paired with the **CursorDriver** property value of **rdUseClientBatch**, manages disconnected recordsets. When the **ActiveConnection** property is set to **Nothing**, the **rdoRecordset** object is effectively disconnected.
BatchCollisionCount	The **BatchCollisionCount** is the number of rows in error as a result of a **BatchUpdate** method. The value is also the number of bookmarks in the **BatchCollisonRows** array. The **Bookmark** property of the **rdoResultset** object can be set to bookmarks in the **BatchCollisionRows** array, which enables positioning to each row that failed the most recent **BatchUpdate** method.
BatchCollisionRows	Returns an array of bookmarks corresponding to the rows that generated collisions during the last batch-mode update.
BatchSize	The **BatchSize** property defines the number of SQL statements sent in each batch. The default value is 15.
BOF, **EOF**	The **BOF** and **EOF** are TRUE respectively for a beginning-of-file or an end-of-file state. Both **BOF** and **EOF** are TRUE, and the **RowCount** property is zero when the returned result set contains no rows. An error occurs with a **MoveNext** when **EOF** is TRUE and correspondingly, an error occurs with a **MovePrevious** when **BOF** is TRUE. Table 14-6 enumerates conditions for different **EOF** and **BOF** states.

continued

TABLE 14-5 RDORESULTSET OBJECT PROPERTIES (CONTINUED)

Property	*Description*
Bookmark	Each row of a *non-forward-only-type* **rdoResultset** object has a unique bookmark. This **Bookmark** property may be stored in a variant, the cursor will return to that row when the variant value is set back into the **Bookmark** property. The **Bookmarkable** property is TRUE if the **rdoResultset** object supports bookmarks.
Bookmarkable	Returns TRUE when bookmarks are supported, FALSE otherwise.
EditMode	Returns the editing state: **rdEditNone** <0>: No editing is in process. **rdEditInProgress** <1>: Editing is in progress and the current row is in the copy buffer. **rdEditAdd** <2>: The **AddNew** method has been invoked and the contents of the copy buffer is a new row, which has not been saved in the database.
hStmt	The **hStmt** property is the exposed ODBC statement handle, which is required for ODBC API calls.
LastModified	The **LastModified** property returns a bookmark to the most recently edited row. Positioning to the new row is accomplished by setting the **Bookmark** property to the **LastModified** property.
LockEdits	Concurrency is managed with the **LockEdits** property. When **LockEdits** is TRUE pessimistic concurrency is in effect and conversely, when **LockEdits** is false optimistic concurrency is in effect. An error occurs with pessimistic concurrency when using the **OpenResultset** method and the page or row is locked. An error also occurs with optimistic concurrency when using the **Update** method and the row or page is locked. When an error occurs, the changes to the row made by the other user can be viewed by setting the **Bookmark** property of the **rdoResultset** object to itself, however, local changes will be lost.
LockType	Manages the concurrency with these intrinsic constants: **rdConcurReadOnly** <1>**:** Default read-only cursor with no updates permitted. **rdConcurLock** <2>**:** Pessimistic concurrency. **rdConcurRowVer** <3>**:** Use Row ID for optimistic concurrency.

Property	*Description*
	rdConcurValues <4>**:** Use row values for optimistic concurrency.
	rdConcurBatch <5>**:** Batch mode optimistic concurrency. A status is returned for each row updated.
Name	The **Name** property of the **rdoResultset** object is the first 256 characters of the SQL query.
PercentPosition	The **PercentPosition** property returns or sets a **Single** variable to the approximate position in the buffer. The **PercentPosition** is relative to the row set population and will not be accurate unless the **rdoResultset** object is fully populated.
Restartable	When the **Restartable** property is TRUE the **rdoResultset** object supports the **Requery** method for refreshing the **rdoResultset** object.
RowCount	The number of rows returned is stored in the **RowCount** property. Referencing the **RowCount** property forces a population of the row set, which is equivalent to a **MoveLast** method. The **RowCount** property is set to <-1> until the query is complete.
Status	Sets or returns the status of the current row. The application will set either **rdRowModified** or **rdRowDeleted** before using the **BatchUpdate** method. Intrinsic definitions include:
	rdRowUnmodified <0>: The row was either updated successfully or is unmodified.
	rdRowModified <1>: The row is modified, however the database is not updated.
	rdRowNew <2>: The row has been inserted with the **AddNew** method, however the database has not been updated.
	rdRowDeleted <3>: The row is marked as deleted, however the row has not been deleted from the database.
	rdRowDBDeleted <4>: The row is marked as deleted and is deleted in the database.
StillExecuting	The **StillExecuting** property is TRUE when the query is still in execution, however, unless the **rdAsyncEnable** option is used, the application will be blocked until the query is complete. **StillExecuting** is set TRUE until a **MoreResults** method completes the population of a subsequent query. The **QueryComplete** event is an alternative method for determining query completion.

continued

TABLE 14-5 RDORESULTSET OBJECT PROPERTIES (*CONTINUED*)

PROPERTY	*DESCRIPTION*
Transactions	The **Transactions** property is TRUE when transactions are supported. The ODBC **SQLGetInfo** API function is called to determine if the ODBC driver is capable of supporting transactions.
Type	ODBC drivers may not support every type of **rdoResultset** cursor type and the ODBC will revert to a supported cursor when an unsupported cursor is requested. RDO supported cursor types include: **rdOpenForwardOnly** <0>: Fixed set, non-scrolling. **rdOpenKeyset** <1>: Updatable, fixed set, scrollable query result set cursor. **rdOpenDynamic** <2>: Updatable, dynamic set, scrollable query result set cursor. **rdOpenStatic** <3>: Read-only, fixed set.
Updatable	The **Updatable** property is TRUE when the **rdoResultset** object contains updateable rows. An updateable row does not mean that a column is updateable and each column should be checked individually before attempting to update the column.
UpdateCriteria	The **UpdateCriteria** property is used to optimize an update using the client batch cursor library (CBCL). The rows to be updated are isolated by an SQL WHERE clause, which is created by the CBCL to isolate the rows in question. This limits the rows referenced to only those rows changed, which minimizes trigger activity on Microsoft SQL Server (triggers are used to enforce referential integrity). Intrinsic values available: **rdCriteriaKey** <0>: Key columns used in the WHERE clause, default. **rdCriteriaAllCols** <1>: Key columns and all columns in the WHERE clause. **rdCriteriaUpdCols** <2>: Key columns and all updated columns in the WHERE clause. **rdCriteriaTimeStamp** <3>: Timestamp columns only. An error occurs with no timestamp columns.
UpdateOperation	This property is only applicable to how rows are modified, since an insert of a new row will always use an INSERT statement and a row deletion will always use a delete statement.

Property	*Description*
	rdOperationUpdate <0>: The client batch cursor library uses an SQL UPDATE statement for each modified row, default.
	rdOperationDelIns <1>: The client batch cursor library uses a pair of DELETE and INSERT statements for each modified row.

TABLE 14-6 CONDITIONS FOR VARIOUS EOF AND BOF COMBINATIONS

	MoveFirst *MoveLast*	*MovePrevious* *Move < 0*	*Move 0*	*MoveNext* *Move > 0*
BOF = TRUE EOF = FALSE	Allowed	Error	Error	Allowed
BOF = FALSE EOF = TRUE	Allowed	Allowed	Error	Error
BOF = TRUE EOF = TRUE	Error	Error	Error	Error
BOF = FALSE EOF = FALSE	Allowed	Allowed	Allowed	Allowed

The rdoColumns Collection

rdoColumns is the default collection of the **rdoQuery, rdoResultset,** and **rdoTable** objects. **rdoColumn** objects need not be closed. They are automatically closed when the **rdoQuery** or **rdoResultset** object is closed.

rdoColumns *Collection Definition*

Methods: **Refresh**

Properties: **Count, Item**

rdoColumn Object

Events: **DataChanged, WillChangeData**

Methods: **AppendChunk, ColumnSize, GetChunk**

Properties: **AllowZeroLength, Attributes, BatchConflictValue, ChunkRequired, KeyColumn, Name, OrdinalPosition, OriginalValue, Required, Size, SourceColumn, SourceTable, Status, Type, Updatable, Value**

The **rdoColumns** keyword is typically not used when referencing a column value. The default property of a **rdoColumn** object is the Value property and all four lines below are equivalent.

```
Debug.Print MyRS!au_fname
Debug.Print MyRS("au_fname")
Debug.Print MyRS.rdoColumns("au_fname").Value
Debug.Print MyRS.rdoColumns(0).Value
```

rdoColumn methods

rdoColumn objects are infrequently used. Quite possibly the only time you'll ever use the **rdoColumns** object is in the management of binary large objects (BLOBS). The size of a BLOB is determined by the **ColumnSize** property. The code snippet below illustrates the essentials of managing a BLOB. The **AppendChunk** method is used for storing blocks of data and is not used in the example below which retrieves data. The chunk size is arbitrary and is set to 512 bytes in the sample code.

```
lColSiz = rdoRes!rdoCol.ColumnSize
if iColSiz = -1 then
   varTmp = rdoRes!rdoCol.GetChunk(512)
   varBlob=Nothing
   while len(varTmp) >0
     varBlob = varBlob & varTmp
     varTmp = rdoRes!rdoCol.GetChunk(512)
   Wend
Else
   If iColSiz > 0 then
      varBlob = rdoRes!rdoCol.GetChunk(iColSiz)
   End If
End If
```

The **BindThreshold** property of the **rdoQuery** object determines the maximum size of a bindable column. Data that exceeds this threshold must be managed with the **GetChunk** and **AppendChunk** methods. The default value for the **BindThreshold** property is 1024 bytes.

AppendChunk, GetChunk

The **AppendChunk** method writes successive blocks of BLOB data to storage. No size argument is required. The target column must have a data type of either **rdTypeLongVARBINARY** or **rdTypeLongVARCHAR**.

The **AppendChunk** method must be used when the **ChunkRequired** property is TRUE.

An error occurs when using **AppendChunk** and there is no current row.

Syntax:

rdoRes.rdoCol.**AppendChunk** *Source*

varBlob = *rdoRes.rdoCol*.**GetChunk**(*Bytes*)

Where:

rdoRes: An object of type **rdoResultset**

rdoCol: An object of type **rdoColumn**

Source: A string expression containing the data

VarBlob: A variable of type **Variant**

Bytes: The size of the requested chunk

ColumnSize

This method returns the size in bytes of either a **rdTypeLongVARBINARY** or **rdTypeLongVARCHAR** variable.

Syntax:

varSize = *rdoRes.rdoCol*.**ColumnSize**

Where:

varSiz: A variable of type **Variant** or **Long**

rdoRes: An object of type **rdoResultset**

rdoCol: An object of type **rdoColumn**

rdoColumn properties

There is very little missing in terms of column properties for the **rdoColumn** object. The only real problem is that the **Status** property is listed as a property of the **rdoColumn** object, yet the intrinsic values are appropriate to a **rdoResultset** object. The properties of the **rdoColumn** object are enumerated in Table 14-7.

TABLE 14-7 RDOCOLUMN OBJECT PROPERTIES

Property	*Description*
AllowZeroLength	TRUE when zero-length strings are permitted, FALSE otherwise.
Attributes	Describes the type of column. Intrinsic options available:
	rdFixedColumn <1>: Fixed column size for column types such as **Char** and **Binary**.
	rdVariableColumn <2>: Variable column size for column types such as **VarChar**, **LongVarChar**, **VarBinary**, and **LongVarBinary**.
	rdAutoIncrColumn <16>: The column value is automatically incremented and cannot be changed. This is a unique value.
	rdUpdatableColumn <32>: The column value is changeable.
	rdTimeStampColumn <64>: A timestamp value set only by **rdClientbatch** cursors.
BatchConflictValue	Returns the newer value when an optimistic batch update conflict occurs.
ChunkRequired	When TRUE the data must be accessed with the **GetChunk** method.
KeyColumn	Returns or sets a Boolean value when the column is a component of a primary key.
Name	Database column name.
OrdinalPosition	The ordinal position of the **rdoColumn** object within the **rdoColumns** collection.
OriginalValue	The value first fetched from the database. Useful in resolving update conflict issues.
Required	When TRUE a **Null** value is not permitted.
Size	Maximum text or numeric data column size.

Property	*Description*
SourceColumn	The database column name, read-only.
SourceTable	The database table name, read-only.
Status	Sets or returns the status of the current row. The application will set either **rdRowModified** or **rdRowDeleted** before using the **BatchUpdate** method. Intrinsic definitions include:
	rdRowUnmodified <0>: The row was either updated successfully or is unmodified.
	rdRowModified <1>: The row is modified, however, the database is not updated.
	rdRowNew <2>: The row has been inserted with the **AddNew** method, however, the database has not been updated.
	rdRowDeleted <3>: The row is marked as deleted, however, the row has not been deleted from the database.
	rdRowDBDeleted <4>: The row is marked as deleted and is deleted in the database.
Type	**rdTypeCHAR** <1>: Fixed-length character string. Length set by **Size** property.
	rdTypeNUMERIC <2>: Signed, exact, numeric value with precision p and scale s (1 p 15; 0 s p).
	rdTypeDECIMAL <3>: Signed, exact, numeric value with precision p and scale s (1 p 15; 0 s p).
	rdTypeINTEGER <4>: Signed, exact numeric value with precision 10, scale 0 (signed: -2^{31} n 2^{31-1}; unsigned: 0 n $2^{32-}1$).
	rdTypeSMALLINT <5>: Signed, exact numeric value with precision 5, scale 0 (signed: -32,768 n 32,767, unsigned: 0 n 65,535).
	RdTypeFLOAT <6>: Signed, approximate numeric value with mantissa precision 15 (zero or absolute value 10^{-308} to 10^{308}).
rdTypeREAL	<7>: Signed, approximate numeric value with mantissa precision 7 (zero or absolute value 10^{-38} to 10^{38}).
	rdTypeDOUBLE <8>: Signed, approximate numeric value with mantissa precision 15 (zero or absolute value 10^{-308} to 10^{308}).

continued

TABLE 14-7 RDOCOLUMN OBJECT PROPERTIES (continued)

Property	Description
	RdTypeDATE <9>: Date, which is data source dependent.
	RdTypeTIME <10>: Time, which is data source dependent.
	RdTypeTIMESTAMP <11>: TimeStamp, which is data source dependent.
	RdTypeVARCHAR <12>: Variable-length character string. Maximum length 255.
	RdTypeLONGVARCHAR <-1>: Variable-length character string. Maximum length determined by data source.
	rdTypeBINARY <-2>: Fixed-length binary data. Maximum length 255.
	RdTypeVARBINARY <-3>: Variable-length binary data. Maximum length 255.
	RdTypeLONGVARBINARY <-4>: Variable-length binary data. Maximum data source dependent.
	RdTypeBIGINT <-5>: Signed, exact numeric value with precision 19 (signed) or 20 (unsigned), scale 0; (signed: -2^{63} n 2^{63}-1; unsigned: 0 n 2^{64}-1).
	RdTypeTINYINT <-6>: Signed, exact numeric value with precision 3, scale 0; (signed: -128 n 127, unsigned: 0 n 255).
	rdTypeBIT <-7>: Single binary digit.
	rdTypeGUID (MSDN documentation is not available).
	rdTypeWCHAR (MSDN documentation is not available).
	rdTypeWLONGVARCHAR (MSDN documentation is not available.)
	rdTypeWVARCHAR (MSDN documentation is not available).
Updatable	TRUE when the column can be updated.
Value	A value that is appropriate for the data type.

The rdoParameters Collection

A collection of the **rdoQuery** object. The **rdoParameter** object encapsulates both input and output parameters of a query. Input parameters are commonly used as query selection criteria and output parameters are the returned results of stored procedures on the remote data source. The returned value is not considered a result set.

Creating a parameter query uses the ODBC syntax of embedding the <?> character in the query text. The position of the <?> determines the relative argument number in the parameters collection. In the SQL string:

```
MySQL = "{ ? = call sp_password (?, ?) }"
```

the first parameter is an output parameter and the last two are input parameters.

Parameters have a **Direction** property that must be set before using the query. This is illustrated below where the **Direction** properties and the default **Value** properties are set.

```
Dim rdoQry as rdoQuery
Set MyPW = rdoQry.CreateQuery("MyPW",MYSQL)
With MyPW
   .rdoParameters(0).Direction = rdParamReturnValue
   .rdoParameters(1).Direction = rdParamInput
   .rdoParameters(2).Direction = rdParamInput
   .rdoParameters(1) = "Yoda"
   .rdoParameters(2) = "Jedi"
End With
```

rdoParameters *Collection Definition*

Methods: **Item**

Properties: **Count**

rdoParameter *Object*

Method: **AppendChunk**

Properties: **Direction, Name, Size, Type, Value**

rdoParameter properties

The **rdoParameter** object supports no methods and only four properties, all of which are enumerated in Table 14-8.

TABLE 14-8 RDOPARAMETER OBJECT PROPERTIES

Property	*Description*
Direction	Sets or returns a value that determines how a parameter is passed to or from a procedure. **rdParamInput** <0>: The default, the parameter is used to pass information to the procedure. **rdParamInputOutput** <1>: The parameter is used for both input and output. **RdParamOutput** <2>: The parameter only returns information from the procedure. **RdParamReturnValue** <3>: Only status information is returned.
Name	**Param***n* where *n* is the ordinal number.
Size	Column size (not documented in MSDN).
Type	(See the **rdoColumn Type** property.)
Value	Returns or sets the value of the object that is appropriate for the data type.

Key Point Summary

This is the last of two RDO chapters. We've learned that RDO has the look and feel of DAO while maintaining the image of a lean and mean database access technology. Required application functionality not available in RDO is immediately available in the ODBC API. Listing 14-1 illustrated mixing RDO and ODBC API functionality.

- Query preparation is automatic with RDO 1.0 and determined by the **Prepare** property of the **rdoQuery** object in RDO 2.0. Query preparation is automatic in DAO when a **QueryDef** object is saved.
- The core processing functionality of RDO is almost identical to that of DAO.
- ODBC API function calls can be intermixed with RDO object statements.
- Microsoft introduced RDO events with RDO 2.0.
- Batch processing was added with RDO 2.0

Applying What You've Learned

The questions below will assess your understanding of the material in this chapter. The questions are not simple and are the type of questions to expect on any Microsoft certification examination. The certification examinations are relatively easy when the related Microsoft product is used and excruciatingly difficult when the product is not used. You have been presented with many RDO programming examples. Success on the certification examinations depends upon both understanding and using the technology. The best teacher is writing applications that use the RDO technology.

The first lab is an extension of the Chapter 13 lab where the ability to update is added to the **RDOClass** class module.

Instant Assessment

1. The **rdoQuery** object has a parallel in the DAO **QueryDef** object. What unique feature is an option with a DAO **QueryDef** object and is built-in with the **rdoQuery** object of RDO?

2. A **Delete** method has failed on a row in a result set. Name six reasons for this problem.
3. An **Edit** method has failed on a row of a result set. Name five reasons for this problem.
4. Your application is using RDO as the database access technology. Which feature of RDO is useful when a grid control must be populated?
5. What useful function is provided by the **MoreResults** method?
6. What is the major difference between RDO 1.0 and RDO 2.0 with respect to **rdoResultset** objects?

For answers to the Instant Assessment questions, see Appendix B.

Lab Exercise

This laboratory is an ongoing expansion of our components that we'll later integrate into Microsoft Transaction Server.

Lab 14.34 *Allowing updates from the RDOClass*

We'll take the ODBC lab of Chapter 13 and change it slightly. We'll add a new method, which is the **RDOClass** class module that supports updates. We'll also add a new method to the **DriverClass** class module to support the update capability.

1. Copy the Chapter 13 lab into a new and empty folder. We'll be modifying the lab of Chapter 13, so you should complete the Chapter 13 lab before attempting this lab. After copying the project to the new folder, you'll want to use Notepad and open ~~RDO.VBP~~. Adjust the file paths as necessary.
2. Open the ~~RDO.VBP~~ project in the new folder.
3. Use the Visual Basic Class Wizard and add the new method **RDOUpdate** to the **RDOClass** class module. The method will have one argument named *UpdateString*, which is defined **ByVal**.
4. Exit the Class Wizard and update the project.
5. Edit the **RDOUpdate** method to read as follows:

```
Public Sub RDOUpdate(ByVal UpdateString As String)
  If mvarStatus = False Then Exit Sub
  On Error GoTo Update_Failure
```

```
    rdoCon.BeginTrans
    rdoCon.Execute UpdateString, Options:=rdExecDirect
    rdoCon.CommitTrans
    mvarStatus = True
    Exit Sub
  Update_Failure:
    rdoCon.RollbackTrans
    mvarStatus = False
    Exit Sub
  End Sub
```

6. Congratulations. You've added the update capability to the **RDOClass** class. Since no intermediate work needs to be accomplished, updates can be accomplished directly from the main application. We'll do that later in the book as our components gradually evolve. As a cross-check on your work, the listing below represents the current version of the **RDOClass** class.

LISTING 13-5 **The RDOClass module code**

```
'(C) 1999 Bruce T. Prendergast
' DBA Prendergast Consulting
' DBA PCS
' IDG Books Worldwide ISBN 0-7645-3314-2
'
' RDO class
'
Option Explicit
Private rdoEnv As rdoEnvironment
Private rdoCon As rdoConnection
Private rdoQry As RDOQuery
Private rdoRes As rdoResultset
Private mvarResponse As Variant
Private mvarStatus As Variant

Public Sub RDOUpdate(ByVal UpdateString As String)
  If mvarStatus = False Then Exit Sub
  On Error GoTo Update_Failure
  rdoCon.BeginTrans
  rdoCon.Execute UpdateString, Options:=rdExecDirect
```

```
  rdoCon.CommitTrans
  mvarStatus = True
  Exit Sub
Update_Failure:
  rdoCon.RollbackTrans
  mvarStatus = False
  Exit Sub
End Sub

Public Property Get Status() As Variant
  Status = mvarStatus
End Property

Public Property Get Response() As Variant
  Response = mvarResponse
End Property

Public Sub RDOQuery(ByVal QueryString As String)
  Dim MyRS As rdoResultset
  Dim RetRows As Variant            ' returned row array
  Dim RetCount As Long              ' returned row count
  Dim i As Integer                  ' scratch integer
  Dim Results() As Variant
  Dim ResultCount As Integer
  '
  '  exit if unable to connect
  '
  If mvarStatus = False Then Exit Sub
  Set MyRS = rdoCon.OpenResultset(QueryString, _
    rdOpenForwardOnly, rdConcurReadOnly)
    '
    ' Pipe the data back. Get the rows 10 at a time
    '
    ReDim Results(2)

    Results(1) = MyRS.rdoColumns.Count
    Results(2) = 0
```

```
    ResultCount = 2
    Do Until MyRS.EOF
      RetRows = MyRS.GetRows(10)
      '
      ' Loop through the records. I am not using the
      ' resultset row count but am depending on the
      ' actual returned rows from a keyset
      '
      RetCount = UBound(RetRows, 2) + 1
      For i = 0 To RetCount - 1
        ResultCount = ResultCount + 3
        ReDim Preserve Results(ResultCount)
        Results(ResultCount - 2) = RetRows(0, i)
        Results(ResultCount - 1) = RetRows(1, i)
        Results(ResultCount) = RetRows(2, i)
      Next i
    Loop
    Results(2) = ResultCount
  mvarResponse = Results()
  Exit Sub
End Sub

Private Sub Class_Initialize()
  mvarStatus = False
  On Error GoTo Initialize_Error:
  Set rdoEnv = rdoEngine.rdoEnvironments(0)
  Set rdoCon = rdoEnv.OpenConnection("", rdDriverNoPrompt, False, _
    "DATABASE=pubs;UID=sa;PWD=;DSN=Thor;")
  mvarStatus = True
  mvarResponse = ""
Initialize_Error:
  Exit Sub
End Sub

Private Sub Class_Terminate()
  If mvarStatus Then rdoCon.Close
End Sub
```

CHAPTER

15

Active Data Objects

About Chapter 15

OLE-DB and the Active Data Objects (ADO), the OLE-DB wrapper, are the two new kids on the block. This chapter provides a thumbnail sketch of the ADO architecture along with a comparative look at Data Access Objects (DAO) and Remote Data Objects (RDO). OLE-DB and ADO are new technologies and the implementations are now reasonably complete. Chapter 15 thumbnail sketches the ADO architecture and enumerates the properties of ADO, while Chapter 16 sketches the methods of various ADO objects along with many examples.

ADO has come a long way in eighteen months. ADO 1.1 was a bit primitive, but functional. ADO 1.5 moved closer to the ultimate implementation, however reliability was an issue with this release. The current version is ADO 2.0, which appears to be a reasonably complete and apparently stable implementation. The performance is outstanding, given the proper environment and there's new functionality such as persisted **Recordset** objects and events for either the ADO **Connection** objects or **Recordset** objects. Another interesting new feature is a Hierarchical Cursor where a child **Recordset** object is defined as the value of a field in the parent **Recordset** object. Microsoft calls this technology *Data Shaping,* which is supported by the ADO Client Cursor Engine. This technology is quite intriguing since the possibility of embedding data within a column is the equivalent of a join operation in the Structured Query Language (SQL) of Microsoft SQL Server.

Batch processing is notably different than that of RDO, which uses the RDO **rdoRecordset** object properties **BatchCollisionCount** and **BatchCollisionRows** to manage optimistic concurrency. The ADO developer sets the **Filter** property of the **Recordset** object to the intrinsic value **adFilterAffectedRecords** and examines the resulting **Status** property.

ADO: Universal Connectivity

ADO and OLE-DB promise to be the universal database access technology. Microsoft finally acknowledged that transaction isolation levels are needed on the client and on the server. Unfortunately, supporting the Atomicity, Consistency, Integrity, and Durability (ACID) properties of a transaction appears to be a vendor-specific issue and the actual implementations may be uneven. Microsoft spin-doctors repeatedly state that OLE-DB/ADO will support the ACID properties of a transaction, but the support is OLE-DB provider specific. The **Connection** object supports the **IsolationLevel** property and the **Field** object does support an **OriginalValue** property, but this doesn't go very far when compared to the functionality of the Microsoft SQL Server write-ahead log. It appears that the ACID properties will remain a provider-specific issue independent of Microsoft marketing hype.

Transaction ACID Properties

Let's start by quickly reviewing the ACID properties of a transaction. These issues were discussed previously in the chapters that covered RDO and ODBC, and are updated here for OLE-DB and ADO, the OLE-DB wrapper.

An important feature of any database is transactions. The **ACID** properties declare the following requirements necessary for consistent transactions:

- **Atomicity** — Either all or none of the transactions changes are present when the transaction completes.
- **Consistency** — The transaction will respect all business rules and referential integrity. Inconsistent updates can be done, but will violate system integrity.
- **Isolation** — The SQL Server transaction isolation levels are maintained for all row sets of the transaction. Transactions are isolated. SQL Server uses the SET statement:

```
SET TRANSACTION ISOLATION LEVEL
READ COMMITTED | READ UNCOMMITTED |
REPEATABLE READ | SERIALIZABLE
```

- **Durability**—Once the commit occurs, the transactions must be present even if the system fails. SQL Server supports this property with a log. Recoverability is guaranteed with SQL Server but not with Microsoft Access.

The issue of ACID properties and OLE-DB/ADO is provider specific. The consumer has the responsibility of determining provider support for OLE-DB and ADO, the OLE-DB wrapper.

Transaction Isolation Levels

Both OLE-DB and ADO support transaction isolation levels. *Transaction isolation* is the degree of interaction between multiple concurrent transactions. There is, however, a simple rule that describes the issue. *Maximum consistency* (highest transaction isolation level) is also the lowest concurrency level. Conversely, the highest concurrency level will yield the lowest consistency level. *Maximum performance* (I'll call it apparent performance) will yield the lowest consistency level. There is no clear answer other than to use the lowest possible transaction isolation level consistent with the application design. An important issue here is that an OLE-DB provider may not support the requested isolation level, but may support transaction at the next highest level. The OLE-DB developer will want to interrogate the DBPROPSET_DBSOURCEINFO structure for the DBPROP_SUPPORTEDTXNISOLEVELS property that defines the supported transaction levels. The ADO developer will want to examine the **IsolationLevel** property of the **Connection** object.

There are four transaction isolation levels. These levels are defined by the occurrence (or lack) of the following phenomena:

- **Dirty Read** is the reading of transaction data of another application before the data is rolled back. The data read is considered dirty if there is a possibility that the transaction can be rolled back. The data may or may not exist within the database even though it was read by an application.
- **Nonrepeatable Read** occurs when the application reads a row and gets a different result each time. Another application updated the row before the second read occurred.
- **Phantom Read** is a row that matches a search criterion but isn't seen by the application. A second application has added a new row that meets the search criterion after the initial rows were read.

Table 15-1 enumerates the various transaction isolation levels.

TABLE 15-1 TRANSACTION ISOLATION LEVELS

Transaction Isolation Level	*Dirty Reads*	*Nonrepeatable Reads*	*Phantoms*
Read Uncommitted	X	X	X
Read Committed		X	X
Repeatable Read			X
Serializable			

Here's a brief definition of the terms used in Table 15-1:

- **Read Uncommitted** — No transaction isolation occurs. Transactions running at this level are typically read-only.
- **Read Committed** — The transaction is forced to wait until write-locked applications release data locks.
- **Repeatable Read** — The transaction waits until write-locks on rows are released by other applications. The transaction holds a read-lock on all rows it returns to the application and write-locks on all rows it changes, deletes, or inserts.
- **Serializable** — The application holds read-locks on all rows affected by a read. A write-lock is placed on all rows affected by a change.

ADO Transaction Isolation Levels

We've seen the optimistic approach in both DAO and RDO. OLE-DB optimistic locking is dramatically different and doesn't support traditional row versioning. Microsoft has discarded the inefficient value-based row versioning in OLE-DB and ADO; however that technology is still supported in RDO and DAO. Value-based row versioning requires a comparison of each field, which can be inefficient.

ADO transaction isolation levels are specified in the **IsolationLevel** property of the **Connection** object and are parallel to those of OLE-DB. Table 15-2 enumerates ADO transaction isolation intrinsic values while Table 15-3 enumerates OLE-DB transaction isolation intrinsic values.

TABLE 15-2 ADO TRANSACTION ISOLATION VALUES

INTRINSIC VALUE	*DESCRIPTION*
adXactUnspecified	The provider is using a different and unknown isolation level.
adXactChaos	Inhibit a transaction overwriting pending changes of a transaction with a higher isolation level.
adXactBrowse	Other transactions may view uncommitted transactions.
adXactReadUncommitted	Same as **adXactBrowse**.
adXactCursorStability	Transaction data cannot be viewed by other transactions until committed (default).
adXactReadCommitted	Same as **adXactCursorStability**.
adXactRepeatableRead	Changes cannot be seen from other transactions; a requery will fetch an updated rowset.
adXactIsolated	Transactions are isolated.
adXactSerialize	Same as **adXactIsolated**.

The OLE-DB transaction isolation level is a parameter of the **ITransactionLocal::StartTransaction** method.

TABLE 15-3 OLE-DB TRANSACTION ISOLATION INTRINSIC VALUES

INTRINSIC VALUE	*DESCRIPTION*
ISOLATIONLEVEL_UNSPECIFIED	Applicable only to **ITransactionJoin::JoinTransaction**. Invalid for **ITransactionLocal** or for setting isolation level while in AUTOCOMMIT mode.
ISOLATIONLEVEL_CHAOS	Cannot overwrite the dirty data of other transactions at higher isolation levels.
ISOLATIONLEVEL_READUNCOMMITTED	
ISOLATIONLEVEL_BROWSE	Synonym for _READUNCOMMITTED.

Intrinsic Value	*Description*
ISOLATIONLEVEL_READCOMMITTED	
ISOLATIONLEVEL_CURSORSTABILITY	Synonym for _READCOMMITTED.
ISOLATIONLEVEL_REPEATABLEREAD	
ISOLATIONLEVEL_SERIALIZABLE	
ISOLATIONLEVEL_ISOLATED	Synonym for _SERIALIZABLE.

Managing Concurrency

RDO, Jet, and ADO each manage optimistic concurrency differently. Jet, for example, sets the property **dbSeeChanges** for each **Recordset** object. This is an error-prone mechanism. Microsoft Access does have the **IsolateODBCTrans** for the **Workspace** object, but that just isolates transactions from each other and does not manage transaction isolation levels.

The situation is different with RDO and ADO where a trappable error occurs with optimistic concurrency. The user then has the responsibility of refreshing the current row with **Move** 0 and then reapplying the **Edit** or **AddNew** methods. In DAO the trappable error doesn't occur unless **dbSeeChanges** is used.

RDO permits reading from locked pages even with pessimistic locking in effect for the **LockEdits** property of the **rdoResultset** object. RDO does not have the **dbSeeChanges** property of Microsoft Access and the possession of this property will still not help matters. Unlike DAO dirty reads and phantoms (see Table 15-1) can be controlled in ADO and OLE-DB. Maximum consistency is always at the expense of concurrency; however it is possible in ADO to eliminate dirty reads since ADO and OLE-DB both support transaction isolation levels. To be fair, any database access technology that uses Microsoft SQL Server transactions will have transaction isolation level support. It's only the local transactions of DAO that do not support transaction isolation levels. Transaction isolation level SUPPORT is not available directly in RDO; however the RDO developer can issue the Transact-SQL (TSQL) statement: `SET TRANSACTION ISOLATION LEVEL`.

OLE-DB has two notification mechanisms. The first notification mechanism is **IRowsetNotify,** which establishes connection sinks for rowset changes and synchronization. This interface is mentioned here because an event occurs with each row and the **IRowsetNotify** interface is not appropriate for a transaction.

The second notification mechanism of OLE-DB uses the **ITransaction OutcomeEvents** as a notification sink. The consumer calls **QueryInterface** for the **IConnectionPointContainer** interface on the session. The returned **IConnection Point** interface for IID_TransactionOutcomeEvent is passed to the consumer **ITransactionOutcomeEvents** interface.

ADO 2.0 supports events for both the **Connection** object and the **Recordset** object (see Chapter 16). These are not events in the strict sense, but notification handlers that report the occurrence or nonoccurrence of events. Two such notifications are the **WillChangeField** and **FieldChangeComplete** events of the **Recordset** object. Concurrency management for a single row is signaled with an error, while no error is signaled for an error within a batch update unless all rows are in error. The developer must test the **Errors** collection after a batch update to ascertain that no errors exist.

When Converting Between ADO, DAO, and RDO

The intrinsic constants relating to optimistic and pessimistic locking for ADO, DAO, and RDO are listed below. The constants illustrate some of the differences between the database access technologies. The fact that there are many common methods such as **Move** or **MoveNext** does not mean that all functionality is comparable. The comparison is started with Table 15-4 enumeration of the intrinsic constants for the **LockEdits** property of a DAO **Recordset** object.

TABLE 15-4 DAO LOCKEDITS INTRINSIC VALUES

Intrinsic Value	*Description*
dbPessimistic	Pessimistic concurrency is always the lowest level locking possible to ensure consistency. This is always at the expense of concurrency.
dbReadOnly	No updates allowed.
dbOptimistic	Record ID based. Compares new and old record ID to see if changes have been made since the record was last accessed.
dbOptimisticValue	Value based. Each field is compared for changes. A very inefficient mechanism.
dbOptimisticBatch	Enables batch optimistic values

Table 15-5 enumerates the intrinsic constants of the **LockType** property of an RDO **rdoOpenResultset** method.

TABLE 15-5 RDO LOCKTYPE INTRINSIC VALUES

Intrinsic Value	*Description*
rdConcurLock	Pessimistic concurrency is always the lowest level locking possible to ensure consistency. This is always at the expense of concurrency.
rdConcurReadOnly	No updates allowed.
rdConcurRowver	Record ID based. Compares new and old record ID to see if changes have been made since the record was last accessed.
rdConcurValues	Value based. Each field is compared for changes, which is a very inefficient mechanism. Lock type is established with the **LockType** parameter of the **Open** method of either an RDO **Connection** object or an RDO **Recordset** object.

The last comparison is the intrinsic values available to the **LockType** property of the ADO **Recordset** object, which are enumerated in Table 15-6.

TABLE 15-6 ADO LOCKTYPE INTRINSIC VALUES

Intrinsic Value	*Description*
adLockReadOnly	No updates allowed, read-only.
adLockPessimistic	Pessimistic concurrency.
adLockOptimistic	Row is locked when the update is attempted.
adLockBatchOptimistic	Optimistic batch updates

Tables 15-4, 15-5, and 15-6 illustrate the point that developers depending upon value-based optimistic or pessimistic locking must redesign their applications for ADO.

Performance

ADO is the newest database access technology from Microsoft. It is an OLE-DB wrapper that is simple and smaller than the DAO or RDO predecessors. A selling pitch for this new technology is its reduced footprint and speed. This is a specious argument because a virtual memory management system is a standard feature of modern operating and desktop systems. The application footprint is not a factor in a virtual memory system. All dynamic link libraries (DLLs) are shared and only one copy of the DLL is loaded irrespective of the number of users. Of course, if you're using Windows 95 you may have a memory problem. After all, what else can be done with a DOS derivative? The bottom line is that memory is cheap and footprint size should never be an issue.

The issue of speed is also highly questionable and it's not the question of literal speed. Visual Basic Programmer's Journal, December 1999, published an article showing the DAO was faster than ADO for local databases. This is an example of the lack of critical thinking that pervades the computer industry today. Yes, DAO is faster than ADO when compared on a line-for-line basis, and differences are expected because DAO and ADO are disparate technologies technologies. ADO is based on COM and must marshal data between interfaces, which certainly adds additional overhead and that is not the case for DAO. On the other hand, ADO is free threaded and supports disconnected **Recordset** objects, which means that ADO is scaleable. DAO is apartment-model threaded and does not support disconnected **Recordset** objects, which means that DAO is anything but scaleable. When bottom of the line personal computer processor speed is in the 300-450 MHz range, the speed of local database access is immaterial and any attempt to measure local database access time is an exercise in futility. A performance test should compare the number of *wire trips,* which is always the limiting factor. A more meaningful benchmark is to compare the best performance of ADO versus DAO independent of environment or protocol. Anything other than that is simply proving that the technologies are indeed different.

Although OLE-DB and the companion ADO wrapper are outstanding technologies, there is always the issue of stability. One can guess that this time next year the new database access technology will be OLE-DB+, or something like that. Microsoft needs to sell software, which means they will continually reinvent the same software. I've previously called these technologies *refried beans* and we've seen examples of this where RDO and ODBCDirect are directly related technologies; RDO is implemented with Microsoft Visual Basic while ODBCDirect is implemented within DAO. Stability only exists with ODBC, which is an ANSI standard. A properly designed ODBC application programming interface (API) application is the correct choice for enterprise applications. Yes, ODBC can be used in a tiered architecture by Microsoft Transaction Server (MTS). Yes, RDO, DAO, and OLE-DB can be used for desktop applications, but enterprise problems need enterprise solutions.

Maybe when Microsoft can demonstrate adequate OLE-DB stability and its implementation of software is executed with the precision necessary for a corporation, and not that of a *Doom II* player, OLE-DB can be considered as a viable database access technology. If you're a *Webbie,* you know that Microsoft Visual InterDev uses ADO by default when creating active server pages (ASP). ODBC is a not a viable choice for this scenario.

RDO, DAO, and ADO

DAO, RDO, and ADO all have the same look and feel. ADO is far simpler for development because it has a smaller number of objects and a correspondingly smaller number of methods and properties. The intrinsic constants have yet to be standardized so you'll find yourself making transliterations of the intrinsic constants depending upon your choice of DAO, RDO, or ADO.

Method names are common. There are some minor transliterations you must make because a DAO **Workspace** object is the equivalent of a **rdoEnvironment** object. An ADO **Command** object is not the equivalent of a DAO **Workspace** object or a RDO **rdoEnvironment** object, but it is a close representation. Table 15-7 enumerates the basic differences between RDO, DAO, and ADO.

TABLE 15-7 Equivalent DAO, RDO and ADO objects.

DAO Object	*Equivalent RDO Object*	*Equivalent ADO Object*
DBEngine	rdoEngine	ADODB
User	N/A	N/A
Workspace	rdoEnvironment	Command
Database	N/A	N/A
Connection	rdoConnection	Connection

Continued

TABLE 15-7 EQUIVALENT DAO, RDO AND ADO OBJECTS. *(continued)*

DAO OBJECT	*EQUIVALENT RDO OBJECT*	*EQUIVALENT ADO OBJECT*
TableDef	rdoTable	N/A
Index	N/A	N/A
Recordset	rdoResultset	Recordset
Table	N/A	N/A
Dynaset	Keyset	Keyset
Snapshot	Static	Static
Dynamic	Dynamic	Dynamic
Forward-Only	Forward-Only	Forward-Only
Field	rdoColumn	Field
QueryDef	rdoPreparedStatement	
Parameter	rdoParameter	Parameter

Binding in DAO is with the **data** control and the equivalent binding in RDO is with the **Remote Data Control** (RDC). Many of the RDO methods have the same name as the corresponding DAO methods. Converting to RDO from DAO is not difficult. Neither is converting an application from DAO or RDO to ADO difficult.

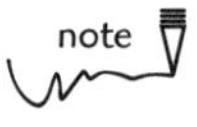

Binding with ADO is with what used to be the Advanced Data Control (ADC). This was renamed recently to Remote Data Service (RDS). Converting to ADO is a trivial exercise when the required functionality exists.

RDO row set, DAO record set, and ADO record sets are discussed below. They are nearly the same except RDO and ADO do not support a table-type cursor. These are the record types supported by the current Microsoft database access technology:

- **Table** — One of the original record set definitions of Microsoft Access and the earlier version of Jet and DAO. RDO and ADO do not support this cursor type
- **Snapshot** — Another original Access DAO record set definition. The data is captured at a point in time and updates or deletions are not visible to the client. The **Snapshot** type cursor is equivalent to an ODBC, RDO, or ADO **Static** cursor or static-type result set.

- **Dynaset**—A key set type result set that may have either pessimistic or optimistic locking. The last of the original three result set definitions. Deleted rows can be detected but newly added rows go undetected. This row set type is a **Keyset** cursor in the ODBC API, in the DAO ODBCDirect, in ADO, and in RDO.
- **Forward-Only**—This is a new result set type that uses the minimum amount of resources. As discussed in Chapter 11, the ODBC default cursor is forward only with a snapshot-type record. The forward-only result set type is equivalent to a snapshot-type without a cursor. A forward-only result set type is available in DAO ODBCDirect, ADO, or RDO, which has only one row visible. Scrolling is only possible at the client when the application caches the result set.
- **Dynamic**—This is a new result set type. It is reserved for access to ODBC-registered data sources. The dynamic-type cursor is limited to ODBCDirect in DAO, ADO, and RDO. It is not available to Jet. A **Dynamic** cursor is equivalent to a Jet **Dynaset** or **Keyset** cursor of ADO or RDO, except that new rows are added to the key set. A simpler way of saying this is that the key set membership is not fixed. Bookmarks are not available with a dynamic cursor.

Figure 15-1 illustrates the basic architecture of DAO, RDO, and ADO.

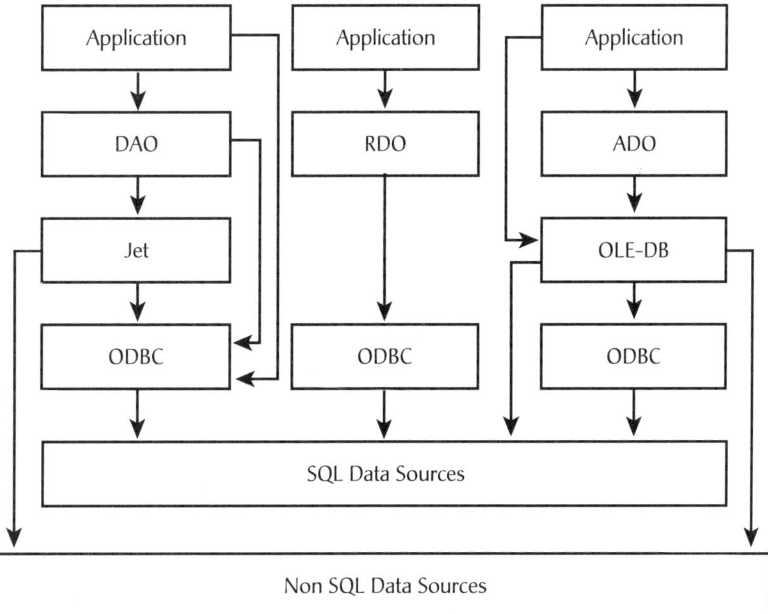

FIGURE 15-1 DAO, RDO, and the ODBC API

The shortest path to a SQL data source is the ODBC API when compared with DAO and RDO. Only one application in Figure 15-1 is illustrated using the ODBC API. In general, the mix and match of ODBC functionality is not possible. The ODBC API is separate from the ODBC desktop driver set of Microsoft Access. It is possible to access the ODBC API from RDO because the ODBC handles are exposed.

Yes, you can use the ODBC API in an application that uses ADO; however, the two technologies do not communicate except through an OLE-DB provider. ADO is an object-oriented technology whereas ODBC is a call-level interface (CLI).

ADO has a reduced footprint, which is meaningless in a multi-user environment. The value of the small ADO footprint is with Web-based applications. The attractiveness of the ODBC API is the **SQLExtendedFetch** or the new **SQLFetchScroll,** which yields optimal performance with column and row binding. RDO approximates this technology with the **GetRows** method. ADO is clever, however the encapsulation of a result set gives it an e-mail flavor. The complexity of OLE-DB far exceeds that of ODBC. ODBC developers wishing to create an OLE-DB application must now learn the COM technology. The new native OLE-DB drivers of OLE-DB 2.0 access the data source directly and OLE-DB is no longer a wrapper for the ODBC API. The optimal OLE-DB driver will be native, and when combined with TCP/IP and forward-only Recordset objects, the performance is very good.

Neither ODBCDirect of DAO nor RDO require a query processor. ADO, which uses OLE-DB, doesn't technically require a query processor; however it does require a provider. Provider resources will vary depending upon the data source.

DAO, RDO, ADO, AND ODBC

ODBC remains a core technology. It is a standard and the technology is not burdened with esoteric programming constructs. DAO is a fat ODBC wrapper, whereas RDO is a very thin ODBC wrapper. I don't mean to say that object-oriented programming isn't useful or valid, but there is a time and a place for everything. The very rich ODBC API function library supports every conceivable database access needed for the enterprise. Of course, if you need animated e-mail, then ADO is a necessary component of the Internet/Intranet equation.

DAO and RDO are both ODBC wrappers. It is not correct to refer to ADO as an ODBC wrapper since OLE-DB supports native drivers. ODBC is a standard over which Microsoft has little control and is ubiquitous in the enterprise today. OLE-

DB is proprietary. Microsoft is busy porting component object model (COM) implementations to different platforms. By the time the implementations are successfully ported, OLE-DB, and its offspring ADO, will be firmly entrenched in the enterprise. Other database access implementations may be developed, but no market will exist. Sane developers do not tinker with software that works.

The ODBC API can be used without objects because it is a call-level interface. Adding objects to an application increases the application volume and application complexity, which in turn increases the potential for application errors. Objects do not enhance ODBC. Objects make it easy to use for someone not skilled in using the ODBC API to access a relational database. Remember that Microsoft is intent on de-skilling jobs and automating tasks. This makes its products usable by a larger community, which increases its sales. ADO is another step in this direction.

What Is ADO?

ADO is the glue of an Internet/Intranet architecture, but Microsoft is trying to use it for everything else. It is COM based and is the necessary flesh to the bones of distributed COM (DCOM), which first appeared in Windows NT 4.0. ADO has its rightful place in the single-user environment, but the original incarnation was far from a proven technology in a multi-user environment. ADO 2.0 is free-threaded, and when used with the TCP/IP protocol, native OLE-DB drivers, and forward only result sets, the performance is outstanding.

ADO is not relational database oriented; it is, however, the promised universal database interface where a query can be constructed to pull data from relational databases, non-relational databases, and non-database sources such as e-mail boxes. Whether that future will be realized is speculative. Release 2.0 of OLE-DB and ADO appears to deliver the promise of universal database access.

ADO is like RDO in that it does not support data definition language (DDL) operations. The supporting OLE-DB does, however, support DDL operations.

ADO shares a kinship with DAO in supporting heterogeneous joins. Microsoft introduced relational database technology to the mass of users who do not understand database design or normalization. When your Internet link slows to a crawl, contemplate all those new ADO users who are doing heterogeneous database joins over the Internet or your Intranet. Microsoft extends this madness still further with Microsoft SQL Server 7.0 now being capable of heterogeneous joins between other databases.

Bound forms are not supported by ADO, RDO, or ODBCDirect; however, a data control is available for each. Both DAO and RDO have a RDC for binding purposes. These controls are not the same with the RDC control in Visual Basic Enterprise Edition named **MSRDC20.OCX** and the RDC of Access 97 named **MSRDC32.OCX**.

Binding is available in ADO with the ADC. The newest version of this ADO/OLE-DB component was renamed RDS and it is backward compatible with ADC. Current features of RDS include data binding in an active hypertext markup language (HTML) environment. This technology is included with the Microsoft Data Access Components SDK 2.0 that is downloadable from Microsoft at: `http://www.microsoft.com/ado`. The SDK is also available from Microsoft press as *Microsoft OLE DB 2.0 Programmer's Reference and Data Access SDK*, ISBN 0-7356-0590-4.

ADO is based upon objects that are roughly parallel to the underlying OLE-DB COM model objects. A hierarchical relationship exists between the ADO objects, but it is not strict. The user can open a **Recordset** object directly, ignoring the need to create a **Connection** object first. ADO automatically creates a default **Connection** object.

RDO objects use the ODBC API implicitly with RDO objects calling the ODBC driver manager. This is quite unlike the call-level interface of ODBC. RDO is an ODBC API wrapper for ODBC functions along with other methods and properties. The use of ODBC functions is implicit, not explicit, in that ODBC functions are not directly called when executing a RDO method.

RDO lacks some of Microsoft Access's flexibility in creating a result set. RDO can create a result set from a table, a SQL string, or a **rdoQueryStatement**. A result set cannot be created from another result set or from another query, both of which are features of Microsoft Access. A different type of flexibility is available with ADO, which can specify the **Source** argument of an **Open** method as a **Command** object variable, a SQL statement, a stored procedure, or a table name.

ADO does not use the ODBC API and depends on an OLE-DB provider for accessing ODBC data sources. This situation is best described by saying that ADO is not an ODBC wrapper, but an OLE-DB wrapper that accesses data sources directly when a native driver is used.

ADO Architecture

The ADO architecture is that of OLE-DB software developer's kit (SDK) version 1.1, and it hasn't changed with either the 1.5 or 2.0 releases of OLE-DB.

Figures 15-2, 15-3, and 15-4 are a look at the respective architectures of DAO, RDO, and ADO. The RDO architecture is simple compared to DAO, and ADO simplifies database access even further.

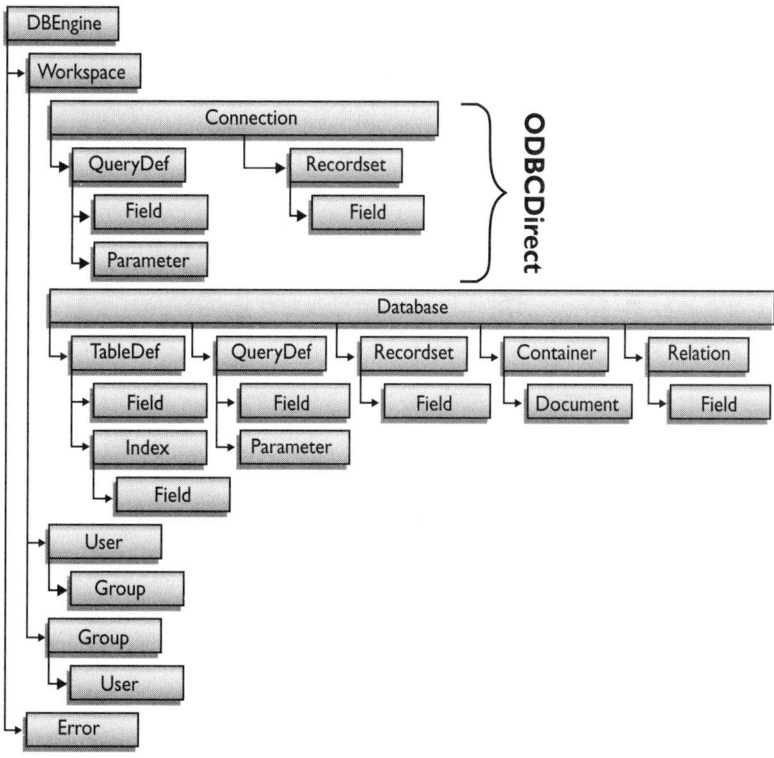

FIGURE 15-2 DAO 3.5 hierarchy

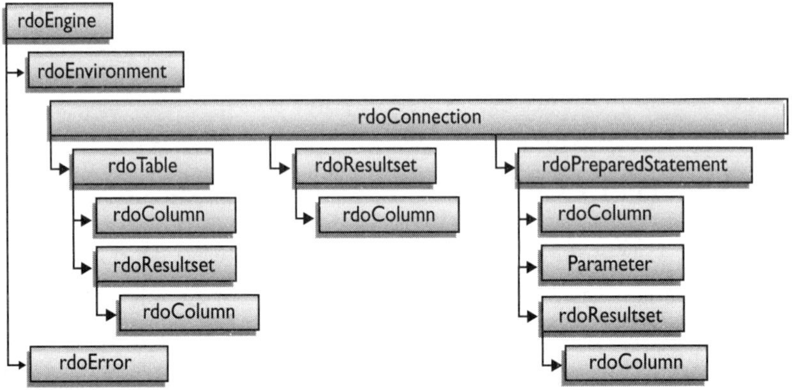

FIGURE 15-3 RDO hierarchy

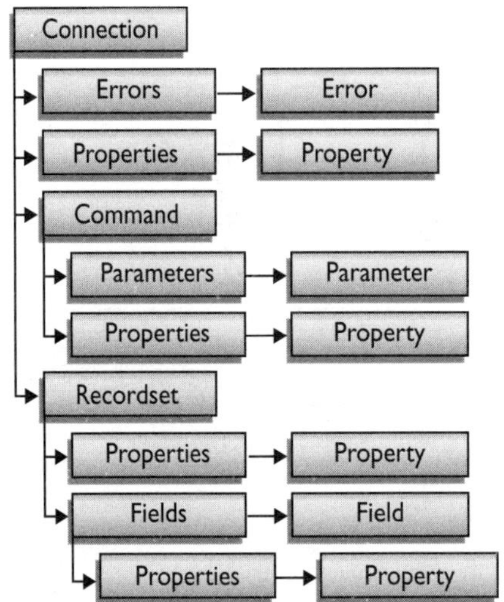

FIGURE 15-4 ADO hierarchy

ADO Architecture Detail

The following is a breakout of the methods and properties of all ADO objects. All objects are listed in their hierarchical order. Each ADO object has a **Properties** collection and the collection is listed only once as a member of the **Recordset** object.

```
Connection Object
  Methods : BeginTrans, Cancel, Close, CommitTrans, Execute, Open, OpenSchema,
```

```
    RollbackTrans
  Properties : Attributes, CommandTimeout, ConnectionString, ConnectionTimeout,
    CursorLocation, DefaultDatabase, IsolationLevel, Mode, Provider, State,
    Version
  Errors Collection
    Method : Clear, Item
    Properties : Count
    Error Object
       Methods : Description, HelpContext, HelpFile, NativeError, Number,
Source,
         SQLState
  Properties Collection
    Method : Item, Refresh
    Properties : Count
      Property Object
        Properties : Attributes, Name, Type, Value
  Command Object
     Methods : Cancel, CreateParameter, Execute
     Properties : ActiveConnection, CommandText, CommandTimeout, CommandType,
       Name, Prepared, State
     Properties Collection
        Method : Item, Refresh
        Properties : Count
        Property Object
          Properties : Attributes, Name, Type, Value
     Parameters Collection
        Methods : Append, Delete, Item, Refresh
        Properties : Count
        Parameter Object
        Method: AppendChunk
        Properties : Attributes, Direction, Name, NumericScale, Precision,
            Size, Type, Value
  Recordset Object
    Methods : AddNew, Cancel, CancelBatch, CancelUpdate, Clone, Close,
      CompareBookmarks, Delete, Find, GetRows, GetString, Move, MoveFirst,
      MoveLast, MoveNext, MovePrevious, NextRecordset, Open, Requery, Resync,
      Save, Seek, Supports, Update, UpdateBatch
```

```
Properties : AbsolutePage, AbsolutePosition, ActiveCommand,
  ActiveConnection, BOF, Bookmark, CacheSize, CursorLocation, CursorType,
  DataMember, DataSource, EditMode, EOF, Filter, LockType, MarshalOptions,
  MaxRecords, PageCount, PageSize, RecordCount, Sort, Source, State, Status,
  StayInSync
Properties Collection
   Method : Item, Refresh
   Properties : Count
   Property Object
     Properties : Attributes, Name, Type, Value
Fields Collection
   Methods : Append, Delete, Item, Refresh
   Properties : Count
   Properties Collection
     Method : Item, Refresh
     Properties : Count
     Property Object
       Properties : Attributes, Name, Type, Value
   Field Object
     Methods : AppendChunk, GetChunk
     Properties : ActualSize, Attributes, DataFormat, DefinedSize, Name,
       NumericScale, OriginalValue, Precision, Type, UnderlyingValue, Value
```

Working with Default Collections

ADO has only four collections: **Errors**, **Fields**, **Properties**, and **Parameters**. Objects of these collections may be addressed in the same manner as illustrated below for the **Field** object. Each of the constructs in each group is equivalent.

Field Object	*Parameter Object*
recordset.Fields.Item(0)	command.Parameters.Item(0)
recordset.Fields.Item("name")	command.Parameters.Item("name")
recordset.Fields(0)	command.Parameters(0)
recordset.Fields("name")	command.Parameters("name")

PROPERTY OBJECT	ERROR OBJECT
recordset(0)	command(0)
recordset("name")	command("name")
recordset![“name”]	command![“name”]
object.Properties.Item(0)	connection.Errors.Item(0)
object.Properties.Item("name")	connection.Item(0)
object. Properties(0)	
object. Properties("name")	
object(0)	
object("name")	
object![“name”]	

Default collections provide a shortcut mechanism for addressing lower-level methods and properties. The **Value** property is the default property for the **Field, Parameter,** and **Property** objects.

Working with Collections

All collections have a **Count** property and the **Item** method. The **For...Each** construct can be used to enumerate ADO collections in the same manner as the RDO and DAO collections. Unlike DAO objects, RDO and ADO objects cannot be saved. Only **Parameter** objects can be appended to the **Parameters** collection.

Append

This method is only available in the ADO **Parameters** collection.

Clear

Clear is only a method of the **Errors** collection, which clears all objects from the **Errors** collection.

Count

Count is the only common property of all collections.

Delete

This is a method of the **Parameters** collection and the **Recordset** object. It deletes a member of a collection or the current record respectively.

Refresh

Refresh is a method of the **Fields, Parameters,** and **Properties** collections. It is not available to the **Errors** collection.

Item

Item is a default method of all collections. The method returns a specific member of a collection when supplied a subscript. It is the default method of all collections.

ADO Properties

This chapter closes with an enumeration of all ADO properties. The properties are in alphabetical order and the applicable ADO object is identified.

AbsolutePage — **Recordset** object. Used in conjunction with the **PageSize** property, which defaults to 10. The consumer sets **PageSize** to the number of records per page. **AbsolutePage** is the absolute page number of the desired record. Useful for Web applications or providers that do not support indexing.

AbsolutePosition — **Recordset** object. Move to a specific record based on a one-based ordinal. It is not to be used in lieu of a record number because delete operations affect absolute position. Cache for the current result set is reloaded starting with the specified record.

ActiveConnection

Command object. Read/write. Setting to **Nothing** disassociates the current **Command** object for reuse with provider-supplied **Parameter** objects cleared and associated data source resources released. Consumer **Parameter** objects are not cleared. Closing a **Connection** object sets the **ActiveConnection** property to **Nothing**.

Recordset object. Read-only when **Source** property is a valid **Command** object. Can be set to a valid **Connection** object or a valid connection string. Provider may return a valid **Connection** object.

ActiveConnection inherits from the *ActiveConnection* parameter of the **Open** method.

ActiveConnection inherits **Command** object **ActiveConnection** when **Source** property is set.

ActualSize

Field object. **ActualSize** may be less than **DefinedSize**. Read-only.

Attributes

Connection object. The values are a power of 2 and represent bit postions. The aggregate properties supported is the sum of the different numbers.

adXactCommitRetaining <1341072 >: CommitTrans starts a new transaction.

adXactAbortretaining <262144>: RollbackTrans starts a new transaction.

Parameter object.

adParamSigned <16>: Accepts signed values, default.

adParamNullable <64>: Accepts **Null** values.

adParamLong <128>: Accepts **Long** binary data.

Field object.

adFldMayDefer <2>: Retrieve only when requested.

adfFldUpdatable <4>: Writable.

adFldUnknownUpdatable <8>: Provider cannot determine if consumer can write field.

adFldFixed <16>: Contains fixed-length data.

adFldIsNullable <32>: Accepts **Null** values.

adFldMayBeNull <64>: Null values may be read.

adFldLong <128>: Long binary and **AppendChunk** and **GetChunk** may be used.

adFldRowID <256>: Field contains some kind of record ID. Type of record ID is not specified.

adFldRowVersion <512>: A date or timestamp field.

adFldCacheDeferred <4096>: Provider caches field.

Property object.

adPropNotSupported <0>: Property is not provider supported.

adPropRequired <1>: Value required before data source initialization.

adPropOptional <2>: Value is optional before data source initialization.

adPropRead <512>: Consumer readable.

adPropWrite <1024>: Consumer writable.

BOF — **Recordset** object. TRUE when before the first record. **EOF** and **BOF** are TRUE when there are no records. No current record when either **EOF** or **BOF** are TRUE. **EOF** and **BOF** remain FALSE after deleting the last record and do not change until an attempt is made to reposition the current record.

Bookmark — **Recordset** object. Returns or sets the bookmark position that identifies the current record position. Bookmarks of the **Clone** method are identical to original bookmarks.

CacheSize — **Recordset** object. Default is 1 for forward-only cursors, 10 for other cursors. **Resync** method refreshes cache. Zero is not a valid value.

CommandText — **Command** object. Sets or returns the text version of a query in a **Command** object. Provider specific. May contain a SQL statement, table name, or a stored procedure call. Zero-length string is the default. The query is prepared when calling either the **Execute** or **Open** methods and the **Prepared** property is TRUE.

CommandTimeout — **Connection** or **Command** object. Elapsed time until ADO declares an error. A zero value is an indeterminate wait.

CommandType — **Command** object. Type of **CommandText** property data.

adCmdText <1>: Textual.

adCmdTable <2>: Table name.

adCmdStoredProc <4>: Stored procedure call.

adCmdUnknown <8>: Unknown, default.

adCmdFile <?>: The **CommandText** property is evaluated as a persisted **Recordset** object.

adCmdTableDirect <?>: Evaluates the **CommandText** field as a table name whose columns are all returned.

ConnectionString — **Connection** object. Five parameters to the connection string: *Provider, Data Source, User, Password,* and *File Name*. String is a series of *arguments = value* statements separated by a semicolon. The connection string cannot have both a *Provider* and a *File Name*.

ConnectionTimeout — **Connection** object. Elapsed time until ADO declares an error. A zero value is an indeterminate wait. Read-only when connection is open.

Count — **Errors, Fields, Parameters,** and **Properties** collections. Object count within collection.

CursorLocation — **Recordset** object. One of:

adUseNone : No cursor services are used.

adUseClient : Use client-side cursors, which replaces the deprecated **adUseClientbatch**.

adUseServer : The default cursor. Uses either the driver supplied or data-provider cursor. Disassociated (disconnected) **Recordset** objects cannot be simulated with server-side cursors.

CursorType

Recordset object. Set to one of:

adOpenForwardOnly <0>: Equivalent to a static cursor with forward-only scrolling.

adOpenKeyset <1>: Cannot see row additions or row deletions by other users. Changes to rows by other users are visible. Supports **adBookmark, adHoldRecords, adMovePrevious,** and **asResync**. See **Supports** method.

adOpenDynamic <2>: Additions, changes, and deletions by other users are visible. Supports **adMovePrevious**. See **Supports** method.

adOpenStatic <3>: Additions, changes, and deletions by other users are not visible. Supports **adBookmark, adHoldRecords, adMovePrevious,** and **adResync**. See the **Supports** method.

DefaultDatabase

Connection object. Resolves to the name of a provider database.

DefinedSize

Field object. Consumer-defined size, which may be greater than **ActualSize**.

Description

Error object. Error description.

EditMode

Recordset object. Returns one of:

adEditNone <0>: Not in edit mode.

adEditInProgress <1>: Current record is modified and not saved.

adEditAdd <2>: Addnew has been invoked but the record hasn't been saved yet.

adEditDelete <?>: Set when the current record is deleted.

EOF

Recordset object. TRUE when after the last record. **EOF** and **BOF** are TRUE when there are no records. No current record when either **EOF** or **BOF** are TRUE. **EOF** and **BOF** remain FALSE after deleting the last record and do not change until an attempt is made to reposition the current record.

Filter

Recordset object. Filtered **Recordset** becomes the current cursor. May affect **AbsolutePosition, Absolutepage, RecordCount,** and **PageCount**. Uses a criteria string with SQL syntax. The criteria string is the equivalent of a SQL WHERE clause without the keyword WHERE. Only <*> and <%> are allowed as wild card characters and they must be the last character in the string. Must not be **Null**.

Sets and returns a **Variant** value, which may be an array of bookmarks, a criteria string concatenated with AND, or one of the following:

adFilterNone <0>: Removes the current filter.

adFilterPendingRecords <1>: View only changed records not yet sent to server. Applicable to batch update mode only.

adFilterAffectedRecords <2>: View records of **Delete, Resync, UpdateBatch,** or **CancelBatch** methods.

adFilterFetchedrecords <3>: View records currently in cache.

HelpContext

Error object. Returns a context ID as a **Long** to a topic in a Microsoft Windows Help file.

HelpFile

Error object. Returns a fully qualified string to a Microsoft Windows Help file.

IsolationLevel

Connection object.

adXactUnspecified <-1>: Indeterminate isolation level.

adXactChaos <16>: Cannot overwrite changes from highly isolated transactions.

	adXactBrowse <256>: Uncommitted transaction may be read.
	adXactReadUncommitted <256>: Equivalent to **adXactBrowse**.
	adXactCursorStability <4096>: Default. Transactions viewable after committing.
	adXactReadCommitted <4096>: Equivalent to **adXactCursorStability**.
	adXactRepeatableRead <65536>: Cannot see other transaction changes; a requery, however, fetches new records.
	adXactIsolated <1048576>: Transactions are isolated.
	adXactSerializable <1048576>: Equivalent to **adXactIsolated**.
Item	**Errors, Fields, Parameters,** and **Properties** collections. Returns a specific member of a collection by name or ordinal number.
LockType	**Recordset** object. **adLockBatchOptimistic** should be either a key set or static cursor. Uses **Supports** method to determine functionality. Provider may substitute lock types. Read/write when closed, read-only when open.
	adLockReadOnly <1>: Read-only.
	adLockPessimistic <2>: Records locked when editing starts.
	adLockOptimistic <3>: Records locked when **Update** method is called.
	adLockBatchOptimistic <4>: Required for batch update mode.
MaxRecords	**Recordset** object. **Long**. Limits the number of records returned by provider. Zero requests all records.
Mode	**Connection** object. Indicates the rules for modifying data of a **Connection**.
	adModeUnknown <0>: Indeterminate permissions.

adModeRead <1>: Read-only.

adModeWrite <2>: Write-only.

adModeReadWrite <3>: Read/write permission.

adModeShareDenyRead <4>: Deny shared reads.

adModeShareDenyWrite <8>: Deny shared writes.

adModeShareExclusive <12>: Deny other reads/writes.

adModeShareDenyNone <16>: Exclude all others.

Name — **Field, Parameter,** or **Property** object. Property name. An ordinal or the property name can be used to retrieve an object.

NativeError — **Error** object. Database-specific error code.

Number — **Error** object. A **Long** that uniquely identifies an error.

NumericScale — **Parameter** or **Field** object. Number of digits to the right of the decimal point.

OriginalValue — **Field** object. The value before any changes or the value before the last **Update** or **BatchUpdate** call. The same value that is returned by a **CancelUpdate** or **CancelBatch** method call.

PageCount — **Recordset** object. Number of pages in the **Recordset** object. See **PageSize** and **AbsolutePage**.

PageSize — **Recordset** object. Determines number of records for a logical page. Useful for Web applications when indexing is not available.

Prepared — **Command** object. Provider compiles and saves a compiled copy of the query before the **Command** object's first execution.

Precision — **Parameter** or **Field** object. Maximum number of digits used to represent a value.

Provider — **Connection** object. Name of the provider for the connection. When there is no provider the default is MSDASQL (Microsoft ODBC Provider for OLE DB).

RecordCount	**Recordset** object. The number of records in a **Recordset** object. When the **Recordset** object does not support approximate position of bookmarks, determining the number of records can be a resource drain. The **RecordCount** method may be very inefficient when **adApproxPosition** is not supported. Use the **Supports** method to verify provider support of the **adApproxPosition** before calling the **RecordCount** method of a **Recordset** object.
Size	**Parameter** object. The maximum size in bytes read or written from the **Value** property of a **Parameter** object.
Source	**Recordset** object. Specifies the **Recordset** source by setting the **Source** property to a **Command** object variable, a SQL statement, a stored procedure, or a table name. The **ActiveConnection** property of a **Recordset** object inherits the **ActiveConnection** property of a **Command** object when the **Source** property is set to a **Command** object variable. **Error** object. The name of the object or application that created the error.
SQLState	**Error** object. Returns a five-character ANSI SQL standard error code.
State	**Connection** object, **Command** object, and **Recordset** object. Describes the state of an asynchronous method, which can be connecting, executing, or fetching. One of: **adStateClosed** : The object is closed. **adStateOpen** : The object is open. **adStateConnecting** : The connection is still in progress. **adStateExecuting** : The object is currently executing. **adStateFetching** : Rows of the **Recordset** object are being fetched.
Status	**Recordset** object. The status of a **Recordset** object as a result of calling **Delete, Resync, UpdateBatch,** or **CancelBatch**.

adRecOK <0>: Record successfully updated.

adrecNew <1>: New record.

adRecModified <2>: Modified record.

adRecDeleted <4>: Deleted record.

adRecUnmodified <8>: Record is unmodified.

None of the following status codes save the record.

adRecInvalid <16>: Invalid bookmark.

adrecMultipleChanges <64>: Affects multiple records.

adRecPendingChanges <128>: Refers to a pending insert.

adRecCanceled <256>: Cancels operation.

adRecCantRelease <1024>: Existing record locks.

adRecConcurrencyViolation <2048>: Optimistic concurrency is in use.

adrecIntegrityViolation <4096>: Integrity constraint violation.

adRecMaxChangesExceeded <8192>: Too many pending changes.

adRecObjectOpen <16384>: Conflict with an open storage object.

adRecOutOfMemory <32768>: Computer is out of memory.

adRecPermissionDenied <65536>: Insufficient permissions.

adRecSchemaViolation <131072>: Violates structure of the underlying database.

adRecDBDeleted <262144>: Already deleted.

Type

Field, **Parameter**, or **Property** object. Parameter is read/write.

adBigInt <20>: 8-Byte unsigned integer.

adBinary <128>: Binary.

adBoolean <11>: Boolean.

adBSTR <8>: Unicode null terminator.

adChapter <?>: Not documented in MSDN.

adChar <129>: String.

adCurrency <6>: 8-Byte signed integer scaled 10,000.

adDate <7>: Date.

adDBDate <133>: *yyyymmdd*.

adDBFileTime <?>: Not documented in MSDN.

adDBTime <134>: *hhmmss*.

adDBTimeStamp <135>: *yyyymmddhhmmss* plus a fraction in the billionths.

adDecimal <14>: Exact numeric with fixed precision and scale.

adDouble <5>: Double precision floating point.

adEmpty <0>: No value specified.

adError <10>: 32-Bit error code.

adFileTime <?>: Not documented in MSDN.

adGUID <72>: GUID.

adDispatch <9>: IDispatch pointer on a COM interface.

adInteger <3>: 4-Byte signed integer.

adIUnknown <13>: IUnknown pointer on a COM interface.

adLongVarBinary <205>: Long binary; Parameter object only.

adLongVarChar <201>: Long string.

adLongVarWChar <203>: Long Null-terminated string; Parameter object only.

adNumeric <131>: An exact numeric value with fixed precision and scale.

adPropVarient <?>: Not documented in MSDN.

adSingle <4>: Single-precision floating point.

adSmallInt <2>: 2-Byte signed integer.

adTinyInt <16>: 1-Byte signed integer.

adUnsignedBigInt <21>: 8-Byte signed integer.

adUnsignedInt <19>: 4-Byte unsigned integer.

adUnsignedSmallInt <18>: 2-Byte unsigned integer.

adUnsignedTinyInt <17>: 1-Byte unsigned integer.

adUserDefined <132>: User-defined variable.

adVarBinary <204>: Binary; Parameter object only.

adVarChar <200>: String; Parameter object only.

adVariant <12>: Automation variant.

adVarNumeric <?>: Not documented in MSDN.

adVarWChar <202>: Null-terminated Unicode character string. Parameter object only.

adWchar <130>: Null-terminated Unicode character string.

UnderlyingValue	**Field** object. The value currently visible to the transaction and which may be the result of an update. The value used by the **Resync** method to replace the Value property.
Value	**Field, Parameter,** or **Property** object. Returns the value of the property.
Version	**Connection** object. Provider version is returned as a dynamic property.

Key Point Summary

Microsoft has stated that ADO will replace DAO and RDO. ADO has the look and feel of both DAO and RDO. Maybe with only one database access technology, we can retreat from this Tower of Babel that Microsoft has been building. ADO is easy to use, and the current common use of ADO is with Web pages. ADO has not yet proved to be scaleable even though Microsoft states that it is their database access technology of the future. These are some of the major issues of this chapter:

- ADO is intended to be the universal database access technology.
- The rigid object implementation hierarchy of RDO and DAO is relaxed in ADO with ADO's automatic creation of default objects as necessary. A

Connection object isn't needed to open a **Recordset** object. One is created by the system automatically.

- Inefficient value-based row is discarded in both OLE-DB and ADO.
- There are only four collections in ADO: **Errors, Fields, Parameters,** and **Properties**.
- ADO supports transaction isolation levels, which means dirty reads and phantom reads can be managed.
- The durability component of the **ACID** properties is not yet visible even though Microsoft states that ADO supports the **ACID** properties. The architecture of OLE-DB/ADO indicates that **ACID** properties support is a provider-specific issue. There is nothing yet available that can be likened to the functionality of the Microsoft SQL Server write-ahead log.
- ADO does not support DDL statements, whereas OLE-DB supports DDL.

Applying What You've Learned

These questions will assess your understanding of ADO. You should be able to answer these questions directly since parallel functionality exists in RDO and DAO.

Instant Assessment

1. What advantages does ADO offer when compared to DAO?
2. Compare RDO optimistic concurrency and ADO optimistic concurrency.
3. Name the ADO objects that support creating a result set.
4. The application starts directly with the ADO **Recordset** object. Explain the events.
5. Which ADO cursor type provides optimum performance in ADO 2.0?
6. What is the default cursor location for ADO 2.0?
7. Explain a *dirty read.*
8. Explain a *non-repeatable read.*
9. Explain a *phantom read.*
10. What is the default property for the **Field, Parameter,** and **Property** objects?

11. Name the collections that support the **Append** method.
12. Name the collections or objects that support the **Delete** method.
13. Name the collections or objects that support the **Clear** method.

For answers to the Instant Assessment questions, see Appendix B.

Lab Exercise

This lab is another variation of Chapter 12, but rather than use a **Variant** array, the result set is returned as an ADO **Recordset** object. Pay close attention to this lab, since it will be the foundation of the tiered component architecture. Another architectural change to the ODBCClass module is to remove the **Response** read-only property. This makes the resulting **ADOClass** class module stateless, which is a requirement for Microsoft Transaction Server (MTS).

Lab 15.35 *Implementing an ADO class*

We'll take the ODBC lab of Chapter 12 and convert it to an ADO lab. An **ADOClass** class will replace the **ODBCClass** class of Chapter 12. The steps below will create the **ADOClass** class.

1. Copy the Chapter 12 lab into a new and empty folder.
2. Start Visual Basic and open the `ODBC.VBP` project in the new folder.
3. Remove the `ODBC.BAS` module from the project.
4. Remove the **ODBCClass** class from the project.
5. Remove the **ODBC.frm** form from the project.
6. Change the project name to **ADODemo** and the default startup form to the **frmLab** form.
7. Save the project as `ADO.VBP`.
8. Use the Visual Basic Class Wizard to create the **ADOClass** class module listed below in Listing 15-1. The SQL Server connection string must be modified to reflect the local SQL Server name, login, and password. The **ADOClass** class module is rather succinct when compared to the previous labs that build RDO and ODBC class modules. The **ADOQuery** function of the **ADOClass** class module returns an ADO **Recordset** object.

LISTING 15-1 **The ADOClass module code**

```
'(C) 1999 Bruce T. Prendergast
' DBA Prendergast Consulting
' DBA PCS
' IDG Books Worldwide ISBN 0-7645-3314-2
'
' ADO class
'
Option Explicit
Private adoCon As ADODB.Connection
Private adoCom As ADODB.Command
Private adoRes As ADODB.Recordset
Private mvarStatus As Variant
Public Property Get Status() As Variant
  Status = mvarStatus
End Property
Public Function ADOQuery( _
      ByVal QueryString As String) As ADODB.Recordset
  Dim adoRS As ADODB.Recordset
  '
  '  exit if unable to connect
  '
  If mvarStatus = False Then Exit Function
  On Error GoTo error_exit:
  mvarStatus = False
  Set adoCom = New ADODB.Command
  adoCom.ActiveConnection = adoCon
  adoCom.CommandText = QueryString
  Set adoRes = adoCom.Execute
  Set ADOQuery = adoRes
  mvarStatus = True
  Set adoCom = Nothing
error_exit:
  Exit Function
End Function
```

```
Private Sub Class_Initialize()
  mvarStatus = False
  On Error GoTo Initialize_Error:
  Set adoCon = New ADODB.Connection
  adoCon.ConnectionString = "DATABASE=pubs;UID=sa;PWD=;DSN=Thor;"
  adoCon.Open
  mvarStatus = True
Initialize_Error:
  Exit Sub
End Sub

Private Sub Class_Terminate()
  If mvarStatus Then adoCon.Close
End Sub
```

9. Edit the **ClassDriver** class module and replace each occurrence of <ODBC> with <ADO>.
10. From **References**, select the appropriate ADO library for your system (ADO 1.1, ADO 1.5, or ADO 2.0) . For Visual Basic 6.0 and ADO 2.0, select: PROJECT ➪ REFERENCES ➪ Microsoft ActiveX Data Objects 2.0 Library. For Visual Basic 5.0 and ADO 1.1, select: PROJECT ➪ REFERENCES ➪ Microsoft OLE DB ActiveX Data Objects 1.0 Library. This lab was tested with both ADO versions.
11. Edit the **ClassDriver** class module to agree with the text in Listing 15-2. The returned recordset supports ADO **Recordset** object properties and methods even though it is disassociated from the ADO **Connection** object.

LISTING 15-2 The ClassDriver module code

```
'(C) 1999 Bruce T. Prendergast
' DBA Prendergast Consulting
' DBA PCS
' IDG Books Worldwide ISBN 0-7645-3314-2
'
' ClassDriver
'
  Option Explicit
  Dim lADOClass As ADOClass
  Dim lDataClass As New DataClass
```

```
  Private mvarStatus As Variant
Private Sub Class_Terminate()
  Set lADOClass = Nothing
End Sub
Public Sub Fill(obj As ComboBox)
  Dim id As DataClass
  For Each id In lDataClass.DataClassCollection
    obj.AddItem id.au_id
  Next id
  obj.ListIndex = -1
End Sub
Public Sub GetOne(ByVal inp As String, txt1 As TextBox, txt2 As TextBox)
  Dim id As DataClass
  Set id = lDataClass.DataClassCollection(inp)
  txt1 = id.au_fname
  txt2 = id.au_lname
  Exit Sub
End Sub
Public Sub RunQuery(ByVal QueryString As String)
  Dim auid As String, aufname As String, aulname As String
  Dim adoRS As ADODB.Recordset
  Set lADOClass = New ADOClass
  Set adoRS = lADOClass.ADOQuery(QueryString)
  mvarStatus = lADOClass.Status
  If lADOClass.Status Then
    While Not adoRS.EOF
      aufname = adoRS!au_fname
      aulname = adoRS!au_lname
      auid = adoRS!au_id
      lDataClass.DataClassCollection.Add auid, _
        aufname, aulname, auid
      adoRS.MoveNext
    Wend
  End If
  Exit Sub
End Sub
```

```
Public Property Get Status() As Variant
  Status = mvarStatus
End Property
```

12. Ascertain that your local copy of Microsoft SQL Server 6.5 is running.
13. Start the project. Congratulations. You've just completed the ADO class lab. We'll change this class slightly later in the book for use in Microsoft Transaction Server.

CHAPTER

16

Working with Active Data Objects

About Chapter 16

Chapter 16 provides thumbnail sketches of all Active Data Objects (ADO) methods along with numerous examples. The chapter starts with a brief discussion of ADO events, which are new to ADO 2.0. An example of an ADO event is presented and the remainder of the chapter discusses ADO methods. The examples use Microsoft Visual Basic 6.0 and were tested with the Microsoft ActiveX Data Object 2.0 Library on Windows 95.

The examples in this chapter are found in the Visual Basic Chapter16.VBP project located in the `EXAMPLES\CHAPTER16` folder of the CD-ROM that accompanies this book. Figure 16-1 is the displayed Visual Basic form from the Chapter16.VBP project.

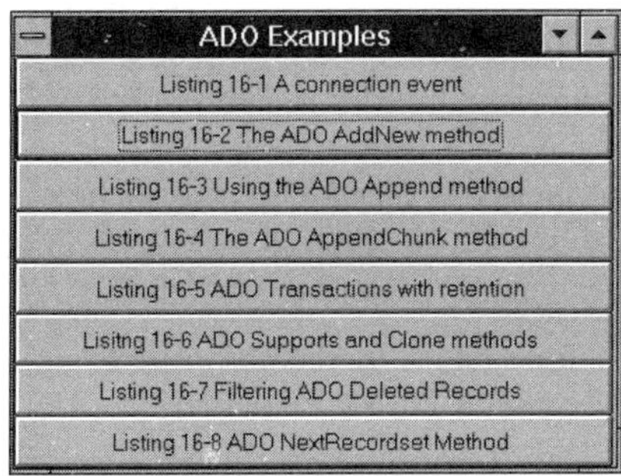

FIGURE 16-1 The Chapter16.VBP Microsoft Visual Basic project.

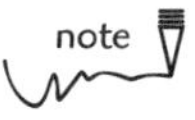

Figure 16-1 was tested on Windows 95 as a client of a Digital Equipment Corporation Alpha running Windows NT 4.0 Server, service pack 3. This book and Figure 16-1 were created on Windows NT Workstation 3.51, which is a different presentation metaphor than Windows 95 or Windows NT 4.0.

ADO Events

Events are not new to the Microsoft architecture, although they are very new to data access. Form events are standard fare for both Microsoft Access and Microsoft Visual Basic. Data access events were introduced with RDO and ADO carries this technology forward. Events are especially useful for slow asynchronous connections.

ADO supports two classes of events. The first class of events reports when a **Command** object executes, starts, or ends (see Listing 16-1). The second class of events reports navigation within rows of a **Recordset** object or any changes to a row or column of the **Recordset** object. Table 16-1 enumerates the details of the ADO **ConnectionEvents** family.

TABLE 16-1 ADO CONNECTIONEVENTS

ConnectionEvent	*When fired*
BeginTransComplete CommitTransComplete RollbackTransComplete	(Transaction Management) Events reporting the different completion stages of a connection transaction.
WillConnect Connect Complete Disconnect	(Connection Management) Events reported when the current connection is about to start, has started, or has ended.
WillExecute Execute Complete	(Command Execution Management) Events reporting the starting or completion of the current connection command.
InfoMessage	(Informational) Additional information, which is not necessarily error information.

Table 16-2 enumerates the details of the ADO **RecordsetEvents** family.

TABLE 16-2 ADO RECORDSETEVENTS

RecordsetEvent	*When fired*
FetchProgress FetchComplete	(Retrieval Status) Event reporting for data retrieval progress and completion.
WillChangeField Field ChangeComplete	(Field Change Management) Event reporting when a column (field) is about to change or has changed.
WillMove MoveComplete EndOfRecordset	(Navigation Management) Events reported when the current row position is about to change, has changed or a **Recordset** object EOF was encountered.

RecordsetEvent	When fired
WillChangeRecord RecordChangeComplete	(Row Change Management) Event reporting when any column (field) in the current row of the **Recordset** object is about to change or has changed.
WillChangeRecordset RecordsetChangeComplete	(Recordset Change Management) Event reporting when any column (field) of any row of the **Recordset** object is about to change or has changed.

Listing 16-1 is an example of using the **ConnectComplete** event of the **ConnectionEvent** family. The event is declared with the **WithEvents** keyword. The last argument of the event handler subroutine call is the **Connection** object that the event supports. Turning the event *on* is accomplished with the statement:

```
Set ConEvent = adoCon
```

This statement is found in the command button **ConnectionEvent_Click** event. Disabling the **ConnectComplete** event is accomplished with the statement:

```
Set ConEvent = Nothing
```

LISTING 16-1 Using the Connection object ConnectComplete event

```
'(C)1999 Bruce T. Prendergast
' DBA Prendergast Consulting
' DBA PCS
' IDG Books Worldwide ISBN 0-7645-3314-2
'
' Listing 16-1 A connection event
'
Option Explicit
Private adoCon As ADODB.Connection
Private WithEvents ConEvent As Connection
Private Sub ConEvent_ConnectComplete( _
  ByVal err As Error, _
  adstatus As EventStatusEnum, _
  ByVal adoCon As Connection)
```

```
    If adstatus = adStatusErrorsOccurred Then
      MsgBox "Connection errors occurred"
    Else
      MsgBox "Surprise, there are no errors!"
    End If
  End Sub
  Private Sub ConnectionEvent_Click()
    Set adoCon = New ADODB.Connection
    On Error GoTo connectionError
    Set ConEvent = adoCon
    adoCon.Open "Driver={SQL Server};Server=Apollo;Uid=sa;Pwd=;Database=pubs"
    Exit Sub
connectionError:
'
' when a connection error occurs, control is returned here after the
' ConEvent_ConnectComplete error notification
'
    Resume Next
End Sub
```

ADO Error Handling

ADO, like DAO, has two sources of errors. The first source is ADO errors and the second source is from the supporting Visual Basic. ADO errors are found in the **Errors** collection of a **Connection** object. This sounds simple and it is when the developer remembers that ADO errors are reported to the **Connection** object. The first example in the following section does not have a **Connection** object. The **Recordset** object is opened directly. Constructs such as:

```
MyCon.Errors(0).Description
```

are meaningless without a **Connection** object. A reasonable construct uses the **ActiveConnection** property to access the implicit **Connection** object created by ADO when a **Recordset** object is opened without an explicit connection. Listing 16-2 uses the **ActiveConnection** property of the **Recordset** object to retrieve errors from the **Connection** object.

Normal Visual Basic error processing involves the **Err** object with the **Description** and **Number** properties. Listing 16-2 also presents an example of the standard Visual Basic error processing.

ADO Methods

With previous database access technologies, the developer knows apriori the support offered by database access technologies such as Data Access Objects (DAO) and Remote Data Objects (RDO). Interrogating the data source was and still is a good programming practice with ODBC. Developing an ADO application requires the ODBC developer mindset since the consumer must interrogate the provider as to the level of support available. This is quite unlike ODBC, which has Application Programming Interface (API) and structured query language (SQL) conformance levels and performance is guaranteed. The consumer interrogated ODBC and knew by conformance level the functionality available. With ADO and OLE-DB, the inquiry is done at the individual feature level. One reason for this is ADO and OLE-DB are proprietary to Microsoft and no standards exist. This means that the level of support from each provider may be uneven. The main reason is that OLE-DB and the companion ADO are universal access technologies. It is not realistic to have conformance levels when comparing an Oracle database to an e-mail box. The ADO developer should use the **Supports** method when applicable to identify provider resources levels. Yes, a provider may support an attribute or resource, but the level of support will not be even. As an example, a provider may support updates, but this support may not extend to a multi-table join.

AddNew

AddNew is a method of the **Recordset** object that adds one or more new records to an existing **RecordSet** object. The consumer should verify that the data source supports the **AddNew** method before attempting to add a new record. The **Recordset** object must be refreshed with the **Requery** method when bookmarks are not supported.

Syntax:

Recordset.**AddNew** *Fields, Values.*

Where:

Recordset: An object of type **Recordset.**

Fields: A **Variant** representing a single name or a **Variant** array of names.

Values: A **Variant** representing a single value or a **Variant** array of values.

When the **AddNew** method uses the optional *Fields* and *Values* parameters, the **Recordset** object is updated immediately and the **Update** method need not be used.

LISTING 16-2 Using AddNew to insert a new record

```
Private Sub AddNew_Click()
'(C)1999 Bruce T. Prendergast
' DBA Prendergast Consulting
' DBA PCS
' IDG Books Worldwide ISBN 0-7645-3314-2
'
' Listing 16-2 Using the ADO AddNew method
'
Dim fldValues(3)
Dim fldNames(3)
Dim MyErr As Error
Dim MyRS As Recordset
'
' declare and create object
'
  On Error GoTo ADO_Error
  Set MyRS = CreateObject("ADODB.Recordset")
'
' open it
'
  MyRS.Open "Select * From Authors", _
    "DATABASE=pubs;UID=sa;PWD=;DSN=APOLLO",adOpenStatic, _
    adLockBatchOptimistic
  If Not MyRS.Supports(adAddNew) Then
    MsgBox "Cannot add new records"
```

```
      Set MyRS = Nothing
      Exit Sub
    End If
'
' build a new record
'
    fldNames(0) = "au_id": _
      fldNames(1) = "au_fname": _
      fldNames(2) = "au_lname": _
      fldNames(3) = "Contract"
  fldValues(0) = "123-45-6789": _
    fldValues(1) = "Sally": _
    fldValues(2) = "Silly": _
    fldValues(3) = 0
'
' add the record (THIS IS IMMEDIATE)
'
  MyRS.AddNew fldNames, fldValues
'
' A requery if bookmarks are not supported
'
  If Not MyRS.Supports(adBookmark) Then
    MyRS.Requery
  End If
'
' this was only a test, delete it.
'
  MyRS.Delete
  MsgBox "ADO AddNew method is a success"
normal_exit:
  Set MyRS = Nothing
  Exit Sub
ADO_Error:
  MsgBox "Error is: " & err.Number & err.Description
'
' note how the ActiveConnection links
```

```
' the recordset back to the Errors
' collection of the connection
'
  For Each MyErr In MyRS.ActiveConnection.Errors
    MsgBox "Error: " & MyErr.Number & " " & MyErr.Description
  Next MyErr
  Resume normal_exit
  Exit Sub
End Sub
```

Append

Append is a method of the **Parameters** collection of a **Command** object. Objects representing query parameters are appended to the **Parameters** collection. The **Type** must be set before the object is appended and the **Size** property must be greater than zero for variable length data. A **Parameter** object is created with the **CreateParameter**, which has the optional arguments *Name Type, Direction, Size,* and *Value*. The example in Listing 16-3 specifies only the *Type* and *Direction*.
Syntax:

Collection.**Append** *Parameter*

Where:

Collection: The **Parameters** collection.

Parameter: An object of type **Parameter.**

LISTING 16-3 Appending a parameter to the Parameters collection

```
Private Sub Append_Click()
'(C)1999 Bruce T. Prendergast
' DBA Prendergast Consulting
' DBA PCS
' IDG Books Worldwide ISBN 0-7645-3314-2
'
' Listing 16-3 Using the ADO Append method
'
```

```
Dim MyCon As Connection
Dim MyCmd As Command
Dim MyPar As Parameter
Dim MyRS As Recordset
Dim MyErr As Error
'
' declare and create a connection
'
  On Error GoTo ADO_Error
  Set MyCon = New ADODB.Connection
  MyCon.ConnectionString = "DATABASE=pubs;UID=sa;PWD=;DSN=Apollo"
'
' switch to no error handling
'
  On Error Resume Next
  MyCon.Open
  Set MyCmd = New ADODB.Command
'
' link command to connection
'
  MyCmd.ActiveConnection = MyCon
'
' build a command
'
  MyCmd.CommandText = "select au_fname, au_lname FROM authors where au_id= ?"
'
' build the parameter
'
  Set MyPar = MyCmd.CreateParameter( , adChar, adParamInput)
  MyPar.Size = 11
  MyPar.Value = "172-32-1176"
  MyCmd.Parameters.Append MyPar
  Set MyPar = Nothing
'
' get the data
'
```

```
  Set MyRS = MyCmd.Execute
'
  If MyRS(0) <> "Johnson" Or MyRS(1) <> "White" Then
    MsgBox "failed to find record"
    Set MyRS = Nothing
    Set MyCmd = Nothing
    Set MyCon = Nothing
    Exit Sub
  End If
  MsgBox "ADO Append method is a success"
normal_exit:
  Set MyRS = Nothing
  Set MyCmd = Nothing
  Set MyCon = Nothing
  Exit Sub
ADO_Error:
  If MyCon.Errors.Count = 0 Then
    MsgBox "Error is: " & err.Number
    MsgBox err.Description
  Else
    For Each MyErr In MyCon.Errors
      MsgBox "Error: " & MyErr.Number & " " & MyErr.Description
    Next MyErr
  End If
  Resume normal_exit
  Exit Sub
End Sub
```

AppendChunk, GetChunk

The **AppendChunk** method appends large amounts of text or binary data to a **Field** or **Parameter object.** The **adFldLong** bit must be set in the **Attributes** property of the **Field** object before the **AppendChunk** method may be used.

GetChunk also requires the **adFldLong** bit set in the **Attributes** property of the **Field** object.

The same condition exists for the **Parameter** object, but the names are different. The **adParamLong** bit of the **Attributes** property of a **Parameter** object has the same bit position as the **adFldLong** bit of the **Field** object **Attributes** property. This bit must be set before **AppendChunk** may be used on a **Parameter** object.

The first instance of **AppendChunk** replaces the original data while subsequent usage functions as an append operation.

Syntax:

{Field | Parameter}.**AppendChunk** Data

Set *Variable* = *Field*.**GetChunk**(*ByteCount*)

Where:

Field: An object of type **Field.**

Parameter: An object of type **Parameter**.

Data: A **Variant** containing the source data.

Variable: A **String** or a **Variant** of type **String**.

ByteCount: The number of bytes to retrieve.

LISTING 16-4 Using AppendChunk on a Parameter object

```
Private Sub AppendChunk_Click()
'(C)1999 Bruce T. Prendergast
' DBA Prendergast Consulting
' DBA PCS
' IDG Books Worldwide ISBN 0-7645-3314-2
'
' Listing 16-4 Using ADO AppendChunk
'
Dim MyCon As Connection
Dim MyCmd As Command
Dim MyPar As Parameter
Dim MyRS As Recordset
Dim MyErr As Error
'
' declare and create a connection
'
```

```
    On Error GoTo ADO_Error
    Set MyCon = New ADODB.Connection
    MyCon.ConnectionString = "DATABASE=pubs;UID=sa;PWD=;DSN=Apollo"
    MyCon.Open

    Set MyCmd = New ADODB.Command
'
' link command to connection
'
    MyCmd.ActiveConnection = MyCon
'
' build a command
'
    MyCmd.CommandText = "select au_id,au_fname, au_lname FROM authors"
'
' build a character glob, or is it blob?
'
    Set MyPar = MyCmd.CreateParameter(, adChar, adParamInput)
    MyPar.Name = "ParamTest"
    MyPar.Size = 4096
'
' make sure AppendChunk will work.
' adParamLong has the same bit number
' as adFldLong of the Field object
'
    MyPar.Attributes = adParamLong
    MyPar.Value = ""
    MyCmd.Parameters.Append MyPar
    Set MyPar = Nothing
'
' get the data
'
    Set MyRS = MyCmd.Execute
'
' build a pile of first and last names
'
```

```
  While Not MyRS.EOF
    MyCmd.Parameters("ParamTest").AppendChunk MyRS(0) & "|" & MyRS(1) & "|"
    MyRS.MoveNext
  Wend
  MsgBox "AppendChunk method is a success"
normal_exit:
  Set MyRS = Nothing
  Set MyCmd = Nothing
  Set MyCon = Nothing
  Exit Sub
ADO_Error:
  If MyCon.Errors.Count = 0 Then
    MsgBox "Error is: " & err.Number
    MsgBox err.Description
  Else
    For Each MyErr In MyCon.Errors
      MsgBox "Error: " & MyErr.Number & " " & MyErr.Description
    Next MyErr
  End If
  Resume normal_exit
  Exit Sub
End Sub
```

BeginTrans, CommitTrans, RollbackTrans

The **BeginTrans, CommitTrans,** and **RollbackTrans** methods manage transactions for a **Connection** object. **BeginTrans** returns a number indicating the current level when nesting transactions. <1> is the top-level transaction. A new transaction is started when the current transaction is committed with **CommitTrans** and the **Attributes** property of the **Connection** object is set to **adXactCommitRetaining.** A new transaction is started when the current transaction is rolled back with **RollbackTrans** and the **Attributes** property of the **Connection** object is set to **adXactAbortRetaining.**

Listing 16-4 sets the **IsolationLevel** property of a **Connection** object to **adXactSerializable**. The transaction retention level in Listing 16-4 is set to **adXactAbortRetaining** and verified.

Syntax:

[*Level* =]*Connection*.**BeginTrans**

Connection.{**CommitTrans** | **RollbackTrans** }

Where:

Level: Optional **Long** returned transaction level.

Connection: An object of type **Connection**.

LISTING 16-5 Using BeginTrans, CommitTrans and RollbackTrans

```
Private Sub BeginTrans_Click()
'(C)1999 Bruce T. Prendergast
' DBA Prendergast Consulting
' DBA PCS
' IDG Books Worldwide ISBN 0-7645-3314-2
'
' Listing 16-5 Using ADO Transactions
'
Dim MyCon As Connection
Dim MyCmd As Command
Dim MyErr As Error
Dim AffectedByMe As Integer
Dim TransactionOpen As Boolean
'
' declare and create a connection
'
  On Error GoTo ADO_Error
  Set MyCon = New ADODB.Connection
  MyCon.ConnectionString = "DATABASE=pubs;UID=sa;PWD=;DSN=Apollo"
  MyCon.Open
'
' set transaction isolation level
'
  MyCon.IsolationLevel = adXactSerializable
'
```

```
' start a new transaction on a rollback
'
  MyCon.Attributes = adXactAbortRetaining

  Set MyCmd = New ADODB.Command
'
' link command to connection
'
  MyCmd.ActiveConnection = MyCon
'
' build a command
'
  MyCmd.CommandText = _
    "insert jobs (job_desc, min_lvl, max_lvl)VALUES('Hacker',10,10)"
  TransactionOpen = True
  MyCon.BeginTrans
'
' Delete the record and check AffectedRecords property
'
  MyCmd.Execute AffectedByMe
  If AffectedByMe <> 1 Then
    MsgBox "Incorrect Add count: " & AffectedByMe
  End If
'
' Roll it back
'
  MyCon.RollbackTrans
'
' lets look at thetransaction retaining status
'
  If (MyCon.Attributes And adXactAbortRetaining) = 0 Then
    MsgBox "Transaction retention status error"
  End If
'
' we're still in a transaction
' reset the retention status and abort it
```

```
'
  MyCon.Attributes = 0
  MyCon.RollbackTrans
  MsgBox "ADO Transaction completed succesfully"
normal_exit:
  Set MyCmd = Nothing
  Set MyCon = Nothing
  Exit Sub
ADO_Error:
  If TransactionOpen Then MyCon.RollbackTrans
  If MyCon.Errors.Count = 0 Then
    MsgBox "Error is: " & err.Number
    MsgBox err.Description
  Else
    For Each MyErr In MyCon.Errors
      MsgBox "Error: " & MyErr.Number & " " & MyErr.Description
    Next MyErr
  End If
Resume normal_exit
  Exit Sub
End Sub
```

CancelBatch

CancelBatch is a method of the **Recordset** object that cancels pending batch updates. An error occurs when the **CancelBatch** method is called and the recordset object is in immediate update mode. The current row is indeterminate after a **CancelBatch** operation and a **MoveFirst** operation is a recommended procedure to reestablish the current row.

Syntax:

*Recordset.***CancelBatch** *AffectRecords.*

Where:

Recordset: An object of type **Recordset**.

AffectRecords: One of:

adAffectCurrent (cancel updates for current row only).

adAffectGroup (cancel updates satisfying the **Filter** property).

adAffectAll (cancel all pending updates including rows hidden by the **Filter** property).

CancelUpdate

CancelUpdate is a method of the **Recordset** object. It cancels changes made to the current record before the **Update** method is called. The prior current record becomes the current record when **CancelUpdate** is called after an **AddNew** call and if **Update** has not yet been called. Changes to a record after an **Update** can only be reversed with the **RollbackTrans** method of a **Connection** object.
Syntax:

Recordset.**CancelUpdate**

Where:

Recordset: An object of type **Recordset**.

Clear

Clear is the only method of the **Errors** collection. ADO automatically clears the collection before logging new errors. The **Filter** property or **Delete, Resync, UpdateBatch,** or **CancelBatch** methods may log warning messages that do not inhibit application execution.
Syntax:

*Collection.***Clear**

Where:

Collection: The **Errors** collection.

Clone

The **Clone** method is a mechanism for creating duplicate **Recordset** objects without requerying the data source. Closing the original **Recordset** object does not close the cloned **Recordset** object and, conversely, closing the cloned **Recordset** object does not close the original **Recordset** object. Changes made to the parent **Recordset** object are available in all cloned copies, independent of cursor type.

note

ADO is unlike Microsoft Access, which allows any form-bound Recordset object to be cloned. The application must ascertain that an ADO Recordset object supports bookmarks or the Recordset object cannot be cloned, as illustrated in Listing 16-5.

Syntax:

Set *Duplicate* = *Original*.**Clone**

Where:

Duplicate: An object of type **Recordset**.

Original: An object of type **Recordset**.

LISTING 16-6 Parent records visible in cloned recordset

```
Private Sub Clone_Click()
'(C)1999 Bruce T. Prendergast
' DBA Prendergast Consulting
' DBA PCS
' IDG Books Worldwide ISBN 0-7645-3314-2
'
' Listing 16-6 Using ADO Supports and Clone methods
'
Dim fldValues(3)
Dim fldNames(3)
Dim MyErr As Error
Dim MyRS As Recordset
Dim MyCS As Recordset
Dim FoundSally As Boolean
'
' declare and create object
'
  On Error GoTo ADO_Error
```

```
  Set MyRS = CreateObject("ADODB.Recordset")
'
' open it
'
  MyRS.Open "Select * From Authors", _
    "DATABASE=pubs;UID=sa;PWD=;DSN=Apollo", _
    adOpenStatic, adLockBatchOptimistic
'
' bookmarks must be supported for cloning
'
  If Not MyRS.Supports(adBookmark) Then
    MsgBox "Cloning not supported on this recordset"
    Set MyRS = Nothing
    Exit Sub
  End If
'
' build the clone recordset
'
  Set MyCS = MyRS.Clone
'
' build a new record
'
  fldNames(0) = "au_id": _
    fldNames(1) = "au_fname": _
    fldNames(2) = "au_lname": _
    fldNames(3) = "Contract"
  fldValues(0) = "123-45-6789": _
    fldValues(1) = "Sally": _
    fldValues(2) = "Silly": _
    fldValues(3) = 0
'
' add the record (THIS IS IMMEDIATE)
'
  MyRS.AddNew fldNames, fldValues
'
' Sally Silly should now be visible on the cloned recordset
```

```
'
  MyCS.MoveFirst
  FoundSally = False
  Do While Not MyCS.EOF
    If MyCS(1) = "Silly" And MyCS(2) = "Sally" Then
      FoundSally = True
      Exit Do
    End If
    MyCS.MoveNext
  Loop
  If Not FoundSally Then
    MsgBox "Error in cloned recordset"
    Set MyRS = Nothing
    Set MyCS = Nothing
    Exit Sub
  End If
  MsgBox "ADO Clone method completed successfully"
normal_exit:
  Set MyRS = Nothing
Set MyCS = Nothing
  Exit Sub
ADO_Error:
  If MyRS.ActiveConnection.Errors.Count = 0 Then
    MsgBox "Error is: " & err.Number
    MsgBox err.Description
  Else
    For Each MyErr In MyRS.ActiveConnection.Errors
      MsgBox "Error: " & MyErr.Number & " " & MyErr.Description
    Next MyErr
  End If
  Resume normal_exit
  Exit Sub
End Sub
```

Close

The **Close** method closes a **Connection** object or a **Recordset** object and all dependent objects.

The actions that occur when a **Connection** object is closed are:

- The **Command** object persists, but the **ActiveConnection** property is set to **Nothing**.
- The command object is reusable at a later time.
- The **Command** object's **Parameters** collection is cleared.
- Any pending changes to an open **Recordset** object are rolled back. Closing a **Connection** object with an outstanding transaction will generate an error.
- Transaction objects are rolled back automatically when the **Connection** object falls out of scope.

The actions that occur when a **Recordset** object is closed are:

- Associated data and exclusive access are released.
- An error is generated when an edit is in progress.
- All changes since the last **UpdateBatch** are lost when closing a **Recordset** object during batch updating.
- Closing a **Recordset** object does not close a cloned **Recordset** object.
- The **Recordset** object remains available for later reuse.

Syntax:

Object.**Close**

Where:

Object: An object of type **Connection** or type **Recordset**.

CreateParameter

The **CreateParameter** method creates a new **Parameter** object.

Syntax:

Set Parameter = Command.**CreateParameter**(Name, Type, Direction, Size, Value)

Where:

Parameter: An object of type **Parameter**.

Command: An object of type **Command**.

Name: A **String** representing the **Parameter** object name.

Type: Optional, a **Long** that specifies the **Parameter** object's data type. One of:

adBigInt <20>: 8-Byte unsigned integer.

adBinary <128>: Binary.

adBoolean <11>: Boolean.

adBSTR <8>: Null-terminator Unicode.

adChar <129>: String.

adCurrency <6>: 8-Byte signed integer scaled 10,000.

adDate <7>: Date.

adDBDate <133>: *yyyymmdd.*

adDBTime <134>: *hhmmss.*

adDBTimeStamp <135>: *yyyymmddhhmmss* plus a fraction in the billionths.

adDecimal <14>: Exact numeric with fixed precision and scale.

adDouble <5>: Double-precision floating point.

adEmpty <0>: No value specified.

adError <10>: 32-Bit error code.

adGUID <72>: Global unique identifier (GUID).

adDispatch <9>: IDispatch pointer on a COM interface.

adInteger <3>: 4-Byte signed integer.

adIUnknown <13>: IUnknown pointer on a COM interface.

adLongVarBinary <205>: Long binary; **Parameter** object only.

adLongVarChar <201>: Long string.

adLongVarWChar <203>: Long **Null**-terminated string; **Parameter** object only.

adNumeric <131>: An exact numeric value with fixed precision and scale.

adSingle <4>: Single-precision floating point.

adSmallInt <2>: 2-Byte signed integer.

adTinyInt <16>: 1-Byte signed integer.

adUnsignedBigInt <21>: 8-Byte signed integer.

adUnsignedInt <19>: 4-Byte unsigned integer.

adUnsignedSmallInt <18>: 2-Byte unsigned integer.

adUnsignedTinyInt <17>: 1-Byte unsigned integer.

aduserDefined <132>: User-defined variable.

adVarBinary <204>: Binary; **Parameter** object only.

adVarChar <200>: String; **Parameter** object only.

adVariant <12>: Automation **Variant.**

adVarWChar <202>: **Null**-terminated Unicode character string; **Parameter** object only.

adWchar <130>: **Null**-terminated Unicode character string.

Size: Optional; a **Long,** the maximum length in bytes or characters.

Value: Optional; a **Variant** specifying the **Parameter** object's value.

See Listing 16-3 for an example of the **CreateParameter** method.

Delete

The **Delete** method deletes the current record of a **Recordset** object or a **Parameter** object from the **Parameters** collection.

The current record is deleted immediately when in immediate mode. If it is marked for deletion from the cache, the actual deletion doesn't occur until **UpdateBatch** is called. Batch updating only exists when the **LockType** property is set to **adLockBatchOptimistic**.

Syntax:

Recordset.**Delete** *AffectRecords*

*Collection.***Delete** *Index*

Where:

Recordset: An object of type **Recordset**.

AffectRecords: One of:

adAffectCurrent <1>: Delete current record only.

adAffectGroup <2>: Delete the records satisfying the **Filter** property.

Collection: An object of type **Collection**.

Index: A **String** identifying the **Parameter** object.

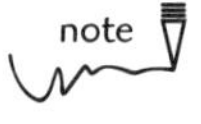

A trappable error only occurs when no records can be deleted. No trappable error occurs when at least one of the intended records can be deleted.

The **Delete** method may not be supported on the **Recordset** object. The consumer has the obligation of calling the **Supports** method to verify record deletion support.

Listing 16-7 is an example of most of the issues involving deleting a record.

- The example starts by creating a complete **RecordSet** object of the original table. A **Recordset** object is created with arguments supplied to both the **Source** and **ActiveConnection** parameters. A **Connection** object is needed for a later transaction.
- The original **Recordset** object is filtered.
- A transaction is opened and the row is deleted.
- The **Errors** collection is interrogated for an error because a delete failure is not usually fatal to application execution.
- The deleted **Recordset** object is filtered and verified.
- The transaction is rolled back because this is only a demonstration.

LISTING 16-7 Deleting a record and verifying the delete with a filter

```
Private Sub Delete_Click()
'(C)1999 Bruce T. Prendergast
' DBA Prendergast Consulting
' DBA PCS
' IDG Books Worldwide ISBN 0-7645-3314-2
'
' Listing 16-7 Filtering deleted rows in ADO
```

```
'
Dim MyCon As Connection
Dim MyCmd As Command
Dim MyPar As Parameter
Dim MyRS As Recordset
Dim MyRSCount As Integer
Dim MyErr As Error
Dim TransactionStarted As Boolean
'
' declare and create a connection
'
  On Error GoTo Filter_Error
  Set MyCon = New ADODB.Connection
  MyCon.ConnectionString = "DATABASE=pubs;UID=sa;PWD=;DSN=Apollo"
'
' switch to no error handling
'
  On Error Resume Next
  MyCon.Open
  Set MyCmd = New ADODB.Command
'
' link command to connection
'
  MyCmd.ActiveConnection = MyCon
'
' this is cleanup from prior efforts
'
  MyCmd.CommandText = "Delete FROM jobs WHERE job_desc ='Hacker'"
  MyCmd.Execute
'
' now for a fresh start
'
  On Error GoTo Filter_Error
  MyCmd.CommandText = _
    "insert jobs (job_desc, min_lvl, max_lvl)VALUES('Hacker',10,10)"
  MyCmd.Execute
```

```
'
' get the data
'
  Set MyRS = New ADODB.Recordset
  MyRS.Open "select * from jobs", MyCon, adOpenKeyset, _
    adLockOptimistic, adCmdText
  If Not MyRS.Supports(adDelete) Then
    MsgBox "Cannot delete records"
    Set MyRS = Nothing
    Set MyCon = Nothing
    Set MyCmd = Nothing
    Exit Sub
  End If
'
' set the filter, a string filter here
'
On Error Resume Next
MyRS.Filter = "job_desc LIKE 'Hack*'"  ' should be one record
'
' Let's look at the filtered set
'
  MyRS.MoveFirst
  MyRSCount = MyRS.RecordCount
  If (MyRS(1) <> "Hacker") Or (MyRSCount <> 1) Then
    MsgBox "Filter original failure"
    Set MyRS = Nothing
    Set MyCon = Nothing
    Set MyCmd = Nothing
    Exit Sub
  End If
  MyCon.BeginTrans
  TransactionStarted = True
'
' delete only filtered records
'
  MyRS.Delete adAffectGroup
```

```
   If MyCon.Errors.Count > 0 Then
     MsgBox MyCon.Errors(0).Description
   Else
   '
   ' filter the deleted records, a filter constant here
   '
     MyRS.Filter = adFilterAffectedRecords
     MyRS.MoveFirst
     MyRSCount = MyRS.RecordCount
     If MyRSCount <> 0 Then
       MsgBox "Filter delete failure"
     End If
   End If
  MyCon.RollbackTrans
  MsgBox "Filtering deleted rows completed successfully"
normal_exit:
  Set MyRS = Nothing
  Set MyCon = Nothing
  Set MyCmd = Nothing
  Exit Sub
Filter_Error:
  If TransactionStarted Then MyCon.RollbackTrans
  If MyCon.Errors.Count = 0 Then
    MsgBox "Error is: " & err.Number
    MsgBox err.Description
  Else
    For Each MyErr In MyCon.Errors
      MsgBox "Error: " & MyErr.Number & " " & MyErr.Description
    Next MyErr
  End If
  Resume normal_exit
End Sub
```

Execute

Execute is a method of the **Command** or **Connection** object. A new **Recordset** object is always returned and the **Recordset** will be closed and can be ignored for action queries that add, delete, or change records. The **RecordsAffected** count is returned only for action queries even though the documentation implies that a query returns a record count.

Input query parameters are optional and can be used to selectively override **Parameter** objects in the **Parameters** collection. Output parameters are not supported.

Defaults for a **Recordset** object created with the **Execute** method are **adOpenForwardOnly** for cursor type and **adLockReadOnly** for lock type.

The **AffectedRecords** property is different than the **RecordCount** property. **AffectedRecords** gives the record count of affected records as a result of an action query. The **RecordCount** property returns the total number of records in a **Recordset** object. If the **Recordset** object supports approximate positioning with the **adApproxPosition** attribute or bookmarks, the returned value will be the exact number of records in the **Recordset** object. This count is independent of **Recordset** object population. If the **Recordset** object does not support approximate positioning, this property may be a significant drain on resources because all records will have to be retrieved and counted to return an accurate **RecordCount** value. The **Supports** method is used to query the **Recordset** object for **adApproxPosition** support.

Syntax:

Set *Recordset* = *Command*.**Execute**(*RecordsAffected, Parameters, Options*)

Command.**Execute** *RecordsAffected, Parameters, Options*

Set *Recordset* = *Connection*.**Execute**(*CommandText, RecordsAffected, Options*)

Connection.**Execute** *CommandText, RecordsAffected, Options*

Where:

Recordset: Object of type **Recordset**.

Command: Object of type **Command**.

Connection: Object of type **Connection**.

RecordsAffected: Optional; **Long**; the number of added, deleted, or changed records.

Parameters: A **Variant** array of input parameters passed to a SQL statement.

Options: One of: **adCmdText<1>, adCmdTable<2>, adCmdStoredProc<4>,** or **adCmdUnknown<8>.**

CommandText: **String**. One of: Table name, SQL statement, or stored procedure name.

Please see Listing 16-4 for an example of the **Execute** method.

GetRows

The **GetRows** method retrieves a block of rows into an array. An optional parameter can be used to identify specific fields.
Syntax:

Set *Array* = *Recordset*.**GetRows**(*Rows, Start, Fields*)

Where:

Array: Returned **Variant** data array. The first subscript identifies the field while the second subscript identifies the row. The array size is automatically calculated by **GetRows**.

Recordset: An object of type **Recordset**.

Rows: Optional. **Long** row count. Default is **adGetRowsRest** (-1).

Start: Optional. A **String** or **Variant** bookmark for the starting record.

Fields: Optional. **Variant** represents an array of one or more field names or ordinal numbers that identify the fields of interest.

Move, MoveFirst, MoveLast, MoveNext, MovePrevious

The **Move** method provides logical navigation between records of a **RecordSet** object. Operation is as expected with moving beyond the last record or before the first record creating the end-of-file (EOF) and beginning-of-file (BOF) conditions, respectively. Attempting to move beyond either the EOF or BOF creates an error.

The **CacheSize** property and the **Move** method can be used to support backward and forward scrolling for forward-only recordsets. The provider replenishes the cache when a **Move** method is executed that is beyond the scope of the current cache.

Syntax:

Recordset.{**MoveFirst | MoveLast | MoveNext | MovePrevious** }

Recordset.**Move** *NumberOfRecords, Start*

Where:

Recordset: An object of type **Recordset**.

NumberOfRecords: **Long** record count.

Start: A **String** or a **Variant** that evaluates a bookmark.

NextRecordset

NextRecordset clears the current **Recordset** object and returns the next **Recordset** object. Multiple **Recordset** objects are created by concatenating at least two SQL statements separated by semicolons. As an example:

```
SELECT * FROM authors;SELECT * FROM titles
```

returns two **Recordset** objects. Multiple recordsets are only available in the **CommandText** property of a **Command** object. Listing 16-8 is an example of processing multiple recordsets.

LISTING 16-8 Processing multiple Recordset objects

```
Private Sub NextRecordset_Click()
'(C)1999 Bruce T. Prendergast
' DBA Prendergast Consulting
' DBA PCS
' IDG Books Worldwide ISBN 0-7645-3314-2
'
' Listing 16-8 Using the ADO GetNextRecordset method
'
Dim MyCon As Connection
```

```
Dim MyCmd As Command
Dim MyPar As Parameter
Dim MyRS As Recordset
Dim MyErr As Error
Dim RecordsAffected As Long
'
' declare and create a connection
'
  On Error GoTo ADO_Error
  Set MyCon = New ADODB.Connection
  MyCon.ConnectionString = "DATABASE=pubs;UID=sa;PWD=;DSN=Apollo"
'
' switch to no error handling
'
  On Error Resume Next
  MyCon.Open
  Set MyCmd = New ADODB.Command
'
' link command to connection
'
  MyCmd.ActiveConnection = MyCon
'
' get the data
'
  MyCmd.CommandText = "Select * FROM authors;SELECT * FROM titles"
  Set MyRS = MyCmd.Execute(RecordsAffected, , adCmdText)
'
' the first recordset
'
  MsgBox MyRS(0) & " " & MyRS(1) & " " & MyRS(2)
'
' the second recordset
'
  Set MyRS = MyRS.NextRecordSet
  MsgBox MyRS(0) & " " & MyRS(1) & " " & MyRS(2)
  MsgBox "NextRecordset completed successfully"
```

```
    MyRS.Delete
  normal_exit:
    Set MyRS = Nothing
    Set MyCmd = Nothing
    Set MyCon = Nothing
    Exit Sub
  ADO_Error:
    If MyRS.ActiveConnection.Errors.Count = 0 Then
      MsgBox "Error is: " & err.Number
      MsgBox err.Description
    Else
      For Each MyErr In MyRS.ActiveConnection.Errors
        MsgBox "Error: " & MyErr.Number & " " & MyErr.Description
      Next MyErr
    End If
    Resume normal_exit
    Exit Sub
  End Sub
```

Open

The **Open** method either opens a connection to a data source using a **Connection** object or opens a cursor using a **Recordset** object.
Syntax:

Connection.**Open** *ConnectionString, UserID, Password*

Recordset.**Open** *Source, ActiveConnection, CursorType, LockType, Options*

Where:

Connection: An object of type **Connection**.

Recordset: An object of type **Recordset**.

ConnectionString: The five parameters to the connection string are: *Provider, Data Source, User, Password,* and *File Name*. String is a series of *argument* = *value* statements separated by a semicolon. The connection string cannot have both a *Provider* and a *File Name*.

UserID: Optional user name; **String**.

Password: Optional password; **String**.

Source: Optional. The *Source* is a SQL statement, table name, stored procedure call, or a **Variant** that evaluates whether a **Command** object is valid.

ActiveConnection: Optional. *ActiveConnection* is a **Variant** that evaluates a **Connection** object or a **String** with connection definitions.

CursorType: Optional. One of: **adOpenForwardOnly <0>** (which is the default), **adOpenKeyset <1>, adOpenDynamic <2>,** or **adOpenStatic <3>.**

LockType: Optional. One of: **adLockReadOnly <1>, adLockPessimistic <2>, adLockOptimistic <3>,** or **adLockBatchOptimistic <4>.**

Options: Optional. One of: **adCmdText <1>, adCmdTable <2>, adCmdStoredProc <4>,** or **adCmdUnknown <8>.**

See Listing 16-2 for an example of opening a cursor on a **Recordset** object and Listing 16-4 for an example of opening a connection using a **Connection** object.

Refresh

The **Refresh** method refreshes a **Fields, Parameters,** or **Properties** collection.

Fields collection

No visible changes occur to the **Fields** collection when using the **Refresh** method. When the **Recordset** object supports bookmarks, changes to the underlying data are retrieved with the **Requery** method or the **MoveFirst** method.

Parameters collection

Using the **Refresh** method on the **Parameters** collection of a **Command** object retrieves either provider-side parameter information for stored procedures or a parameterized query specified in the **Command** object. The collection is empty when the provider does not support stored procedure calls or parameterized queries. Accessing a **Parameter** object automatically refreshes the **Parameters** collection.

The following conditions should exist before using the **Refresh** method on a **Command** object's **Parameters** collection.

- A valid **Command** object and a valid **Connection** object must exist.

- The **ActiveConnection** property of the **Command** object must be set to a valid **Connection** object.
- The **CommandText** property of the **Command** object must be set to a valid command.
- Unless the consumer initially sets the **Size** property to a nominal value, ADO allocates the maximum possible space for variable-length objects in the **Parameters** collection.

Properties collection

The provider populates the **Properties** collection with exposed dynamic properties. This functionality is beyond ADO built-in property support.
Syntax:

Object.**Refresh**

Where:

Object: One of: **Fields, Parameters,** or **Properties** collections.

Requery

The **Requery** method refreshes the current cursor. This is because cursor properties such as **CursorType, LockType,** and **MaxRecords** are read-only when the cursor is open. The **Requery** method is equivalent to calling **Close** immediately followed by a call to **Open**.
Syntax:

Recordset.**Requery**

Where:

Recordset: An object of type **Recordset**.

Resync

The **Resync** method resynchronizes records in the current **Recordset** object. This method lets a consumer see underlying changes made by other consumers when the **Recordset** object is either a static or forward-only cursor. New rows will not be seen by the **Resync** method. Deleted rows return an error and the consumer must check the **Errors** collection for deleted rows after executing a **Resync** method. **Resync** cancels any pending batch updates and the **Resync** method is not available to client-side cursors.

Syntax:

Recordset.**Resync** *AffectRecords*

Where:

Recordset: An object of type **Recordset** object.

AffectRecords: One of:

adAffectCurrent <1>: Refreshes current record.

adAffectGroup <2>: Refreshes records satisfying the **Filter** property.

adAffectAll <3>: Refreshes all records in the **Recordset** object independent of the **Filter** property setting.

Supports

The **Supports** method determines functionality of a **Recordset** object. There is no guarantee that a provider will support a particular feature. The developer determines the supported functionality by querying the **Recordset** object with the **Supports** method

Syntax:

Boolean = *Recordset*.**Supports(***CursorOptions***)**

Where:

Boolean: A variable of type **Boolean.**

Recordset: An object of type **Recordset.**

CursorOptions: One of:

adAddNew <16778240>: AddNew method is permitted.

adApproxPosition <16384>: AbsolutePosition and **AbsolutePage** are permitted. A record count is the physical reading of each record without this support.

adBookmark <8192>: Bookmarks are supported.

adDelete <16779264>: Record deletion is permitted.

adHoldRecords <256>: Record retrieval and manipulation are permitted without committing pending changes.

adMovePrevious <512>: Move and **MovePrevious** are permitted.

adResync <131072>: Cursor may be updated with visible data from underlying database.

adUpdate <16809984>: Update method is permitted.

adUpdateBatch <65536>: Batch updating is permitted.

See Listing 16-2 for an example of this method.

Update

The **Update** method updates the underlying database with accumulated changes to a record. Using the **Update** method isn't necessary with a single record because ADO automatically calls **Update** when positioning to a new record. This is the *immediate mode* supported by the underlying OLE-DB.

The **Update** method provides optional updating capabilities for multiple fields.

Because ADO does not support an **Edit** mode it is quite unlike prior database access technologies such as Microsoft Access. Consequently, pessimistic locking starts when the **Recordset** object is created and not when editing starts. This may be a bit confusing and more than one database may operate in an almost exclusive mode until developers fully understand the different update strategy. Changes made before the **Update** method is called may be canceled with the **Cancel Update** method.

Syntax:

Recordset.**Update** *Fields, Values*

Where:

Recordset: An object of type **Recordset**.

Fields: Optional. *Fields* is a **Variant** variable or array of one or more field names or field ordinal numbers.

Values: Optional. *Values* is a **Variant** variable or array of one or more field values that correspond to the ordinals or names of the *Fields* argument.

UpdateBatch

The **UpdateBatch** method infers that the **Recordset** object is operating in the *deferred mode* supported by the underlying OLE-DB. Batch mode is established when the **Recordset** object is created by setting the **LockType** property of the **Recordset** object to **adLockBatchOptimistic.** Setting both the **CursorType** and **LockType** properties of the **Recordset** object **Open** method to **adOpenKeyset** and **adLockBatchOptimistic** respectively creates a fully scrollable and batch-updateable **Recordset** object.

Batch operations can only be used with a static or **Keyset** cursor. Batch updating is the preferred update mechanism for records with multiple key fields because batch updating eliminates the inconsistent states that occur during partial updates.

The provider caches multiple changes in batch update mode and only writes the accumulated changes to the underlying data source only when the client calls the **UpdateBatch** method. The process starts with the client calling the **AddNew** method without arguments. This sets the **EditMode** property to **adEditAdd**. ADO will now cache any column changes locally. When the client calls the **Update** method a new row is added to the row set (result set) and the **EditMode** property is reset to **adEditNone**. The changes are still not posted to the underlying database. The client eventually posts the changes to the underlying database with the **UpdateBatch** method.

The **UpdateBatch** method may generate errors and the consumer must check the **Errors** collection for error messages. A run-time error only occurs when none of the records can be updated. The errors in the **Recordset** object can be located by setting the **Filter** property to **adFilterAffectedRecords**. The **Status** property of each record in the resulting **Recordset** is then examined to determine the record status. A good choice is to wrap the update within a transaction and have the complete update roll back when conflicts cannot be resolved.

Syntax:

*Recordset.***UpdateBatch** *AffectRecords*

Where:

Recordset: An object of type **Recordset**.

AffectRecords: Optional. One of:

adAffectCurrent <1>: Writes current record changes only.

adAffectGroup <2>: Writes changes satisfying the **Filter** property.

adAffectAll <3>: This is the default. It writes all pending changes.

This finishes the thumbnail sketch of the ADO. We've covered the fundamentals. Chapter 17 is next, which is the first of four chapters that address 70-100 objectives. Persevere.

Key Point Summary

ADO has many of the familiar methods and properties of both DAO and RDO but there are significant differences. The ADO developer must be vigilant and must always test for support of a resource with the **Supports** method before attempting to use that resource. Interrogating for resources is a commonplace practice for ODBC programmers who use ODBC catalog functions.

- ADO does not support an edit method. Changes to a record are immediate after moving off the record unless in batch mode.
- The **Errors** collection is a collection of the **Connection** object. When an error occurs the **ActiveConnection** property of a **Recordset** object provides the link to the appropriate **Connection** object.
- Row versioning is implicit in optimistic locking. Row versioning by record ID, which was introduced in RDO, is not available in ADO.
- Transaction isolation levels are supported giving the developer the ability to accurately manage consistency.

Applying What You've Learned

These questions assess your understanding of ADO objects, properties, and methods. There are subtle differences between ADO and the predecessor RDO and DAO technologies.

Instant Assessment

1. Name the four ADO collections.
2. What is the issue when the **Recordset** object attribute **adApproxPosition** is not supported?
3. What role does the **ActiveConnection** property of a **Recordset** object play in error analysis?
4. Identify and describe the two classes of ADO events.
5. Describe creating an ADO event routine.
6. How are ADO events enabled or disabled?
7. Identify the basic difference between editing a record in DAO and ADO.
8. What is batch mode?
9. How is batch mode initiated?
10. What determines when a **Recordset** object is fully scrollable and updatable?
11. What common characteristic does the DAO **Errors** collection share with the ADO **Errors** collection?
12. Explain the use of the **Supports** method.
13. What is the common issue for the **Delete, Resync, UpdateBatch,** or **CancelBatch** methods?

For answers to the Instant Assessment questions, see Appendix B.

Lab Exercise

This lab is not another variation of Chapter 12, but rather a lab that illustrates an architectural error. I recently attended Microsoft course 1298, which is the recommended curriculum for core Microsoft Certified Solution Developer certification exam 70-100. The instructional material from that class espouses what I and many others believe is an architectural error. Apparently the course authors don't have practical experience developing applications. The architectural error will be discussed in detail in the forthcoming chapter on Distributed COM (DCOM, Chapter 21). Until then attempt to decipher the problem. The code is clean, and unfortunately quite deceiving. Good luck.

Lab 16.36 *Implementing an ADO class*

This lab presents an architectural error. The code is straightforward and is a bit deceiving when the Microsoft guidelines are followed. The problem consists of a form with supporting code (presentation services), a data class (business rules), and a database class (data services). The steps below will create the QUESTION.VBP project.

1. Place a combo box on the form and label it *cmbau_id*.
2. Enter the code shown in Listing 16-9 in the form **Declaration** section.

LISTING 16-9 The form code of the ArchitecturalQuestion project

```
'(C) 1999 Bruce T. Prendergast
' DBA Prendergast Consulting
' DBA PCS
' IDG Books Worldwide ISBN 0-7645-3314-2
'
' ADO form for DataClass and adoDatabaseClass
'
Option Explicit

Private DataEngine As New DataClass

Private Sub cmbAU_ID_Click()
Dim col As Collection
  For Each col In DataEngine.GetRow("Au_fname, Au_lname", "Authors", _
    " WHERE au_id = '" & [cmbAU_ID] & "'")
    txtAu_fname = col("au_fname")
    txtAu_lname = col("au_lname")
    Exit For
  Next
End Sub
Private Sub Form_Load()
Dim col As Collection
  On Error GoTo NoSQLServer*
  For Each col In DataEngine.GetRow("au_id", "authors", "")
    cmbAU_ID.AddItem col("au_id")
```

```
    Next
    cmbAU_ID.ListIndex = 0
    Exit Sub
  NoSQLServer:
    Resume Next
    MsgBox "SQL Server is not available"
    Stop
  End Sub
```

3. Edit the code of the new class to agree with listing 16-10.

LISTING 16-10 The DataClass class code of the ArchitecturalQuestion project

```
'(C) 1999 Bruce T. Prendergast
' DBA Prendergast Consulting
' DBA PCS
' IDG Books Worldwide ISBN 0-7645-3314-2
'
Public Function GetRow( _
  ByVal strCols As String, _
  ByVal strTable As String, _
  ByVal strWhere As String) As Collection
Dim myRs As adodb.Recordset
Dim DBC As adoDatabaseClass
Dim myList As New Collection
Dim MySubList As New Collection
Dim i As Integer

  Set DBC = New adoDatabaseClass
  Set myRs = DBC.SelectQuery( _
    "SELECT " & strCols & " FROM " & strTable & " " & strWhere & ";")
  While Not myRs.EOF
    For i = 0 To myRs.Fields.Count - 1
      MySubList.Add myRs(i).Value, myRs(i).Name
    Next i
    myList.Add MySubList
```

```
      myRs.MoveNext
      Set MySubList = Nothing
    Wend
    Set GetRow = myList
    Set myRs = Nothing
    Set myList = Nothing
End Function
```

4. Edit the code of the new class to agree with listing 16-11.

LISTING 16-11 The adoDatabaseClass class code of the ArchitecturalQuestion project

```
'(C) 1999 Bruce T. Prendergast
' DBA Prendergast Consulting
' DBA PCS
' IDG Books Worldwide ISBN 0-7645-3314-2
'
Public Function SelectQuery(ByVal strSQL As String) As adodb.Recordset
Dim adoCon As adodb.Connection
Dim adoRS As adodb.Recordset

  On Error GoTo ErrorEncountered
  Set adoCon = New adodb.Connection
  adoCon.Open "Database=pubs;DSN=Thor;Uid=sa;pwd=;"
  Set adoRS = New adodb.Recordset
  adoRS.Open strSQL, adoCon
  Set SelectQuery = adoRS
  Set adoRS = Nothing
  Set adoCon = Nothing
  Exit Function
ErrorEncountered:
  Resume Next
  Set SelectQuery = Nothing
  Set adoRS = Nothing
  Set adoCon = Nothing
End Function
```

5. Save the project as `QUESTION.VBP`

PART

Designing a Tiered Architecture Application

III

This group of four chapters is dedicated to Exam 70-100 objectives.

Chapter 17: Conceptual Design - This chapter addresses the Exam 70-100 objective section ***Analyzing Business Requirements***.

Chapter 18: Logical Data design - This chapter address the Exam 70-100 objective section ***Developing Data Models***.

Chapter 19: System Design - This chapter addresses the Exam 70-100 objective sections ***Defining the Technical Architecture for a Solution, Developing the Conceptual and Logical Design for an Application,*** and ***Deriving the Physical design***.

Chapter 20: Solution Interface Issues - This chapter addresses the Exam 70-100 objective section ***Designing a user Interface and User Services.***

CHAPTER 17
Conceptual Design

About Chapter 17

Welcome to Chapter 17 and conceptual design, which is the most important chapter in this book. The success of any computer application depends upon a thorough understanding of the problem at hand.

Chapter 17 is the first of four chapters that specifically address 70-100 objectives. The chapter is divided into three sections:

- The first section draws upon a traditional framework to build the models that represent the different steps of application design. (We'll use the same framework in Chapter 18 for logical design, and in Chapter 19 for physical design.)
- The second section deals with collecting application requirements. Collecting requirements raises many tangential issues such as local politics, hidden agendas, corporate strategy, budget and time restrictions, and resources available.
- The third section is a case study from a Fortune 1000 company (name expunged to protect the innocent) that we'll use for a series of labs on conceptual design issues.

I think you'll like this chapter. You'll find in this chapter a methodology that is unique, but borrows from the masters of the past and creates a useful tool for analyzing and building the new architectures of today.

Classical Models

Let's start building our framework. The application design framework that I'll present is based on a classical model, which is the Zachman Framework (*IBM Systems Journal,* Volume 26, No.3). In this chapter we'll combine the Zachman Framework with the IDEF1X Information Models, which is a Department of Defense data modeling standard (see Thomas A. Bruce, *Designing Quality Databases with IDEF1X Information Models*). The application model we'll use here employs concepts from IDEF1X and the Zachman Framework, along with some new models of my own. I call the result an Augmented Zachman Framework.

Every application implementation requires a model to be successful unless it is a trivial system. A model can be described as:

- An abstraction of a real-world phenomenon.
- A tool to measure conformance to implementation standards.
- A tool to measure conformance to user requirements.
- Models place bounds on features preventing *feature-creep.* A model prevents developers from adding unwarranted and unnecessarily clever features. A model discourages customers from adding poorly thought out new features during development. Design oversights are incorporated by reviewing and revising the model. All stake holders are expected to agree on model revisions along with the expected budgetary changes.
- Models signal when the application is complete by defining the application completion requirements.
- Models are effective project management tools to keep a project on schedule and reasonably within budget. When a user wants a feature added, the user can be informed of what other features must be removed to keep the project on schedule and reasonably within budget.

Models can be roughly categorized as conceptual models, logical models, physical models, or results models. Many software projects fail if the designers use models that are wrong or incomplete, or the developer assumes that the problem is relatively simple and no model is needed. These simple rules should give you some insight to the value of modeling and why software projects fail:

- ***A model cannot be built unless the designer understands the problem.*** This sounds reasonable, however the context is the business environment, and things that happen in business aren't always reasonable. The Information Model depends upon a correct Business Model. This means that normalization of entities within the Information Model may be incorrect unless the business rules of the Business Model are understood. Unfortunately Microsoft Visual Modeler does not support a Business Model and modeling starts with the Information Model, which is incorrect. Rational Rose from Rational Corporation starts modeling with the Business Model, which is correct (see Chapter 18).
- ***An application cannot be built without a model.*** This is also a deceptively simple statement. The value of a model is incalculable. A model gauges conformance to user requirements and implementation standards. It also serves as a limiter to feature-creep.
- ***Models prevent us from falling into the trap of thinking about*** how ***to solve a problem rather than*** what ***the problem is.*** An example is the time-old image of a technically oriented person that invents a very clever gadget and then looks for a gadget market. The resulting business enterprise that is established with the technically oriented mindset eventually goes bankrupt. A successful enterprise will identify a market need and then develop a product that satisfies the market need. The technically oriented approach is to invent a clever gadget and then look for a use for the gadget. The *how* and not the *what* all too often absorb technically oriented individuals. You'll learn shortly that distinguishing between the *how* and the *what* is the key to successful software application development (see Figure 17-1).
- ***I believe that programmers work very long hours, not because they need to but because they want to.*** This explains to some degree why the how takes on such importance in the design cycle. This preoccupation with implementation techniques disrupts the design cycle. My own personal experience is that the C/C++ language is one of the most intellectually satisfying languages ever developed; yet it is one of the least cost-effective languages in use today. Because of this preoccupation with implementation techniques, systems are designed in terms of the how and not in terms of business needs.

WHEN THE *HOW* COMES BEFORE THE *WHAT*

I had a recent experience that illustrates this point very well. I was listening to a vice president of a multi-national corporation tell me where he wanted pull-down lists and pop-ups on the screen. He should have been discussing the business aspect of the problem at hand. He was discussing implementation issues rather than problem issues, which is the *how* and not the *what*. The mistake is to place too much emphasis on *how* to solve the problem rather than answering the question: "*What* is the problem?" It's illogical to discuss *how* to solve a problem when the problem isn't known.

The preoccupation with implementation techniques also changes the order of phases in a product lifecycle with the population of the database occurring after application development. The actual cycle steps should be to design the database, populate it, create reports for it, and then develop the required application. There are third-party tools available today that will let you do this. These include InfoModeler from Asymetrix and ER*win*/Desktop from Logic Works, Inc. for VisualBasic/Powerbuilder. A relational database can be designed, tested with queries and data entry tested before any coding is done in C/C++, Visual Basic, Power Builder, or Access. The resulting tables can then be exported to a database for application development. This approach puts the *what* before the *how* which is correct.

The preoccupation with the *how* and not the *what* is driven by management that wants immediate results. Compounding the problem is a new crop of developers (users) who do not know how to model data or how to normalize it. The problem is further exacerbated by the very nature of development tools which use the graphical user interface that promotes the *how* aspect with their ease of use.

- ***Models enable the designer to formulate the problem in business terms and not resources available or implementation techniques***. This is another deceptively simple statement. In a typical scenario, management gives a directive to implement a system using the current infrastructure. The system fails within a few short months after delivery because of performance issues. The other scenario is that user needs are not fulfilled because of inadequate infrastructure.

The architectural model I offer is called an Augmented Zachman Framework. It is not a single model but a series of models based upon the Zachman Framework. I've replaced one model from the Zachman Framework with two IDEF1X models, and I've added two more models: the Requirements Model and the Business Rules Model. I've also renamed the Zachman Objectives/Scope Model as the Business Scope Model.

Information Systems Architecture, Zachman Framework

The Zachman Framework (Figure 17-1) identifies the *what, how,* and the *where*. The original Zachman Framework names are *data, function,* and *network*. The remainder of this chapter is only interested in the *what* or the Zachman Framework *data*, which is the conceptual design aspect. There is a great deal of detail missing from Figure 17-1, but for now all that is necessary is the identification of the different models. We'll get into the details later in the chapter, but for now, let's borrow some concepts from IDEF1X.

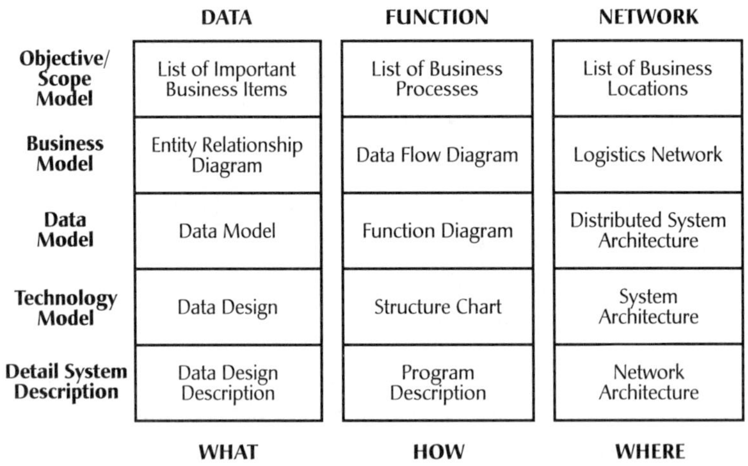

	DATA	FUNCTION	NETWORK
Objective/ Scope Model	List of Important Business Items	List of Business Processes	List of Business Locations
Business Model	Entity Relationship Diagram	Data Flow Diagram	Logistics Network
Data Model	Data Model	Function Diagram	Distributed System Architecture
Technology Model	Data Design	Structure Chart	System Architecture
Detail System Description	Data Design Description	Program Description	Network Architecture
	WHAT	HOW	WHERE

FIGURE 17-1 The Zachman Framework

IDEF1X Information Models

As you can see there is a clear distinction between the *how* and the *what* within the Zachman Framework. The Zachman Framework gives us that starting point by delineating the difference between the *how* and the *what*. Using it, we'll focus only on the *what* and develop a methodology for it. The methodology has a basis in IDEF1X Information Models, which is illustrated with the hierarchy of models shown in Figure 17-2. Figure 17-2 is also a detailed representation of the *what* from a Zachman Framework. The order of the models in the hierarchy is the order of application of our methodology for our eventual Application Model.

Figure 17-2 illustrates the IDEF1X model types. You should immediately recognize that there is no Business Model within this architecture. That's okay because we're only going to borrow the concept of the Key Based Model (KBM) and the Fully Attributed Model (FAM). The entity-relationship diagram (ERD), KBM, and FAM are logical models and they are introduced here only to complete the framework. Each of these three logical models is discussed in Chapter 18, Logical Design. Physical models are discussed in Chapter 19, Physical Design. The Area and Project models are included only because of IDEF1X notation and will be ignored for our purposes.

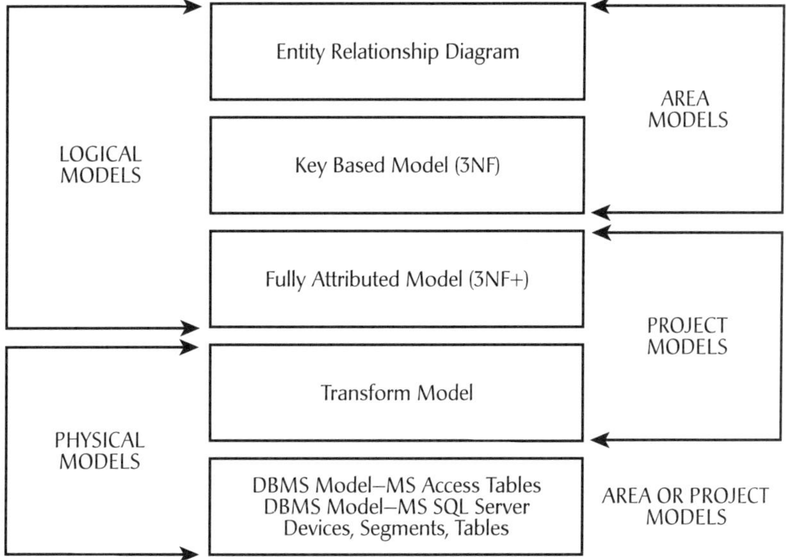

FIGURE 17-2 IDEF1X Model Types

Defining the Application Model

The application model consists of a series of models based upon the IDEF1X architecture and the Zachman Framework. When the *Augmented Zachman Framework* is implemented, there are identifiable deliverables at each level of the architecture. The architecture is designed so that each progressive model has links back to a prior model. This enables an analyst to trace back from a stored procedure, trigger, or intelligent agent to the information model and identify the relevant business rule, constraint, or related entity. If tracing is done back to the Requirements Model, then the related Definition, Fact, Constraint, or Derivation in the Requirements Model (see below, Requirements Model) is identified. Tracing back further yet, we can identify which user requirement caused the creation of the current Definition, Fact, Constraint, or Derivation. The last trace back level is the identification of the affected items from the Objective/Scope level of our Modified Zachman Framework.

I define the Application Model as the collection of all related models. The Application Model deliverables are easily identified. Except for the Requirements Model, the models parallel very closely the Zachman Framework. Table 17-1 outlines the Zachman Framework deliverable models.

TABLE 17-1 ZACHMAN FRAMEWORK DELIVERABLE MODELS

Zachman Framework Level	*Deliverable*
Objectives/Scope	Business Scope Model
Business Model	Entity-Relationship Model (Diagram)
Information Model	Data Model
Technology Model	Access database, SQL Server devices/tables
Detailed Representation Model	Business Implementation Model

The Application Model in Table 17-1 is defined in Zachman Framework terms. I want to redefine it in IDEF1X terms. As you'll see later in this chapter, this approach simplifies the implementation process. Table 17-2 is the Augmented Zachman Framework or the Applications Model. Let's look at the changes to the Zachman Framework:

- A new Requirements Model is added. The models are arranged in hierarchical order and the Requirements Model is placed between the Business Scope Model and the combination of the entity-relationship diagram (Entity Relationship Model).
- The Business Rules Model is added in parallel with the Entity Relationship Model.
- The Data Model is decomposed into the KBM and FAM, neither of which are deliverables.
- The Technology Model is renamed Transform Model and corresponds to the IDEF1X Transform Model.

That's it! Figure 17-3 represents the Augmented Zachman Framework or Application Model.

TABLE 17-2 AUGMENTED ZACHMAN FRAMEWORK DELIVERABLE MODELS

Augmented Zachman Framework	*Deliverable*
Objectives/Scope	Business Scope Model
	Requirements Model
Business Model	Entity Relationship Model (Diagram), Business Rules Model
Key Based Model	Not Applicable
Fully Attributed Model	Data Model
Technology Model	Transform Model (Access database, SQL Server devices/tables, or other database)
Detailed Representation Model	Business Implementation Model

Figure 17-3 represents the work we've done so far in constructing the Application Model. That is my name for the aggregation of all models. It is also the Augmented Zachman Framework.

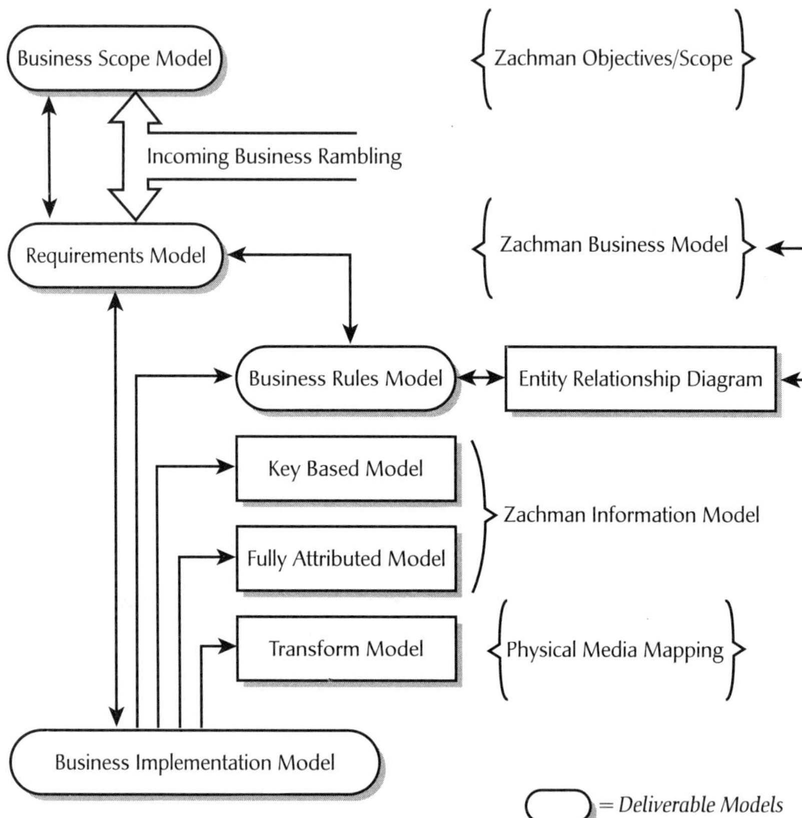

FIGURE 17-3 The Application Model or the Augmented Zachman Framework

When the methodology is followed the analyst will be able to trace back through all prior models identifying the dependencies. The Business Scope Model, Requirements Model, Business Rules Model, and Business Implementation Model are all implemented as one or more tables in a relational database. This enables an analyst to identify dependencies between different models.

With the different models, we have made a difficult problem manageable and reduced it down to bite-sized chunks. Let's create a thumbnail sketch of each of the different models. We'll step through the different models in a logical order that pursues the *what* before the *how* is even considered. You'll note that we're primarily discussing conceptual models here so the entity-relationship diagram, KBM, FAM, and Transform Model are not discussed to any great length until the logical design phase of our application.

AN EDITORIAL

I disagree with Microsoft on two counts. I do this because Microsoft is not an application development entity, but a tool company. Tool companies always have a bottom-up perspective. They create a tool and then look for a problem. Microsoft Solutions Frameworks (MSF) is a perfect example of this mindset since MSF espouses bottom-up design along with commencing programming before the problem at hand is completely understood.

The first issue where I disagree with Microsoft is the Microsoft Certified Solution Developer certification track. Simply put, Microsoft does not understand application skill sets. The legacy world does it right with three distinct skill sets: coder, programmer, and analyst. The coder is fluent with languages and tools. There are degrees to this skill set with rankings ranging from apprentice to skilled coder. While functioning as a coder, the individual acquires and develops analytical skills. Many beginning coders do not know how to formulate an approach to a problem. I taught advanced programming topics at the University of California, Irvine, California and I recall a student with a Masters degree that could not formulate an approach to a problem.

Another common problem is in not knowing how to take a logical approach to locating program errors. The beginning coder will invariably make program changes based upon symptoms and not the actual problem. Program logic is slowly perverted and over time the original program structure is lost. Eventually the coder acquires the necessary analytical skills and becomes a programmer. There are also degrees of skill for programmers, and eventually the programmer may become an analyst, however a good programmer doesn't necessarily make a good analyst. An analyst has a business-oriented mindset, and the requirements for being an analyst do not always require programming skills, but business skills. The problem is that Microsoft has tried to shoehorn each of these three distinct skill sets into the Microsoft Certified Solution Developer certification track. It just doesn't happen. Most will make the transition from coder to programmer, but very few programmers have a business-oriented mindset.

The second issue where I disagree with Microsoft is the 70-100 certification exam. The Microsoft 70-100 certification objectives are a rather extensive list of topics related to application development. The objectives enumerate the topics, however nothing is said about how to collect the data. Collecting the data is far from easy and a failure to understand user requirements can be catastrophic. As a rule, users can always tell you what they don't want, but they can never tell you what they do want. Collecting application requirements requires special skills and is a task best suited to the role of an analyst and not that of a programmer.

This contrasts with other design methodologies, which start with data normalization (a step in logical design) as the very first step. By this I mean that the database normalization phase may proceed incorrectly when it is the starting point. The developer is given a list of entities and attributes and is expected to normalize them and commence application development. The developer relies on intuitive judgment that is occasionally wrong, and proceeds to normalize the database. We'll see later in Chapter 18 that proper database normalization requires an intimate understanding of the conceptual model before proceeding to database normalization in the logical model.

All too often database normalization is an intuitive process. Formal database normalization requires knowledge of functional *dependence* (in the mathematical sense). *Something* depends upon *something else*. That dependency cannot be known unless the conceptual model is known and understood, and the very difficult issue is that conceptual models change with time.

Business Scope Model

In this model we try to capture the business rules that define scope. Our goal is the identification of strategies, processes, and constraints (limitations) that define a scope. The source of this information is the user requirements (which we will call the *business rambling*). Information for the Business Scope Model is collected at the same time we are collecting information for the Requirements Model. In computer terms, the incoming user supplied specifications are parsed with some information placed into the Business Scope Model and the remainder in the Requirements Model.

Requirements Model

We try to complete the business essence with this model. The analyst deconstructs the rambling into succinct, non-compound English sentences that are stated in business terms and not in programmer terms. The related rambling is placed in a *Rambling* table and the related business rules are placed in a *Requirements* table. Within the latter table is our analysis and reasoning for the derived business rule. It in turn is linked back to the text of the original business rambling. All business rules from the business rambling appear in this model.

The analyst also identifies scenarios, which are action sequences such as ordering new inventory stock, and places them within a *Scenario* table in the Requirements Model. Each entry in the *Scenario* table contains a back-link to the related business rambling.

Building the Business Model

The Business Model consists of the entity-relationship diagrams (ERD, see Chapter 18) and the Business Rules Model. The ERD does not contain enough information since we also want to capture the original assumptions, comments, and examples of usage of the attribute or entity. This ancillary information is placed in the Business Rules Model. Capturing this type of information is a relatively recent feature of data modeling tools. You'll want to evaluate your data-modeling tool in terms of capturing this ancillary information. The Business Rules Model can be thought of as an augmented ERD.

The ERD and the Business Rules Model comprise the two elements of the Business Model. This is a very key point. The ERD is a model of the business and not yet a model of data structures even though there is some resemblance to a data model. Tools such as Erwin confuse the separation of logical models slightly since Erwin supports both the physical and logical models even though the ERD is a logical model.

The entity-relationship diagram (ERD) and the Business Rules Model comprise the two elements of the Business Model.

We really can't store any information in the ERD since it is a structure, so the Business Rules Model is the bridge between the ERD and the Requirements Model. It provides the mapping between the Business Rules Model and the ERD. We recall that the Requirements Model gave us definitions, facts, constraints, and derivations. Facts and definitions are the only business rules incorporated in the Business Rules Model. Not every definition will become an entity and some definitions may be synonyms for other definitions. To recap, this model is a mapping between the Requirements Model facts and definitions. It also provides the reasoning for the decisions of how this model is implemented. It will include:

- Examples of usage.
- Hidden or underlying assumptions. Documentation is quite often only that information which is stated explicitly in the program implementation. What are the assumptions made when decisions are made? Some of this information is captured in the *Reason* attribute of the Requirements Model database.

- Comments about the attribute or entity.
- Links back to the Requirements Model. From there a link exists back to the original business rambling and the Business Scope Model.

Business Implementation Model

There are two logical and one physical intervening models sandwiched between the Business Implementation Model and the Business Rules Model. These intervening models consist of the KBM, FAM, and the Transform Model, which is the physical mapping to the storage media.

The Business Implementation Model represents documentation for all aspects of the application. It includes:

- The logical to physical mapping of the database.
- Triggers and procedures (if used) to enforce constraints and derivations from the Business Rules Model.
- Backward links to the Business Rules Model identify the relevant fact, definition, constraint, or derivation and a second link exits back to the referenced entity.
- The final application system documentation.

There are some very important statements made in the thumbnail sketches above. One of the more profound statements is the capturing of the hidden or underlying assumptions in place when a model is defined. Business models do change with time and it is important to know the underlying assumptions when the attribute or entity was defined. These may change with a passage of time.

Capturing the Essence

The most important step in analyzing user requirements is capturing the essence of an application. Unfortunately it is a step ignored by the 70-100 MCSD certification exam. I'll propose a strategy that is effective, but before I do that, let's look at different strategies available (Table 17-3).

TABLE 17-3 DATA GATHERING ALTERNATIVES

TECHNIQUE	ADVANTAGES	DISADVANTAGES
Business Rambling	The user writes the specification. The user provides in written form every aspect of the system in user terms. This is done over a period of 1-2 weeks so that all aspects are considered.	No user contact.
Interviews	Detailed information often provided.	Too time intensive. Very special skills are required to prevent the interviewer from leading the user.
Facilitated Sessions	A popular approach that can be motivational.	A strong and outspoken individual with an agenda often leads meetings. Some attendees may be intimidated.
Prototyping	Quick results are often available.	This is definitely the *how* and not the *what* paradigm. Very inflexible and expensive.
Focus Groups	Often provides very specific information. Usually a user perspective.	See *Facilitated Sessions* above.
User Survey	Easy to implement.	Too shallow. No user contact. A survey may not reveal the real issues.
Users Teaching	You'll find system quirks that are not otherwise known.	Very time consuming. Only the user perspective and the immediate tasks.

Problems Obtaining User Specifications

The first order of business is to understand the user's needs. There are different philosophies of how to acquire the systems specifications. The common technique is to interview the user, and this is not always successful. A failure at this point is often catastrophic. According to *Computerworld* (February 24, 1997), "What many analysts lack...are the communication skills and people skills needed for such key tasks as eliciting system requirements from users."

The analyst interviewing the user is faced with these obstacles:

- The user does not correctly understand his or her role within the corporation. The role is interpreted from a personal perspective.
- The user understands a portion of his or her role correctly, but only as far as the role is known. There may be facets of the role that are not understood because role training was incomplete and informal. The complete picture was not given.
- The interviewer is limited to the interviewer's personal experiences. The interviewer asks questions within the scope of personal experiences and translates user responses in terms of personal experiences.
- The programmer/analyst may not know how to ask open-ended questions. Poorly worded questions may lead the user to a particular answer.
- The programmer/analyst often interviews within the context of resources currently available. This includes using favorite rapid application development (RAD) tools, defining the problem within the context of hardware resources, or even encouraging the user to discuss the *how* aspect of the problem.

Having programmers interview users doesn't work. An example of good interview techniques is in the artificial intelligence area. A person is specifically trained to interview knowledgeable individuals. This information is then placed in a knowledge base and forms what is known as an expert system. Answers to queries of the expert system represent a composite opinion of the experts in the field. For example, expert systems are used in operating rooms during surgery. A query of an expert system validates the doctor's decision. Expert systems operate at the eighty-five percent correctness level, whereas the best doctors are only right seventy-five percent of the time. This is based on long-term averages. But don't worry. The doctor always makes the ultimate decision. The point of this discussion on expert systems is that care must be taken during the interview.

note **If you have an interest in expert systems and artificial intelligence, these books can serve as a starter:**

- *The Handbook of Artificial Intelligence,* Volumes 1–4 Barr, Cohen, and Feigenbaum, published by Addison-Wesley Publishing Company, Inc., 1982 – 1989.

- *Artificial Intelligence*; Luger and StubbleField, published by The Benjamin/Cummings Publishing Company, Inc., 1993.
- *Artificial Intelligence*; Rich and Knight, published by McGraw-Hill, Inc., 1991

Obtaining User Specifications

The solution to the problem is simple. The user writes the specification by creating a document known as a *business rambling* ("The Never-Ending Search for Knowledge," Barbara Von Halle, *Database Programming and Design;* February 1996). The scenario goes like this:

- The user approaches you with an interest in having a system developed.
- You ask the user to place on paper every fact the expected system should address. No stone is to be left unturned; ask the user to include every small detail relating to the proposed system.
- You emphasize to the user that the required needs are always to be stated in business terms and not implementation terms.
- You also emphasize to the user that the required needs are not to be stated in terms of current resources.
- You also emphasize that this procedure is very informal and the user shouldn't worry about organization.

Solitary individuals do not plan systems. A representative sample of users should take part in the process, and each user who participates should write separate business ramblings. Each business rambling will be unique because it is the user's individual perspective on the business processes. No attempt should be made to pull the individual ramblings together into a master rambling. It is the analyst's responsibility to analyze each business rambling independently.

Don't expect your user-supplied requirements to make sense. Sentences may be unclear, ambiguous, and possibly untrue. Sentences may be incomplete, and they may be unauthorized, meaning that they may exceed the writer's job scope. The sentences probably violate the supplied guidelines. Be prepared to find that the authors of the rambling do not understand the enterprise business. To give you an example of what to expect in terms of business rambling, Listing 17-1 is an actual business rambling from a client. (The names have been changed to protect the innocent.)

LISTING 17-1 A sample user-supplied specification (business rambling)

```
MEMORANDUM

To: Bruce Prendergast
From: ABC Corporation
Subject: Contract Tracking Business Rambling

Potential fields to include in the ABC Contract Tracking database
I. Areas to track
   A. Name on the file folder and in the current list
   B. Links to other contracts ???? do we really want or need this, is
      it too difficult to do?
      1. by name ????
      2. by tracking number
   C. Tracking Number (assigned by Access)
      1. What procedure do we use if there is a need to put an
         additional contract into the same folder as the main contract?
      2. What if a codicil is added?
   D. Title of contract (which may be different from the name on he folder
      and in the current list).
   E. Address of Party.
      1. Address of location if different from the address of the party or
         principle
         a) (Vendor, Property, etc.)
   F. Contract status
      1. Currently in force.
      2. Expired.
         a) What is the disposition of the actual contract after expiration?
            (1) Stored?
            (2) Destroyed?
II. Who are the parties to the contract? (entities pull down list of
         ABC and affiliates - Mexico, H. K., U. K., DRD, etc.)
   A. Address of each party
      1. Comes down automatically for the ABC entities??
      2. Capability to modify?
         a) If modified, an automatic indicator to show that it is modified.
```

B. Principal(s) of each party

C. Signatories (for each party name(s) and title(s))

1. Pull down list of main signatories

2. What is the process for adding another name?

a) Contract administrator?

b) Data entry person?

c) Notification to the contract administrator?

III. Is this contract the original?

A. Is it signed?

1. If it is not signed, where is the signed original or copy?

2. Is there a copy at all?

B. If it is a copy, where is the original?

C. Are there multiple signed copies?

1. If so where or who has the other copies?

D. The file folder is empty apply the above criteria, where, who?

IV. What department is the contract from?

A. Who is the head of the Dept. / or who is responsible for the contract??? which/both??

V. Major terms of the contract

A. Dollar value of the contract.

B. Major terms of the contract.

C. Are there specified consequences of noncompliance?

1. For ABC Corporation

2. For other party(ies).

D. Is the contract affected by a change in ownership of either party?

1. How?

VI. Term of the contract

A. Effective date of the contract.

B. Termination data of the contract (if any).

1. Has the contract already expired?

C. Terms of renewal

1. Can it be renewed?

2. Does it renew automatically?

a) When does it renew?

b) What is necessary to prevent it from being renewed?

D. Termination provisions

```
        1. Automatically expires? (If so, on what date?)
        2. Actions ABC must take to terminate.
           a) Steps.
           b) Timing.
        3. Actions other party must take to terminate.
VII. Attachments (note field or fields)
VIII. Other items in the same folder as the main contract that relate
        to the contract (list).
    A. Law firm(s) involved in writing the contract.
    B. Litigation
        1. Reference to other contracts.
    C. What.
IX. Fields to flag
    A. Key violations
    B. Renewal date
    C. Term date
    D. Payment either due to or from ABC corporation.
    E. Other?
    F. "Things" to notify Sally Silly about in relation to 10K and other
        reporting requirements.
X. What else?
XI. Things to cross-relate for reporting
        1. Create a reporting checklist as a guide (see Sally Silly)
    A. What?
    B. Keywords (to provide the ability for a person(s) to sort contracts
        by type or subject to aid in writing new contracts that address issues
        that include these topics.
        1. Dividends
        2. Compensation
        3. What else?
XII. Fields or determining factors that would indicate that a department
        action would be in violation of an already existing contract that
        is in the process of negotiation.
    A. What?
XIII. Key indicators ((((((WHAT))))))
    A. What?
```

XIV. Special "Use" contracts (set up a window that allows the entry of a preselected type from a pull down list. This would then bring up a special window(s) for contract specific information.

- A. Banking agreements
  - 1. Schedules
  - 2. Amendments
  - 3. Subsets
- B. Sales rep groups
- C. Leases
- D. What else?

XV. Sales Agreements

XVI. Does this contract need to be serviced in multiple languages?

XVII. What else?

XVIII. Contract tracking (a limited access check list to let all involved with the contract administration program know what the status is of any particular contract or group of contracts.)

- A. It would need to consist of buttons and fields for status and additional information.
  - 1. It is signed.
  - 2. Where it is now.
    - a) At the lawyers
    - b) At our office
      - (1) With what person or department

XIX. Future needs

- A. Tracking of status of new contracts
  - 1. Who can sign the contract?
  - 2. What is the approval process?
  - 3. What is the dollar limit for each signatory?
  - 4. Who is the key contact?
    - a) In ABC corporation
    - b) At the other party
  - 5. Autonotification via E-mail
    - a) Flags (discussed above)
    - b) What is the routing of the contract in the chain - who, where, for how long, what next, who next?
      - (1) New contract administration

```
            (2) Renewal of existing contract
            (3) Changes in terms to an existing contract
            (4) What else?
   B. Is a copy of the executed contract back to our attorney?
   C. Is a copy or additional signed original at the office of the other
      party involved?
   D. Log of who accesses the contract
      1. Who has permission to check a contract out?
      2. What is the approval process for special needs?
      3. Is the original ever to be checked out or only copies?
         a) If so who does the duplicating and has responsibility for the
            process?
         b) Where is the original?
         c) Where is the copy?
      4. Special situations in which the contract may be read but not copied.
         (restricted access issues)
XX. Reporting
   A. Searching for contract by:
   B. Name
   C. Date
   D. Company
   E. Type of contract
   F. Key word
   G. Etc.
XXI. Ease of use is paramount
   A. The entire interface to the program needs to be form driven. A learning
      curve of as close to zero for the person entering the data is what I
      would like you to strive for.
```

Distillation Repositories

Analyzing the business rambling is a distillation process. Two models are created in parallel during the distillation process. The first is the Business Scope Model, which is at the top of our Augmented Zachman Framework. The second model is the Requirements Model, which is also a member of the Augmented Zachman Framework. The relationship of these two models is illustrated in Figure 17-4.

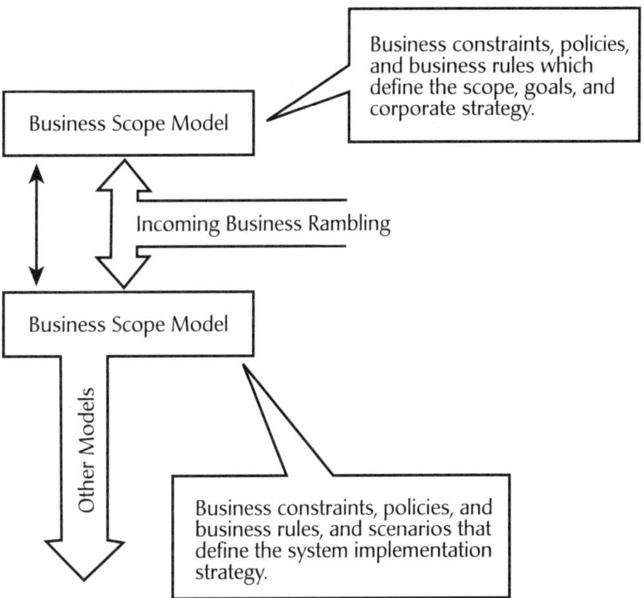

FIGURE 17-4 **The relationship between the Requirements Model and the Business Scope Model.**

This section outlines the basic contents of each of these models. There are no hard rules and tables in a relational database represent these models. Feel free to add additional tables or attributes as dictated by your requirements.

The context here is that of supporting a system implementation and not business process reengineering. Consequently, the models may not fulfill all the requirements for business process reengineering, and are not designed to do so.

Business Scope Model

Let's start with the Augmented Zachman Framework of Figure 17-3. This is our anchor as we start from the top and build our Application Model. Although the intent of modeling process is the processing of the *what*, we break the rules slightly and include both the *what* and *how* from the Zachman Framework. The goal of this model is a detailed statement of business strategy, goals, assets, and processes.

There can be more than one goal. Of course, the enterprise can lose focus if there are too many goals. There may be intermediate goals or subgoals. If such goals exist, they are an element of a strategy.

The enterprise may already deliver products so those current products can be categorized as an achieved goal; on the other hand, the increasing of production may be an unachieved goal.

Intangible assets should also be included. These are not dollars and cents in the bank or tangible assets such as equipment, but an enterprise skill-pool enumeration. They are assets in terms of the anticipated system implementation. Enumerating the existing skill pool is enough to question the feasibility of even considering a new system for a business process. The recommendation is to always have the skill pool catalogued and available.

What we're looking for is a description of the enterprise. The statement should identify goals and the processes that the skill pool (labor force) performs to achieve those goals. This implementation definition provides a natural hierarchy for a database representation. This hierarchy is defined as:

1. Stated goal.
2. Intermediate subgoals.
3. Strategy to implement the goal. There may be multiple strategies.
4. Processes used to realize the goal. There may be multiple processes for a unique strategy.
5. Assets utilized in process. Multiple assets may be used for a process.

A goal of the distillation process is to build a relational database uniquely identifying each goal, strategy, process, or asset. The Requirements Model is linked back to the Business Scope Model. This forms a cross-check on business requirements that are not supported by existing corporate strategies or existing resources.

The tables that follow are only suggestions. Any level of detail may be kept. The important issues are:

Strategies support goal achievement.

Processes implement a strategy.

Assets are consumed in the processing.

Tables 17-4, 17-5, 17-6, and 17-7 are elementary and only serve as guidelines. The user is expected to add additional attributes to these tables.

TABLE 17-4 GOALS TABLE DEFINITION

ATTRIBUTE	DATA TYPE	DESCRIPTION
Identifier	Counter	
Description	Text	
Reference	Text	Foreign key. Link to rambling entry in the rambling table.
<Other Attributes>		

TABLE 17-5 STRATEGIES TABLE DEFINITION

ATTRIBUTE	DATA TYPE	DESCRIPTION
Identifier	Counter	
Description	Text	
Goal	Text	Foreign key (Goal)
Reference	Text	Foreign key. Link to rambling entry in the rambling table.
<Other Attributes>		

TABLE 17-6 PROCESSES TABLE DEFINITION

ATTRIBUTE	DATA TYPE	DESCRIPTION
Identifier	Counter	
Description	Text	
Strategy	Text	Foreign key (Strategy)
Reference	Text	Foreign key. Link to rambling entry in the rambling table.

TABLE 17-7 ASSETS TABLE DEFINITION

Attribute	*Data Type*	*Description*
Identifier	Counter	
Description	Text	
Process	Text	Foreign key (Process)
Reference	Text	Foreign key. Link to rambling entry in the rambling table.
<Other Attributes>		

Reports from these tables resemble a traditional bill-of-materials expansion.

Reference is the link to the rambling table of the Requirements Model. This is the link between the models of Figure 17-4. I'll define the rambling table in the next section.

The incoming business rambling from a user is parsed. Scope parameters move the rambling up toward the Business Scope Model, and implementation of business rules moves the rambling down toward the Requirements Model. The Requirements Model provides the input for the subsequent Business Model.

The Business Scope Model is not a model for business process reengineering. If it were, we would attempt to define all business processes within this model. What we use it for is the tracking of requirements within our Application Model. A business rambling in the Requirements Model is linked to a business strategy, constraint, or asset in the Business Scope Model. For our purposes, we will not generate an actual Business Scope Model, but will augment one with strategies and constraints and possibly assets or process requirements that we encounter in analyzing the business rambling. It is not within our scope to build a Business Scope Model, but only to augment one for tracking purposes. It might be more accurate to call this a *limited* Business Scope Model.

Requirements Model

The Requirements Model is constructed in tandem with the Business Scope Model. We already know that the IDEF1X model type does not include a Requirements Model. Other than that, IDEF1X models closely parallel the Zachman Framework. This is the second model in the Augmented Zachman Framework.

Before building our Requirements Model, we should state our goals. The output from the Requirements Model will be used as input for an Information Model. Within that model, you will find the IDEF1X entity relationship diagram (ERD). An interesting transformation occurs with this model. *Facts* from the Requirements Model are transformed into information within the Information Model. We don't do that in this phase. We only catalogue facts within the Requirements Model. Facts with a context and/or relation become information. We discuss the Information Model in greater detail later but for now let's look at the Requirements Model.

Apart from requiring an expert on linguistics, building a Requirements Model is difficult. We want to parse both the business requirements and the user requirements. In Listing 17-1 the user and business requirements are combined in the business rambling. Where do you start? Probably with a high-level list of business functions and then add sentences to that. Once the business rambling is complete, we can start construction of a Requirements Model by defining tables in which to save our information. Just as with the Business Scope Model, there is no limit to the amount of information to be stored in the Requirements Model. At a minimum, this database should have a derived requirements table, ramblings table, and a scenarios table as described in tables 17-8, 17-9, and 17-10.

TABLE 17-8 RAMBLING TABLE DEFINITION

Attribute	*Data Type*	*Description*
Identifier	Counter	
Reference	Text	Referenced location within the business rambling text.
Rambling	Text	User supplied statement.

TABLE 17-9 REQUIREMENTS TABLE DEFINITION

Attribute	*Data Type*	*Description*
Identifier	Counter	
Reference	Text	Foreign key (Rambling Table)
DerivedSentence	Text	
SentenceIdentifier	Number	Unique. Assigned when derived sentence is accepted. There may be derived sentences that are not accepted. No SentenceIdentifier is assigned for those cases.
Type	Text	Rule type. One of Definition, Fact, Constraint, Derivation, or Implementation.
Reasoning	Text	The analytical reason for accepting or rejecting the derived sentence.

TABLE 17-10 SCENARIOS TABLE DEFINITION

Attribute	*Data Type*	*Description*
Identifier	Counter	
Reference	Text	Foreign key (rambling table)
DerivedSentence	Text	The derived text is in the form of a use case scenario.
SentenceIdentifier	Number	Unique. Assigned when derived sentence is accepted. There may be derived sentences that are not accepted. No SentenceIdentifier is assigned for those cases.
Reasoning	Text	The analytical reason for accepting or rejecting the derived sentence.

Our analysis of a business rule is very informal; in fact, one of the listed types is not a rule type, but a *How* identifier. Implementation techniques have no place in modeling, but they are a hot button with users. This allows easy tracking of the implementation requirements.

These are the rule types as defined within the requirements table. Note that all of them are not business rules, but we declare then as pseudo-rules so we can track all the requirements of the original business rambling. The Requirements Model serves two purposes. The first is as the repository for distilled business rules from the business rambling and the second is to track all issues identified in the business rambling, even if they are not business rules. I offer the following informal business rule categories (feel free to augment these with categories of your own):

- Definitions — These will eventually be entities, but for the requirement model they remain definitions.
- Facts — Fact business rules may represent connections between definitions or between a definition and attributes.
- Scenarios — A scenario is an action and is represented in the Universal Modeling language (UML) as an actor with a use case scenario such as *Get Account Information*. A scenario may also be a set of sequenced steps. Not all use case scenarios are visible during conceptual design and additional use case scenarios will be derived in logical design (see Chapter 18).
- Constraints — Constraints are mandatory. The condition must be satisfied. "A new customer cannot be invoiced for more than $1,000" is an example of a constraint. Constraints as defined here could be, but are not necessarily, referential integrity constraints.
- Inferences/derivations — This is really a form of a not required constraint. Typical usage might be with "If **. . .** Then **. . .**".
- Implementation (pseudorule) — This is really not a business rule but it is an implementation technique. Declaring implementation techniques as informal rules just gives us some way to track them. I am sure you have talked to users who say, "Yeah, I want a combo box here and a list box over there." Because it is a tracking issue, an implementation technique can be placed in the Business Requirements Model.
- Process, strategy, asset, or goal (pseudorules) — These are not business rules, but they are essential elements of a Business Scope Model.

So far we've defined two models: the Business Scope Model and the Business Requirements Model. These models are logically linked to enable tracking.

Distilling the Essence

We've identified the repositories for the business rambling distillation and described the recommended minimal information content. This section provides some guidelines on the distillation and a presentation of the distillation rules. The section closes with a distillation of a few ramblings from Listing 17-1.

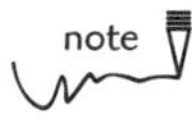

I define a *business rambling* as the complete user document and a *rambling* as a sentence or line from that document.

Distilling the essence of the user-supplied specifications requires significant skill. The ultimate reward is a specification in which:

- The Requirements Model will be business driven.
- Requirements are stated in business terms and not implementation terms.
- It is an unambiguous specification of what is wanted, and not what currently exists.

Unfortunately, these goals listed are still not clear. This is because the enterprise owner, the data modeler, the user, and the programmer/analyst all view the model differently. More than one business rambling may be necessary: one from the enterprise ownership perspective and the other from the user perspective. In this chapter we only step through the process of analyzing a single business rambling. Additional business ramblings are analyzed and the resulting specifications are applied to the same model because it represents another view of the same business process.

Distillation Guidelines

Viewed casually, the user-supplied specification of Listing 17-1 appears reasonable. However, when we look at it closely we find that the writer does not understand the business processes. In particular, near the beginning of the specification a reference to *codicil* is made. This is wrong for a business because a *codicil* is a legal instrument for a will.

There are also too many unanswered questions. This is an indicator that the business process does not yet exist in a manual form. I learned many years ago that if you don't have a good manual system, computerizing the process will not solve the problems.

The rambling makes many references to the *how* and this project can be looked upon as an experiment. The business rambling is preoccupied with presentation style (*how*) and an inadequate problem analysis (*what*). The clue to the experiment was the user's request that the resulting application mimic an Apple computer. A good manual system did not exist and the business processes were incomplete.

Are there guidelines that will help us? Yes. Consider these:

1. ***Understand the enterprise.*** You must understand the customer's enterprise operations and processes to distill the business rambling accurately. Take it upon yourself to understand the enterprise operations. Always cross-check your information with more than one source. No single individual always has a complete understanding of all the processes within an enterprise. As demonstrated in the user specification in Listing 17-1, enterprise operations are not always clearly understood by employees within the enterprise, even when they are in responsible positions. A vice president supplied listing 17-1.
2. ***Understand the objectives.*** Clearly understand the objectives or goal of the required task. Go as high as possible within the enterprise to determine the source for the requirement. The CEO may only want one number on a report at the end of the month, but as the requirement filters down through various departments more baggage is added. The original goal becomes obscured and the project may fail because of other infrastructure issues.
3. ***Understand your probabilities for success.*** After you understand the enterprise operations and the stated goal or objective for the endeavor, ask these questions:
   - Is there a manual system that the new project replaces? If there is a bad manual system, then computerizing it won't solve any problems. A bad system is always a bad system. A good rule of thumb is that system implementations of bad business process models inevitably fail. Build a good business process first, even if it is manual before attempting a computer-system implementation.
   - Is this type of project common within the industry? When you are a pioneer there are always unanticipated problems that threaten the project.
   - Has this project been attempted before within the enterprise? If so, analyze the reason for failure. The real reasons are never obvious and may surprise you.
   - What is the success rate for this type of project? If the proposed system is high-risk, why do it unless the life of the corporation is at stake?

- Is the new system a replacement for an existing system? If so, what are the differences in the business processes? There is a significant advantage when the business processes are already in place.

4. ***Understand the resource requirements.*** Resource requirements should only be addressed after the system is designed. One of the more common mistakes is for management to direct that a business process be implemented on existing facilities.

THE RISKS OF RELYING ON ASPIRATIONS

Organizations often do not consider issues such as five-year business plans when implementing WinTel-class systems. What I find amazing is that WinTel-class systems are implemented on an architecture whose growth potential is stated as an aspiration. The WinTel systems are implemented on the blind faith that a faster and bigger box will always be available. As a CIO, I would consider it a serious mistake to implement a system that utilizes one hundred percent of an existing architecture and to have future expansions based on aspirations and possibly unreal expectations. Microsoft promises scalability of enterprise applications with a tiered architecture that is a software approach to scalability. The tiered architecture concept holds promise, but the maelstrom of change represented by a component architecture, and the unreliability of Microsoft software, makes a tiered architecture questionable.

An example of a limited architecture is the Compaq Proliant, which is currently the leader in Intel-class boxes for the enterprise. The limit of the Compaq Proliant architecture is where the architecture of the Digital Equipment Corporation Alpha starts. Fortunately for Compaq, they now own Digital Equipment Corporation.

If the project has been done before, what are the resource requirements? Are there enough resources for the project? This is a very difficult issue. Enterprises have been know to reach too far in building a system and ended up with no funds for ongoing maintenance.

5. ***Understand the reasons for failure.*** A project may fail for many different reasons. Knowing the typical reasons for project failure can be an aid in avoiding failure on your own project. The most common single factor leading to project failure is incomplete or changing requirements. Other common reasons for failure include:

- Lack of user involvement
- Lack of resources

- Unrealistic expectations
- Lack of executive support
- Lack of planning
- Lack of experience with a particular technology

In summary, the project has a high probability of failure when:

- The developers fail to completely understand the business processes when gathering the system requirements.
- The developers fail to construct a business model or construct an incomplete business model.
- The new system is defined in terms of current resources, which ignores user requirements that cannot be supported.

If you followed the steps above, you completed a feasibility study. Management wants the project and the key questions have been answered. The probability for success is reasonable because the resource requirements are not yet known. The next task is to build the Requirements Model and Business Scope Model from a business rambling.

Distillation Rules

I now define informal business rule categorizations. These definitions are quite informal, and you may add new rule types as desired.

The analyst starts by looking at the ramblings that can generate information. A compound rambling is parsed until the rambling is stated as a single sentence that represents a single issue. The sentence must always be stated in business terms and never in implementation terms. The resulting sentence is then categorized as to its content. An example of ramblings stated in business terms is:

```
E. Address of Party.
   1. Address of location if different from the address of the party or
      principle
      a) (Vendor, Property, etc.)
```

This is an example of several ramblings that discuss implementation issues, which should not be in a business rambling:

```
II. Who are the parties to the contract? (entities pull down list of
```

```
ABC and affiliates - Mexico, H. K., U. K., DRD, etc.)
A. Address of each party
   1. Comes down automatically for the ABC entities??
   2. Capability to modify?
      a) If modified, an automatic indicator to show that it is modified.
B. Principal(s) of each party
C. Signatories (for each party name(s) and title(s))
   1. Pull down list of main signatories
   2. What is the process for adding another name?
      a) Contract administrator?
      b) Data entry person?
      c) Notification to the contract administrator?
```

The first rambling fragment is stated in business terms, but the second fragment has numerous ramblings that are implementation terms.

Sentences are categorized as follows:

- Sentences that contain facts, business terms, or definitions.
- Sentences that identify connections between singular terms. Don't associate a fact with a context yet, but only identify business terms that are related.
- Sentences that identify business rules or policies and that will be constraints upon the business practice.
- Sentences that identify actions or processes.
- Sentences that deal with the infrastructure of implementing the solution.

Sentences are constructed in accordance with these rules:

- Sentences must be atomic and address only one issue such as a fact, definition, constraint, or condition.
- Sentences must not be redundant.
- Sentences must be declarative. Inferred entities are explicitly identified.
- Sentences must be expressed in business terms and not database or implementation terms.
- Sentences must be consistent with each other.
- Sentences must be expressed precisely in terms of other aspects of the data/knowledge environment.

I enumerate the possible contents of sentences below at the risk of confusing you. Yes, entities do exist within sentences. At this time we only wish to record the business rambling text along with the distilled sentence in the rambling table and requirements table, respectively. Later, when building the information model, we return and examine the rule types and make decisions on entities and attributes. For now, here is the *what* to expect in a sentence:

- Entities — We have a very poor model if it doesn't have any entities. Entities are abstractions of real-world things and are different than real-world things. Entities within a model are only abstractions. An entity may be a person, concept, place, event, or thing. It has lasting value and data about it can be stored. It can be uniquely identified.
- Inferred entities — These are entities that are not referenced directly but whose existence may be inferred from context.
- Entity instances — There is a difference between an instance of an entity and the entity. Spot the dog is an instance of the entity dog.
- Attributes — Attributes describe a specific occurrence of the data (instance). Quite often these are confused with entities. Be careful in your analysis. The table below includes attributes, entities, entity instances, and relationships as *a, e, ei,* and *r,* respectively. Note the differences between each.

animal — e,ei	fruit — e,ei	mineral — e,ei
cabbage — ei	dog — e,ei	dog named Spot — ei
selling — r	car type — a	car door — e,ei
salesperson — e	owner — e	Joe the owner — ei

- Implementation techniques — This is the *how* we discussed above. It falls into the area of user requirements and should not color our thinking. I always give this topic special attention because it is usually a user hot button. Sift out all the implementation issues. They are really not part of the model, but they are important to the user and must be addressed. We can't afford to overlook them or our user will consider us unresponsive. Even though we categorize implementation issues, we must not let them influence our thinking or they will confuse the issues.

Parsing the Business Rambling

Let's use the business rambling of Listing 17-1 from ABC Corporation to start the construction of our Requirements Model. We build the model by stating the value of each field in the different tables as we progress. The distillation below steps through the first few lines of the business rambling. We are fortunate in that most sentences are already atomic and decomposition isn't necessary.

Study the example distillation in Table 17-11 carefully. Note the inferences that are made. Note also that other interpretations are possible. The goal of the distillation process is to obtain context-free facts that are unencumbered with resource issues or implementation techniques. The syntax of the notation is *Model.Table.Field*. The syntax *.Field* assumes the previous model and table. Information is being placed in both the rambling table and requirements table.

Table 17-11 represents the distillation of the first five statements of Listing 17-1. Attribute entries in Table 17-11 for the **.Rambling** value correspond to actual business rambling text of Listing 17-1.

TABLE 17-11 A PARTIAL DISTILLATION OF LISTING 17-1, THE BUSINESS RAMBLING

Model.Table.Attribute	*Value*
ReqModel.Rambling.Reference	I
.Rambling	Areas to track
ReqModel.Requirements.Reference	I
.DerivedSentence	Active contracts exist
.SentenceIdentifier	1
.Type	Definition
.Reasoning contracts	Tracking infers that there are active
.Reference	I
.DerivedSentence	Related contracts exist
.SentenceIdentifier	2
.Type	Fact
.Reasoning	An area isn't very specific, so there must be related contracts.

Model.Table.Attribute	*Value*
ReqModel.Rambling.Reference	I A
.Rambling current list.	Name on the current folder and in the
ReqModel.Requirements.Reference	I A
.DerivedSentence	Active contracts exist.
.SentenceIdentifier	
.Type	Fact
.Reasoning	A current list is probably a list of active contracts. The sentence is rejected because it is redundant under rule 2 and SentenceIdentifier 1.
ReqModel.Requirements.Reference	I A
.DerivedSentence	Related contracts exist.
.SentenceIdentifier	
.Type	Fact
.Reasoning	In doing business with another entity, related contracts are kept in the same file folder. A single contract does not require a folder. Rule 2 and SentenceIdentifier1 reject the sentence.
ReqModel.Rambling.Reference	I B
.Rambling	Link to other contracts. Do we really want or need this? Is it too difficult to do?
ReqModel.Requirements.Reference	I B
.DerivedSentence	Related contracts exist.
.SentenceIdentifier	
.Type	Fact
.Reasoning	Redundant under rule 2 and SentenceIdentifier 2.
ReqModel.RamblingReference	I B 1
.Rambling	By name?
ReqModel.Requirements.Reference	I B 1
.DerivedSentence	Contract is identified by name.

Continued

TABLE 17-11 *(continued)*

MODEL.TABLE.ATTRIBUTE	VALUE
.SentenceIdentifier	3
.Type	Fact
.Reasoning	This is a fact, but eventually it will become an entity attribute.
ReqModel.Rambling.Reference	I B 2
.Rambling	By tracking number.
ReqModel.Requirements.Reference	I B 2
.DerivedSentence	Contract is identified by number.
.SentenceIdentifier	4
.Type	Fact
.Reasoning	This is a fact that eventually will become an entity attribute.

What have we collected so far from paragraph I of the business rambling of Listing 17-1? Only the first four sentences listed below. Continuing on derives additional sentences, but the sentences listed below do not constitute a complete list for Listing 17-1.

Some derived sentences from Listing 17-1:

1. Active contracts exist.
2. Related contracts exist.
3. Contract is identified by name.
4. Contract is identified by number.
5. Group-related contracts.
6. Contract group has a name.
7. Contract party exists.
8. Contract other party exists.
9. Party has address.
10. Other party has address.
11. Real estate contracts exist.

12. Party is a principal.
13. Other party is a principal.
14. Purchase contracts exist.
15. Contract has status.
16. Expired contracts exist.
17. Expired contracts have disposition.

Unfortunately, analyzing paragraph I of the business rambling of Listing 17-1 yielded no Business Scope Model entries. Quite a few of the later rambling entries are candidates for the Business Scope Model, including:

- XIX A 1: Who can sign the contract?
- XIX A 2: What is the approval process?
- XIX A 3: What is the dollar limit for each signatory?

The first and last ramblings are constraints while the second rambling qualifies as a process. I'll leave these as an exercise for you.

We have completed the Requirements Model and now we move to the Business Model in the Zachman Framework. This is where ERD and the Business Rules Model are constructed.

Applying the Distillation

The issue of parsing the business rambling is to obtain facts, definitions, derivations, and constraints that are context-free. The task is not easy because the English language is not context-free. One wishes for a context-free grammar such as used in computer compiler language theory, but such a language is useless to users.

The goal of the parsing phase is to collect the facts in a context-free manner. Here we'll return to the Requirements Model and analyze each fact, definition, derivation, and constraint. During this review we'll build the Business Rules Model. Output from the rules model creates an ERD. The general data flow is shown in Figure 17-5.

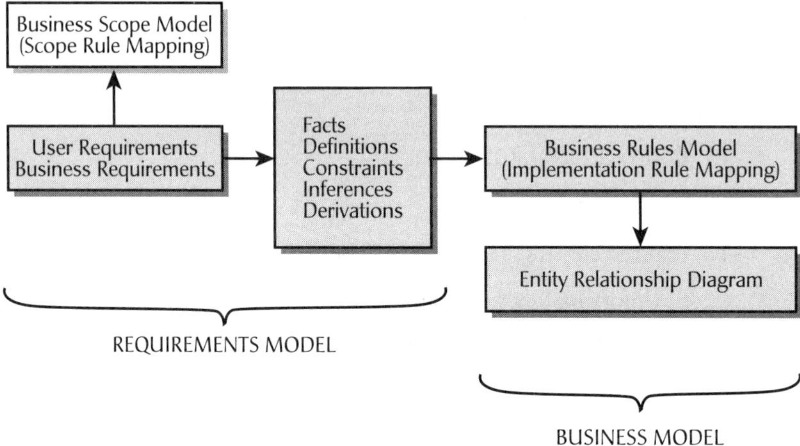

FIGURE 17-5
The Requirements Model and Business Model relationship.

Remember, complete the parsing phase (building the Requirements Model) before starting construction of the Business Rules Model.

The output of the Business Rules Model completes the distillation phases of building the Application Model. The output of the Business Rules Model can be directed to a commercial tool and the Key-Based Model, Fully Attributed Model, and Transform Model can be generated directly.

Business Rules Model

This is one of the more important models. This model holds all the fact and definition business rules that eventually become either attributes or entities in the entity-relationship diagram. The model is represented as a table in a relational database.

Each entry fact or definition entry in this table should parallel an entry in the ERD. Feel free to add anything you wish to the list that will be helpful to you. The table below can be your starting point. The attributes currently defined in Table 17-12 are essential, but others can be added as necessary.

TABLE 17-12 BUSINESS RULES

Attribute	*Data Type*	*Description*
Identifier	Counter	
Reference	Text	Foreign key. Link to rambling entry in the rambling table.
EntityDescription	Text	
UniqueIdentifier	Text	Entity or attribute name.
BusinessExamples	Text	Examples of usage.
Comments	Text	Any comments necessary for a complete history.
UnderlyingAssumptions	Text	Assumptions of how used in the enterprise. This may change slowly with time, so the original assumptions are very important.
Type	Text	Rule type. One of Definition, Fact, Constraint, or Derivation. Pseudorules do not appear here.

There are two critically important issues here. The first is to document business examples of how the entity is used and where it is used. The second issue is that of identifying and documenting the underlying assumptions. Programs always have two contexts, explicit and implicit. Analyzing the program structure can derive the explicit context. The implicit context is all too often not stated in any program notes and may change with time. Programmers, given enough pressure, will document a program. This quite often isn't enough because they typically document what the program does. The data model is rarely documented, and what documentation that does exist may be buried within a program, which is where a programmer might look for it. There may be some hidden assumptions about the entity. Put that information here. It will be invaluable for maintenance at some future date. (For those who have some legacy experience, this is somewhat analogous to a data dictionary or a data repository on the mainframe.)

When the Distillation Is Complete

One can't take a distillation and proceed to build a system. We've discussed the distillation in terms of a single *business rambling*. There should be more than one rambling if the system has a reasonable size. Management should supply a business rambling and more than one user should supply a business rambling. Each of these ramblings must be distilled. When all distillations are complete, the business model is formally documented. The business analysts report back to the user with a formal statement of the business. The user either states that "yes, that is the correct business model," or amends the rambling.

It is easy to derail a context-free distillation with a few hurried questions. It is very important to not ask the user any questions at this stage since questions will lead the user. Everything must be stated in business terms and not implementation terms. Remember that the user will attain additional insight as the system is being built. You need an initial Business Model that is extremely accurate, since the project scope will creep as the user attains further insight.

All of this sounds fanciful, and to some degree it is. The context of the distillation made no mention of turf wars or local politics, but both are common. The results of the distillation may change when hidden agendas become known. Either factor in the political component and distill the business rambling again, or continue with Chapter 18 and build the data model.

Key Point Summary

Microsoft has provided an invaluable checklist for application design requirements, however collecting the data is always the weak link. There are many obstacles to delivering a successful system, but the most insidious one is hidden agendas and not all project participants are always forthcoming with the necessary information. Invariably a user will arrive with a new requirement within days of the final buyoff. One is often left with feeling of *deja vu* and a sense that the project is being sabotaged.

Nothing of any value is ever free. An analysis of the requirements and a logical design are always required for a successful application. RAD tools are too easy to use and promote development before the problem is understood. Unfortunately Microsoft also supports the initiation of the development cycle before there is a complete buyoff on all specifications. Some successful systems are delivered, but these are all too often systems modeled on successful existing systems. Productivity of corporate information systems (CIS) continues to decline and has been steadily declining since 1987 in spite of the use of RAD tools. I call this time frame "the Microsoft epoch." I expect this epoch to end when CIS productivity becomes a net loss. At that time I expect very fundamental changes to occur in the computing industry.

The most important lesson that I can convey is that in spite of the hard work in analyzing specifications, users never know what they want. They only know what they *don't* want. The safest procedure is to break a system implementation into two separate and distinct contracts, (projects when the work is done for an internal sister organization). The first contract is only for the design and specification, while the second contract is the implementation.

One of the problems that we have today is that development tools are too easy to use and some aspects of the application can be implemented too quickly. I say "too quickly" because there must be a minimum gestation time for the specifications. Develop the specifications too quickly and invariably some aspects of the system are left out. Implement those specifications too quickly and you hear that all too familiar: "Oh, I forgot to tell you, but we must have ...". That's the advantage of a legacy specification. In spite of being protracted along with a lot of work, no stone was left unturned. I call applications developed today with RAD tools *apparent* applications since they only fulfill the perspective of the moment. Two contracts separate the design from the implementation and provide the gestation time that is necessary for a successful system. It is only fair to mention that a bad design remains a bad design even when the gestation period is lengthened.

Applying What You've Learned

The Microsoft *Analyzing Requirements and Defining Solution Architectures* examination requires a significant knowledge of conceptual design. We'll forego the normal *instant assessment* section found at the end of the preceding chapters and replace it with a series of labs based on a real-life case study. Each lab corresponds to one conceptual design objective of the 70-100 certification test.

Answers to the labs are found in Appendix C.

Lab Exercises

This is a series of laboratories constructed from the real world business rambling found in Listing 17-1. You will be asked to respond to each of the 70-100 conceptual design objectives and the related topics. If the business rambling doesn't provide explicit answers to a particular lab, feel free to make inferences. Some of the topics of a particular objective are not applicable. You'll find an analysis of all conceptual design labs in Appendix C.

Kudos to Microsoft for identifying the issues related to analyzing business requirements. The identification of the issues is quite valuable even though Microsoft presents no methodology for collecting the data. The identification of the requirements issues can serve as a tool beyond just the 70-100 certification exam. Constructing a checklist from the 70-100 *Analyzing Business Requirements* section is recommended for anyone directly involved with designing software to satisfy user requirements.

The labs thus far in the book were about *doing* something. Not so with analyzing user requirements. We're making analytical choices based on information, which is different than *doing* something that requires a step-by-step formula. The answers to the labs are succinct and are based strictly upon the client at hand, which is the real world business rambling from Chapter 17. I'll give the direct answer related to the real world issues, followed by a brief discussion of alternatives. Many of the objectives, but not all, have different answers depending upon the perspective. Participants in a project include the developer, the user, CFO, CIO, and CEO, and their perspectives can vary dramatically.

Case Study

The client is a Fortune 1000 international company. I was hired as a consultant to construct a contract management system for the ABC Corporation (a fictitious name). The corporation has approximately 1,000 contracts that are managed manually. My initial interview with the Director of Information Systems revealed that he was newly hired and apparently wanted to make an impression with his new employer. He has significant Microsoft Access skills and became a hero with his last employer when he constructed an Access application that tracked Workman's Compensation lawsuits. The Access applications identified lawyers frequently involved in lawsuits and eventually broke a fraud ring.

I never met ABC's comptroller, but her husband works as a consultant to the corporation and prepared the business rambling found in Listing 17-1. (I'll call the husband Fred, another fictitious name.) This is obviously a pet project of the comptroller, which her husband is undertaking. I am not allowed to converse with the staff and all contact is through Fred. Fred is not an active employee; hence many contract management details are unknown to him.Fred has significant Apple Computer skills and is somewhat remiss with the difficulty he perceives with the Microsoft Windows paradigm. In other words, he wants a Windows application that looks like an Apple Computer application.

The goal of the project is to manage the legal exposure when state, federal, or international laws change. Currently there is no simple means to measure legal exposure when such laws change. With the system in place, a simple search is made across all relevant contracts.

The secondary issue is to track the source of different paragraphs within a contract and the lawyer responsible for that portion of the contract. A contract may involve many different amendments and lawyers over time, and each of these amendments is unique to a specific lawyer. Lawyers die or change firms and it is important to know the status and location of each lawyer.

It's interesting that the MIS director has more Microsoft programming skills than the ABC Corporation programming staff. The ABC Corporation is mainframe-centric, although many users have Windows 95 and use Microsoft Word, Access, or Excel. The ABC programming staff is only involved with bound Access forms, which is an application construct typically used by beginners. Microsoft SQL Server is not installed at ABC Corporation and no database administrators are on staff.

LAB 17.37 *Analyze the scope of a project*

Using the case study and business rambling in Listing 17-1, analyze each of the following. Considerations include:

- Existing applications
- Anticipated changes in environment
- Expected lifetime of solution
- Time, cost, budget, and benefit trade-offs

Lab 17.38 *Analyze the extent of a business requirement*

Using the case study and business rambling in Listing 17-1, analyze each of the following. Considerations include:

- Establish business requirements.
- Establish type of problem, such as messaging problem or communication problem.
- Establish and define customer quality requirements.
- Minimize Total Cost of Ownership (TCO).
- Increase Return on Investment (ROI) of solution.
- Analyze current platform and infrastructure.
- Incorporate planned platform and infrastructure into solution.
- Analyze impact of technology migration.
- Plan physical requirements, such as infrastructure.
- Establish application environment, such as hardware platform, support, and operating system.
- Identify organizational constraints, such as financial situation, company politics, technical acceptance level, and training needs.
- Establish schedule for implementation of solution.
- Identify audience.

Lab 17.39 *Analyze security requirements*

Using the case study and business rambling in Listing 17-1, analyze each of the following. Considerations include:

- Identify roles of administrator, groups, guests, and clients.
- Identify impact on existing environment.
- Establish fault tolerance.
- Plan for maintainability.
- Plan distribution of security database.
- Establish security context.
- Plan for auditing.

- Identify level of security needed.
- Analyze existing mechanisms for security policies.

Lab 17.40 *Analyze performance requirements*

Using the case study and business rambling in Listing 17-1, analyze each of the following. Considerations include:

- Transactions per time slice
- Bandwidth
- Capacity
- Interoperability with existing standards
- Peak versus average requirements
- Response-time expectations
- Existing response-time characteristics
- Barriers to performance

Lab 17.41 *Analyze maintainability requirements*

Using the case study and business rambling in Listing 17-1, analyze each of the following. Considerations include:

- Breadth of application distribution
- Method of distribution
- Maintenance expectations
- Location and knowledge level of maintenance staff
- Impact of third-party maintenance agreements

Lab 17.42 *Analyze extensibility requirements. Solution must be able to handle the growth of functionality*

Analyze the extensibility requirements of the application required for the case study and business rambling in Listing 17-1.

Changing productions systems if fraught with risk. Analyze extending the functionality of a production system, which may be a mission critical to the enterprise.

Lab 17.43 *Analyze availability requirements*

Using the case study and business rambling in Listing 17-1, analyze each of the following. Considerations include:

- Hours of operation
- Level of availability
- Geographic scope
- Impact of downtime

Lab 17.44 *Analyze human factors requirements*

Using the case study and business rambling in Listing 17-1, analyze each of the following. Considerations include:

- Target users
- Localization
- Accessibility
- Roaming users
- Help
- Training requirements
- Physical environment constraints
- Special needs

Lab 17.45 *Analyze the requirements for integrating a solution with existing applications*

Using the case study and business rambling in Listing 17-1, analyze each of the following. Considerations include:

- Legacy applications
- Format and location of existing data
- Connectivity to existing applications
- Data conversion and data enhancement requirements

Lab 17.46 *Analyze existing methodologies and limitations of a business*

Using the case study and business rambling in Listing 17-1, analyze each of the following. Considerations include:

- Legal issues
- Current business practices
- Organizational structure
- Process engineering
- Budget
- Implementation and training methodologies
- Quality control requirements
- Customer's needs

Lab 17.47 *Analyze scalability requirements*

Using the case study and business rambling in Listing 17-1, analyze each of the following. Considerations include:

- Growth of audience
- Growth of organization
- Growth of data
- Cycle of use

CHAPTER

18

Logical Data Design

About Chapter 18

Chapter 18 builds the Application Model using the Augmented Zachman Framework introduced in Chapter 17. The approach is *top-down,* which means that the problem must be fully understood before resources are expended to solve a problem that isn't known. The chapter discusses only those steps necessary to design and construct the data-modeling portion of the Application Model. *How* is not a topic of discussion for this chapter, although it's been discussed in nearly every chapter of this book.

The previous chapter was the most important chapter in this book; this chapter is the most difficult. Most developers deal with an intuitive sense of what proper data normalization is and have no formal rule mechanism to apply for complex situations. In this chapter we introduce normalization rules that can be used when the intuitive sense of data normalization fails.

An intuitive sense of data normalization works well when building a small application on the desktop from scratch. The developer works through all the stages and typically never goes beyond the third normal form. This approach does not work when the developer is trying to place an OLE-DB wrapper around legacy databases. Legacy databases can be flat-file structures where no consideration was given to relational database issues. The intuitive sense of database normalization will often fail with this scenario.

This chapter introduces the concept of functional dependence, which is used in all data normalization phases. The concept of functional dependence is characterized by something *depending on* something else. This dependence may be incorrect unless the developer clearly understands the business rules.

Entities and IDEF1X

Chapter 17 defined an entity (see Chapter 17, Distillation Rules) somewhat prematurely with a warning to not consider entities during the distillation phase. The goal of the distillation phase is only data collection. Before we move on, let's review the definition of an entity:

- *Entities* — Entities are abstractions of real-world things and are different than real-world things. Entities within a model are only abstractions. An entity may be a person, concept, place, event, or thing. It has lasting value and data about it can be stored. It can be uniquely identified.
- *Inferred entities* — These are entities that are not referenced directly but whose existence may be inferred from context.
- *Entity instances* — There is a difference between an instance of an entity and the entity. Spot the dog is an instance of the entity dog.
- *Attributes* — Attributes describe a specific occurrence of the data (instance).

An entity is typically represented in a database as a table and relationships exist between different tables. To say that a table is a relation is not correct and is an over simplification of the issue. Table 18-1 defines the formal structural properties of a relation. Not all tables form a relation. This formal definition of a relation is introduced before we introduce the notation for a relation, which is the graphical ERD. The graphical ERD oversimplifies a relation and does not accurately portray all properties of a relation.

TABLE 18-1 Structural Properties of a Relation

	Structural Property
1	Columns represent fields and each column has a unique name.
2	Each column contains data of the same type; that is, the data is homogeneous.
3	Each column has a domain. This is the set of possible values that can be used in a column.
4	A row is a record in common terminology. It is a tuple and is also called an *n*-tuple when there are *n* columns.
5	The order of the rows and columns is unimportant.

Continued

TABLE 18-1 *(continued)*

	Structural Property
6	No duplicate rows are allowed. This is not to be confused with *resultsets,* which may have duplicate rows.
7	*Repeating groups* are not allowed. All values are scalar or atomic.
8	A *candidate key* is an attribute or a set of attributes that uniquely identify a row. A candidate key must uniquely identify a row and have the *non-redundancy* property. If a key is *non-redundant,* then no attribute in the key may be discarded without destroying the unique identification property of the key.
9	A primary *key* is a candidate key selected as the unique identifier. Each relation must have a primary key.
10	A *superkey* is any set of attributes that identifies a row. The *non-redundancy* property is not required for a *superkey.* Another name for *superkey* is *natural key.*
11	A *foreign key* is an attribute that appears as a non-key attribute in one relation and as a *primary key* in another relation.
12	A *composite key* contains more than one attribute.
13	A *relational schema* is a set of attributes, dependencies, and constraints that characterize a relation.
14	An *instance* is a set of rows that populate the *relation.* An update to the *relation* is valid only if all dependencies and constraints are honored.

We now know the properties of a relation and we need a notation to represent the relation. Assume a table with two columns: *A* and *B*. We'll use the notation R(A, B) for the relation where *A* and *B* are the column names in a two-dimensional table and no structural properties of Table 18-1 are violated.

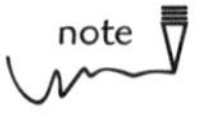

A data table is not always a relation. For example, a table with a duplicate row is not a relation because structural property six of Table 18-1 is violated.

Let's move on to the construction of an ERD. We have the formal definition of a relation in our pocket and won't be seduced by the simplicity of an ERD diagram. Within the Application Model, the ERD is not a standalone model. It is very closely coupled with the Business Rules Model. I did this because there is additional information I wished to capture such as assumptions, examples of usage, reasoning, and comments. Commercial ERD tools function as standalone models and capturing historical information is not always on their agenda. This explains the relationship between the Business Rules Model and the ERD.

Numerous tools on the market can be used to create an ERD. Most data-modeling tools have the capability to create an IDEF1X ERD. The IDEF1X ERD features are sketched briefly below after which Ill show you how to construct an ERD of your own without using a commercial tool. Your company may own a tool such as ER*win*, which we'll use later in this chapter. ER*win* from Platinum Technologies, Inc. is the data modeling standard. This tool is a must have for every serious data modeling project.

IDEF1X Entity Perspective

Chapter 17 completed the Requirements Model. We have all the business rules and possibly some pseudo-rules, all of which rules were placed in the Requirements Model. Rules that mapped to business scope issues are placed in the Business Scope Model while rules that mapped to business rule implementations are placed in the Business Rules Model. However, we only have facts and definitions. Moving to the Business Model, we will turn facts and definitions into information. We do that with relations. Before we can do that, let's look at the IDEF1X definition of a relation in Figure 18-1.

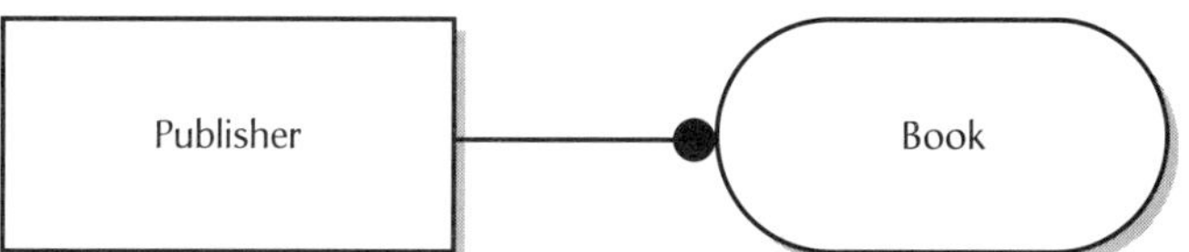

FIGURE 18-1 **IDEF1X relationship representation for a publisher that publishes books.**

Entity naming is not precise and the parent entity is also known as an *independent entity,* and on occasion as a *kernel* entity. All of these names convey a sense of independence. The formal name is *independent* entity.

The child entity also exhibits name confusion because it is known by surrogate names of *dependent entity* and *characteristic entity*. The formal name is *characteristic entity,* which we'll adopt. Figure 18-1 illustrates an independent entity and a characteristic entity. The black dot represents a one-to-many relationship in that many characteristic entities exist for a single independent entity.

From the IDEF1X representation and Figure 18-1, we can discern these business rules:

- *Definition* — Publisher exists.
- *Definition* — Books exist.
- *Fact* — Publisher publishes many books.
- *Fact* — Book is published by publisher.

An IDEF1X relation is a collection of business rules from the Requirements Model, in particular definitions and facts. *Book* and *Publisher* are entities within an entity relation diagram (ERD), but are facts in the Requirements Model. The distillation phase does not allow the combining of definitions into facts until the distillation phase is complete. The combining of definitions into facts occurs during the construction of the ERD. Heretofore disjoint information becomes knowledge when definitions are combined to form entities with relationships. Definitions are potential entities and not every definition becomes an entity. An entity doesn't exist until a relationship is established, which is a *fact*. Business rules are managed with cardinality and by the choice of IDEF1X entity type, each of which is discussed below:

- *Independent entity* — An entity that is not dependent upon another entity. It is sometimes referred to as a *kernel entity.* The **Publisher** in Figure 18-1 is an *independent entity* while **Book** is a *characteristic entity*. An independent entity is graphically represented by a rectangle. A relationship for an independent entity is described with an *active* sentence. For example, the independent entity relationship is characterized as *Publisher publishes books*.
- *Characteristic entity* — A characteristic entity is a group of attributes that occurs many times for an entity. An example is the many sides of a one-to-many relation. The parent entity may be an independent entity, a category entity, an associative entity, or another characteristic entity. A characteristic entity is graphically represented by the rectangle with rounded corners. A relationship for a characteristic entity is described with a *passive* sentence.

For example the characteristic entity relationship is: *Books are published by publisher*.

- *Associative entity* — An associative entity (there is an association) is an entity that inherits its primary keys from two or more entities. This is the mechanism used to resolve what is referred to as a "many-to-many" relation. Figure 18-2 illustrates a many-to-many relationship that does not exist in IDEF1X. A patient has many doctors and a doctor has many patients. Figure 18-3 is the equivalent of Figure 18-2, which consists of an associative entity and two independent entities. Note that the primary keys from each of the independent entities are combined to form the compound key of the associative entity. Everything below the horizontal line in the associative entity of Figure 18-3 represents attributes, and everything above the bisecting line represents the primary key.

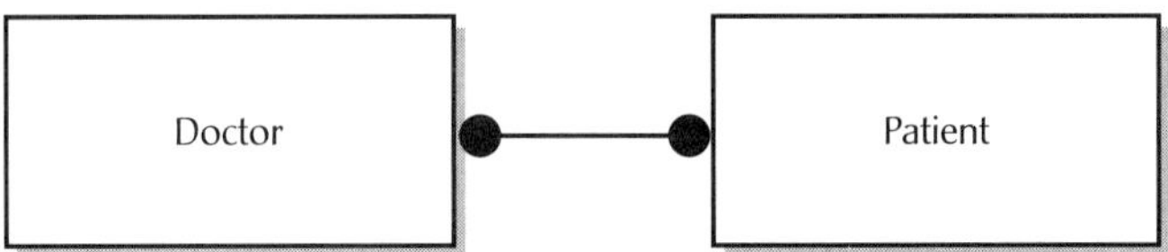

FIGURE 18-2 A many-to-many relationship (invalid in IDEF1X).

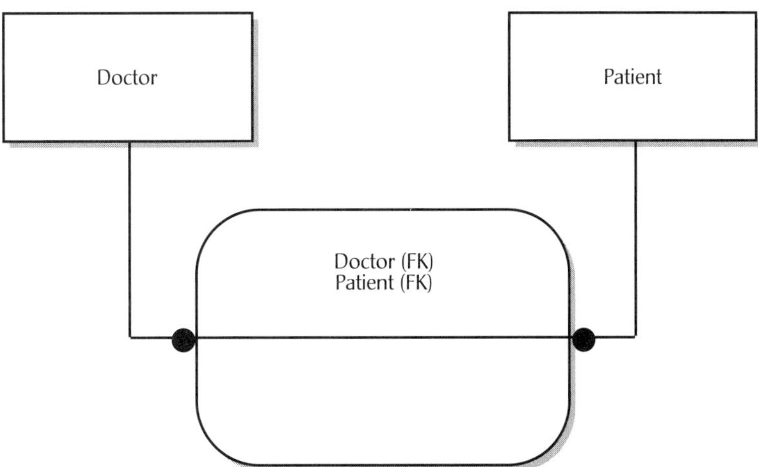

FIGURE 18-3 An associative entity with two independent entities (Figure 18-2 equivalent).

- *Category entity* — A category entity is a subset of instances of a generic parent. A *generalization hierarchy* is formed by a set of *category* entities whose parent is a *generalization* entity. A *category discriminator* distinguishes the different instances of a generic parent. In Figure 18-4, *account type* is the *category discriminator.*

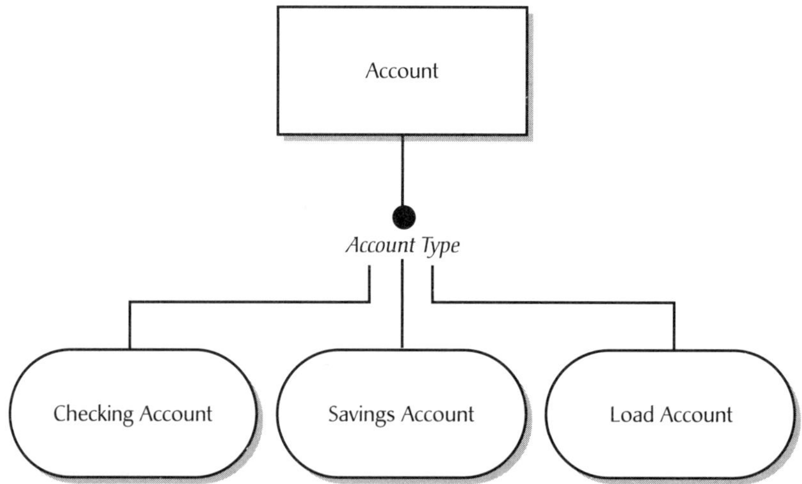

FIGURE 18-4 Category entities in a generalization hierarchy.

An *identifying relationship* occurs when the characteristic (child) entity subsumes the primary key of the independent (parent) entity as a component of the child entity primary key. A *non-identifying relationship* is unique to IDEF1X and the foreign key migrates as an attribute rather than as a primary key constituent. A *non-identifying relationship* does not support referential integrity while an *identifying relationship* does support referential integrity. Figure 18-5 illustrates both an *identifying relationship* and a *non-identifying relationship*. The dashed line in Figure 18-5 is a notation for a *non-identifying relationship*, which is explained in Table 18-2.

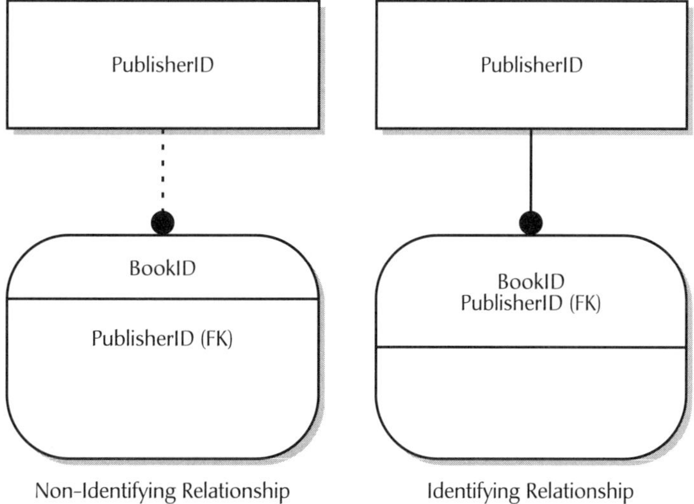

Figure 18-5 Identifying and non-identifying relationships.

An independent entity with a *non-identifying* relationship may have a NULL foreign key, which means the independent entity instance (row) does not have a characteristic entity. This means that the characteristic entity may or may not be *existence-dependent* (see Table 18-2) upon the independent entity. A characteristic entity of a non-identifying relationship is not *identification-dependent* upon the independent entity.

So far we've been a bit glib about relationships and cardinality. Not every relationship is a one-to-many as shown in Table 18-2.

TABLE 18-2 IDEF1X RELATIONSHIPS AND RELATED CARDINALITY NOTATION

Cardinality Description	*Identifying Relationship*	*Non-Identifying Relationship*
One to exactly N	– – – – –(N	------------(N
One to zero, one, or more	– – – – –(	------------(
One to one or more	– – – – –(P	------------(P
One to zero or one	– – – – –(Z	------------(Z
Zero or one to zero, one, or more		(---------(
Zero or one to zero or one		(---------(Z

There is one last notational issue that needs to be discussed before we build an ERD. The issue involves recursive relationships in legacy software and is only supported for non-identifying relationships. A classic example is a company that is the parent of another company. This structure is hierarchical and the recursion attribute is NULL for the top most entity. The value of the recursive field is the primary key, which means that the primary key for an entity and the recursion field must be distinct. Such a relationship is invalid since a company cannot be it's own parent. Another way of stating the problem is that an attribute cannot appear twice in the same entity under the same name. This is because the *CompanyID* that identifies each instance of the entity is not the same *CompanyID* that migrates through the relationship that identifies the parent company. Solving this problem is accomplished with a rolename, which is the *OwnerID* of Figure 18-6. Table 18-3 represents a sample table with a recursive relationship instance that is based on the Figure 18-6 recursive relationship.

TABLE 18-3 EXAMPLE RECURSIVE RELATIONSHIP TABLE

CompanyID OwnerID	*CompanyName*
C1 NULL	Monster Book Company
C2 C1	Smaller Book Company
C3 C1	Other Smaller Book Company
C4 C2	Big Subsidiary
C5 C2	Small Subsidiary
C6 NULL	Independent Company

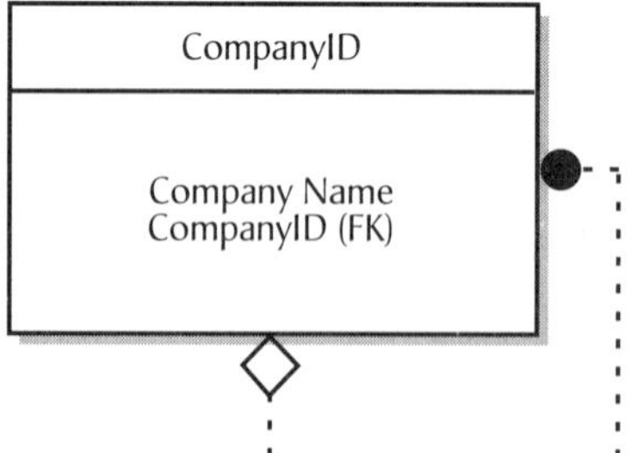

FIGURE 18-6 A recursive relationship in IDEF1X.

Rolling uur wn ERD

Relations have a primary definition and an inverse definition. The primary definition is represented by an active verb such as: *Publisher publishes books*; the inverse relation is represented by a passive verb such as: *Books are published by publisher*. If you don't have a commercial data-modeling tool for building entity relationship diagrams (ERDs), I'll show you how to make your own, which will have the same characteristics as an IDEF1X ERD. Because this is a manual process, it isn't feasible to build your own ERD with a large number of entities. The concept is very simple. Create an N x N symmetric matrix where each column and row contains the same entity as illustrated below. Figure 18-7 is an ERD with four entities.

	Publisher	**Author**	**Book**	**Employee**
Publisher		Pays 1-M	Prints1-M	Employs 1-M
Author	Paid by 1-1		Writes1-M	
Book	Printed by 1-1	Written by 1-M		
Employee	Employed by publisher 1-1			

FIGURE 18-7 A manual ERD of a very small business model.

Figure 18-7 identifies the two main features of an ERD: the cardinality and the relationships. The <M> represents *many* and 1-M represents *one-to-many* in Figure 18-7, which is the cardinality. Using the ERD of Figure 18-7, the business rules along with the cardinality are stated in the following list. Note that nothing is entered on the diagonal. The business rules of Figure 18-7 include:

1. Publisher pays many authors.
2. Publisher prints many books.
3. Publisher employs many employees.
4. Author is paid by publisher.
5. Author writes many books.
6. Book is printed by publisher.
7. Book is written by many authors (coauthors).
8. Employee is employed by publisher.

These business rules were applied to a commercial data-modeling tool. The tool is limited to the verb *has* and the results appear in Figure 18-8, which appears to be a distortion of the ERD in Figure 18-7. That is not completely true and the original entities remain; however, the business rule *Publisher pays authors* becomes *Publisher has* authors. Other business rules are also changed. Content is lost. The issue here is that commercial modeling tools are useful in creating the Key-based Model, the Fully Attributed Model, and the Transform Model of Figure 17-3. Not all data-modeling tools accurately model the Business Scope Model, the Requirements Model, or the Business Rules Model of Figure 17-3. A commercial modeling tool is not always the panacea for all modeling needs. Figure 18-8 illustrates the ERD of Figure 18-7 with lost content. The data-modeling tool used for Figure 18-8 applied business rules directly. The problem in Figure 18-8 occurs when there is no mechanism to express cardinality other than to pluralize the characteristic entity. ER*win,* the data-modeling standard, uses graphical IDEF1X notation; hence there is no cardinality ambiguity.

	Publisher	**Author**	**Book**	**Employee**
Publisher		Has 1-M	Has 1-M	Has 1-M
Author	Has 1-1		Has 1-M	
Book	Has 1-1	Has 1-M		
Employee	Has 1-1			

FIGURE 18-8 An ERD with lost content.

Figure 18-9 is created in Access 97 by opening the Microsoft Access `Northwind` database and selecting *Relationships* from the **Tools** menu. Figure 18-9 is an ERD for the Microsoft Access `Northwind`database. What we see is a metaphor change with the infinity symbol (sideways eight) representing the *many* sides of entity relationships.

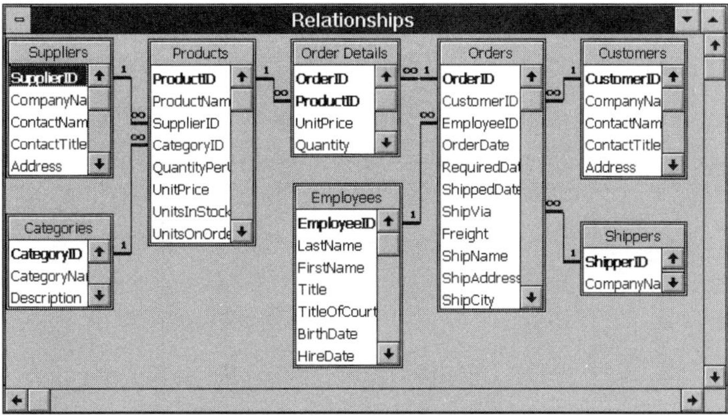

FIGURE 18-9 The Microsoft Access Northwind database relationships.

We'll use ER*win* from Platinum Technologies, Inc. to reverse engineer the Pubs database of Microsoft SQL Server 6.5. We're using the reverse engineering feature of ER*win* to create an ERD of an existing database. This procedure assumes that SQL Server is currently running. If SQL Server is not started, use the SQL Service Manager to start SQL Server. Follow these steps to reverse engineer the Pubs database using ER*win*:

1. Select `Reverse Engineer` from the ER*win* Task menu.
2. Select `PROGRESS`
3. Select `NEXT`
4. Select `SQL Server` and `6.X`.
5. Select `NEXT`
6. Select `NEXT` (We're using the defaults.)
7. Enter the SQL Server UID, PWD, the database name (Pubs for this example), and the server name.
8. Select `Connect`
9. The Pubs database is reverse engineered and Figure 18-10 is displayed.

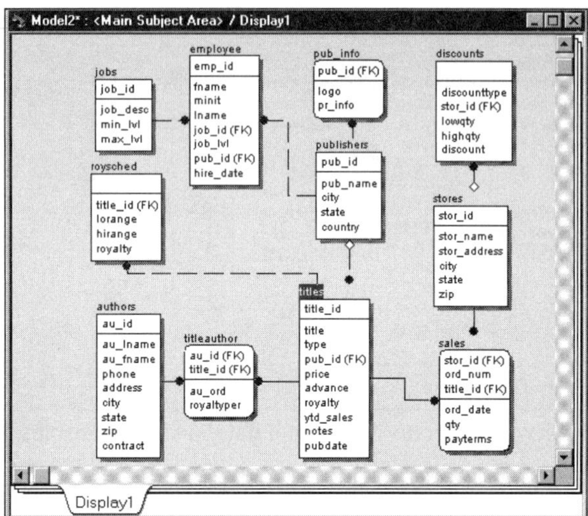

FIGURE 18-10 Reverse engineering the SQL Server Pubs database with ER*win* 3.5.2.

Note in Figure 18-10 that ER*win* presents the ERD of the Pubs database in IDEF1X notation. There is not confusion over metaphor.

Building the Key-based Model

As we work our way through the Augmented Zachman Framework shown in Figure 17-3, the Key-based Model (KBM) is next. We'll construct the KBM from the ERD we defined previously; however, the defined database must be in third normal form (3NF) to qualify as a KBM. We do not add attributes when constructing the KBM, only the primary keys. We only want to create the relationships among all the entities. This approach compartmentalizes normalization into two phases: normalizing the underlying database structure and normalizing the enhanced structure when attributes are added. The data normalization that occurs in the first phase is the base structure. When this phase is finished and you move to the next phase, the fully attributed model, you may have to do additional normalization when the attributes are added. Not all the attributes are added in one step. It's an iterative cycle of adding attributes and normalizing.

The first step of building the KBM is entity recognition and identifying entity relationships. Figure 18-11 illustrates this interim step, which shows the entities and relationships of the SQL Server Pubs database. Follow these steps to recreate Figure 18-11 using ER*win*:

1. Select `Reverse Engineer` from the ER*win* **Task** menu.
2. Select `SAMPLE`
3. Select `NEXT`
4. Select `SQL Server` and `6.X`.
5. Select `NEXT`
6. Select `NEXT` (We're using the defaults.)
7. Enter the SQL Server UID, PWD, the database name (Pubs for this example), and the server name.
8. Select `CONNECT`
9. Select `PHYSICAL` from the combo box on the ER*win* toolbar.
10. Select `ENTITY` at the bottom of the dialog box.
11. Figure 18-11 is recreated, which are the entities and relationships of the SQL Server Pubs database.

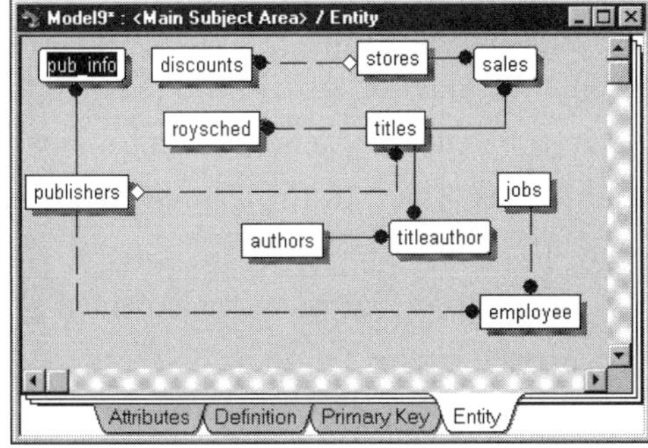

FIGURE 18-11 **Entities and relationships of the SQL Server Pubs database.**

Let's take a peek at our KBM goal before addressing the nitty-gritty process of identifying primary and foreign keys. Figure 18-12 is created when the **Primary Key** tab is selected in step 10. Figure 18-12 represents the KBM for the SQL Server Pubs database, while Figure 18-10 represents a Fully Attributed Model (FAM) version of the Pubs database. This section is about building the KBM, and we'll look more closely at the FAM later in this chapter.

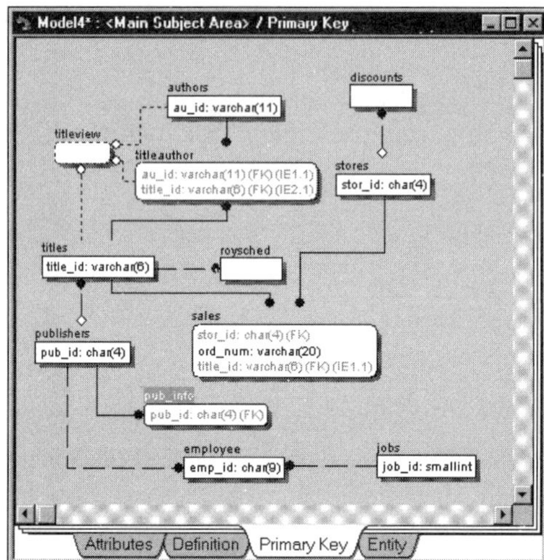

FIGURE 18-12 The KBM of the SQL Server Pubs database.

Functional Dependence

A database cannot be normalized unless the developer understands the Business Model. Functional dependency requires an understanding of the business process, and functional dependency is the tool for normalizing a database. Function dependency is when something *depends on* something else. This relationship may not be inferred accurately when content is missing such as in Figure 18-8. Nearly all developers use an intuitive approach to data modeling, but intuition fails when faced with complex normalization issues. The intuitive approach works well if you're very experienced or if you are designing a new database. It doesn't work well when you're trying to access legacy databases that were implemented as flat-file structures with no normalization considerations.

The purpose of functional dependence is the identification of primary keys. Before we embark on that search, a few comments are in order about primary keys. These considerations are apart and separate from functional dependence and include:

- A primary key should be an attribute that does not change its value over the life of each entity instance, a row.
- Primary keys should be relatively small. When a primary key consists of more than one attribute, the designer must ascertain that each key value is supplied, that is, there are no NULL constituents.

- Avoid the use of intelligent keys in which characters or digits represent groupings, dates, or classifications. Changing an intelligent key violates first normal form (see below).
- Use keys to enforce constraints that govern the existence of entity instances. An example is an identifying relationship where the independent entity contributes a primary key to the characteristic entity's primary key.

The problems of normalization and functional dependency center on the ambiguous nature of the English language and the fact that statements are not context-free.

Functional dependence between attributes in a relation is not unlike functional dependence in mathematics. In the equation $y = x^2 - 2x - x$, we can say that y *depends on* x. X is the independent variable and y is the dependent variable. But functional dependence is not limited to mathematics. Table 18-4 illustrates the concept of functional dependency.

TABLE 18-4 ILLUSTRATING FUNCTIONAL DEPENDENCY WITH AIRPORTS AND CITIES

Airport Name	*City*
SeaTac	Seattle/Tacoma
Stapleton	Denver
J. F. Kennedy	New York
LaGuardia	New York
LAX	Los Angeles
Portland International	Portland

Airport names are unique, but more than one airport is identified with a city. We can state that city *depends on* name, but name *does not depend on* city. Functional dependence is the key database design tool. As later examples show, primary key determination uses functional dependence.

We need to adopt a notation for functional dependence. We can use mathematical notation for our example above and state city = *f*(name). I prefer instead to use the notation Airport Name → City, or City depends on Airport Name.

Defining a schema

Table 18-4 defines a relation. The definition of a primary key is *something that can be depended upon*. A schema is defined as the combination of the relation and the related dependencies and constraints. Using our adopted notation, the schema for the example in Table 18-4 is:

R (Airport Name, City), Airport Name → City

Functional dependency inference axioms

W. W. Armstrong developed a set of functional dependency inference axioms ("Dependency Structures of Database Relationships," Proceedings, IFIP Congress, 1974). C. Berri, R. Fagin, and J. H. Howard published "A Complete Axiomatization for Functional and Multivalued Dependencies in Database Relations," Proceedings 1977 ACM SIGMOD International Conference on Management of Data, Toronto, August 1977. These axioms are collectively known as the *Armstrong axioms* and are tools that are used in the normalization process. All possible functional dependencies implied by a given set can be generated using these axioms:

1. *Reflexivity rule*— If B is a subset of A then A → B. A → A is also implied, which is the *Self-Determination* rule.
2. *Augmentation rule*— If A → B, then AC → BC.
3. *Transitivity rule*— If A → B and B → C, then A → C.
4. *Union rule*— If A → B and A → C, then A → BC.
5. *Decomposition (projection) rule*— If A → C, then A → B where B is a subset of C; or restated as if A → BC then A → B and A → C.
6. *Composition rule*— If A → B and C → D, then AC → BD.
7. *Pseudotransitivity rule*— If A → B and CB → D, then AC → D.

Axioms 1, 2, and 3 are derived from the definition of functional dependence. Axioms 4, 5, 6, and 7 are derived from axioms 1, 2, and 3.

Finding candidate keys and superkeys with functional dependence

Our discussion now focuses on finding candidate keys and superkeys using functional dependency. By definition, a table with duplicate rows does not have candidate keys and are not a topic of discussion. This is not an issue for the key-based model that contains only primary keys. A key-based model only exists if a new database is being constructed. The techniques outlined here using functional dependency fall within the realm of constructing the Fully Attributed Model. Functional dependence is the tool used in all normalization steps. These steps can be loosely categorized as:

- Removing groups of repeating data.
- Removing duplicate data.
- Removing columns of a table that do not depend on the primary key.
- Placing independent multiple relationships in separate tables.
- Placing dependent multiple relationships in separate tables.

We'll always use succinct notation. These rules are guide to the notation issues:

- Rather than spelling out a table name, <R*n*> is used to indicate a relation. When the table is not a relation or is unknown a superscript notation is used. For R^{maybe} indicates that the table may not be a relation.
- Functional dependencies are indicated as FD.
- Single uppercase letters indicates columns in a table. Occasionally a superscript will be used to illustrate an issue. An example is $B^{repeats}$. The reader should know immediately that the attribute violates first normal form.
- The primary key of a relation is always underlined. When no underline exists, the primary key has not yet been selected even though one may exist. Consider the relation $R(\underline{A}, B)$. A is the primary key and B depends upon A.

Let's move on and use our notation and the new notion of functional dependence. The Armstrong axioms have an immediate and practical consequence for key selection. A relation R with attributes A, B, C, D and the functional dependencies illustrate this:

$A \rightarrow D$

$CD \rightarrow B$

$AD \rightarrow C$

This example is artificial and only serves to illustrate the issue. Before proceeding, several definitions must be made so we can understand the objective. These definitions are a repeat of Table 18-1 (structural properties of a relation).

- Superkey—A superkey is an attribute or set of attributes that identify an entity uniquely.
- Candidate key—A candidate key is a superkey such that no proper subset of its attributes is itself a superkey.
- Primary key—A candidate key that is used to identify tuples (formal row definition) in a relation.

Our interest is in determining candidate keys. We have three choices for a candidate key: A, CD, and AD. We look first at AD to see if it is a candidate key. To do that we want to compute AD^+ using the following algorithm. The algorithm is iterative, and as long as the result set changes, it loops until there are no further result set changes. The term *determinant* is what is depended on. A is the *determinant* and B is the *dependent* for the functional dependency $A \rightarrow B$.

To determine candidate keys, follow these steps:

1. Initialize the algorithm and place AD in the result set. The selection of the determinant to place in the result set is not arbitrary. We must apply this algorithm to all determinants.
2. Look at the FDs. Is there an FD whose determinant is in the result set? We find that there is an FD whose determinant is in the result set with $AD \rightarrow C$. Augment the result set with C. AD is in the result set because we initialized it with AD.
3. Look at the FDs again. The result set is now ACD. Is there another FD whose determinant is found in the result set? The answer is yes, $CD \rightarrow B$. Augment the result set with B. The result set AD^+ now contains all attributes of R and we conclude that AD is a superkey.

We have found one superkey. To find the next superkey, we'll need to compute A^+. To do that, we'll use the same algorithm we used above.

1. Assign A to the result set A^+.
2. Look for an FD whose determinant is contained in the result set. We find one in $A \rightarrow D$. Augment the result set with D. A^+ now contains AD.

3. Search the FDs for a determinant that is contained in the result set. We find one in AD → C. Augment the result set with C. A^+ now contains ACD.
4. Search the FDs again. CD → B is an FD whose determinant is contained A^+ so augment A^+ with B. All attributes of R are now in A^+. We conclude that A is a superkey since the result set A^+ includes all attributes of R. A is also a candidate key, and that is because it has no proper subset that is also a superkey.

AD was the first candidate key we found. We found another candidate key in A. We now know that AD is not a candidate key because the definition of a candidate key is that it has no proper subset of attributes that are superkeys. A is a superkey and is a proper subset of AD. AD still remains a superkey key; it is just not a candidate key.

There is one last FD to consider in our search for a candidate key or superkey, the FD CD → B.

1. Initialize CD^+ to CD.
2. Search for an FD whose determinant is contained in CD^+. We find one, CD → B. Augment CD^+ with B.
3. Search for a FD whose determinant is contained in CD^+. There isn't one, so we can conclude that CD is not a superkey because A is not contained in CD^+, and therefore is not functionally dependent upon it.

Congratulations. You've just found your first candidate key and your first super key.

A minimal covering: removing redundant functional dependencies

We now have a technique for key determination, but we shouldn't apply our algorithm until a *minimal covering* is built; that is, we remove redundant FDs using the Armstrong axioms. To illustrate removing redundant FDs, consider the relation R with attributes A, B, C, D and FDs:

A → CD

A → C

CD → B

AD → C

Reducing by *decomposition* we have:

A → C

A → D

A → C

CD → B

AD → C

A → C is redundant and the FDs reduce to:

A → C

A → D

CD → B

AD → C

Let me digress for a moment from the business of removing redundant functional dependencies. A relational database supports the `Select`, `Project`, and `Join` operators. These are features of a relational database; flat-file systems do not support these operators. The decomposition above uses Armstrong's axiom 5 but it is also the `Project` operator of a relational database. We'll use the `Project` operator in each of the normalization steps in the remainder of the chapter. This is the formal term; decomposition is the commonly used term.

After the FDs are reduced to a single term by decomposition, we can build the *irreducible* set. The irreducible set is a set of candidate keys that do not include any attributes that are irrelevant for unique identification purposes. We do that with the following algorithm:

Let's define an algorithm for creating the *irreducible set*. Pick an FD. Place the determinant of the selected FD in the result set, but remove that FD from the selection list. Search for a determinant whose value is in the result set. If one is found, include the dependent variable in the new result set. If at any time a determinant is found that is ***not*** in the result set, then it has been shown that the original dependent variable is not in the result set and we can conclude that the FD under attack is not redundant.

1. Select the FD A → C and place A in the result set.
2. Remove the FD A → C from the selection list of candidates. This will be a non redundant FD, if after examining all FDs, the dependent variable is not found in the result set.
3. Locate another FD whose determinant is in the result set. We find the FD A → D. Place D in the result set that now contains AD.
4. Locate another FD whose determinant is in the result set. We find the FD AD → C. Place C in the result set which now contains ACD. However, this variable is the same dependent variable for the FD A → C. The conclusion is that A → C ***is redundant*** because C is in the result set.
5. Start again and select the FD A → D for evaluation. Place A in the result list and remove the FD from the list of FD candidates.
6. Start again and select the FD CD → B to evaluate. Place CD in the result set.
7. Select an FD whose determinant is in the result set. There is none and the FD CD → B ***is not redundant*** because B is not in the result set.
8. Start again and select the FD AD → C to evaluate. Place AD in the result set and remove the FD AD → C from the selection list.
9. We find the determinant of A → D is in the result set. However, the dependent variable is already there, and because there are no other FDs with a determinant in the result set, the FD AD → C ***is not redundant*** because C is not in the result set. We didn't consider A → C because we already know it is redundant. It should also be obvious that A → C is equivalent to AD → C by augmentation (see the Armstrong axioms).

Practicing Recognizing Functional Dependency

Functional dependency is the tool we need to resolve normalization issues. In this section we'll provide a few problems (with answers) to test your functional dependence recognition skills. How about some practice identifying a functional dependency? I used cities and airports in Table 18-4 when I initially introduced functional dependence. Now we'll just use columns of numbers. After all, getting dirty with the data is what it is all about.

We start first with Table 18-5. For part one of the question, identify all possible dependencies. For part two of the question, identify the invalid dependencies. The answers are below so don't peek.

TABLE 18-5 PROBLEM 1

A	*B*	*C*
3	5	2
5	5	4
7	5	4
9	4	8
11	2	10

The second problem is to identify all the valid dependencies in Table 18-6.

TABLE 18-6 PROBLEM 2

A	*B*	*C*
2	3	4
2	4	5
3	4	6
5	6	6
7	6	6

Our last problem is slightly different. Before you answer the question, go back and reread the fourteen structural properties of a relation. Is Table 18-7 a relation?

TABLE 18-7 PROBLEM 3

A	*B*	*C*	*D*
6	7	9	10
2	11	4	3
4	8	21	16
36	23	8	19
6	7	9	10
5	3	2	1

Problem 1 answers: a → b, a → c, ac → b, and ab → c are the only valid dependencies since a is a unique column, which means that any combination with a in the determinant can be depended upon. All possible dependencies are a → b, a → c, b → a, b → c, c → a, c → b, ab→ c, ac → b, bc → a, c → ab, b → ac, and a → bc.

Problem 2 answers: The only valid dependencies are a combination of two different columns, which yields the valid dependencies ac → b and ab → c. Combining bc as a determinant of a dependency is not valid since duplicate rows exist.

Problem 3 answer: No; rows 1 and 5 are duplicates.

Normalization

Using our newly acquired knowledge of functional dependencies and relations, we can make these statements:

- First normal form — All domains must contain atomic values only, be scalar, or contain no repeating groups.
- Second normal form — Each nonkey domain must be functionally dependent upon the primary key.
- Third normal form — Nonkey domains cannot be functionally dependent on any other non-key values, which is transitive dependency.

To help you remember these rules, remember:

```
"The key,
the whole key,
and nothing but the key,
so help me Codd."
```

It pays homage to the inventor of relational database technology, Dr. E. F. Codd and is derived from:

"The rules leading to and including third normal form can be summed up in a single statement: Each attribute must be a fact about the key, the whole key, and nothing but the key." (*DB2 Design and Development Guide*, Wiorkowski and Kull.)

First normal form

First normal form (1NF) requires that all values be atomic or scalar. There are no repeating values. Let's start with the employee table in Table 18-8 that is not in 1NF.

TABLE 18-8 EMPLOYEE TABLE

ID	NAME	PAYDATE
1	Silly, Sally	10 Jan 1999
		10 Feb 1999
		10 March 1999
2	Doright, Dudley	10 Jan 1999
		10 Feb 1999
		10 March 1999

Although the personnel record contains more than just the three fields shown above, these three fields are enough to illustrate the issue. Also the repeated values may extend further but the three values suffice. Recall that a table and a relation are equivalent if the fourteen rules we discussed previously are satisfied. Although they are not satisfied in this illustration because rule 7 is violated for repeating groups, we'll describe the table in relation notation for now. Table 18-8 is not a relation, but we'll name it R and script it. The underscore indicates the primary key in our notation. Let's start by defining the relation in terms of the table attributes. The superscripts indicate that the **PayDate** attribute repeats and there is not yet a relation. I illustrate this relation this one time before moving to a succinct notation.

$\text{Relation}^{\text{Maybe}}$ ($\underline{\text{ID}}$, Name, $\text{PayDate}^{\text{Repeat}}$).

We move to the succinct notation by using a synonym for the attributes (columns) we have:

R^{Maybe} ($\underline{I}$, N, P^{Repeat}).

A relation, the functional dependencies, and constraints determine a schema. There are no constraints here, but there is at least one dependency because there is a primary key, ID. What are the dependencies?

$I \rightarrow NP$ This is the primary key dependency.

So our schema is:

R^{Maybe} ($\underline{I}$, N, P^{Repeat}), $I \rightarrow NP^{\text{repeat}}$

Using decomposition (projection) the dependency $I \rightarrow NP^{\text{repeats}}$ is decomposed to $I \rightarrow N$, $I \rightarrow P^{\text{repeats}}$. The specific steps of the decomposition are shown below for Tables 18-9 and 18-10. Decomposition is used on all our normalization steps so it's advantageous to note the decomposition strategies available:

- When the determinant of the dependency that is being decomposed is unique, the determinant becomes the primary key in the new child table and the primary key from the parent table becomes the foreign key in the new child table.
- When the determinant of the dependency is not unique, the primary key of the parent table and the determinant become the primary key in the new child table. The determinant in our example is not unique and that requires a projection of both the primary key and the determinant as the new primary key in the child table. Tables 18-9 and 18-10 illustrate the decomposition.
- Identify the repeating attribute within the parent relation. In our example, *P* is the attribute of interest.

Table 18-9 is the newly created *PayDate* table.

TABLE 18-9 PAYDATE TABLE

PayDate
10 Jan 1999
10 Feb 1999
10 Mar 1999
10 Jan 1999
10 Feb 1999
10 Mar 1999

The *PayDate* table really isn't a relation yet, just a table. The rows are not unique but creating unique rows will transform the table into a relation. We have decomposed the parent table by removing a column from it. To relate the new table back to the parent table, we add the primary key of the parent relation. Attributes within a relation that are primary keys of another relation are foreign keys. Table 18-10 represents the augmented *PayDate* table.

TABLE 18-10 PAYDATE TABLE

ID	*PayDate*
1	10 Jan 99
1	10 Feb 99
1	10 Mar 99
2	10 Jan 99
2	10 Feb 99
2	10 Mar 99

In the new *PayDate* table there are no functional dependencies. The table only has a primary key. Because each row is unique we can now call it a relation.

We'll name the new relation R1 and provide the new schema. Note that we dropped the script on R because it now is a relation.

$R(\underline{I}, N), I \rightarrow N$

$R1(\underline{I}, \underline{P})$

Both relations are now in 1NF because no repeated values exist.

Second normal form

A relation is in second normal form (2NF) when it is 1NF and all attributes fully depend on the whole key, not just a portion of it. The simple order detail record shown in Table 18-11 demonstrates this. Table 18-11 has attributes that do not depend upon the complete key.

TABLE 18-11 ITEM TABLE

OrderID	*ItemID*	*Description*	*OrderDate*	*Quantity*
1	1	Gadget	10 Jan 1999	100
1	2	Widget	10 Jan 1999	120
2	1	Toy	10 Jan 1999	120

We have the relation:

$R(\underline{OrderID}, \underline{ItemID}, Description, OrderDate, Quantity)$

$OrderID \rightarrow OrderDate, OrderID\ ItemID \rightarrow Quantity, ItemID \rightarrow Description$

It is obvious that *Quantity* is the only attribute that is functionally dependent upon the complete primary key. Moving this relation to a more succinct notation we have:

$R(\underline{A}, \underline{B}, C, D, E)\ AB \rightarrow E, A \rightarrow D, B \rightarrow C$

(where: A = OrderID; B = ItemID; C = Description; D = OrderDate; E = Quantity)

Our solution to this problem is to use the Armstrong's decomposition axiom to create a 2NF schema. We do this by projecting the FD $A \rightarrow D$ and the FD $B \rightarrow C$ to new relations. Our new schema becomes:

R($\underline{A}$, $\underline{B}$, E) AB → E

R1($\underline{A}$, D) A → D

R2($\underline{B}$, C) B → C

The net result of the projections are three relations that are in 2NF.

Third normal form

A relation is in third normal form (3NF) when it is in 2NF and each non-key attribute depends on the entire key and not another non-key attribute. Restated, a relation is in 3NF if there are no transitive dependencies. A → B, B → C represents the transitive dependency A → C. An example is Table 18-12 that represents a transitive dependency where the *Rate* column depends upon the column *Code* and not the column *ID*.

TABLE 18-12 EMPLOYEE TABLE

ID	*NAME*	*CODE*	*RATE*
1	Silly, Sally	P	5
2	Doright, Dudley	T	4
3	Whiplash, Snidley	F	3

The schema of Table 18-12 is represented by:

R($\underline{I}$, N, C, R), I → NC, C → R

Decomposing (projecting) the C → R dependency into a new child table results in the two relations:

R($\underline{I}$, N, C), I → NC

R1($\underline{C}$, R) C → R

The third-normal form normalization problem is solved by creating a simple look-up table. By now I hope the benefits of functional notation are obvious.

Steps in Building the Key-based Model

Normalizing a database is an iterative process. So far we've discussed 1NF, 2NF, and 3NF, which are all we need to build a KBM. The following procedure is offered as a guideline for building the Key-based Model. Remember that we are only building the base structure here. This means that attributes that are not keys or foreign keys are not included in the KBM construction process. Non-key attributes are added during the construction of the Fully Attributed Model, which occurs in the next phase. Also recall that a KBM is only normalized through 3NF, so advanced normalization techniques are not yet applied.

1. The first step is to define the attributes to be used as keys or foreign keys. You probably already know them from the Business Rules Model and the entity relationship diagram.
2. Logically related attributes are grouped into relations.
3. Candidate keys are identified for each relation.
4. A primary key is selected for each relation.
5. The relations are placed in 1NF by identifying and removing all repeating groups.
6. Relations with identical foreign keys are combined. This is still 1NF. Look carefully at the primary keys because there may be synonyms.
7. Continue the normalization process to 2NF by identifying all functional dependencies. Consider reviewing the "Functional Dependence" section above until you have more experience.
8. Decompose (*project*) relations until each non-key attribute is dependent on all the attributes in the key.
9. Complete 2NF normalization by combining all relations with identical primary keys.
10. Start 3NF normalization by identifying all transitive dependencies. You want to check for relations where one non-key attribute depends on another non-key attribute. Don't limit this checking to just non-key attributes. Check for instances where an attribute in the key depends upon another attribute in the key.
11. Decompose (*project*) relations until there are no transitive dependencies.
12. Complete 3NF normalization by combining all relations with identical primary keys *as long as no transitive dependencies occur.*

Fully Attributed Model

Completing the fully attributed model almost completes the Augmented Zachman Framework. In this phase we add attributes that were not a part of the base structure; that is, they were not primary keys or foreign keys. There is nothing wrong with including all the attributes during the KBM phase, because this phase is only a methodology for developers who do not have database design tools.

The actual normalization process for a FAM proceeds much like that of a KBM. Add some attributes, and then normalize. However, because we are adding only attributes, special situations can develop. We discussed dependencies earlier, but as attributes are added, multi-valued dependencies may occur. When this does occur, an additional normalization step must take place.

Boyce Codd Normal Form

We are going beyond our KBM requirement slightly. We've built the KBM, which was only normalized to 3NF. Boyce Codd Normal Form (BCNF) errors occur with overlapping, multiple, composite keys, which are not apparent in 1NF, 2NF, or 3NF normalization. Update anomalies, which are BCNF errors, may develop slowly over time as the developer creates new indexes to access the data or to improve performance.

Composite keys are a source for business rules and are a necessary element of the logical database design. Composite keys are also a source for BCNF errors when the keys are not designed properly. An example of a composite key with an inferred business rule is the relation:

R(SalesPerson, Product, City, Quantity)

A relation is in BCNF by ensuring that it is 3NF for any feasible choice of candidate key as a primary key. More formally stated, a relation is in BCNF if for every $X \rightarrow A$, A does not belong to X. In that event, X is a superkey. A relation is also in BCNF if and only if *each determinant of each dependency in the relation is a candidate key*. That is, all attributes are fully determined by each full candidate key and not by any subset of a candidate key.

Let's use some Star Wars characters to illustrate BCNF errors. Table 18-13 illustrates a BCNF error.

TABLE 18-13 BCNF ERRORS

Class	*Student*	*Teacher*
Planets100	Luke	Anakin
Planets100	Han	Anakin
Planets100	Leia	Winter
Stars100	Lando	Jaina
Stars100	Yoda	Jaina
Stars100	Chewbacca	Jacen

Let's create all the possible relations with composite keys for Table 18-13.

Relation 1 (<u>Class</u>, <u>Student</u>, Teacher) R1(<u>C</u>, <u>S</u>, T)

Relation 2 (<u>Teacher</u>, <u>Student</u>, Class) R2(<u>T</u>, <u>S</u>, C) S → C

Relation 3 (<u>Teacher</u>, <u>Class</u>, Student)

Relation 4 (<u>Teacher</u>, <u>Student</u>, <u>Class</u>)

By inspection *Relation 1* and *Relation 4* are normalized to 3NF. *Relation 3* isn't a valid relation since duplicate primary key values exist. *Relation 2* is not in 3NF because *Class* depends upon *Teacher*, which is a 2NF error. Therefore *Relation 2* is not in BCNF because it is not in 3NF for any feasible choice of candidate keys. We therefore conclude that Table 18-13 violates BCNF. We solve this dilemma with a projection, just as we did for 1NF, 2NF, and 3NF normalization.

R2(<u>T</u>, <u>S</u>, C) S → C

becomes

R5(<u>S</u>, C)

R6(<u>T</u>, <u>S</u>)

Relations R5 and R6 are now normalized to BCNF.

Fourth Normal Form

Fourth normal form (4NF) is the next logical step after BCNF. 4NF errors are illustrated in Table 18-14. However, before we can discuss 4NF, we must understand the meaning of *multi-valued* dependency. Multi-valued dependencies occur when there are attributes within a relation that are not logically related.

TABLE 18-14 ILLUSTRATING 4NF ERRORS

Name	*Occupation*	*Sports Interest*
Tom	Bookkeeper	Hiking
Tom	Bookkeeper	Biking
Tom	Finance	Hiking
Tom	Finance	Biking
Dick	Finance	Swimming
Dick	Real Estate	Running
Dick	Real Estate	Swimming

If you look carefully, you'll note that there are two independent dependencies:

Name → Occupation

Name → Sport

These are multi-valued dependencies and the first one is represented by:

Name > Occupation

The instances of this multi-valued dependency are:

Tom → Bookkeeper, Finance

Dick → Finance, Real Estate

The second multi-valued dependency is represented by:

Name > Sport

This multi-valued dependency has similar instances with:

Tom → Biking, Hiking

Dick → Running, Swimming

The original schema is:

Relation (Name, Occupation, Sport) Name > Occupation, Name > Sport

or

R(N, O, S) N > O, N > S

This is converted to 4NF by using our old friend projection (decomposition) to create the new relations:

R1(N, O)

R2(N, S)

which is in 4NF. A relation is 4NF if it is in BCNF and there are no independent multi-valued dependencies. Another way of saying this is that a relation is in 4NF if the implying set X of every nontrivial multi-valued X > Y is a superkey. Here N is a superkey and the relation is in 4NF.

Fifth Normal Form or Projection-Join Normal Form

This is the final database normalization step. A relation is in fifth normal form (5NF) if it has the lossless join property. Recall that a relational database has three operators, a *select,* which determines rows, a *project,* which determines columns, and a *join,* which joins tables (relations). We start first by using a relation that does not exhibit the lossless join property. We start with a relation R1(A, B, C) and create projections R2(A, B), R3(A, C), and R4(B, C). We attempt to reconstitute the original relation with the joins (R2 X R3) X R4 and find that the data is invalid. 5NF errors cannot be corrected.

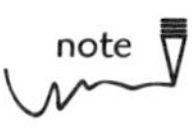

Two relations will have a lossless join if a foreign key is the primary key for one of the relations.

TABLE 18-15 DECOMPOSING A LOSSY RELATION (LOSSLESS JOIN PROPERTY NOT EXHIBITED)

R1(A, B, C)			*R2(A, B)*		*R3(A, C)*		*R4(B, C)*	
A	**B**	**C**	**A**	**B**	**A**	**C**	**B**	**C**
3	6	4	3	6	3	4	6	4
3	7	10	3	7	3	10	7	10
4	6	10	4	6	4	10	6	10

The 5NF problem is illustrated by attempting to reconstitute the original relation with the joins (R2 X R3) X R4 to find that the data is invalid. R5 has an extra row that is not valid.

TABLE 18-16 FAILING TO EXHIBIT THE LOSSLESS JOIN PROPERTY

R2(A, B)X		*R3(A, C)*					*X R4(B, C)*		= *R5(A, B, C)*		
A	**B**	**A**	**C**	**A**	**B**	**C**	**B**	**C**	**A**	**B**	**C**
3	6	3	4	3	6	4	6	4	3	6	4
3	7	3	10	3	6	10*	7	10	3	6	10*
4	6	4	10	3	7	4*	6	10	3	7	10
				3	7	10			4	6	10
				4	6	10					

As can be seen, this relation does not exhibit the lossless join property and therefore is not in 5NF. Relation R5 is not identical to relation R1.

A relation that exhibits the lossless join property is said to satisfy a projection-join dependency. In our relation R(A, B, C) the projection-join dependency between AB and BC holds if and only if B > A (a multi-valued dependency exists). This can only occur if B is a superkey, which it is not, and hence our example does not have the lossless join property and the projection-join dependency is not satisfied. In our example, if A is a primary key, then AB must be a superkey for the join-dependencies to hold. When this is true, 4NF is satisfied by definition. It's not true in our example because neither A nor B are a primary key. For all projection-join dependencies to hold, *each* implying set of multi-valued dependencies must be a superkey.

5NF is just an itch to scratch. 5NF normalization errors occur when dealing with multi-valued dependencies. However, there is no formal methodology for dealing with the issue. Decomposition can be used with other normalization issues, but you run the risk of losing dependencies when applying decomposition to 5NF normalization problems.

With that said, let's look at a 5NF example. You'll note that the data looks much like that of a BCNF error. Recall that a BCNF error is overlapping keys. A 5NF error is different than a BCNF error and is manifested by paired cyclical dependencies within a compound key. Table 18-17 is an abstract and easy to recognize representation of a 5NF error with paired cyclical dependencies in the primary key.

TABLE 18-17 REPRESENTING 5NF ERRORS

A (PK)	*B(PK)*	*C(PK)*	*T*
A1	B1	C1	T1
A1	B1	C2	T2
A1	B2	C1	T3
A1	B2	C2	T4
A2	B1	C1	T5
A2	B1	C2	T6
A2	B2	C1	T7
A2	B2	C2	T8

The pairings in Table 18-17 include (A, B), (A, C), and (B, C). Table 18-17 is artificial and an idealization because I used all combinations. In actual practice all combinations will not be used and a 5NF error is difficult to detect.

The issue with Table 18-17 is that four updates must be made when any value of the primary key is changed. Using our notation, we can write the schema for Table 18-17 as:

R($\underline{A}$, $\underline{B}$, $\underline{C}$, T) $\underline{ABC} \rightarrow T$

A decomposition will yield:

R1(A, B)

R2(B, C)

R2(A, C)

R(A, B, C, T) ABC → T

This reduces the update count to three. This may be good, however the fact that Table 18-17 has a compound key means that one or more business rules are inferred from the table. As an example, lets rewrite our schema as: R(SalesPerson, Product, City, Quantity) SalesPersonProductCity → Quantity

We are now stating that a salesperson has access to individual products in a city. This is acceptable, since the original entity R was preserved. In the schema below business rule information may be lost since the original entity was not preserved:

R3(A, B, T) AB → T

R4(B, C, T) BC → T

R5(A, C, T) AC → T

Normalizing to 5NF is not an abstract procedure, but a procedure that must be done with a firm understanding of the business rules. Normalization to 5NF is not a necessity. Knowing that a 5NF error exists should be sufficient to avoid semantic disintegrity.

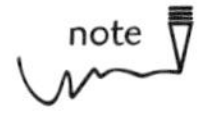

Semantic disintegrity refers to resultsets with errors that may occur when using relational database query languages. Semantic disintegrity exists when joins are created without the lossless join property.

Advanced Normalizations

Domain-key normal form (DKNF, DK/NF) cannot have update, insertion, or deletion anomalies. Even though the concept of DKNF is easy to understand, there is no proven method of converting a database design to this form. DKNF normalization isn't practical and remains an academic issue and an ideal. There is still another esoteric normalization form known as Restriction Union normal form (RUNF). A discussion of DKNF or RUNF is beyond the scope of this book.

In summarizing normalization, we've discussed 1NF, 2NF, 3NF, BCNF, 4NF, and 5NF. A well-designed database typically needs normalization to only 3NF. BCNF and 4NF normalization are used when necessary, however applying 5NF normalization may result in lost information. All normalization forms use decomposition (Armstrong axiom 5), which is also the `Project` operator of a relational database.

When To Stop Normalization

I've been told many times, "You don't need to go beyond 3NF." This is absolutely *not* true. Although in designing a database you build the KBM to 3NF and the statement is true. You proceed to the point where no further normalization is practical and no normalization errors exist. At that point the database is ready for performance denormalization, but only when necessary. You want to know the perfect normalization model or something very near to it, from which to start performance denormalization. At issue is the understanding of what normalization errors exist in a denormalized database. So when does the normalization process stop? It stops when:

- The performance goals are met.
- The number of individual relations becomes too large, and the resulting joins will incur far too much overhead for the database management system.
- Further decomposition will not preserve FDs.

Consider the relation R(<u>Name</u>, City, Street, City, State, Zip). It has the FD Zip → City, State. It becomes a matter of choice to decompose further with the FD Codes(<u>Zip</u>, City, State). A join must occur for each complete address.

Managing Denormalization and the Dependency Model

When our database is denormalized, we must take special precautions to prevent update anomalies or queries with false output. We can do this by building a complete list of dependencies that exist within the database. The database is normalized to the point where further decomposition will not preserve an FD. We now have our dependency model.

The dependency model is very important for ongoing maintenance and is the schema we discussed earlier, an example being the relation R(A, B, C, D) with the FD AB → C, D. At this point, denormalization can start. As we denormalize, we must "tag" each FD that is no longer valid because of the denormalization. The database administrator's (DBA) task is to limit/control updates or queries to these FDs. Either limit access by using a view on SQL Server or a query on Microsoft Access. Both the SQL Server view and the Microsoft Access query can be managed with permissions. A SQL Server trigger is another tool for alerting the user of the invalidity of the query.

Unless you are the architect of a Structured Query Language (SQL) database, maintenance of an existing database is difficult, if not impossible, without a schema that includes the dependencies. Simply having an ERD is not sufficient. The dependencies must also be known. This is because nearly all production database systems are denormalized, and adding dependencies to an existing system where the dependencies are not normalized and are unknown will not necessarily result in proper operation.

The first step to denormalization is deceptively easy and a potential trap. A computed column represents a denormalized database. The other deceptively easy and potential trap is overlapping keys, which creates a Boyce-Codd Normal Form (BCNF) error. A BCNF error is typically not designed into the database, but occurs when the DBA adds additional keys to improve performance.

Building the Transform Model

The Transform Model is the creation of tables in the database of your choice. There is no discussion of this model since the Transform Model represents the physical files, devices, and segments. Data-modeling tools create the Transform Model (required tables) automatically. Figure 18-13 represents the Transform Model of the SQL Server Pubs database, which is the physical mapping of the logical database. The logical view (Fully Attributed Model) is illustrated in Figure 18-10. Follow these steps to create Figure 18-13, the Transform Model of the SQL Server Pubs database:

1. Select `Reverse Engineer` from the ER*win* **Task** menu.
2. Select `PROGRESS`

3. Select NEXT
4. Select `SQL Server` and `6.X`.
5. Select NEXT
6. Select NEXT (We're using the defaults.)
7. Enter the SQL Server UID, PWD, the database name (Pubs for this example), and the server name.
8. Select `Connect`
9. Select `PHYSICAL` from the combo box on the ER*win* toolbar.
10. The Pubs database physical model is displayed, which is shown in Figure 18-13.

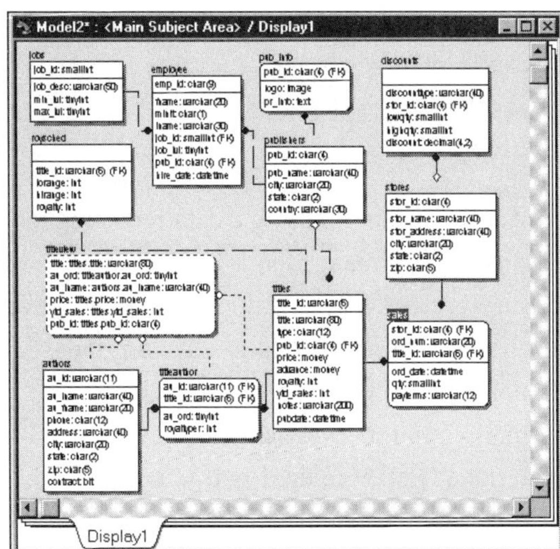

FIGURE 18-13 The Transform Model of the SQL Server Pubs database.

BUSINESS IMPLEMENTATION MODEL

This is our last stop. I won't bore you with a lot of minutiae, but this is where we place all of the remaining documentation. We captured information for the Business Scope Model, the Requirements Model, and the Business Rules Model but that information said nothing about physical implementation. The Business Implementation Model consists of all the documentation required to build the system. In this context, I am not referring to program documentation, but all requirements, specifications, and programming notes. The purpose of the Business Implementation Model is to capture the business rules, the reasoning behind the business rules, and the programmatic manifestation of the business rules. Business rules change with time and it is important to capture the original reasoning and assumptions related to the business rules. This information is linked with a foreign key to the Requirements Model. Documentation we should consider includes:

- Programmatic manifestations of our business rules.
- Physical mapping of the transform model and why the choices were made.
- Complete documentation of the denormalization model.
- Other issues pertinent to the application.

Key Point Summary

Data modeling does not start with purchasing a data-modeling tool and proceeding to normalize relations. The normalization is suspect when the developer does not understand the business rules. Normalization is not an intuitive ad hoc procedure. Normalization relies on the Armstrong axioms, an understanding of business rules, and functional dependence.

A database is normalized to the level necessary to remove normalization errors. Typically a well-designed database does not go beyond third normal form. After the necessary normalization is complete, the database may be denormalized for performance. Legacy databases were not designed as relational databases; hence normalizing a legacy database often goes beyond third normal form.

Applying What You've Learned

The Microsoft *Analyzing Requirements and Defining Solution Architectures* examination requires a significant knowledge of logical data design. We'll forego the normal *instant assessment* section at the end of this chapter and replace that with a series of labs based on a real-life case study that was introduced in Chapter 17. Each lab corresponds to one logical data design objective of the 70-100 certification test.

Answers to the laboratories are found in Appendix C.

Lab Exercises

This is a series of labs constructed from the real world business rambling found in Listing 17-1 and the case study found at the end of Chapter 17. We won't repeat the case study here, however you are asked to respond to each of the 70-100 logical data design objectives and the related topics. You'll find all the answers for these labs in Appendix C. Figure 18-14 represents a portion of the entities derived from the case study and Listing 17-1.

LAB 18.48 *Group data into entities by applying normalization rules*

The goal of this objective is to measure your understanding of entities and the use of normalization rules. Approximately half of the questions deal with entity types with the remainder of the questions dealing with normalization issues.

1. Describe an *independent* entity. Name an *independent* entity in Figure 18-14.
2. Describe a *characteristic* entity. Name a *characteristic* entity in Figure 18-14.
3. What is an *associative* entity? How is an *associative* entity used? Name an *associative entity* in Figure 18-14.
4. What is a *categorization* entity? Name a *categorization* entity in Figure 18-14.
5. What is the schema for the 5-tuple (OrderID, ItemID, Description, OrderDate, Quantity)? You may assume that OrderID and ItemID represent a composite key.
6. What is the normalization error in question five?
7. Describe a Boyce Codd normal form error.
8. Describe a third normal form error.
9. Describe a second normal form error.
10. Describe a first normal form error.

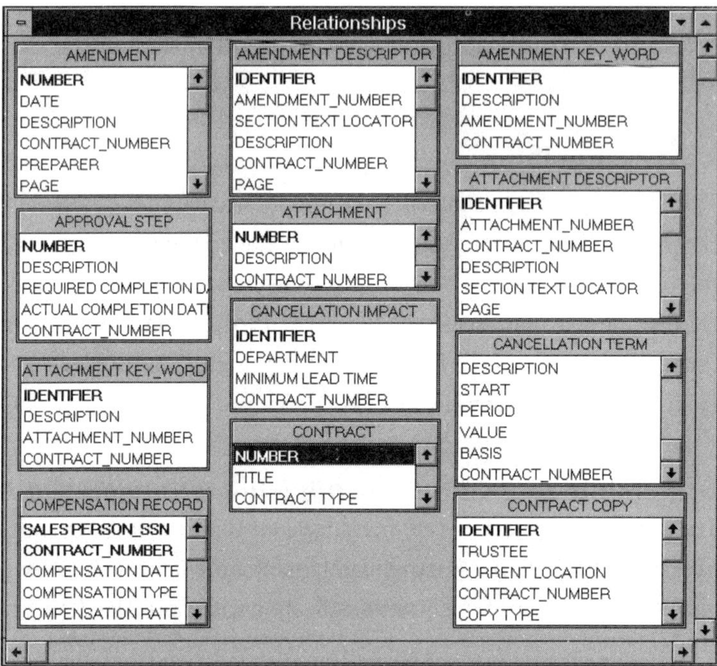

FIGURE 18-14 A few entities from the case study.

LAB 18.49 *Specify the relationships between entities*

These questions will measure your understanding of the relationships between entities.

1. What is common about the relationships of the characteristic entities shown in Figure 18-14?
2. Describe the relationship between the *Contract* entity and the *Compensation Record* entity shown in Figure 18-14.
3. Describe the relationship between the *Contract* entity and the *Approval Step* entity shown in Figure 18-14.
4. Describe the relationship between the *Contract* entity and the *Attachment entity* shown in Figure 18-14.
5. What important factor does a relationship between entities determine?
6. Describe the semantic, (not graphical) rules for describing a relationship between entities (hint: consider only formal entities and not a many-to-many).

LAB 18.50 *Choose the foreign key that will enforce a relationship between entities and will ensure referential integrity*

Foreign keys enforce relationships. These questions will measure your understanding of foreign keys.

1. How is a foreign key derived (hint: Recall the Armstrong axioms)?
2. What is a characteristic of a foreign key?
3. What is the prevalent use of foreign keys in Figure 18-14?
4. What is the foreign key issue of Figure 18-14?
5. Characterize the creation of a foreign key.
6. What can be said formally about a foreign key?
7. Discuss the issue of *identifying* versus *non-identifying* relationships with respect to foreign keys.

LAB 18.51 *Identify the business rules that relate to data integrity*

Discuss the objective. This objective requires revisiting Chapter 17 and the business rambling found in Listing 17-1. The answer to this objective requires an understanding of the analysis process that is applied to a business rambling.

LAB 18.52 *Incorporate business rules and constraints into the data model*

The answer to this objective is easy if you've read and understood this chapter and Chapter 17. How are business constraints and rules incorporated into the data model? The term *data model* is generic within the objective context and does not refer to a specific model discussed in this chapter. The answer to the objective is rooted in understanding how business rules and constraints are incorporated into a tiered-component architecture.

LAB 18.53 *Identify appropriate level of denormalization*

Denormalization is accomplished to improve performance. Too many table joins induces poor database performance. These questions will measure you understanding of denormalization.

1. Does denormalization exist in Figure 18-14?
2. Discuss inadvertent denormalization.
3. Discuss planned denormalization and give an example.

LAB 18.54 *Develop a database that uses general database development standards and guidelines*

Of course the short answer to this objective is to use presented methodology. However, that's too much of a simplification. Discuss in detail how to develop a database that uses general database development standards and guidelines. Consider both Chapters 17 and 18 in your answer.

Application Design

CHAPTER

19

About Chapter 19

Welcome to Chapter 19 and application design. This is the third of four chapters devoted exclusively to the Microsoft 70-100 certification exam. Chapter 17 is the most important chapter in the book, and I believe Chapter 18 is the most difficult chapter for you, the reader. This chapter is the most difficult for me. My challenge is to make you an accomplished programmer in a handful of pages. This is a formidable challenge and I hope that I'm up to the task at hand.

This chapter addresses application design, which consists of conceptual, logical, and physical design. The labs for this chapter address the corresponding 70-100 objective sections entitled "Developing the Conceptual and Logical Design for an Application," "Developing the Technical Architecture for a Solution," and "Deriving the Physical Design."

Conceptual Design

This section uses the system requirements collected in Chapter 17 and distills those requirements into a conceptual and logical system design. Rational Rose 98 Enterprise from Rational Rose Corporation is the tool used in this section to both create the conceptual and logical application design. Rational Rose expresses the conceptual design model in the Universal Modeling Language (UML). Microsoft Visual Modeler is an entry-level modeling tool that is a subset of Rational Rose, which only supports logical modeling and not conceptual modeling. To start modeling at the logical level places the intended system at risk since a conceptual model doesn't exist and the logical model depends upon the conceptual model.

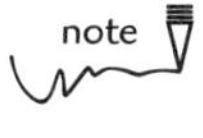

Conceptual modeling is the user perspective defined in business terms. Logical or physical model aspects are not a consideration of conceptual design and will taint the conceptual design model validity. The corruption occurs with the inclusion of logical or physical model aspects that are not defined in user or business terms.

Why Model?

A model is a reality check on our understanding of the world around us, since a model is a representation of real-world phenomena. The model is derived from either the spoken or written word, and therefore it is subject to misunderstanding and misinterpretation. One way to test the model's validity is to present the model to the source that supplied the original information. The model is considered valid when the feedback obtained from the source matches the original material.

Our vision doesn't always serve us well. The mind combines the visually observed images with those of an a priori expectation and the result is often less than reality. I've raced bicycles for many years, and I've witnessed this visualization problem many times. A motorist driving up to an intersection stops, looks left and right for other automobiles, and then proceeds through the intersection. This motorist is oblivious to the fact that I'm within one hundred feet of the intersection and approaching at a speed slightly over twenty miles per hour. There's a sudden look of shock on the motorist's face as I cave in the driver-side door. The motorist was unaware of my presence until impact. Even though I wear florescent spandex to make myself more visible, the motorist had the a priori expectation of other cars, not cyclists.

Likewise if I place my car keys in the same spot every day, I always expect to find them there. If on only one day I place the keys in another obvious location, I won't be able to find them because I expect to find them in the normal location. It's only after I'm able to purge the expected location from my mind that the keys reappear.

There's the simple lack of communication. This occurs when the developers are not immersed in the customer's corporate culture. We saw an example in Chapter 17 where the manager used the term "back-office system." The developer, not immersed in the culture, assumed the manager was referring to Microsoft SQL Server. In reality, last year's benefit plan data was the "back-office system." This project did not use visual modeling for conceptual design. It started directly from the specifications with the logical design phase using Microsoft Visual Modeler. The project failed because the manager was *too busy to provide the necessary interviews* and communicated only through an intermediary. The project should have been stopped immediately once the manager started refusing interviews. The second reason the project failed was because the developer did not do visual modeling, which would have validated the requirements analysis phase.

note

I recall an interview with a client in the 70s for a turnkey system that consisted of receivables, payables, inventory, and order-entry. As I was interviewing the president of this small distributorship, he made the comment. "Why are you asking me questions? You're supposed to be the expert." From the client's perspective, I was no different from the air-conditioning maintenance man. That perspective still prevails today in smaller companies.

Let's review very briefly the primary reasons a system fails. I introduced these reasons in Chapter 17 as the primary sources of system failures. As we examine each of these reasons for system failure you'll see that the lack of communication is a significant factor in project failures.

- ***Changing or incomplete requirements*** — The users are unable to accurately articulate their needs and the developers are not able to articulate their understanding of the issues. The design iterations are occurring during the coding phase rather than the requirements analysis phase. Microsoft Solution Frameworks (MSF) is a methodology that allows development to start before there is complete buyoff on the project. Microsoft reports many successes using MSF, however they never report the failures. Some have been colossal with losses in terms of many millions of dollars.
- ***Users' lack of involvement*** — The lack of user involvement in the system design can be traced back to several root causes. The first may be that management did not give strong enough marching orders that the new system was strategically necessary for the business entity.
  - Fear of change on the part of users is always an issue. Users with a currently inadequate system often assume the role of hero or heroine by solving problems not addressed by current system inadequacies. The new system can take away their sense of identity and perceived entrepreneurial role.
  - Lack of user involvement is a certain sign that the developers are not immersed in the culture.
  - User intimidation by the developers is always a possible reason for the lack of user participation. The user's computer skill level will be less than that of the developers and it important that conceptual design issues always be discussed in business terms user needs. Technological issues are not addressed in conceptual design.
  - There is always the risk that the developers feel they've "done this before." That may be true, but a cocky attitude will always freeze out the users. Since the developers have done this before, there is a risk that the developers will not listen to the users and will implement their own version of the system. The delivered system may be technically correct, however the users will find some means of rejecting it.

- *Inadequate resources* — There are two definitions of *inadequate resources*. The first is a poor system design that uses inappropriate or inadequate hardware. This occurs when a system is designed for the existing hardware. The correct approach is to design the system and then determine the hardware required. The second definition of *inadequate resources* is the shortage of developers. The real lack of resources can be a lack of development skills. Yes, there are many pretenders, but there is a significant difference between reciting minutiae and being able to deliver a system that is viable, satisfies user requirements, and is scalable. We have shrink-wrapped software, users expect shrink-wrapped solutions, and unfortunately many developers have shrink-wrapped certifications. (My definition of a shrink-wrapped certification is one that is not supported by relevant experience.)
- *Unrealistic expectations* — This should never be a reason for system failure. Users need to clearly articulate their requirements. Nothing can be assumed. The developers should address these requirements during the conceptual design phase. Conceptual design always starts with the topmost business objectives as articulated by the CEO, CIO, or CFO. Corporate goals for the system establish the limiting parameters. System failures of this category occur when systems are designed from the bottom up. System failures due to unreal expectations occur when the topmost business objectives are not articulated clearly. For example, suppose a company's management assumed their new e-mail system would be a collaborative design tool, but to users it was just another e-mail system. Clear articulation of the requirements must occur at all levels within the enterprise.

  The worst type of unreal expectation occurs when a project sponsor intentionally sets an unrealistically low budget and an optimistic project manager is afraid to say no.
- *Lack of management support* — Either intentional or unintentional, the lack of management support is the death knell of any project. Maybe there's a hidden agenda and the project is targeted for failure, which is the case for the example discussed above. We're left with two other choices. Either the manager is too busy, in which case it's a management failure not to delegate responsibility or the manager is incompetent. In either situation, the manager should be dismissed.

- *Poor or minimal planning*— Rapid Application Development (RAD) tools encourages an environment where the development of code is too easy. The pressure to create *apparently* useful code comes at the expense of not analyzing a proper choice of technology, deployment strategy, or maintenance strategy. Even when deployment and maintenance plans are considered, there is still the problem of contingency plans and business continuation when a failure occurs. Failing to plan for adequate or parallel testing contributes to system failure. Planning requirements extend beyond the constructing of modules.
- *Lack of experience with required technologies*— This is not a communication failure but a failure on the part of management. Failures of this category can't be blamed on the developers because team selection is management's responsibility. Many organizations today believe that they can survive without an Information Systems (IS) department, something unheard of ten or fifteen years ago. As a Microsoft Solution Provider (MSP), I received a referral from Microsoft. The referral was to a regional sales office of a Fortune 1000 international company. The sales manager had asked the corporate IS department for a sales management database system. None was forthcoming, not because it couldn't be done, but because of budgetary constraints. The regional sales manager then sent his secretary to a Microsoft Authorized Training and Education Center (ATEC) for a one week course on Microsoft Access. Time passed and six months later I got a call from Microsoft about a locked database. I cannot adequately describe the horror that existed within that database. The regional sales manager was incredulous when I quoted a fee of thousands of dollars to preserve the current data and completely redo the whole system. Unfortunately with shrink-wrapped software comes an expectation of shrink-wrapped solutions.

Before we move on to creating a conceptual design with the Universal Modeling Language (UML), let's state the value of the conceptual design. *A conceptual model is a mechanism that provides feedback to the user and ensures that the developers understand the problem at hand.* When the feedback from the developer's conceptual model matches the user's original requirements, it can be assumed that the developers understand the issues. A conceptual design is defined in both user and business terms, which enables users to calibrate the developer's understanding of the issues. The conceptual design model bridges the gap between the logical design and the requirements analysis phase of a project.

Building the Conceptual Design Model

The conceptual model consists of five distinct elements. Taken together, these five models provide a clear statement of the business as it currently exists, along with the business strategies, goals, and proposed policies of the new system. The five models are:

- *Context Model*—A description of the current environment that includes all policies and procedures. Also included are organization or physical constraints and any other issues. The Context Model starts with a mission statement and includes all external and internal influences.
- *Process Model*—UML use case diagrams, which are representations of the scenarios derived from business rambling distillations, constitute the Process Model. UML use case diagrams should clearly model how the business functions today. Both *before* and *after* versions of this model give a better perspective of the proposed project. The Process Model depicts a use case scenario in which actors interact with UML use cases.
- *Task Sequence Model*—UML sequence diagrams are used to represent the different phases of a multi-task process. A Task Sequence Model represents the ordered steps of a use case scenario.
- *Workflow Process Model*—This is not a UML model, but a Microsoft model that is an aggregation of use case scenarios. Figure 19-8 is an example of use case aggregation. The model is manually constructed and represents the complete workflow process. This model is decomposed into use cases, which are in turn represented by various task sequence models.
- *Physical Environment Model*—The physical environment does not always change for a software application. When the physical environment changes, this model should reflect all physical environment changes. Some changes may be to plant and equipment that may fall outside the purview of software application development, however new equipment such as computers, office furniture, and fixtures are included in this model.

This section will look at each of these models more closely.

Context model

The Context Model represents the developer's understanding of the enterprise including goals, strategies, and processes. The developer starts the Context Model by including the contents of the Business Scope Model from Chapter 17. The Business Scope Model is built during the business rambling distillation and is a detailed statement of business strategy, goals, assets, and processes.

The Organizational Model is a subset of the Context Model, which is the enterprise perspective. Let's start first with the Organizational Model perspective. We'll want to include:

- Enterprise Architecture issues
- Infrastructure Issues
- Organizational Charts
- Policy and Procedure manuals
- Mission statements and Directive memos

The Implementation ContextModel is a description of the implementation environment, which is also a subset of the Context Model. The model describes the current environment and the proposed changes to the current environment. Implementation issues to consider include:

- Business Processes
- Process Constraints
- Worker Process Participation (This will overlap the Process Model outlined below.)
- Current Process Deliverables
- Expected deliverables from new processes

In summary, the Context Model is a detailed statement of the enterprise mission, goals, culture, and processes as they currently exist. The Context Model is also a statement of the expected changes to current mission, goals, culture, and processes. The goal of the Context Model is to provide feedback of the developer's understanding of the *big picture* and not just a perspective of writing program code.

Process model (UML use case diagrams)

The Process Model is UML based. The source for the Process Model is the Requirements Model of Chapter 17, which is a distillation of the business rambling into atomic sentences. The Requirements Model describes the *what* perspective and not the *how* perspective. This means that the Process Model describes business processes and not program processes. The sentences within the Requirements Model can be further distilled with these rules:

- Active sentences that describe the relationship of the independent data entity (see Chapter 18). *Publisher publishes books. Publisher* is the independent entity.
- Passive sentences that describe dependent (characteristic) data entities (see Chapter 17). *Book is published by publisher. Book* is the dependent or characteristic entity.
- Transitive verbs and verb phrases that describe or hint at relationships with objects (a scenario). *Clerk rents rooms. Clerk* is an actor in a use case scenario (see Figure 19-4 or Figure 19-5 for an example of a use case).
- Declarative verbs or procedural statements that describe or hint at services. *Checkout time is 11:00 AM.* A *checkout* procedure exists. This procedure is sequenced (see Task Sequence Model).
- Adjectives and possessive noun phrases describe or hint at object attributes. *The daily room rate is $175.* The room has a *rate* attribute.

We used ER*win* from Platinum Technology in Chapter 18. The ER*win* product is very easy to use once you make an investment in understanding the IDEF1X notation. The same is true of UML and Rational Rose 98 from Rational Corporation — we must first master the notation. There are complete books devoted to UML, so I'll only sketch the highlights of the language. Your authoritative source for UML is *The Unified Modeling Language Guide* Addison Wesley, October 1998 by Grady Booch, James Rumbaugh, and Ivar Jacobson (the three amigos). It is my understanding that this was the most popular computer book on Amazon.com in 1998.

UML has nine different types of diagrams. We're only interested in the behavior of a system for the Process Model and not the system implementation. The Process Model we're building will only have UML use case diagrams and UML sequence diagrams. Although a UML collaboration diagram is classified as a behavior type diagram, I'm omitting the UML collaborative diagram from the Process Model since users will not relate to objects. Remember that the importance of the

Process Model is to model system behavior in user terms, not abstract developer terms. Table 19-1 enumerates the different UML diagrams.

TABLE 19-1 UML DIAGRAM TYPES

UML Diagram Type	*Description*
Class Diagram	An implementation diagram that shows a set of classes, interfaces, and collaborations along with their relationships.
Object Diagram	An implementation diagram that shows a set of objects and their relationships.
Use Case Diagram	A behavior diagram that shows use cases and special classes (actors).
Sequence Diagram	A behavior diagram is an interaction diagram that shows the message sequences in time-order.
Collaboration Diagram	A behavior diagram that shows the structural organization of objects that send and receive messages.
Statechart Diagram	An implementation diagram, which is a state machine. The state machine consists of states, transitions, events, and activities.
Activity Diagram	An implementation diagram that illustrates the flow from activity to activity within the system.
Component Diagram	An implementation diagram that illustrates component organization and dependencies.
Deployment Diagram	An implementation diagram that shows the node configuration and the components that reside on the different nodes.

Actors and use cases

UML use case diagrams model the behavior of a system. The first UML concept we'll need for a use case diagram is that of an actor. An actor in the UML sense is something or someone that interacts with the system and exchanges data. Before we create our actors and use cases, let's take a peek at Rational Rose. Figure 19-1 is a view of Rational Rose 98 Enterprise edition. Actors or use cases can be created by right clicking *Use Case View* and then selecting NEW | Actor or New Use Case. Double clicking *Main* under *Use Case View* displays the use case diagram.

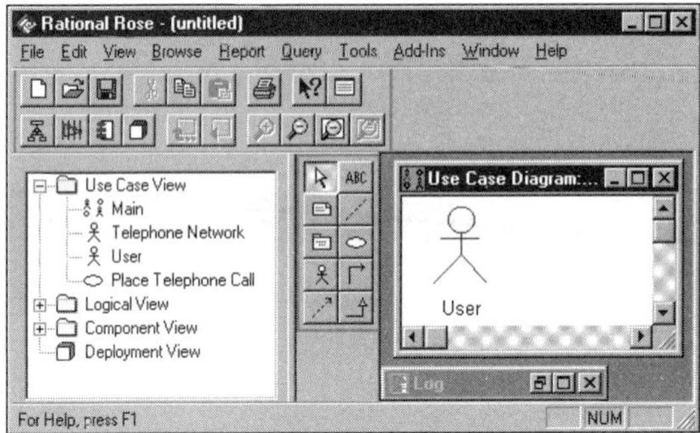

FIGURE 19-1 Rational Rose 98 Enterprise Edition with an actor displayed.

Actors assume roles. The actor need not be an individual as shown in Figure 19-2 where an actor represents both an individual and a system. Use cases are determined by examining all aspects of an actor.

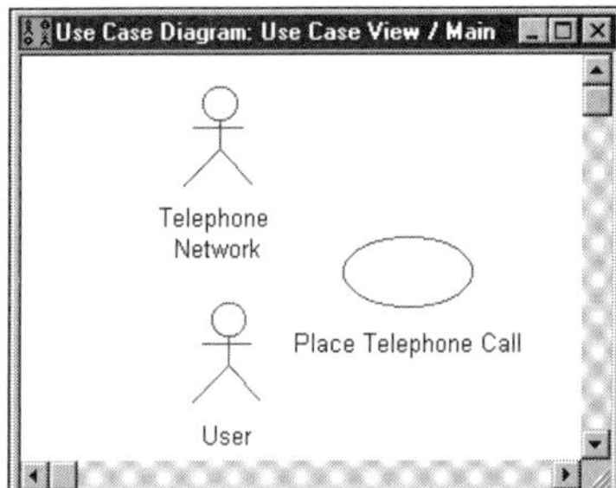

FIGURE 19-2 Two actors with a use case.

Actor relationships

Relationships exist between actors and use cases, but no relationships (Table 19-2) are defined in Figure 19-2 since only a use case and two actors are defined. A relationship between an actor and a use case *communicates association*. The association determines the direction of navigation, which can be from the actor to the use case, from the use case to the actor, or bi-directional. Figure 19-3 illustrates two associations that communicate both to and from an actor. Note that Figure 19-3 accurately models a specific behavior, which is something that cannot be done with logical modeling tools such as Microsoft Visual Modeler. Selecting *Unidirectional Association* from the **Use Case** toolbar and using the mouse to draw between the actor and use case creates directed associations. The arrow direction represents the drawing direction and the communication direction.

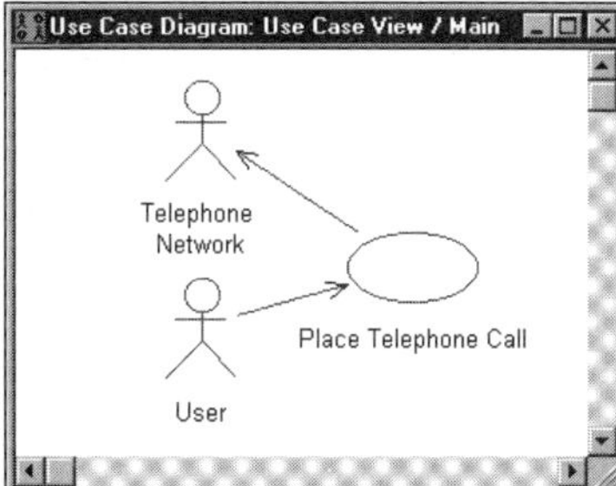

FIGURE 19-3 Modeling directed associations in a use case diagram.

Figure 19-3 does not depict all UML relationships. There are four different types of relationships in the UML, but only generalizations and associations are elements of a use case diagram. The other relationships model implementation aspects of a system and not behavioral aspects. Table 19-1 enumerates the UML relationships.

TABLE 19-2 UML RELATIONSHIPS

RELATIONSHIP	*DESCRIPTION*
Dependency	Symbolized by: ---------> A dependency is a semantic relationship between two things. This is equivalent to a data dependency discussed in Chapter 18, however the dependency is between *things*, which may not be data entities. A dependency is rendered as a dashed line with an optional label and may not be directed.
Association	Symbolized by:(0..1 ______ * An association is a link between objects. The link may be directed and optionally may include multiplicity (cardinality). This is a structural relationship with optional labels. An association is the only relationship permitted between an actor and a use case. Multiplicity is expressed as: 1 Exactly one 0..* Zero or more 1..* One or more 0..1 Zero or one 5..7 Specific range (5, 6, or 7) 5..7,10 Combination (5, 6, 7, or 10)

Continued

TABLE 19-2 UML RELATIONSHIPS (continued)

RELATIONSHIP	DESCRIPTION
	Aggregations are a special type of association that represents a relationship between a whole and its parts. Aggregations also have an optional cardinality and labels. Aggregations are not an element of a use case diagram and are represented by the association symbol prefaced with a ♫.
Generalization	Symbolized by: ————▷
	A generalization establishes a parent-child relationship. The child shares the structure and behavior of the parent.
Realization	Symbolized by: ----------▷
	A realization is a semantic relationship that occurs between interfaces and components or between use cases and collaborations. A realization is a guaranteed contract in the COM sense (see Chapters 1-10). A realization is an element of UML but is not defined in Microsoft Visual Modeler since Microsoft Visual Modeler does not support conceptual modeling.

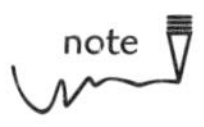

UML only defines the relationships of Table 19-2. A UML aggregation is not a relationship but a special form of an association relationship and is therefore not represented in Table 19-2.

Now that all the relationships are defined, let's expand Figure 19-3 with a generalization relationship. In Figure 19-4 the actors *Private User* and *Corporate User* share a generalization relationship with the actor *User*.

Use case relationships

Use cases can be shared and extended with a special version of a generalization relationship. UML defines the concept of *stereotype* that either *extends* or *uses* an existing use case. A stereotype is included within guillemets {<< >} and is placed along the relation line. Figure 19-4 is expanded in Figure 19-5 with two stereotypes, one of which *extends* a use case and the other *uses* a use case. The Verify Phone Card use case is a *uses* stereotype that is reused by the Place telephone Call use case. The Place Collect Call use case extends the Place Telephone Call use case. Figure 19-5 illustrates the two stereotypes.

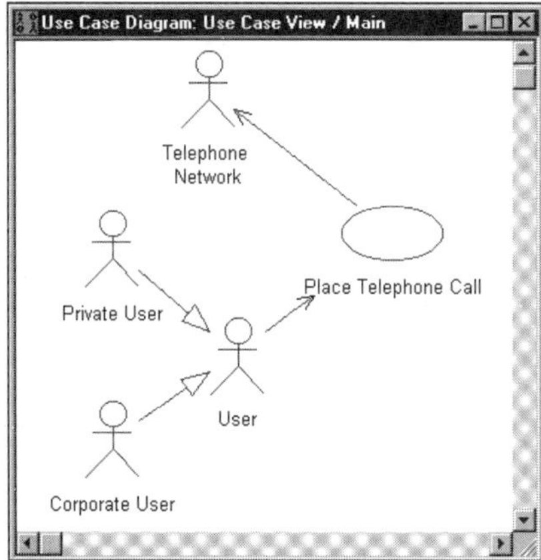

FIGURE 19-4 Modeling a generalization in a use case diagram.

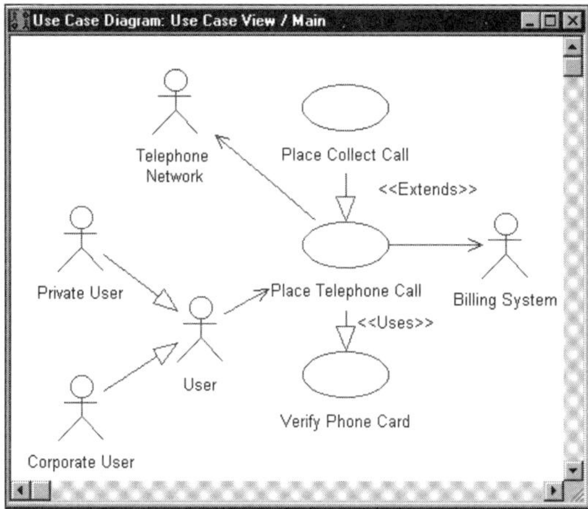

FIGURE 19-5 A use case relationship with two stereotypes.

That completes the sketch of the use case diagrams. There are no hard and fast rules to the contents of a use case diagram. A complex system will have many use case diagrams. Just remember that the goal of the use case diagram is to demonstrate to users that you, the developer, understand the system requirements.

I've added an additional actor in Figure 19-5 for the purpose of illustrating our UML sequence diagram, which is next. Let's move on to the Task Sequence Model, which is a collection of UML sequence diagrams.

Task Sequence Model (UML Sequence Diagrams)

A UML Sequence Diagram illustrates scenario interactions in a time sequence, which are steps that an actor (not necessarily a person) executes in performing a task. Sequence diagrams represent the developer's understanding of the scenarios. User acceptance of the UML sequence diagrams is the user's acknowledgement that the developers understand the processes.

UML sequence diagrams represent use case scenarios. Figure 19-6 is a Rational Rose browser view after right-clicking *Place Telephone Call* and selecting NEW | Sequence Diagram. Sequence diagrams are an exploded view of a use case scenario. Each use case that involves more than one operation should have a sequence diagram.

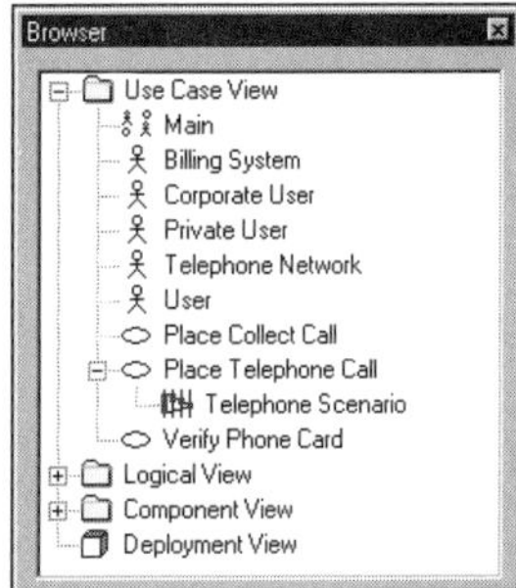

FIGURE 19-6 A view of the Rational Rose browser window.

Let's create a UML sequence diagram with only two objects. The sequence diagram in Figure 19-7 is for illustrative purposes only. The Telephone Scenario can involve more than two objects.

Figure 19-7 was created with these steps:

1. Double-click the sequence diagram in the browser.
2. Click and drag the **User** icon to the sequence diagram.
3. Click *Object* on the **Sequence Diagram** toolbar and paint the object on the sequence diagram. Enter the object name while it is selected.
4. Repeat the above procedure for the second object.
5. Click and drag the **Billing System** icon to the sequence diagram.

6. Connect the objects by selecting *Object Message* on the **Sequence Diagram** toolbar and connect the objects. The painting direction determines the message direction. Enter the message text while the *Object Message* is selected.
7. Click the **Message to Self** icon on the **Sequence Diagram** toolbar and drop the icon at the second object. Enter the message.

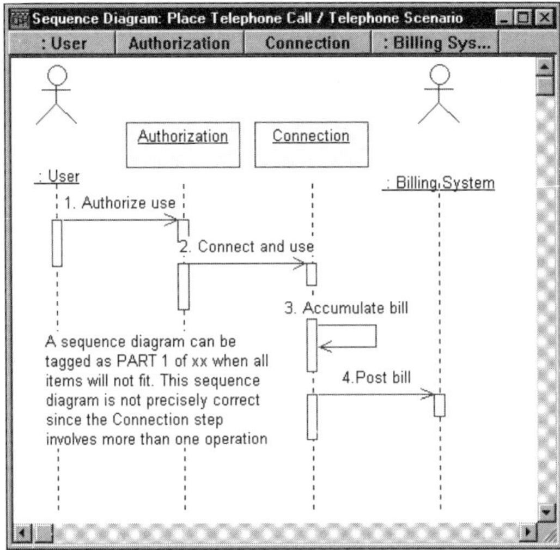

FIGURE 19-7 Our use case example as a UML sequence diagram.

There's not too much to a UML sequence diagram. The issue is to mirror back to the users the developer's understanding of the scenarios. Let's move on to the next step in building the Conceptual Model, which is the Workflow Process Model.

Workflow process model

This model is the fourth in our series of scenario types constructed during a project's conceptual design phase. Rational Rose does not support a Workflow Process Model. The Workflow Process Model is an aggregation of use case scenarios, each of which represents some stage of the overall process. There are three distinct use case scenarios in the Workflow Process Model of Figure 19-8.

The Workflow Process Model is constructed manually using a Visio(c) drawing tool. The Workflow Process Model does not exist within the scope of UML diagrams and any workflow or process-modeling notation can be used to create the model. Microsoft uses the notation of a circle to represent a person and a square to represent an artifact. Artifacts are objects that are either informational or real world objects. Flow between the artifacts is indicated with a directed arrow. Flow is through a medium and is labeled as such. Mediums of transfer typically include paper, fax, disk, or a network.

A UML Task Sequence Diagram should represent each artifact. UML Task Sequence Diagrams are a direct result of applying decomposition to the Workflow Process Model. Figure 19-8 illustrates a Workflow Process Model with a cash receipts artifact. This is the artifact that was decomposed into the UML Task Sequence Diagram in Figure 19-7. The medium type is not indicated and is implied disk transfers.

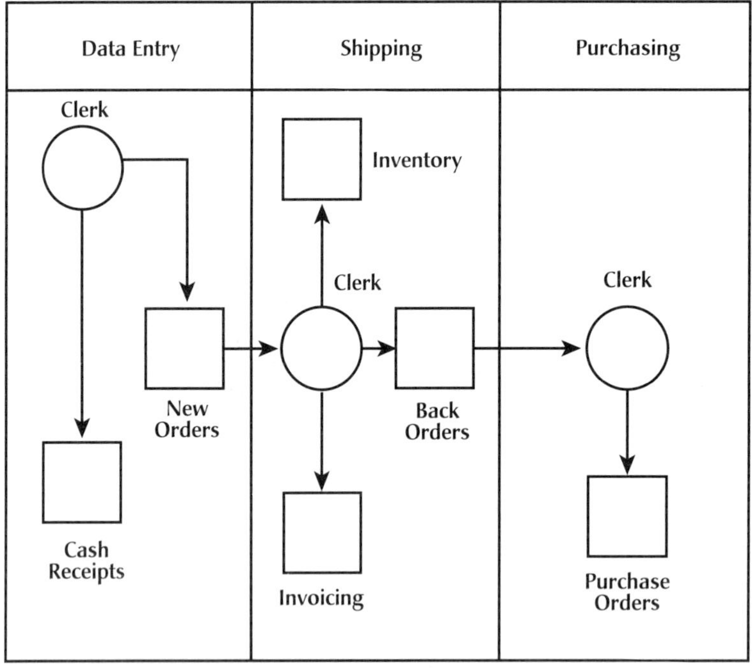

FIGURE 19-8 Workflow Process Model of an order-entry system.

Only informational artifacts are illustrated in Figure 19-8, but artifacts are anything that plays a part in the workflow process. This includes departments and external customers with linkages, such as an Extranet. The purpose of a Workflow Process Model is to:

- Identify the number of artifacts consumed.
- Calculate the cost per artifact and aggregate that sum.
- Calculate the unit time required for each artifact.

This is not a book on reprocess engineering, but modeling the workflow is a necessary step in the conceptual design of a project. There is significant risk involved in reprocess engineering. Any efforts in that direction should be tempered since the local dynamics of hidden agendas and local politics may doom such an effort. In general, individuals are resistant to change. I've had the unhappy experience of a system being sabotaged by client staff members that perceived a new system as a threat.

Physical Environment Model This is the last of the conceptual design scenarios. The Physical Environment Model is only mentioned for closure. Plant and equipment do not normally change for a software application. What can and often does change is process workflow, which should be thoroughly documented. The documentation should contain a statement of the workflow as it presently exists and the proposed changes. Care must be taken so that a proposed workflow does not interrupt an existing workflow that is not being replaced.

As with the previous model, UML does not support a Physical Environment Model. A Physical Environment Model is an ad hoc model that illustrates the physical, environmental, and ergonomic conditions that either constrain or support the proposed project. The model can include:

- Geographic site locations of resources and personnel.
- Work area layouts that are represented by floor plans or photographs.
- Artifacts that are used in the workflow process. These can be the same artifacts discussed in the Workflow Process Model.
- Create a resource inventory by identifying the physical plant and facility. The inventory will identify equipment, computers, furniture, lighting, telephone, and network resources. New buildings are often pre-wired for a local area network, while older buildings may require installing a complete network.

There is no particular format suggested for the Physical Environment Model. The important issue is that the developers communicate their understanding of the environment for the proposed new project.

The five models tie together all aspects of the enterprise and define the enterprise as it exists today, the expected changes to processes, workflow patterns, and the corporate culture. The models also identify the consequences of implementing a new system. Too often developers are unaware of the consequences of their actions.

Logical Design

Logical design is the second step of application design. The conceptual design represents the user's perspective while the logical design represents the developer's perspective. The process of logical design is to construct a logical model that mirrors the user requirements using both the UML use case diagrams and the UML sequence diagrams. This section defines logical design, presents a brief historical perspective, and then builds an illustrative logical design.

Basics

A logical model is a hierarchical model. At the top is the definition of a system, which consists of one or more subsystems. Within each subsystem are applications that consist of one or more modules. Within the modules are objects that encapsulate functions, methods, and attributes. The logical arrangement and relationships between the various system elements constitute a logical design. The purpose of logical design can be summarized as:

- *Grouping by Category* — The objects, modules, and subsystems are defined in the logical design phase. Objects are grouped into modules, modules are grouped into applications, and applications are grouped into subsystems.
- *Grouping by Function within a Category* — Objects grouped within a module should have a natural affinity. Communication is between objects and not between modules. Unrelated objects should not be grouped together.

- *Interface Design* — Logical design describes the relationship between the various elements of the system and how the components interact. How objects communicate is critical to the success of the system. Data should flow smoothly between objects with few transformations.

note **I never start the coding of a system unless I can visualize the data flowing like water from one object to the next throughout the complete system. I want to visualize data that does not undergo perturbations or transformations in any way during the flow. Perturbations are only acceptable for reports, which are dead-end flows. It takes supreme will power to resist coding until I've reached this visualization state.**

We'll create the logical design from the UML sequence diagrams, which are derived from the scenarios. The Microsoft strategy is to create the logical design directly from the scenarios. Such an approach is very high risk since the Microsoft approach doesn't demonstrate to the users that the problem at hand is understood. We already have a user buy off on our logical design since the users approved the UML sequence diagrams. All we have to do is translate the UML sequence diagrams into objects in architecture, which is a relatively easy task.

Logical program design is not a new programming topic. The Microsoft approach is iterative decomposition during the logical design phase, which is independent of user approval. In my opinion this is wrong and engenders risk. The design approach presented in this book is an iterative decomposition during the conceptual design phase with the results of the decomposition mapped into UML sequence diagrams. The user approves and understands the UML sequence diagrams, which is an indirect approval of the logical design phase. Users must have faith with the Microsoft approach, and of course a very large budget.

The Historical Perspective

The art of designing an application was lost with the advent of the RAD tool and the Microsoft epoch, which started in approximately 1987-1988. The easy to use RAD tool promotes an environment that's *too* easy to use. Too many developers today pile code into form events thereby recreating the spaghetti code that the industry strove for 30 years to eradicate.

NO GESTATION PERIOD

The problem is that RAD tools are too easy to use today and the time between collecting system requirements and writing code is too short. The legacy COBOL specification was a protracted effort. You knew by the time that the specification was complete that all alternatives were considered. Not so today. The applications today are *apparent applications*, which reflect only today's view of the problem. Forty-two percent of all technology projects are abandoned before completion (*Computer World*, March 22, 1999, "Bad Management is to Blame for the IT Skills Crunch"). Maybe the proposed system is not an application at all but a *half-baked idea*, which should be abandoned. Lengthening the conceptual design phase will lengthen the gestation period, which in turn causes *half-baked ideas* to be discarded early in the process. Lengthening the gestation period also means that all alternatives will be considered, which also eliminates *apparent applications* or *today's view of the application*. The conceptual design phase is lengthened when the system decomposition is moved back to the conceptual design phase, which provides the necessary gestation period. A bad design will always remain a bad design even when the gestation period is lengthened.

Microsoft is promoting an n-tier architecture paradigm, which is not new. Tiered architectures have been with us for thirty years. The tiered legacy application does not have a user interface tier, which is the only difference with current architectures. Figure 19-9 illustrates the various application architectures. When all architectures are compared, it is obvious that Microsoft created the ultimate monolithic application architecture with Microsoft Access.

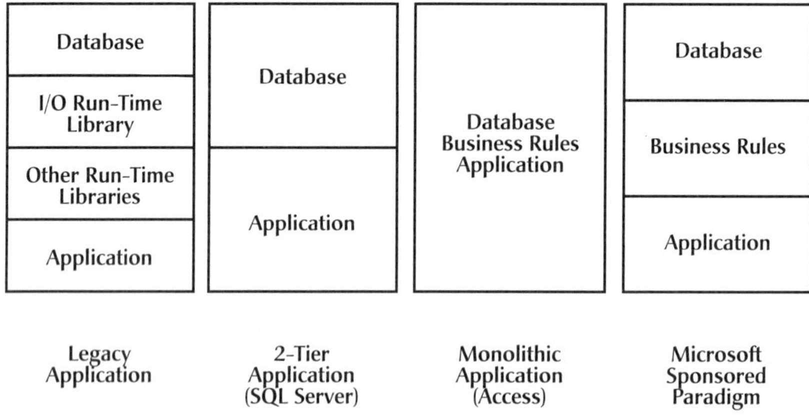

FIGURE 19-9 Various application architectures.

The only similarity between a legacy application and the Microsoft sponsored paradigm is that both represent tiered applications. While Microsoft Access represents the ultimate monolithic application architecture, a legacy application is monolithic since the application is compiled and linked into an immutable binary mass. That is to say, Microsoft Access is a monolithic architecture, while a legacy application is a monolithic program. The Microsoft tiered-application that you run today is not the same tiered application that you ran yesterday. Since the Microsoft architecture depends upon COM (see Chapters 1-10), aggregation and delegation are used to replace dynamic link libraries whenever new software is installed. Think of it as the grim reaper visiting your DLL library. No changes were made to the application, but because the system and the application share DLLs there's always a chance that you're using new code. Another perspective is that the application is rebuilt every time it is run. No so with the legacy application since it is an immutable binary mass. Legacy applications are not always immutable binary masses, but many of them are. I have clients that are running VAX/VMS systems with binaries that have survived many operating system updates without being recompiled.

The differences don't stop there. Imagine each of the hundreds or possibly thousands of components in the Microsoft architecture being connected by an invisible umbilical cord, because that in reality is a fact. COM must marshal data between interfaces and there is a proxy for data that is outgoing from one component and a stub in the receiving component. Let's stop a moment and consider the complexity. First, the application is never stable. DLLs will be replaced at the most inopportune time. I'm sure you know that Murphy's law still reigns supreme. Secondly, the connection mechanism is outlandishly complex and very fragile (see DCOM, Chapter 21). The end result is the developer ends up writing a custom API for each component interface.

I'm confident that you've accepted that fact that there is complexity in the Microsoft sponsored paradigm. Let's look at another Microsoft paradigm that has failed. Client/server technology is the hallmark of the Microsoft epoch with the highest failure rates in the low seventy percent range. The current client server failure rate is approximately fifty percent. Considering the fact that the client/server architecture is only two-tier, and probably an order of magnitude less in complexity than a tiered architecture paradigm (TAP), I have serious doubts about the ultimate success of the Microsoft sponsored TAP. I believe that TAP failure rates will easily exceed those recorded for the client/server paradigm, which reach a high of seventy percent.

It can be argued that the current situation is not Microsoft's fault. I believe it is. Poor design on the part of developers is a direct consequence of the *dumbing-down* approach that Microsoft has taken to software development. The *dumbing-down* approach broadens the software market at the expense of increased project failure rates.

It can also be argued that there is an abrogation of management's responsibility to manage. Technically that's true, but management cannot keep up with the maelstrom of change that emits from the Redmonians. The only individuals that are able to keep up with the technology maelstrom are the loyal certification zealots, which means that many enterprises today are managed from the trenches.

I have a dark foreboding that tier-component architecture failure rates will far exceed those of the client/server paradigm because the new paradigm is much more complex than the client/server paradigm and when coupled with a *dumbed-down* developer community, chaos may ensue.

Both the legacy architecture and the Microsoft sponsored tiered architecture can have an indefinite number of tiers. There is no tier limit for either architecture. In the case of the legacy architecture it's a question of an additional run-time library, while additional components create another tier in the Microsoft sponsored architecture.

Logical Design Goals

Logical design is a top-down process, which is hierarchical. We'll look at logical design from a universal perspective, which is that of an accounting system. The user says, "I want an accounting system." Common subsystems of an accounting system include accounts payable, accounts receivable, payroll, order-entry, a general ledger, and inventory. When the user asks for an order-entry system, the list of subsystems is nearly the same, except for the omission of a payroll system. Figure 19-10 is manually constructed using the Visual Basic TreeView control and illustrates the hierarchical nature of logical system design.

Out goal is to create objects (components) and assimilate those objects into modules of an application. We want to do that in a way that future developers can perform maintenance and at the same time we want a logical and consistent (and hopefully succinct) design that is efficient. We haven't said anything about tiers and we don't need to. Tiers are just a level of support and are equivalent to the legacy run-time library. Tiers (run-time libraries) represent a compartmentalization of common functionality into a public accessible region of the environment. Windows developers have been using DLLs for many years. The only difference is that today Distributed COM (DCOM, see Chapter 21) allows those libraries to be accessed remotely.

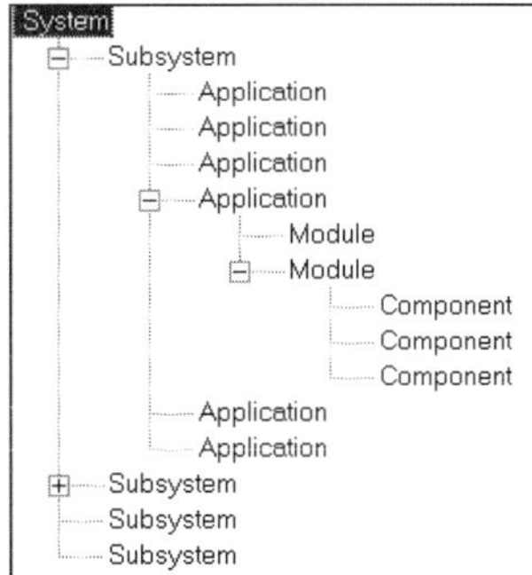

FIGURE 19-10 The hierarchical order of a system.

Logical Design Concepts

The key point of this section is the understanding of the modular design principles of abstraction, encapsulation, cohesion, and coupling. The raw material for creating a logical model comes from the Chapter 17 Requirements Model, which is a repository of semantic distillations. We've used the repository before, and at the risk of being redundant the following is available in the repository:

- Active sentences that describe the relationship of the independent data entity (see Chapter 18). *Publisher publishes books. Publisher* is the independent entity.
- Passive sentences that describe dependent (characteristic) data entities (see Chapter 17). *Book is published by publisher. Book* is the dependent or characteristic entity.
- Transitive verbs and verb phrases that describe or hint at relationships with objects (a scenario). *Clerk rents rooms. Clerk* is an actor in a use case scenario (see Figure 19-4 or Figure 19-5).
- Declarative verbs or procedural statements that describe or hint at services. *Checkout time is 11:00 AM.* A *checkout* procedure exists. This procedure is sequenced (see Task Sequence Model).

- Adjectives and possessive noun phrases describe or hint at object attributes. *The daily room rate is $175*. The room has a *rate* attribute.

We've already identified the logical hierarchy and organizational structure of a system along with the source to fill the structure. What's left to discuss is abstraction, encapsulation, cohesion, and coupling, which are the concepts of how data and services are combined with an interface to create an object and how to place that object in the system structure.

Abstraction

Abstraction is a generalization from the specific to the generic. A customer account is an abstraction that allows the specification of unique customer information, and yet retains the generality of a classification. The properties and attributes of an object are distilled to the point where a general classification occurs. Distinguishing features are maintained as properties or attributes.

We define an object as an abstraction that models behavior, has attributes, and can communicate. An object is an aggregation of services and data, some of which may be encapsulated (see below, Encapsulation). The services model the object's behavior while the object's attributes are defined by the object's data. The object offers the use of selected services through an interface, which is a COM contract.

Identifying objects is the first order of business. If we've done our conceptual design properly, many of the system objects are already identified as elements of a UML Task Sequence Diagram, well maybe not all but most of them.

Creating an object that doesn't exist in a UML Task Sequence Diagram is often intuitive. Assume that there is a collection of services and data attributes. Attributes include **LastPaymentDate, LastPaymentAmount,** and **LongDistance Charges**. The payment attributes are generic. The **LongDistanceCharges** attribute suggests that the object is related to telephones and an object identification such as **TelephoneBill** is a reasonable object identification.

Not all objects are intuitively apparent. The real problem is sifting through the user's expected services (the Requirements Model) and combining related services and data into a meaningful design. Not everything can be combined. The process takes work and the primary goal of any logical design is modularity, which reduces errors and simplifies maintenance. An ancillary benefit of logical design is the reuse of modules. You'll find an example of class reusability in the two classes discussed in Chapter 21, a Data class, which supports the second tier while the Database class supports the third tier. These classes support data creation, reading, updating, and deletion (CRUD). CRUD classes are normally generic and reusable, which means that the classes can often drop directly into either a prototype or a final system version. You'll find these two CRUD classes quite complete with transacted cascading deletes and transacted insertions of parent-child data. I've intentionally left a wart in the classes, and one of the labs in Chapter 21 involves removing that wart.

Encapsulation

Encapsulation is an objected-oriented design technique that hides functionality. Hiding functionality facilitates the creation of abstractions and the notion of black boxes, which promotes modular replacement of components. The only requirement is that both black boxes (components) have the same interface requirements, which may be independent of internal operations. This means that each black box is an independent self-contained unit. Hiding functionality manages complexity and simplifies interfacing with only the minimal functionality exposed. The designer's task is to hide all internal functionality and only expose an interface that supports the necessary services and attributes.

Cohesion

Function cohesion is how closely the services are related. An example of poor functional cohesion is a cash receipts method in a reports component. When we're discussing a general accounting system, reports are often placed in a reporting subsystem. What's not normally done is to define a large system that contains unrelated functionality such as input forms and reports. It's true that cash receipts do require reports, but that's a user interface issue. The reports are still placed in their own subsystem. You'll quickly find that you can leverage many reports since the sign-on dialogs and setup routines may be almost identical.

Cohesion also occurs at the module level. Since we're dealing with related functionality, you can use your newfound skill of using functional dependence (see Chapter 18) in identifying related services and data. Be open to the fact that you might want to create another tier. A good example is addresses within an accounting system. Let's assume that there is a relatively primitive accounting system where the account master only supports two addresses, a bill-to address and a ship-to address. How do you handle drop shipments? What about alternative ship-to addresses? In this case you create a separate tier for addressing operations. You'll quickly find that the purchasing subsystem, accounts payable subsystem, and the accounts receivable subsystem can utilize this new tier.

When cohesion is strictly applied the end result is that one unit (subsystem, module, or component) does one task. The net result is high reliability. The cash receipts data entry program does not create a report. As long as I can remember, which is quite a few years, the dictum is one routine performs only one task. Along with that dictum was another that said any function greater than fifty lines was a design error and should be decomposed into two or more functions.

Functional cohesion is the primary goal of logical design. There are other forms of cohesion, which may or may not yield a benefit:

- *Sequential Cohesion* — Grouped operations share the same data and must be performed sequentially. I do not consider this a violation of functional cohesion.
- *Communicational Cohesion* — Operations in a unit share the same data, but are not related. This violates functional cohesion but minimizes communication overhead.
- *Temporal Cohesion* — Operations are combined in the same unit because they are all done at the same time. I do this all the time with either an end-of-year close or an end-of-period close in a general ledger subsystem. There are many discrete jobs to do in a general ledger close and I provide copious comments in the code as well as allowing a rollback if there's a failure half way through the close operation. I combine these operations because the very last thing I want is a naive user crashing the general ledger, which is the lifeblood of any business.
- *Procedural Cohesion* — Grouped operations that must execute in a specific order and do not share common data. This violates functional cohesion and is undesirable.
- *Logical Cohesion* — Unrelated operations are grouped together and selected through program logic constructs such as IF or CASE. This violates functional cohesion and is undesirable.
- *Coincidental Cohesion* — Unrelated operations are grouped and no discernible relationship exists. This violates functional cohesion and is undesirable. Developers that use coincidental cohesion require remediation, which means they can be fired, retrained, or promoted into management positions.

At least seventy-five percent of my 71-100 beta version of 70-100 certification test questions involved cohesion and coupling issues. These topics are important in both the 70-100 certification test and in a successful system.

Coupling Cohesion occurs within a tier while coupling is between tiers. Coupling defines the characteristics of object interfacing. Coupling is the interfacing of components or the creation of a connection to another object. Tight cohesion and loose coupling are traits of a good design. Loose coupling is illustrated with an addressing tier that can be used by accounts payable, purchasing, and accounts payable. An example of tight coupling is a tier that can only be used by accounts payable. Figure 19-11 illustrates the relationship of cohesion and coupling in a tiered architecture.

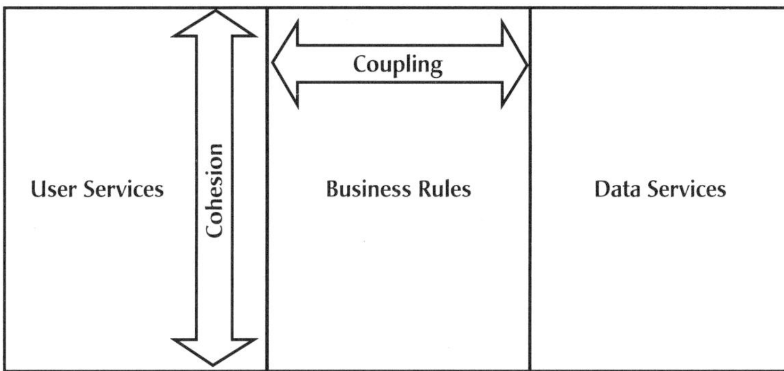

FIGURE 19-11 The relationship of coupling and cohesion.

Loose coupling between objects is obtained by:

- Minimizing the number of connections between objects. The goal is small and simple interfaces.
- Use explicit data with a direct connection between objects. The data should be passed *ByVal* (see Chapter 21) as a parameter whenever possible. Passing either global data or database records to an object will result in concurrency problems.
- Public connections that are explicitly defined.
- Generic connections that support the black-box concept of replaceable modules.

I mentioned earlier in this chapter the term *flowing like water,* which is a metaphor that describes the coupling between objects. Chapter 21 has a good example of this concept. A form global collection is initialized to NULL at form startup. Whenever data is entered into a control on the form, the data field name and the data value are appended to the collection. When the user selects the **Save** command button, the collection count is interrogated. When a count exists, the collection is passed to the CRUD class, which is the middle tier **Data** class in Chapter 21. There's not a long parameter list to export. The data flow is smooth but this technique does have limitations, all of which are discussed in Chapter 21. An alternative is custom marshaling with user defined data types (UDT), however this requires Windows NT service pack 4.

Coupling between objects in a tiered architecture leaves much to be desired. The problems of coupling objects in a tiered architecture should not be underestimated. You'll find the coupling problems discussed in detail in Chapter 21, which deals with DCOM. Let's move on and look at some design issues before we apply the mechanics of building objects with Rational Rose 98 Enterprise edition, which is my design tool of choice.

Logical Design Considerations

We know how to do a logical design, but what type system should be designed? There are issues to be considered that include performance, maintainability, extensibility, scalability, availability, and security. Let's start first by identifying the different classes of applications that can be created.

- *Desktop* — Desktop applications are monolithic applications that are not scaleable. Microsoft Access is the classic monolithic application with user services, business services, and data services all located on the same system. The desktop system is included in this list as an antithesis of an enterprise application.
- *Enterprise* — An enterprise application is a scaleable multi-user application that is available to groups of users within the enterprise. An enterprise application overlaps a distributed application and a centralized application, both of which are discussed below. An enterprise application is commonly deployed using the Microsoft Windows Distributed InterNet Applications (DNA) framework. This is an architecture that uses any browser, Internet

Explorer 4.0 or later with Dynamic Hypertext Markup Language (DHTML), and Microsoft Windows with Distributed COM (DCOM) for the user services layer. The business services layer consists of COM components managed by Microsoft Transaction Server (MTS). The data services layer consists of Microsoft SQL Server, Microsoft Messaging Queue (MSMQ), and Microsoft Internet Information Server (IIS). Lumping everything together; this technology collection is often referred to as an *n-tier* application.

Enterprise applications are not limited to the DNA architecture. The *improve-the-return-on-investment* initiative fostered the thin-client technology. Thin-clients require a fat-server, which is a box with a massive amount of memory where all the applications are installed. The thin-clients are relatively inexpensive terminals that have more intelligence than the dumb-terminals used with legacy mainframe applications. This architecture is somewhat limited and ten to fifteen thin-clients are the maximum that can be supported by one fat-server.

- ***Distributed Application*** — A distributed application is an enterprise application that has distributed resources or processing. Another definition is any application that is not monolithic or client/server, however in the very strictest sense a client/server application is distributed. Microsoft SQL Server 7.0 supports heterogeneous joins between remote databases. As an example the Seattle sales office database of company XYZ can be joined to the corporate database in San Francisco.

  Multiple data sources are not the only definition of a distributed application. The larger view of a distributed application is distributed computing, which is the connectivity of all enterprise computer systems. Interconnection of computer systems is defined by the Open Software Foundation (OSF) in its Distributed Computing Environment (DCE) product, which is a set of specifications and tools. Microsoft operating systems support OSF-DCE compatible services.

  The choice of technology also determines the type of application. As an example, an application is considered distributed when either Distributed COM (DCOM), Microsoft Transaction Server (MTS), or Microsoft Message Queue (MSMQ) is incorporated in the solution. A special version of MTS is the COM Transaction Integrator (COMTI), which extends MTS as a wrapper for IBM programs that use the Advanced Program-to-Program

Communication (APPC) protocol to communicate with another transaction processor.

In summary multiple data sources, the choice of technology, or the interconnection of diverse enterprise computers determines a distributed application.

- *Centralized Application* — A centralized application is still an enterprise application. The data comes from one source, however tiers may still exist in a centralized application. An example of a centralized application is the traditional client/server two-tier system. Another example is the new thin-client/fat-server paradigm where all applications are installed on the server and the clients use what are euphemistically called dumb-terminals.
- *Collaborative Application* — Microsoft Internet Explorer, Microsoft Outlook, and Microsoft Exchange Server are scaleable collaborative tools. Microsoft Internet Explorer also includes Microsoft Outlook Express and Microsoft NetMeeting. There is intelligence within these tools. A universal inbox is included, along with public folders, server-based rules, and advanced calendaring.

  At the low end these tools are designed for users that need e-mail, newsgroup access, the ability to chat, Internet telephony, and simple application collaboration. At the high end these are full-scale collaboration tools that provide forms applications, workflow capability, group voting, and routing.

Performance

Microsoft states that the maximum number of Microsoft Access users should be limited to fifteen. This is independent of the fact that Microsoft Access does not support the ACID properties of a transaction.

Microsoft further states that a useful upper limit to the two-tier architecture that uses Microsoft SQL Server is one hundred users. The number of clients can be increased to no more than two hundred clients by writing SQL Server stored procedures.

When the number of users significantly exceeds the two-tier limits, Microsoft recommends an n-tier architecture that includes Microsoft Transaction Server (MTS) and DCOM. MTS pools components and threads, however the thread limit of MTS is one hundred. This limit corresponds closely to the upper limit of a two-tier architecture, however since the resources are shared an n-tiered architecture should be able to handle many more users.

The user upper limit for a MTS application is a direct function of the design. The MTS upper limit is found during performance and acceptance testing. As a rule-of-thumb, I would personally suggest that any application that must support five hundred or more users be Internet/Intranet based.

Maintainability

Maintainability is synonymous with ease of deployment. Is a single-tiered architecture maintainable? Yes from an academic perspective, but deploying a single-tier application requires copying a new version of a monolithic application to every user, which is a manual operation.

The same maintainability problems exist with a two-tier application and the fat-client. Every fat-client must be updated, which is not a scaleable process.

Is an n-tiered application maintainable? Yes, MTS significantly simplifies application deployment with the concept of packages where logically related components are grouped, which are managed by the Microsoft Management Console (MMC). The other half of an n-tiered (distributed) application is the Web server. User applications are updated by updating components on the server. MTS supports transactions with a rollback when the transaction fails. MTS components must be stateless, which facilitates transaction rollback.

Web-based n-tiered applications are also easy to maintain. The developer updates components on the Web server and the user automatically downloads the next version when the page is used.

Scalability

A distributed (n-tiered) application is the only scaleable application in the Microsoft architecture. Both the monolithic and two-tiered applications lack scalability. ODBC 3.0 and beyond pools database connections and MTS pools threads and components, which yields a distributed architecture that is scaleable. ODBC connection pooling provides a small amount of scaling in the two-tiered architecture, but this is minimal when compared to the scalability of a distributed application.

Availability

Microsoft Message Queue (MSMQ) is a distributed architecture technology and is used with slow or unreliable networks. Messages sent through MSMQ can be transacted, which provides reliable communications. MSMQ supports its own transaction mechanism or the transaction mechanism of MTS can be used. The value of MSMQ is that the intended recipient may be offline, in which case the message is queued for later delivery.

A Microsoft distributed application supports availability in the positive sense with just-in-time component activation within MTS, which provides a short response time. A Microsoft distributed application supports availability in the negative sense that messages will be queued for recipients that are temporarily unavailable.

Availability is also defined in terms of access to external resources such as mainframe applications. A gateway server becomes a component in a distributed architecture.

Security

A monolithic application (Microsoft Access) supports traditional group and user level security. This security is form, view, or table based.

Two-tier applications support security, however business rules may be exposed on the client. SQL Server supports user and group security on all SQL Server objects. This security mechanism is of the same type as the monolithic application.

The distributed application has a finer grain of security with security specified at the component level. This approach is simplified with a common infrastructure that supports a role-based security mechanism. This mechanism means that the Windows NT administrator does not have to create component-specific Windows NT user accounts for each component. Managing security is simplified with the middle-tier component secured centrally.

Building the Logical Design Model

We'll use the pragmatic perspective of logical design with a typical phrase that you might find is a business rambling: "We post the checks in the morning after mail is delivered. We give standard discounts and the checks are deposited in the afternoon."

Let's examine the requirements statement from the UML perspective. Figure 19-12 identifies an actor and three use cases. No reports are included since this is only a very small fragment of a subsystem within a larger accounting system.

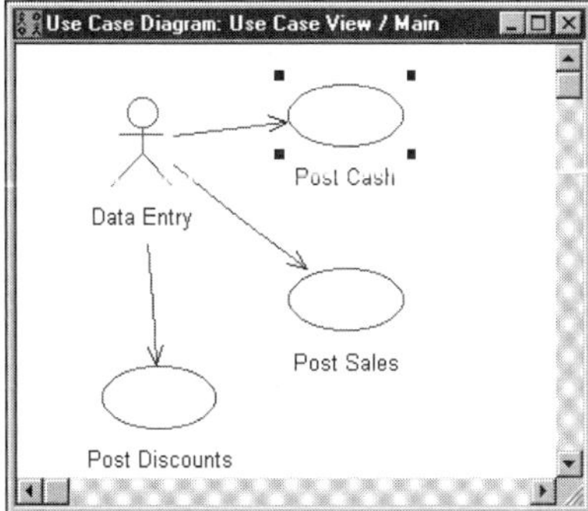

FIGURE 19-12 The Actor and use cases for our cash receipts example.

Let's pause and review some accounting fundamentals before we start the construction of our system fragment with Rational Rose 98 Enterprise edition. Understanding the general ledger mechanisms is essential so let's look at the some general ledger mechanics:

- The check is applied to an invoice. The invoice remains open when the check is insufficient to close the invoice, which includes cash discount considerations. A general ledger *Cash* asset debit account is debited by the check amount and the general ledger *Accounts Receivable* asset account is credited with the payment amount. *Shipped Sales* (a credit sales account) is debited by the payment amount. The transaction to *Shipped Sales* is offset by a credit to *Completed Sales,* which is also a credit sales account.
- When the check amount exceeds the invoice amount the excess cash is posted to a general ledger *Unapplied Cash* asset account with a debit. This is offset with a credit to a general ledger *Unapplied Cash* liability account in the amount of the excess cash. A general ledger *Cash* asset account is debited by the check amount and the general ledger *Accounts Receivable* asset

account, also an asset account, is credited with the payment amount. *Shipped Sales* (a credit sales account) is debited by the payment amount. The transaction to *Shipped Sales* is offset by a credit to the *Completed Sales* credit account, which will be less any cash discount. The cash discount is credited to a *Cash Discount* sales contra account, which is a credit sales account that functions like a debit account. The invoice is marked closed.

- When a check with the cash discount included equals the invoice amount, all operations of step two are completed with the exception of the *Unapplied Cash* postings since none exists.
- Credit memos are treated like a check. A credit memo may be applied against an invoice. When the amount of the credit memo exceeds the invoice amount, the excess credit memo amount is posted to the two *Unapplied Cash* accounts.
- Unapplied cash may be applied against any invoice. All the steps of 2 above are performed except that the *Unapplied Cash* account postings are reversed. The asset *Unapplied Cash* asset account is credited and the *Unapplied Cash* liability account is debited.

Moving back to our water flow concept, it's crucial that the data flow smoothly. From the various general ledger operations described above it should be obvious that the posting of one check against an invoice may involve a dozen or more general ledger postings. The strategy for implementing the posting mechanism is the same mechanism mentioned previously, a collection of collections. Each element of the outer collections is a leg of a general ledger posting. This collection of collections is passed to the Chapter 21 CRUD **Data** class as a single collection. All general ledger postings are an aggregate transaction and postings are not transacted individually, but as a total group. This means that when the *Cash Discount* posting fails, all other general ledger postings are rolled back. I suggest studying the CRUD **Data** class in Chapter 21 in detail so you understand the mechanism involved. Figure 19-13 is a portion of the UML sequence diagram for the cash receipts example. What's missing is the CRUD **Database** class, which is generic reusable software.

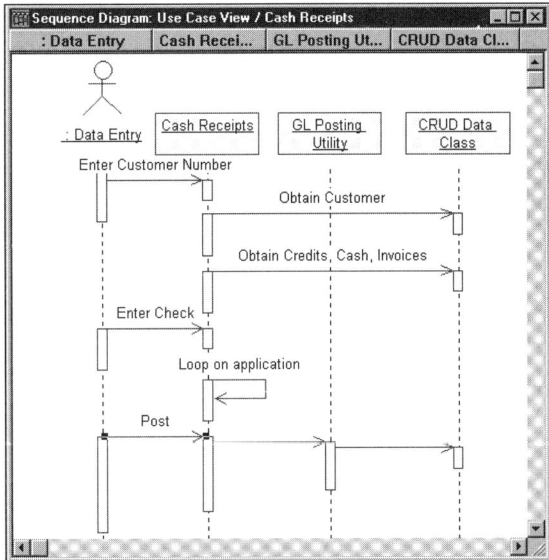

FIGURE 19-13 The UML sequence diagram for the cash receipts example.

There are other features missing from Figure 19-13 such as the loop back to another check for the same customer, or the outer loop back to a new customer. These issues should be intuitively apparent to the developer and need not be represented on the UML sequence diagram. Figure 19-14 is an alternative view of Figure 19-13. A UML collaboration diagram is an alternative way to view a scenario. Figure 19-14 is equivalent to Figure 19-13.

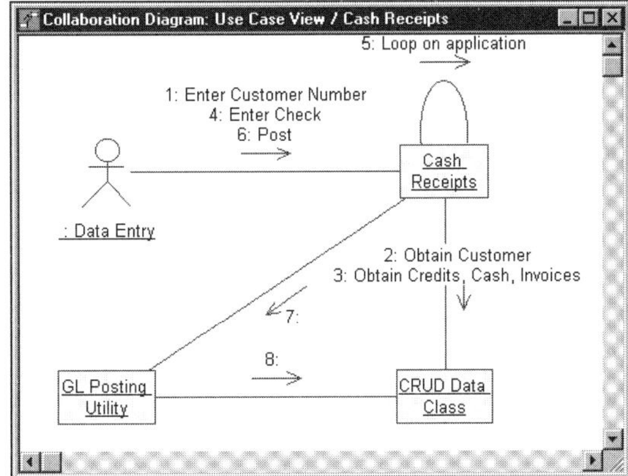

FIGURE 19-14 A UML collaboration diagram for the cash receipts example.

From both Figure 19-13 and Figure 19-14, the logical design should be obvious. The beauty of both the UML sequence diagram and the UML collaboration diagram is that logical design is fed back to the user in user terms. We're still in conceptual design for our cash receipts example, but the step to logical design is very small. Figure 19-15 is a UML class diagram, which represents a logical design view of the cash receipts example.

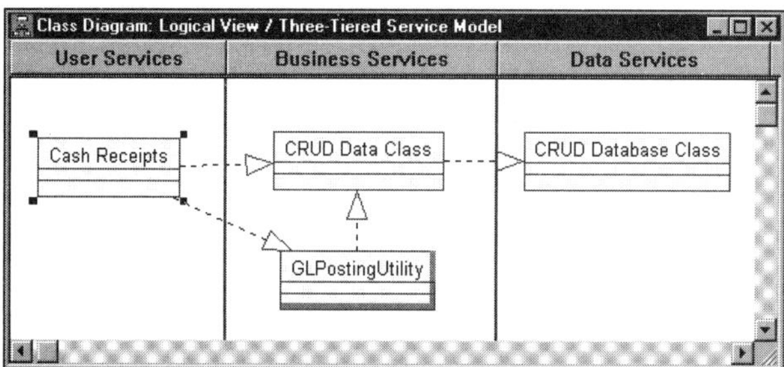

FIGURE 19-15 A UML class diagram for the cash receipts example.

We won't go any further with Rational Rose. The goal was to move to the point of logical design and laying down code does not fall within the purview of this chapter. The classes need both methods and interfaces defined. The CRUD classes of Chapter 21 should be studied in detail for the techniques used. It's not that those techniques must always be used, but the continuity of data flow with the *water concept*. The last step is the automation creation of the objects by Rational Rose, which we won't do. After that the developer enters the specific fix-up code.

Physical Design

You probably have been to a Microsoft *show-and-tell* where the presenter dazzles the audience with the capability of a new software release. Such is the case with an n-tiered architecture. Apparently the Redmonians have only built birdhouse examples, because a tiered architecture is a literal minefield to implement. The booby-traps are wire trips, component binding, and parameter declarations. These and other issues are discussed in far greater detail in Chapter 21, which is DCOM. We'll skip discussing esoteric issues such as component blocking in a handcrafted component architecture, since that class of problems is solved by using MTS.

The physical design is determined by the application type, which is discussed above in *Logical Design Considerations*. Physical design issues are manageable in either a monolithic architecture or a client/server architecture when Microsoft suggested user limits are not exceeded. As discussed previously, maintainability, extensibility, and security are easily managed in an n-tiered architecture. Microsoft touted scalability and performance of the n-tiered architecture is difficult to achieve. It's not difficult to imagine an n-tiered application with performance less than that of a two-tier application. Let's look at some reasons why this can occur.

Wire Trips

Performance is the major n-tiered architecture issue. DCOM instantiates network objects, which is a source of DCOM performance issues. Instantiation issues don't exist with MTS components, which use a just-in-time strategy of component reuse.

The primary goal is to minimize the number of wire trips, (network traverses) for a DCOM object or a MTS component. As an example, a method call with three parameters will require a wire trip for each parameter. The three wire trips will occur with either a DCOM component or a MTS component. The solution is custom marshaling where parameters are packed into a **Variant** or into a **User Defined Type** (UDT) and only one object is transmitted. Visual Basic 6.0 supports UDT marshaling, however Windows NT service pack 4 is required.

Collection objects are a very poor choice for communicating with remote components. When a **For Each** construct is used to enumerate a **Collection** object a new connection is created to the remote client object for each member of the **Collection** object. This is certainly not tolerable and collections are only useful when used with in-process servers. Even then collections are relatively slow, although this is offset to some degree by their ease of use.

Starting with Chapter 12, I attempted to illustrate the different types of marshaling. You'll recall the example that used a string with the pipe <|> characters for marshaling. Other examples used variants and collections for parameter passing. Those laboratories were designed to prepare you for the marshaling issues of a tiered architecture and to provide some insight into custom marshaling.

The net result of minimizing wire trips is that each n-tiered component has at most a single input and a single output parameter. All parameters are custom marshaled with a variant, a string, or a UDT. This is equivalent to writing a custom API interface for each component, which defeats many of the modularity goals that we've been striving to reach.

Component Binding

The **IDispatch** interface is the least desirable component binding interface, however there are situations where no other choice is available. The desirable interface is **IUnknown** since access is through a Vtable. Vtable binding is many orders of magnitude faster than the **IDispatch** interface. Late binding and **IDispatch** are slow, but are an accommodation to clients that cannot process custom Vtable bindings (*dispinterfaces* and the **IUnknown** interface).

The **IDispatch** interface is inefficient. **GetIDsOfNames** is called to resolve the name and a second call is made to **Invoke**. **Invoke** only accepts an array of variants and results are only returned as a **Variant**. **Variants** are the least desirable data type.

Early binding occurs with an **IDispatch** only interface and a type library must exist for the object. There is no need to call **GetIDsOfNames** at execution time because the DISPIDs were embedded at compile time. Early binding is faster than late binding, but it still lags far behind a Vtable binding in terms of performance.

Automation objects are only able to use an object's default interface since an Automation client cannot call **QueryInterface**. This is because VB only supports Automation clients by hosting public methods in a createable class, which means that Automation clients will always use the **IDispatch** interface.

Vtable binding is always the fastest component binding mechanism. Microsoft Visual Basic applications can use Vtable binding when:

- A reference to the appropriate type library exists.
- The reference is typed to an interface or a creatable class, which is the default interface.
- The object exposes Vtables and is not an **IDispatch** only interface.

There are four alternatives available to the Visual Basic programmer with respect to component binding.

- Dual interfaces improve the situation somewhat but parameters must still be passed as variants. VB 5.0 and VB 6.0 automatically create a dual interface.
- The VB **Implements** statement creates a Vtable. (See the lab at the conclusion of Chapter 1 and Chapter 21). This can be taken as an admonition to always create user-defined interfaces. The improved performance will easily offset the additional effort.
- The VB developer can create a type library directly. The Enterprise version of Visual Basic creates a type library automatically when the component is compiled and the project's **Remote Server Files** property is set. Before compiling the component, select PROJECT| PROPERTIES| COMPONENT| REMOTE SERVER FILES. Normally type libraries are internal to VB components. The **OLE View** tool of Microsoft Visual Studio can also be used to create a library. The task is a bit cumbersome, but using **OLE View** tool may be the only choice. A lab at the conclusion of Chapter 21 creates a type library using the **OLE View** tool.
- **CreateObject** can be used to bind an application object directly to an interface's Vtable. The restriction is that the **Object** data type cannot be used. The code snippet below illustrates such a binding.

```
Function GetAuthor(ByVal NerdBook as String) as IAuthor
  Dim ProgID as String
  ProgID = "IDGAuthor." & NerdBook
  Set GetAuthor = CreateObject(ProgID)
End Function
```

Parameter Declarations

We already know that each parameter of a method in a DCOM or MTS component architecture is a wire trip. The parameter *ByVal* declaration type pushes data to the component in one wire trip. The most efficient DCOM component marshaling mechanism is to package all the parameters into one package (*custom marshaling*) and use *ByVal* as the declaration type. But this isn't always possible and on occasion *ByRef* must be used. The problem with *ByRef* is that data is marshaled both ways, both from and to the component. The developer's only choice to prevent unwanted data from being marshaled back to the client is to erase the data array before exiting the component's method. This means that at most an empty array is marshaled back to the client.

Key Point Summary

A software project has three clear phases, which are conceptual, logical, and physical design. An inadequate design at one level dooms the succeeding level to failure.

Starting the project is always difficult. Improper or lack of communication is often the primary reason for failure. Inadequate communication between developers and users during conceptual precipitate design changes in a project's later phases. Changing specifications is the most common reason for project failure. There are other reasons for project failure such as unreal budget expectations from the project's sponsor.

The leap from requirements analysis and conceptual design phase to Microsoft Visual Modeler (VM) is too great. What's missing is feedback to the user in business and user terms, which communicates the developer's understanding of the project. The Universal Modeling Language (UML) is the bridge between requirements analysis and VM. The move to logical modeling is not made until the developers demonstrate with UML models that all business requirements are satisfied. When you're developing within the Microsoft paradigm, Rational Rose is the design tool of choice.

The final phase of the project is the construction of the physical model, which is not easy. A DCOM architecture is very fragile and the developers must exercise caution when using the services of a DCOM component. The net result is that custom marshaling is used for each service of a component.

This chapter completes the search for the Holy Grail of scalability. ODBC 3.0 pools connections, MTS pools components and threads, and Internet/Intranet or MTS applications both have scaleable deployment. The cost of MTS scalability comes with a high price. The relational database is removed data from the process. We've had about twenty-five years of context-free processing until Microsoft, through MTS, reintroduced security and data to the process. Processing is no longer context-free and we're now in an era of application fragility that we've not seen since the COBOL File Definition (FD) was replaced by a relational database. The Microsoft 491 courseware states that data entities are created by discarding object methods and mapping the results to data entities. If you've understood what I've said in Chapters 17, 18, and this chapter, then you'll realize that this is not my definition of the *what* and the *how*. Microsoft continues to promote the *how* before the *what,* which says that developers get to program before they know what they're programming. This is bottom-up design, which is something that is expected from a tool company such as Microsoft.

Applying What You've Learned

The Microsoft *Analyzing Requirements and Defining Solution Architectures* examination requires a significant knowledge of application design. Many of the questions on the 71-100 beta exam use the four principles of modular development.

We'll forego the normal *instant assessment* section at the end of this chapter and replace that with a series of labs based on a discussion of the 70-100 objectives related to application design. Some objectives pose questions related to the real-life case study that was introduced in Chapter 17. Each lab corresponds to one application design objective of the 70-100 certification test.

Answers to the labs are found in Appendix B.

Lab Exercises

This is a series of labs constructed from the real world business rambling found in Listing 17-1 and the case study found at the end of Chapter 17. The case study will not be repeated here, however you are asked to respond to each of the 70-100 logical data design objectives and the related topics. You'll find the answers for these labs in Appendix B.

Defining the Technical Architecture for a Solution

Lab 19.55 ***Given a business scenario, identify which solution type is appropriate. Solution types are single-tier, two-tier, and n-tier.***

Choose a solution type for the project described in the Chapter 17 business rambling. Discuss the limitations of each solution type.

Lab 19.56 ***Identify which technologies are appropriate for implementation of a given business solution***

Considerations include:

- Technology standards such as EDI, Internet, OSI, COMTI, and POSIX
- Proprietary technologies

- Technology environment of the company, both current and planned
- Selection of development tools
- Type of solution, such as enterprise, distributed, centralized, and collaborative

Discuss each of the above bulleted issues and then choose the appropriate technology for the project described in the Chapter 17 business rambling.

Lab 19.57 *Choose a data storage architecture*

Considerations include:

- Volume
- Number of transactions per time increment
- Number of connections or sessions
- Scope of business requirements
- Extensibility requirements
- Reporting requirements
- Number of users
- Type of database

Discuss the above bulleted items with respect to the Chapter 17 business rambling. Be very careful of your information source since the metrics depend upon reliable data.

Lab 19.58 *Test the feasibility of a proposed technical architecture*

- Demonstrate that business requirements are met.
- Demonstrate that use case scenarios are met.
- Demonstrate that existing technology constraints are met.
- Assess impact of shortfalls in meeting requirements.

Discuss each of the bulleted items with respect to demonstrating the feasibility of a proposed technical architecture. Each of the items represents different aspects of the proposed technical architecture.

Lab 19.59 *Develop appropriate deployment strategy*

Discuss the various deployment strategies. Emphasis should be placed on scaleable deployment. Choose a deployment strategy for the project discussed in the Chapter 17 business rambling.

Developing the Conceptual and logical Design for an Application

Lab 19.60 *Construct a conceptual design that is based on a variety of scenarios and that includes context, workflow process, task sequence, and physical environment models.*

Types of applications include:

- SDI, MDI, console, and dialog desktop applications
- Two-tier, client/server, and Web applications
- N-tier applications
- Collaborative applications

Discuss each of the application types identified in the bulleted items above. Briefly discuss the **Context Model, Workflow Process, Task Sequence,** and **Physical Environment** models and identify the relationships between these models. Identify primary actors of the Chapter 17 business rambling. Build a **Workflow Process** model for a simple accounting application.

Lab 19.61 *Given a conceptual design, apply the principles of modular design to derive the components and services of the logical design.*

Discuss the four principles of modular design, which includes identifying the desirable design characteristics when these principles are applied.

Lab 19.62 *Incorporate business rules into object design.*

This is a relatively simple lab and is trivial within the tiered architecture paradigm. Discuss how business rules are incorporated into object design.

Lab 19.63 *Assess the potential impact of the logical design on performance, maintainability, extensibility, scalability, availability, and security.*

The choice of application type affects the logical design. All application types have different characteristics. Discuss the potential impact of the logical design on performance, maintainability, extensibility, scalability, availability, and security.

Deriving the Physical Design

Lab 19.64 *Assess the potential impact of the physical design on performance, maintainability, extensibility, scalability, availability, and security.*

The application type affects the physical design. This lab is related to lab 19-9. Extend the discussion of lab 19-9 by discussing potential impact of the physical design on performance, maintainability, extensibility, scalability, availability, and security.

Lab 19.65 *Evaluate whether access to a database should be encapsulated in an object.*

The material for this object is found in Microsoft course 491. Decide when access to a database should be encapsulated.

Lab 19.66 *Design the properties, methods, and events of components.*

Discuss the issues of designing properties, methods, and events of components in a tiered architecture. Special considerations are required for components in a tiered architecture.

CHAPTER

20

Solution Interface Issues

About Chapter 20

This is the last of four chapters dedicated to exclusively to the 70-100 certification test. Chapter 17 collected the requirements, Chapter 18 designed the database, and Chapter 19 designed and built the application. This chapter is an extension of the conceptual design phase of Chapter 19 since the application type determines to some degree the presentation style. We'll look at the presentation style along with some user interface guidelines. The goal of this chapter is a user interface that is both intuitive and helpful. Chapter 17 and 18 discussed the *what* whereas this chapter and Chapter 19 discuss the *how* aspects of an application.

This Chapter addresses the 70-100 objective section *Designing a User Interface and User services*.

Choosing the Metaphor

In many ways the presentation layer of an application is the most important aspect of an application since it is the user's application portal. There's not always a clear answer as to the choice of presentation tier technology, but Table 20-1 presents the salient issues: understanding the target audience, deployment and maintenance concerns, user interface texture, and ease of development.

TABLE 20-1 PRESENTATION LAYER ISSUES

Issue	*Consideration*
Target Audience	Corporate standards for presentation style can be used when the users are employees of a corporation. There is still the need to recognize that a spectrum of users exists with computer skills ranging from the novice to the experienced power users. Users will reject any application where the interface is perceived as awkward or difficult. A successful application interface follows Microsoft recommended guidelines as to component, menu, and toolbar placement. When all elements are in the Microsoft recommended standard position, the novice uses menu bars for navigation while the power-user navigates with short-cut keys. A conservative approach is to understand the client capabilities and accommodate all classes of clients. Corporate browser standards should exist for Intranets but when the application is the Internet, no assumptions can be made about the users. Different users will have different browsers and browser version levels will vary.
Deployment and Maintenance	Deployment and maintenance are life-cycle costs that must be factored into the total system cost. A frequently updated application is a candidate for an HTML or DHTML application. DHTML is particularly effective with an Intranet since corporate standards exist and all clients will use a compatible browser. Frequently updated applications should be designed with the minimum number of components in the presentation layer. When that's not possible, a web-based application that automatically downloads components is desirable.

Continued

TABLE 20-1 *(continued)*

Issue	*Consideration*
Interface Texture	When the user demands a rich interface, the developer has no choice other than a Win32 application. The deployment of a Win32 application is not scalable. A Win32 application must be downloaded and updated manually.
Development Effort	The choice of tool plays a role in the choice of technology for the presentation layer. The developer should consider tools that have integrated support for the selected technology. Visual Studio 6.0 is probably the tool set of choice. *Time to Market* is very critical in the currently rapidly moving economy and a hand-coded technology is not always cost effective.

The different presentation tier technologies offer unique benefits and characteristics, but what are the choices? Again, there are issues and considerations with no clear answer. The important issue is an understanding of the target audience. Table 20-2 enumerates several presentation tier technology choices and the issues they raise.

TABLE 20-2 SELECTING THE PRESENTATION TIER TECHNOLOGY

Technology	*Considerations*
Static HTML	This type of Web-based application is universal. HTML is a standard and is supported by all browsers. Rendering is done at the client and deployment issues do not exist for standard HTML applications. The target audience is any Intranet/Intranet user.
Static DHTML	Dynamic HTML (DHTML) is not yet a standard. DHTML is a richer interface than HTML. DHTML implementations vary between browsers, which means that the intended effect is not always created. The technology is suitable for a corporate Intranet with uniform browsers. Carefully coded DHTML applications can degrade gracefully when the client browser does not support DHTML. The target audience is limited with DHTML as the presentation tier technology.

TECHNOLOGY	CONSIDERATIONS
Active Server Pages browser with either HTML or DHTML	Active Server Pages (ASP) can interrogate the client and send back the appropriate HTML, DHTML, ActiveX control, or Java applet. The target audience is any Intranet/Intranet user.
Java Applets	Java applets require the Java language. The audience includes nearly all browsers, however the Java Virtual Machine may vary between implementations. This is Microsoft's doing because Java was to be the universal web scripting language. Sun successfully sued Microsoft for varying from the Java specification.
ActiveX controls, ActiveX Documents	This technology is for a corporate Intranet with uniform browsers on a Win32 platform. Deployment is automatic with components downloaded automatically from the Web server. Not all browsers support ActiveX and the audience is limited.
Win32 Applications	Win32 applications require a platform that supports COM. Applications can be written in any language that supports COM. Deployment is not scalable and installations or updates are a manual process. The Win32 application has a very rich user interface.

In summary, choosing a technology is not a simple task even when the target audience is identified. There are still scalabilty concerns such as ease of deployment and maintenance. Win32 applications are the least desirable since they're not scalable even though a Win32 application has the richest interface.

User Interface Guidelines

This section illuminates the Microsoft application interface standards. A successful Windows application is not a clever application; it is an application that adheres to standards. The goal of defining user interface guidelines is to provide a consistent user interface. A consistent user interface is intuitive since the user can guess how to use the functionality based on prior experience. A good example is the paradigm of double-clicking an object to start an operation. Change that paradigm and the user is confused.

How does one measure a good interface? A simple test is to ask the user of a new system to perform a task without explaining how the task should be accomplished. When a new user can perform a task without assistance, the interface is a success. If a system is designed for a group of elite power-users, new and inexperienced employees will find the interface difficult and not intuitive.

A rule of thumb is that a clever application is not a good application. The primary issue is the application's "look and feel." In this section I'll address some basic design issues based on Microsoft Press's *The Windows Interface Guidelines of Software Design*. I'll look at guidelines for window interfaces, control interfaces, dialog boxes, and menu interfaces.

Windows Interface Guidelines

Let's start with a disclaimer. We're about to start a discourse on interfacing Win32 applications. Microsoft has insisted for years, and rightly so, that Win32 applications should have a standard look and feel. Not so with the Internet. It's as clever as the technology will permit. Some Internet applications do have a semblance of a Win32 application, but in general there are no rules. We can distinguish between the Internet and an Intranet by noting that an Intranet supports enterprise internal applications that are scalable. An Internet site delivers content and no training is associated with the site. Intranet developers should try to follow Microsoft sponsored guidelines as much as possible, since this will reduce application training costs.

I start with the window, which is the host container for all objects. It is also the environment know as the desktop. Every application has a window except for special cases such as COM windowless controls.

In brief, the basic interface design guidelines for creating and displaying windows include:

- The primary window, where most of the editing and viewing takes place.
- Multiple or supplemental secondary windows, which may be included to allow users to specify parameters or options.
- Primary window components:
  - Window Frame: A sizable window has a distinct border that provides a control point for resizing the window using direct manipulation with the mouse.

- Title Bar: Clicking on the title bar with mouse button 2 will display the pop-up menu for the window. Double clicking will maximize it. Windows are moved by dragging the title bar or using the Move command from the window pop-up menu.
- Title bar Icon: The title bar icon appears in the upper-left corner of the title bar. If it is a tool (if it does not create, load, or save separate date files), then the smaller version of the icon is used. There are two sets of icons and windows buttons when an MDI window is minimized. When maximized, the MDI icon and buttons are merged onto the menu bar.
- Title Text: The document name appears in the title bar. A placeholder is supplied in the title text when a document has no name. The full path name is not displayed when the title is a filename. The title can optionally hold the application name in use. For Windows 3.1 the name of the document appears followed by a hyphen and the application name. For Windows 95/98 and Windows NT the application name is first followed by the document name. The title text is always kept up to date.
- Windows buttons always appear on the right side of the title bar.
- Task Bar: A task bar entry will be created for primary windows when they are opened. Window activation and deactivation is accomplished with ALT + TAB shifts between windows while SHIFT + ALT + TAB shifts between windows in the reverse order.
- Scroll Box: Sometimes known as an elevator, thumb, or slider. When scrolling allow one unit of overlap from previous view. When scrolling horizontally, scroll in units greater than a single character to prevent discontinuous or uneven scrolling. Always scroll in the direction of drag. The scrolling lock is an option for keyboard scrolling.
- Split Box: The split box is located at the top of the up arrow or at the left of the right arrow on the right side of the window. Move the mouse just above the top of the right up arrow and pull the small bar down. A split box will appear. A split box must be at least one pixel wide.

Control Interface Guidelines

Controls are graphical objects that represent the properties or operations of other objects. Controls are the vehicle by which a developer expresses a solution for a problem. Appropriate control use is critical in an environment where users do not have the time or desire to study an operations manual, but prefer to "wing it." The following are the common controls with their intended usage:

- ***Buttons*** — Users change properties or initiate actions with buttons. There are three basic types of buttons: command buttons, option buttons, and check boxes. Buttons are read from left to right and from top to bottom. Always place the default button at the top or the left. This is a general rule and there are occasions when the rules are broken. A button named *Left* will appear on the left even though the button at the right, which is labeled *Right,* is the default button.
  - ***Command Buttons*** — Include ellipsis points (. . .) as a visual cue for buttons that require additional information. You can use command buttons to enlarge a secondary window and display additional options. Command buttons used in this context are known as *unfold buttons*. When enlarging a secondary window, include the chevron (>) as part of the button's label. A secondary window has neither a menu bar nor min/max buttons.
  - ***Menu Button*** — A menu button displays a pop-up menu; when used for this purpose, it includes a triangular arrow. This triangular arrow is similar to that found in cascading menus.
  - ***Option Buttons*** — An option button (also known as a radio button) represents a single choice from a set of mutually exclusive choices. The option button can be mixed mode (multiple values) in which case the first click selects, the second click clears, and the third click returns everything to mixed mode. Normally part of a group that can have its own label, option buttons should be limited to small groups. There should be at least two choices, but never more than six.
  - ***Check Boxes*** — Check boxes are used for nonexclusive choices. Always express the check box label in terms of the choice available. Related check boxes should be grouped.

    A check box may be mixed mode. Selecting the check box the first time places a check mark in the check box. The second selection removes the check mark, and the third selection causes the check box to revert to mixed mode.

- ***List Boxes*** — Used for displaying a large number of choices. List boxes do not include their own label. Keep everything in a natural order. Use numeric or alphabetical order when a natural order is not available. Use ellipsis points (. . .) in long text strings to shorten them. Use a horizontal scroll bar if necessary.
    - ***Single Selection List Box*** — The list box is a fixed size and only one entry may be selected.
    - ***Drop-down list box*** — Width is a few spaces more than the average width. Normally, there are three to eight entries in a drop-down list box. Use Alt + up arrow and Alt + down arrow for navigation. A drop-down list box is used to conserve screen real estate.
- ***Extended Selection*** and ***Multiple Selection List Boxes*** — These list boxes support the selection interface for contiguous and disjoint selection. Extended selection list boxes are optimized for individual item or range selection, and multiple selection list boxes are optimized for independent selection. Simple multiple selection list boxes are not visually distinct from extended selection list boxes. You may want to consider designing the multiple selection list box to have the appearance of a scrollable list of check boxes. See the *Windows Interface Guidelines for Software Design* published by Microsoft Press for additional details.
- ***List View Box*** — Displays a set of objects and is often used with a tree control. More than one item may be selected at a time. The list view box is also known as a *Column Headings* control. The list view control supports drag-and-drop.
- ***Tree Control Box*** — Displays a set of objects in an indented outline based on their logical hierarchical relationship.
- ***Text Fields*** — No labels included; editing and validation are possible. Can be read-only.
- ***Text Boxes*** — Individual font or paragraph properties are not supported. Text boxes for fixed length entry support auto-exit.
- ***Rich Text Box*** — Support for individual character, font, and paragraph formats.
- ***Combo Box*** — Combines a list box with a text box. Auto-scrolling to the nearest entry is supported. Up arrow and down arrow are supported.
- ***Drop-Down Combo*** — Combines the characteristics of a text box with a drop-down list box. Operates like a combo box.

- ***Spin Box*** — Similar to a text box but with a limited range of input. The values are ordered and make up a circular loop. The user may enter a value or the buttons can be used to increment or decrement the value. An example of spin boxes is a spin box for setting hours, minutes, and seconds.
- ***Static Text Field*** — Dates, page number (that is, read-only).
- ***Horizontal/Vertical Scroll Bars*** — Scroll bars are used for scrolling context only. A common mistake is to set values with a scroll bar.
- ***Sliders*** — Sliders are used for setting values of a continuous range such as volume or brightness. A slider does not include its own label. The developer should provide a static label to help the user interpret the scale and range of the control.
- ***Status Bars*** — Status bars only appear at the bottom of the primary window. Secondary windows do not have status bars. A status bar may include controls. Always provide ToolTips for controls placed in a toolbar or status bar that do not have labels.
- ***Progress Bar*** — Progress bars are not interactive. Static text should be provided to indicate the overall purpose of the progress indicator.
- ***Tab Control*** — Similar to a notebook divider. Used for dividing logical pages. Left arrow or right arrow is used to navigate between tabs. CTRL+TAB also moves between tabs.
- ***Wells*** — Used for displaying color, pattern, or image used as a property. An example is the color palette displayed when setting either background or foreground colors.
- ***Group Boxes*** — Another name for *Frame*. Commonly used to group option buttons.

Dialog Box Interface Guidelines

Whenever possible, use familiar titles for dialog. This practice is consistent with the theme of presenting familiar formats and familiar themes. Common dialog box titles include *Open, Save, Find and Replace, Print, Print Setup,* and *Font*. These are the guidelines to follow when using dialog box interfaces:

- Position controls in a dialog box in the same way people read information, which is left to right and top to bottom.

- Always make the dialog box title identical to the command that it refers to. For example, the **Print** command on the **File** menu should use the title *Print* and not *Print...* or *Print File.*
- Lay out the major command buttons either stacked along the upper-right border of the dialog box or across the bottom.
- Position the **Default** button first, followed by the **Cancel** button. The **Help** button is last.
- Optionally, use double-clicking on a selection control to select the option and the **Default** button.
- Use common system dialog boxes whenever possible rather than creating new dialog boxes. Common dialog box interfaces include: *Open, Save, Find and Replace, Print, Print Setup,* and *Font* dialog box

Menu Interface Guidelines

Menus are a means of presenting commands. The user is not faced with the issue of knowing the correct spelling or syntax of a command. A menu bar is not a requirement, although it is a common convention. Interface standards are evolving toward unified toolbars, which are toolbars with menu controls.

Study Microsoft menus before implementing your own. When your menu uses a common command such as **Exit,** ensure that it is placed last. Also ensure that each command is placed in the proper menu. The **Exit** command is always the last entry on the **File** menu. This means that applications must have a **File** menu for an **Exit** command even though there may be no other commands in the **File** menu.

Be accurate with menu commands. When an object remains active even though the window is closed, use the **Close** command rather than the **Exit** command.

Menus come in three forms: drop-down menus, pop-up menus, and cascading menus:

- ***Drop-Down Menus*** — Dragging downward and releasing over an item "chooses" an entry from the menu. Alternately, the Alt key can be used followed by cursor positioning keys. There are five classes of drop-down menus:
  - ***File Menu*** — Commands such as **Open**, **Save**, **Send,** or **Print**. If an **Exit** is used, place it at the end.
  - ***Edit Menu*** — Commands such as **Undo, Repeat, Find and Replace, Delete,** and **Duplicate**.

  - ***View Menu*** — Includes commands for changing the user's view of data in the window.
  - ***Window Menu*** — Used in multiple-document interface (MDI)-style applications.
  - ***Help Menu*** — Include the **About** *<application name>* here.
- ***Pop-Up menus*** — A pop-up menu is similar to a drop-down menu except there is no title. A pop-up menu is contextual to the selected object(s). A pop-up menu is displayed when an object is right-clicked. The right-click establishes the pop-up menu context. A control can support a pop-up menu. When a control supports a pop-up menu, the pop-up menu is contextual to what the control represents, rather than to the control itself. Therefore, do not include commands such as **Set, Check,** or **Uncheck**. The exception is in forms design or window layout context, where the commands on the pop-up menu can apply to the control itself.

  Commands in a pop-up menu may not always be supplied by the object but may be a combination of commands from the object and from the container. **Properties** is last in a pop-up menu. **What's This?** is next to last in a pop-up menu.

  Your pop-up menu should follow conventional command ordering. The rule of thumb is that the most frequently referenced items are placed first in the menu. Some generic pop-up menus are offered below as a design guideline:

  - Pop-up menu command order:

    Open, Play, Print

    Cut, Copy, Paste, Paste Link
  - Application file pop-up menu:

    Cut, Copy, Create Link, Delete, What's This?, Properties
  - MDI application pop-up menu:

    Close (or Exit), Save All, Insert New, Find, What's This?, Properties
- ***Cascading Menus*** — Cascading menus should be limited to a single level. The visual cue is the side arrow. User interaction is the same with a cascading menu as with that of a drop-down menu except that the cascading menu displays after a short timeout to avoid a flashing effect.

Accelerated (Shortcut) Keys

Accelerated keys are keys or key combinations that provide rapid access to functionality without the use of the mouse. The Microsoft architecture contains many standard accelerated key such as CTRL N in the **File** menu. Accelerated keys are a requirement for power-users. Factors to consider when implementing accelerated keys:

- Always assign single letters when possible.
- Modified-letter assignments should be case insensitive. *CTRL N* or *CTRL n* should initiate the same action.
- "Look and feel" issues apply to accelerated keys. Use the Microsoft conventions for standard menu features such as *CTRL N* or *CTRL O* for **New** and **Open** respectively in the file menu.
- Use SHIFT to complement an action. An example is the Microsoft defined ALT+TAB combination that switches between windows in a top to bottom order. SHIFT+ALT+TAB reverses the functionality and switches between windows from bottom to top. SHIFT+*text* may conflict with international keyboards and should be avoided.
- Amplify effects with CTRL+*key*. An example of this is HOME move to the start of a line; CTRL+HOME moves to the beginning of the text.

  CTRL is used for access to commands with a single letter. For example CTRL+I places text in italics. Pressing CTRL+I again returns the text to normal.
- Do not use ALT+*key* sequences. Such a sequence may conflict with Microsoft defined ALT sequences such as ALT+TAB, ALT+ESC, or ALT+SPACEBAR.
- Letter keys can only be assigned once. Once CTRL+N is defined in the **File** menu, the sequence cannot be used in other menus.
- When possible, give the power-user the opportunity to change a shortcut key. Accelerated keys are created at run time within Microsoft Visual Basic by prefixing the **Caption** property with the ampersand <&> character and are corresponding removed by deleting <&> from the **Caption** property.
- Use the ESC key as the standard key to stop a function. The ESC key is equivalent to the **Cancel** button.

Help for The User Interface

When a user clicks on **Help,** your intuitive interface has failed. User help is your last line of defense before the application is relegated to that class of loaded but never-used applications.

User help should be simple, efficient, and relevant. More than that, help shouldn't insult the user. (We'll discuss techniques of writing good help dialogs shortly.) Remember: At this point the user is frustrated, and some of that frustration may be your fault.

Application errors fall into three general categories. The first category consists of mechanical errors of spelling, omissions, or incorrect type declarations. The next category is plain old logic bugs. The last and most common error category is that the developer's perception of the problem does not match the user's perception. The clash is between how the user wants to use the application and how the developer thinks the application should be used. This gap can be huge.

In the legacy world, the user had very little choice. The user was forced to accept whatever was provided. The paradigm today is that the developer is no longer in control. It's the user who is in control, and if the developer doesn't do the application correctly, there is a high probability that the user will implement his or her own version. I've made light of everyone from vice presidents to secretaries programming Microsoft Access. It's not a joke — they do!

There are different categories of help, each designed for a particular purpose. The categories are Context Sensitive Help, ToolTips, Status Bar Help, Help Command Buttons, Task Help, and Reference Help:

- ***Context Sensitive Help*** — Selecting *What's This?* from a menu puts the user in context-sensitive mode. Context-sensitive help is available by clicking *What's This?* from the **Help** menu and then moving the mouse pointer over the object and clicking the left mouse button. During this operation the mouse pointer is considered a contextual pointer. The mouse will change to a combined question mark and arrow. If a user selects a menu title after selecting *What's This?*, keep the mode until something is selected.

  Context-sensitive help is also available by clicking the right mouse button. When the right mouse button is clicked over an object that supports a pop-up menu, maintain the context-sensitive mode until the user chooses something from the menu or cancels the menu.

The developer should always remember that context-sensitive information is written to answer a question. A good practice is to start context-sensitive help with a verb, such as *Adjusts the speed of your mouse*. The information should be brief. Reference-related help should be deferred to task-oriented help.

Pressing F1 is the shortcut key that presents contextual information for the object that has the input focus.

- ***Tooltips*** — Small pop-ups that display the name of a graphical icon. ToolTips do not have a label. Drag the mouse pointer over an object and hesitate for several seconds. The ToolTip will display the object name.
- ***Status Bar Help*** — Use the status bar to provide descriptive information about a menu or toolbar button that the user chooses. Always begin a message with a verb and in the present tense. Use only familiar terms and avoid jargon. Be specific when describing a command. Be constructive and not descriptive. Your goal is to inform the user about the command. The message should be brief, yet not truncated.
- ***Help Button*** — The help button is different from *What's This?*'s summary assistance, overview, or explanatory information. A help button is used for help from a property sheet, dialog box, or message box. The help button is included in the window. When the user presses the **Help** command button, the help information is displayed in a Help secondary window and not in a contextual pop-up window. A wizard is always implemented in a secondary window. Selecting a help command from the **Help** command button starts a Help wizard. This, in turn, starts the Help Browser after the indexes and content are initialized.
- ***Task Help*** — Task help enumerates the steps for carrying out a task. The preferred window type is a primary window that the user can resize, move, maximize, or minimize. The window can support shortcut buttons and has command buttons that support access to the index and content pages of the Help Browser. The developer should use the default system windows colors for the task help window. This distinguishes the task help window from other application windows. The task help window standard has changed slightly. Microsoft added the "Clipit" wizard to the task help menu in Office 97. A task-related help example is found by selecting HELP | CONTENTS and INDEX | CONTENTS from the Microsoft Word toolbar. All entries will start with a verb.

- ***Reference Help*** — Reference help serves as the application's on-line documentation. Reference help is also presented in a primary window and the developer should use the default system colors for the window. The common use of this help style is from an explicit menu item in the Help drop-down menu with *Contents and Index* as the typical command. The user is initially presented the primary window of the Help Wizard. The bottom of the Help Wizard has the buttons *<Back>, Next, Finish,* and *Cancel.* Stepping through the different steps initializes the Help Browser. The user is presented with the Help Browser in a primary window and within the primary window are three tabs: Contents, Index, and Find.

  Reference help is written in the first person directly to the user. Use personal pronouns such as "you" or "your." Write the text in the user's vernacular and do not use jargon. The developer should realize that there are two different classes of users: beginning users and advanced users. Different key words should be provided for each class of users. Describe the topic generally for beginning users and specifically for advanced users. Don't insult the users, and keep the writing simple, clear, concise, and not condescending. Be succinct, yet clear, with an economy of style.

  A reference-related help example is found by selecting `HELP | CONTENTS and INDEX | INDEX` from the Microsoft Word toolbar. Enter a keyword such as *spelling* and select `DISPLAY`. Reference-related help will be displayed.

The window is the primary viewing and editing environment. Secondary windows (MDI) provide for editing of parameters or options, or for additional object detail. We'll start with the primary window.

Windows are opened when a task starts execution. Selective activation of loaded windows is controlled by executing Alt + Tab, which shifts focus to another window. Shift + Alt + Tab shifts between windows in the reverse order.

Dragging the title bar or using the move command from the window pop-up menu moves a window.

A task bar entry is created for primary windows when they are opened within Windows NT 4.x or Windows 95. The task bar concept does not exist for Window NT 3.51, Windows NT 3.5, Windows 3.11, or Windows 3.1.

The application window should mimic the placement of Microsoft Windows's required features. Primary window components are listed as follows (a toolbar isn't included because it is a feature of an application and not a basic window requirement):

- ***Window Frame***—A sizable window has a distinct border that provides a control point for resizing the window using direct manipulation with the mouse.
- ***Title Bar***—Clicking on the title bar with the right mouse button displays the pop-up menu for the window. Double-clicking maximizes it.
- ***Title Bar Icon***—The title bar icon appears in the upper-left corner of the title bar. If it is a tool (that is, it does not create, load, or save separate data files), then the smaller version of the icon is used.
- ***Title Text***—The document name appears in the title bar when opened. If a document has no name, then it supplies a placeholder in the title. A full path name is not supplied when the title is a filename.
- ***Windows Buttons***—Windows buttons always appear on the right side of the title bar. This is different than Windows 3.1 or Windows NT 3.51. These buttons replace the control menu of the older Windows 3.1 paradigm.
- ***Scroll Bar***—A scroll bar is optional and is sometimes known as an elevator, thumb, or slider. A scroll bar control consists of scroll arrows, a scroll box, and a scroll bar shaft. When scrolling vertically, allow one unit of overlap from previous view. When scrolling horizontally, scroll in units greater than a single character to prevent discontinuous or uneven scrolling. Always scroll in the direction of drag.
- ***Split Box***—If no split box is present, then it is typically located at the top of the up arrow of the vertical scroll bar at the left of the window. A split box is a special control contained in the scroll bar. Split bars must be at least one pixel wide.
- ***MDI Window***—When an MDI window is maximized, the icon and buttons are merged onto the toolbar of the parent MDI form There is no icon on either the child tool or the parent MDI form.

  A child form of a MDI application functions as a primary window in that it can be moved, resized, minimized, or maximized. The only limitation is that all interactions occur within the limits of the parent MDI form.

note **Recall that ALT + TAB shifts focus to another primary window, while SHIFT+ ALT + TAB shifts between primary windows in the reverse order. CTRL + TAB (or CTRL + F6) moves focus between child windows of an MDI application.**

Accessibility Requirements

Another important aspect of the user interface is accessibility for users with disabilities. You do not need to program accessibility features into your application. Rather, be aware that tools are available for impaired individuals. The tools include:

- ***Screen Enlargement Utilities*** — This is a screen magnifier. The enlarger must track the current position and readjust the screen accordingly.
- ***Screen Review Utilities*** — A screen reviewer utility scans the screen and renders the information in a different medium. This can be a refreshable Braille display or synthesized speech.
- ***Voice Input Utilities*** — These utilities are useful when the individual has a mobility impairment. It is also a useful tool for boosting productivity of individuals who are not impaired.
- ***In-Screen Keyboards*** — There are a number of variations for this type of aid. A Morse code-type system, a system of pointing and clicking, and a system of clicks-only are different types of input systems for impaired individuals. The system that is selected will depend upon the impairment of the individual.
- ***Keyboard Filters*** — Keyboard filters accommodate impaired dexterity. Windows 95 keyboard filters help by providing some compensation for erratic motion, tremors, or slow response time. In this category of tools are aids such as abbreviation expansion utilities, add-on spelling checkers, and word prediction utilities. These tools are often used to improve the productivity of individuals not impaired.
- ***Customizing the Mouse Pointer*** — Windows 95 supports a customizable mouse pointer display for the visually impaired. High contrast color schemes are also an aid for the visually impaired.
- ***Keyboard Emulation of the Mouse***--Keyboard emulation of the mouse is accomplished by assigning keyboard keys such as left and right arrow to mouse movement. This is another feature of Windows 95.

General Interface Guidelines

The Internet, a Windows 16-bit application, and a Windows 32-bit application each have a different look and feel. The primary rule is to keep the look and feel that is appropriate to the platform. There are no standards for either the Internet or Intranet and some Internet sites are as garish as *midnight at the gaslight district*. Web developers should use the Browser Capabilities Component since browser functionality is not uniform. For example, a browser may support VBScript and not Jscript. The converse may be true. Another consideration is that not all browsers support ActiveX.

There are interface standards for both Windows 95/98 and Windows 3.1. Windows 95/98 for example, uses context menus and the right mouse button extensively. There are common interface factors for 16-bit and 32-bit platforms such as the use of controls, control placement, menu placement, and contents. The look and feel of Windows 3.1 changed to 3-D (edged controls) with Windows 95/98 and Windows NT 4.0. Windows NT 3.51 still maintains the Windows 3.1 look and feel.

Windows 95/98 and Windows NT have two main areas of abuse. Microsoft did not anticipate the abuse in *The Windows Interface Guidelines for Software Design*. The first is overloading the desktop with unneeded graphical constructs advertising an application. The other area of abuse is cluttering the **Start** menu with application shortcuts. The **Start** menu should have only one application link and shortcuts should maintained in their own folder.

Each platform also has bandwidth considerations. Internet applications are typically limited to 28.8, 33.6, or 56 Kb for downloading. This means that considerations must be give to the amount of information downloaded, and to download asynchronously. Windows 3.1 and 16-bit applications have limitations that are inherent in the platform. This limitation is the 64 Kb GDI, KERNEL, and USER stack sizes. Within Windows 3.1, the *out of memory* message that occurs is not an exhaustion of physical memory, but the exhaustion of one of the aforementioned stacks. The experienced Windows 3.1 user limits the number of windows open simultaneously, thereby avoiding the *out of memory* message.

32-bit platforms such as Windows 95/98 and Windows NT utilize a Registry. This is a system-wide database of hardware and software parameters. The corresponding information Windows 3.1 information is stored within the *SYSTEM.INI* and *WIN.INI* files, with some applications owning private .INI files.

The bottom line is to stay within the paradigm for the platform. For example, don't add right context mouse button usage to either Windows 3.1 or Window NT 3.51. It is not an integral feature of the interface and will confuse the user.

Web Site Interface Design

I don't think I'll get an argument when I say that many Web sites have that *garish* look that borders on being rude. Consistency of design and purpose serves a different audience with a Win32 application. A benefit of a consistent Win32 design is reduced training costs and employees with higher productivity. Placement of menus and controls is standardized as is the content of menus. The goal is a consistent look and feel.

Within a Web site, it's not an issue of common look and feel with consistent control layout and placement of graphical controls, but of metaphor and theme consistency. A Web site selling books should use book metaphors. For example, entering a library is a useful metaphor for a Web book reseller. Web site design focuses on presentation and interaction of content. This is done with consistent themes and metaphors that are implemented with graphics and color.

Color can be an asset and a liability. Special colors that do not map to the standard palette require a longer download time. Inappropriate color choices can make text very hard to read.

Inappropriate use of fonts can also be a liability. As in e-mail, using all capitals is the equivalent of shouting. Italics lose their significance when used too often. Too many font size changes confuse the potential client. Boldface should be used sparingly if at all.

Web site aesthetics are directly related to download time. Graphics require download time and a Spartan Web site with minimal graphics will download quickly. Graphics should be small and tasteful. Users have no patience with pages that require long load times. A user will select another URL and move on to another site rather than wait for a long download.

What's extremely critical in Web site design is page navigation. Web pages should be designed on the basis of ease of use and predictability. Not all browsers function identically and I know personally that my CompuServe browser will not always move to the previous page, although Microsoft Internet Explorer functions flawlessly given the same page. It's a function of page content and of course Microsoft does have a bit of a reputation for pushing Web page content beyond commonly accepted standards. The remedy is navigation buttons on every page to accommodate inconsistencies between browsers since the **Back** button action is not always predictable.

In summary, a good Web site has a professional touch. The user never encounters page dead-ends or under construction pages, and is warned when leaving the site. There is no limit to what can be done with a Web site, however taste, style, economy of presentation, and ease of use all contribute to a successful Web site. Garish Web site presentations are self-fulfilling disasters.

Application Internationalization

There is no simple answer to internationalization. Companies that market software products internationally must adjust the software product to different locales. One of the key steps of localization is language translation for each locale. Translating to the target language is never enough. There are also cultural issues to consider. Let's define the character sets before we discuss other internationalization issues.

Translating the Character Sets

There are obvious language differences between the United States versions of software and the versions for other countries. The problems extend far beyond mechanical translation of languages and can involve religious and cultural issues. Internationalizing an application is not a simple task for the fainthearted. It is complex, very costly, time consuming, and iterative. The translation starts with an *input method editor* (IME) that translates text entered on a 101-key keyboard to the target character set. When you don't know Japanese, and if you have access to an IME, names like "Toyota" or "Suzuki" can be typed. The appropriate double-byte character is created and the results are displayed immediately. To understand what's involved in the translation, let's start with the definition of the character sets used today. Table 20-3 maps the support for the different character sets and Table 20-4 illustrates the various implementations of the character `A`, each of which is unique.

TABLE 20-3 ANSI, DBCS, AND UNICODE IMPLEMENTATIONS

ENVIRONMENT	*CHARACTER SET(S)*
Visual basic	Unicode
32-bit object libraries	Unicode
16-bit object libraries	ANSI and DBCS
Windows NT API	Unicode
Automation in Windows NT	Unicode
Windows 95 API	ANSI and DBCS
Automation in Windows 95	Unicode

TABLE 20-4 CHARACTER CODES FOR "A" IN ANSI, UNICODE, AND DBCS

THE CHARACTER <A>	*HEXADECIMAL EQUIVALENT*
ANSI character "A"	&H41
Unicode character "A"	&H41 &H00
DBCS character that represents a Japanese wide-width "A"	&H82 &H60
Unicode wide-width "A"	&H21 &HFF

Let's mention a few kind words about each of the character sets:

- ***ANSI*** — ANSI represents the traditional American Standard Code for Information Interchange (ASCII) character set. It is the most popular and is the legacy character set. The implementation is eight bits.
- ***Unicode*** — Unicode is a standard and not an invention of Microsoft.

  The Unicode standard is defined in two volumes: *Worldwide Character Encoding* Version 1.0, Volume 1 and Volume 2. Additional Unicode information may be found at `ftp://unicode.org`.

  Unicode is a character-encoding scheme that uses two bytes to represent every character. This scheme is capable of encoding all known characters and is used as a worldwide character-encoding standard. Unicode is supported by all 32-bit versions of Microsoft Windows and by 32-bit OLE technology. All versions of Microsoft Access after Version 2.0 are component-based (OLE) and by definition support Unicode. The same is true for Visual Basic 4.0 and later. Unicode is relatively new even though it is a standard. Legacy applications do not use Unicode.

- ***DBCS*** — The double-byte character set is used with Windows operating systems that are distributed in most regions of Asia. For example, Japanese has four alphabets, each of which is encoded in DBCS:
  - Kanji — Ideograms or meaning not related to pronunciation.
  - Hiragana — Phoenetic alphabet that is used for Japanese words.
  - Katakana — Phoenetic alphabet used for foreign words.
  - Romanji — Latin letter alphabet.

The name *double-byte character set* is a misnomer. It is possible to combine a *single-byte character set* (SBCS) with a DBCS. The result is a character string that is relatively complex to scan. Figure 20-1 illustrates the different character combinations. The current cursor position in each string is noted. Position a cursor at the wrong position in a DBCS string and chaos ensues. The SBCS range is limited to the inclusive values of 20 hexadecimal (hex) to 7F hex. The lead DBCS character is always an extended character that is always greater than 7F hex. The trailing character is not limited in value and may be either a SBCS or a DBCS character.

Character strings 3 and 4 for Figure 20-1 illustrate that the trailing byte may assume any value. This makes DBCS string parsing difficult. Microsoft supplies the function **IsDBCSLeadByte,** which returns a `TRUE` only when the lead byte is a candidate lead byte. Lead-byte determination is also based on the context of the character. An example is the second character of String 4, which is a candidate lead byte and is a trailing byte. **IsDBCSLeadByte** will return `TRUE` for this character but the context is that of a trailing byte. The Visual C++ operators ++ and -- are no longer safe with DBCS character strings. **CharNext** and **CharPrev** are the 32-bit implementations of character positioning, while **AnsiNext** and **AnsiPrev** are the 16-bit implementations.

A DBCS is not case sensitive.

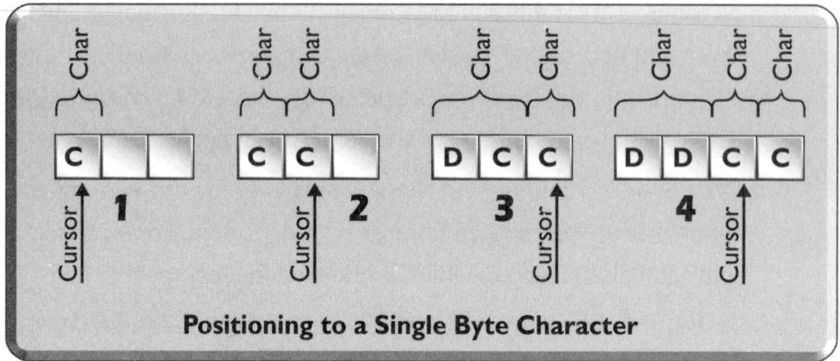

Legend: D > 7F, C >= 20 and <= 7F

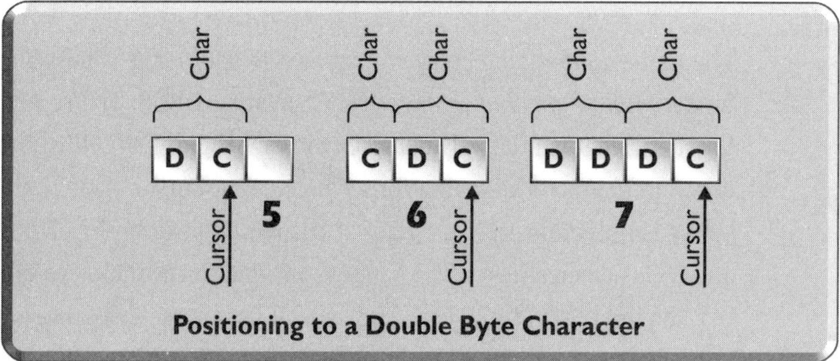

FIGURE 20-1 Double-byte and single-byte character combinations.

Internationalization Issues

The internationalization issues mentioned in thss section are not inclusive, but should form a starting point for internationalizing your application.

Internationalization starts by isolating localizable resources. Developers identify these localizable program elements (localizable resources) before the application is completed and in tandem with normal application development. The list of program elements that require localization is more than the traditional bitmaps and character strings. The program elements that require localization include: special algorithms, messages, constants, prompts, dialogs, sounds, macro languages, status bars, menus, icons, and toolbars.

One of the goals of localizing is to reduce production costs of internationalization. Rather than a system per locale, localization isolates the core software from elements that require localization. This means that the core software is compiled independently of resources that must be localized. Resources are normally placed in a `.RC` file. When the localized resource is placed in a DLL, it need not be linked with the core software, but must be linked at execution time. The goal is one core module and a locale-specific DLL for each locale.

- Use good coding practices. It is not uncommon to find a statement such as:

```
case '0':
DoClose();
```

  This is an example of a literal embedded in code and in general is not a good coding practice. Localize all constants and don't be clever with messages. By that I mean don't try to construct messages on the fly from fragments, but define complete messages that can be localized.

- Make sure your buffers are large enough to hold the translated text. The word *Edit* in German is *Bearbeiten*. The size consideration doesn't apply to just data buffers. Menu bars, status bars, toolbars, title bars, and dialog boxes should all be designed for an increased text size.
- Use system functions for sorting, character typing, and string mapping. Always use system dialog boxes.
- Use extreme caution with keyboard shortcut-key combinations. Not all keyboards are the same and characters map differently. Consider using the function keys such as F4 or F5 rather than a shortcut-key combination.
- Avoid special effects and be culturally sensitive. The beep of the computer wanting the next installation diskette will embarrass a Japanese user. A *beep* may embarrass a Japanese user by drawing attention to a blunder even though a *beep* signaling the next diskette is not a blunder.
- Avoid metaphors. Some languages read from right to left. A pointing arrow to the left signifying an *undo* operation might be confusing to an Arabic or Hebrew speaker.
- Do not include text in bitmaps unless the text will not be translated. A company name is an example of text that will not be translated.

Input Validation

Input for an application can come from many sources. The common inputs are from the keyboard or mouse. Other application inputs include voice, PIN, bar codes, graphics tablets, query-based input, and imported files. Validation issues exist for each of these input types, as shown in Table 20-5.

TABLE 20-5 INPUT VALIDATION CONSIDERATIONS

Type of Input	*Consideration*
Keyboard	Complete validation of all keyboard input is necessary. This includes both domain and range tests.
Mouse	Mouse input is not validated
Voice	Voice input is not 100% accurate. The system must echo back the intended operation on the screen with a speech synthesizer.
PIN	Personal Information Numbers must be accepted. PIN numbers do not have check sums, but the number of digits can be counted.
Bar Code	Bar codes normally have a built-in checksum. The wand will not accept data when the checksum fails. The only remaining issue is the transportation of bar code information via a serial interface. The developer should checksum bar code buffers.
Graphics Tablet	A graphics tablet is a hardware device. Validating the data is not necessary, however mapping the data to the screen or a storage device is required.
Query-Based Input	Data in a database is normally already validated. The only issue is adequate security to access the data. Some systems contain inconsistent and invalid data, which requires validation.
Imported Files	Scrubbing the data of imported files is recommended, unless the files are under system control. Files can be created offline with tools such as Microsoft Notepad. Such files are subject to user data-entry errors.

The primary concern is data entered from the keyboard. There is a natural dichotomy of data-entry with data entered from a Win32 application or from an HTML type form in a browser. Let's consider data validation of Win32 applications first.

Win32 data validation

The elegance of design occurs with a Win32 application and not with a Web-based application. Data validation with a Web-based application uses the brute force approach. The Win32 application uses a *state* machine that controls the content of and positioning between data entry fields. A *state* machine is best described by enumerating the necessary parameters:

- ***Next Field*** — When data is successfully entered into a data entry control or text box, the *next field* is the control number counting from top to bottom and left to right. All controls are initially disabled except the first control that can accept data. When valid data is entered, the control identified by *next field* is enabled and the cursor is positioned to that field. *Next field* values are stored in an array sized to the number of controls.
- ***Default Values*** — An array of default values exists. The system initializes the specified controls to the default values. Default values are initialized when the form is opened and when a record is saved. However the user must be given the option of preserving the current screen values. This is useful for repetitive entries.
- ***Required*** — Each field is tagged as required or not required. Fields that are not required and which do not have a default value are by definition NULL.
- ***Type*** — An array that describes the data types for each field. Typically the values are either numeric or string.
- ***Max*** — An array of maximum values exists for numeric fields. For simplicity the array is the same size as the number of controls, and entries in the array that correspond to data types other than numeric are NULL.
- ***Min*** — An array of minimum values exists for numeric fields. For simplicity the array is the same size as the number of controls, and entries in the array that correspond to data types other than numeric are NULL.
- ***NULLPermitted*** — Applicable only to string fields.

- ***ZeroLengthPermitted***—Applicable only to string fields.
- ***ToDoFields***—A collection that is initialized to the field numbers of the required fields. As data is successfully entered into a field, the field number is removed from the collection. When the collection is empty the fields on the screen may be saved into a file. Optional fields are not entered into the **ToDoFields** collection. The **Save** command button is enabled when the collection count is zero.
- ***Sequence***—A numeric array with field input sequence numbers. When data is successfully entered into a control, this array provides the next control number. The control is enabled and the cursor is positioned to the control.

The general operating strategy is to start with only one control enabled and with the **ToDoFields** collection initialized to all the required field numbers. Data entry starts with the first field number. This is the only control that is enabled and the user has no choice other than to enter data in that control. When data is entered successfully into a control, the field number of the control is removed from the **ToDoFields** collection by the *state* engine. The *state* engine also determines the next sequential field for data entry, enables the control, and positions the cursor to that field awaiting user input. In essence, the user is led through the fields in the proper order. When a user re-enters data into a field that was previously validated, the *state* engine will invalidate the field by placing the field number back into the **ToDoFields** collection.

Microsoft has improved the process of field validation with the new **CausesValidation** property of a Visual Basic 6.0 text box, which is by default TRUE. A **Validate** event occurs when the user attempts to change focus with the **Tab** key. The code snippet below illustrates using the **Validate** event. Each **Validate** event is specific to a control and must be individually coded, which makes this approach useful for small forms but not for large forms with many fields. The *state* engine is a better choice for larger forms.

```
Private Sub txtPartNumber_Validate(KeepFocus As Boolean)
   If Not IsNumeric(txtPartNumber.Text) then
         KeepFocus = True
         Msgbox "Please enter a valid part number"
   End If
End Sub
```

Browser-based data validation

Not all data validation should be done at the browser. Proprietary data validation algorithms are exposed for all to see on the browser and are protected from view on the server. Browser-based data validation is limited to simple sanity tests or domain value checks such as; is the data numeric or is the data string?

As mentioned previously, validating browser input fields requires a brute force approach. The application designer can validate with the Internet Explorer **OnSubmit** event, which occurs when the **Submit** button is clicked. The **OnSubmit** event of Internet Explorer also occurs when the form has a single text box and the user presses the **Enter** key. This means that a PIN number is only checked for numeric digits. Listing 20-1 illustrates using the **OnSubmit** event to validate fields. The **OnSubmit** event returns a FALSE when errors exist and Microsoft Internet Explorer does not submit the page to Internet Information Server (IIS).

LISTING 20-1 **Validating a form with the OnSubmit event of Microsoft Internet Explorer**

```
<SCRIPT LANGUAGE = "VBScript">
  Function MyForm_OnSubmit
    Dim msgErrors
    Dim fRef
    Set fRef = Document.MyForm
   msgErrors = ""
    '
    ' Validate every field
    '
    If Not IsNumeric(fRef.txtPartnumber.Value) Then
      msgErrors = msgErrors & _
        "Part number is not numeric" & Chr$(13)
    End If

    If Not IsDate(fRef.txtOrderDate.Value) Then
      msgErrors = msgErrors & _
        "Order date is invalid" & Chr$(13)
    End If
    '
```

```
    ' continue with other field validations
    '
    If msgErrors <> "" Then
      MsgBox msgErrors
      MyForm_OnSubmit = False
    Else
      MyForm_OnSubmit = True
    End If
  End Function
</SCRIPT>
```

Listing 20-2 is similar to Listing 20-1. The difference is that the user selects a button for validation and the button code submits the form if all fields are correct.

LISTING 20-2 **Validating a form without the OnSubmit event of Microsoft Internet Explorer**

```
<SCRIPT LANGUAGE="VBScript">
<!--
   Sub btnValidate_OnClick
        Dim msgErrors
        Dim fRef
        Set fRef = Document.MyForm
        msgErrors = ""
        '
        ' Validate every field
        '
        If Not IsNumeric(fRef.PartNumber.Value) Then
             msgErrors = msgErrors & _
              "Part number is not numeric" & Chr$(13)
        End If

        If Not IsNumeric(fRef.Quantity.Value) Then _
             msgErrors = msgErrors & _
             "Part number is not numeric" & Chr$(13)

        If Not val(fRef.Quantity.Value) < 0 Then _
             msgErrors = msgErrors & _
```

```
            "Invalid quantity" & Chr$(13)

        If Not val(fRef.Quantity.Value) = 0 Then _
            msgErrors = msgErrors & _
            "Invalid quantity" & Chr$(13)

        If Not IsDate(fRef.OrderDate.Value) Then
            msgErrors = msgErrors & _
            "Order date is invalid" & Chr$(13)
        End If
        '
        ' continue with other field validations
        '
        If msgErrors <> "" Then
             MsgBox msgErrors
        Else
             MyForm.OnSubmit
        End If
End Sub
//-->
</SCRIPT>

<FORM  METHOD= "POST" NAME= MyForm  ACTION="myAsp.asp"  >
   PartNumber: <INPUT TYPE="text" NAME="PartNumber" >
   Quantity:  <INPUT TYPE="text" NAME="Quantity">
   Description:  <INPUT TYPE="text" NAME="Description" >
   OrderDate:  <INPUT TYPE="text" NAME="OrderDate" >
   Quantity:  <INPUT TYPE="text" NAME="Quantity" >
   <INPUT TYPE="button" NAME="btnValidate"  VALUE="Enter">
</FORM>
```

Server-based Validation

Listing 20-3 is precisely what shouldn't be done, which is server-based validation of domain values. The form posts information to itself by specifying *myAsp.asp* in the ACTION attribute.

LISTING 20-3. **Overloading the server with server-based form validation**

```
<FORM  METHOD= "POST" NAME= MyForm  ACTION="myAsp.asp"  >
   PartNumber: <INPUT TYPE="text" NAME="PartNumber" >
   Quantity:  <INPUT TYPE="text" NAME="Quantity">
   Description:  <INPUT TYPE="text" NAME="Description" >
   OrderDate:  <INPUT TYPE="text" NAME="OrderDate" >
   Quantity:  <INPUT TYPE="text" NAME="Quantity" >
   <INPUT TYPE="submit" VALUE="Enter">
</FORM>

<% If IsNumeric(Request.QueryString("PartNumber")) then %>
  <p>Part Number: <%=Request.QueryString("PartNumber")%>
<%Else %>
  <p>Please enter a valid part number.
<%End If %>
```

Avoiding input validation

Input need not be validated when input is created by selecting items from a list or a combo box. The selected entry is placed in a read-only text box that the user cannot change. The only choice is to select another entry from the list or combo box. Such a technique only ascertains the domain values, and the context still needs to be validated.

Key Point Summary

Microsoft espouses a "common look and feel" approach that is intuitive and also reduces training costs. Microsoft promotes development standards, which is admirable because one of the more difficult tasks in this world is to get developers to write documentation. Good user documentation isn't just about what to click, it's about the user's whole business process. Unfortunately good user documentation is a relic of the past. We appear to be moving towards an era of intuitive throw-away software where the programmer is off the hook for documentation when the application has an intuitive interface and supports the Microsoft-sponsored initiatives.

Standards reduce training costs. Users always expect a context menu with a right-button click. Unique, clever, and non-standard applications invariably increase training and maintenance costs.

The issue of localization is a Microsoft issue and an issue of software development companies. I do not market shrink-wrapped software, and I am reasonably sure that you don't either. The issue is discussed only for closure since the 70-100 objectives do not consider localization.

The ongoing theme of this book is scalabilty. Not all applications are scalable and the choice of user navigation determines the scalabilty of an application. Win32 applications are not scalable.

Applying What You've Learned

The Microsoft *Analyzing Requirements and Defining Solution Architectures* examination requires a significant knowledge of application construction details. I recall fifty or more questions that specifically addressed user interface issues such as control use and control layout. We'll forego the normal *instant assessment* section at the end of this chapter and replace that with a series of labs based on a user interface issues.

Answers to the labs are found in Appendix C.

Lab Exercises

This is a series of labs that deal with user interface issues. These labs address the issues of the *Designing a User Interface and User Services* section of the 70-100 objectives. Each laboratory corresponds to one objective from the *Designing a User Interface and User Services* section of the 70-100 certification test. You'll find all the answers for these labs in Appendix C.

Lab 20.67 *Given a solution, identify the navigation for the user interface*

Identify the following:

1. The most scalable type of navigation.
2. The least scalable type of navigation.
3. The navigation metaphor with the minimum functionality.

4. The navigation metaphor with the maximum functionality.
5. Two types of navigation suitable for the application described by the business rambling in Chapter 17.

Lab 20.68 *Identify input validation procedures that should be integrated into the user interface*

Discuss the issues concerning user interface validation procedures.

Lab 20.69 *Evaluate methods of providing online user assistance, such as status bars, ToolTips, and Help files*

Briefly describe each of the following items that provide help for the user interface:

- Context Sensitive Help
- ToolTips
- Status Bars
- Help Button
- Task Help
- Reference Help

Lab 20.70 *Construct a prototype user interface that is based on business requirements, user interface guidelines, and the organization's standards*

1. Establish appropriate and consistent use of menu-based controls.
2. Establish appropriate shortcut keys (accelerated keys).
3. Discuss the different types of menu-based controls and when these controls should be used.
4. Discuss the shortcut key issues. Explain how shortcut keys within Microsoft Visual Basic are created or deleted dynamically.

Lab 20.71 *Establish appropriate types of output. Types of output include paper-based reports, HTML, screen, disk, and export of data to other applications*

Discuss the issues of application output.

PART

Building a Tiered Architecture Application

IV

DCOM is the glue of the distributed application. This section addresses DCOM's performance issues. Marshaling data to or from remote servers is a major DCOM issue and Chapters 12 through 16 experimented with different types of marshaling as a precursor to this chapter. The developer no longer has the freedom of calling methods with the prescribed parameters when using DCOM. To do so invites pitifully poor performance since each parameter of a method call requires a wire trip. The type of parameter is also a performance issue. These issues and others are discussed in detail and the chapter closes with a significant lab that builds a CRUD class.

The QUESTION.VBP project in a lab at the end of Chapter 16 posed a tiered architecture error question. That question is answered in this chapter.

Chapter 21: Distributed COM (DCOM) - Windows NT 4.0 delivers distributed COM, which provides COM communication between diverse systems.

CHAPTER

21

Distributed COM (DCOM)

About Chapter 21

Chapter 21 is about extending COM. This chapter examines DCOM from several perspectives. The first perspective is the DCOM evolution path. This is followed by a quick peek at DCOM architectural issues including threading. I also take a close look at DCOM performance issues.

The first ten chapters of this book dealt with COM, which is ubiquitous in the Microsoft architecture. The next six chapters discussed database access technologies. I made sure that the labs of each chapter except Chapter 11 built at least one class. Chapter 12 included an elegant ODBC class that manages a Unicode query of any size. I also introduced various custom marshaling techniques in the labs. Chapters 17 through 20 addressed the 70-100 objectives.

This chapter puts it all together using DCOM. The labs of this chapter construct a three-tier application using a CRUD class, which is discussed in the 491 courseware. Knowledge of CRUD classes is essential for several 70-100 objectives.

Your acquired custom marshaling knowledge is an asset for this chapter. DCOM is not easy to use, and the developer must be very careful — a DCOM application will have pitifully poor performance unless custom marshaling is used. There are other DCOM programming vagaries, each of which is discussed in this chapter.

The chapter closes with a presentation of several classes. These classes are robust and I use them for both system prototyping and final client system delivery. Building a component application is not easy. The main problem is deciding upon an architecture and then deciding where to locate specific functionality within that architecture.

The examples in this chapter are found in the Visual Basic Chapter21.VBP project located in the `EXAMPLES\CHAPTER21` **folder of the CD-ROM that accompanies this book.**

About DAO

I use DAO in this chapter since many readers will not have access to Microsoft SQL Server. DAO is used to create, read, update, and delete (CRUD) classes, which are discussed in Microsoft Course 491.

DAO is not a tiered architecture building block for these reasons:

- DAO consumes significant system resources.
- The object instantiation hierarchy is rigid.
- DAO does not support server-side cursors.
- DAO does not support a disconnected **Recordset** object, something that is required in a tiered architecture.
- DAO does support stored-procedure output parameters or return codes.
- DAO queries against Microsoft SQL Server are synchronous.
- DAO cannot limit the number of returned rows. Limiting the returned row count is especially useful when a complete table is inadvertently returned because of inferior SQL statements.

The Road to DCOM

The availability of COM defines the first step to a component architecture. Only after COM matured was Remote Automation introduced as the second step, which coincided with the release of Microsoft Visual Basic 4.0. Microsoft Windows NT 4.0 hosted the first release of distributed COM (DCOM), which is the third step to a component architecture. Before Windows NT 4.0 was released, COM was limited to either an *in-process* server or an *out-of-process* server on the same machine. Distributed COM makes remote *out-of-process* servers transparent to the client, which is aptly named *location transparency*. Parallel to the third step is the Distributed Transaction Coordinator (DTC) of Microsoft SQL Server. DTC evolves into the fourth step, which is the current Microsoft Transaction Server.

Useful software must satisfy three distinct criteria: *extensibility, maintainability,* and *reusability*. Let's look at each of these criteria. COM and DCOM are used interchangeably since DCOM is a distributed version of COM.

- ***Extensible*** — COM/DCOM is extensible. The COM contract is maintained with the client and the object is extended following COM versioning rules. Either aggregation or delegation is used for the extension and the original client is unaware of the new services, which new clients can use (see Chapter 1).
- ***Maintainability*** — COM is maintainable since COM uses interfaces as an abstract data type to isolate implementation details from the client. COM uses interface inheritance where no actual code is inherited, but the developer is required to implement the interface. This can be compared to C++ implementation inheritance. When a developer makes a change in a C++ superclass, all the subservient subclasses break. This is known as the *superclass problem*. Such a problem doesn't occur with COM/DCOM since the implementation is isolated from the user, and if the object's signatures (methods and properties) are not modified, the client is unaware of any changes. Interfaces represent a functional binary encapsulation. Binary encapsulation is not possible in C++; that is, the only encapsulation available in C++ is syntax-based.
- ***Reusability*** — Reusability in COM is a given since COM supports the client/server paradigm. Different clients each have their own instance of a server, hence the reusability.

We can get a better perspective of COM usability by examining various application models. Figure 21-1 is an age-old model. The architecture has two tiers with a monolithic client application. This application model is present in both the legacy era and in the current Microsoft Windows epoch. Such an application is limited in scaleability and maintainability.

The classic application of the Microsoft epoch is the two-tier architecture, which is illustrated in Figure 21-2. The application is distributed to the extent that business rules reside in stored procedures on the server. This client/server paradigm shift started in the early 90s and is still popular today. This paradigm will remain popular for quite some time considering the zeal with which Database Administrators (DBAs) protect their turf. Many DBAs do not allow the placement of COM objects within Microsoft SQL Server and have assumed roles not unlike those of holy priests protecting the sacred scrolls of relational database scripture.

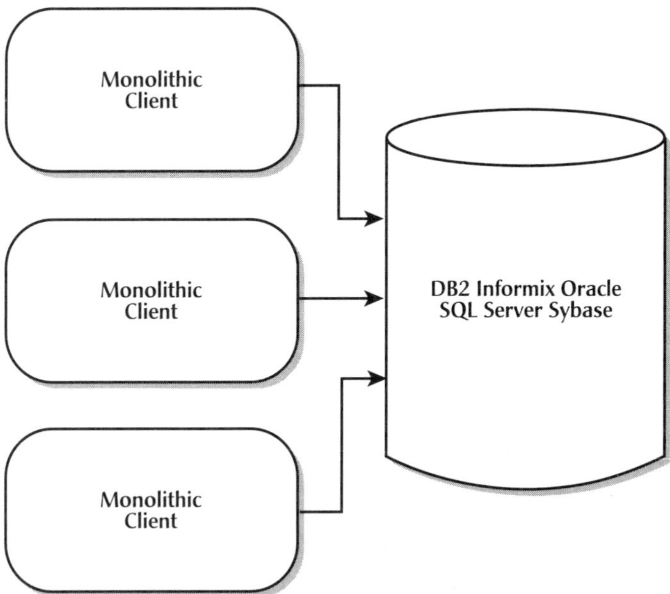

FIGURE 21-1 A monolithic application.

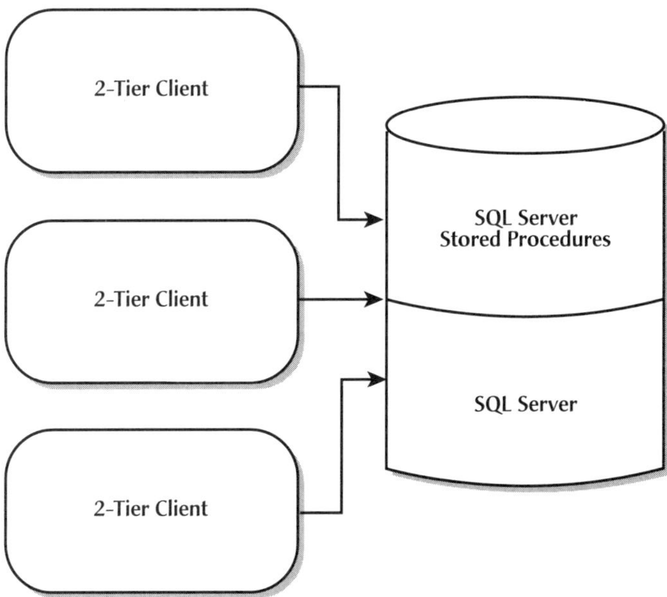

FIGURE 21-2 The classic Microsoft client/server architecture.

Microsoft again improved client/server scaleability with connection pooling in Open Database Connectivity (ODBC) 3.0. Prior to ODBC 3.0 connections were always maintained since the cost of acquiring a connection was prohibitive. Maintaining a continuous connection limits scaleability. The two-tier architecture has several limiting factors:

- The number of connections that can be established with the server limits a two-tier architecture. Scaling a two-tier architecture is always an issue of increasing the server size. A point of diminishing returns is always reached after which increasing server size does not improve scaleability.
- Placing stored procedures on the server improves scaleability to some degree.
- Pooling connections also improves scaleability, however the ultimate issue is always increasing server size.
- Moving application code to intelligent clients improves scaleability, however this is offset by a loss of central software control and the difficulty in deploying new applications.

Combining connection pooling with stored procedures on the server still does not supply enough scaleability. Distributed COM delivered in Windows NT 4.0 starts another paradigm, which is the distributed application. The first step in distributing an application is to decompose a possibly monolithic application into generic components. Figure 21-3 represents the monolithic application of Figure 21-1 decomposed into generic functionality.

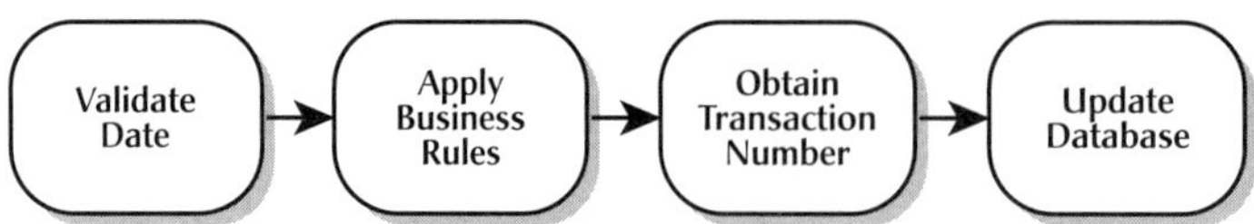

FIGURE 21-3 A decomposed monolithic application.

A COM server is defined for each of the decomposed functions illustrated in Figure 21-3. More than one server may exist and load balancing occurs betwseen servers. Such an architecture is illustrated in Figure 21-4. Clients instantiate a server instance and release the instance when processing is complete. This architecture is created and maintained by the developer. The objects may retain *state* (information). Scaleability is improved, however *stateless* objects improve scaleability still further. The remainder of this chapter deals with objects that may or may not retain maintain state since MTS is not a requirement for every application.

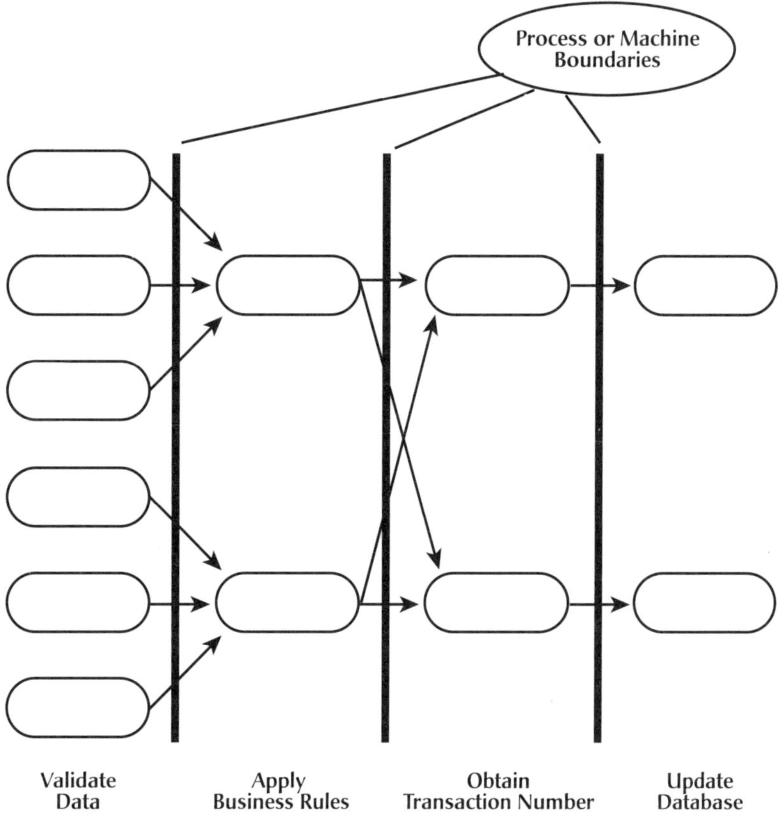

FIGURE 21-4 Distributing a monolithic application.

Under the Hood with DCOM

The two major DCOM topics are marshaling (see Chapter 1) and the Microsoft threading model. Marshaling and threading are related, but the first order of business is to understand a *message pump* in the context of the Windows architecture. Microsoft Windows is message-based. Messages are continually sent to applications and it is the application's responsibility to process these messages. An example of a message pump is this classic Windows code fragment:

```
MSG msg;
While(getMessage(&msg, NULL, 0, 0))
      DispatchMessage(&msg);
```

The Windows architecture is event driven and messages are sent to the *WinMain* function, which is the main entry point of a Windows application. The logic inside *WinMain* spins in a continuous loop processing messages. Figure 21-5 illustrates the basic architecture of a Windows application. Nearly all the work accomplished is in response to events.

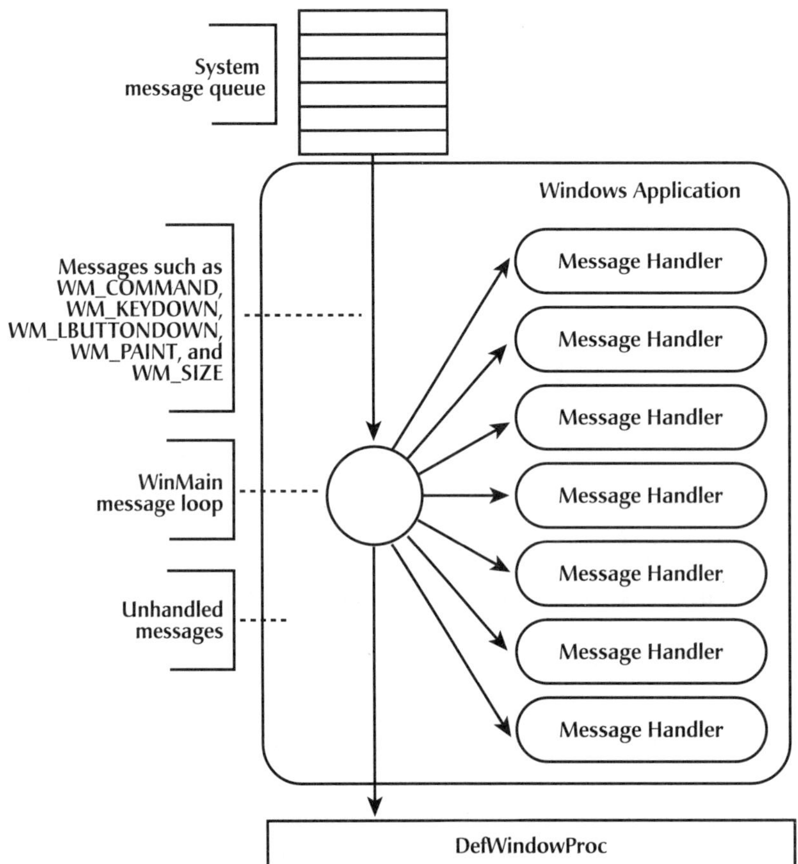

FIGURE 21-5 The Windows message pump architecture.

Message pumps are related to *single-threaded apartments* and *single-threaded main,* so let's define the threading models.

Threads are an execution path of the host operating system. Each thread maintains local storage that is inaccessible by other threads. An *apartment* is defined as a logical grouping of objects that share common concurrency and reentrancy constraints. Apartments that host a thread that is not safe outside the confines of the apartment are aptly named *single-threaded* apartments (STA). Such a thread cannot be trusted and is limited to the confines of the apartment (house arrest). Apartments hosting threads that obey strict concurrency and reentrancy rules are correspondingly named *multi-threaded* apartments (MTA). These threads are known collectively as the *free-threading* model, which is a rigid adherence to concurrency and reentrancy rules.

Threads are created with the Win32 function **CreateThread.** A thread context is created with the functions **CoInitializeEx, CoInitialize,** or **OleInitialize**. Creating a thread context is illustrated with:

```
HRESULT hr = CoInitializeEx(0, COINIT_MULTITHREADED)
HRESULT hr = CoInitializeEx(0, COINIT_APARTMENTTHREADED)
```

In-process servers run in the process of the client and do not call **CoInitializeEx** to establish a threading context. An application may have any number of STAs, but only one MTA. Table 21-1 enumerates the various Microsoft thread models.

TABLE 21-1 MICROSOFT THREAD MODELS

Thread	*Description*
Single	Legacy application. Only one thread allowed within the application. Objects can be marshaled to private threads from this thread.
Apartment	One thread per apartment, however there may be more than one apartment within the application. The same thread is used for all calls. Objects can be marshaled to private threads from this thread type.
Free	Can only be used in one MTA. Multiple threads may exist for each instance. Objects cannot be marshaled to private threads from this thread type.
Both (Mixed)	This thread may be used in any number of STAs or within one MTA. Objects can be marshaled to private threads from this thread type.
Rental	The equivalent of a MTA (free threading), however all method calls are serialized. This type of thread is very suitable for thread-safe classes. Objects cannot be marshaled to private threads from this thread type.

We now have the necessary background to examine DCOM marshaling. There are two versions of marshaling. The first is the free-threaded marshaling, which we won't discuss since we're interested in performance issues. The second is single-threaded apartment (STA) marshaling. The context here is the cost of STA marshaling, which is required by Microsoft Visual Basic. Every STA requires a message pump.

Figure 21-6 illustrates the architecture of STA marshaling. A total of four threads are required for STA marshaling, two on the client side and two on the object side. When marshaling VB STA components is a performance issue, the only other alternative is Microsoft C++ MTA components and the *free-threaded marshaler*.

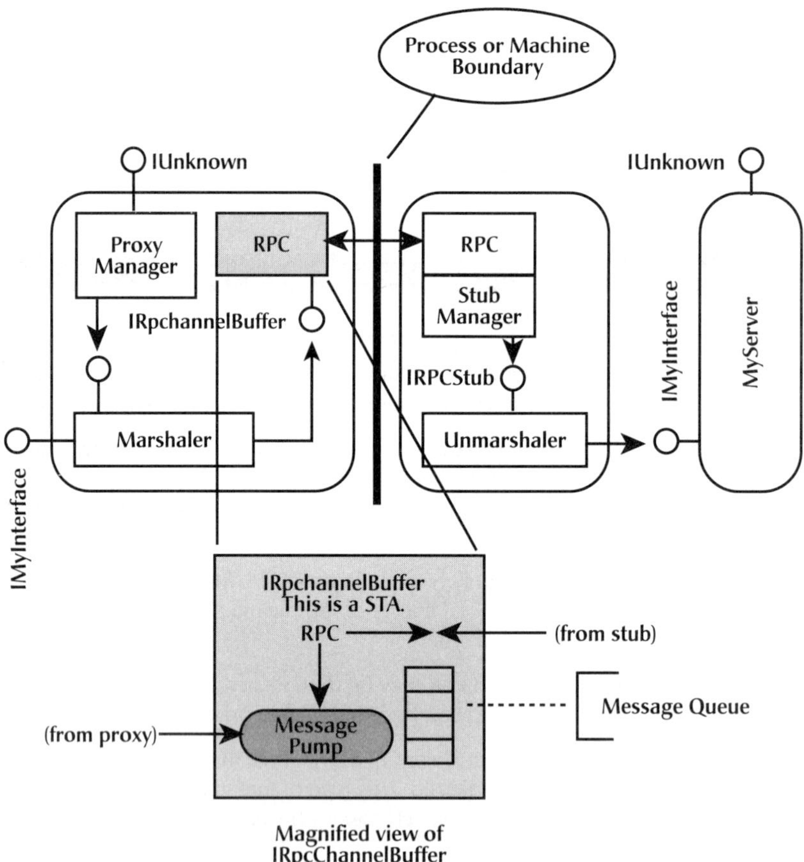

FIGURE 21-6 Microsoft Visual Basic STA marshaling.

DCOM Performance Issues

Microsoft promised a transparent implementation of DCOM. From an implementation perspective, DCOM is transparent. However DCOM components exist on a network and techniques used for COM in-process servers are not applicable to DCOM components. This section addresses DCOM performance issues.

Scaling a DCOM Application

Scaling an application is not the indiscriminate adding of new components. Bottlenecks can result without a planned approach. Bottlenecks will occur as the application illustrated in Figure 21-4 is scaled. A solution to the bottlenecks problem is a *broker* component that returns the *best choice* component. Figure 21-7 illustrates the best choice broker strategy.

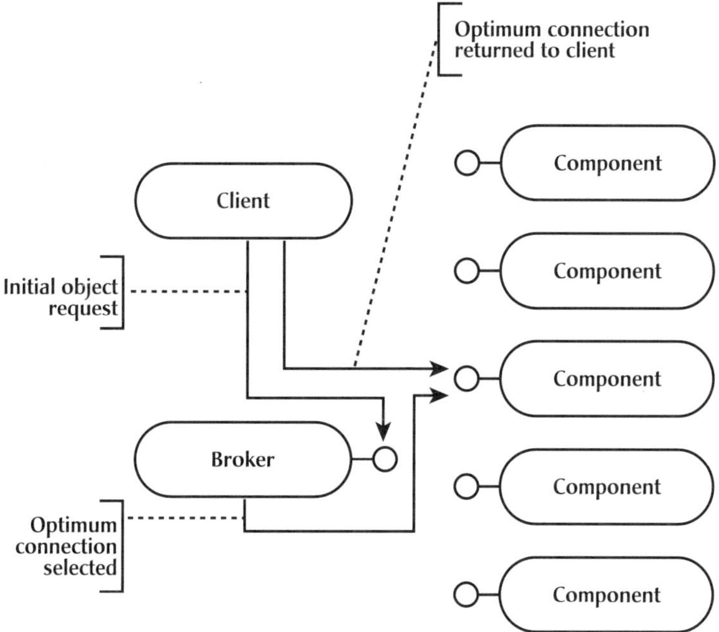

FIGURE 21-7 Solving the bottleneck problem.

Wire Trips

Performance is the major DCOM issue. DCOM instantiates network objects, which is the main source of DCOM performance issues. The primary goal is to minimize the number of wire trips, (network traverses) for a DCOM object. As an example, a method call with three parameters will require a wire trip for each parameter. The solution is custom marshaling where parameters are packed into a **Variant** or into a User-Defined-Type (UDT) and only one object is transmitted. Collection objects are not a viable choice for communicating with remote components. Listing 21-1 is from a **DataClass** class that is discussed later in this chapter. The client calls the **UpdateRows** method of the **DataClass** class with a **Collection** object that is a collection of collections. Each item in the outer collection is another collection that consists of the table name and name-value pairs. This makes the techniques shown in Listing 21-1 very useful, since a parent table and a child table can both be updated within the same transaction. Although this technique is used within an in-process server, the technique is not recommended when the component is an out-of-process server.

LISTING 21-1 **The InsertRows method. Using collections as DCOM parameters**

```
Public Function InsertRows( _
     ByVal colInsertRows As Collection) As Long
'(C) 1999 Bruce T. Prendergast
' DBA Prendergast Consulting
' DBA PCS
  Dim NewRow As Collection
  Dim strColumns As String, strValues As String
  Dim strComma As String * 1
  Dim strSQL As String
  Dim i As Integer, ActionCount As Long
  Const UserIDSize = 31
  Dim UserID As String * UserIDSize, _
     lngSize As Long, Status As Long
  If colInsertRows.Count < 1 Then Exit Function
  InitializeErrorLog
  On Error GoTo NewRowError
  UserID = String$(UserIDSize, 0)
```

```
lngSize = UserIDSize - 1
Status = GetUserName(UserID, lngSize)
DBC.DBBeginTransaction
For Each NewRow In colInsertRows
  strColumns = ""
  strValues = ""
  strComma = ""
  For i = 2 To NewRow.Count - 1 Step 2
    strColumns = strColumns & Trim$(strComma & _
      NewRow.Item(i))
    Select Case VarType(NewRow.Item(i + 1))
      Case vbDate
        strValues = strValues & strComma & "#" & _
      NewRow.Item(i + 1) & "#"
      Case vbString
        strValues = strValues & Trim$(strComma & "'" & _
      NewRow.Item(i + 1) & "'")
      Case Else
        strValues = strValues & strComma & NewRow.Item(i + 1)
    End Select
    strComma = ","
  Next i
'
' user id
'
  strColumns = strColumns & "," & "UserID"
  strValues = strValues & ",'" & Left$(UserID, lngSize - 1) & "'"
'
' insert time
'
  strColumns = strColumns & "," & "UserDate"
  strValues = strValues & ",'" & Format(Now, _
    "dd-mmm-yyyy hh:mm:SS AMPM") & "'"
  strSQL = "INSERT INTO " & NewRow(1) & _
    " (" & strColumns & ") VALUES (" & strValues & ");"
  ActionCount = DBC.ActionQuery(strSQL)
```

```
        If ActionCount <> 1 Then
          DBC.DBRollBackTransaction
          InsertRows = 0
          Exit Function
        End If
      Next
      DBC.DBCommitTransaction
      InsertRows = colInsertRows.Count
      Exit Function
    NewRowError:
      Resume Next
      DBC.DBRollBackTransaction
      LogDataClassErrors
      InsertRows = 0
      Exit Function
    End Function
```

Component Binding

The **IDispatch** interface is the least desirable component binding interface, however there are situations where no other choice is available. The desirable interface is **IUnknown** since access is through a Vtable. Vtable binding is many orders of magnitude faster than the **IDispatch** interface. Late binding and **IDispatch** are slow, but are an accommodation to clients that cannot process custom Vtable bindings (*dispinterfaces* and the **IUnknown** interface).

The **IDispatch** interface is inefficient. **GetIDsOfNames** is called to resolve the name and a second call is made to **Invoke**. **Invoke** only accepts an array of variants and results are only returned as a **Variant**. **Variants** are the least desirable data type because of the excessive overhead.

Early binding occurs with an **IDispatch**-only interface and a type library must exist for the object. There is no need to call **GetIDsOfNames** at execution time because the DISPIDs were embedded at compile time. Early binding is faster than late binding, but it still lags far behind a Vtable binding in terms of performance.

Automation objects are only able to use an object's default interface since an Automation client cannot call **QueryInterface**. This is because VB only supports Automation clients by hosting public methods in a creatable class, which means that Automation clients will always use the **IDispatch** interface.

Vtable binding is always the fastest component binding mechanism. Microsoft Visual Basic applications can use Vtable binding when:

- A reference to the appropriate type library exists.
- The reference is typed to an interface or a creatable class, which is the default interface.
- The object exposes Vtables and is not an **IDispatch** only interface.

There are four alternatives available to the Visual Basic programmer with respect to component binding.

- Dual interfaces improve the situation somewhat but parameters must still be passed as variants. VB 5.0 and VB 6.0 automatically create a dual interface.
- The VB **Implements** statement creates a Vtable. (See the lab at the conclusion of Chapter 1 and this chapter). This can be taken as an admonition to always create user-defined interfaces. The improved performance will easily offset the additional effort.
- The VB developer can create a type library directly. The Enterprise version of Visual Basic creates a type library automatically when the component is compiled and the project's **Remote Server Files** property is set. Before compiling the component, select: PROJECT | PROPERTIES | COMPONENT | REMOTE SERVER FILES. Normally type libraries are internal to VB components. The **OLE View** tool of Microsoft Visual Studio can also be used to create a library. The task is a bit cumbersome, but using **OLE View** tool may be the only choice. A lab at the conclusion of this chapter creates a type library using the **OLE View** tool.
- **CreateObject** can be used to bind an application object directly to an interface's Vtable. The restriction is that the **Object** data type cannot be used. The code snippet below illustrates such a binding.

```
Function GetAuthor(ByVal NerdBook as String) as IAuthor
       Dim ProgID as String
       ProgID = "IDGAuthor." & NerdBook
       Set GetAuthor = CreateObject(ProgID)
End Function
```

Developer Issues

Nothing is more dreaded than the VB message *expression is too complex*. The expression is invariably very simple and the real problem is a memory leak. The best defense against a memory leak is always an aggressive offense.

- Write tight code.
- Destroy any objects created as soon as possible by setting the object values to **Nothing**.
- Use strict data typing. Avoid **Variants** if at all possible.
- Never use bound controls. Your skills as a developer are measured in inverse proportion to the number of bound controls within your application. It goes without saying that beginning developers use Microsoft Access and bind all controls.
- Use the **End** keyword in the main form's **Unload** event.
- Use the **ClassTerminate** event to destroy data collections and other objects.
- Erase arrays that are no longer in use.

Parameter Declarations

We already know that each parameter of a method in a DCOM architecture is a wire trip. The parameter declaration type is also important. The *ByVal* declaration pushes data to the component in one wire trip. The most efficient DCOM component marshaling mechanism is to package all the parameters into one package (*custom marshaling*) and use *ByVal* as the declaration type. But this isn't always possible and on occasion *ByRef* must be used. The problem with *ByRef* is that data is marshaled both ways, both from and to the component. The developer's only choice to prevent unwanted data from being marshaled back to the client is to erase the data array before exiting the component's method. This means that at most an empty array is marshaled back to the client.

Listing 21-1 is an example of a method designed for an *in-process* class. This is because every iteration of a *For Each* construct creates a new connection to the client object. This is not tolerable in an out-of-process environment, especially when the client object is remote.

COURSE WRITERS DON'T DEVELOP APPLICATIONS

I got a chuckle from Microsoft class 1298, which presents collections as a technique for implementing a 3-tier architecture. The *For Each* construct is used to enumerate a returned collection of a component. No mention is made of the cost engendered of accessing each object in a collection that is not local. Collections are owned by another component and an *in-process* server is the only environment where the overhead is acceptable. The example is from the Executive Air application of course 1298.

Component Communication

The success of a DCOM component architecture hinges upon component communication. We've discussed component communication using parameters and methods, however there are two other DCOM component communication mechanisms. The first is *callbacks* and the other is *events*. You'll find a *callback* lab at the conclusion of Chapter 10 and an *event* (advisory-sink) lab at the conclusion of Chapter 6.

The **Raise** statement is another DCOM tool that is useful for communicating error information back to the client. The **Raise** statement takes advantage of an intrinsic feature of Microsoft Visual Basic. This feature is based on the fact that a VB error handler cannot handle errors created within the error handler. Such errors are always passed back up the call-tree to the prior level. The prior level of the call tree will process the error, but only if an error handler exists. The application stops when the application does not possess an error handler at the top level. Each level adds additional information as the error message is passed back up the call-tree to the client. This is known as *unwinding the stack*. The examples that follow retain state to the extent that error messages are retained in a class variable. When an error occurs, the client instantiates an error processing component passing a reference to the object in which the error occurred. The error component retrieves the last error message with the **RetrieveErrors** method. Retaining error information within a component isn't necessary and the example code may appear to be artificial, however this was done to illustrate the issue of a component maintaining state.

In the Trenches with DCOM

Building a component architecture is not a simple task. There are many factors to consider. Interaction rates, dispersion, and component size are issues to consider when creating a distributed architecture. A high interaction rate dictates a local component that is best implemented as an in-process server.

Component size may reduce the flexibility of deployment. The component may not be large when compared with a monolithic application, but ease and speed of deployment are essential. Remember that components are not anchored to a particular system — the deployment costs should be considered. The last issue is that smaller components increase network traffic. Validation of data and business rules can be combined within one component, however the choice is specific to the problem at hand.

DatabaseClass Class

This section presents a class based on Data Access Objects (DAO). This class is easily converted to either a Remote Data Objects (RDO) or Active Data Objects (ADO) class. The choice was made to create a DAO class since you may not have Microsoft SQL Server, and it is assumed that you are familiar with Microsoft Access.

The software that I'm about to present is an in-process server. A lab at the conclusion of this chapter will convert this class to a DCOM .EXE server suitable for deployment. The **DatabaseClass** class adheres to the previously stated DCOM component rules: only one parameter is passed to a method and the parameter is passed by value. Table 21-2 enumerates the methods of **DatabaseClass** class module and Listing 21-2 contains the code for this class.

TABLE 21-2 DatabaseClass Class Methods

Method	*Description*
ActionQuery()	Called only from the instantiator **DataClass** class. SQL statement(s) are passed in for execution. Multiple statements are separated by a semicolon. The RecordsAffected property is returned for analysis. <-1> is returned on an error.

Method	*Description*
ClassInitialize()	The **DataClass** class instantiates this component. The DAO **Workspace** object and **Database** object are created.
ClassTerminate()	The **DataClass** terminates this object by setting the instance to **Nothing**. An error is issued for an open transaction and the DAO **Workspace** object and the **Database** object are both set to **Nothing**.
DBBeginTransaction()	Called only from the instantiator **DataClass** class. An error is returned when an active transaction already exists. Both Microsoft Access and Microsoft SQL Server support nested transactions, however Open Database Connectivity (ODBC) does not support nested transactions. The choice is arbitrary if ODBC is not used. Disallowing nested transactions simplifies the conversion to other technologies such as RDO or ADO.
DBCommitTransaction()	Called only from the instantiator **DataClass** class. An error is returned when an active transaction does not exist.
DBRollBackTransaction()	Called only from the instantiator **DataClass** class. An active transaction is rolled back. An error is returned when no active transaction exists.
LogSoftError()	A private method called only by methods of the **DatabaseClass** class. A string message is logged to the dynamic error array.
LogDatabaseClassErrors()	A private method called only by methods of the **DatabaseClass** class. All errors in the DAO error collection are logged to the local dynamic array.
RetrieveErrors()	Called only from the instantiator **DataClass** class. Errors are retrieved from a dynamic array.
SelectQuery()	Called only from the instantiator **DataClass** class. A SQL statement is passed to the Jet engine and a result set is returned.

LISTING 21-2 **The DatabaseClass class**

```
'(C) 1999 Bruce T. Prendergast

' DBA Prendergast Consulting

' DBA PCS

'
```

```
' IDG Books Worldwide ISBN 007645-3314-2
'
' DCOM DatabaseClass class
'
  Option Explicit
  Private Const DatabasePath = _
     "E:\70-100\CH21\Examples\DCOMDAO.mdb"
  Private wrkJet As Workspace
  Private dbsDataV As Database
  Private TransactionActive As Boolean
  Private DatabaseClassErrors()

Public Function RetrieveErrors() As Variant
  RetrieveErrors = DatabaseClassErrors()
  InitializeErrorLog
End Function
Private Sub InitializeErrorLog()
  ReDim DatabaseClassErrors(1)
  DatabaseClassErrors(1) = "No errors occurred in Database Class"
  Exit Sub
End Sub
Private Sub LogSoftError(strErr As String)
  ReDim DatabaseClassErrors(2)
  DatabaseClassErrors(2) = "Database Class software error: " & strErr
End Sub

Private Sub LogDatabaseClassErrors()
  Dim DB As DBEngine
  Dim dbError As Error
  Dim s As String, i As Integer
  s = ""
  i = UBound(DatabaseClassErrors())
  DatabaseClassErrors(1) = "Errors occurred in Database Class"
  For Each dbError In DB.Errors
    s = s & "DatabaseClass error Number: " _
      & Str$(dbError.Number) _
```

```
      & " " & dbError.Description
    i = i + 1
    ReDim Preserve DatabaseClassErrors(i)
    DatabaseClassErrors(i) = s
  Next
End Sub

Public Function ActionQuery(ByVal strSQL As String) As Long
  InitializeErrorLog
  On Error GoTo ActionQueryError
  dbsDataV.Execute strSQL
  ActionQuery = dbsDataV.RecordsAffected
  Exit Function
ActionQueryError:
  Resume Next
  LogDatabaseClassErrors
  ActionQuery = -1
End Function

Public Function DBRollBackTransaction() As Boolean
  InitializeErrorLog
  If Not TransactionActive Then
    LogSoftError "No Transaction available to rollback"
    DBRollBackTransaction = False
    Exit Function
  End If
  On Error GoTo RollbackFailure
  wrkJet.Rollback
  DBRollBackTransaction = True
  TransactionActive = False
  Exit Function
RollbackFailure:
  Resume Next
  LogDatabaseClassErrors
  DBRollBackTransaction = False
End Function
```

```
Public Function DBCommitTransaction() As Boolean
  InitializeErrorLog
  If Not TransactionActive Then
    LogSoftError "No Transaction available to commit"
    DBCommitTransaction = False
    Exit Function
  End If
  On Error GoTo UnableToCommit
  wrkJet.CommitTrans
  TransactionActive = False
  DBCommitTransaction = True
  Exit Function
UnableToCommit:
  Resume Next
  LogDatabaseClassErrors
  wrkJet.Rollback
  TransactionActive = False
  DBCommitTransaction = False
End Function

Public Function DBBeginTransaction() As Boolean
  InitializeErrorLog
  If TransactionActive Then
    LogSoftError "Transaction is already active"
    DBBeginTransaction = False
    Exit Function
  End If
  On Error GoTo UnableToStart
  wrkJet.BeginTrans
  DBBeginTransaction = True
  TransactionActive = True
  Exit Function
UnableToStart:
  Resume Next
  LogDatabaseClassErrors
  DBBeginTransaction = False
```

```
End Function

Public Function SelectQuery(ByVal strSQL As String) As Recordset
  Dim myRS As Recordset
  On Error GoTo SelectError
  InitializeErrorLog
  Set myRS = dbsDataV.OpenRecordset(strSQL, _
     dbOpenForwardOnly, dbReadOnly)
  Set SelectQuery = myRS
  strSQL = ""
  Set myRS = Nothing
  Exit Function
SelectError:
  Resume Next
  LogDatabaseClassErrors
End Function

Private Sub Class_Initialize()
  Set wrkJet = CreateWorkspace("", "admin", "", dbUseJet)
  Set dbsDataV = wrkJet.OpenDatabase(DatabasePath, True)
End Sub

Private Sub Class_Terminate()
  If TransactionActive Then
    DBEngine.Rollback
    MsgBox "Warning: Transaction rolled back on class termination"
  End If
  Set dbsDataV = Nothing
  Set wrkJet = Nothing
End Sub
```

DataClass Class

The DataClass class is the second of three classes presented in this section. This class uses **Collection** objects extensively and is only suitable for deployment as an in-process server. The DataClass class stands between the presentation layer and the data services layer. This is the *business rules* layer using Microsoft nomenclature. I prefer to call it the *infrastructure* layer.

Using collections of in-process servers leads to succinct and very readable code. The code fragment below uses the **DataClass** component of Listing 21-3 and Table 21-3 to load a combo box and to retrieve master holidays for a master calendar. (Clients have plus and minus calendars, which are additions or deletions to the master calendar.)

```
For Each MyCol In DataEngine.GetRows( _
     "cust_num, CompanyName", "tblCustomers", "")
  cmbCust.AddItem MyCol("CompanyName")
  cmbCust.ItemData(cmbCust.NewIndex) = MyCol("cust_num")
Next
cmbCust.ListIndex = 0
cmbCust.Enabled = True
For Each MyCol In DataEngine.GetRows( _
     "HolidayDate", "tblHolidays", _
     " WHERE Cust_Num = 'BASE';")
 HolidayCount = HolidayCount + 1
 ReDim Preserve Holidays(HolidayCount)
 Holidays(HolidayCount - 1) = _
     Format(MyCol("HolidayDate"), "dd-mmm-yyyy")
 lstHolidayMaster.AddItem Holidays(HolidayCount - 1)
Next
```

TABLE 21-3 DATACLASS CLASS METHODS

Method	*Description*
CascadingDelete()	Called directly from the presentation layer. The input argument is a collection of table names and SQL WHERE expressions, which are presented in child-to-parent order.
ClassInitialize()	Called indirectly by the presentation layer when the class is instantiated. The **DatabaseClass** class is instantiated.
ClassTerminate()	Called indirectly by the presentation layer when the class is terminated. The **DatabaseClass** class is terminated.

Method	*Description*
DeleteRows()	Called from the presentation layer. An action query is constructed from the supplied table name and WHERE clause. The DELETE transaction is aborted when the count returned from the **DatabaseClass** class fails to match the row count supplied by the presentation layer.
GetColumn()	Called from the presentation layer. Returns a collection of values based on a supplied WHERE clause and table name.
GetCount()	Called from the presentation layer. The row count is returned for a SELECT COUNT(*) from a supplied table name and a supplied WHERE clause.
GetRows()	Called from the presentation layer. Returns a collection of collections based on a supplied WHERE clause. Each subcollection is based on name-value pairs.
GetIdentifier()	Called from the presentation layer. Concurrency is value-based. This method returns the next concurrency identifier. The concurrent identifier is a special table where each row is padded to approximately 1800 or more bytes. This is because locks in Microsoft Access are based on 2048 byte pages as are the Microsoft SQL Server pages. Row locking does NOT work in Microsoft SQL Server 6.5, hence row locking is not a consideration in Microsoft SQL Server 6.5. Microsoft SQL Server 7.0 supports row level locking.
InitializeErrorLog()	Private method called by the **DataClass** class. The class error variable is initialized.
InsertRows()	Called from the presentation layer. The supplied input is a collection of collections. Each subcollection consists of a table name and name-value pairs. The subcollection count is compared to the count returned from the **DatabaseClass** and the INSERT transaction is committed when these counts match. For auditing purposes each row is appended with a UserID and a UserDate.
LogSoftError()	Private method called by the **DataClass** class. Logs software errors to the class variable.
LogDataClassErrors()	Private method called by the **DataClass** class. Logs data errors to the class variable.
RetrieveErrors()	Called from the presentation layer. The **DatabaseClass RetrieveErrors** method is called and those errors are appended to those found in the local error variable and returned to the presentation layer.

continued

TABLE 21-3 DATACLASS CLASS METHODS (CONTINUED)

Method	Description
UpdateRows()	Called from the presentation layer. The supplied input is a collection of collections. Each subcollection consists of a table name, a WHERE clause that includes the concurrency expression and name-value pairs. The subcollection count is compared to the count returned from the **DatabaseClass** and the UPDATE transaction is committed when these counts match. For auditing purposes each row is appended with a UserID and a UserDate.

LISTING 21-3 The DataClass class

```
'(C) 1999 Bruce T. Prendergast
' DBA Prendergast Consulting
' DBA PCS
'
' IDG Books Worldwide ISBN 0-7645-3314-2
'
' DCOM DataClass class
'
Option Explicit
Private DBC As DatabaseClass
Private DataClassErrors()
Private TransactionActive As Boolean
Private Declare Function GetUserName & Lib "advapi32.dll" _
    Alias "GetUserNameA" ( _
    ByVal lpBuffer As String, nSize As Long)

Public Function CascadingDelete( _
    ByVal colDelete As Collection) As Boolean
  Dim ActionCount As Long, DeleteCount As Long
  Dim i As Integer
  Dim MyCol As Collection
  InitializeErrorLog
  CascadingDelete = False
```

```
  On Error GoTo CascadingDeleteError
  DBC.DBBeginTransaction
  For Each MyCol In colDelete
    DeleteCount = GetCount(MyCol("Table"), MyCol("Where"))
    If DeleteCount <> 0 Then
      ActionCount = DBC.ActionQuery( _
          "DELETE " & MyCol("Target") & _
          " FROM " & MyCol("Table") & " " & MyCol("Where"))
      If ActionCount <> DeleteCount Then
        DBC.DBRollBackTransaction
      End If
    End If
  Next
  DBC.DBCommitTransaction
  CascadingDelete = True
  Exit Function
CascadingDeleteError:
  Resume Next
  LogDataClassErrors
  CascadingDelete = False
End Function

Private Sub InitializeErrorLog()
  ReDim DataClassErrors(1)
  DataClassErrors(1) = "No errors occurred in Data Class"
  Exit Sub
End Sub

Public Function GetCount( _
     ByVal strTable As String, _
     ByVal strWhere As String) As Long
  Dim myRS As Recordset
  InitializeErrorLog
  On Error GoTo GetCountError
  Set myRS = DBC.SelectQuery("SELECT Count(*) " & _
    " as RowCount FROM " & strTable & " " & strWhere)
```

```
    GetCount = myRS(0).Value
    Set myRS = Nothing
    Exit Function
GetCountError:
    Resume Next
    LogDataClassErrors
    GetCount = -1
End Function

Public Function RetrieveErrors() As Variant
    Dim CapturedErrors As Variant
    Dim i As Long, j As Long, k As Long
    CapturedErrors = DBC.RetrieveErrors
    i = UBound(DataClassErrors)
    j = UBound(CapturedErrors)
    For k = 1 To i
      j = j + 1
      ReDim Preserve CapturedErrors(j)
      CapturedErrors(j) = DataClassErrors(k)
    Next
    RetrieveErrors = CapturedErrors
End Function

Private Sub LogSoftError(strErr As String)
    ReDim DataClassErrors(2)
    DataClassErrors(1) = "Errors occurred in Data Class"
    DataClassErrors(2) = "Data Class software error: " & strErr
End Sub

Private Sub LogDataClassErrors()
    Dim DB As DBEngine
    Dim dbError As Error
    Dim i As Integer
    i = UBound(DataClassErrors())
    DataClassErrors(1) = "Errors occurred in Data Class"
    For Each dbError In DB.Errors
```

```
      i = i + 1
      ReDim Preserve DataClassErrors(i)
      DataClassErrors(i) = _
        "DataClass Error Number: " _
        & Str$(dbError.Number) _
        & " " & dbError.Description
    Next
End Sub

Public Function UpdateRows( _
     ByVal colUpdateRows As Collection) As Long
  Dim Status As Boolean
  Dim i As Integer
  Dim UpdateRow As Collection
  Dim strColumns As String
  Dim strValues As String
  Dim strComma As String * 1
  Dim strSQL As String
  Dim ActionCount As Long
  Const UserIDSize = 21
  Dim UserID As String * UserIDSize
  Dim lngSize As Long, APIStatus As Long
  If colUpdateRows.Count < 1 Then Exit Function
  InitializeErrorLog
  On Error GoTo UpdateRowsError:
  UserID = String$(UserIDSize, 0)
  lngSize = UserIDSize - 1
  APIStatus = GetUserName(UserID, lngSize)
  Status = DBC.DBBeginTransaction()
  For Each UpdateRow In colUpdateRows
    strComma = ""
    strColumns = ""
    For i = 3 To UpdateRow.Count Step 2
      strColumns = strColumns & strComma & UpdateRow(i) & "="
      Select Case VarType(UpdateRow(i + 1))
        Case vbDate
```

```
          strColumns = strColumns & "#" & UpdateRow(i + 1) & "#"
        Case vbString
          strColumns = strColumns & "'" & UpdateRow(i + 1) & "'"
        Case Else
          strColumns = strColumns & UpdateRow(i + 1)
      End Select
      strComma = ","
    Next i
    strColumns = strColumns & strComma & _
           "UserID='" & Left$(UserID, lngSize - 1) & "'"
    strColumns = strColumns & strComma & _
           "UserDate='" & Format(Now, _
           "dd-mmm-yyyy hh:mm:ss AMPM") & "'"
    strSQL = "UPDATE " & UpdateRow(1) & _
           " SET " & strColumns & " " & UpdateRow(2) & ";"
    ActionCount = DBC.ActionQuery(strSQL)
    If ActionCount <> 1 Then
      Status = DBC.DBRollBackTransaction()
      UpdateRows = 0
      Exit Function
    End If
  Next
  Status = DBC.DBCommitTransaction()
  UpdateRows = colUpdateRows.Count
  Exit Function
UpdateRowsError:
  Resume Next
  Status = DBC.DBRollBackTransaction()
  LogDataClassErrors
  UpdateRows = 0
End Function

Public Function GetIdentifier(ByVal strTable As String) As Long
  Dim MyCol As Collection
  Dim ActionCount As Long
  On Error GoTo GetIdentifierError
```

```
  InitializeErrorLog
  If TransactionActive Then
    LogSoftError "Transaction open when identifier requested"
    GetIdentifier = -1
    Exit Function
  End If
  DBC.DBBeginTransaction
  ActionCount = DBC.ActionQuery( _
     "UPDATE tblAssignConcurrency" & _
     " SET Identifier=Identifier + 1 WHERE TableName = '" & strTable & "'")
  Set MyCol = DataEngine.GetColumn("Identifier", _
     "tblAssignConcurrency", " WHERE TableName = '" & strTable & "'")
  DBC.DBCommitTransaction
  GetIdentifier = MyCol(1)
  Set MyCol = Nothing
  Exit Function
GetIdentifierError:
  Resume Next
  LogDataClassErrors
  GetIdentifier = -1
End Function

Public Function InsertRows(ByVal colInsertRows As Collection) As Long
  Dim NewRow As Collection
  Dim strColumns As String, strValues As String
  Dim strComma As String * 1
  Dim strSQL As String
  Dim i As Integer, ActionCount As Long
  Const UserIDSize = 31
  Dim UserID As String * UserIDSize, lngSize As Long, Status As Long
  If colInsertRows.Count < 1 Then Exit Function
  InitializeErrorLog
  On Error GoTo NewRowError
  UserID = String$(UserIDSize, 0)
  lngSize = UserIDSize - 1
  Status = GetUserName(UserID, lngSize)
```

```
DBC.DBBeginTransaction
For Each NewRow In colInsertRows
  strColumns = ""
  strValues = ""
  strComma = ""
  For i = 2 To NewRow.Count - 1 Step 2
    strColumns = strColumns & Trim$(strComma & NewRow.Item(i))
    Select Case VarType(NewRow.Item(i + 1))
      Case vbDate
        strValues = strValues & strComma & "#" & _
              NewRow.Item(i + 1) & "#"
      Case vbString
        strValues = strValues & Trim$(strComma & "'" & _
              NewRow.Item(i + 1) & "'")
      Case Else
        strValues = strValues & strComma & NewRow.Item(i + 1)
    End Select
    strComma = ","
  Next i
'
' user id
'
  strColumns = strColumns & "," & "UserID"
  strValues = strValues & ",'" & Left$(UserID, lngSize - 1) & "'"
'
' insert time
'
  strColumns = strColumns & "," & "UserDate"
  strValues = strValues & ",'" & Format(Now, _
        "dd-mmm-yyyy hh:mm:SS AMPM") & "'"
  strSQL = "INSERT INTO " & NewRow(1) & _
        " (" & strColumns & ") VALUES (" & strValues & ");"
  ActionCount = DBC.ActionQuery(strSQL)
  If ActionCount <> 1 Then
    DBC.DBRollBackTransaction
    InsertRows = 0
```

```
      Exit Function
    End If
  Next
  DBC.DBCommitTransaction
  InsertRows = colInsertRows.Count
  Exit Function
NewRowError:
  Resume Next
  DBC.DBRollBackTransaction
  LogDataClassErrors
  InsertRows = 0
  Exit Function
End Function

Public Function DeleteRows(ByVal strTable As String, _
     ByVal strWhere As String, RowCount As Long) As Long
  Dim ActionCount As Long
  InitializeErrorLog
  On Error GoTo DeleteRowsError
  DBC.DBBeginTransaction
  ActionCount = DBC.ActionQuery("DELETE * FROM " & _
     strTable & " " & strWhere)
  DeleteRows = ActionCount
  If ActionCount <> RowCount Then
    DBC.DBRollBackTransaction
  Else
    DBC.DBCommitTransaction
  End If
  Exit Function
DeleteRowsError:
  Resume Next
  LogDataClassErrors
  DeleteRows = 0
End Function

Public Function GetColumn(ByVal strCols As String, _
```

```
    ByVal strTable As String, ByVal strWhere As String) As Collection
  Dim myRS As Recordset
  Dim myList As New Collection
  InitializeErrorLog
  On Error GoTo GetColumnError
  Set myRS = DBC.SelectQuery("SELECT " & strCols & " FROM " & _
    strTable & " " & strWhere)
  While Not myRS.EOF
    myList.Add myRS(0).Value
    myRS.MoveNext
  Wend
  Set GetColumn = myList
  Set myRS = Nothing
  Set myList = Nothing
  Exit Function
GetColumnError:
  Resume Next
  LogDataClassErrors
End Function

Public Function GetRows(ByVal strCols As String, _
    ByVal strTable As String, ByVal strWhere As String) As Collection
  Dim myRS As Recordset
  Dim myList As New Collection
  Dim MySubList As New Collection
  Dim i As Integer
  InitializeErrorLog
  On Error GoTo GetRowsError
  Set myRS = DBC.SelectQuery("SELECT " & strCols & " FROM " & _
    strTable & " " & strWhere)
  While Not myRS.EOF
    For i = 0 To myRS.Fields.Count - 1
      MySubList.Add myRS(i).Value, myRS(i).Name
    Next i
    myList.Add MySubList
```

```
    myRS.MoveNext
    Set MySubList = Nothing
  Wend
  Set GetRows = myList
  Set myRS = Nothing
  Set myList = Nothing
  Exit Function
GetRowsError:
  Resume Next
  LogDataClassErrors
  Set GetRows = Nothing
End Function

Private Sub Class_Initialize()
  Set DBC = New DatabaseClass
End Sub

Private Sub Class_Terminate()
  Set DBC = Nothing
End Sub
```

ErrorClass class

As stated previously, both the **DatabaseClass** and the **DataClass** classes maintain state, which is artificial and is used for illustration purposes only. The state is comprised of any error messages generated by the component. The code fragment below illustrates the relationships between the **ErrorClass** and **DataClass** classes. Note that a reference to the **DataClass** class (*DataEngine*) is passed to the **ErrorClass** component, since the error messages exist within the **DataClass** as state.

The code fragment of Listing 21-4 builds a collection of collections. The subcollection consists of the table name and name-value pairs. Listing 21-4 also illustrates the **ErrorClass** component instantiation mechanism. The complete **ErrorClass** class is illustrated in Listing 21-5.

LISTING 21-4 **Showing the collection of collections construction for the InsertRows method**

```
insCol.Add "tblHolidays"
insCol.Add "Cust_Num": insCol.Add txtCustNum
insCol.Add "BMP": insCol.Add "M"
insCol.Add "HolidayDate": insCol.Add NewDate
insRow.Add insCol
InsertCount = DataEngine.InsertRows(insRow)
Set insCol = Nothing
Set insRow = Nothing
If InsertCount <> 1 Then
      Set ErrorEngine = New ErrorClass
      Status = ErrorEngine.LogError(DataEngine, _
      "Unable to add client calendar deletion date", 4)
      Set ErrorEngine = Nothing
      Exit Sub
End If
```

The **ErrorClass** component has several distinctive features, which include:

- On any given day the maximum number of errors is limited to one thousand. This is an arbitrary value and accommodates situations where a network disconnects or there is a catastrophic server failure.
- Each error message is tagged with a UserID and a UserDate. This identifies specific application features or helps to isolate unreliable hardware or software components.
- The user is given the opportunity to skip the reading of the error messages, and the errors are logged independent of user choices.

LISTING 21-5 **The ErrorClass class that uses a reference to the errant DataClasscomponent.**

```
'(C) 1999 Bruce T. Prendergast
' DBA Prendergast Consulting
' DBA PCS
'
' IDG Books Worldwide ISBN 0-7645-3314-2
'
```

```
' ErrorClass class
'
Option Explicit
Public Function LogError( _
     ByRef oObject As DataClass, _
     ByVal ErrorMessage As String, _
           Operation As Integer) As Boolean
  Dim i As Integer, k As Integer, state As Integer
  Dim ErrorObject As DataClass
  Dim ThisDate As Date
  Dim curCol As Collection
  Dim ErrorList As Variant
  Dim msg, Style, Title, Response
  Dim ActionCount As Long
  Dim LoggedErrorCount As Integer

  LogError = False
  Set ErrorObject = oObject
  ErrorList = ErrorObject.RetrieveErrors
  If Operation > 3 Then
    i = UBound(ErrorList) + 1
    ReDim Preserve ErrorList(i)
    ErrorList(i) = "Row count error"
  End If
  i = UBound(ErrorList)
  state = 2 * Operation + Abs(i > 2)
'
' state codes
'
' 0   No errors and no row returned ' indeterminant state
' 1   No row and errors were returned
' 2   Rows returned with no errors
' 3   Rows returned with errors
' 4   Row Count error on UPDATE or INSERT
'     with no errors returned
' 5   Row Count error on UPDATE or INSERT
```

```
'     with error messages returned
' 6   Row count error on DELETE
'     with no error messages returned
' 7   Row count error on DELETE
'     with error messages returned
'
  If state = 0 Or state = 2 Then
    LogError = True
    Exit Function
  End If

  If state \ 2 <> state / 2 Then
    msg = ErrorMessage & ", which resulted in errors. " & vbCr
    msg = msg & "Do you wish to see the error messages? " & vbCr
    Style = vbYesNo + vbCritical
    Title = "Errors Encountered"
    Response = MsgBox(msg, Style, Title)
    If Response = vbYes Then
      For i = 1 To UBound(ErrorList)
        MsgBox ErrorList(i)
      Next i
    End If
  Else
    msg = ErrorMessage & ", which resulted in no errors. " & vbCr
    msg = msg & "An error exists in the expected row count. " & vbCr
    msg = msg & "Please consider retrying the operation"
    Style = vbOK + vbCritical
    Title = "Row Count Discrepancy Encountered"
    Response = MsgBox(msg, Style, Title)
  End If
  ThisDate = Format(Now, "dd-mmm-yyyy")
  Set curCol = ErrorObject.GetColumn( _
     "CurrentErrorCount", "tblErrorLogControl", _
     " WHERE ErrorDate = '" & ThisDate & "'")
'
' no more than 1000 aggregate errors per day
```

```
' Prevents a runaway error log when the server
' or the wire breaks
'
  If curCol.Count > 0 Then
    If curCol(1) > 1000 Then
      MsgBox "System stopping because of an excessive error rate"
      Stop
    End If
  End If
  Dim insCol As New Collection
  Dim insRow As New Collection
  For i = 1 To UBound(ErrorList)
    insCol.Add "tblErrorLog"
    insCol.Add "Message"
    insCol.Add ErrorList(i)
    insRow.Add insCol
    Set insCol = Nothing
  Next i
  ActionCount = ErrorObject.InsertRows(insRow)
  If ActionCount <> UBound(ErrorList) Then
    MsgBox "Unable to log errors. System is stopping"
    Set insRow = Nothing
    Stop
  End If
  Set insRow = Nothing
  If curCol.Count = 0 Then
    insCol.Add "tblErrorLogControl"
    insCol.Add "CurrentErrorCount"
    insCol.Add UBound(ErrorList)
    insCol.Add "ErrorDate"
    insCol.Add ThisDate
    insRow.Add insCol
    ActionCount = ErrorObject.InsertRows(insRow)
    If ActionCount <> 1 Then
      MsgBox "Unable to create error log date header. " &
          "System is stopping"
```

```
      Stop
    End If
    Set insCol = Nothing
    Set insRow = Nothing
  Else
    Dim updcol As New Collection
    Dim updRow As New Collection
    updcol.Add "tblErrorLogControl"
    updcol.Add " WHERE ErrorDate = '" & ThisDate & "'"
    updcol.Add "CurrentErrorCount"
    updcol.Add curCol(1) + UBound(ErrorList)
    updRow.Add updcol
    ActionCount = ErrorObject.UpdateRows(updRow)
    If ActionCount <> 1 Then
      MsgBox "Unable to update error log date header. " & _
        "System is stopping"
      Stop
    End If
    Set updcol = Nothing
    Set updRow = Nothing
  End If
  Set curCol = Nothing
  LogError = True
End Function
```

Confusion Now Reigns

I don't know how to explain how chaotic the tiered-component architecture is today. No one knows how to build one. Microsoft says do it this way, which is patently wrong. Someone else says do it this way, but that's not right either. To compound matters still further, the tiered-component material is not being taught correctly. Common sense is being overlooked and any trick that will help solve the scaleability issue is acceptable. The long-term consequences of many of these changes have not been properly thought out. All the problems resolve down to two basic issues: data is now being bound to the process, which introduces application fragility, and Microsoft Visual Basic is not suitable for enterprise applications. Let's start by examining the process issue.

Relational databases: freeing data from the process

The defining point in the evolution of computers and computing was the creation of relational database technology by Dr. E. F. Codd. Relational databases maintain the definition of data within the data, which forever separates data from the process. A major limiting factor to the early COBOL programs was the definition of data (files) within the process. All applications had to be recompiled when the definition of the data changed. Not so with a relational database, which maintains the data definitions within the data. Data was now free from the process, but not for long. Microsoft entered the computer evolution timeline and now threatens to move the evolution of computer processing back 25 years.

This chapter uses **Collection** objects as an introduction to a component-based architecture, however collections are limited to use within in-process servers. The problem is that collections cannot be passed to the client, only a collection pointer can be marshaled to the client. Figure 21-8 uses **Collection** objects to define data relationships. There is no inherent problem with storing data in collections, however collections should never infer data relationships. To do so embeds data relationships within the process. Shades of 1966 and a COBOL File Division (FD) with embedded file definitions, we're back to embedding definitions of data within the process! Change the data architecture and all associated applications with the embedded relationship collapse. Microsoft's self-interest in the role of process is likened to the *how*, which represents the process, while the *what* represents the data. An example of the *what* is the Oracle relational database, which focuses exclusively on the *what*.

The issue is just not collections. Course 491, which is a suggested course for the 70-100 objectives, proposes creating database entities from process objects. Take a process object, discard the methods, and the remaining properties become columns in a database entity with the same name. This is binding data to the process in the crassest form. Such an application is bound to eventually fail. This is application fragility that we've not experienced for twenty-five years!

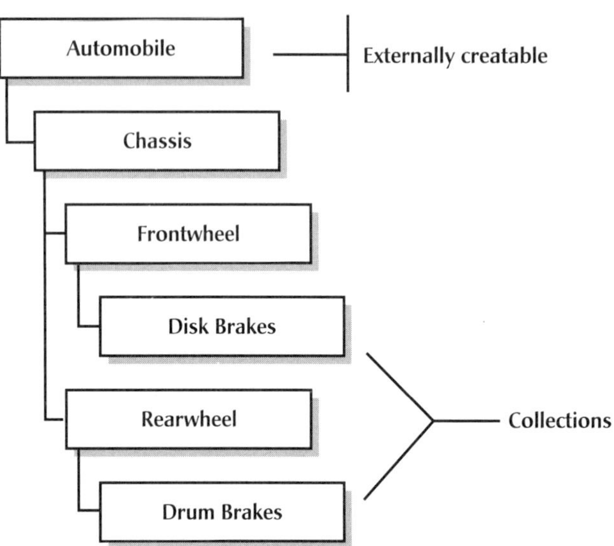

FIGURE 21-8 When collections are used for inferring data relationships.

MTS and data binding

Let's look at the flip side of the coin. I was at a presentation recently where a system was described that is diametrically opposite to the Course 491 approach. The developers wait until the data entities are defined and a process object is defined from each data entity. Is this right? Certainly not! It's still the binding of data to the process. During the discussion after the presentation, a quiet but firm voice in the back row said: "We use ADO **Recordset** objects to transport data." Very few understood the import of that profound statement. I don't mean ADO queries, but ADO **Recordset** objects used in lieu of binding to process objects or defining collections as surrogate data entities. Is this the answer? Yes! There is no binding to the process and the definition of the data is stored within the data, or more precisely within the ADO **Recordset** object. Some binding must occur that is not to the process, but to data controls on the user form. This is a very important but subtle point. Before Microsoft Transaction Server (MTS), binding was to data controls, now binding is to process objects when MTS is present.

Ignoring training issues, is MTS to blame for the mass confusion that permeates the Microsoft software architecture? Probably. Before MTS appeared SQL Server was the security host. Users and or groups were assigned security permissions on SQL Server objects. Enter MTS. Users are now given access to MTS servers but not direct access to SQL Server objects. Only MTS packages have access to SQL Server objects. Security is applied to MTS user roles. Security is assigned directly to exposed properties of MTS objects when a finer degree of user security is necessary. This means that MTS is now the security host and not SQL Server. That's the answer! When MTS is included in the software architecture, detailed security is available only through exposed properties. Developers have no choice and must bind data to the process when MTS is incorporated in the architecture.

MTS and Visual Basic threading models

Whence MTS? To understand MTS, we must step back and look at Microsoft Visual Basic (VB) threading models. VB is an apartment model threaded tool that creates either apartment model or multi-threaded objects. Apartment model treading is just a term concocted by the Microsoft spin-meisters. An apartment model thread is a single thread in a domain. You put the monster in a room and lock the door and you're safe as long as the door is locked. Monsters can't be shared, hence there's no scaleability for apartment model threads.

The developer can define multi-threaded objects, but the management of these objects is far from simple and certainly not scaleable. Microsoft has committed two architectural blunders:

- All objects should be multi-threaded, which means that developers shouldn't be given the choice of thread type. Letting developers define thread types creates the traditional Tower of Babel. Thread type is an operating system prerogative and single-threaded objects in a multi-threaded objects environment are an open invitation to a disaster.
- Thread management functionality is exposed to C^{++} applications, but not to VB applications. The VB developer is forced to create overly complex thread management code, which is not scaleable, hence MTS. The apparent mistake is in not exposing thread management functionality to VB, but maybe that exacerbates an already bad situation. VB is starting to resemble a *Frankenstein monster* (see *Visual Basic Programmers Journal,* April 1999, "Confessions of a VB Beta Tester") The real error is in trying to solve a problem with a language that is not suitable and solving that unsuitability with bolt-ins that are covered with five pounds of sugar.

Microsoft appears willing to do anything to solve the problem of scaleability and that includes committing the unpardonable sin of binding data to the process.

Biography

Certification books have to cover so much material that there isn't much time for us to get to know each other. As the book draws to a close, I'd like to tell you a little about myself and why I'm so passionate about my work. My passion is bicycling, and that includes bicycle racing. I've been racing bicycles for many years. My United States Cycling Federation (USCF) license is L008412 and the USCF is currently issuing licenses in the six-digit range, which gives you an idea of how long I've been at it. My favorite race is a criterium (closed circuit race), where I specialized in lapping the field. Of course that doesn't happen every race. I broke the national forty kilometer time-trial record for my age group in 1988 and 1992. I didn't hold either of the records long enough to go down in the record books, but I plan to change that. I'm sixty-two and currently training for an assault on the forty kilometer time-trial record when I'm sixty-five in three years. Let's not call it an assault; I plan to annihilate the record.

Let me share a small part from one of my innumerable special days. The alarm goes off at 4:00 AM. I turn it off and sleepily climb out of bed. I dress in my bicycling gear, grab a glass of orange juice, load my bicycling equipment, and am driving to Glendora Mountain Road by 4:15 AM. I park in a residential neighborhood. I always park in front of the same house so no one thinks I'm a burglar on the prowl.

It's still dark as I start the long climb. My leg muscles are cold and I'm in my lowest gear. My breath hangs in the air as something that refuses to die. Many switchbacks later I'm still climbing. The legs are now warmed up and I've moved up a couple of gears. As the road swings left I glance to my right and can see the serpentine road along the far ridge, which is still about two miles distant as the crow flies.

The road eventually swings back to the right with almost perfect timing and the sun is starting to rise. The sun is making its normal ascension, but as I'm nearing the top of the ridge, the sun appears to jump into the sky in slow motion as if it were launched from an infernal trampoline.

I'm on the ridge now. The grade has dropped to about three percent and I'm making good time. I see a vixen up ahead with her young. They're poking their heads out of the scrub brush watching me as I come up the gentle grade. Just before I get there, they disappear.

I'm on top now. I stop, drink some water, and redress. It'll be cold on the backside of the mountain, which is still shaded from the sun. I start my descent as I swing to the left at the Y in the road. I remember to keep my legs moving even though I'm not pedaling, which keeps the blood circulating.

Some nine miles later I arrive at the valley floor and the east fork of the San Gabriel River. I immediately turn around and start up the backside of the mountain. It's still cold here and I'm now in my lowest gear. Somewhere beyond the halfway point coming up the backside of the mountain, I arrive at a rock wall. As the wall and the road curve left, I can see the distant ridge. The setting reminds me of Andy Hampsten climbing L'Alpe-d'Huez in the Tour de France. I shift up two gears and stand up. Yes, yes! Today I'm Andy Hampsten as I gently rock the bicycle in a slow rhythm up the remainder of the mountain. Life is good!

Its not quite 9:00 AM and I'm back home. Before showering, I check my e-mail and note that I've got twenty-four messages. Yes, today is a great day.

I also mountain bike with my buds *JR, The Glenoid,* and *RoboMan*. They call me *Yoda-of-the-North*. My buds renamed my favorite mountain bike ride Yoda's Revenge after I trashed them thoroughly. I was honored when a local bicycling club scheduled an annual Yoda's Revenge ride. It's a thirty-three mile loop with a seventeen mile climb. I took a good friend, Dr. Laura Thomas, on the ride and she was totally awesome. After the ride I complimented her on such a great ride. She replied "Bruce, I was terrified. My brakes didn't work!"

My last comment is a recommendation to buy the book *The Art of Living* by Sharon Lebell (ISBN 0-06-251322-2). The book is a new translation of the Greek philosopher Epictetus, a proponent of the philosophy known as stoicism. His philosophy helps me deal with issues over which I have no control such as death and the chaotic world situation.

To *JR, The Glenoid,* and *RoboMan*: *Yoda-of-the-North* says "keep the rubber side down". To each of my many loyal fans: I award in absentia the *Jolt Cola and Cold Pizza* award. Persevere.

Key Point Summary

Microsoft delivered DCOM with Windows NT 4.0. As expected, the implementation was transparent to existing applications, except for performance.

- The type of DCOM interface now becomes important. Developers should strive to use **IUnknown** rather than the **IDispatch** interface.
- The number of parameters passed to a method of a DCOM interface plays a factor in DCOM performance. A separate wire trip must be made for each parameter. This promotes the concept of *custom marshaling* where parameters are packaged together.
- The type of DCOM parameter is also a performance issue. Parameters defined as *ByVal* are pushed to the server, while parameters defined as *ByRef* are marshaled both to and from the DCOM server.
- Collections should only be used with in-process DCOM servers. Only a **Collection** object pointer is marshaled and the *For Each* construct must establish a new object connection for each member of the collection.
- Developers must be fastidious about releasing objects and erasing arrays. Lack of due diligence in releasing objects and erasing arrays will invoke the dreaded *Expression is too complex* message.

Applying What You've Learned

The questions that follow measure your comprehension of this chapter. The primary issue addressed is DCOM performance.

Instant Assessment

1. What is the *fragile super class* problem?
2. COM supports a model of binary encapsulation where the interface isolates the client from the implementation. Explain binary encapsulation in Microsoft C^{++}.
3. What are the primary limiting factors of two-tier applications?

4. What are the disadvantages of shifting processing to the client layer in a two-tier architecture?
5. What threading model is used by Microsoft Visual Basic?
6. What is the relationship between a message pump and a single-threaded apartment?
7. What is the threading issue regarding Microsoft Visual Basic and marshaling data with respect to DCOM components?
8. Parameters can be passed to a DCOM component either by value or by reference. Explain the actions when data is passed by value to a DCOM server.
9. Explain the actions when data is passed by reference to a DCOM component.
10. What is the issue relating to the use of collections in a DCOM architecture?
11. What is the context of custom marshaling?
12. Explain the context of *state* with respect to DCOM.
13. Please explain the value of using the **Implements** statement.
14. Please explain the meaning of *unwinding the stack*.
15. What was the architectural error of Chapter 16?

For answers to the Instant Assessment Questions, see Appendix B.

Lab Exercises

There are three labs in this chapter. The first lab peeks at a type library embedded within a Microsoft Visual Basic ActiveX component. The second lab presents an application that implements the **DataClass, DatabaseClass** and **ErrorClass** components of this chapter. The third and final lab rebuilds the application, but this time the **DatabaseClass** component becomes a DCOM server.

Lab 21.72 *DCOM performance*

Performance is an issue with DCOM. The first half of this lab builds a simple ActiveX DLL that implements an interface with the **Implements** statement. The DLL is examined with the **OLE View** tool and the resulting display indicates that the implementation is with *dispinterfaces* (**IUnknown**).

The **OLE View** tool reveals that this implementation uses the **IUnknown** interface, which can be orders of magnitude faster that the **IDispatch** interface. The importance of using the **Implements** statement with DCOM components cannot be over emphasized.

1. Start a new ActiveX DLL project in Visual Basic 5.0 or 6.0.
2. Rename the project to **vTableInterface.**
3. Rename the class module to **vTableDLL.**
4. Add a class module to the project. Name the class module **ICheckBook**. This will be an interface class.
5. Enter the following code into the declaration section of the **ICheckBook** Interface class:

```
'(c) 1999 Bruce T. Prendergast
'  DBA Prendergast Consulting
'  DBA PCS
'  IDG Books WorldWide
'
' Interface Class Name: ICheckbook
'
Option Explicit
'
Public Property Get Balance() As Currency
'
End Property

Public Sub Withdrawal(Amount As Currency)
'
End Sub

Public Sub Deposit(Amount As Currency)
'
End Sub
```

6. Verify that the class is set to **PublicNotCreatable** in the **Properties** window and exit the class designer.
7. Enter the following code in the **vTableDLL** class **Declaration** section.

```
'(c) 1999 Bruce T. Prendergast
'  DBA Prendergast Consulting
'  DBA PCS
'  IDG Books WorldWide
'
Option Explicit
Implements ICheckbook

Private m_curBalance As Variant

Private Property Get ICheckBook_Balance() As Currency
  ICheckBook_Balance = m_curBalance      .
End Property

Private Sub ICheckbook_Withdrawal(Amount As Currency)
  m_curBalance = m_curBalance - Amount
  MsgBox "Balance is: " & m_curBalance
End Sub

Private Sub ICheckbook_Deposit(Amount As Currency)
  m_curBalance = m_curBalance + Amount
End Sub
```

8. Exit the class code window.
9. Compile the **vTableInterface** .DLL.
10. Start the **OLE View** tool, which is found in Visual Studio 6.0.
11. Select: FILE | VIEW TYPELIB. Open the **vTableInterface** DLL. Figure 21-9 verifies that the **Implements** statement does indeed implement *dispinterfaces* (**IUnknown**).

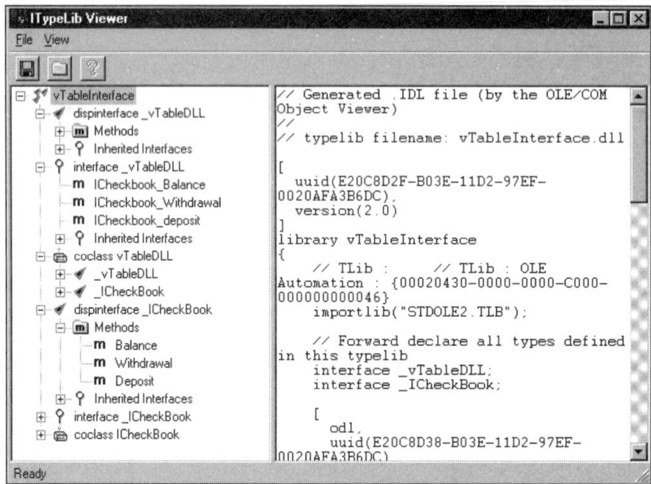

FIGURE 21-9 OLE View from Visual Studio 6.0

12. The text in the right window of the **OLE View** tool can be copied to Notepad and from there pasted into to a file with the proper .IDL extension.
13. Use the Microsoft Interface Definition Language (MIDL) compiler to compile the .IDL file into a type library.

Lab 21.73 *Using the DataClass, DatabaseClass and ErrorClass components*

The software for this lab is located in the Chapter21 folder of the CD-ROM that accompanies this book. This is the first of two related labs. This lab builds an application that uses the **ErrorClass**, **DataClass,** and **DatabaseClass** components. The second lab constructs a distributed application that uses a DCOM server constructed from the **DatabaseClass** class.

1. Move the Chapter 21 folder on the CD-ROM to a suitable folder on a hard disk.
2. Start Visual Basic 5.0 or 6.0 and open the DCOMDAO.vbp project
3. Open the DatabaseClass class. Edit the statement below found in the Declaration section of the DatabaseClass class to reflect the project's folder path.

```
Private Const DatabasePath = _
 "E:\70-100\CH21\Examples\DCOMDAO.mdb"
```

4. Run the project. Listing 21-6 contains the complete DCOMDAO.frm code for this lab.

LISTING 21-6 An application using the DatabaseClass, DataClass, and ErrorClass components

```
'(C) 1999 Bruce T. Prendergast
' DBA Prendergast Consulting
' DBA PCS
'
' IDG Books Worldwide 0-7645-3314-2
'
' An example using DataClass, ErrorClass, and DatabaseClass
'
Option Explicit

Private ApplicationMode As String
Private lngConcurrency As Long
Private InputCol As New Collection

Private Sub LogChanges(ByVal strName, ByVal varValue As Variant)
  Dim wrkCol As New Collection
  If ApplicationMode = "" Then Exit Sub
  wrkCol.Add strName
  wrkCol.Add varValue
  On Error GoTo AlreadyExists
  InputCol.Add wrkCol, strName
  Set wrkCol = Nothing
  Exit Sub
AlreadyExists:
  InputCol.Remove strName
  InputCol.Add wrkCol, strName
  Set wrkCol = Nothing
End Sub

Private Sub LoadCustomer()
  Dim myRow As Collection
```

```
Dim MyCol As Collection
Dim strCustNum As String
Dim strWhere As String
Dim i As Integer
strCustNum = ExtendField(txtCustomerNumber, 4)
strWhere = " WHERE CustomerNumber ='" & strCustNum & "'"
Set myRow = DataEngine.GetRows( _
  "CustomerNumber, FirstName, Lastname, " & _
  "YearlyPurchases, Concurrency", _
  "tblCustomers", strWhere)
Set InputCol = Nothing
If myRow.Count = 0 Then
  cmdReset_Click
  txtCustomerNumber = strCustNum
  EnableAll
  txtFirstName.SetFocus
  txtCustomerNumber.Enabled = False
  ApplicationMode = "Insert"
  Exit Sub
Else
'
' found customer
'
  DisableAll
  Set MyCol = myRow(1)
  Set myRow = Nothing
  txtFirstName = MyCol("FirstName")
  txtLastName = MyCol("LastName")
  lngConcurrency = MyCol("Concurrency")
  txtYearlyPurchases = CCur(MyCol("YearlyPurchases"))
  ApplicationMode = "Update"
  EnableAll
  txtFirstName.SetFocus
  txtCustomerNumber.Enabled = False
End If
End Sub
```

```
Private Sub DisableAll()
  txtCustomerNumber.Enabled = False
  txtFirstName.Enabled = False
  txtLastName.Enabled = False
  txtYearlyPurchases.Enabled = False
End Sub

Private Sub EnableAll()
  txtCustomerNumber.Enabled = True
  txtFirstName.Enabled = True
  txtLastName.Enabled = True
  txtYearlyPurchases.Enabled = True
End Sub
Private Sub cmbCust_Click()
  If cmbCust.ListIndex = -1 Then Exit Sub
  txtCustomerNumber = ExtendField(cmbCust.ItemData(cmbCust.ListIndex), 4)
  LoadCustomer
End Sub

Private Sub cmdDelete_Click()
  Dim ActionCount As Long
  Dim ErrorEngine As ErrorClass
  Dim Status As Boolean
  Dim MyCol As Collection
  If cmbCust.ListIndex = -1 Then Exit Sub
  If ApplicationMode = "" Then Exit Sub
  ActionCount = DataEngine.DeleteRows( _
    "tblCustomers", " WHERE CustomerNumber= '" & _
     txtCustomerNumber & "'", 1)
  If ActionCount <> 1 Then
    Set ErrorEngine = New ErrorClass
    Status = ErrorEngine.LogError(DataEngine, _
      "Unable to delete customer", 6)
    Set ErrorEngine = Nothing
  '
  ' nothing is cleared on an error
```

```
'
    Exit Sub
  End If
  ApplicationMode = ""
  DisableAll
  txtCustomerNumber = ""
  txtFirstName = ""
  txtLastName = ""
  txtYearlyPurchases = ""
  Set InputCol = Nothing
  txtCustomerNumber.Enabled = True
  cmbCust.Clear
  For Each MyCol In DataEngine.GetRows("CustomerNumber, FirstName, _
       Lastname",   "tblCustomers", "")
    cmbCust.AddItem MyCol("FirstName") & " " & MyCol("LastName")
    cmbCust.ItemData(cmbCust.NewIndex) = MyCol("CustomerNumber")
  Next
  End Sub

Private Sub cmdReset_Click()
  Dim i As Integer
  Dim MyCol As Collection
  ApplicationMode = ""
  DisableAll
  txtCustomerNumber = ""
  txtFirstName = ""
  txtLastName = ""
  txtYearlyPurchases = ""
  Set InputCol = Nothing
  txtCustomerNumber.Enabled = True
  cmbCust.Clear
  For Each MyCol In DataEngine.GetRows("CustomerNumber, FirstName, _
      Lastname", "tblCustomers", "")
    cmbCust.AddItem MyCol("FirstName") & " " & MyCol("LastName")
    cmbCust.ItemData(cmbCust.NewIndex) = MyCol("CustomerNumber")
  Next
```

```
  If MyCol Is Nothing Then
    cmbCust.ListIndex = -1
  Else
    cmbCust.ListIndex = 0
  End If
End Sub
Private Sub cmdSave_Click()
  Dim ErrorEngine As ErrorClass
  Dim ReturnedCount As Long
  Dim Status As Boolean
  Dim i As Integer
  Dim lngNewConcurrency As Long
  Dim InsertRow As New Collection
  Dim wrkCol As New Collection
  Dim UpdateRow As New Collection
  Dim MyCol As Collection
  '
  ' The system will respond with an error when
  ' required field is not entered. Don't check
  ' for required fields.
  '
  ' were there any changes?
  '
    If ApplicationMode = "Update" Then
      ApplicationMode = ""
      If InputCol.Count < 1 Then Exit Sub
  '
  ' Update
  '
  ' The collection passed to the DataClass component
  ' consists of the table name, WHERE clause and
  ' name-value pairs with appended concurrency.
  '
      wrkCol.Add "tblCustomers"
      wrkCol.Add " WHERE CustomerNumber ='" & _
        txtCustomerNumber & "' AND Concurrency = " & lngConcurrency
```

```
      For Each MyCol In InputCol
        wrkCol.Add MyCol.Item(1)
        wrkCol.Add MyCol.Item(2)
        Set MyCol = Nothing
      Next
      Set MyCol = Nothing
    '
    ' insert the new concurrency identifier
    '
      lngNewConcurrency = DataEngine.GetIdentifier("tblCustomers")
      wrkCol.Add "Concurrency"
      wrkCol.Add lngNewConcurrency
      UpdateRow.Add wrkCol
      Set wrkCol = Nothing
      ReturnedCount = DataEngine.UpdateRows(UpdateRow)
      Set UpdateRow = Nothing
      If ReturnedCount <> 1 Then
        Set ErrorEngine = New ErrorClass
        Status = ErrorEngine.LogError(DataEngine, _
          "Unable to update customer", 4)
        Set ErrorEngine = Nothing
        ApplicationMode = "Update"
    '
    ' nothing is cleared on an error
    '
        Exit Sub
      Else
        cmdReset_Click
        Exit Sub
      End If
    Else
    '
    ' Insert
    '
    ' The collection passed to the DataClass component
    ' consists of the table name and name-value pairs
    ' with the concurrency appended.
```

```
'
    If InputCol.Count < 1 Then Exit Sub
    Set wrkCol = New Collection
    wrkCol.Add "tblCustomers"
    wrkCol.Add "CustomerNumber"
    wrkCol.Add ExtendField(txtCustomerNumber, 4)
'
' append changed columns (name-value pairs)
'
    For Each MyCol In InputCol
      wrkCol.Add MyCol(1)
      wrkCol.Add MyCol(2)
    Next
    Set MyCol = Nothing
'
' Insert the new concurrency
'
    lngNewConcurrency = DataEngine.GetIdentifier("tblCustomers")
    wrkCol.Add "Concurrency"
    wrkCol.Add lngNewConcurrency
    InsertRow.Add wrkCol
    Set wrkCol = Nothing
    ReturnedCount = DataEngine.InsertRows(InsertRow)
    Set InsertRow = Nothing
    If ReturnedCount <> 1 Then
      Set ErrorEngine = New ErrorClass
      Status = ErrorEngine.LogError(DataEngine, _
        "Unable to insert new customer", 4)
      ApplicationMode = "Insert"
      Set ErrorEngine = Nothing
'
' nothing is cleared on an error
'
      Exit Sub
    Else
      ApplicationMode = ""
```

```
        cmdReset_Click
      End If
    End If
End Sub

Private Sub Form_Load()
  Dim MyCol As Collection
  For Each MyCol In DataEngine.GetRows("CustomerNumber, _
    FirstName, Lastname", "tblCustomers", "")
    cmbCust.AddItem MyCol("FirstName") & " " & MyCol("LastName")
    cmbCust.ItemData(cmbCust.NewIndex) = MyCol("CustomerNumber")
  Next
  If MyCol Is Nothing Then
    cmbCust.ListIndex = -1
  Else
    cmbCust.ListIndex = 0
  End If
  DisableAll
  txtCustomerNumber.Enabled = True
End Sub

Private Sub Form_Unload(Cancel As Integer)
  Set DataEngine = Nothing
End Sub

Private Sub txtCustomerNumber_KeyPress(KeyAscii As Integer)
  If (KeyAscii < 49 Or KeyAscii > 57) And _
    (KeyAscii <> 13) Then KeyAscii = 0
  If KeyAscii <> 13 Then Exit Sub
  LoadCustomer
End Sub

Private Sub txtFirstName_Change()
  LogChanges "FirstName", txtFirstName
End Sub

Private Sub txtLastName_Change()
```

```
  LogChanges "LastName", txtLastName
End Sub

Private Sub txtYearlyPurchases_Change()
  LogChanges "YearlyPurchases", CCur(Val(txtYearlyPurchases & ""))
End Sub
```

Lab 21.74 *Building a DCOM Server*

This lab uses all the elements of Lab 21-2 to construct a DCOM application. This lab was tested on Windows NT 4.0 Server, service pack 3 with Visual Studio 6.0 Enterprise Edition installed.

1. Start a new Visual Basic ActiveX .EXE project.
2. Import the **DatabaseClass** class of Lab 21-2.
3. Delete the **Class1** class.
3. Change the project name to DCOMSRVR.
4. Create a reference to the Microsoft DAO 3.51 Object Library. Select: Project | References | Microsoft DAO 3.51 Object Library.
5. Set the **Instancing** properties of the **DatabaseClass** class to *multiuse*.
6. Set the project's **Component** properties to *Remote Server Files*. Select: Project | Properties | Component.
7. Compile the project. The project should compile with no errors.
8. Save the project.
9. Remove the project and start a new **Standard** .EXE project.
10. Remove Form1.
11. Rename the project to DCONCLNT.
12. Add the DCOMDAO form of Lab 21-2 to the project.
13. Add the DataClass class of Lab 21-2 to the project.
14. Add the ErrorClass class of Lab 21-2 to the project.
15. Create a reference to the recently created DCOM server. Select: Project | References | DCOMSRVR, which is the recently created server.
16. Create a reference to the Microsoft DAO 3.51 Object Library. Select: Project | References | Microsoft DAO 3.51 Object Library.
17. Verify that the startup object is the **DCOMDAO** form.
18. Run the project. Congratulations! You've just completed a DCOM server project created in steps 1-8.

Lab 21.75 *Building stateless components*

Both the **DatabaseClass** and the **DataClass** class maintain what I call a *weak* state in that the classes remember the last error information. Other than error information, no state is maintained. When an error code is returned to the application calls the **ErrorClass** with the object reporting the error code. The **ErrorClass** in turn interrogates the passed object for error messages. The **ErrorClass** expects an object of type **DataClass**, since the **DataClass** class will in turn interrogate the **DatabaseClass** class for error messages.

Microsoft Transaction Server (MTS) does not support the **Err.Raise** statement. If MTS is not being used, implementing the **Err.Raise** statement in both the **DataClass** and **DatabaseClass** classes will result in stateless components.

When the components are implemented within MTS, returning error message information is implemented by function return values. Functions only return a single value and when additional error information is required, the developer must use custom-marshaling.

The objective of this lab is to convert both the **DataClass** and the **DatabaseClass** classes to stateless components. This is a programming assignment and there is no step-by-step procedure. It is your choice as to the type of stateless component: either implement the **Err.Raise** statement or modify all methods to return functional values.

Resources

APPENDIX

A

Analyzing Requirements and Defining Solution Architectures Exam Objectives

EXAM 70-100: ANALYZING REQUIREMENTS AND DEFINING SOLUTION ARCHITECTURES

This appendix lists the Microsoft objectives for the Analyzing Requirements and Defining Solution Architectures examination. The objectives represent goals that require a knowledge of collecting application requirements. The requirements are used to create a conceptual, logical and physical design. Completing the Analyzing Requirements and Defining Solution Architectures examination will identify you as a skilled professional.

Credit Toward Certification

A passing score on this exam counts as core credit toward *Microsoft Certified Solution Developer* certification and achieves the *Microsoft Certified Professional* status.

Skills Being Measured

The Analyzing Requirements and Defining Solution Architectures certification exam measures your ability to collect requirements and implement business solutions, which requires the ability to perform conceptual, logical, and physical application design.

Exam Objectives

Analyzing business requirements

Analyze the scope of a project. Considerations include:

- Existing applications
- Anticipated changes in environment
- Expected lifetime of solution
- Time, cost, budget, and benefit trade-offs

Analyze the extent of a business requirement:

- Establish business requirements.
- Establish type of problem, such as messaging problem or communication problem.
- Establish and define customer quality requirements.
- Minimize Total Cost of Ownership (TCO).
- Increase Return on Investment (ROI) of solution.
- Analyze current platform and infrastructure.
- Incorporate planned platform and infrastructure into solution.
- Analyze impact of technology migration.
- Plan physical requirements, such as infrastructure.
- Establish application environment, such as hardware platform, support, and operating system.
- Identify organizational constraints, such as financial situation, company politics, technical acceptance level, and training needs.
- Establish schedule for implementation of solution.
- Identify audience.

Analyze security requirements:

- Identify roles of administrator, groups, guests, and clients.
- Identify impact on existing environment. Establish fault tolerance.
- Plan for maintainability.
- Plan distribution of security database.

- Establish security context. Plan for auditing.
- Identify level of security needed.
- Analyze existing mechanisms for security policies.

Analyze performance requirements. Considerations include:

- Transactions per time slice
- Bandwidth
- Capacity
- Interoperability with existing standards
- Peak versus average requirements
- Response-time expectations
- Existing response-time characteristics
- Barriers to performance

Analyze maintainability requirements. Considerations include:

- Breadth of application distribution
- Method of distribution
- Maintenance expectations
- Location and knowledge level of maintenance staff
- Impact of third-party maintenance agreements

Analyze extensibility requirements. Solution must be able to handle the growth of functionality.

Analyze availability requirements. Considerations include:

- Hours of operation
- Level of availability
- Geographic scope
- Impact of downtime

Analyze human factor requirements. Considerations include:

- Target users
- Localization
- Accessibility

- Roaming users
- Help
- Training requirements
- Physical environment constraints
- Special needs

Analyze the requirements for integrating a solution with existing applications. Considerations include:

- Legacy applications
- Format and location of existing data
- Connectivity to existing applications
- Data conversion
- Data enhancement requirements

Analyze existing methodologies and limitations of a business. Considerations include:

- Legal issues
- Current business practices
- Organization structure
- Process engineering
- Budget
- Implementation and training methodologies
- Quality control requirements
- Customer's needs

Analyze scalability requirements. Considerations include:

- Growth of audience
- Growth of organization
- Growth of data
- Cycle of use

Defining the technical architecture for a solution

Given a business scenario, identify which solution type is appropriate. Solution types are single-tier, two-tier, and n-tier.

Identify which technologies are appropriate for implementation of a given business solution. Considerations include:

- Technology standards such as EDI, Internet, OSI, COMTI, and POSIX
- Proprietary technologies
- Technology environment of the company, both current and planned
- Selection of development tools
- Type of solution, such as enterprise, distributed, centralized, and collaborative

Choose a data storage architecture. Considerations include:

- Volume
- Number of transactions per time increment
- Number of connections or sessions
- Scope of business requirements
- Extensibility requirements
- Reporting requirements
- Number of users
- Type of database

Test the feasibility of a proposed technical architecture.

- Demonstrate that business requirements are met.
- Demonstrate that use case scenarios are met.
- Demonstrate that existing technology constraints are met.
- Assess impact of shortfalls in meeting requirements.

Develop appropriate deployment strategy.

Developing the conceptual and logical design for an application

Construct a conceptual design that is based on a variety of scenarios and that includes context, workflow process, task sequence, and physical environment models. Types of applications include:

- SDI, MDI, console, and dialog desktop applications
- Two-tier, client/server, and Web applications

- N-tier applications
- Collaborative applications

Given a conceptual design, apply the principles of modular design to derive the components and services of the logical design.

- Incorporate business rules into object design.
- Assess the potential impact of the logical design on performance, maintainability, extensibility, scalability, availability, and security.

Developing data models

Group data into entities by applying normalization rules.

- Specify the relationships between entities.
- Choose the foreign key that will enforce a relationship between entities and will ensure referential integrity.
- Identify the business rules that relate to data integrity.
- Incorporate business rules and constraints into the data model.
- Identify appropriate level of denormalization.
- Develop a database that uses general database development standards and guidelines.

Designing a User Interface and User Services

- Given a solution, identify the navigation for the user interface. Identify input validation procedures that should be integrated into the user interface.
- Evaluate methods of providing on-line user assistance, such as status bars, ToolTips, and Help files.
- Construct a prototype user interface that is based on business requirements, user interface guidelines, and the organization's standards.
- Establish appropriate and consistent use of menu-based controls.
- Establish appropriate shortcut keys (accelerated keys).
- Establish appropriate type of output.

Deriving the physical design

- Assess the potential impact of the physical design on performance, maintainability, extensibility, scalability, availability, and security.

- Evaluate whether access to a database should be encapsulated in an object.
- Design the properties, methods, and events of components.

Exam Objectives Cross-Reference Chart for Study Purposes

Table A-1 lists the objectives for exam 70-100, Analyzing Requirements and Defining Solution Architectures, in a cross-reference chart for study purposes. Use this table to help you determine the specific chapters in this book you should study, as well as the lab exercises you should review to prepare for the exam.

TABLE A-1 ANALYZING REQUIREMENTS AND DEFINING SOLUTION ARCHITECTURES CROSS-REFERENCE CHART

Exam Objective	*Chapter*	*Lab(s)*
Analyzing Business Requirements Analyze the scope of a project.	Chapter 17, Conceptual Design	Lab 17.37
Analyze the extent of a business requirement.	Chapter 17, Conceptual Design	Lab 17.38
Analyze security requirements.	Chapter 17, Conceptual Design	Lab 17.39
Analyze performance requirements.	Chapter 17, Conceptual Design	Lab 17.40
Analyze maintainability requirements.	Chapter 17, Conceptual Design	Lab 17.41
Analyze extensibility requirements. Solution must be able to handle the growth of functionality.	Chapter 17, Conceptual Design	Lab 17.42
Analyze availability requirements.	Chapter 17, Conceptual Design	Lab 17.43
Analyze human factor requirements.	Chapter 17, Conceptual Design	Lab 17.44
Analyze the requirements for integrating a solution with existing applications.	Chapter 17, Conceptual Design	Lab 17.45
Analyze existing methodologies and limitations of a business.	Chapter 17, Conceptual Design	Lab 17.46
Analyze scalability requirements.	Chapter 17, Conceptual Design	Lab 17.47
Group data into entities by applying normalization rules.	Chapter 18, Logical Data Design	Lab 18.48

Continued

TABLE A-1 *(continued)*

Exam Objective	Chapter	Lab(s)
Specify the relationships between entities.	Chapter 18, Logical Data Design	Lab 18.49
Choose the foreign key that will enforce a relationship between entities and will ensure referential integrity.	Chapter 18, Logical Data Design	Lab 18.50
Identify the business rules that relate to data integrity.	Chapter 18, Logical Data Design	Lab 18.51
Incorporate business rules and constraints into the data model.	Chapter 18, Logical Data Design	Lab 18.52
Identify appropriate level of denormalization.	Chapter 18, Logical Data Design	Lab 18.53
Develop a database that uses general database development standards and guidelines.	Chapter 18, Logical Data Design	Lab 18.54
Defining the Technical Architecture for a Solution	Chapter 19, Application Design	Lab 19.55
Given a business scenario, identify which solution type is appropriate. Solution types are single-tier, two-tier, and n-tier.		
Identify which technologies are appropriate for implementation of a given business solution.	Chapter 19, Application Design	Lab 19.56
Choose a data storage architecture.	Chapter 19, Application Design	Lab 19.57
Test the feasibility of a proposed technical architecture.	Chapter 19, Application Design	Lab 19.58
Develop appropriate deployment strategy.	Chapter 19, Application Design	Lab 19.59
Developing the Conceptual and Logical Design for an Application	Chapter 19, Application Design	Lab 19.60
Construct a conceptual design that is based on a variety of scenarios and that includes context, workflow process, task sequence, and physical environment models.		

Exam Objective	*Chapter*	*Lab(s)*
Given a conceptual design, apply the principles of modular design to derive the components and services of the logical design.	Chapter 19, Application Design	Lab 19.61
Incorporate business rules into object design.	Chapter 19, Application Design	Lab 19.62
Assess the potential impact of the logical design on performance, maintainability, extensibility, scalability, availability, and security.	Chapter 19, Application Design	Lab 19.63
Deriving the Physical Design	Chapter 19, Application Design	Lab 19.64
Assess the potential impact of the physical design on performance, maintainability, extensibility, scalability, availability, and security.		
Evaluate whether access to a database should be encapsulated in an object.	Chapter 19, Application Design	Lab 19.65
Design the properties, methods, and events of components.	Chapter 19, Application Design	Lab 19.66
Designing a User Interface and User Services	Chapter 20, Solution Interface Design	Lab 20.67
Given a solution, identify the navigation for the user interface.		
Identify input validation procedures that should be integrated into the user interface.	Chapter 20, Solution Interface Issues	Lab 20.68
Evaluate methods of providing online user assistance, such as statusbars, ToolTips, and Help files.	Chapter 20, Solution Interface Design	Lab 20.69
Construct a prototype user interface that is based on business requirements, user interface guidelines, and the organization's standards.	Chapter 20, Solution Interface Design	Lab 20.70

APPENDIX

B

Answers to Instant Assessment Questions

Chapter 1: COM

1. **What is the unique difference between a traditional application library service call and that of a client accessing a COM server object interface?**

   A traditional application library publishes service interfaces. This is different than COM that only publishes generic infrastructure interfaces. Interrogation of the COM object determines the services available.

   COM components do not publish the services available. New features can be added to a COM component and the component installed in the enterprise with no application impact. The installation is transparent to the application. The application cannot interrogate an **IUnknown** interface about features that it doesn't know about. The COM model handles version issues. The server object recognizes an older version of the application and emulates features of a prior version.

2. **What interface is required of all COM objects?**

   IUnknown is the interface which must be supported by all COM objects. The interface supports the **QueryInterface** method for interrogation of services available and the methods **Release** and **AddRef** for object management.

3. **Name the three basic standards for interoperability of COM.**

   The COM specification details show:

   - how an object is instantiated from a class
   - how the client accesses features of the instantiated object
   - how the instantiated object is responsible for destroying itself upon termination and the object is no longer in use

4. **What feature does Aggregation or Delegation support?**

   Aggregation and Delegation support Interface Inheritance. This is a conceptual model that ensures code reusability. Interface Inheritance should not be confused with Implementation Inheritance of C++.

5. **What is another name for an Application Programming Interface (API)?**

   Application Programming Interface (API) is a synonym for Windows Operating System Extensions.

6. **What is an SPI and who uses it?**

   The Service Provider Interface (SPI) is a programming interface that insulates the client application from the different features of various service providers. The client application is written to one API. This model is valuable in a heterogeneous enterprise where there are multiple service providers. The same application program can communicate with Microsoft MSMail, IBM Profs, or Digital Equipment All-In-One.

   The SPI model is the other half of the equation and is used by third-party vendors to provide services to a client application. The MAPI model is a good example of service providers and the MAPI SPI. MAPI service providers are free to create and market store, address book, and transport services.

   The API/SPI model is a key element of the Microsoft Consistent and Unified Interface. The client uses the API model to develop a Consistent and Unified interface to *use* a MAPI service. The service provider uses the SPI model to *offer* a MAPI service.

7. **Name four benefits of the COM model.**

   - The COM model of component pluggable components reduces software development costs. Off-the-shelf components may be used.
   - A component architecture is easy to change as the business model changes.

- The COM model insulates the Enterprise from the traditional problem of updating all applications whenever a library is changed. New or revised COM components can be installed in the Enterprise with no impact. Older versions are emulated saving the expense of updating the application.
- The COM model is a binary interface specification and is language independent. A COM model may be shared across diverse platforms.
- COM interfaces are rigid. As new interfaces are added, the original interfaces remain unchanged.
- All COM objects share the same consistent interface of **IUnknown.** A distributed COM component application can be built since the objects and interfaces are uniquely identified.

8. **What is Emulation?**

   Emulation occurs when the COM server objects detect a prior version of a client application. A prior version of the server is emulated.

9. **What is a benefit of Emulation?**

   Emulation in the COM model is the server object emulating an older server version when it detects a client expecting an older server version. This feature can significantly reduce software costs. Emulation means that not all machines in an enterprise need to be synchronized simultaneously. The logistics are reduced and the enterprise can be upgraded in a controlled manner. Emulation reduces client software updating costs and promotes code reuse.

10. **What is Aggregation?**

    Aggregation is an expression of interface inheritance. An aggregated object is passed the **IUnknown** reference of the controlling object at creation time. The control object is given the responsibility of managing the services available in the aggregated object. The services of the aggregated object are directly available to the client, however the client interrogates the **IUnknown** of the control object to determine the services available from the aggregated object. The **IUnknown** of the aggregated object is encapsulated.

11. **Describe Delegation.**

    Delegation is a form of interface inheritance where the control object calls the delegated object. The control object is a client of the delegated object. The delegated object does not know that it plays the role of a delegated object and cannot distinguish between a call from the client or the control object.

The delegated object is a publicly accessible COM object and is also directly accessible from the client. An example is any version of Microsoft Word using a drawing tool. The drawing tool is either an OLE control (OCX) or an ActiveX(tm) control in the current technology. Microsoft Word has access to a spell checker object, however the drawing control also has access to the same spell checker object. I am using Visio(r) as the drawing tool for this book. When I installed it the setup program asked me if I wanted to use the spell checker of Microsoft Word.

12. Describe Containment.

Containment is a variation on delegation where the delegated object is contained within the control object and is not accessible by the client application. Delegation encapsulates the **IUnknown** of the delegated object, while containment encapsulates the complete delegated object.

13. What characteristic of COM is not supported by Visual Basic?

Aggregation in the COM sense is not supported by Microsoft Visual Basic. This is because Visual Basic can export pointers but Visual Basic cannot be the recipient of COM pointers. This limitation is at the developer level since Visual Basic supports the passing and receipt of pointers internally.

14. Describe Encapsulation.

Encapsulation is the isolation of data or properties from the client. Methods of the object must be used for indirect data access. The client cannot directly access the data. Encapsulation is not limited to data. Containment is an example of object encapsulation.

15. What are the three commonly accepted criteria for object orientation?

I'll assume that the object is a class with methods and properties. Commonly accepted criteria for object orientation are Encapsulation, Inheritance, and Polymorphism. Other answers in this section describe each of these criteria with respect to the COM model.

16. Explain the differences between inheritance in C++ and inheritance in the COM model.

Interface inheritance is a concept of the COM model. By definition all COM objects support the **IUnknown** interface. This does not mean that an object will use existing code for **IUnknown** but that the **IUnknown** methods are always available in any COM object. This technique differs from implementation inheritance where code is inherited from a base class. Each model demonstrates a different type of inheritance, however both models realize the same goals of reusable code.

17. **What is Polymorphism?**

    Polymorphism is the access of multiple and different objects through the same interface. Aggregation, Delegation, and Containment are examples of Polymorphism.

18. **What is the *fragile base-class* problem?**

    The *fragile base-class* problem is a phenomenon of implementation inheritance associated with an object-oriented language such as C++. Change the base class and the project must be recompiled and relinked.

    This problem doesn't occur with COM, which uses generic, and universal interfaces and doesn't publish the services available, while C++ class publishes the services available.

19. **How does the COM model avoid the *fragile base-class* problem?**

    COM avoids the fragile base-class problem by not publishing service interfaces. Only generic and universal infrastructure interfaces are published. A client must interrogate the **IUnknown** interface to locate a service.

Chapter 2: Object Interfacing

1. **What is a vtable?**

   A vtable is a virtual function pointer table. The client knows only the address of the table. The interface **IUnknown::QueryInterface** is the first entry and is used to locate other interfaces.

2. **What interface must all COM objects support?**

   All COM objects must support the **IUnknown** interface.

3. **What is the minimum number of interfaces for a COM (OLE) object? Name the interfaces.**

   The minimum number of interfaces that constitutes a COM object is two. They are **IUnknown** and **IClassFactory.** This has been relaxed with ActiveX(tm) requiring only the **IUnknown** interface and the ability to be self-registering.

4. **Name the three IUnknown methods.**

   QueryInterface, AddRef, and **Release.**

5. **Name two unique characteristics of the IDispatch interface.**

   The **IDispatch** interface is only used by OLE Automation (Automation) and it supports a DISPID for function and parameter referencing.

6. **What is a dual interface?**

   A dual interface is an **IDispatch** interface which supports a vtable entry for a function and a DISPID for the same function.

7. **Under what condition might you use a dual interface?**

   A dual interface is only useful for an in-process server. Marshaling the proxy and stub consumes a disproportionate amount of resources, consequently a remote or local server will see no benefit from a dual interface.

8. **What function is it that the COM library cannot do?**

   The COM library cannot initialize an object. The object must initialize itself. The client calls **IUnknown::QueryInterface** requesting a pointer to **IPersistFile.** If the request is successful, the client asks the object to initialize itself by calling **IPersistFile::Load.**

9. **What is the role of the Service Control Manager?**

   The Service Control Manager (SCM) is responsible for locating the requested server. This task may involve setting up an RPC. If the request server is not local, SCM sends a message to the target machine and requests the SCM on the target machine to start the server.

10. **What is the role of IUnknown::AddRef and IUnknown::Release?**

    AddRef and Release manage the in-use count for an object and the subsequent life of an object. The object cannot be destroyed when the usage count is non-zero.

11. **Which component in the COM architecture is responsible for using IUnknown::AddRef and IUnknown::Release?**

    There really isn't one component responsible for managing **IUnknown::AddRef.** It is actually the responsibility of any method that creates a pointer. Those methods are **IUnknown::QueryInterface, IOleContainer::GetObject, IOleContainer::EnumObjects,** and **IClassFactory::CreateInstance.**

12. **Identify the COM library component used to start a server.**

    The COM library function **CoGetClassObject** is the function which starts the server load process. Actually most of the work is passed off to the Service Control Manager.

13. **Identify the information which must be supplied to the COM library component identified in question 12 in order to successfully start a server.**

    The client must supply the CLSID of the requested server and the IID of the **IClassFactory** interface to COM library function **CoGetClassObject.**

Chapter 3: Interface Issues

1. **What is the global name space problem?**

   The global name space problem is the issue of creating unique names in a global environment. The local directory named *temp* that you'll find in your Windows has the same local name on all Windows systems. Our problem is that each of these directories may be unique locally but not globally.

2. **How is the global name space problem solved?**

   The Open Software Foundation (OSF) proposed a Unique Universal Identifier (UUID) in their Distributed Computing Architecture (DCE) specification. Microsoft adopted that concept.

3. **Explain the differences between a UUID, a GUID, and an IID.**

   The differences are enumerated as follows:

   - A Unique Universal Identifier (UUID) is an OSF DCE concept.
   - A Globally Unique Identifier (GUID) is the 128-bit Microsoft implementation of a UUID.
   - A COM object Class Identifier (CLSID) is a GUID.
   - A COM object Interface Identifier (IID) is a GUID.

4. **Name three methods of creating a UUID.**

   A GUID may be created by using the program UUIDGEN, the graphic program GUIDGEN, the COM library function COCreateGUID, or the WIN32 RPC_EntryUuidCreate. Visual Basic 5.0 generates them automatically.

5. **What is the unique requirement of an Insertable Object?**

   All insertable objects require a GUID. Insertable objects are identified by selecting the Insert menu from a Microsoft product such as Word, Access, Excel, or any other product and selecting Object from the resultant menu.

6. **When doesn't an object require a GUID?**

   A GUID is not required for all objects. If an object was not created by the COM library, then it is not required to have a CLSID. However, that does not mean that a non-COM object cannot use COM objects. Indeed they can, and a non-COM object using an OLE Automation server is a an example.

7. **What is the difference between the ODL compiler MKTYPLIB.EXE and the IDL compiler MIDL?**

   The MKTYPLIB compiler is now obsolete and has been replaced by the newer Microsoft Interface Definition Language (MIDL). MIDL is the compiler of choice for a 32-bit platform.

8. **Name four types of information created by an ODL or IDL compiler.**

   The MIDL or MKTYPLIB compilers produce a type library, (.TLB extension), C++ header files, proxy code, and stub code. The Proxy and stub code are used for marshaling interfaces for local or remote servers.

9. **Name two instances where a GUID is necessary.**

   A Globally Unique Identifier is required for COM Model object and interface identification.

10. **Name at least three ways a type library is registered.**

    Server registration with a type library can take several forms:

    - Registering CLSIDs at object installation through a setup file.
    - A self-registering object which is downloaded from the Internet.
    - Dynamically registering objects at runtime with MFC.
    - Compiling a Visual Basic ActiveX component.
    - Selecting References ➪ Browse and selecting an ActiveX object from a VBA editor.

    Registering a new server is necessary before a client can locate and use your new server. All server CLSIDs must be registered, which is normally done at installation time. The object setup file provides this information. Either system defaults are assumed at object installation, or, at the very minimum, the CLSID key and AppID key information is required. Important information is the designation of type, which can be in-process, out-of-process local, or out-of-process remote. **RemoteServerName** and **ActivateAtStorage** are also important attributes because they let a client instantiate a server with no built-in server knowledge.

11. **Where is the type library for a Visual Basic ActiveX(tm) component located?**

    The type library for a Visual Basic ActiveX component is located within the component. Local registration is automatic at compilation time.

12. **What is Persistent data?**

    Persistent data is non-volatile data that is available to COM objects. The lifetime of persistent data does not depend upon the lifetime of the object. Data stored in the Registry is persistent since it is still available after the COM object terminates and the object is released when the usage count goes to zero. Files contain persistent data. The object's type library entry in the Registry will have the actual type library file name.

Chapter 4: Structured Storage

1. **What is the difference between structured storage and compound files?**

   Structured storage is a model and compound files are the implementation of that model.

2. **Name the four objects of structured storage.**

   The structured storage objects are **LockBytes, RootStorage, Storage,** and the **Stream** object. These objects implement a file system within a file system. The basic functionality can be described as:

   - LockBytes — A transparent interface to the underlying file system or global memory.
   - RootStorage — This object is equivalent to a master directory. Very little functionality is provided at this level.
   - Storage — The storage object can be thought of as a directory. It is always a substorage object to a parent storage. Transactions and locking are supported at this level but not at the stream level.

- Streams — Streams are analogous to files. Locking and transactions are not supported in the OLE compound file implementation.

3. **Which interface uses the ILockBytes interface?**

   The **ILockBytes** interface is used transparently by the **IStorage** and **IStream** interfaces. Methods of the **ILockBytes** interface are not used directly.

4. **Are there any restrictions on the ILockBytes Interface? If there are, what are they?**

   As stated above, the **IStream** and **IStorage** interfaces use the **ILockBytes** interface transparently. This means that the marshaling of the **IStream** or **IStorage** interfaces to another process will automatically include the **ILockBytes** interface. This can be prevented by implementing a custom **IMarshal** interface, which will prevent the automatic marshaling of the **ILockBytes** interface.

5. **What is the purpose of the one IRootStorage method?**

   SwitchToFile is the only method of the **IRootStorage** interface. Its purpose is to switch to another file and do a full save when low memory conditions occur. It is not intended to be used as a save-as mechanism and such an operation may not be supported in future releases of COM.

6. **Name two issues when marshaling a stream object to another process.**

   The first issue is that the current stream pointer is marshaled to the other process. An alternative is using the method **IStream::Clone** with the resulting pointer passed to the other process. There is still one copy of the data, however there are two different pointers to the data.

   The second issue is that the underlying **ILockBytes** interface is also marshaled to the other process. The alternative is a custom **IMarshal** interface.

7. **What are the IStream interface limitations?**

   The OLE implementation of compound files does not support transactions or locking for the **IStream** interface. The **IStream** methods affected by this limitation are **LockRegion, UnlockRegion, Commit,** and **Revert.**

8. **What is the role of IPersistMoniker?**

   IPersistMoniker signifies an asynchronous object. Binding URL monikers in the background is an example. The synchronous objects interfaces **IPersistFile, IPersisnStreamInit,** or **IPersistStorage** use **IMoniker::BindToObject.**

9. **Compare the role of IPersistMoniker and persistent data as compared to IMoniker::BindToObject and persistent data.**

   The difference in techniques is that the **IPersistMoniker** implementation allows control to be given to the object being instantiated. This technique is used for binding URL monikers in the background after the application has regained control.

   This compares with the **IPersistStream, IPersistStorage,** and **IPersist Stream[Init]** interfaces which use **IMoniker::BindToObject** to bind persistent data to the object.

10. **Describe using the IPersistPropertyBag interface**

    This is a shared labor. The object decides what to save or load with the **IPersistPropertyBag** interface and the client saves the information in any manner it deems proper with the **IPropertyBag** interface. The client reports errors back to the object with the **IErrorLog** interface.

11. **What is the primary use of IPersistStream, IPersistStorage, and IPersist Memory?**

    IPersistStorage is associated with files, **IPersistStream** is associated with monikers, and **IPersistMemory** is associated with global memory.

12. **What valuable service does IStorage::CopyTo perform besides performing the utilitarian role of copying a storage object?**

    IStorage::CopyTo defragments a storage object by creating a contiguous stream object in the target compound file. All lost space between stream objects in the source compound file is recovered in the new compound file.

Chapter 5: Monikers

Monikers

1. **Which interface must be supported for all item monikers?**

   The **IOleItemContainer** interface must be supported by all item monikers. The interface includes the functionality necessary for parsing object names and communicating with the object or with the object's storage.

2. **In binding a composite moniker, which moniker is responsible for determining the pointer for the original IID passed in by the client?**

   The simplest answer is the last moniker or the top moniker in the push down stack. The binding process has each item moniker invoking **BindToObject** on the left context object with the IID of the **IOleItemContainer** interface. These addresses are then cascaded back down the stack and the last item moniker executes the required **QueryInterface.**

3. **What is the first action the client performs related to binding a moniker?**

   The very first action is to create the binding context with the global API CreateBindCtx. This allocates and initializes a binding context for later use by the **IMoniker** interface. A simple moniker can be bound directly with the global API **BindMoniker.**

4. **What is the second step?**

   The client starts the binding process by invoking **IMoniker::BindToObject** with the moniker pointer and a pointer to the bind context previously created.

5. **Which important interface does IMoniker inherit besides IUnknown?**

   IMoniker inherits both the **IPersist** and the **IPersistStream** interfaces. These interfaces are necessary for reading and writing monikers to or from a stream.

6. **What is the Running Object Table?**

   The Running Object Table (ROT) is a global table of active objects. The moniker provider is responsible for ROT table maintenance. Entries are removed when objects are no longer running. The ROT table optimizes the binding process. It's not necessary to bind running objects and **IMoniker** can invoke **IOleItemContainer::GetObject** rather than **<LeftContext>:: BindToObject.**

7. **What restrictions are there on the global API GetRunningObjectTable call?**

   The Running Object Table should only be accessed from within the context of the bind operation. A moniker class will invoke **IBindCtx::GetRunningObjectTable.** Failure to do this could result in a severe bug such as the bug that occurred with Access 95 where there were two instances of the same memory data.

8. **What is the unique characteristic of the IOleLink interface?**

   Only a linked object implements this interface. The container object uses this interface for locating the presentation data, activating the link to the native data, and for locating the link source.

9. **What is the unique characteristic of the IOleUILinkContainer interface?**

   The **IOleUILinkContainer** must be implemented by container objects when the global API OleUIEditLinks is used to display a dialog box. This includes the Links dialog box, the Change Source dialog box, and Update Links dialog box, and the Object Properties dialog box.

10. **Explain the relationship between MkParseDisplayName, IParseDisplay Name, and IMoniker::GetDisplayName.**

    MkParseDisplayName indirectly uses **IParseDisplayName** which is the inverse of **IMoniker::GetDisplayName.**

Marshaling

1. **What is the general meaning of marshaling within the COM context?**

   Marshaling is the packaging of data by a proxy before being sent by an RPC or LPC to a destination stub.

2. **What are the generic names for the COM functions which perform marshaling?**

   The generic names are proxy and stub. The proxy packages the data on the local system and sends it to another site which may be remote. The data is unpacked there by a stub before it is passed to the target server.

3. **What feature of COM requires marshaling?**

   Marshaling is required for late binding.

4. **Default marshaling is accomplished with the IStdMarshal interface. Name four reason for custom marshaling.**

   - Custom marshaling is a consideration when the target server object itself is a proxy for some other object.
   - Some objects store their entire state in shared memory. Creating a custom proxy gives immediate access to the storage.

- Some objects have an immutable state after creation, that is, the object cannot change. A custom proxy can create a copy of this immutable state without the overhead of an RPC channel.
- A custom proxy can be used to batch cached data until such time as a commit operation is performed.

Chapter 6: Uniform Data Transfer

Uniform Data Transfer

1. **When is an application using uniform data transfer?**

   Any object implementing the **IDataObject** interface is using uniform data transfer. **IDataObject** is responsible for graphic rendering.

2. **Discuss the benefits of uniform data transfer.**

   Uniform Data Transfer (UDT) provides a wrapper function for the various clipboard protocols and adds support for additional protocols. The most direct benefit to the user is that object I/O is no longer limited to global memory.

3. **Identify the data structures associated with uniform data transfer and describe the contents of each structure.**

   There are three data structures associated with Uniform Data Transfer. The first structure is FORMATETC, which stores the object format type and the aspect (view), which can be native data, an icon, a thumbnail sketch, or preformatted printer output.

   The object storage type is stored in FORMATETC. The type can be global memory, a disk file, a storage object, a stream object, a bitmap, or a metafile.

   A pointer to the DVTARGETDEVICE structure is also stored in the FORMATETC structure.

   The DVTARGETDEVICE is the second structure that describes the target device with a driver name, a device name, a port name and a device mode.

The STGMEDIUM structure is the third of the three data structures and stores the filename, a pointer to the stream object, and a pointer to a storage object.

4. **Describe the programming restriction when implementing your own version of the IAdviseSink interface.**

   IAdviseSink is an asynchronous interface. Synchronous methods cannot be called from an asynchronous method.

5. **What interfaces are required to implement an advisory connection?**

   An advisory connection is implemented with the **IDataObject** and **IAdvise Sink** interfaces.

6. **Explain the role of the interfaces IDataAdviseHolder and IOleAdviseHolder.**

   IDataAdviseHolder manages the advisory connections for **IDataObject** while **IOleAdviseHolder** manages the advisory connections for **IOleObject.**

7. **What interfaces define an embedded object?**

   Each embedded object requires the interfaces **IOleObject, IPersistStorage,** and **IDataObject** for each type of embedded object that is supported.

8. **You are building a container application. What are the three nontrivial methods of the IOleObject interface which must be implemented?**

   This interface has twenty-one methods and the three required and nontrivial interfaces to implement are **DoVerb, SetHostNames,** and **Close. SetExtent, InitFromData, GetClipboardData, SetColorScheme, SetMoniker,** and **GetMoniker** provide optional functionality.

9. **What method activates an embedded object?**

   DoVerb activates an embedded object. Other methods include **SetHostNames** which communicates container application and document names, and Close which moves an embedded object from the running state to the loaded state. **The SetExtent, InitFromData, GetClipBoardData, SetColorScheme, SetMoniker,** and **GetMoniker** methods of **IOleObject** are optional and need not be implemented.

10. **Explain the difference between IViewData and IDataObject.**

    The **IViewObject** interface is implemented by object handlers and in-process servers that manage their own presentations. The **IViewObject** is functionally equivalent to **IDataObject,** however the difference is that **IViewObject** places a data representation on a device context(hDC), while a data representation is placed on a transfer medium by **IDataObject.**

11. **What is a limitation of the IViewObject interface?**

    Device contexts are only valid within the context of a process. This means that **IViewObject** cannot be marshaled. This seems quite logical since a bitmap on the screen is a local rendering dependent upon local attributes and characteristics.

12. **What is the relationship between the IAdviseSink and IConnectionPoint interfaces?**

    IAdviseSink and **IConnectionPoint** are asynchronous communication mechanisms. A client can only pass a single **IAdviseSink** pointer to **IDataObject.** This can be contrasted to the **IContainerPointContainer** interface which can return a pointer to more than one interface. The client then provides advisory sink pointers to each of the **IConnectionPoint** pointers returned by **IConnectionPointContainer.**

13. **What defines a connectable object?**

    Connecting to a connectable object starts by invoking **IUnknown::Query Interface** with an IID of **IID_IconnectionPointContainer.** A pointer is returned to **IConnectionPointContainer** when the object is connectable.

Drag and Drop

1. **What does drag and drop eliminate?**

   Drag and drop eliminates traditional application borders. Inter-window dragging moves objects from one application window to another application window.

2. **Drag and drop is an extension of what Microsoft operating system feature?**

   Drag and drop is an extension of the clipboard.

3. **Name the two interfaces responsible for drag-and-drop operations and indicate when they should be implemented.**

   IDropSource is implemented by any object containing data which can be dropped onto another object.

   IDropTarget is implemented by any object which can accept data.

4. **What is a requirement of the drag-and-drop target object?**

   The drag-and-drop target object must be registered with **RegisterDragDrop**.

5. **What is the function of DoDragDrop?**

   DoDragDrop is used to initiate a drag-and-drop operation. Called by the drag source when a drag drop operation starts. **DoDragDrop** calls **IDrop Target::DragEnter** when the mouse pointer passes over a window that is a registered drop target.

   DoDragDrop calls **IDropSource::QueryContinueDrag** during each loop iteration to determine if the operation should continue. Consistent operation is assured with **IDropTarget::DragOver** and **IDropSource::GiveFeedback** paired, giving the user the most up-to-date feedback information.

Chapter 7: Document Linking

1. **What is an OLE Documents representation?**

   OLE Documents represents an interaction model. Objects can be spreadsheets, charts, drawings, forms, and video or sound clips. These objects may be linked to or embedded in an OLE Document for interactive use by the user.

2. **What is the definition of an OLE component?**

   An OLE component is an object which uses COM and communicates with other objects.

3. **What is the definition of an OLE Document?**

   An OLE Document is a COM component which supports either or both linking and embedding.

4. **Explain COM model compound document embedding.**

   The persistent state of an object is maintained locally within the document. The document exists within a container and may be nested. Editing this document does not affect other users. An embedded object may be edited in place.

5. **Explain COM model compound document linking.**

   The persistent state of an object is stored with the document source. Only meta-data (presentation data) exists within a container.

A linked object is edited in its own window. Other linked users will see the changes immediately.

6. **What is the compelling reason to use linked OLE Documents as compared to embedded documents?**

   Linked OLE Documents use minimum resources since the original document is stored with the source object. A meta-file presentation copy only exists at the client site.

7. **What is an adaptable link?**

   The linked object can always locate a linked source which has not moved or when both the linked source and object are moved but the same relative path was maintained. Linked source locations are stored in the Registry. The Links dialog box can be used when the Registry is not current.

8. **An object is selected. When can editing start?**

   Only active objects may be edited.

9. **What is outside-in activation?**

   Outside-in activation is an explicit action by the user such as double-clicking.

10. **What is inside-out activation?**

    Inside-out activation is associated with embedded objects. No overt action on the part of the user is necessary to activate an object. The best example of this is an OLE control (OCX) now known as ActiveX(tm). Inside-out objects are indistinguishable from native data and require very close cooperation between the container and the object.

11. **Name an example of a full server.**

    Microsoft Excel is an example of a full server. It is free standing, supports both embedded and linked objects, and is implemented as an EXE.

12. **When is a mini-server used?**

    A mini-server only supports embedded objects and runs within the context of a container application as an EXE. It does not access the disk and cannot support linking.

13. **What is an in-process server?**

    An in-process server is a mini-server implemented as a DLL. It runs within the address space of the object application.

14. What is an in-process object handler?

An in-process object handler exists simply to display an object. It reduces the overhead of loading a server.

15. The presence of what interface indicates a linked object?

The object is linked when the **IOleLink** interface is present.

16. What are the three non-trivial interfaces required for an object handler implementation?

The three required non-trivial interfaces for an object handler are:

- **IExternalConnection** — Supports correct shutdown of links to embedded objects.
- **IRunnableObject** — Determines when to transition between running state and when to become a contained object.
- **IOleObject** — The primary interface through which a linked or embedded object provides functionality to the container.

Chapter 8: Document Embedding

1. What is another name for in-place activation?

Visual editing

2. Explain the difference between an embedded document and a linked document.

An embedded object is a copy of the native date. It is edited in-place with visual editing and does not affect other users. A linked document is edited in its own window. The data is maintained at the source and editing the document will affect all attached users.

3. What interface does the object request of the container when in-place activation starts.

The object calls **IOleClientSite::QueryInterface** looking for **IOleInPlaceSite.** The **IOleInPlaceSite** container interface must exist for in-place-activation.

4. Assume for the moment that the interface IOleInPlaceSite exists. What is the next logical step for in-process activation?

The next logical step is the object application asking permission to in-place activate by calling **IOleInPlaceSite::CanInPlaceActivate.**

5. **You have implemented an embedded application. The user complains that the screen flashes too much. What interface is faulty, or which did you forget to implement?**

   The **IOleInPlaceSiteEx** which inherits from **IOleInPlaceSite** avoids unnecessary screen flashing.

6. **Explain a windowless object implementation.**

   A windowless implementation is an object which can be activated without consuming windows resources. The container provides all windows services for the windowless object. A windowless object is an extension of normal compound documents.

7. **What type of object is a candidate for a windowless object implementation?**

   A control is a candidate for a windowless object implementation. Small controls do not need a window and a window prevents the control from being non-rectangular.

8. **What container interface must exist before an object can do a windowless activation?**

   The container interface **IOleInPlaceSiteWindowless** must exist before an object can do a windowless activation.

9. **When will a windowless control activate as a normal object?**

   The object will activate as a normal compound document when the call **IOleInPlaceSiteWindowless::CanWindowlessActivate** fails.

10. **When will edited data of an embedded object be saved?**

    OLE embedded data is edited in the container. Embedded objects retain their native, full-featured editing and operating capabilities in the new container and are edited in-place within the container. Edits made to the data become a part of the container immediately and automatically, just like edits to native data. OLE embedded objects participate in the undo stack of the window in which they are activated. Changes can be abandoned if the topmost container includes an explicit command that prompts the user asking to abandon the container update.

Chapter 9: Automation

1. **What is the definition of Automation?**

   Automation is the exposing of methods and properties by an OLE component for manipulation by another OLE component.

2. **What distinguishes Automation from OLE Documents?**

   Automation does not support linking or embedding. Note however that a component using Automation may also support the linking and embedding of OLE Documents.

3. **Explain a dual interface.**

   A dual interface is actually the **IDispatch** interface which supports the methods of **IUnknown** which include **QueryInterface, AddRef,** and **Release. IDispatch** also supports the methods **GetIDsOfNames, GetTypeInfoCount, GetTypeInfo,** and **Invoke.** What makes the interface dual is that vtable pointers to private methods are included in the interface as well as the DISPIDs of the methods. Early binding can use a vtable and late binding can use the dispinterface. Objects without vtable support can use the dispinterface while objects supporting a vtable can use the vtable interface.

4. **Explain the term *"Being a good OLE client is a requirement for being an OLE Automation application controller."***

   A good OLE client supports numerous services and cooperates closely with the server. The fact that the OLE client can support in-place activation, visual editing, and drag –and drop indicates significant support of COM functionality. This type of OLE client is an excellent OLE Automation controller candidate. As an example, Microsoft Word does not support drag and drop and is a very poor OLE Automation controller candidate.

5. **Explain why Microsoft Visual Basic cannot be an OLE Automation server.**

   Neither Microsoft Access nor Microsoft Visual Basic can be manipulated. This means they cannot be an OLE Automation server, however they are both good Automation clients in that they can manipulate an OLE Automation server such as Excel, Project, or Word.

6. **Name the three non-trivial tiers of an architecture which are candidates for Automation.**

   The three non-trivial tiers of an architecture which are candidates for Automation are data services which is SQL Server or back-end services, business services, which is where business rules are implemented, and user services, which is the client interface. Data services and business services should be shared, however the sharing of user services is not required.

7. **I mentioned that business rules are very primitive. In what way are they primitive?**

   Business rules are primitive since the business rule is embedded in the process, that is, it is embedded in code. Initially data was embedded in the process in a dim and distant past. Data has now evolved from being embedded in the process to the point today where the definition of the data is embedded in the data. Business rules always evolve after data and it is reasonable to not expect their evolutionary cycle to be as current as that of data. A tiered architecture isolates business rules, however they are still embedded in the process.

Chapter 10: OLE Controls: Using it All (Well, Almost!)

1. **Name a new feature of OLE controls.**

   The new feature of OLE controls is property pages. Properties existed in the COM model before OLE controls, but they were only ad-hoc definitions with no formalized structure and protocol.

2. **OLE controls are considered the pinnacle of COM technology in that they use nearly all COM features. What key COM feature is missing with OLE controls?**

   An OLE control does not support linking.

3. **What is the limitation of using Visual Basic 5.0 for creating ActiveX(tm) Controls?**

Visual Basic 5.0 cannot control threading. Visual Basic 5.0 does not replace Microsoft C++ as the tool for creating an ActiveX(tm) control. It functions as a proof of concept until a later implementation is done in either J++ or C++ with thread control.

4. **How are events implemented within OLE controls?**

   Events in an OLE control are a method calling an advisory sink. Events are the formalizing of method calls on a state change.

5. **What activation method is used for OLE controls?**

   In-place activation is used by OLE controls.

6. **What is the purpose of the IPointerInactive interface?**

   IPointerInactive enables drag-and-drop operations over inactive objects. The interface adds intelligence to object activation. A reduced active object count is a performance boost.

7. **What is an ActiveX Document and what are the advantages of using them?**

   An ActiveX Document is an OLE Document hosted by a browser. The advantage to this is that existing applications can be used on the Web. Non-HTML files can be opened with an ActiveX-aware Web browser. A Word document may be dropped into Microsoft Internet Explorer.

8. **How does the ICategorizeProperties interface help a container?**

   A control implements **ICategorizeProperties.** The container interrogates this interface for properties supported.

9. **What is unique about the IOleCommandTarget interface?**

   The **IOleCommandTarget** interface is used by both an Active Document server and an Active Document client for communication with each other. The interface supplies **IDispatch** functionality to active documents with less overhead than that of **IDispatch** interface.

10. **Explain the usage of -1, -1, -1, -1 in the version field of an HTML Object tag.**

    The HTML OBJECT tag with a version value of -1 -1, -1, -1 forces **CoGetClass ObjectFromURL** to always download the latest version of an ActiveX control from the Internet or Intranet.

Chapter 11: ODBC

1. **Name the major components of the ODBC architecture.**

   The major components of ODBC architecture are the application, the driver manager, the driver, and the data source.

2. **Name six benefits of the ODBC architecture.**

   - ODBC is vendor neutral. Drivers with the same specifications may be used interchangeably.
   - ODBC permits heterogeneous connection of diverse databases from a single application program.
   - ODBC insulates the application from data source and network versioning issues.
   - ODBC simplifies application development. The same application program can communicate with different databases. The only change necessary is the selection of a different ODBC driver.
   - ODBC is a portable application programming interface. The same interface and access technology exists on different platforms.
   - ODBC is open. It has the support of the SQL Access Group (SAG) and is the preferred connectivity tool for many Web tools.

3. **What role does the ODBC driver play in the Microsoft Windows Architecture?**

   The ODBC driver has the role of service provider within the framework of the Microsoft Windows Architecture.

4. **Explain the roles of each component in the ODBC architecture.**

   The client uses the application to formulate queries and either display or update data in a data source.

   The driver manager is the interface between the application and the ODBC driver. The driver manager communicates with the client, and manages the ODBC driver.

   The ODBC driver establishes the connection with the data source, issues user formulated queries, and returns result sets to the client application. The driver may manage both cursors and transactions when necessary, but the task will be transparent to the user.

5. **Explain the purpose of conformance levels.**

   API and SQL grammar conformance exist to guarantee an open architecture. ODBC drivers for the same DBMS may be used interchangeably if the conformance levels agree.

6. **Discuss ODBC driver functionality versus client application requirements.**

   ODBC drivers are written to API and SQL grammar conformance levels. The application must supply the missing functionality when the driver does not support functionality required by the client.

7. **The application design requires a time stamp for transactions. Which conformance level is required?**

   The TIMESTAMP data type is only supported with Extended SQL Grammar.

8. **The client wishes to do a browse connect. Which conformance level is required?**

   This is an API conformance issue and the driver must support a Level 2 API conformance level for a browse connect.

9. **The client wants optimal performance with prepared SQL statements. Which API conformance level is required?**

   This is an API conformance issue. Prepared SQL statements are supported by a core API conformance level. This is the minimum API conformance level and is supported by all ODBC drivers.

10. **Which ODBC API conformance level supports a scrollable cursor?**

    A scrollable cursor is supported by the Level 2 API Conformance level.

11. **Explain a single-tier driver.**

    A single-tier driver supports xBase or flat file systems. The driver has the responsibility of converting the SQL statements to file I/O statements. The driver directs the resulting file I/O statements to the data source which may not be local. Results are then returned to the client application. A single-tier driver is the only ODBC driver architecture where the driver processes the SQL requests.

12. **What is the difference between a single-tier and a two-tier ODBC driver?**

    A two-tier driver passes SQL statements to a data source. The statements may be partially parsed, however the driver takes no responsibility for retrieving the data. That is the responsibility of the data source.

A two-tier driver may be SQL-based or non-SQL-based. The non-SQL-based ODBC driver architecture will have an ODBC bridge and it may have either a client-based SQL engine or a data source-based SQL engine.

13. **What is the basic difference between a two-tier and a three-tier ODBC?**

    The three-tier driver architecture has gateway software on an intermediary system.

14. **What is a driver-leveling library?**

    Not all ODBC drivers adhere to the same conformance level. A driver-leveling library presents a uniform interface to the application task by providing missing driver functionality. This gives all drivers the appearance of having the same API and SQL Grammar conformance levels.

Chapter 12: ODBC Applications

1. **Explain the concept of a search-limited expression. Give several examples of search-limited expressions.**

   A search-limited query has an expression, which evaluates to a limiting value. The search for equality is search-limited since the complete table need not be searched. An obvious corollary is that a table without an index is not search-limited. A search-limited query requires an index

2. **What is the fastest processing technique for a single SQL statement? What about statements that are repeated?**

   SQLExecDirect will always be the fastest execution technique for a single SQL non-repeated statement. SQLPrepare followed by repeated SQLExecute statements provides the fastest execution for repeated SQL statements.

3. **Explain why an SQL query with the NOT IN operator is not search-limited.**

   The issue here is to understand that SQL returns a result set. Members not in the returned result set are by definition in the NOT IN set. The first pass is made creating the result set. Another pass is then made selecting only those elements NOT IN the original result set.

4. **What is the problem with calculations in a query expression?**

The index can't be used since each row must be retrieved and the required expression calculated before the selection criteria can be applied.

5. **What is unique about an SQL expression containing an OR clause?**

   An SQL expression containing the OR operator is decomposed by the SQL parser into two distinct queries connected with a UNION statement.

6. **What advantage does preparing an SQL statement offer?**

   Microsoft SQL Server and other relational database servers use query optimization. The optimization is cost-based and follows numerous heuristic rules. The resulting query plan is saved and associated with an SQL statement. The advantage to this is that the query plan may be reused and saves recompilation time. This is great stuff, however there are some occasions where you might not want to use reuse your query plan.

   Recall the concept of search limited strings and that the expression LIKE %<character string> is not search-limited while the expression like <character string>% is search-limited. The issue is client supplied character strings where no control is placed on wild-card characters. Preparing a statement and preserving the query plan is of little value if there are no limits placed on the user provided input. One query may be a specific value which is search-limited while the next input value may have a leading wild-card character which is not search-limited.

   There are other examples such as the data itself. Orders to an order-entry system may be batched. Query plans are made for existing data. New batches of data may skew and invalidate existing query plans. Microsoft is right is recommending that SQL statements should be prepared, however some thought must be given to creating new query plans when the characteristics of the data change. There is also the related issue of UPDATE STATISTICS on SQL Server, but that is not a topic for this book.

7. **What is a state transition error?**

   A state transition error occurs when API functions are either called in the wrong order or are not in the proper state. The three handles, environment, connection, and statement each have three states, which are unallocated, allocated, and connected. A state error occurs when calling an API function which is not in the proper state. A simple example is setting connection attributes when not connected to a data source.

8. What is a fat cursor?

A fat cursor is a synonym for a block cursor. A block cursor is a set of rows (result set), that has a cursor that can be positioned to any given row in the result set.

9. What is the unique characteristic of a static cursor?

Static cursors are equivalent to snapshots. It is a copy of a rowset at a point in time. No changes to the underlying tables are detectable.

10. Explain the operating principles of a dynamic cursor?

A dynamic cursor can detect all underlying table changes. It is not an easy cursor to implement. For example the keyset-driven cursor technique can determine deleted rows in the underlying table. Changed rows can be identified with timestamps, but new rows added are much more complex. A possible implementation mechanism is to notify all attached processes when new rows are added to the underling table. There must be a qualification since an application only wants notification when the newly added row is of interest.

11. What are the limitations of a keyset-driven cursor?

A keyset-driven cursor cannot detect newly added rows, even though it can detect deleted rows. It detects the deleted rows when the cursor is positioned to the row. A read request is issued for the row, and an error status is returned if the row doesn't exist.

12. Name a limitation of the Microsoft implementation of ODBC in C/C++.

Column binding in ODBC utilizes the data types of the implementation language. Microsoft states that the ODBC specification is language independent, however the Microsoft implementation of ODBC is C/C++ based which does not support either the new Unicode or the SQL Server data type VARCHAR. This is by no means a negative statement about ODBC which is an open and very powerful database connection tool. These issues are only minor irritations, which as you'll see shortly, are solved with wrappers providing a higher level of functionality.

13. What important function must be performed after an environment handle is allocated?

The behavior of ODBC must be established. **SQLSetEnvAttr** is used to set SQL_ATTR_ODBC_VER before a connection is made to the data source. This is used to change the behavior of ODBC 3.0 to ODBC 2.x.

14. Describe the differences between the ODBC 2.x SQLFetch and the ODBC 3.0 SQLFetch.

The SQLFetch function of ODBC 2.x returns a single row while the same function in ODBC 3.0 returns a result set. This could give unexpected results to an application not expecting multiple rows.

15. Name a new and very useful connection attribute that enhances performance.

ODBC 3.0 supports connection pooling. The connection example in the topic "Debugging an ODBC Application" illustrates the cost of establishing a connection to a data source.

16. Describe long data and how to process it.

Long data is Binary Large Objects (BLOBs). The data can be either characters or binary data. The issue is the stripping of null termination characters before recombining the data buffers.

17. SQLGetData has a unique property. What is it?

SQLGetData retrieves data for unbound columns. The function must be called in order of increasing column number. Columns are numbered starting with one on the left.

18. What new binding feature is not supported for ODBC 2.0? Is it a performance issue?

ODBC 3.0 provides binding offsets. A pointer to an offset is a parameter and the client application changes the offset without rebinding the columns. This is not a feature of ODBC 2.0.

19. What is a catalog function?

A catalog function is an ODBC API function that returns a result set.

20. Name the catalog functions.

The catalog functions are: **SQLTables, SQLColumns, SQLStatistics, SQLSpecialColumns, SQLPrimaryKeys, SQLForeignKeys, SQLTable Privileges, SQLColumnPrivileges, SQLProcedures, SQLProcedure Columns,** and **SQLGetTypeInfo.**

21. When is SQLDescribeCols used?

SQLDescribeCols is used in the column binding loop. The client first invokes **SQLNumResultCols** which determines the number of result columns. The application then loops on **SQLDescribeCol** and **SQLBindCOL** for the binding. **SQLDescribeCol** isn't necessary when the column attributes are known a priori by the application.

22. **When is the ODBC API function SQLEndTran used?**

    The ODBC API function is only used in manual-commit mode.

23. **What happens to an SQL statement which cannot be translated by the ODBC driver?**

    An SQL statement which cannot be understood by the ODBC driver is passed directly to the data source without translation. The Microsoft SQL Server statement USE *Pubs* is an example.

24. **What is the scope of a transaction?**

    The connection is the scope of a transaction. All statements for the connection will either be committed or rolled back.

25. **Describe using the API function SQLExecute.**

    SQLExecute is paired with **SQLPrepare** and executes the query plan prepared by **SQLPrepare.**

26. **What is the default transaction mode for ODBC?**

    The default transaction mode for ODBC is auto-commit.

27. **What determines cursor behavior for commit or rollback operations?**

    The data source determines cursor behavior for commit or rollback operations. **SQLGetConnectAttr** is interrogated with an attribute of SQL_CURSOR_COMMIT_BEHAVIOR or SQL_CURSOR_ROLLBACK_BEHAVIOR.

28. **When is a cursor closed automatically?**

    A cursor is closed automatically when a statement times out or the cursor behavior mode for the connection attribute SQL_CURSOR_COMMIT_BEHAVIOR or SQL_CURSOR_ROLLBACK_BEHAVIOR is set to either SQL_CB_DELETE or SQL_CB_CLOSE.

29. **Describe a performance issue with manual-commit transactions.**

    The problem is with the cursor in SQL_CB_PRESERVE mode where the cursor and query plan are preserved even though the transaction has been committed. This leaves a read lock on the server which may block other users.

30. Discuss optimistic concurrency versus pessimistic concurrency.

Optimistic concurrency assumes that few collisions will occur and locks the data only when an update is eminent. Pessimistic concurrency locks the data at the beginning of the transaction.

31. Describe ODBC cursor library support.

ODBC 3.0 cursor library supports only static and forward-only cursors. It supports block scrollable cursors for any driver that is Level 1 API compliant.

Chapter 13: RDO

1. Name the first object in the RDO hierarchy.

The first object in the RDO hierarchy is the **rdoEngine.** This is a single object and it can only be initialized.

2. Name a property of all collections.

Count is a property of all collections.

3. Which RDO object does not have a default collection?

Neither the **rdoColumn** object not the **rdoParameter** object have a default collection.

4. Give an example of a default collection.

```
MyRS!au_fname
     MyRS("au_fname")
     MyRS.rdoColumns("au_fname").Value
MyRS.rdoColumns(0).Value
```

5. Name an object which is automatically appended to a collection.

All new objects are automatically appended to a collection.

6. When does RDO ignore the Close method?

RDO ignores the **Close** method for the default **rdoEnvironments**(0) object.

7. Name a collection where objects cannot be removed with the Close method.

Nothing can be removed from the **rdoTables** collection.

8. **Name three objects that share the same collection.**

   The **rdoPreparedStatement, rdoTable,** and **rdoResultset** objects have in common the **rdoColumns** collection.

9. **Name two DAO and Jet features not available in RDO.**

   RDO does not support updatable joins, heterogeneous joins, or DDL statements, all of which are supported in Microsoft Access. RDO uses the DDL statements of the remote server. Updatable joins, heterogeneous joins, or DDL statements are functions of a database and Microsoft SQL Server 7.0 now supports heterogeneous joins. RDO depends upon DDL statements of the data source.

10. **What is the default collection of the rdoEngine object?**

    The **rdoEnvironments** collection is the default collection of **rdoEngine.**

11. **Explain the difference in optimistic concurrency in RDO as compared to DAO.**

    Both DAO and RDO have the same intrinsic constants, although the names differ. DAO requires the intrinsic constant **dbSeeChanges** to create trappable optimistic concurrency errors, while RDO trappable optimistic concurrency errors occur automatically.

12. **You have two rdoConnection objects, each with a result set. The rdoEnvironment object is not the default environment. What happens when it is closed?**

    You will probably lose data. Objects should always be closed in their inverse hierarchical order. Close the result set, then the connection, and finally the environment.

13. **You are attempting to register a data source using RDO. It fails and you can find nothing wrong with your VB. code. What is your probable problem?**

    The SQL Server driver is not registered. This must be registered before the data source can be registered.

14. **What is a unique characteristic of the rdoEnvironments(0) object?**

    The **rdoEnvironments(0)** object cannot be closed.

15. **You have an error. There are many error messages and it is quite confusing since every layer of the system has their own interpretation of the problem. Where is the primary RDO error message located?**

    The primary error is located at **rdoErrors(0).**

16. **What must be done before accessing the rdoTables collection?**

    It must be populated with the Refresh method.

17. **What is the scope of a transaction?**

    An **rdoEnvironment** object is the scope of a transaction started in an object other than an **rdoConnection** object. RDO 2.0 now supports transactions local to a connection.

18. **Why is RDO a good choice for heterogeneous connection of the enterprise?**

    RDO is designed to support only ODBC data sources. This gives connectivity to foreign relational databases. RDO is not a good choice for flat-file operations or for Microsoft Access.

19. **You have developed this killer application which uses RDO. What must be done to license the software?**

    RDO cannot be licensed. Your client must purchase Microsoft Visual Basic Enterprise Edition. The exception to this rule is RDO technology encapsulated within an Automation server.

Chapter 14: RDO Queries

1. **The rdoQuery object has a parallel in the DAO QueryDef object. What unique feature is an option with a DAO QueryDef object and is built-in with the rdoQuery object of RDO?**

   A DAO **QueryDef** object is prepared automatically when it is saved. The intrinsic constant **dbQPrepare** must be used with ODBCDirect while the **rdoQuery** object of RDO prepares SQL statements automatically in RDO 1.0, however the Prepared property must be set in RDO 2.0.

2. **A Delete method has failed on a row in a result set. Name six reasons for this problem.**

   A delete may fail for numerous reasons. Factors to consider on a delete failure include:

   - There is no current row.
   - The **rdoConnection** object or the **rdoResultset** object is read-only.
   - Columns in the row are not updatable.

- The row doesn't exist, it has already been deleted.
- The row or data page is locked by another user.
- The user permissions do not allow a delete operation.

3. **An Edit method has failed on a row of a result set. Name five reasons for this problem.**

   The Edit method will fail when:

   - A current row doesn't exist.
   - The **rdoConnection** or **rdoResultset** object is read-only.
   - Columns in the row are not updatable.
   - The **EditMode** property indicates an edit is already in process.
   - The row or data page is locked by another user.

4. **Your application is using RDO as the database access technology. Which feature of RDO is useful when a grid control must be populated?**

   The **GetClipString** method, which is the string equivalent of the **GetRows** method, will return a delimited string for populating the grid control.

5. **What useful function is provided by the MoreResults method?**

   The **MoreResults** method signals that at least one more additional **rdoResultset** object waits to be processed.

6. **What is the major difference between RDO 1.0 and RDO 2.0 with respect to rdoResultset objects?**

   In RDO 1.0 the original **rdoResultset** object was not closed when a new **rdoResultset** object was created with the same name. In RDO 2.0 the prior **rdoResultset** object is closed automatically.

Chapter 15: Active Data Objects (ADO)

1. **What advantages does ADO offer when compared to DAO?**

ADO, when compared to DAO has four distinct advantages:

- ADO 2.0 is free-threaded. This is a significant advantage with respect to scalabilty.

- ADO 2.0 supports disassociated result sets. This means that the connection may be released and the **Recordset** object remains instanitated. That is not the case for DAO. Release the DAO **Connection** object and everything is lost.
- ADO has a smaller footprint, which is of value for enterprise applications, but is not too meaningful for desktop applications when 64 Mb of memory for the client is the norm.
- ADO relaxes the rigid object instantiation requirements of both RDO and DAO with a minimal ADO application instantiating only the **Connection** object. ADO will automatically instantiate a Connection object when the application attempts to connect to a data source with either a **Command** or **Recordset** object.

2. **Compare RDO optimistic concurrency and ADO optimistic concurrency.**

   Both DAO and RDO support either value-based or record ID-based optimistic concurrency. ADO supports optimistic concurrency, and the type of optimistic concurrency is not explicitly stated. It can be surmised that the ADO supported optimistic concurrency is record ID-based, since value-based optimistic concurrency is very inefficient.

3. **Name the ADO objects that support creating a result set.**

   An ADO result set may be created from a **Connection** object, a **Command** object, or a **Recordset** object.

4. **The application starts directly with the ADO Recordset object. Explain the events.**

   ADO automatically obtains a **Connection** object when the application attempts to connect to a data source directly with a **Recordset** object.

5. **Which ADO cursor type provides optimum performance in ADO 2.0?**

   The **CursorType** property of the **Recordset** object available cursor types. The optimum choice for ADO is the intrinsic value **adOpenForwardOnly,** which is equivalent to a static cursor with forward-only result scrolling.

6. **What is the default cursor location for ADO 2.0?**

   The default cursor location is defined by the **CursorLocation** property of the **Recordset** object. The default value is **adUseServer,** which uses either the driver-supplied or data source-supplied cursor. **adUseServer** does not support disassociated result sets, which are supported by **adUseClient** or the deprecated **adUseClientBatch**.

7. **Explain a *dirty read*.**

   An application is permitted to read transaction data that is later rolled back.

8. **Explain a *non-repeatable read*.**

   A non-repeatable read occurs when other applications update the same row before the second read occurs.

9. **Explain a *phantom read*.**

   A phantom read occurs when a row that matches the selection criteria is added by another application. This event occurs after the initial rows were read by the first application.

10. **What is the default property for the Field, Parameter, and Property objects?**

    The **Value** property is the default property for the **Field, Parameter,** and **Property** objects.

11. **Name the collections that support the Append method.**

    Only the **Parameters** collection supports the **Append** method.

12. **Name the collections or objects that support the Delete method?**

    The **Delete** method is only supported by the **Parameters** collection and the **Recordset** object.

13. **Name the collections or objects that support the Clear method.**

    The **Clear** method is only supported by the **Errors** collection.

Chapter 16: Working with Active Data Objects

1. **Name the four ADO collections.**

   The four ADO collections are the Errors, Fields, Parameters, and Properties collections.

2. **What is the issue when the Recordset object attribute adApproxPosition is not supported?**

   Counting records in the **Recordset** object requires the reading of each record which may be resource intensive.

3. **What role does the ActiveConnection property of a Recordset object play in error analysis?**

   The **ActiveConnection** property of the **Recordset** object is necessary since errors are stored in the Connection object and the **ActiveConnection** property is the **Recordset** object link to the Connection object.

4. **Identify and describe the two classes of ADO events.**

   ADO supports two classes of events. The first class of events reports when a Command object executes, starts, or ends and is aptly named the **Connection Events** family. The second class of events reports navigation within rows of a **Recordset** object or any changes to a row or column of the **Recordset** object and is name the **RecordsetEvents** family.

5. **Describe creating an ADO event routine.**

   An ADO event is declared with the **WithEvents** keyword (see Listing 16-1).

6. **How are ADO events enabled or disabled?**

   The **ConnectionEvents** family of events are enabled by setting the declared event object to the **Connection** object of interest. Correspondingly, the **RecordsetEvents** family is enabled by setting the declared event object to the **Recordset** object of interest. Both families of events are disabled by setting the declared event object to **Nothing.**

7. **Identify the basic difference between editing a record in DAO and ADO.**

   An edit mode is not required with ADO. The record is edited and moving to the next record will save the changes.

8. **What is batch mode?**

   Batch mode is a form of record editing where changes are accumulated and submitted collectively. The method **UpdateBatch** submits batch changes while the method **CancelBatch** will revert all changes since the last **Update Batch** call.

9. **How is batch mode initiated?**

   Batch mode is initiated by setting the **LockType** property of the **Recordset** object to the intrinsic constant **adLockBatchOptimistic.**

10. **What determines if a Recordset object is fully scrollable and updatable?**

    Setting both the **CursorType** and **LockType** properties of the **Recordset** object Open method to **adOpenKeyset** and **adLockBatchOptimistic** respectively creates a fully scrollable and batch-updateable **Recordset** object.

11. **What common characteristic does the DAO Errors collection share with the ADO Errors collection?**

    The ADO Errors collection is only for ADO errors and the DAO Errors collection is only for DAO errors. VBA errors will not be found in either collection.

12. **Explain the use of the Supports method.**

    ADO and OLE-DB are not fully implemented, provider support may be uneven, there are no standards, Microsoft might make unexpected changes, and the **Recordset** object may not be appropriate are some of the reasons the consumer must always verify the support for a particular feature. For example before deleting a record the consumer should verify that the record can be deleted. Such a prototype statement might be:

```
if MyRS.Supports(adDelete) then
MyRS.Delete
else
```

13. **What is the common issue for the Delete, Resync, UpdateBatch, or CancelBatch methods?**

    A run-time error will not occur if at least one operation is performed successfully. As an example a run-time error will not occur if one record was successfully deleted and twenty-four records were not deleted. The consumer must check the Errors collections for error messages.

Chapter 21: Distributed COM1.

1. **What is the *fragile super class* problem?**

   The fragile super class problem occurs with implementation inheritance and Microsoft C++. Changing any feature of the super class will break all dependent sub classes. This does not occur with COM interface inheritance.

2. **COM supports a model of binary encapsulation where the interface isolates the client from the implementation. Explain binary encapsulation in Microsoft C++.**

Microsoft C++ does not support binary encapsulation. The only encapsulation supported by Microsoft C++ is syntax-based and is dependent upon the language.

3. **What are the primary limiting factors of two-tier applications?**

   Two-tier applications are not scalable with respect to additional connections. The server size can be increased but this reaches a point of diminishing returns.

4. **What are the disadvantages of shifting processing to the client layer in a two-tier architecture?**

   Application logic is decentralized and is difficult to manage. Deploying new applications is also difficult.

5. **What threading model is used by Microsoft Visual Basic?**

   Microsoft Visual Basic uses the single-threaded apartment threading model.

6. **What is the relationship between a message pump and a single-threaded apartment?**

   Every single-threaded apartment requires a message pump.

7. **What is the threading issue regarding Microsoft Visual Basic and marshaling data with respect to DCOM components?**

   Marshaling from Microsoft Visual Basic requires four threads, two on the client side and two on the server side.

8. **Parameters can be passed to a DCOM component either by value or by reference. Explain the actions when data is passed by value to a DCOM server.**

   Data with the *ByVal* type designation is pushed to the server during marshaling. No data is returned from the server.

9. **Explain the actions when data is passed by reference to a DCOM component.**

   The data is marshaled in both directions, both to and from the server. Return marshaling is prevented by erasing the array or object.

10. **What is the issue relating to the use of collections in a DCOM architecture?**

    Collections are owned by a component. Collections are not marshalled to another component. The *For Each* construct establishes a new connection with the server for each item. This behavior is not tolerable for any environment other than an in-process server.

11. **What is the context of custom marshaling?**

    Each parameter of a component method reference requires an individual wire trip. Custom marshaling is the packing of all parameters into a complex data structure such as a Variant or a user-defined data type (UDT). This reduces the wire trips to one for the parameters.

12. **Explain the context of *state* with respect to DCOM.**

    Chapter 21 presented *stateful* components. State is residual context information, which relates to scalability. The component cannot be reused reliably with residual state.

13. **Please explain the value of using the Implements statement.**

    The Implements statement uses *dispinterfaces* and **IUnknown** to implement the fastest possible interface. (See the first laboratory at the conclusion of this chapter.)

14. **Please explain the meaning of *unwinding the stack*.**

    A Visual basic error cannot process errors created within the error handler. Such errors are always passed back up the call-tree to the prior level. The prior level of the call-tree will process the error, but only if an error handler exists. The application stops when the application does not possess an error handler at the top level. Each level adds additional information as the error message is passed back the call-tree to the client, which is known as *unwinding the stack*.

15. **What was the architectural error of Chapter 16?**

    Only use Collection objects with in-process DCOM servers.

APPENDIX

C

Lab Objectives

Chapter 17 Labs

This appendix provides detailed discussion of the exam objectives covered in chapters 17-20.

Lab 17.37 *Analyze the scope of a project.*

Using the case study and business rambling in Listing 17-1, analyze each of the following.

The case study has no *existing applications*. However, when related applications exist, there are a significant number of issues to consider. Is data shared between applications? If so, will the new application provide output or receive input from an existing application? Does prior data exist? Is conversion required for existing data? If so, what are the anticipated data conversion costs? Does the new application replace an existing application? What are the issues related to the existing application? Is there a salvage factor on the existing application?

The case study requires minimal changes to the environment. The project will require larger display terminals since 13 or 14-inch monitors are not suitable for the simultaneous viewing of more than one document. The other environmental issue to consider is existing workflow patterns. Will the new application create new workflow patterns? Will the new application be disruptive to existing workflow patterns?

The *expected lifetime of the solution* to this case study application will be indefinite. This means that the application should be implemented with technologies and tools that are based on standards. This makes Microsoft SQL Server a better choice than Microsoft Access as the repository of the contract documents. Microsoft SQL Server supports the American National Standards Institute (ANSI) Structured Query Language (SQL) 1992 standard. Microsoft Access is a combination of SQL 1989, SQL 1992, and proprietary Microsoft SQL implementations. The developers should be given guidelines concerning the use of proprietary and nonstandard SQL implementations. Conversion costs are minimized when applications adhere to standards.

Factors to consider when choosing a technology are the revision rate, the relative age of the technology, the existence of standards, and the stability of the technology. Technology that is revised once a year is not a candidate for a stable environment. For example, Microsoft intentionally withholds revisions in an effort to maximize revenue. The example is Microsoft SQL Server. The update to the ANSI SQL 92 standard came in two distinct and different releases of Microsoft SQL Server, which is certainly less than desirable.

No time, budget, or cost *constraints* or benefit trade-offs were included in the case study business rambling. Since this is an *unofficial* project the actual budget amounts will be minimal. In many areas, especially cost, the business rambling does not address reality.

It's a mistake to set budgets before the issues are completely understood and the project designed. A fixed budget can be set for the design phase, assuming that you're not using Microsoft Solution Frameworks that allow design during development. After the system is designed, costs can be estimated. Budget slack time and spare funds into the project. You'll need both of these downstream when some component falls behind schedule. Invariably some comfort zone (budget) will be violated in terms of both cost and time. At that time a reduction in features can be negotiated that will reduce the anticipated cost and implementation time. Don't negotiate out the slack built into the project. You still need that. Negotiate out a hard feature along with the anticipated benefits. Just remember that when benefits are dropped because of time or budget constraints, you're also dropping some of the justification for the system. When you're in the development phase and the user wants a new feature, charge for it. When you decide to incorporate a new feature, charge 3-4 times the normal rate, since the project is now at risk. Tell the user up front that features added during the implementation phase cost X times normal because they put the project at risk.

Lab 17.38 *Analyze the extent of a business requirement*

Using the case study and business rambling in Listing 17-1, analyze each of the following. Considerations include:

The case study *business requirements* were established with the business rambling in Listing 17-1. The project is an effort to manage exposed risk on existing contracts when applicable laws change. The business requirements include tracking contract changes by sentence. There is also a document-tracking requirement for primary copies or master copies. All copies are numbered and must be tracked.

Capturing and understanding the business requirements minimizes risks. As stated earlier in the book, a successful project requires a buy-in by all related parties. Depending upon the scope of the project, this can include the CEO, CFO, CIO, department managers, the development team, and the users.

A project failed this week. It was not a large project nor was it a small project. A Microsoft Solution Provider (MSP) signed a contract to develop a retirement benefit system. The problem was that the responsible manager on the client side "was always too busy for an interview." I fault the MSP for not stopping the project at that point, however they subscribe to the Microsoft Solution Frameworks paradigm, which allows development in parallel with design. Clearing the obstacles assumed the trappings of a death march.

Eventually everything progressed and two modules were completed with quite a bit of pain. The final module was half completed when the project was stopped because "we're out of funds." That may or may not be true, however in retrospect, the project was set up for failure. The manager never provided the necessary interview and information came through a third party that was not always correct. That manager is probably now talking to the CEO saying: "Yeah, we couldn't do it with Microsoft technology, so it appears that we'll have to do it with Oracle." It is very obvious in retrospect that the manager had a hidden agenda and was only following marching orders in dealing with the MSP.

It's amusing to surmise what new obstacles would be encountered had the MSP successfully completed the last module. Maybe the project was stopped because there was a significant possibility that the MSP could make the system work, in spite of the obstacles. A successful project requires that everyone must buy in, and there must be a complete buy-off of the project concept by all parties before the project starts, not during project development. This is contrary to the

Microsoft Solution Frameworks paradigm, but experience has proven that this is the prudent course to follow.

Establish the *type of problem,* such as a messaging problem or a communication problem. The case study application is a text management system. Once the problem is identified, the choice of technology can be an issue. The resulting solution is often a hybrid of different technologies. The basic structure of the case study application is Microsoft SQL Server supporting clients using a text-processing engine with integrated security. A custom text-processing engine needs to be built since the SQL language is not suitable for searching text. Each row in a SQL Server table represents either an atomic string or a single sentence, which supports the case study tracking requirement.

Establish and define *customer quality requirements***.** The case study advocate demands a system that is self-tutoring and as easy to use as an Apple Computer.

The case study system falls into the realm of zero-defects. There cannot be an error on a contract. Such a system typically doesn't have a parallel test period. It is tested on the basis of scenarios. This is quite different from accounting systems, which are a different class of application that require extensive testing and should be run in parallel for a fixed period of time. It's not pleasant to switch over to a new system on Monday and have the system fail by noon because "someone forgot about ...". Additional staff is an absolute necessity during the parallel testing period. The current staff will be stressed and the error rate too high when dual duties are imposed.Minimize *Total Cost of Ownership (TCO)***.** The case study is not a production system and TCO is not applicable.

TCO is a mythical Holy Grail and everyone has a different TCO interpretation. That can be illustrated with a marketing example. A salesman books a sale when a customer displays interest, the sales manager books a sale when the contract is received, and the comptroller books a sale when the money is received. It's a bit more complicated since the players in the TCO game include the CEO, CFO, CIO, the responsible department managers, the users, and the developers.

Is TCO the ultimate answer? I think not, and hardware is a good example. Yes, you can buy cheap hardware, but is the hardware reliable and stable? It's a question of being penny-wise and pound-foolish. Yes, it can be demonstrated that TCO has been reduced, however saving ten, twenty, or even fifty thousand dollars can leave the corporation at risk. The issue will become very significant in days to come with desktop systems eclipsing the 400 MHz mark. You won't be able to go to your local dealer and procure boxes with clone motherboards and memory from an unknown source that operate reliably. Such a system is adequate for a Doom II player, however corporate America needs reliability. At 400 MHz, matching the CPU to the memory is a job best done by the manufacturer.

My advice is simple. TCO is a marketing issue since there are too many perspectives and the real issue is reliability, which may be sacrificed in the interest of TCO. TCO is a Pandora's box of infrastructure costs. The bottom line is to manage costs prudently while managing risks. Undue price cutting often engenders unwarranted risks, which means that minimum TCO often corresponds to maximum risk. This policy applies to all infrastructure costs, not just equipment costs.

Increase *Return on Investment (ROI)* of solution. The case study project is considered a necessity for corporate well being. It can be assumed that precluding just a single lawsuit will pay for the system implementation, possibly many times over. Does the solution have business value? If not, then implementation is highly questionable. It's not enough to just realize a return on investment when an implementation has business value. The anticipated system should have a high benefit to cost ratio, not just a simple ROI but a multiplier. This is because risks are engendered in system development. A major success can offset the losses of other failed projects. Sacrificing features and benefits halfway through the project to maintain the schedule will also reduce the return on investment.

Analyze the *current platform and infrastructure.* The current platform is not adequate for the case study project. Both the network and the platform must be upgraded.

This is not a difficult task when accomplished in the post-design phase. The platform and infrastructure should not be analyzed before the task at hand is completely understood and a system is designed. Doing so results in a system designed for the current infrastructure, which is often limited and inadequate. Analyze the current platform and architecture after the system is designed, not before, and don't let the current platform or infrastructure influence the design.

Incorporate the planned platform and infrastructure into the solution. The case study infrastructure must be upgraded to a secure network that supports both Microsoft Windows NT and Microsoft SQL Server. Virtual Private Network (VPN) and the Point-To-Point Tunneling protocol (PPTP) are choices to consider when communicating with foreign subsidiaries. However at this point, foreign subsidiaries are in stage II of the implementation.

As stated in the analysis for the previous objective, design the system first and then analyze the current platform and infrastructure. Incorporate new platforms and infrastructure when the current platforms and infrastructure are inadequate.

Analyze the impact of *technology migration.* Windows 95 is currently installed for all case study users and there is no impact due to technology migration. Both Windows NT 4.0 and Microsoft Windows 95 use the same paradigm.

That's the short answer. Windows 2000 will not run applications developed under either Windows 95, 98 or Windows NT 4.0. The best choice is a year 2000 compliant version of Windows NT 4.0. Maintain that system for several years until the new Microsoft technology stabilizes. By then migration tools should be available to migrate to Windows 2000.

There are stable and unstable technologies. Open Database Connectivity (ODBC) is a stable technology that adheres to the ANSI SQL 92 standard. OLE database (OLE-DB) is a new Microsoft technology with no standards that is undergoing a maelstrom of change. An enterprise needs a stable and reliable technology.

Plan *physical requirements,* such as infrastructure. Although the case study initially planned using Microsoft Access, this project requires Microsoft SQL Server for text storage. The only problem is that the corporation does not at this time have the necessary infrastructure to support Microsoft SQL Server.

Planning physical requirements is not a difficult task when accomplished in the post-design phase. Budgetary problems arise when a budget is established before the system is designed and the final design requires additional infrastructure.

Establish *application environment,* such as hardware platform, support, and operating system. The case study system will require a dedicated Windows NT installation that is secure from other portions of the network. The administrator will not have a significant security problem.

Establishing the platform is not a difficult task when accomplished in the post-design phase. This task is a function of recognizing the requirements. Microsoft SQL Server 6.5 requires Windows NT, however that is relaxed with SQL Server 7.0. Both Windows 95 and 98 emphasize client support, but neither support user level security. The major features of Windows NT and Windows 95 or 98 include:

- ***Windows NT***—MAPI, TAPI, Security, Named Pipes, Sockets, Unicode, multiple CPUs, and Win32 API are supported. Plug-and-Play and direct hardware access is not supported.

- ***Windows 95/98*** — MAPI, TAPI, direct hardware access, Named Pipes, Plug-and-Play, Sockets, single CPU, ANSI/DBCS, and a limited Win32 API. Security and Unicode are not supported.

Identify *organizational constraints,* such as financial situation, company politics, technical acceptance level, and training needs. The case study project is very political. There are significant company politics and the success of this venture cannot be guaranteed. An unreal expectation exists as to the capabilities of Microsoft Access. The initial expectation is a system developed in Microsoft Access that is self-teaching.

Each of the items identified in this objective can cause a system implementation to fail, and none of the issues are developer related. Just writing good code on a timely basis is not enough. The first objective of this section chronicled a situation where the manager did not want the system and only paid lip service to the implementation, which guaranteed an implementation failure. Unfortunately that manager is still employed and he is probably now considered an astute individual by upper management, which is far from the truth.

It's not possible to establish a schedule for the case study at this point since the initial project is considered a pilot. Given that the project is successful, there is now the question of deploying the application on an international basis. This means code localization, which is not an aspect considered in the original business rambling.

Establishing an implementation schedule is a post-design task. Unfortunately too many systems are developed today with a rigid time schedule that was established before system design. Defining an unrealistic implementation schedule before the system is designed is a contributing factor in the high reported system failure rates. An accurate schedule cannot be established unless all the tasks of the implementation are understood. Establishing a premature schedule is driven by marketing pressures, however when the system fails, the pressures still exist, only more so. The problem is a management issue and not an implementation issue.

Identify the *audience*. The case study audience consists of the officers, division managers, designated signers, and key staff members that will maintain the system. The system is a fiduciary tool for the accounting and legal departments.

It's not just a question of identifying the audience, but one of developing user profiles. This information is distilled from the business rambling. Developers need to be immersed into the organization's culture. There was a miscue on a project recently where a customer referred to *back-end system*. The developer thought it was Microsoft SQL Server, when in actuality it was the data from the last fiscal year.

The issue of user profiles is very important since many users are not formally trained in their jobs. Their training often consists of passed-on training from former users, who are moving on to new jobs that may be outside the company. Often the users have their own interpretation of the job, which may not match that of upper management. Experience, education, and training all help a user when presented with a new system paradigm. Can the user adapt?

Attitudes and a comfort factor with computers also play a significant role in system acceptance. I've had systems sabotaged by users that were fearful of change. Your best defense against such issues is to get active user participation. A nice touch is to work into the system a feature specifically requested by the user. The feature may not be needed from a functionality perspective, but it's a way to get the user to buy into the new system.

Lab 17.39 *Analyze security requirements*

Using the case study and business rambling in Listing 17-1, analyze each of the following. Considerations include:

Identify *roles* of administrator, groups, guests, and clients**.** The case study system will not support the concept of guests although Microsoft SQL Server and Windows NT both support guests. The SQL Administrator will also be the application administrator. With no other services intended for the platform, it is possible for the administrator to be responsible for Windows NT, SQL Server, and the application. The administrator's primary skill set should be that of SQL Server.

The system will support groups that can read, print, or edit contracts. The system clients are the designated contract signers, corporate officers, division managers, and key employees of both the legal and accounting departments.

Roles are key to system operation. A role is associated with a set of business activities and scenarios are derived from these activities. We use Rational Rose, (Microsoft Visual Modeler is a subset of Rational Rose), in Chapter 19 to construct components from scenarios using the Universal Modeling Language (UML).

Roles also determine a security context. This is managed with Windows NT user level security and with user profiles, which allows the administrator to manage access to both data and resources.

The case study system presents no impact on *the existing physical environment* except for space to accommodate the new platform. Users of this system should be upgraded to large video display terminals (VDTs).

There is little physical impact on the existing environment, however the work environment must be considered. An important issue for any new system is workflow patterns. Factors to consider include:

- Will the new system establish new workflow patterns?
- Will the new system disrupt existing workflow patterns?
- Will the new system replace existing workflow patterns?

Establish *fault tolerance*. Every system requires a contingency plan, even the case study project. The type of contingency plan depends upon what might be called a *mission-critical* index. Those systems with the highest ranking will have warm-spares ready to be switched in when the primary systems fail. This class of systems also takes advantage of hardware redundancy features such as clustering, mirrored disks, and arrays of redundant disks.

Systems with a low *mission-critical* index can often be left offline until the malfunction is repaired. In our case study, contracts can be typed manually until the system is restored.

Maintenance is not planned for the case study system other than the normal service packs for both Windows NT and SQL Server. Application errors will be handled with the shipment of a new version that is self-installing.

Microsoft supports several infrastructures for application maintenance. The first is a Web-based application. Updated components can be uploaded to the Web server. Most Internet Service Providers (ISP) do not normally allow the installation of COM components on the Web server. This type of application is best suited for an Intranet or a company that hosts their own Web site.

The second type of application maintenance is with Microsoft's Systems Management Server (SMS, originally code-named Hermes). SMS is best suited for large corporations that have many desktop installations. SMS provides complete remote management of a desktop, including the remote installation of software.

The third type of infrastructure is the ubiquitous **Setup** program. New versions of the application are created and delivered to the user site. Unfortunately this type of installation is for what is known as a monolithic application, which is a self-contained application that runs on the client desktop. This type of installation can be managed by SMS, but not every company has SMS installed.

Another type of supported infrastructure is the downloading of signed ActiveX controls over the Internet (Intranet). The application can be updated on a modular basis with the Internet Download Component (IDC). Web-based applications using Active Server Pages (ASP) use IDC whenever an **Object** tag is encountered in an ASP script.

The last type of infrastructure that I'll mention is the Active Documents paradigm. COM continues to evolve and Active Documents (Document Objects or Doc Objects) are a recent extension of COM. A Doc Object is a full-scale (complete) document that is embedded in a container. An Active Document is illustrated by dropping a Microsoft Word Document onto Microsoft Internet Explorer. The interface created should be very familiar to a Microsoft Word user. Microsoft Internet Explorer provides the basic menus, status bars, and tool bars and Word merges all of its menus, status bars, and tool bars with those of Microsoft Internet Explorer.

There is a significant intrinsic benefit with an Active Document application, which is reducing the Total Cost of Ownership (TCO). A run-time engine need not be distributed with an Active Document since Microsoft Internet Explorer can be the run-time engine.

Another Active Document issue is software control and licensing. It is difficult to enforce licensing over the Internet, however an alternative is to provide a freely downloadable Active Document server and to license the Active Document container. Of course this involves constructing a proprietary Active Document container.

The type of application architecture selected plays a significant role in the application updating mechanism.

Security of the case study system depends upon Windows NT integrated security. The Windows NT security database will be distributed to either primary domain controller (PDC) or a backup domain controller. Guest accounts will not be accommodated.

Client system specifications are sometimes vague to the developer who is used to dealing with issues in precise terms. The term "real-time" can have several different meanings depending upon the needs of the client. Consider the different scenarios for a financial reporting system. Each scenario is "real-time" because that is the stated time period, which is satisfactory.

- Financial data is captured from an on-line service and placed in a Microsoft SQL Server database. Replication occurs immediately to outlying offices that are also Microsoft SQL Server systems. Think of the system as being in constant replication mode. Such a system is useful to financial analysts.

- Financial data is captured and stored in a Microsoft SQL Server database, however the replication cycle is on an hourly basis. Consider a large international food-processing corporation that must monitor financial markets and commodity markets for prices and exchange rates.
- This is the same scenario however replication only occurs once every twenty-four hours. This is a major newspaper chain and the captured information will be printed in the next morning's newspaper.

Database replication distributes copies of the database to various locations, updates the copies independently, and keeps the copies synchronized. Each of these systems operates in "real-time" mode with Microsoft SQL Server replicating to other Microsoft SQL Servers. To borrow a manufacturing term, information is delivered "just-in-time."

Don't volunteer more than is necessary to do a complete job. A shorter information delivery time frame always corresponds to higher cost. Another good piece of advice is don't send a boy to do a man's work. Don't use Microsoft Access; use Microsoft SQL Server when the task is mission critical. Recall that Microsoft Access does not support the ACID properties of a transaction and doesn't have a write-ahead log like Microsoft SQL Server. (This may change with Microsoft Office 2000.) The Microsoft SQL Server log ensures that a restart will provide a complete database recovery. With Microsoft Access the choice is between a prayer wheel and a prayer rug. Yes, when Microsoft Access is restarted most of the time the data is there, however Murphy's law reigns supreme and Microsoft Access will fail at the most inopportune time with a maximal loss of data. The choice is yours. I would certainly NEVER put financial transactions in a Microsoft Access database.

The rule is simple. Never use Microsoft Access for mission critical applications. An example is sales orders that are collected in the field and transmitted to the central office. The central system is mission critical; hence Microsoft SQL Server is used. Access cannot replicate to SQL Server but only to other replica databases. Orders can be transmitted as desired. Field personnel will manually synchronize the data when necessary. Only the central system is mission critical in this scenario. Collecting and transmitting the data is not mission critical since data can be transmitted by fax or telephone when laptops are not able to contact the server.

In a different scenario, neither the central site nor the dependent sites are mission critical. An example is a service organization that uses replicated databases on laptops to transmit the service orders for the day. Completion reports are transmitted to the central site by synchronizing with the central site at the end of the day. This scenario has a Microsoft Access replica copy of the database on each laptop and a major system failure is not catastrophic. The benefit of this architecture is that many users can make data changes and reduce the load on the central server. The only issue is the scheduling of synchronization periods.

The case study system will use Microsoft Windows NT integrated security. As best as possible the system should be self-auditing with external checks. Since contracts represent legal documents, each page should be numbered. This means that each printed page is accountable. Each line on the page is also numbered.

There are several different aspects of security within the Microsoft Windows architecture. The first is that neither Microsoft Windows 95 nor Microsoft Windows 98 supports user-level security, although each support shares on network files. Microsoft Windows NT supports user-level security and has a Department of Defense C2 rating.

The next security issue is that Microsoft Windows NT 4.0, Internet Explorer 3.0 and later, Windows 98, and Windows 95 OEM service release 2 and support the CryptoAPI. This API provides all the necessary functionality to create Cryptographic Service Provider (CSP) components. The caveat with this is that the United States Government restricts exporting of cryptographic software.

The third issue of security is the security level of Internet downloads with code signing. Microsoft Internet Explorer can be configured to prompt the user with a dialog box when leaving an insecure site.

The last security issue is that the Microsoft architecture supports the Secure Socket Layer (SSL). This is necessary for transactions such as credit cards. A SSL connection is established by using "https://" rather than "http://" in the URL.

Our case study requires significant *auditing*. This includes a complete change history along with the original text that allows older versions of the contract to be recreated.

Auditing can be a performance issue, which often doubles the volume of disk traffic. The case study maintains old data, which cannot be deleted. There is a modest storage space requirement of old data.

Identify the *level of security* needed. User access to the case study text processing system requires Microsoft Windows NT integrated security. User level security along with server based mandatory profiles establish the user access security.

Physical security requires local backups, which are stored in a secured vault with cycled copies stored offsite in a secured location. The latest backup copy is moved immediately moved to another server in the event that the primary server experiences a catastrophic storage failure. A data storage vault company picks up backup copies on a regular basis. Two levels of backups exist: periodic permanent copies and cycled pool copies.

Analyze existing mechanisms for *security policies*. Existing case study security policies are inadequate and somewhat ad-hoc.

The developer should use caution in advising the client about security policies, since the developer is not a business consultant or security consultant. Simple statements can be made that don't engender risk, such as "Microsoft Windows NT supports integrated security" or "Microsoft Windows 98 does not support user-level security". The risk comes when the client is presented with a survey of security policies. The client assumes that the developer is a security expert, and when a security breach occurs the developer might be held liable. The developer should analyze existing mechanisms for security policies relative to only the needs of the new application. Analyzing beyond the security required for the new application is not recommended.

Lab 17.40 *Analyze performance requirements*

This objective merits a lecture. Estimating system performance is almost a useless exercise. Metrics gathered from an existing system are valid, but anything beyond that is a guess, both on the part of the client and the developers. It's also foolish to project performance of a new system. The performance delivered by a new system is pure alchemy. No one knows the response time or capacity until the system is tested. The tried and true approach is to measure the new system's capacity and performance, identify bottlenecks, and address the issues. Often the problem is application code and not the underlying infrastructure. For example, it's not uncommon to realize a thousand percent increase in Microsoft SQL Server performance by rewriting developer SQL statements. Of course that statement is not always true since many developers can write good SQL, but when there's a performance problem, always look to the application first.

Extra funds should be included in the budget for performance tuning of a transaction-based system. This goes beyond making the system operational. Often performance tuning will reveal a design flaw, that can result in a budget overrun. Budget overruns are very common on transaction-based systems.

When the application is transaction based, scalability is a major problem. The peak volume is often only a calculated guess. On-line stock market transactions are a good example. Whatever you think is adequate in terms of resources should be doubled, and doubled again for good measure. Frequently new systems go on-line and exhaust their initial capacity within a few months. When a company is fighting for market share and name recognition, the last thing it wants is a Web site that cannot accommodate the traffic.

Using the case study and business rambling in Listing 17-1, analyze each of the following. Considerations include:

- The project is not a transaction-based system and *transactions per time slice* are not applicable.
- Transactionsper time slice is not a valid metric. Microsoft SQL Server performance is measured with a TPC rating from the Transaction Processing Council (see http://www.tpc.com). The problem is that transactions per time slice cannot be measured because whenever a thread initiates an I/O request, control is given up and the thread is placed on the scheduling queue. The thread is given a new time slice when it is rescheduled and possibly a priority boost.
- The amount of data transferred over the network for the case study is very low and *bandwidth* issues do not exist.
- The case study has no anticipated *capacity* limitations. The number of users is relatively low, the quantity of data is easily managed, and infrastructure-processing capabilities are adequate.
- Regarding *interoperability* with existing standards, no standards exist, however the case study system will maintain the current workflow patterns and processes.
- The anticipated case study application volume is such that *peak versus average requirements* is not a meaningful metric.
- The anticipated case study problems with *response-time expectations* will be in document searches. The SQL language is not suitable for text processing and a search engine must be developed and installed on the server.

Search times will be prohibitive if all rows are pulled down the wire to the client and searched locally.

- Applicable case study response-time characteristics do not exist.
- The case study has *no performance barriers.* The only potential barrier to performance will be a dedicated printer. This is because each page is numbered and accountable. If necessary an additional dedicated printer can be installed.

Lab 17.41 *Analyze maintainability requirements*

Using the case study and business rambling in Listing 17-1, analyze each of the following. Considerations include:

The case study system will be installed at corporate headquarters. There are less than a dozen foreign subsidiaries; hence the *breadth of application distribution* is minimal with one installation per subsidiary.

The breadth and scope of application is an influence on application design. Web based applications are desirable when deployment is in terms of thousands. A Web-based system is significantly easier to maintain since new components are installed once on the server rather than at each user site, which can be problem when there are thousands of users. Microsoft Visual Basic 6.0 supports a new class of Web application, which is called an *IIS Application*.

As for *method of distribution,* members of the case study Information Systems (IS) department will use the traditional setup and install mechanism, however there are other methods of application deployment that include:

- ***Systems Management Server*** — Only useful when users are connected on a network. SMS clients include Microsoft Windows 3.1, Windows 95, Windows 98, Windows for Workgroups 3.11, Windows NT Workstation 3.5 or later, MS-DOS 5.0 and later, IBM OS/2 2.*x* and OS/2 Warp, and Macintosh System 7.
- ***Internet*** — SMS is not Internet enabled. There may be situations in which deploying an Access database with e-mail is satisfactory
- ***Network*** — The developer builds a network installation and notifies all users.

- ***Setup*** — Build a traditional diskette-based installation with the Setup Wizard of Visual Basic or use the Access Developers Toolkit. A disk installation procedure follows strict guidelines as to where new files will be installed. The Registry must be used for recording installation parameters and WIN.INI or SYSTEM.INI files must not be used. Application files are never to be copied to either the WINDOWS or SYSTEMS directory unless they are system-wide shared files.
- ***Internet*** — Software is installed or updated by including a .CAB file reference within the CODEBASE attribute of an HTML OBJECT tag.

  Software deployment on Internet/Intranet is with the Internet Download Component. The component is prepackaged for downloading over the Internet. An Internet download occurs when the CODEBASE attribute in an HTML OBJECT tag points to a COM object. An HTML OBJECT tag is shown below:

```
<OBJECT
CODEBASE="/MyWeb/MyBillBoard.CAB#version=8,0,0,8
      WIDTH=570
      HEIGHT=70
      DATA="/MyWeb/Controls/MyBillBoard.ods"
      CLSID=clsid:11111111-2222-3333-4444-555555555555">
</OBJECT>
```

The example above indicates a .CAB file as the source of the COM object. There are two other possible packaging mechanisms for Internet downloads:

- ***PE*** — A portable executable such as a .OCX, .DLL, or .EXE. A single executable is downloaded, installed, and registered in one operation. The file category may be code-signed. The Internet Download Component will try to start self-registration for those components marked as such. The Internet Download Component ignores the "OleSelfRegister" flag if the main URL code points directly at a .EXE file. This type of file will not be platform independent except with HTTP.
- ***CAB*** — A .CAB file has the advantage of compression and can be code-signed. A .CAB file required component is a .INF file, which contains the packaging instructions. A .CAB file will not be platform independent with-

out HTTP format negotiation. The accompanying .INF file may point to the URL of the component or to another .CAB file. DIAMOND.EXE from the Microsoft Internet SDK will build a .CAB file using a .DDF file.

- ***INF***—A .INF file cannot be code-signed, but it is platform independent. The .INF file is a map of all required files. This file download category is still useful in an Intranet environment, but is unsafe on the Internet. The simplest multiple platform support mechanism is a single .INF file in a .CAB file and the .INF file points to separate .CAB files for each platform. But as stated, this is not safe.

When the version is -1,-1,-1,-1 the Internet Download Component will always try to download the latest version. The Internet Download Component will download and install the file only if the specified version is more recent than any version of the same file that is currently installed in the system. When a version is not specified, any version is considered acceptable.

Maintenance expectations for the case study application are low, however Microsoft SQL Server and Windows NT are both high maintenance products.

The case study staff is not currently capable of *maintaining* Microsoft SQL Server and Windows NT. Each subsidiary that implements this system must have a Windows NT administrator and a SQL Server administrator.

It's quite possible that the deployed system is not maintainable by the resident computer staff. There is always a problem when a company needs technology that it cannot support. The problem is always one of budget and unrealistic expectations. Such is the case with Microsoft SQL Server, which requires competent professionals and not relatively inexperienced individuals.

When the resident computer staff is relatively inexperienced, the developers can expect a telephone call when the system malfunctions. This includes not only software, but also the hardware platform and the supporting infrastructure. The customer simply knows that the system doesn't work and their staff can't make it work. The point is this: When the system doesn't work it's always your fault unless you can prove otherwise. For this reason it's not advisable to develop applications for small and emerging companies unless there is a significant service contract in hand. You'll find that many service calls are handholding for problems other than your application.

No *third-party* ***maintenance*** agreements exist with respect to the case study and none are anticipated.

Third-party maintenance agreements are difficult from the perspective of the developer. The maintenance company will want access to the source code, which can be warranted. There is the issue of protecting trade secrets plus the issue of the maintenance company being capable of providing application support. It's common for maintenance companies to provide hardware support along with help-desk support for common products. Realistically, a third-party maintenance company should not maintain proprietary software. The customer should have the ability to perform the required software maintenance, or be expected to sign a maintenance contract with the developers.

Lab 17.42 *Analyze extensibility requirements. Solution must be able to handle the growth of functionality*

Analyze the extensibility requirements of the application required for the case study and business rambling in Listing 17-1.

Changing production systems if fraught with risk. Analyze extending the functionality of a production system, which may be mission critical to the enterprise.

The case study system is not generally extensible and no growth of functionality is anticipated. Occasionally a new feature may be added to the editing engine, however there is no planned upgrade path.

Analyze extensibility requirements, analyze extensibility requirements, ... Stop, stop, and stop. The growth of functionality is not a user requirement but a vendor plan to create an additional revenue stream. The first question that should be is asked is quite simple: Does the design support the current user and corporate requirements and also accommodate the strategic interests of the company? If that answer is yes, then no additional functionality is required until the company changes business rules or strategic plans. One cannot safely guess the ultimate path of a corporation, except in very broad terms. A corrected version of this objective should ask the question: "Can the solution accommodate changes or additions to business rules?" Business rules in this context are not the supporting infrastructure between the data tier and the presentation tier in three-tier application architectures, but business rules in the sense of corporate business rules. Corporations don't change paths very often, and business rules should be reexamined only at that point. The new software generation has not learned "If it ain't broken don't fix it."

OF TOOLS AND APPLICATIONS

Microsoft may be viewed as a tool company, which means that Microsoft is not an application development enterprise. In my opinion, Microsoft may design products that are never complete. This paradigm is acceptable for tools since not all features are ever used or even wanted, and the features that you use may not be the features that I use. Microsoft seemingly withholds functionality for release in the next version. Microsoft presents this as managing the product. However, in my opinion it's managing the revenue stream. The classic example is that it took two complete releases of Microsoft SQL Server to deliver all the ANSI SQL 92 updates.

The problem is that Microsoft may be construed as trying to impose their mode of software tool development on corporate America, which builds applications and not tools. When corporate business rules dictate a required functionality, leaving a portion of that functionality out until the next version is not acceptable. Try telling the CIO that new account credit checks are scheduled for the next release and you'll quickly find that you are looking for a new job. Either the application supports the corporate business rules or it doesn't. There is no middle road with versioned application releases. This is why the growth of functionality is oxymoronic for business applications.

Very few of the newer members to the computer community have an appreciation of computer science. Using complex mathematical formulas I can compute both the *volume* and *complexity* of an application. Each of these metrics is related to reliability. As either metric increases, so does the error rate. The increase is not linear, but exponential. The problem is not with the application, but with the supporting infrastructure. Microsoft Windows NT is measured in millions of lines of code. Windows NT 5.0, (renamed to Windows 2000) has somewhere between thirty and forty million lines of code. In my opinion thirty-five million lines of code will never be debugged. It won't happen in this millenium, or the next, or the one after that. The point is that when you have systems that try to do everything, ("kitchen sink, hold the mayo"), the complexity becomes unmanageable and the error rate can be intolerable. As long as common features are always used, it will have the appearance of being debugged, but chaos is invited when other than popular features are used.

There's a new kid on the block name Linux. It's touted as a reliable alternative to Windows NT, but is it? I don't think the reliability rate for Linux is any different than that of Microsoft Windows NT and the supporting infrastructure. I'm reasonably certain that the Linux error rate per lines of code is quite close to that of Microsoft Windows NT. The difference is in size and Linux is a very small succinct system that doesn't carry the baggage of trying to do everything. Microsoft literally dumps everything they can find into their products. Their products are marginal and barely tolerable because of the unreliability. I'm writing this book on Microsoft Word 6.0a (OfficePro 4.3). I still get general protection faults (GPFs) from Microsoft Word 97 of Office 97 with Service Pack 2 installed, and the risk is just too high to use it.

How do we use Microsoft software if it's so unreliable? That's a good question. I liken it to threading a needle through a minefield. Once you get something that works, you don't change it, which brings up an interesting issue. How to you crash a system? Simply put a new user on it. The new user will attempt to use advertised features. They don't yet know what doesn't work. My last book examined the Microsoft architecture. I found complete sections of Microsoft code that had never been tested, however the features are obscure and not commonly used.

Software is becoming unmaintainable. Fix a bug for me and you create a bug for ten thousand other users. In my opinion even though Microsoft is staffed with bright and creative coders, their products do not exhibit an understanding of basic computer science.

Lab 17.43 *Analyze availability requirements*

Using the case study and business rambling in Listing 17-1, analyze each of the following. Considerations include:

The *hours of operation* of the case study system are limited to normal business hours. The server and related database are secured from any access after normal business hours. During this period a full database dump is made and stored off site.

This is a seemingly obvious topic, however hours of operation can have a profound impact on budget. I recall developing a mainframe communication link between different cities. I was given a half-hour of computer time at night immediately following system backups. The scheduled time was 2:30 AM, and if system backups were late, I missed the window of opportunity.

Another type of operation is a Web site or a SQL Server database that has a 24X7 schedule, which is every hour of every day. When is the development done?

Evaluate very carefully the hours of operation. Limited availability will protract the implementation schedule and negatively impact the budget.

The case study system *level of availability* is restricted. It is only available to selected employees of the accounting and legal department during normal business hours.

Typically the level of availability isn't an issue when the system is available. That's not a self-defining statement, but a simple statement that the system is available or it isn't. Level of availability can depend upon the basic system being available even though all aspects of the infrastructure are not available. This is a fallback mode of operation that occurs with contingencies.

Regarding *eographic scope,* ABC is a multi-national corporation. All subsidiaries speak English, however medium of exchange varies between countries.

Geographic scope requires that the application roll out occur in stages. The application should be stable before international versions are rolled out. The budget should accommodate the additional cost of localization. This is not an issue with the case study, which is only a pilot project. The system is not mission critical so the *impact of downtime is not a factor in the case study.* Contracts can be typed manually with the data entered at a later date.

Downtime is a factor for mission critical-systems and significant contingency plans are a necessity for mission-critical systems. The degree of criticality will determine the scope of contingency plans. Is any downtime acceptable; is one hour acceptable, or even two hours? The impact of downtime falls into the category of capacity planning. An acceptable threshold of financial loss must be established for system failures. The contingency plan maintains at least this threshold until full operation is restored.

Lab 17.44 *Analyze human factors requirements*

Using the case study and business rambling in Listing 17-1, analyze each of the following. Considerations include:

The *target users* of the case study are identified as select corporate staff individuals, designated signers, and corporate officers. General employees will not have access to the system.

Targeting users is useful for many reasons. Users are a benefactor of the new system and are already participants in the conceptual design. Additional factors include:

- User levels of expertise.
- Job functions and workflow patterns that may change with the new system.
- Should training be delivered before or after roll out?

- What type of training should be delivered? The case study has two types of training. Inquiry for management and using the system for those deemed responsible for contract management.
- What are the training logistics?
- Are special needs required?

Localization is a future problem for the case study project. At this point all foreign subsidiaries use English as the primary language. A localization issue exists in terms of the local currency. Not all foreign subsidiaries exist in countries that use the American dollar as a medium of exchange.

The goal of localizing is to reduce production costs of internationalization. Rather than a system per locale, localization is isolating the core software from elements that require localization. This means the core software is compiled independently of resources that must be localized. Resources are normally placed in a .RC file. When the localized resource is placed in a DLL, it need not be linked with the core software, but linked at execution time. The developer's goal is one core module and a locale-specific DLL for each locale.

- Use good coding practices. Don't embed literals in code (not a good coding practice).
- Localize all constants and don't be clever with messages. By that I mean don't try to construct messages on the fly from fragments, but define complete messages that can be localized.
- Make sure your buffers are large enough to hold the translated text. The word *Edit* in German is *Bearbeiten*. The size consideration doesn't apply to just data buffers. Menu bars, status bars, tool bars, title bars, and dialog boxes should all be designed for an increased text size.
- Use system functions for sorting, character typing, and string mapping. Always use system dialog boxes.
- Use extreme caution with keyboard shortcut-key combinations. Not all keyboards are the same and characters will map differently. Consider using the function keys such as F4 or F5 rather than a shortcut-key combination.
- Avoid special effects and be culturally sensitive. The beep of the computer wanting the next installation diskette will embarrass a Japanese user. A Japanese user is embarassed when a beep calls attention to blunders even though a beep signaling the next diskette is not a blunder.

- Avoid metaphors. An arrow pointing might be confusing to an Arabic or Hebrew speaker.
- Do not include text in bitmaps unless the text will not be translated. A company name is an example of text that will not be translated.

The case study has no known *accessibility* requirements.

Accessibility requirement issues are addressed with tools that include screen enlargement utilities, screen review utilities, voice-input utilities, in-screen keyboards, keyboard filters, customizing the mouse pointer, and keyboard emulation of the mouse.

The case study project requires the ability to serve *roaming users*.

Roaming users is an issue of infrastructure. Microsoft Windows NT supports sever-based profiles, which accommodate roaming users. Microsoft Windows NT replicates the security database of the primary domain controller (PDC) to backup domain controllers (BDC).

There is a very strict requirement that the case study system be very easy to use. This requires various *help* implementations that include:

- ***Context Sensitive Help*** — Selecting *What's This?* from a menu puts the user in context sensitive mode. Context sensitive help is available by clicking *What's This?* from the **Help** menu and then moving the mouse pointer over the object and clicking mouse button 1. During this operation the mouse pointer is considered a contextual pointer. If a user selects a menu title after selecting *What's This?*, keep the context sensitive mode until something is selected.

  Context sensitive help is also available by clicking mouse button 2. When the right mouse button is clicked over an object that supports a pop-up menu, maintain the context sensitive mode until the user chooses something from the menu or cancels the menu.

  The developer should remember that context sensitive information is written to answer a question. A good practice is to start context sensitive help with a verb — for example, "Inserts a table." The information should be brief. Reference related help is placed in task-oriented help.

  Depressing F1 is the shortcut key that presents contextual information for the object that has the input focus.

- ***ToolTips*** — Small Pop-Ups that display the name of a graphical icon. ToolTips do not have a label. Drag the mouse pointer over an object and hesitate for several seconds. The ToolTip will display object name.
- ***Status Bar Help*** — Use the status bar to provide descriptive information about a menu or toolbar button that the user chooses.
- ***Help Button*** — Different from *What's This?*. The **Help** button is for summary assistance, overview, or explanatory information. A help button is used for help from a property sheet, dialog box, or message box. The help button is included in the window. When the user presses the Help command button, the help information is displayed in a Help secondary window and not in a contextual pop-up window. A wizard is always implemented in a secondary window. Selecting a help command from the **Help** command button starts a Help wizard. This starts the Help Browser after the indexes and contents are initialized.
- ***Task Help*** — Task help enumerates the steps for carrying out a task. The preferred window type is a primary window that the user can resize, move, maximize, or minimize. The window can support shortcut buttons and will have command buttons that support access to the index and content pages of the Help Browser. The developer should use the default system windows colors for the task help window. This distinguishes the task help window for other application windows. The task help window standard has changed slightly. Microsoft added the "Clipit" wizard to the task help menu in Office 97.
- ***Reference Help*** — Reference help serves as the application on-line documentation. Reference help is also presented in a primary window and the developer should use the default system colors for the window. The common use of this help style is from an explicit menu item in the Help drop-down menu with *Contents and Index* as the typical command. The user is initially presented the primary window of the Help Wizard. The bottom of the Help Wizard will have the button <Back >, Next, Finish, Cancel. Stepping through the different steps initializes the Help Browser. The user is next presented with the Help Browser in a primary window and within the window will be three tabs: Contents, Index, and Find.*Training requirements* for the case study require two levels: a Windows NT administrator and a SQL Server administrator. These are overhead costs, which will be

significant. Training on the delivered contract management system is not expected to exceed a workday.

In general, the user profiles should identify the levels of user expertise. Should the training be performed before or after roll out? Are different types of training required? Are there any training constraints such as geographical, functional, or resource limitations? If geography is a factor, will there be international training? How will it be managed?

The case study has *no physical environment constraints*.

Physical environment constraints do not apply just to computer systems. Will the work current environment accommodate the new work flow patterns? Is there space for the temporary staff required during parallel testing? Is there office space for the developers?

Special needs are not anticipated for the case study. Special needs are not something that the developer must program. Rather, the developer should be aware that there are tools available for impaired individuals. The tools include:

- ***Screen Enlargement Utilities*** — This is a screen magnifier. The enlarger must track the current position and readjust the screen accordingly.
- ***Screen Review Utilities*** — A screen reviewer utility scans the screen and renders the information in a different medium. This can be a refreshable Braille display or synthesized speech.
- ***Voice Input Utilities*** — These utilities are useful when the individual has a mobility impairment. It is also a useful tool for boosting productivity of individuals who are not impaired.
- ***In-Screen Keyboards*** — There are a number of variations for this type of aid. A Morse code-type system, a system of pointing and clicking, and a system of clicks-only are different types of input systems for impaired individuals. The system that is selected will depend upon the impairment of the individual.
- ***Keyboard Filters*** — Keyboard filters accommodate impaired dexterity. Windows 95 and Windows 98 keyboard filters help by providing some compensation for erratic motion, tremors, or slow response time. In this category of tools are aids such as abbreviation expansion utilities, add-on spelling checkers, and word prediction utilities. These tools are often used to improve the productivity of individuals not impaired.

- ***Customizing the Mouse Pointer*** — Windows 95 and Windows 98 support a customizable mouse pointer display for the visually impaired. High contrast color schemes are also an aid for the visually impaired.
- ***Keyboard Emulation of the Mouse*** — This is another feature of Windows 95 and Windows 98.

Lab 17.45 *Analyze the requirements for integrating a solution with existing applications*

Using the case study and business rambling in Listing 17-1, analyze each of the following. Considerations include:

The case study has no existing *legacy applications*.

What's the definition of legacy application? Is it a COBOL program on an IBM mainframe or a Microsoft Access 2.0 application running on Windows 3.1? When a new application must communicate with a legacy application, a network provides the necessary normalization factor.

When the legacy application is being replaced, a strategy must be developed that details a step-by-step process of how the legacy application will be retired. The plan should include provisions for parallel testing and a strategy for cut over to the new application. It's prudent management to keep the legacy application in place for contingencies until other contingency plans are developed and deployed.

Dealing with the *format and location of existing data* in the case study application requires entering old contract data into the new system, which is a significant effort. Scanning the data is possible, however the scanned text must still be reviewed. A reasonable process is to scan the existing contracts, which preserves the original format and then scan again using optical character recognition (OCR) equipment.

Legacy data by definition exists on an outdated architecture. The legacy data may be located on magnetic tape reels, a medium not commonly supported in the Microsoft architecture. The location, format, and storage play a significant role in data conversion costs. Converting legacy data is expensive. It's not just a question of converting the data, but also scrubbing it so that no errors remain.

The case study does not require *connectivity to existing applications*.

Connectivity to legacy applications is with a *wrapper* function. The wrapper's role is that of an intermediary between the legacy application and the new application. Software AG simplifies connecting to legacy systems with a release of

Distributed COM (DCOM) for both the IBM (MVS) and UNIX (Solaris) operating systems.

The case study has no *data conversion or enhancement requirements.*

Data enhancement includes scrubbing the data as discussed above. Data enhancement can involve much more than just conversion and scrubbing. An example is data that exists in flat-file legacy systems that does not conform to the relational data model (see Chapter 18). The converted and scrubbed results must then be edited to conform to Microsoft SQL Server storage characteristics.

Lab 17.46 *Analyze existing methodologies and limitations of a business*

Using the case study and business rambling in Listing 17-1, analyze each of the following. Considerations include:

There are no *legal issues* surrounding the case study project, however a primary goal of the project is to anticipate legal issues relating to contracts.

Legal issues shouldn't be a problem when the application project is approached professionally. There are two potential problem areas. The first is Microsoft licensing practices. Send a letter to the client outlining the necessary licenses, however offer those licenses at a discount to the client. Every developer should understand the Microsoft Open Licensing (MOL) program. It can be a secondary source of revenue.

The other issue is encryption and exporting software with embedded encryption technology. Laws are currently in a flux in this area, so be especially careful when you're dealing with a multi-national company or when you are marketing software internationally.

The case study *current business practices* do not change other than to the extent that a manual process is being automated.

The current business practices should be understood with respect to the enterprise. The business practices can be distilled from the business rambling, an example of which is found in Listing 17-1. Business practices (read that as business rules) do change. The system should be able to accommodate changes in business practices without completely redesigning the software. Business practices are used within a business process, and the process per se isn't subject to change, just occasional business rules. For example, managing credit should not consist of rigid and fixed rules, but rules that can be changed or substituted without software engineering changes.

The case study *organizational structure* does not change.

A software project should not change organizational structure. Changing the organizational structure for an application falls in the realm of business process reengineering, which we're not about. The issue is to understand the organization and the role that each participant plays in the organizational structure. There are bit players and major role players and the problem is to identify each along with their agenda.

The case study has an existing manual contract system in place. There are no reported problems with the manual contract system and consequently no *process reengineering* is expected.

There are two very important points. The first is to separate process reengineering from application development. Yes, processes can be changed but new processes are always an experiment. This task is best left to companies that specialize in process reengineering.

There are three choices for processes:

- The proposed process is new, in which case there is a significant chance that the designed system will not satisfy user needs. This should not come as a surprise in spite of significant conceptual design efforts. It happens because building the application simply gives a better understanding of the nature of the problem. It may turn out that the proposed system is dealing only with a symptom and not the actual problem. There are no existing processes that can be modeled and the resulting workflow may be less than amenable. Such systems are always high-risk when new processes are being designed.
- The process to be replaced exists, but is a mess. The existing process can be manual or an outdated computerized system. Regardless, of the original type of process, computerizing a mess results in a computerized mess. As a self-employed mercenary, I do not build applications where the existing system is a mess. I've tried to build such systems, but there are always cost overruns, which the client believes are always the developer's fault. Not every company has a bottomless-pit budget like Microsoft's.
- What's left? Processes that work. A process model exists and costs can be controlled. The problem with both building a new process and with reengineering a mess is that costs cannot be controlled. It should be pointed out that reprocess engineering doesn't necessarily deal with messes, but with making existing and working processes more efficient.

A *budget* doesn't exist for the case study and the project is being expensed as an overhead item.

How about a rule for budgets? Here's one: *Whatever you think it will cost, double that number*. It's not just the software development costs, but all the hidden costs such as extra staff during parallel testing or the lost revenue when the new system crashes. And there are other costs such as training, data conversion and enhancement, and additional infrastructure. New systems should have a high benefit to cost ratio because hidden costs will creep in and erode the ratio, which in turn erodes the justification.

Regarding *implementation and training methodologies,* the case study business rambling states that the system is to be self-tutorial. This is an unreal expectation.

Training is a not always effective. An example is large companies that sell major systems. Training is offered, but it expects all users to be at the same skill level, which is not always the case. The end result is that the training is often less than effective.

The user profiles present an opportunity to address user skill levels. Training classes can be developed based on specific user's needs. The first example is different levels of classes such as introductory, intermediate, and advanced. Another perspective is separate classes for users and management.

Many users have a fear of change, and a segmented introduction of the new system will help manage that fear. A suggested approach is small introductory classes either before of after the system is installed. Once the users have acquired a minimum skill level, an advanced class can be offered. The issue is to take the necessary training and break it down into smaller steps. Presenting everything at one time is not always effective. Power users are bored while other users won't comprehend the material when the material is presented in a single class or series of classes.

Case study requirements do not exist for *quality control* other than the professional conduct of the developers.

The issue is not "What are the quality control requirements?" but "What is the maximum level of financial loss that the client is willing to absorb when the new system fails?" When no financial loss is tolerable, the proposed system falls into the zero-defects category. Anything other than zero-defects is a matter of degree. The degree of financial loss governs the quality control requirements.

The financial system should be run in parallel with an existing system. When a parallel system doesn't exist, scenarios should be planned and run for all conceivable situations.

The case study has several primary *customer needs*. A need that is inferred is the tracking of the original contract and each contract copy. The current mechanism is to *sign out* a folder, however that mechanism probably fails occasionally. A second need is the ability to track contract revisions by lawyer and firm. A third need is the ability to scan contract text for key phrases when state, federal, or international laws change. Tracking these needs is done with the Requirements Model database discussed in Chapter 17. It's the customer's needs and not the developer's cute little tricks and snazzy controls that count here. This means a user-centric design (see Chapter 20). The user must be able to relate to the system and perform their perceived tasks intuitively. Note that I said *perceived* tasks, and not *required* tasks. You may find yourself dealing with a power-user that demands too much. The line has to be drawn at some point, but the system still must be easy to use. When the user interface is awkward, the system is perceived as a failure even though the under-the-hood software does an outstanding job of addressing the issues.

It is possible that the user has unwarranted but perceived needs that stem from a lack of training. Categorize the needs as to application-related and system-related. Make absolutely sure that your users know exactly how you've addressed their needs. When they demand a feature that you don't deem necessary, it's best to put it in anyway. Not a lot of them, but putting in a single unwarranted feature goes a long way with respect to public relations. As I've said previously, disgruntled users can sabotage a system easily.

Lab 17.47 *Analyze scalability requirements*

Using the case study and business rambling in Listing 17-1, analyze each of the following. Considerations include:

The *growth of audience* for the case study is nearly fixed. It consists of key members of the corporate staff, division managers, and designated contract signers. The only corporate growth will be through acquisition and that is not currently on the event horizon. Scalability of an application is addressed in Chapter 19 with a tiered component architecture. Independent of a scalability requirement, an application should be tiered to manage complexity. This means that scalability of the application is free. Tiering an application occurs when logically related functionality is encapsulated into classes.

Growth of organization of the case study is not expected to be a factor. The company is currently a multi-national corporation. Approximately 1000 contracts exist in aggregate between all divisions of the corporation. Doubling the size of the corporation will not necessarily double the number of contracts. .

The growth of an organization places scalability into several dimensions. The first dimension is domestic deployment. Deploying an application on a nationwide basis is a significant undertaking when compared to deploying an application over a local Intranet. The second dimension is entered when an organization becomes an international entity. Localization between the various mediums of exchange and language become a significant issue. Roll outs of new applications are now dependent upon many complex factors, some of which may be international politics.

The *data growth* for the case study is not significant and some contracts have been in place for nearly ten years. However within the concept of a Microsoft SQL Server managing gigabytes of data, the amount of newly created data will not be a problem.

Mass storage is very cheap today. There is no excuse for not having enough mass storage and growth of data should never be a factor, unless the application is exceptional, such as a multiple terrabyte Visa or MasterCard database.

Cycle of use is not a factor for the case study.

This was not a problem, until the advent 24X7 Web sites (24 hours/day, 7 days/week). Hours of operation affect maintenance of an existing system. I previously mentioned the communication system that I developed for mainframes, where I was given a half-hour of block-time at 2:30 AM for testing. The cycle of use can dramatically protract a project's development cycle causing costs to escalate. I suppose it's time for my own personal horror story, so here it is. In the 1970s I bid on and won a contract to write a numerical-control system that managed a machine tool. The language was 8008 assembler and the task was to manage a tape-laying machine that laid down Boron tape for F-111 aircraft wings (when I see an F-111, I tell myself "Those are my wings!"). The tape was laid down in multiple and very precise layers on the wing frame. I had no problem writing the software or making the application work. I have a keen understanding of electronics and worked directly with the engineers. (I had designed my own computer until I found that it was cheaper to buy one.)

Well, where is the horror? The horror is that the system was a Texas Instruments mini-computer and the only input/output was with paper tape. When I bid the project, I did not take into account how long it took to load/unload the paper tape. I only looked at the technical aspects of the project. I had previous numerical-control experience and thought I knew what I was doing. I didn't go broke, but I certainly got very poor, and all because I didn't examine all aspects of the prospective project. I survived that debacle because of the generosity of my contract supplier, who continued to pay me until the project was finished.

Chapter 18 Labs

LAB 18.48 *Group data into entities by applying normalization rules*

The goal of this objective is to measure your understanding of entities and the use of normalization rules. Approximately half of the questions deal with entity types. The remainder of the questions address normalization issues.

1. Describe an independent entity. Name an independent entity in Figure 18-14.

   Contract is the primary independent entity. An independent entity is the parent of a parent-child relationship.

2. Describe a *characteristic* entity. Name a *characteristic* entity in Figure 18-14.

   There are many characteristic entities in Figure 18-14. A few include *Amendment, Attachment,* and *Approval Step*.

3. What is an *associative* entity? How is an *associative* entity used? Name an *associative entity* in Figure 18-14.

   An associative entity is used for mapping many-to-many relationships. The associative entity inherits a primary key from each of the respective independent entities. These keys are combined into a compound key within the associative entity. *Compensation Record* is an associative entity in Figure 18-14.

4. What is a *categorization* entity? Name a *categorization* entity in Figure 18-14.

   Categorization entities along with a generalization entity and a category discriminator form a generalization hierarchy. A generalization entity is an independent entity that is the root entity of a generalization hierarchy. *Contract Copy* is a categorization entity in Figure 18-14.

5. What is the schema for the 5-tuple (OrderID, ItemID, Description, OrderDate, Quantity)? You may assume that OrderID and ItemID represent a composite key.

   The schema is represented as:

   R(<u>OrderID</u>, <u>ItemID</u>, Description, OrderDate, Quantity)

   OrderID (OrderDate, OrderIDItemID (DescriptionQuantity

6. What is the normalization error in question 5?

   This is a second normal form error and where an attribute does not depend upon the whole key. *OrderDate* does not depend upon *ItemID*.

7. Describe a Boyce Codd Normal Form error.

   A BCNF error is a result of overlapping keys. This usually occurs after the database is normalized. The database administrator adds additional keys for performance, and a BCNF error occurs when keys overlap.

8. Describe a third normal form error.

   A third normal form error occurs when an attribute depends upon another attribute and not the primary key. This is also known as transitive dependency.

9. Describe a second normal form error.

   A second normal form error occurs when an attribute depends upon a portion of the primary key and not the complete key.

10. Describe a first normal form error.

    A repeating group is a first normal form error.

LAB 18.49 *Specify the relationships between entities*

These questions will measure your understanding of the relationships between entities.

1. What is common about the relationships of the characteristic entities shown in Figure 18-14?

   All characteristic entities of Figure 18-4 are represented by non-identifying relationships.

2. Describe the relationship between the *Contract* entity and the *Compensation Record* entity shown in Figure 18-14.

   The *Compensation Record* entity is an associative entity. It is a component of a many-to-many relationship between the Contract entity and another hidden entity.

3. Describe the relationship between the Contract entity and the *Approval Step* entity shown in Figure 18-14.

   The *Approval Step* entity is a characteristic entity.

4. Describe the relationship between the Contract entity and the Attachment *entity* shown in Figure 18-14.

   The Attachment entity is a characteristic entity.

5. What important factor does a relationship between entities convey?

   A relationship determines cardinality and the type of entity.

6. Describe the semantic, (not graphical) rules for describing a relationship between entities (hint: consider only formal entities and not a many-to-many).

   A sentence describing a relationship from the *independent* entity is always written in the active tense, that is, an action verb is used. Sentences describing relationships from the *characteristic* entity perspective are passive. Respective examples include: "... sells ..." and "... is sold by ..."

LAB 18.50 *Choose the foreign key that will enforce a relationship between entities and will ensure referential integrity*

Foreign keys enforce relationships. These questions will measure your understanding of foreign keys.

1. How is a foreign key derived (hint: Recall the Armstrong axioms)?

   A foreign key (FK) is initially a primary key of an *independent* entity. The FK migrates to the *characteristic* entity during the decomposition process (Armstrong axiom number 5).

2. What is a characteristic of a foreign key?

   A foreign key is a primary key of the related *independent* entity.

3. What is the prevalent use of foreign keys in Figure 18-14?

The foreign keys of Figure 18-14 are all used for *non-identifying* relationships, which does not enforce referential integrity.

4. What is the foreign key issue of Figure 18-14?

   Figure 18-4 does not maintain referential integrity.

5. Characterize the creation of a foreign key.

   A foreign key is not created per se, but is a primary key of an independent entity that migrates to the characteristic entity.

6. What can be said formally about a foreign key?

   Since a foreign key is a primary key of an independent entity, the fourteen properties of a relation (Table 18-1) are not violated.

7. Discuss the issue of identifying versus non-identifying relationships with respect to foreign keys.

   Non-identifying relationships do not enforce referential integrity, while identifying relationships enforce referential integrity.

LAB 18.51 *Identify the business rules that relate to data integrity*

Discuss the objective. This objective requires revisiting Chapter 17 and the business rambling found in Listing 17-1. The answer to this objective requires an understanding of the analysis process that is applied to a business rambling.

Recall that the distilled business rambling of Chapter 17 isolated facts, definitions, constraints, and derivations. Definitions are things that exist. Facts are verb phrases that associate (in the connective sense, not an associative entity) two entities that used to be things (definitions). In this context the fact becomes a relationship. Two entities with a relationship represent knowledge, while simple facts and definitions only represent information. The third aspect of identifying business rules is the derivation, which is equivalent to an *if ... then ...* construct. A derivation is not a literal *if ... then ...* construct, but a statement of condition that the business rule may or may not always exist. Business rules are identified as facts and derivations of the distilled business rambling that relate to definitions with applied constraints. A business rule is a fact, derivation, or constraint that defines a relationship between definitions (entities).

LAB 18.52 *Incorporate business rules and constraints into the data model*

The answer to this objective is easy if you've read and understood this chapter and Chapter 17. How are business constraints and rules incorporated into the data model? The term *data model* is generic within the objective context and does not refer to a specific model discussed in this chapter. The answer to the objective is rooted in understanding how business rules and constraints are incorporated into a tiered-component architecture.

Business rules are incorporated into the data model as identifying, non-identifying, and category constraints between entities. The existence and identification of business rules is managed with these constraints. The entity type and cardinality model constraints. The choice of entity relationship determines how business constraints are incorporated into the data model. As an example, referential integrity cannot be maintained with non-identifying relationships. Related to constraints are *derivations,* which are statements of business rule conditional existence.

LAB 18.53 *Identify appropriate level of denormalization*

Denormalization is accomplished to improve performance. Too many table joins induce poor database performance. These questions will measure your understanding of denormalization.

1. Does denormalization exist in Figure 18-14?

   Significant denormalization occurs in Figure 18-14 with the foreign key *Contract_Number*. A specific example is the *Amendment Key_Word* entity, which is an associative entity of the *Amendment Descriptor* entity.

2. Discuss inadvertent denormalization.

   Inadvertent denormalization occurs when additional keys are added for performance. When keys overlap, a Boyce Codd Normal Form error occurs.

3. Discuss planned denormalization and give an example.

   Planned denormalization is done for performance. Denormalization that occurs at the column or table level intentionally violates principles of normalized design. A denormalized database assumes prior normalization. Assuming that the database is denormalized, how will the database be updated? Updating a denormalized database can be a problem when the denormalized data is volatile. Updating denormalized data is maintained with SQL Server triggers and stored procedures, however if the data is volatile, the updating may offset any gains made by denormalization. Possible denormalization techniques include:

- ***Duplicating Columns*** — Exact copies of a column can be made or new columns defined that are derived from aggregated data.
- ***Redefining Columns*** — Contrived key columns are a consideration when the primary key size exceeds eight bytes.
- ***Column Abstracts*** — The best example of this is binary large object (BLOB) data stored in a flat file with relative path pointers maintained in a SQL Server table.
- ***Splitting Tables*** — Splitting tables is a consideration when the table is too large. Although it's possible to have a ten million-row table in Microsoft SQL Server, such a table is not considered good design.
- ***Splitting Columns*** — Every table will have frequently referenced columns. Move the infrequently referenced to another table. The remaining table is now narrower.
- ***Duplicating Foreign Keys*** — Figure 18-14 is an example of duplicating foreign keys, which reduces the number of joins necessary to access the data.
- ***Duplicating Attributes*** — This is a common technique that reduces the number of joins, however candidate attributes should be nonvolatile data.
- ***Duplicating Entire Tables*** — This is a common denormalization technique for decision support systems (DSS) where the data is not updated. Data is refreshed on a regular basis by SQL Server replication. This denormalization technique divides the users into two groups. One group updates data with on-line transaction processing (OLTP) while the other group creates reports and queries from another server, the DSS system, that is refreshed from the OLTP server.

LAB 18.54 *Develop a database that uses general database development standards and guidelines*

Of course the short answer to this objective is to use the presented methodology. However, that's too much of a simplification. Discuss in detail how to develop a database that uses general database development standards and guidelines. Both Chapters 17 and 18 should be considered in the discussion.

Building a database that conforms to development standards and guidelines is a normalized database. A denormalized database is created only after the production system exhibits performance problems. Database performance problems are nearly always the result of poor SQL statement design by application developers. To denormalize a database before tuning the application's SQL statements is a serious mistake.

The first issue of a database design is a thorough understanding of the organization's business rules. A database cannot be normalized when the business rules are not understood. A common mistake is to start data modeling with a tool such as ER*win* when the business rules are not completely understood.

Business rules and the organization's business model change with time. It is essential that as much information as possible is collected when designing the database. Of utmost importance is a narrative statement describing reasoning and understanding of each fact, definition, constraint, and derivation. Given that the business rules are understood, the Key Based Model (KBM) is constructed. When the KBM fully represents the data architecture, then and only then does the data designer move to the Fully Attributed Model (FAM). Attributes are slowly added to the FAM with normalization at each incremental level. Eventually the FAM is complete and the Transform Model (physical database) is created.

Chapter 19 Labs

Lab 19.55 *Given a business scenario, identify which solution type is appropriate. Solution types are single-tier, two-tier, and n-tier.*

To tier or not to tier, that is the question. The choices presented by Microsoft are single-tier, two-tier, and n-tier. The application suggested by the business rambling of Chapter 17 is a two-tier system, which is the classical client/server paradigm. There are very few users in the proposed system hence Microsoft Transaction Server is not needed for component pooling. The final choice is a classical two-tier system that incorporates Microsoft SQL Server.

There are three primary reasons for tiering an application. For example, the classical client/server architecture is called two-tier even though there may be more than two tiers. We've just mentioned two different interpretations of tiering.

There is a tiering of the architecture such as browser, MTS, SQL Server, and IIS. There is also tiering within an application.

Let's start first with tiered applications and complexity management. Every application should be tiered, even desktop applications. A tiered application is robust and maintainable. Create as many tiers as necessary following the concepts of abstraction, cohesion, and coupling that were discussed earlier in this chapter.

Now let's look at the other perspective of architectural tiering. There's still the need to manage complexity, however tiering also enhances the scalability of an application. Microsoft states that the traditional client/server two-tier applications are only viable up to 100 users. Anything beyond 100 users requires a tiered solution. Tiering enhances scalability. ODBC 3.0 and later versions automatically pool database connections and the last element of the scalability equation is the pooling of components with MTS.

The last tiering issue requires the question: "Where is the work being done?" Let's assume that the application is e-commerce. Work is done on the Web server, the SQL Server site, and at the client site. We have three distinct locations where processing occurs plus we add another transparent layer for scalability. This gives us a four-tier architecture without further analysis.

In summary, tiering manages complexity and promotes scalability. Tiering at the processing source is always cheaper than passing massive tables down the wire to the client and processing the data locally.

One very important point must be made. Components in a tiered architecture must not maintain state. This is not a resource issue, but one of data consistency. After data is updated in a database a data copy cannot exist in a component without creating a concurrency issue. You'll revisit this problem in Chapter 21, DCOM.

Lab 19.56 *Identify which technologies are appropriate for implementation of a given business solution.*

Considerations include:

Technology standards such as EDI, Internet, OSI, COMTI, and POSIX. These standards simplify interconnection between systems. The Chapter 17 business rambling has no external system interconnection requirements, hence the above standards are not applicable to the ABC corporation contract management system. Let's discuss the value of each of these standards and when each should be used.

- ***EDI*** — EDI is the acronym for electronic data interchange. EDI is defined as *Content Type P35 (1990 X.435 -EDI)* as an amendment to the 1988 X.400 standard, which forms the basis for messaging. Microsoft implementation of messaging has many names since Microsoft renames technologies on a regular basis to give the impression of innovation. The various aliases for Microsoft messaging include Messaging API (MAPI), OLE Messaging, Active Messaging, and the current name, which is Collaborative Data Objects (CDO). Microsoft Exchange Server 5.0 shipped with the Active Messaging Library 1.1, while Microsoft Exchange Server 5.5 shipped with Collaborative Data Objects (CDO) 1.2.

  EDI is a standard for transmitting documents over a network. EDI is the preferred technology when dealing with business or trading partners and there is the need to transmit insurance forms, invoices, or purchase orders electronically. An Extranet is a good example of when EDI should be used. (An Extranet is an Intranet to which selected business partners or suppliers have been given access.) Uniformity of document transfer is essential.
- ***Internet*** — Standards are essential with the Internet. ActiveX controls are acceptable for an Intranet, but not all users own Microsoft Internet Explorer. When the Internet is used for commerce, standards are essential to maximize market potential. An Internet application should only use protocols that are standards. An example of something that is quite non-standard is the new Internet Information Server (IIS) application of Microsoft Visual Basic 6.0. Very few Internet Service Providers (ISP) will allow objects to be installed on their server.

  Another example is Dynamic Hypertext Markup Language (DHTML), which is sponsored by Microsoft as a future Internet standard. DHTML is not yet a standard, and a new potential standard is Extensible MarkupLanguage (XML). The point is that both of these protocols offer viable and useful futures, but which one is a dead-end, or do they both become Internet standards? The bottom line is that you can do whatever you want for an Intranet, however standard protocols are *de rigueur* for Internet commerce applications.
- ***OSI*** — OSI is the acronym for Open System Interconnect Reference Model document, which was started in 1980 and delivered in 1984. The document is published by the International Standards Organization (ISO). The docu-

ment describes a layered protocol that supports the communication between computer systems. There are seven layers that start with the physical layer and the application layer as the topmost.

The Internet model has four layers, which means that the Transport Control Protocol/Internet Protocol (TCP/IP) maps into the seven OSI layers. The OSI model is the basis for work done by the IEEE 802 project that redefined the OSI model data link level into the logical link control (LLC) and media access control (MAC) layers. The IEEE 802 project produced these documents: *802.1 OSI Model and Network Management, 802.2 Logical Link Control, 802.3 CSMA/CD (Ethernet), 802.4 Token Bus,* and *802.5 Token Ring*. Microsoft expands the IEEE 802 model with a standard Network Driver Interface Specification (NDIS), which defines standardized network card interfacing. Microsoft also added another layer immediately before the network layer, which is the Transport Driver Interface (TDI). This means that the redirector has only one interface and transport protocols are easily switched.

The bottom line to this is that Microsoft products conform to protocol standards. Windows NT is NDIS compliant. When you're using ODBC, you're using the OSI model. ODBC is an industry that is based on the OSI document, which simplifies heterogeneous computer interconnection. ODBC is the glue that allows Microsoft applications to communicate with diverse systems such as the IBM DB2 database. Developers should not develop their own protocols.

- ***COMTI*** — The COM Transaction Integrator (COMTI) brings data from IBM programs that use the Advanced Program-to-Program Communication (APPC) protocol to the Windows desktop. This means that any COM enabled Windows application now has access to the IBM mainframe. Microsoft Visual Basic, Web pages through Microsoft Active Server Pages (ASP), and even Microsoft Word have access to data stored on an IBM mainframe. COMTI functions as a wrapper that enables application developers to easily create COM components that can expose and extend CICS and IMS transaction programs. The initial version of COMTI shipped with Microsoft SNA Server 4.0.

  COMTI is an extension of Microsoft Transaction Server (MTS), that uses the Microsoft Distributed Transaction Coordinator (DTC) to provide distributed two-phase commit support. A two-phase commit occurs when all parties to the transaction signal agreement. A no vote by any party to the transaction causes the transaction to roll back.

- ***POSIX***— The Portable Operating System Interface (POSIX) standard promotes portability of applications. The standard was initially for UNIX operating, however Windows NT 3.51 is compliant with the current POSIX standard. Windows NT 4.0 is currently under test and one can assume that the system will pass.

  There are thirteen different POSIX specifications and POSIX.1 defines a C-language source-code-level application programming interface (API) to an operating system environment. POSIX.5 defines the ADA language specification and POSIX.9 defines the FORTRAN language specification. The Windows NT implementation is C-based and only supports POSIX.1. Other than C, ADA, or FORTRAN other application development languages are not applicable. POSIX will often be found in government Requests for Proposals (RFP). Vendors not compliant with the specifications cannot submit proposals in response to an RFP.

The Chapter 17 business rambling business requires the *proprietary technology* of an editing engine tailored specifically to legal documents. The "make or buy" decision is yet to be made.

Proprietary technologies are very high risk. Proprietary technology must always interface existing standard technology. Can the proprietary technology vendors update their products at the same rate as standardized technology? Probably not. The system that uses proprietary technology has a good chance of being orphaned, which is behind the technology curve.

How much can the proprietary vendor support? The proprietary technology vendor may not be able to support all the required standardized technology. Key standard features are often missing.

The proprietary software may be unproven. Is proposed installation the alpha or beta test for proprietary technology? When a vendor offers free or reduced price software in exchange for an endorsement, watch out! You are being asked to either alpha test or beta test new software. The concepts are unproven.

The *technology environment* of ABC corporation described in the Chapter 17 business rambling is on the low side of technology. ABC corporation must home grow a SQL Server database administrator before their system can go on-line. The current technology environment of the ABC corporation is desktop oriented. It can be described as a Microsoft Windows 95—Microsoft Office environment. Both the tool set and the staff must be upgraded to support an enterprise application. The ABC corporation requires the security of Windows NT. No Windows NT systems are currently installed at ABC corporation.

The issue is to not install a system that does not fall in the strategic path of the enterprise. The entity will not be able to support the system and the system may be forcing the unexpected hiring of computer support personnel. Many systems are envisioned without understanding the support requirements. Such a situation is a candidate for outsourcing. A financially responsible organization builds and maintains the system for a fixed term with a negotiated fee.

There is a factor that I call *corporate ego*. A company must have a particular type of system because the golfing buddy of the CEO has one. This attitude creates the environment for *half-baked ideas,* which is discussed elsewhere in this book. An appropriate gestation period and UML sequence diagrams along with UML collaboration diagrams will help eliminate *half-baked ideas* before significant funds are committed.

The *type of solution,* (such as enterprise, distributed, centralized, and collaborative systems) suggested by the Chapter 17 business rambling of ABC corporation is a small enterprise application. The system may have some overtones of a collaborative application, but not necessarily in the true collaborative sense.

Recall the hierarchical nature of a system that was further divided into subsystems, modules, and components. Solutions can be categorized and the simple categorizations are desktop, enterprise, distributed, centralized, and collaborative. The type of solution answers the question "What is it?" Each of the solution types is discussed below.

- ***Desktop***—Desktop applications are the monolithic applications that are not scaleable. Microsoft Access is the class monolithic application with user services, business services, and data services all located on the same system. The desktop system is included in this list as an antithesis of an enterprise application.
- ***Enterprise***—An enterprise application is a scaleable multi-user application that is available to groups of users within the enterprise. An enterprise application overlaps a distributed application and a centralized application, both of which are discussed below. An enterprise application is commonly deployed using the Microsoft Windows Distributed InterNet Applications

(DNA) framework. This is an architecture that uses any browser, Internet Explorer 4.0 or later with Dynamic Hypertext Markup Language (DHTML), and Microsoft Windows with Distributed COM (DCOM) for the user services layer. The business services layer consists of COM components managed by Microsoft Transaction Server (MTS). The data services layer consists of Microsoft SQL Server, Microsoft Messaging Queue (MSMQ), and Microsoft Internet Information Server (IIS). Lumping everything together, this technology collection is often referred to as an *n-tier* application.

Enterprise applications are not limited to the DNA architecture. The *improve the return on investment* initiative fostered the thin-client technology. Thin-clients require a fat-server, which is a box with a massive amount of memory where all the applications are installed. The thin-clients are relatively inexpensive terminals that have more intelligence than the dumb-terminals used with legacy mainframe applications. This architecture is somewhat limited and ten to fifteen thin-clients are the maximum that can be supported by one fat-server.

- ***Distributed Application*** — A distributed application is an enterprise application that has multiple data sources. Microsoft SQL Server 7.0 supports heterogeneous joins between remote databases. As an example the Seattle sales office database of company XYZ can be joined to the corporate database in San Francisco.

  Multiple data sources is not the only definition of a distributed application. The larger view of a distributed application is distributed computing, which is the connectivity of all enterprise computer systems. Interconnection of computer systems is defined by the Open Software Foundation (OSF) in its Distributed Computing Environment (DCE) product, which is a set of specifications and tools. Microsoft operating systems support OSF-DCE compatible services.

  The choice of technology also determines the type of application. As an example, an application is considered distributed when Distributed COM (DCOM), Microsoft Transaction Server (MTS), Microsoft Message Queue (MSMQ). A special version of MTS is the COM Transaction Integrator (COMTI), which extends MTS as a wrapper for IBM programs that use the Advanced Program-to-Program Communication (APPC) protocol to communicate with another transaction processor.

In summary a distributed application is determined by multiple data sources, the choice of technology, or the interconnection of diverse enterprise computers, which is a distribution of processing.

- ***Centralized Application*** — A centralized application is still an enterprise application. The data comes from one source, however tiers may still exist in a centralized application. An example of a centralized application is the traditional client/server two-tier system. Another example is the new thin-client/fat-server paradigm where all applications are installed on the server and the clients use what are euphemistically called dumb-terminals.

- ***Collaborative Application*** — Collaborative systems have grown up. It wasn't too many years ago when a collaborative application was your typical e-mail system. That has changed and Microsoft now has a suite of scaleable collaborative tools that include Microsoft Internet Explorer, Microsoft Outlook, and Microsoft Exchange Server. Microsoft Internet Explorer also includes Microsoft Outlook Express and Microsoft NetMeeting. There is intelligence within these tools. A universal inbox is included, along with public folders, server-based rules, and advanced calendaring.

  At the low end these tools are designed for users that need e-mail, newsgroup access, the ability to chat, Internet telephony, and simple application collaboration. At the high end these are full-scale collaboration tools that provide forms applications, workflow capability, group voting, and routing.

Lab 19.57 *Choose a data storage architecture*

Considerations include:

- Volume
- Number of transactions per time increment
- Number of connections or sessions
- Scope of business requirements
- Extensibility requirements
- Reporting requirements
- Number of users
- Type of database

The platform

This is not a simple objective. Many systems fail because of inappropriate hardware choices or data storage architecture. All Intel class systems are not alike even after scale factors are considered. There is a difference between an Intel desktop system and an Intel-based server. Simply adding memory and additional disk drives does not qualify a desktop system as a server. I was the co-author of *Microsoft SQL Server Survival Guide*, published in 1996. In that book I referred to Intel class systems as "elongated calculators with a fancy instruction set and an impressive cycle speed." That's still true to some degree, but a few companies do produce Intel class systems that are worthy of the name server. The impressive cycle speed is nice, but the main factor missing in most systems is bandwidth. Fortunately companies like IBM produce systems that look like mainframes that run Microsoft Windows NT. These are enterprise level systems and not the clone boxes cobbled together at your local computer emporium.

Enterprise problems require enterprise solutions. The system of choice is still a Digital Equipment Corporation (DEC) Alpha Server. (DEC was purchased by Compaq corporation.) When compared to a DEC Alpha, the Intel architecture is generally not scaleable. This does not mean that Intel system benchmarks are not impressive. On the contrary, they are quite impressive. I used to do benchmarks for a venerable company named Univac that is now deceased. The real issue is a benchmark using your own data with your own enterprise applications.

The enterprise architect who builds an Intel network does so on the blind faith that a bigger and faster box is available within a year to eighteen months, in other words, blind faith that Moore's law is still in effect. I recall being a value-added reseller (VAR) at various times for DEC, IBM, and Control Data Corporation (CDC) in the 70s. The systems were turn-key and included order-entry and general accounting along with the hardware. System capacity was planned for a five-year life. Not today. Many systems today exceed their maximum capacity soon after installation. To paraphrase an old adage, it's *penny-wise and pound-foolish* to save ten, twenty, or even thirty thousand dollars and place your enterprise at risk. Computers are very cheap today and the undue risk is not necessary.

Choosing a database The type of database plays a major factor in the enterprise hardware equation. We're discussing enterprise solutions so databases such as Microsoft Access are not applicable. The first rule-of-thumb for Microsoft SQL Server 6.5 is that tables in the 2-4 million row range are acceptable for on-line transaction processing (OLTP) systems without a loss in performance. This is a general rule and the system is expected to be first normalized and then denormalized as required for performance. Indexes are picked very carefully. This is different than a data-warehousing (DW) type database where rule-of-thumb estimates are approximately five-hundred thousand rows per table being the maximum to maintain performance of a DW application. A DW database is read-only and heavily indexed to optimize queries. A DW database is not updated on a regular basis and users only create reports from a DW database. The numbers for either type of database are only guidelines and do not take into account performance degradation that occurs with poor application design or database design.

Microsoft SQL Server 7.0 is still fairly new and statistically valid experiences are yet to be reported. In many areas version 7.0 performance is superior to version 6.5, which implies that version 7.0 performance in general is superior to that of version 6.5. Version 6.5 can be considered a minimal baseline.

Estimating hardware requirements Estimating hardware requirements is almost folly. There are too many variables and estimates always expect a near perfect level of software performance. The problem is to determine a plan of attack for the enterprise hardware architecture. This plan can be distilled down into these distinct steps:

- Determine the required logistics such as number of users, transaction rates, number of connections.
- Build the system on prototype hardware that is far less than enterprise level hardware such as a DEC Alpha. Don't buy the enterprise level hardware until the system is running on prototype hardware, which we'll do in the following steps.
- Review the required resources such as connection counts, users, transaction rates, and other logistics.
- Use the estimated logistics to acquire enough licenses to test the system. We're not talking about a complete system, but only enough licenses to support twenty-five percent or less of the fully deployed system.
- Start testing the system with performance measurement tools. Remember that no system operates as expected. It's almost as if systems have a mind of their own. Some performance issues will be outstandingly good while others will be embarrassingly bad.

- Redesign, code, and continue testing as necessary to bring the system to an acceptable level of performance. Continue plotting the performance curve during this phase. The performance curve will ramp up gradually and then eventually go asymptotic. You want to be testing the system in the portion of the performance curve that is increasing on a linear basis. If the performance curve test point is not linear than the testing hardware is inadequate. You can roughly determine the performance parameters by testing at the five, ten, fifteen, twenty, and twenty-five percent system load levels.
- When the system reaches an acceptable level of performance and a linear section of the performance curve is established, extrapolate how much hardware is required for a full deployment based on the required logistics. Now is the time to acquire your enterprise level hardware. Disks are cheap and virtual memory systems such as Windows NT will use all the memory supplied. Don't skimp on memory. Uninterruptible Power Supplies (UPS) and redundant arrays of independent disks (RAID) arrays are derigueur in today's world of 24X7 Web servers
- Don't be surprised if the enterprise level system must be upgraded. The original extrapolation that used the prototype hardware was an educated guess as to the resources required. The real performance curve is determined on the final enterprise level system.

Lab 19.58 *Test the feasibility of a proposed technical architecture*

Demonstrate that business requirements are met.

There are two stages to feasibility testing. The first test is a walk-through of project scenarios. The primary goal of the scenario walk-through is to verify that all business requirements are met. The second goal of the walk-through is to identify design weakness and dependencies that include:

- Triggering events must be identified, which are preconditions of a service.
- Identify objects that depend upon the consistency of existence of other objects. These objects can be a source of system errors.
- Are there any concurrency issues? Concurrency issues are minimized by writing stateless objects. Do any sequencing issues exist?

- Are there any timing issues? MSMQ can be used for communicating with unreliable sources. Can an activity be suspended or must it be responded to immediately?
- Evaluate transactions. Do transactions span more than one functional area? Is a two-phase commit required?
- Identify transaction dependencies. Does the object controlling the transaction depend upon services of still another object?
- Identify business rules that cross objects. Coordination events may be necessary to keep the objects synchronized.
- What is the frequency of the scenario? Is it uniform or periodic?

The second stage of feasibility testing is with a pilot or a prototype system. Testing of the pilot or prototype system validates the implementation of the business requirements. Testing is thorough and is divided into different stages. The testing stages are as follows:

- Deployment testing is stage one. This occurs before complete system testing is scheduled. The reason this is done first is that new versions must be deployed during testing as coding errors and design problems are resolved.
- The next stage is error recovery from communication failures. A distributed application will use a least one wire and recovery from communication failures should be graceful.
- The third stage is testing application error recovery in general. We're verifying that errors are managed properly. It's important to have error recovery in place and functional before starting stress testing.
- There's always the issue of integration with existing applications. We'll assume that this is an enterprise-wide application with a dedicated server. If the application must be integrated with existing applications on a server, the recommended approach is to completely debug the application on a stand-alone server before integrating the application with existing server applications.
- This is the next step in testing, which is end-to-end testing. All parts of the system are tested as an integrated whole. The testing can start with a single client and the testing of all services. Additional clients are added in a controlled fashion. During the testing phase, performance monitoring should

be in place. System through-put projections can be made from the collected performance data.

- Testing security is the last step. The system is distributed and not monolithic. In a distributed application the users should only have access to the servers that support the application. The users should not have direct access to any other servers.

Demonstrate that use case scenarios are met.

Use case scenarios were built in the conceptual design stage and demonstrated in the walk-through discussed above. Chapter 17 described a Requirements Model (RM) that is a database. Use case scenarios are uniquely identified and that identification is placed in the RM database. Constructed components are also uniquely identified and placed in the RM database. A report can be generated from the RM database that links a business rambling sentence to a use case scenario, the components used in that use case scenario, and the form responsible for activating those components. It's possible to include a certification test that verifies the specific requirement, but this is not always necessary. With user buyoff on the use case scenario, and user buyoff on component unit testing, which may require temporary scaffolding, the system will probably be a success barring any performance issues. The problem with this approach is that the implementation time frame is often unrealistic and there's no time for scaffolding code.

Demonstrate that existing technology constraints are met.

Existing technology constraints are demonstrated with stress testing during the end-to-end testing phase discussed above. The system is instrumented and performance data is collected that should validate expected performance. It goes without saying that this test only occurs after many hours of performance testing to remove locking, blocking, or deadlocks. This demonstration occurs after the developers know the system will work and this is the final buyoff.

Assess impact of shortfalls in meeting requirements.

What's almost never considered in a software project is the potential project failure. Both technology and changing market conditions are in a constant flux today, a situation that did not exist in the past. The Internet is an example of a rapidly changing market, while the rate of technology change (I didn't say "innovation"), is directly attributable to Microsoft. Every software project requires a risk-assessment plan and the key plan points include:

- ***Project Goals*** — The plan starts with a definition of the project's goals. Companies sell goods and or services and these goals may be market expansion, to establish new markets, or on-going system maintenance to preserve the current market share. The project, possibly combined with other options, is part of the strategy to attain these goals. When a project fails there is either a loss of market share, failure to enter a new market, or additional costs are incurred to maintain market share.
- ***Project Benefits*** — A project must have benefits. If the benefits are not significant then the project is not worthy of implementation. It's a known fact that forty-two percent of all projects are cancelled (*ComputerWorld,* March 22, 1999, "Bad management is to blame for IT skills crunch"), which means that a new project has a forty-two percent chance of failure. This means that the derived benefits must be at least double the implementation costs.

  In spite of the best planning and budgeting, project delivery schedules and budgets will invariably not be met. My own personal rule is to multiply expected implementation costs by two. This means that a project's benefits must exceed the implementation costs by a factor of four to be considered a viable project.
- ***Defining Project Failure Points*** — Goals are often defined, but failures are not. The analogy is a person that has invested in the stock market. The selected stock keeps going down, and down, and finally there's nothing left. Too many project leaders and managers are guilty of believing that somehow the project can be implemented. Rather than continuing to believe in unreal expectations, definite failure points need to be established. Budget and time considerations are obvious candidates for defining failure points. Exceed either the budget or time allotted and a failure point is reached. Another candidate for quantifying a project failure point is business rules. Too many business rule changes portend of either poor requirements analysis or changing business rules. Track the number of business rule changes. Define a failure point as that point when the number of business rule changes exceed a specified level.

  Failure points are not limited to the development phase of a project and failure points can occur during acceptance testing. Failing to meet minimal performance levels can be defined as a failure point. This can be defined as the number of active connections, the number of transactions per unit time, or any other quantifiable metric. Good examples of failing to meet required performance levels are the Web sites that offer stock market services. Numerous complaints have been filed with the Securities Exchange Commission concerning the inability of the Web sites to complete transactions during very busy stock market trading sessions.

System failure tolerance levels must be set. Failures may be acceptable when business losses can be managed. The obvious question is, "What is the acceptable maximum business loss that can be incurred?" When a loss limit is defined, a strategy must be defined that restores operations within the specified loss limit. Some systems such as a 24X7 Web site may have a zero tolerance for failure.

- ***Analyzing a Project Failure Point***—A failure point is incurred and the project is now at risk. Depending upon the type of failure point, there are many questions to ask. When the failure point is a time or budget constraint, the question can be asked, "Was the failure incurred on a high-risk component?" If not, then there may be serious project problems and the failure should be analyzed extensively. After the analysis, the questions should be asked, "Are the remaining project milestones in jeopardy?" The failure may be an aberration, however a new risk analysis must still be performed. The issue is to cut losses short and not deal with unreal expectation.

  Software can be looked at as an iterative approach to a problem solution. Software always fails to completely solve a problem because a completed solution provides better insight to the apparent problem. The software development iterations only bring us closer to the perceived problem. An imperfect view of the problem and knowing that the business model will change before the software is deployed, is a recipe for a disaster. It should not be a surprise when a new application fails to meet business requirements. When business rule changes exceed a failure point threshold, there are two controllable sources and one uncontrollable source of business rules changes.

  The first source of controllable business rule changes is an inadequate requirements analysis. If this is the type of business rule changes that are occurring, the system should be stopped at this point and the requirements analysis phase revisited. The project is guaranteed to fail at this point, and the only salvage point is to revisit the requirements analysis phase.

Users are the second source of controllable business rule changes. *Users will be defining the requirements for the new system within the scope and framework of the older system*. Users do not understand the capability of the new proposed system during the requirements collection phase. As development proceeds, the users acquire insight as to the capability of the new system, which begat the business rule changes. Preventive medicine is to thoroughly educate users as to the capability of the proposed new system before the requirements collection phase. User-sourced business rule changes must be analyzed and categorized before acceptance.

A changing business environment is the source for uncontrollable business rule changes. Today is an era of rapidly changing technology. What's overlooked is that business environments also change very rapidly, and the Internet is an example. To date we've not developed a suitable technology that permits business requirements to change during the software development process. The best we can do is pause, consider the consequences, and retrofit changes that accommodate the new business rules. *Incomplete or changing* business requirements is one of the primary reasons for project failure. I conjecture that of the forty-two percent of technology-based projects that are cancelled (*Computer World,* March 22, 1999, "Bad management is to blame for IT skills crunch"), some are cancelled because the business model and business climate has changed. Such cancellation should not reflect upon developers.

Measuring Project Progress — Monitoring the project carefully is the only way to avoid surprises on delivery day. Use as many project milestones as possible to monitor performance.

Microsoft sponsors a paradigm that is known as iterative development in which the developer iterates on the component until it functions. The iteration paradigm is an element of Microsoft Solution Frameworks (MSF). The iterative development approach negates managing with either a time or budget constraint. Developer iterations can be symptomatic of design flaws and iterations. In my opinion iteration during software development is a mistake. Iterations make it difficult to measure project progress. Is this the first iteration, the second, or the third? Iterative software development can only be done by companies like Microsoft that have a bottomless-pit budget.

Lab 19.59 *Develop appropriate deployment strategy*

There are several deployment mechanisms, some of which are simple. The list below presents the deployment alternatives available to the developer.

- ***Systems Management Server*** — Only useful when users are connected on a network. SMS clients include Windows 3.1, Windows 95/98, Windows for Workgroups 3.11, Windows NT Workstation 3.5 or later, MS-DOS 5.0 and later, IBM OS/2 2.*x* and OS/2 Warp, and Macintosh System 7. SMS is not Internet enabled. There may be situations where deploying an Access database with e-mail is satisfactory.
- ***Network*** — The developer builds a network installation and notifies all users.
- ***Setup*** — Build a traditional diskette-based installation with the Setup Wizard of Visual Basic or use the Access Developers Toolkit. A disk installation procedure follows strict guidelines as to where new files will be installed. The Registry must be used for recording installation parameters and WIN.INI or SYSTEM.INI files must not be used. Application files are never to be copied to either the WINDOWS or SYSTEMS directory unless they are system-wide shared files. Application files are placed as follows:
  - ***Application Files*** - ...\ProgramFiles\<app>
  - ***Shared Files*** - ...\ProgramFiles\CommonFiles\System
  - ***Ancillary Support Files*** - ...\ProgramFiles\<app>\System
- ***Internet*** — Software is installed or updated by including a .CAB file reference within the CODEBASE attribute of an HTML OBJECT tag. Software deployment on Internet/Intranet is with the Internet Download Component. The component is prepackaged for downloading over the Internet. An Internet download occurs when the CODEBASE attribute in an HTML OBJECT tag points to a COM object.

I won't discuss Win32 deployment since it is not generally scaleable. A thorough analysis of Win32 deployment issues can be found in *Windows Architecture I & II MCSD Study Guide* published by IDG Books Worldwide.

Scaleable deployment comes in two flavors. The first type of scaleable deployment is with Microsoft Transaction Server (MTS). Software is deployed in packages on a MTS server, which isolates users from direct database access. MTS also isolates the user from system maintenance activities, which makes a MTS deployment scaleable.

Internet applications represent the ultimate in scalability and HTML is the common denominator. When Active Server Pages (ASP) are used at the server, the application can intelligently manage the user's browser. The ASP can interrogate the user's browser with standard HTML and return either standard HTML or Dynamic HTML (DHTML), which depends upon the browser's response to the query. The ASP page may also return Java applets or ActiveX controls, which is browser dependent.

Internet downloads are tools that support content. The server must know the client capabilities before a download is possible. Even if one is possible, is it useful? I'll try to integrate the discussion of the Internet Download Component with a practical application. We'll start with Listing F-1, which is ASP script looks at the browser type. The second example in Listing F-2 is also ASP script that asks if the browser can support ActiveX controls. The Internet Download Component is invoked only when the browser supports ActiveX controls. This is almost like ADO programming where the developer uses the **Supports** method to verify that the requested functionality is supported.

LISTING F-1 Using the Marquee Control for Internet Explorer

```
<%
        '
        '     Use HTML Marquee if Internet Explorer
        '
        Set MyObj = Server.CreateObject("MSWC.BrowserType")
        if (MyObj.browser = "IE") Then
%>
              <marquee
              bgcolor="#00005B"
              direction="LEFT"
              behavior="SCROLL"
              >
              Thank you for buying Solution Architectures
```

```
		</marquee>
<%Else%>
		<center>
		 Thank you for buying Solution Architectures
		</center>
<%End If%>
```

We're adding some intelligence to our Active Server Page. Listing F-1 uses the Browser Capabilities component to determine the type of browser. When Microsoft Internet Explorer is the client browser, the HTML marquee element is used by the browser, otherwise a text message is displayed. Most browsers probably support the HTML Marquee element, so this example is merely illustrative.

The type of browser is not the only issue. Does the browser support ActiveX controls? Listing 19F-2 raises the functionality a notch by deciding between downloading an ActiveX control and displaying a message of the Billboard Rotator Component of Internet Information Server. The Billboard Rotator Component rotates advertising images on a Web page and can be configured so the browser gets a new message each time the ASP is requested. (If that's not clear, then remember that the MSWC .Adrotator control is an Internet Information Server component, and only an image can be downloaded.)

LISTING F-2 Deciding between the Adrotator control and a custom control

```
<%
   '
   '    Use HTML Marquee if Internet Explorer
   '
   Set MyObj = Server.CreateObject("MSWC.BrowserType")
   if MyObj.ActiveXControls =TRUE Then
%>
        <OBJECT
CODEBASE="/MyWeb/MyBillBoard.CAB#version=8,0,0,8
        WIDTH=570
        HEIGHT=70
        DATA="/MyWeb/Controls/MyBillBoard.ods"
        CLSID=clsid:11111111-2222-3333-4444-555555555555">
        </OBJECT>
```

```
<%
   Else
        Set MyAD=Server.CreateObject(MSWC.Adrotator")
        Response.Write(MyAD.GetAdvertisement("/MyWeb/ad.txt"))
   End If
%>
```

The script is busy making download decisions. When the script encounters the CODEBASE attribute of the HTML OBJECT tag, **CoGetClassObjectFromURL,** is invoked directly. All the URL Moniker machinations we previously discussed in Chapter 5 now come into play.

#version=8,0,0,8 is a URL fragment of Listing F-2 that represents the version number. This portion of the URL is pivotal in the load process because it determines if the component will be downloaded. When this value is `-1,-1,-1,-1` a new version of the component is always downloaded. When no version is present, the currently loaded version is considered acceptable, otherwise the Internet Download Component will download a new version only when the requested version is more recent than the existing version. When no component is loaded, and no version is present, the URL path is searched for the component.

The Internet Download Component processes three file categories:

- *PE*—A portable executable such as a `.OCX`, `.DLL`, or `.EXE`. A single executable is downloaded, installed, and registered in one operation. The file category may be code-signed. The Internet Download Component will try to start self-registration for those components marked as such. The Internet Download Component ignores the `OleSelfRegister` flag if the main URL code points directly to an `.EXE` file. This type of file is not platform independent except with HTTP.
- *CAB*—A `.CAB` file has the advantage of compression and can be code-signed. A `.CAB` file-required component is an `.INF` file which contains the packaging instructions. A `.CAB` file is not platform independent without HTTP format negotiation.
- *INF*—An `.INF` file that cannot be code-signed, but it is platform independent. The `.INF` file is a map of all required files. This file download category is useful in an Intranet environment but is unsafe on the Internet.

Developers should always use a `.CAB` file because it uses compression, reduces component download time, and increases client satisfaction. The `CAB-`

SDK.EXE, CABVIEW.EXE tool, and the code-signing tool AUTH2SDK.EXE are all downloadable from http://www. microsoft.com/. Once you are connected to Microsoft.com, go to the developer page and search for AUTH2SDK.EXE. You'll be presented with the current download URL

The Internet/Intranet is the only deployment strategy that does not suffer from a lack of scalability. SMS has limitations and suffers the least, but when compared to automatic updating from a Web page, SMS deployment is not scaleable.

In summary, there are many ways to deploy an application and the main issue of deployment is scalability. An Internet/Intranet solution is scaleable and should be the application type of choice when deployment is an issue. Developers deploy updates only to the Internet/Intranet server and not directly to the clients. MTS applications improve scalability, but not to the degree of an Internet/Intranet application.

Lab 19.60 *Construct a conceptual design that is based on a variety of scenarios and that includes context, workflow process, task sequence, and physical environment models*

Types of applications include:

- SDI, MDI, console, and dialog desktop applications
- Two-tier, client/server, and Web applications
- N-tier applications
- Collaborative applications

The first issue is to define each of the applications types:

- ***SDI***—A single document interface is defined as a SDI application and such an application has only one form, hence the SDI classification.
- ***MDI***—An application that supports many forms has a multiple document interface. The developer has the option of letting the child forms float, or be contained completely within the parent window. An application is allowed only one MDI form, all the remaining forms are child forms. MDI applications typically support many applications. The child forms are typically accessed from a menu bar on the parent form.
- ***Console***—The Win32 API supports a character-based I/O interface for character-mode applications. The console interface is processor-independent. A console consists of an input buffer and one or more screen buffers. Buffers

are queued and each buffer contains information about an event. Events include key-press, key-release, and mouse events. A screen buffer is a two-dimensional array of character and color data.

There are two different levels of console access. High-level is the equivalent of standard input to retrieve data stored in a character buffer. The second level of access is low-level with the application receiving detailed information about keyboard and mouse events.

- ***Dialog Desktop*** — These applications fit into the category of useful tools. Standard interfaces are available allowing access from other developer applications.
- ***Two-Tier*** — An application that is partitioned into two layers. The remote layer is typically a database. The two-tier architecture is characterized by a fat client that embodies both presentation services and business services.
- ***Web*** — Web applications are often n-tier application affairs that include Internet Information Server (IIS), SQL Server, both or either of Microsoft Message Queue (MSMQ) or Microsoft Transaction Server (MTS), and the client layer. MTS or MSMQ are not necessary but are highly recommended.
- ***N-Tier*** — A Web application is certainly an n-tiered application, but that is not the only type of n-tiered application. N-tiered applications can be built using Distributed COM (DCOM, see Chapter 21).
- ***Collaborative*** — Microsoft supports a suite of scaleable collaborative tools that include Microsoft Internet Explorer, Microsoft Outlook, and Microsoft Exchange Server. Microsoft Internet Explorer also includes Microsoft Outlook Express and Microsoft NetMeeting. There is intelligence within these tools. A universal inbox is included, along with public folders, server-based rules, and advanced calendaring.

  At the low end these tools are designed for users that need e-mail, newsgroup access, the ability to chat, Internet telephony, and simple application collaboration. At the high end these are full-scale collaboration tools that provide forms applications, workflow capability, group voting, and routing.

Completion of this objective requires the construction of the Context Model, Workflow Process Model, Task Sequence Model, and Physical Environment Model. There is inadequate information for the reader to complete either the Context Model or the Physical Environment Model from the Chapter 17 business rambling.

Chapter 19 builds a sample Context Model, Workflow Process Model, and Task Sequence Model. Let's review the models:

- ***Context Model***—A description of the current environment that includes all policies and procedures. Also included are organization or physical constraints and any other issues. The Context Model starts with a mission statement and includes all external and internal influences.
- ***Process Model***—This model is represented by UML use case diagrams, which are representations of the scenarios derived from business rambling distillations. UML use case diagrams should clearly model how the business currently functions and the expected future processes. Both before and after versions of this model give a better perspective of the proposed project. A use case scenario is depicted with actors interacting with use cases

We won't present any other models from the Chapter 17 business rambling since scenarios are very straightforward. Chapter 19 has an example of a UML Task Sequence Model and a Workflow Process Model.

- ***Task Sequence Model***—UML sequence diagrams are used to represent the different phases of a multi-task process. A Task Sequence Model represents the ordered steps of a use case scenario.
- ***Workflow Process Model***—This is not a UML model, but a Microsoft model that is an aggregation of use case scenarios. The model is manually constructed and represents the complete workflow process. This model is decomposed into use cases, which are in turn represented by various task sequence models.
- ***Physical Environment Model***—The physical environment does not always change for a software application. When the physical environment changes, this model should reflect all physical environment changes. Some changes may be to plant and equipment that may fall outside the purview of software application development. This model should reflect the environment as it exists before the project is started along with the projected changes. New equipment such as computers, office furniture, and fixtures are included in this model.

Lab 19.61 *Given a conceptual design, apply the principles of modular design to derive the components and services of the logical design*

Abstraction, encapsulation, cohesion, and coupling are the principles of modular design (see Chapter 19 for a detailed discussion of these principles). These principles are applied against the Requirements Model of Chapter 17, which is a repository of semantic distillations. The semantic rules used to identify attributes, services, or other logical design parameters include:

- Active sentences that describe the relationship of the independent data entity (see Chapter 18). *Publisher publishes books. Publisher* is the independent entity.
- Passive sentences that describe dependent (characteristic) data entities (see Chapter 17). *Book is published by publisher. Book* is the dependent or characteristic entity.
- Transitive verbs and verb phrases that describe or hint at relationships with objects (a scenario). *Clerk rents rooms. Clerk* is an actor in a use case scenario.
- Declarative verbs or procedural statements that describe or hint at services. *Check-out time is 11:00 AM*. A *check-out* procedure exists. This procedure is sequenced (see Task Sequence Model).
- Adjectives and possessive noun phrases describe or hint at object attributes. *The daily room rate is $175*. The room has a *rate* attribute.

Abstraction

Abstraction is a generalization from the specific to the generic. A *customer account* is an abstraction that allows the specification of unique customer information, and yet retains the generality of a classification. The properties and attributes of an object are distilled to the point where a general classification occurs. Distinguishing features are maintained as properties or attributes.

We define an object as an abstraction that models behavior, has attributes, and can communicate. An object is an aggregation of services and data, some of which may be encapsulated (see below, Encapsulation). The services model the object's behavior while the object's attributes are defined by the object's data. The object offers the use of selected services through an interface, which is a COM contract.

If we've done our conceptual design properly, many of the system objects are already identified as elements of a UML task diagram, well maybe not all but most of them. When an object is not defined in a UML Task Sequence Diagram, creating an object is often intuitive. Assume that there is a collection of services and data attributes. Attributes include **LastPaymentDate, LastPaymentAmount,** and **LongDistanceCharges**. The payment attributes are generic, however the **LongDistanceCharges** attribute suggests that the object is related to telephones and an object identification such as **TelephoneBill** is a reasonable choice.

Not all objects are intuitively apparent. The real problem is sifting through the user's expected services and attributes (the Requirements Model) and combining related services and data into a meaningful design. Not everything can be combined. The goal of any logical design is modularity, which reduces errors and simplifies maintenance. An ancillary benefit of logical design is the reuse of modules.

So far I've not been too specific about objects, but here are some general rules that can be used to define objects.

- Define the scope of the objects that are candidates for refining. Accounts payable objects are out of scope when payroll objects are considered. Ignore irrelevant objects.
- Identify redundant objects and combine them. Review all the objects that are within scope. Do any have a name that is a synonym for another object? Compare the functionality and attributes of each object. A synonym exists when two objects have comparable functionality and attributes.
- Objects cannot be vague. An object must have a clear identity with specific functionality and attributes. Rename the object if necessary and include the necessary functionality and attributes to support the object's mission.
- Be very careful about distinguishing between objects and attributes. It's possible that some scenario nouns are attributes of another object. When an attribute must exist independently, it should be defined as an object and not as an attribute.
- Transactions are managed with a control object that controls the transactions. Create a control object when none exists.
- Actors and roles are not objects. Nouns that represent actors or roles should not be modeled as objects.

An object model now exists. This model can be normalized with a set of rules much as a database is normalized. The purpose of object normalization is to remove redundancy and isolate functionality with respect to cohesion and coupling. Object normalization rules include:

- ***Identify and isolate repeating patterns*** — The task is to search for repeating patterns of attributes, which is relatively easy. An **Address** object is a good example of a repeating pattern. The search is expanded for patterns that differ by a small degree such as objects that differ by one attribute. The question must then be asked, "Will the design become too complex when each caller is expected to supply the distinguishing attribute along with the input parameters?" The problem is to attain a smooth interface design without engendering unnecessary complexity.
- ***Identify and isolate disparate functionality*** — Disparate functionality does not contribute to the single activity of the object. When the remaining functionality contributes to the single activity of the object; the object is said to have *tight cohesion* (see below, Cohesion).
- ***Identify and isolate independent functionality*** — Independent functionality is independent of the remainder of the object. *Loose coupling* (see below, Coupling) is a characteristic of independent functionality that is not tightly bound to any object.
- ***Identify and isolate cross-object dependencies*** — Dependencies exist in object parent/child relationships. The issue is to ascertain that objects such are **Customer** or **Product** do not call each other, but are only called from the parent **Order** object. Both **Customer** and **Product** are child objects of an order object

Continue the distillation process on the objects until all interfaces are smooth and the objects are clearly defined. Applying the distillation criteria is an iterative process. It's very difficult to say when the process ends, but the developer should guard against *over-objectification* where the distillation process has created too many objects. There is no clear example of either and I use the personal criteria of *flowing like water with no hindrance*. It's all intuitive.

Encapsulation

Encapsulation is an objected-oriented design technique that hides functionality. Hiding functionality facilitates the creation of abstractions and the notion of black boxes, which promotes modular replacement of components. The only requirement is that both black boxes (components) have the same interface requirements, which may be independent of internal operations. This means that each black box is an independent self-contained unit. Hiding functionality manages complexity and simplifies interfacing with only the minimal functionality exposed. The designer's task is to hide all internal functionality and only expose an interface that exposes the minimal but necessary services and attributes.

Cohesion

Function cohesion is how closely the services are related. An example of poor functional cohesion is a cash receipts method in a reports component. When we're discussing a general accounting system, reports are often placed in a reporting subsystem. What's not normally done is to define a large system that contains unrelated functionality such as input forms and reports. It's true that cash receipts require reports, but that's a user interface issue. The reports are still placed in their own subsystem. You'll quickly find that you can leverage many reports since the sign-on dialogs and setup routines may be almost identical.

Cohesion also occurs at the module level. Since we're dealing with related functionality, you can use your new found skill of using functional dependence (see Chapter 18) in identifying related services and data. Be open to the fact that you might want to create another tier. A good example is addresses within an accounting system. Let's assume that there is a relatively primitive accounting system where the account master only supports two addresses, a bill-to address and a ship-to address. How do you handle drop shipments? What about alternative ship-to addresses? In this case you create a separate tier for addressing operations. You'll quickly find that the purchasing subsystem, accounts payable subsystem, and the accounts receivable subsystem can utilize this new tier.

When cohesion is strictly applied the end result is that one unit (subsystem, module, or component) does one task. The net result is high reliability. The cash receipts data entry program does not create a report. As long as I can remember, which is quite a few years, the dictum is one routine performs only one task. Along with that dictum was another that said any function greater than fifty lines was a design error and should be decomposed into two or more functions.

Functional cohesion is the primary goal of logical design. There are other forms of cohesion, which may or may not yield a benefit:

- ***Sequential Cohesion*** — The operations in the unit share the same data and must be performed sequentially. I do not consider this a violation of functional cohesion.
- ***Communicational Cohesion*** — Operations in a unit share the same data, but are not related. This violates functional cohesion but minimizes communication overhead.
- ***Temporal Cohesion*** — Operations are combined in the same unit because they are all done at the same time. I do this all the time with either an end-of-year close or an end-of-period close in a general ledger subsystem. There are many discrete jobs to do in a general ledger close and I provide copious comments in the code as well as allowing a back out if there's a failure halfway through the close operation. I combine these operations because the very last thing I want is a naive user crashing the general ledger, which is the lifeblood of any business.
- ***Procedural Cohesion*** — Operations that must execute in a specific order are grouped together and do not share common data. This violates functional cohesion and is undesirable.
- ***Logical Cohesion*** — Unrelated operations are grouped together and selected through program logic constructs such as IF or CASE. This violates functional cohesion and is undesirable.
- ***Coincidental Cohesion*** — Unrelated operations are grouped and no discernible relationship exists. This violates functional cohesion and is undesirable. Developers that use coincidental cohesion require remediation.

Coupling

Cohesion occurs within a tier while coupling takes place between tiers. Coupling defines the characteristics of object interfacing. *Tight cohesion* and *loose coupling* are traits of a good system design. Loose coupling is illustrated with an addressing tier that can be used by purchasing and accounts payable.

Loose coupling between objects is obtained by:

- Minimizing the number of connections between objects. The goal is small and simple interfaces.

- Using explicit data with a direct connection between objects. The data should be passed *ByVal* (see Chapter 21) as a parameter whenever possible. Passing either global data or database records to an object will result in concurrency problems.
- Connections are public and are explicitly defined.
- Connections are generic, which supports the black-box concept of replaceable modules.

Let's go back to the Chapter 17 business rambling and identify some attributes and objects. There are very few transitive verbs, consequently identifying objects based on required services is difficult.

Demonstrating cohesion using the Chapter 17 business rambling is difficult since there are very few services and many attributes. We'll start with some obvious objects and their attributes from the Chapter 17 business rambling:

- ***Contract Object***— This object is supported by a **Name**, **TrackingNumber, Title, ExpirationDate, StartDate,** and **Status** attribute. There are other attributes, but these attributes justify the **Contract** object definition. These attributes do not exhibit a high cohesion level when considered apart from the **Contract** object. The attributes were selected after first determining that a **Contract** object definition was a necessary element of the logical design. Given the existence of a **Contract** object, the attributes do exhibit high cohesion. Attributes with high cohesion independent of an object will invariably suggest the proper object name.

  The choice of attribute names affects cohesion. For example by changing the generic **Status** attribute to **SignedStatus** changes the cohesion.
- ***ContractCopy Object***— **Location, CopyNumber,** and **SignedStatus** are **ContractCopy** attributes. These attributes justify the **ContractCopy** object definition and exhibit a very high cohesion level.
- ***Address Object***— This object has major justification with the **Party, OtherParty, Principle, Signatory,** and **LawFirm** objects as parents of the **Address** object. Loose coupling allows the **Address** object to be shared with other objects.

Lab 19.62 *Incorporate business rules into object design*

Incorporating business rules into the object design is very simple. Microsoft calls infrastructure issues business rules, which is not completely true. Within the Microsoft context business rules represent infrastructure issues that are packaged and moved to another layer (tier). The CRUD **DataClass** class of Chapter 21 represents business rules within the Microsoft concept. Formal business rules are a subset of Microsoft's loosely defined business rules.

The formal business rules of the Chapter 17 business rambling are pretty sparse. Most issues involve security, however who can be a signatory to a contract is a managed business rule. Two other managed business rules are the amount and duration of the contract. The other issues are related directly to security and are not business rules per se. The application will include the standard infrastructure layers, which follows Microsoft's loosely defined concept of business rules.

Lab 19.63 *Assess the potential impact of the logical design on performance, maintainability, extensibility, scalability, availability, and security*

The type of application is determined in logical design. Performance, maintainability, extensibility, scalability, availability, and security are each dependent upon the type of application.

Performance Microsoft Access is a monolithic application, which is a single-tier architecture. Microsoft states that the maximum number of Microsoft Access users should be limited to fifteen. This is independent of the fact that Microsoft Access does not support the ACID properties of a transaction.

Microsoft further states that a useful upper limit to a two-tier architecture that uses Microsoft SQL Server is one hundred users. The number of client can be increased to no more than two hundred clients by writing SQL Server stored procedures.

When the number of users significantly exceeds the two-tier limits, Microsoft recommends an n-tier architecture that includes Microsoft Transaction Server (MTS) and DCOM. MTS pools components and threads, however the thread limit of MTS is one hundred. This limit corresponds closely to the upper limit of a two-tier architecture, however since the resources are shared an n-tiered architecture should be able to handle many more users.

The user upper limit for an MTS application is a direct function of the application design. The MTS upper limit is found during performance and acceptance testing. As a rule-of-thumb, I would personally suggest that any application that must support five hundred or more users be Internet/Intranet based.

Maintainability

Maintainability is synonymous with ease of deployment. Is a single-tiered architecture maintainable? Yes, from an academic perspective, but deploying a single-tier application requires copying a new version of a monolithic application to every user.

The same maintainability problems exist with a two-tier application and the fat-client. Every fat-client must be updated, which is not a scaleable process.

Is an n-tiered application maintainable? MTS provides the concept of packages where logically related components are grouped. The packages are managed by the Microsoft Management Console (MMC), which greatly simplifies installation and maintenance. The other half of an n-tiered (distributed) application is the Web server. User applications are updated indirectly by updating components on the Internet Information Server (IIS).

Scalability

A distributed (n-tiered) application is the only scaleable application in the Microsoft architecture. Both the monolithic and two-tiered applications lack scalability. ODBC 3.0 and beyond pools connections and MTS pools both threads and components, which yields a distributed architecture that is scaleable. ODBC connection pooling provides a small amount of scaling in the two-tiered architecture, but this is minimal when compared to the scalability of a distributed application.

Availability

Microsoft Message Queue (MSMQ) is a distributed architecture technology and is used with slow or unreliable networks. Messages sent through MSMQ can be transacted, which provides reliable communications. MSMQ supports its own transaction mechanism or the transaction mechanism of MTS can be used. The value of MSMQ is that the intended recipient may be offline, in which case the message is queued for later delivery.

A Microsoft distributed application supports availability in the positive sense with just-in-time component activation within MTS, which provides a short response time. A Microsoft distributed application supports availability in the negative sense that messages will be queued for recipients that are temporarily unavailable.

Availability is also defined in terms of access to external resources such as mainframe applications. A gateway server becomes a component in a distributed architecture.

Security

A monolithic application (Microsoft Access), supports traditional group and user level security. This security is form, view, or table based.

Two-tier applications support security, however business rules may be exposed on the client. SQL Server supports user and group security on all SQL Server objects. This security mechanism is of the same type as the monolithic application.

MTS supports the concept of packages that contain related components. MTS automatically creates a user account for each package, rather than an account for individual users or groups. This approach makes each package a virtual user. The users are only given access to the MTS server, while the packages only have access to the database, which isolates users from direct database access. Management of security is simplified with a common infrastructure that supports a role-based security mechanism that is managed centrally. This mechanism means that the Windows NT administrator does not have to create component-specific Windows NT user accounts for each component. When a finer degree of security is required, the managed can define security at the service level of a component by user. Role based security is certainly scaleable, but declarative security at the component service level is not scaleable.

Our Chapter 17 business rambling is a client/server architecture that will use SQL Security along with domain security of Window NT workstations. The application is not scaleable, however there are very few users.

Lab 19.64 *Assess the potential impact of the physical design on performance, maintainability, extensibility, scalability, availability, and security*

A tiered architecture that uses MTS has improved performance, maintainability, extensibility, scalability, and availability. However it's not clear that security issues are scaleable. For example, declarative security lets the system manager manage access to a component at the service level, which is not scaleable.

Lab 19.65 *Evaluate whether access to a database should be encapsulated in an object*

A two-tier (client/server) architecture will be used for application described by the Chapter 17 business rambling. The application will have more than two tiers even though the architecture is technically called two-tier. Several of the tiers are create, read, update, and delete (CRUD) classes, which are generic classes. For example a CRUD DAO class is used for prototyping and testing. The delivered system will have the CRUD DAO class replaced by a CRUD RDO class. No programming is necessary other than to ascertain that a data source name (DSN) is defined. You'll find examples of using CRUD classes in Chapter 21.

CRUD classes represent significant reusability. Microsoft espouses component reusability, but this is system reusability. A reusable CRUD class is an asset in any developer's toolkit.

This objective is misleading and access to a database should always be encapsulated. The Microsoft 491 courseware recommends building a CRUD class for all applications.

Lab 19.66 *Design the properties, methods, and events of components*

Designing components in a tiered architecture with physically remote servers requires special consideration. A tiered architecture is scaleable, but when implemented incorrectly, the performance may be less than that of a two-tier architecture. The goal is logical design with tiered components is that the components do not retain state. MTS supports transactions with a rollback when the transaction fails, which is facilitated with stateless components.

Events

Events can be used for error declaration. When an error occurs in a Visual Basic error handler, the error is not processed locally but is passed back up the call tree to the next level, which is often the client. This is done with the **Err.Raise** method, which returns an error to the previous call level. This technique doesn't work with components managed by MTS since MTS passes its own error information back to the client.

Events must be used when business rules cross objects. This keeps the object synchronized. If possible, business rules should be contained within one object.

Methods

Each parameter of a method in a DCOM or MTS component architecture is a wire trip. The parameter declaration type is an important factor in method design. The *ByVal* declaration pushes data to the component in one wire trip. The most efficient DCOM component marshaling mechanism is to package all the parameters into one package (*custom marshaling*) and use *ByVal* as the declaration type. But this isn't always possible and on occasion *ByRef* must be used. The problem with *ByRef* is that data is marshaled both ways, both from and to the component. The developer's only choice to prevent unwanted data from being marshaled back to the client is to erase the data array before exiting the component's method. This means that at most an empty array is marshaled back to the client.

Properties

The Microsoft 491 courseware espouses creating data entities by discarding the methods of objects and mapping the resulting objects into data entities. The resulting entities are then normalized. What happens is that the data architecture is now bound to the process, which makes it fragile.

Accessing a property on a remote server requires a wire trip. Properties should be encapsulated with custom marshaling and returned to the requesting client in one wire trip. The remote component should expose the minimum functionality and properties.

Chapter 20 Labs

Lab 20.67 *Given a solution, identify the navigation for the user interface*

Let's start by enumerating the possible navigation metaphors:

- ***Static HTML*** — This type of Web-based application is universal. HTML is a standard and is supported by all browsers. Rendering is done at the client and deployment issues do not exist for standard HTML applications. The target audience is any Intranet/Intranet user. Functionality is minimal.

- ***Static DHTML***—Dynamic HTML (DHTML) is not yet a standard. DHTML is a richer interface than HTML. DHTML implementations vary between browsers, which means that the intended effect is not always created. The technology is suitable for a corporate Intranet with uniform browsers.

  Carefully coded DHTML applications can degrade gracefully when the client browser does not support DHTML. The target audience is limited with DHTML as the presentation tier technology.
- ***Active Server Pages (HTML or DHTML)***—Active Server Pages (ASP) can interrogate the client browser and send back the appropriate HTML, DHTML, ActiveX control, or Java applet. The target audience is any Intranet/Intranet user. The supported functionality is significantly more than the HTML paradigm.
- ***Java Applets***—Java applets require the Java language. The audience is nearly all browsers, however the Java Virtual Machine may vary between implementations. This is Microsoft's doing because Java was to be the universal web scripting language. Sun successfully sued Microsoft for varying from the Java specification.
- ***ActiveX Control/Documents***—This technology is for a corporate Intranet with uniform browsers on a Win32 platform. Deployment is automatic with components downloaded automatically from the Web server. Not all browsers support ActiveX and the audience is limited.
- ***Win32***—Win32 applications require a platform that supports COM. Applications can be written in any language that supports COM. Deployment is not scaleable and installations or updates are a manual process. The Win32 application has a very rich user interface.

The selection of a presentation metaphor is always a compromise between functionality and scalability. Maximum functionality always yields minimum scalability.

Identify the following:

1. **The most scaleable type of navigation.**

   The most scaleable type of application is an Active Server Page (ASP) application
2. **The least scaleable type of navigation.**

   The least scaleable type of application is a Win32 application.

3. **The navigation metaphor with the minimum functionality.**

   The navigation metaphor with the minimum functionality is an HTML application.

4. **The navigation metaphor with the maximum functionality.**

   The navigation metaphor with the maximum functionality is a Win32 application.

5. **Two types of navigation suitable for the application described by the business rambling in Chapter 17.**

   Either an Active Document application or a Win32 application is suitable for the application described in the Chapter 17 business rambling.

Lab 20.68 *Identify input validation procedures that should be integrated into the user interface*

All input data must be validated. The question of where the data is validated is a function of the application type. Browser applications are limited to domain validation of input fields. All fields are checked for domain values when a Microsoft Internet Explorer **OnSubmit** event occurs. The approach lacks elegance and a message box informs the user of input errors. Data validation with a Web-based application uses the brute force approach for client-side validation. Other validation is performed on the server. For example, the browser can only report that *PartNumber* is correctly numeric, however the server can report that the part number doesn't exist.

The elegance of design occurs with a Win32 application and not with a Web-based application. Win32 applications can validate data on a field by field basis. Microsoft has improved the process of field validation with the new **CausesValidation** property of a Visual Basic 6.0 text box, which is by default TRUE. A **Validate** event occurs when the user attempts to change focus with the **Tab** key. Each **Validate** event is specific to a control and must be individually coded, which makes this approach useful for small forms but not for large forms with many fields, a custom validation engine is a better choice.

Input data validation is minimized for either type of application when input is created by selecting items from a list or a combo box. The selected entry is placed in a read-only text box that the user cannot change. The user's only choice is to select another entry from the list or combo box. Such a technique only ascertains the domain values, and the context still needs to be validated.

Lab 20.69 *Evaluate methods of providing online user assistance, such as status bars, ToolTips, and Help files*

Each help type is listed below and each has a specific purpose:

- ***Context Sensitive Help*** — Selecting *What's This?* from a menu puts the user in context-sensitive mode. Context-sensitive help is available by clicking *What's This?* from the **Help** menu and then moving the mouse pointer over the object and clicking the left mouse button. During this operation the mouse pointer is considered a contextual pointer. The mouse will change to a combined question mark and arrow. If a user selects a menu title after selecting *What's This?*, keep the mode until something is selected.

  Context-sensitive help is also available by clicking the right mouse button. When the right mouse button is clicked over an object that supports a pop-up menu, maintain the context-sensitive mode until the user chooses something from the menu or cancels the menu.

  Context sensitive help should adhere to the look and feel within the system. Neither Windows NT 3.51 nor Windows 3.1 supports selecting *What's This?* from a menu.

  Depressing F1 is the shortcut key that presents contextual information for the object that has the input focus.
- ***Tooltips*** — Small pop-ups that display the name of a graphical icon. ToolTips do not have a label. Drag the mouse pointer over an object and hesitate for several seconds. The ToolTip will display the object name.
- ***Status Bar Help*** — Use the status bar to provide descriptive information about a menu or toolbar button that the user chooses. Always begin a message with a verb and in the present tense. Use only familiar terms and avoid jargon. Be specific when describing a command. Be constructive and not descriptive. Your goal is to inform the user about the command. The message should be brief, yet not truncated.
- ***Help Button*** — The help button is different from *What's This?*'s summary assistance, overview, or explanatory information. A help button is used for help from a property sheet, dialog box, or message box. The help button is included in the window. When the user presses the Help command button,

the help information is displayed in a Help secondary window and not in a contextual pop-up window. A wizard is always implemented in a secondary window. Selecting a help command from the **Help** command button starts a Help wizard. This, in turn, starts the Help Browser after the indexes and content are initialized.

- ***Task Help*** — Task help enumerates the steps for carrying out a task. The preferred window type is a primary window that the user can resize, move, maximize, or minimize. The window can support shortcut buttons and has command buttons that support access to the index and content pages of the Help Browser. The developer should use the default system windows colors for the task help window. This distinguishes the task help window from other application windows. The task help window standard has changed slightly. Microsoft added the "Clipit" wizard to the task help menu in Office 97.
- ***Reference Help*** — Reference help serves as the application's on-line documentation. Reference help is also presented in a primary window and the developer should use the default system colors for the window. The common use of this help style is from an explicit menu item in the Help drop-down menu with *Contents and Index* as the typical command. The user is initially presented the primary window of the Help Wizard. The bottom of the Help Wizard has the buttons *<Back>, Next, Finish,* and *Cancel.* Stepping through the different steps initializes the Help Browser. The user is presented with the Help Browser in a primary window and within the primary window are three tabs: **Contents**, **Index**, and **Find**.

  Reference help is written in the first person directly to the user. Personal pronouns such as "you" or "your" should be used. The text is written in the user's vernacular and jargon should not be used. The developer should realize that there are two different classes of users. Key words should be provided for beginning users and advanced users. The topic should be described generally and also described specifically. Don't insult the users and keep the writing simple, clear, concise, and not condescending. Be succinct, yet clear, with an economy of style. Watch for unneeded prepositional phrases.

Lab 20.70 *Construct a prototype user interface that is based on business requirements, user interface guidelines, and the organization's standards*

Prototyping is a useful adjunct to application when controlled. Not all systems require prototypes, but prototypes can address specific issues. Prototyping must have defined goals. Some useful prototyping goals include:

- A prototype can demonstrate the feasibility of the project. The risk is that the prototype model becomes the production system.
- Prototypes are useful tools for interacting with the user. The prototype in this case is merely a vehicle of expression that developers use to communicate concepts to the user. Interface prototypes are very useful. The contents behind the screens are immaterial, what's important is how the user interacts with the system.
- Programming is an iterative process. There's a very old saying that states: "Programming an application never solves the problem. It just gives us better insight to the nature of the problem." This class of prototyping confirms requirements and may discover new requirements.
- Prototypes are useful tools to either prove the technology or to develop an implementation approach. I have a current client that has a calendar scheduling system that I developed. The task required several prototypes to arrive at a satisfactory solution. Even after the algorithms were satisfactory, there was still the problem of mapping the prototype to the production model. This is the risk with fixed price software. You really can't afford to experiment since prototyping is an expensive proposition.
- Another use of prototyping is the evolution of a system. I prefer to call it scaffolding, which is temporary functionality. As production components are delivered, the scaffolding is removed on a piecemeal basis until the system consists of production components only. I used this technique for a major Univac 1108 operating system project in the late 60s, so the concept of prototyping as scaffolding is not new.

Establish appropriate and consistent use of menu-based controls

Application menus should mimic Microsoft functionality. Study Microsoft menus carefully before implementing your own menu system. When your menu uses a common command such as **Exit,** ensure that it is placed last. Also ensure that the command is placed in the proper menu. The **Exit** command is always the last entry of the **File** menu. This means that applications must have a **File** menu for an **Exit** command even though there may be no other commands in the file menu.

Be accurate with menu commands. When an object remains active even though the window is closed, use the **Close** command rather than the **Exit** command.

Menus come in three forms: drop-down menus, pop-up menus, and cascading menus:

- ***Drop-Down Menus*** — Dragging downward and releasing over an item "chooses" an entry from the menu. Alternately, the Alt key can be used followed by cursor positioning keys. There are five classes of drop-down menus:
  - ***File Menu*** — Commands such as **Open, Save, Send,** or **Print**. If an **Exit** is used, place it at the end.
  - ***Edit Menu*** — Commands such as **Undo, Repeat, Find and Replace, Delete,** and **Duplicate**.
  - ***View Menu*** — Includes commands for changing the user's view of data in the window.
  - ***Window Menu*** — Used in multiple-document interface (MDI)-style applications.
  - ***Help Menu*** — Include the **About** *<application name>* here.
- ***Pop-Up menus*** — A pop-up menu is similar to a drop-down menu except there is no title. A pop-up menu is contextual to the selected object(s). It is not to be used for general purposes. A control can support a pop-up menu. When a pop-up menu is supported, it is contextual to what the control represents, rather than to the control itself. Therefore, do not include commands such as **Set, Check,** or **Uncheck**. The exception is in forms design or window layout context, where the commands on the pop-up menu can apply to the control itself.

  Commands in a pop-up menu may not always be supplied by the object but may be a combination of commands from the object and from the container. **Properties** is last in a pop-up menu. **What's This?** is next to last in a pop-up menu.

Your pop-up menu should follow conventional command ordering. The rule of thumb is that the most frequently referenced items are always placed first in the menu. Some generic pop-up menus are offered below as a design guideline:

- Pop-up menu command order

  Open, Play, Print

  Cut, Copy, Paste, Paste Link

- Application file pop-up menu

  Cut, Copy, Create Link, Delete, What's This, Properties

- MDI application pop-up menu

  Close (or Exit), Save All, Insert New, Find, What's This?, Properties

- ***Cascading Menus*** — Cascading menus should be limited to a single level. The visual cue is the side arrow. User interaction is the same with a cascading menu as with that of a drop-down menu except that the cascading menu displays after a short timeout to avoid a flashing effect.

Establish appropriate shortcut keys (accelerated keys)

Accelerated keys are keys or key combinations that provide rapid access to functionality without the use of the mouse. The Microsoft architecture contains many standard accelerated keys such as CTRL N in the **File** menu. Accelerated keys are a requirement for power-users. Factors to consider when implementing accelerated keys:

- Always assign single letters when possible.
- Modified-letter assignments should be case insensitive. *CTRL N* or *CTRL n* should initiate the same action.
- Look and feel issues apply to accelerated keys. Use the Microsoft conventions for standard menu features such as *CTRL N* or *CTRL O* for **New** and **Open** respectively in the file menu.
- Use SHIFT to complement an action. An example is the Microsoft defined ALT+TAB combination that switches between windows in a top to bottom order. SHIFT+ALT+TAB reverses the functionality and switches between windows from bottom to top. SHIFT+*text* may conflict with international keyboards and should be avoided.

- Amplify effects with CTRL+*key*. An example of this is HOME moves to the start of a line; CTRL+HOME moves to the beginning of the text.

  CTRL is used for access to commands with a single letter. For example CTRL+I places text in italics. Pressing CTRL+I again returns the text to normal.
- Do not use ALT+*key* sequences. Such a sequence may conflict with Microsoft defined ALT sequences such as ALT+TAB, ALT+ESC, or ALT+SPACEBAR.
- Letter keys can only be assigned once. Once CTRL+N is defined in the **File** menu, the sequence cannot be used in other menus.
- When possible, give the power-user the opportunity to change a shortcut key. Accelerated keys are created at run time within Microsoft Visual Basic by prefixing the **Caption** property with the ampersand <&> character and are correspondingly removed by deleting <&> from the **Caption** property.
- Use the ESC key as the standard key to stop a function. The ESC key is equivalent to the **Cancel** button.

Lab 20.71 *Establish appropriate type of output. Types of output include paper-based reports, HTML, screen, disk, and export of data to other applications*

The type of application determines the type of application output, which is determined during requirements analysis. The word scalability is an ongoing theme in this book. Scalability issues also apply to application output. Let's look at the types of application output defined by this objective:

- ***Paper-Based Reports*** — Typically this is a Win32 application, but that's not necessarily correct. Microsoft Access has a very rich report writer, however Microsoft Access is not scaleable.

  Microsoft Visual Basic ships with Crystal Reports, a third-party report writer. Crystal Reports is commonly used with Visual Basic applications. Visual Basic programs are scaleable to the degree permitted by Microsoft Transaction Server, but is a paper-based output Visual Basic application scaleable? Possibly if its an Intranet application.

  Microsoft Windows NT Option Pack 4 installs Active Server Pages (ASP), Windows Scripting Host (WSH), and Microsoft Visual Basic Scripting

Edition (VBScript). These technologies, when combined, allow an ASP application to create printed reports. The code below, although incomplete, illustrates the general technique of ASP printing. The code snippet below assumes that the HTTP POST method supplied the *printerpath* **Form** element.

```
<%
      strPrintPath = Request.Form("printerpath")
      strUsername = Request.Form("username")
      strPassword = Request.Form("message")
      Set objFs = CreateObject("Scripting.FileSystemObject")
      Set objWSHNet = CreateObject("WScript.Network")
      objWSHNet.AddPrinterConnection "LPT1", _
           strPrintPath, False, strUsername, strPassword
      Set objPrinter = objFs.CreateTextFile("LPT1: ", True)
            objPrinter.Write(strMessage) ' Print the message
      %>
```

This is not a secure mechanism, but it does illustrate the issue of printing to network printers over an Intranet. The only issue is that the network connection should be a Secure Sockets Layer (SSL), which protects the user name and password.

In summary, paper-based output is not scaleable. Either each user must have a printer, or there is the additional effort of creating accounts and assigning print permissions to the network printer.

- ***HTML*** — HTML applications are scaleable, at least to the degree of compatibility between browsers. The ASP can adjust the outgoing HTML for browser differences. Since we're only discussing output and not input, Internet catalogs or Yellow Pages are a good example of HTML output that is scaleable.
- ***Screen*** — Screen-based output is loosely interpreted as a Win32 application, which is not scaleable. The user can preserve screen data by using the mouse and copying and pasting the data to a file. This is not desirable since the data is not managed. The only realistic use of screen output is the monitoring of volatile real-time data such as a ticker-tape.

- ***Disk*** — Applications don't normally write directly to the disk and the context is disk files. Is disk file output acceptable? No, disk files are not scaleable. The only acceptable output to a disk must be managed, which implies a database. Access to a database is scaleable within the constraints of the selected architecture.
- ***Exporting Data*** — We know that access to a database is scaleable within the constraints of an architecture. Exporting disk files to another application is certainly not scaleable, but there are other choices. Active Data Objects (ADO) is the universal data access mechanism. Data can be exported in ADO **Recordset** objects. Another export mechanism is Microsoft SQL Server. I'm not talking about replication, since that's not scaleable, but the e-mailing of a query to an intended recipient. The neat fact about this architecture is that the recipient receives the SQL Server query without establishing a connection to the database; the surrogate established the connection. The exporting of data is scaleable when properly managed.

APPENDIX

D

About the CD-ROM

CD-ROM Contents

The CD-ROM included with this book contains the following materials:

- Adobe Acrobat Reader
- An electronic version of this book, *Solution Architectures MCSD Study System,* in .pdf format
- BeachFront Quizzer exam simulation software
- Code examples from the book
- Microsoft Internet Explorer version 5.0
- *Micro House Technical Library* (demo)
- Microsoft TechNet (trial version)

Installing and Using Items on the CD-ROM

The following sections describe each product and include detailed instructions for installation and use.

The Adobe Acrobat Reader Version of *Solution Architectures MCSD Study System*

Adobe's Acrobat Reader is a helpful program that will enable you to view the electronic version of this book in the same page format as the actual book.

To install and run Adobe's Acrobat Reader and view the electronic version of this book, follow these steps:

1. Start Windows Explorer (if you're using Windows 95/98) or Windows NT Explorer (if you're using Windows NT), and then open the `Acrobat Reader` folder on the CD-ROM.
2. In the `Acrobat Reader` folder, double-click `rs40eng.exe` and follow the instructions presented onscreen for installing Adobe Acrobat Reader.
3. To view the electronic version of this book after you have installed Adobe's Acrobat Reader, start Windows Explorer (if you're using Windows 95) or Windows NT Explorer (if you're using Windows NT), and then open the `Book` folder on the CD-ROM.
4. In the `Book` folder, double-click the chapter or appendix file you want to view

BeachFront Quizzer

The version of BeachFront Quizzer software included on the CD gives you an opportunity to test your knowledge with practice questions. The BeachFront Quizzer product has many valuable features, including:

- Study session
- Standard exam
- Adaptive exam
- New exam every time
- Historical analysis

The questions in the BeachFront Quizzer product included on the CD-ROM are based on Chapters 1 through 16 of this book. If you want more simulation questions, you can purchase the full retail version of the BeachFront Quizzer software from BeachFront Quizzer. See the BeachFront Quizzer ad in the back of the book.

To install and run BeachFront Quizzer, follow these steps:

1. View the contents of the BeachFront folder
2. Execute `ExamName`.exe, whereas `ExamName` is the name of the exam you wish to practice.
3. Follow the directions for installation.

(Authorship by Bruce Prendergast does not imply affiliation with, or endorsement of, BeachFrontQuizzer)

Code Examples

All of the code examples for this book are located on the CD-ROM. The parent folder name is EXAMPLES and an example folder is <unit>\EXAMPLES\CHAPTER1. In general the examples are not code fragments, but small working pieces of code that illustrate functionality. All functions run unless otherwise stated. The code examples on the CD are inventoried in table D-1.

TABLE D-1 CODE EXAMPLE INVENTORY

Folder	*Description*
Chapter1	This chapter has two Visual Basic 5.0/6.0 labs. The first lab illustrates *creating an interface* and the second lab illustrates *delegation* to a base class. The CHECKBOOK.VBP project builds a Visual Basic interface class. The CUSTOMER.VBP project delegates to a base class.
Chapter3	The Visual Basic 5.0/6.0 Enterprise Edition project ICHECKBOOK.VBP is located in this folder. This is the ActiveX control example developed within the chapter.
Chapter4	The PROPERTY.VBP project illustrates building a property bag (**IPropertyBag** interface).
Chapter6	The CUSTOMER.VBP project illustrates an advisory sink (**IAdviseSink** interface) with the Microsoft Visual Basic **RaiseEvent** keyword.
Chapter8	This is not an executable example. The file BLOB.BMP located in this folder is used with the laboratories of Chapter 8.
Chapter9	There are many Automation examples in this folder. The examples are in an Access 97 AUTO.MDB database or in the Visual Basic 5.0/6.0 Enterprise Edition AUTO.VBP project.
Chapter10	The CALLBACK.VBP demonstrates a Microsoft Visual Basic *callback*. The PROPPAGE.VBP project builds a component property page.

continued

TABLE D-1 CODE EXAMPLE INVENTORY *(continued)*

FOLDER	*DESCRIPTION*
Chapter12	This chapter is dedicated to the ODBC API examples. The ODBC examples were developed using ODBC 3.0 and Microsoft Visual Basic 6.0 Enterprise edition. The examples within the ODBC.VBP project demonstrate an ODBC API function from each logical grouping of ODBC API functions. The folder also contains the ODBC class and the ODBC class driver components. These components are used in a lab to build a project that processes Unicode queries transparently. In the ODBC.VBP project modify the connection string within the **Initialize** event of the **ODBCClass** class: BTPSQLConnect(hdbc, "Thor", 4, "sa", 2, "", 0) to reflect the DSN of the local SQL Server.
Chapter13	This is the first of two RDO chapters. The chapter examples are located in the Visual Basic Enterprise Edition 6.0 CHAPTER13.VBP project. The lab at the conclusion of the chapter is found in the RDO.VBP project. In the CHAPTER13.VBP project modify the connection string within each of the **Command** button **Click** events to reflect the proper local DSN connection string: **Starting_rdoEngine_Click** event: "DATABASE=Pubs;UID=sa;PWD=;DSN=Thor;" **Register_DataSource_Click** event: "Address=\\Thor\PIPE\SQL\QUERY" **Transactions_Click** event: "DATABASE=Pubs;UID=sa;PWD=;DSN=Thor;" **Asynchronous_Click** event: "DATABASE=Pubs;UID=sa;PWD=;DSN=Thor;" **RdoTables_Click** event: "DATABASE=Pubs;UID=sa;PWD=;DSN=Thor;" In the RDO.VBP project modify the connection string within the **Initialize** event of the **RDOClass** class: "DATABASE=pubs;UID=sa;PWD=;DSN=Thor;" to reflect the DSN of the local SQL Server.
Chapter14	The chapter examples are located in the Visual Basic Enterprise Edition 6.0 CHAPTER14.VBP project. The lab at the conclusion of the chapter is found in the RDO.VBP project.

Folder	*Description*
	In the CHAPTER14.VBP project modify the connection string within each of the **Command** button **Click** events to reflect the proper local DSN connection string: **GetRows_Click** event: "DATABASE=Pubs;UID=sa;PWD=;DSN=Thor;" **MoreResults_Click** event: "DATABASE=Pubs;UID=sa;PWD=;DSN=Thor;" **ODBC_API_Click** event: "DATABASE=Pubs;UID=sa;PWD=;DSN=Thor;" **Updating_Rowsets_Click** event: "DATABASE=Pubs;UID=sa;PWD=;DSN=Thor;" In the RDO.VBP project modify the connection string within the **Initialize** event of the RDOClass class: "DATABASE=pubs;UID=sa;PWD=;DSN=Thor;" to reflect the DSN of the local SQL Server.
Chapter15	This is the first of two ADO chapters. There are no chapter examples in this folder and the lab at the conclusion of Chapter 16 is found in the Visual Basic Enterprise Edition 6.0 ADO.VBP project. In the ADO.VBP project modify the connection string within the **Initialize** event of the **ADOClass** class: "DATABASE=pubs;UID=sa;PWD=;DSN=Thor;" to reflect the DSN of the local SQL Server.
Chapter16	The chapter examples are located in the Visual Basic Enterprise Edition 6.0 CHAPTER16.VBP project. The QUESTION.VBP project is the lab at the conclusion of Chapter 16. In the QUESTION.VBP project modify the connection string within the **adoDatabaseClass** class **SelectQuery** function connection string: "Database=pubs;DSN=Thor;Uid=sa;pwd=;" to reflect the DSN of the local SQL Server. In the CHAPTER16.VBP project modify the connection string within the **ConnectionEvent_Click** event of the CHAPTER16 form: "Server=Apollo;Uid=sa;Pwd=;Database=pubs" to reflect the DSN of the local SQL Server.

continued

TABLE D-1 CODE EXAMPLE INVENTORY *(continued)*

FOLDER	*DESCRIPTION*
Chapter21	Chapter 21 is the last chapter of the book, which is distributed COM. This folder contains the VTABLEINTERFACE.VBP project, which verifies that the Microsoft **Implements** statement creates a vTable. The second project in this folder is the DCOMDAO.VBP project, which is an extensive create, read, update, and delete (CRUD) class for the Chapter 21 lab. In the DCOMDAO.VBP project, the path in the **DatabaseClass** module **Declarations** section must be modified to reflect the current EXAMPLES folder installation. Modify the statement fragment: "G:\Examples\CHAPTER21\DCOMDAO.MDB" to reflect the current path to the EXAMPLES folder.

The Host Environment

I used more than one operating system while writing this book. All examples were developed using Windows NT, and the standard Windows NT hardware requirements should be satisfactory. The minimum suggested memory is 64 MB although I've had Automation errors that disappeared only after converting to 128 MB. The development systems are:

- ***Windows NT Workstation 3.51 SP 5*** — This system is a 133MHz and131MB system. The examples were initially developed on this system in Visual Basic 5.0 Enterprise edition. Visual Studio 6.0 had not yet shipped when the examples were developed.
- ***Windows NT Server 4.0 SP 4*** — This is the primary development system, which is a 128 MB dual-processor Pentium 90. Microsoft Visual Studio 6.0 Enterprise edition and Microsoft Office 97 are installed on this system.
- ***Windows 95*** — This is a 48 MB Pentium 90 that served as the client for Microsoft SQL Server operations.
- ***Windows NT Server 4.0 SP 3*** — This is a Digital Equipment Corporation Alpha with SQL Server 6.5 SP 3 installed. The Windows 95 clients access Microsoft SQL Server 6.5 over a network.

Installing the Examples

No installation procedure is required. These examples do not modify the registry and are designed to run stand-alone. The only installation procedure recommended is to open File Manager and drag the EXAMPLES folder of the CD-ROM to a root directory of a hard disk. The EXAMPLES folder requires 7.9MB of space on your hard drive. This places an EXAMPLES folder in the root of your hard drive and the book examples may be run from there.

Running the Examples

There isn't a need to run the examples since each example normally demonstrates a specific issue. Just copy and paste the code for use in your own applications. Running the Visual Basic Examples is relatively easy. Start Visual Basic 5.0 or 6.0. (You'll need the Enterprise Edition for the RDO examples.) To start:

1. From the **File** menu select *Open Project*
2. Browse for the Visual Basic project of interest
3. Select OK

   After the project is loaded, Select *Start with Full Compile* from the **Run** menu.

When the Examples Don't work

Many examples require SQL Server. When SQL Server is available, the login to SQL Server must be changed to reflect your SQL Server. Code for the examples is normally behind a command button. In Visual Basic, double-click the command button and modify the login.

The expected problems with Visual Basic will be with missing type libraries, missing controls, or the wrong version when Visual Basic 5.0/6.0 is not the Enterprise Edition. If the Visual Basic project reports an error on opening, exit Visual Basic without saving the project. Open the .VBP project in Notepad and examine the first few lines. Some example lines from the CHAPTER14.VBP are shown below:

```
Type=Exe
Reference=*\G{00020430-0000-0000-
C000-000000000046}#2.0#0#I:\NTWS351\System32\STDOLE2.TLB#OLE
Automation
```

```
Reference=*\G{EE008642-64A8-11CE-920F-
08002B369A33}#2.0#0#I:\NTWS351\System32\MSRDO20.DLL#Microsoft
Remote Data Object 2.0
Form=Chapter14.frm
Startup="Chapter14"
```

You can see that Chapter 14 requires the MSRDO20.DLL. In the **Tools** menu of Visual Basic Code Editor, you'll want to select *References* and browse for MSRDO20.DLL on your own system.

My email address for this book is bruce@prendergast.com. I will provide help with running the examples and updated examples if necessary. Just remember that I am not a company with a help desk.

Microsoft Internet Explorer Version 5.0

A complete copy of Microsoft Internet Explorer is included on the CD-ROM. You can use Internet Explorer to browse the Internet if you have an Internet connection.

To install and run Microsoft Internet Explorer, follow these steps:

1. Start Windows Explorer (if you're using Windows 95/98) or Windows NT Explorer (if you're using Windows NT), and then open the `\Msie40` folder on the CD-ROM.
2. In the `\Msie40`, double-click `Setup.exe` and follow the instructions presented onscreen for installing Microsoft Internet Explorer.
3. To run Microsoft Internet Explorer, double-click the Internet Explorer icon on the desktop.

Micro House Technical Library (Demo)

Micro House Technical Library is a useful CD-ROM-based set of encyclopedias that contains hardware-configuration information. This evaluation copy of *Micro House Technical Library* includes only the Encyclopedia of I/O cards. Use this evaluation copy to determine whether or not you want to purchase the full version of the *Micro House Technical Library*.

To install and access the *Micro House Technical Library,* follow these steps:

1. Start Windows Explorer (if you're using Windows 95/98) or Windows NT Explorer (if you're using Windows NT), and then open the `Micro House` folder on the CD-ROM.
2. In the `Micro House` folder, double-click `Install.exe` and follow the instructions presented onscreen for installing the *Micro House Technical Library*.
3. To run the *Micro House Technical Library,* select Start ➪ Programs ➪ MH Tech Library ➪ MTL Demo Edition.

Microsoft TechNet (Trial Version)

The Microsoft TechNet CD subscription product delivers the most complete and current source of Microsoft technical information right to your desktop. A one-year subscription includes an initial shipment of more than 20 CDs, thereafter a minimum of three CD updates are sent monthly. That's a total of more than 50 CDs included with a one-year subscription.

The trial version of TechNet located on this CD is a 30-day evaluation copy of the January 1999 Technical Information CD, one of the 50+ CDs a one-year TechNet subscription delivers. Check out the trial version to evaluate a portion of the content TechNet CD subscribers receive monthly.

Annual subscribers receive:

- The complete Microsoft Knowledge Base, the same database of technical support information developed and used by Microsoft support engineers
- Troubleshooting tips, workarounds and technical notes
- Microsoft Resource Kits, deployment guides and compatibility lists
- Current service packs, drivers and patches, utilities and 3rd party tools
- Strategy and white papers, case studies and training materials
- And much more

A subscription is a must have for any IT professional who evaluates, deploys or supports Microsoft products. To subscribe in the US or Canada, call (800) 344-2121 ext. 3442 or click to `http://www.microsoft.com/technet/cd/`.

System requirements include:

- PC with a 386DX/33 MHz or higher processor
- Microsoft Windows 3.1 or later operating system or Windows NT Workstation operating system version 3.51 or later
- 8 MB of RAM for Windows 95 or Windows 3.1; 16 MB for Windows 98 or Windows NT Workstation 3.51 or later operating system
- 2 MB of available hard-disk space
- CD-ROM drive compatible with MPC Level 1 specifications
- Microsoft Compact Disc Extensions (MSCDEX) version 2.2 or later and compatible CD-ROM driver
- VGA or higher-resolution video adapter
- Microsoft Mouse or compatible pointing device

To install and access TechNet from Windows 95, Windows 98 or Windows NT Workstation 4.0, TechNet Setup will start automatically when the CD is inserted into the CD-ROM drive.

To install and access TechNet from Windows 3.1, Windows for Workgroups version 3.11 or Windows NT Workstation 3.51:

1. Insert the CD into the CD-ROM drive.
2. Start File Manager.
3. In File manager, select the CD-ROM drive, double-click SETUP.EXE and follow the directions that appear on the screen.

Component Technology Glossary

This COM glossary contains common terms or terms that represent an architectural issue. By architectural issue I mean only the common terms in relation to an application. An interface such as **IUknown** represents an architectural issue, while methods of an interface do not represent an architectural issue. For this reason methods are not included in this glossary, and many methods such as **CreateFileMoniker** are self-explanatory. This rule is bent a bit because some of the ubiquitous methods such as **QueryInterface** are included in this glossary.

There are many COM interfaces not mentioned in this glossary. The goal is to give you, the reader, an understanding of the core terminology. For specific object and interface implementation details, see the Microsoft platform software development kit (SDK) for further documentation.

The (::) is known in C++ as the scope resolution operator and is used in different contexts within this glossary. **IUnknown::QueryInterface** is an example, which is read as: Use the **Query Interface** method of the class **IUnknown**.

Activation Activation is the conversion of an object to a running state with binding, or the invoking of an operation on the object such as editing or playback. (See *primary verb*.)

Active One of the four states of object presentation, the other three states are *inactive*, *open*, and *selected*. These states apply to an OLE 2.0 server object or to an ActiveX(tm) component acting in the role of a server object. An active object is identified by the diagonal hatched border along with eight sizing handles surrounding the object. Object presentation states are different than object states, which may be *passive*, *loaded*, or *running*.

ActiveX™ A stand-alone component with methods, properties, and events that are used to perform a unique task. These components (controls) are contrasted with DLLs that only contain methods. ActiveX™ and OLE controls are both COM based. OLE controls was renamed ActiveX™ for marketing reasons.

ActiveX™ Client An OLE Automation controller is now known as an ActiveX™ client. The client manipulates the exposed methods of an ActiveX™ component (OLE Automation server) resulting in programming of the component.

ActiveX™ Component ActiveX™ Components were formally known as OLE Automation Servers. Today they are known as an ActiveX™ components acting in the role of servers.

ActiveX™ Control See OLE Control.

ActiveX™ Object Synonym for an ActiveX™ component.

Adaptable links A feature of OLE technology. The link to the link source is maintained when an object is moved to another location. This presupposes that when the object is moved, the link source remains in the same or relative location. An example is a Word document with an embedded spreadsheet. The links remain intact when the document is moved to another location as long as the location of Microsoft Excel remains unchanged. An object may be linked to a complete or a partial object. A link to a partial object is known as a pseudo object. An example is selected rows and columns from an Excel spreadsheet.

Advisory Sink The ActiveX™ interface **IAdviseSink** supports user notification of embedded object changes while the interface **IAdviseSink2** supports user notification of linked object changes.

Aggregate object The aggregate object is the object implementing **IUnknown**, a pointer of which is supplied to the created (aggregated) object at creation time. The aggregate object is designated the controlling **IUnknown** object.

Aggregation Aggregation is the reuse of an object and requires support from the inner aggregated object. The controlling (aggregate) object passes it's **IUnknown** pointer to the control (aggregated) object at creation time. This will be a pointer to the controlling object **IUnknown** interface and is done by either **CoCreateInstance** or **IClassFactory::CreateInstance** when creating the aggregated object. When done, **IUnknown** of the control object reports all interfaces through the **QueryInterface** method. This means that the aggregated object must provide an **IUnknown** interface that is separate from all other interfaces. With such an interface, the parent (controlling) object can call **IUnknown::QueryInterface** of the aggregated object and expose those interfaces as if they belonged to the parent object. This is the reporting of the InterfaceX and InterfaceY along with the inherited InterfaceZ shown in Figure GL-1. The control object was delegated the responsibility of reporting InterfaceZ by the aggregated object. Aggregation can be likened to a shell or wrapper where the internal functioning does not change, but a unified interface of all services is presented to the client. A common example of aggregation is **IPersistFile::QueryInterface** where the **IPersistFile** interface is aggregated with the **IUnknown** interface and **QueryInterface** is a method of the **IUnknown** interface. The **QueryInterface** method appears as a service of the **IPersistFile** interface to the client even though it is a method of the **IUnknown** interface.

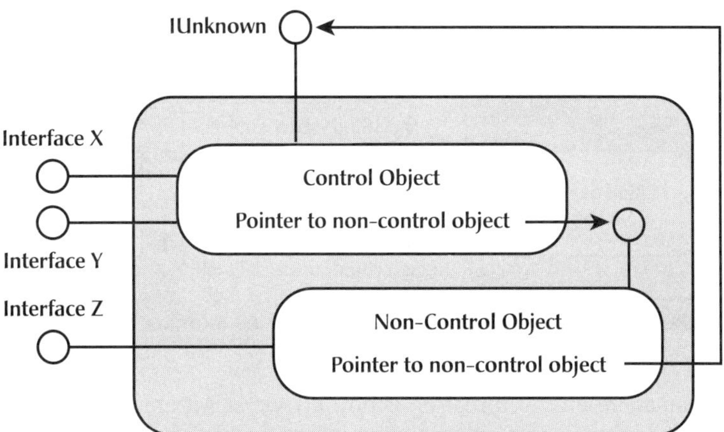

FIGURE GL-1 The internal structure of an aggregate.

Ambient property A container property that is exposed to hosted embedded objects. Controls retrieve and set the ambient properties supported by the container.

Apartment model COM objects were single-threaded before Windows NT 4.0, hence the name apartment model. *Fre-threading* or *multi-threading* is now available with Windows NT 4.0.

Artificial reference counting The life of the object is controlled by the reference count that is increments with **AddRef** and decrements with **Release**. Artificially setting the reference count high safeguards the object when a destructive function call is made. (Great way to disguise a bug!)

Asynchronous call A function call which returns control immediately to the caller. Some of the functions implementing asynchronous calls are **IAdviseSink**, **OnDataChange**, and **OnViewChange**.

Asynchronous moniker A moniker that returns control to the client before the binding process is complete, as in URL binding. The client registers the **IBind StatusCallback** interface for asynchronous binding as illustrated in Figure GL-2 below. (See Synchronous Moniker.)

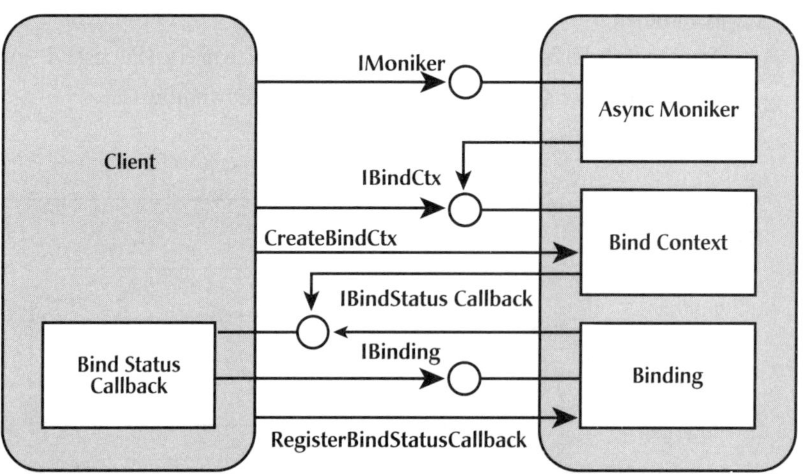

FIGURE GL-2 The relationship of asynchronous moniker interfaces.

Automation OLE Automation is now known as Automation. An Automation application exposes its methods and properties for programmability through dispinterfaces for manipulation by a client.

Automation Controller A tool such as Microsoft Visual Basic or Microsoft Access which can control the exposed properties and methods of another object. Typically an Automation controller cannot be controlled, but this is not a limitation with VBA ubiquitous in the Microsoft architecture. Access and Excel are good Automation controllers since they support drag-and-drop along with in-place editing. None of these features are supported by Microsoft Word, hence Microsoft Word is a good Automation server, but not a good Automation controller.

Binding The process of activating an object or placing the object in a running state. Binding uses the **IMoniker** interface.

Cache Presentation data is stored in cache as a metafile and is rendered by the default object handler. See the **IOleCache2** interface.

Class factory table The storage location for an object's registered CLSID.

Class identifier (CLSID) A unique 128-bit identifier associated with an ActiveX™ or OLE object. Clients can locate and load objects identified by a CLSID maintained in a registration database.

Client A container by definition and any program that uses OLE or ActiveX™ controls.

Clipboard The clipboard is a cut-copy-paste model for simple data sharing between Microsoft Windows applications. It is a loosely coupled exchange medium where the applications only agree on the data format. The providing application places the data on the clipboard and the receiving application chooses from the available formats.

CoCreateGUID A helper function for creating a GUID. Other useful helper functions include **IsEqualGUID**, **IsEqualIID**, and **IsEqualCLSID**.

CoCreateInstance A method of the COM library for creating a single object. The client provides a CLSID and COM delegates the work of creating the object to the Service Control Manager.

CoCreateStandardMalloc See IMalloc.

CoGetMalloc See IMalloc.

COM OLE and ActiveX™ are both based on COM. OLE is an older term for ActiveX™. OLE technology now refers only to linking and embedding technology and all other technologies are known as ActiveX™. The infrastructure of COM includes: interface negotiation, memory management, error and reporting status, communication, structured storage, data transfer, naming, and binding. COM uses a binary interface specification that is language independent.

COM library Every implementation of COM requires a COM library. Starting a server is the primary purpose of the COM library. COM library functions start with the character sequence <co>.

COM object COM objects are always implemented within a server. The object may be implemented within an in-process server, a local server, or a remote server. All COM objects must support the **IUnknown** interface and all interfaces to a COM object are derived from the **IUnknown** interface that consists of three methods: **QueryInterface**, **AddRef**, and **Release**. The life of the object is controlled by the reference count that is increments with **AddRef** and decrements with **Release**. The client determines the services available with the interface **QueryInterface**. Implementation inheritance is not supported and reuse of objects occurs with aggregation or containment (delegation).

Compound documents See OLE.

Compound files A file consisting of a Root object and an indeterminate number of stream and storage objects. Common usage is to store all the embedded objects of a container in a compound file. OLE applications are not required to use structured storage. (See structured storage.)

Connectable objects Connectable objects can communicate back to the client object. An additional interface other than **IAdviseSink** is used to implement the **IConnectionPointContainer** interface. The **IConnectionPoint** interface is the server outgoing connection and the client outgoing connection **IOutgoing** pointer of Figure GL-3 is passed to the server via the **IConnectionPoint Container** interface. Figure GL-3 represents the basic architecture of connectable objects.

The **IAdviseSink** - **IDataObject** advisory architecture is limited in that a client can only pass an **IAdviseSink** interface pointer to **IDataObject**. Compare this with the **IContainer** interface, which can pass the pointer of any interface to the **IConnectableContainer** interface. An **IConnectionPointContainer** may support more than one **IConnectionPoint** interface and more than one **IConnection Point** interface may use the same **IConnectionPointContainer** interface. Figures GL-4 and GL-5 represent the one-to-many and many-to-one relationships of connectable objects.

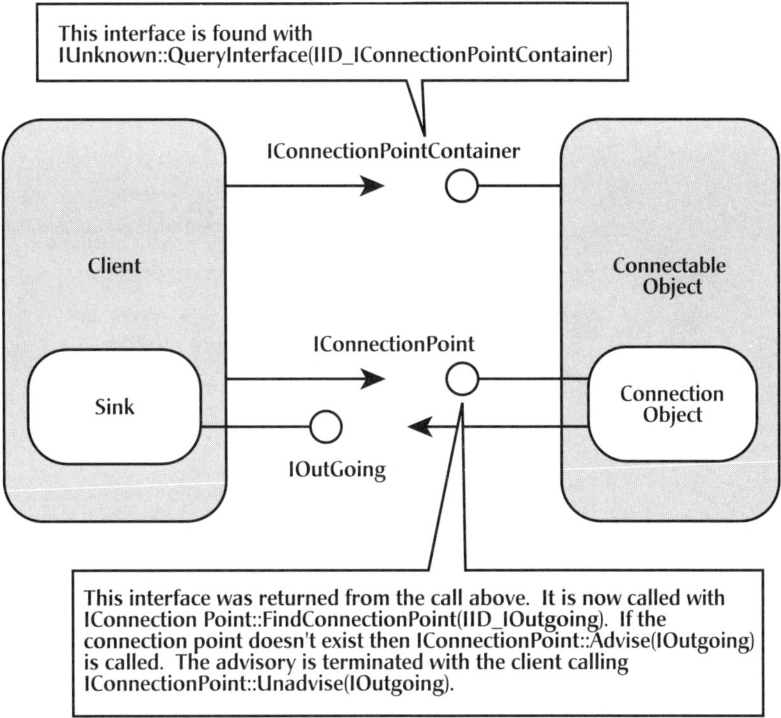

FIGURE GL-3 The mechanics of a connectable object.

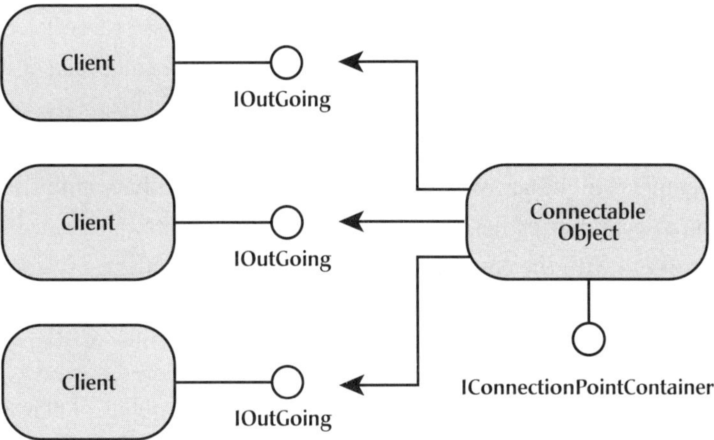

FIGURE GL-4 A many-to-one connectable object relationship.

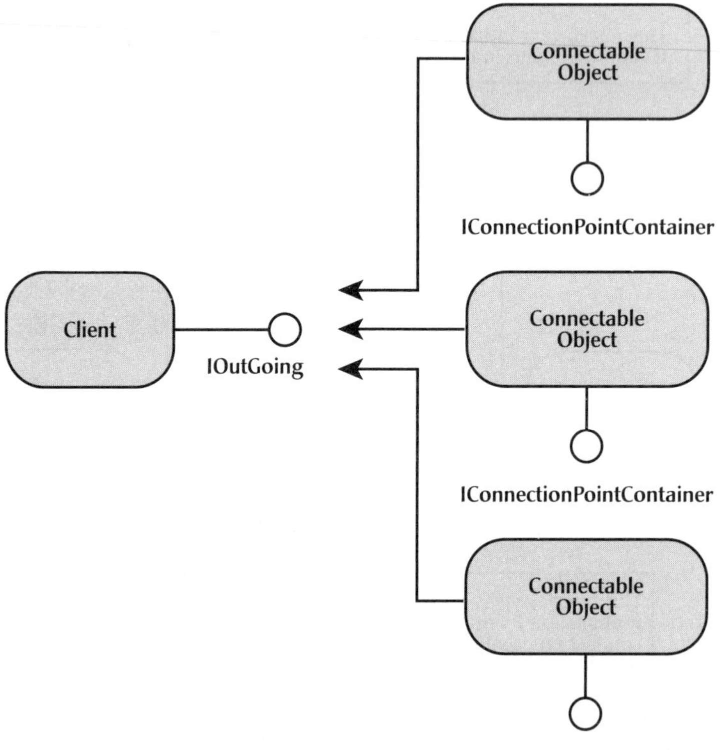

FIGURE GL-5 A one-to-many connectable object relationship.

Container A container offers sites to ActiveX™ controls or DocObjects (formally known as an OLE Document). The DocObject may be embedded or linked in a container object or it can be imbedded in another DocObject. Restated in the current vernacular, a container may be embedded within another container. Only one document will be active at any given time. Containers have ambient properties. The object inherits these properties and transforms its appearance to be more consistent with the object's container.The container offers services to the object. A special example is a windowless object where all interactive services are supplied by the container.

Containment Figure GL-6 illustrates delegation of a contained object and a public accessible object. InterfaceY, a contained and delegated object, is a client of the control object and direct user access is not possible. InterfaceY cannot distinguish control between client access or access by the control object and does not know that direct client access is impossible. Containment is the encapsulation of a delegated object. There is no specific requirement that a delegated object be encapsulated. The delegated object can be any publicly accessible COM component, as illustrated with InterfaceZ of Figure GL-6. Both InterfaceY and InterfaceZ of Figure GL-6 are delegated by the control object. The parent object in Figure GL-6 calls **CoCreateInstance** on CLSID_<inner object> asking for IID_InterfaceY of the contained object when the parent object is created. The parent object implements and maintains interfaces of delegated and contained objects. InterfaceZ is a public object and the interface is known or obtainable.

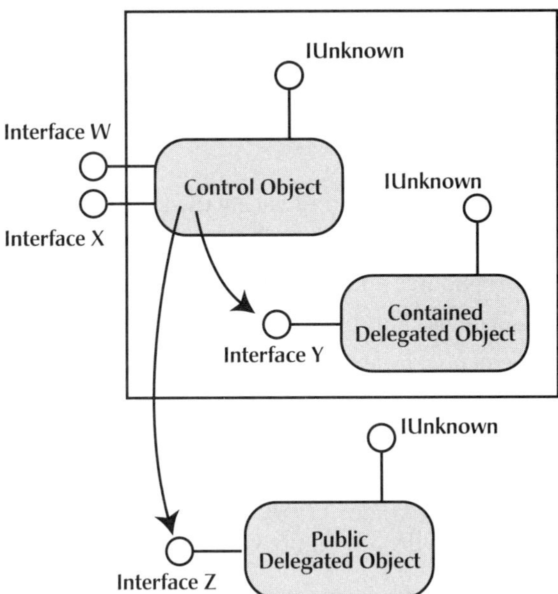

FIGURE GL-6 The delegated object is a client of the controlling object.

Contract A contract is said to exist between a COM object and a client. Once published, the interface cannot change.

CreateBindCtx Creates an instance of a bind context and returns an **IBindCtx** pointer.

Data transfer object An object that implements the interface **IDataObject** for the transfer of data between the clipboard, drag and drop, or Automation operations. Objects conforming to the Uniform Data Transfer model implement the **IData Object** interface.

Default object handler A default handler provided by the OLE/ActiveX™ SDK that provides support for basic tasks such as rendering.

Delegation See containment.

Direct mode All changes are immediately committed. (See transacted mode.)

DISPID An index identifying a dispinterface method or function.

Dispinterfaces Another name for an **IDispatch** interface. These interfaces use a DISPID integer for identifying the method.

DocObject Synonym for OLE Document. See OLE.

Document See OLE.

Drag and drop Drag and drop is the most widely used method for transferring data between applications and the Clipboard. Drag and drop is implemented with the two interfaces **IDropSource** and **IDrop Target**. **DoDragDrop** is an API function which implements a loop used for tracking mouse and keyboard movement. **IDropSource** is implemented by any object containing data which can be dropped onto another interface. **IDropTarget** is implemented for all applications that can accept data.

Dual Interface An **IDispatch** interface which implements both a vtable and the **Invoke** method using a DISPID. See Figure GL-7.

Early binding Early binding is done at compile time for the object. This approach is faster for the user since type checking and conversions are not necessary at run time. It cannot always be done and early binding is used for static OLE Controllers or ActiveX™ clients. It is very easy to do late binding with the **IDispatch** interface and conversely, it is very difficult to do early binding with **IDispatch**. As a general rule early binding uses a vtable and late binding uses **IDispatch**.

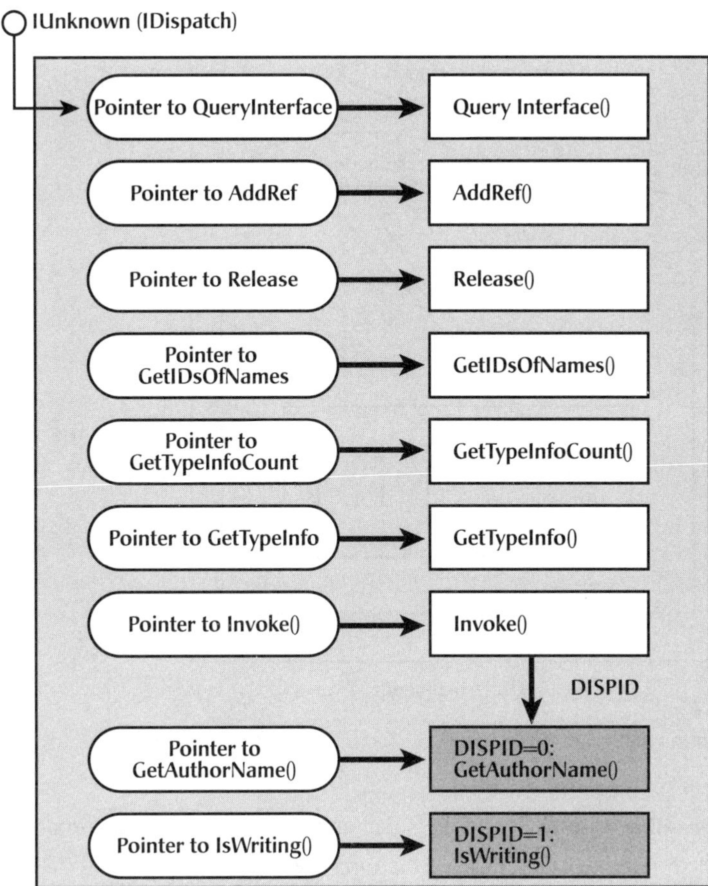

FIGURE GL-7 A dual IDispatch interface.

Embedded In-place activation initiates visual editing of an embedded object. The embedded object interacts with the container temporarily replacing existing features such as menus, toolbars, and possibly other controls of the active window. Documents may be embedded within another document as illustrated below, however only one level of the document will be active at any given time. The example below illustrates multiple levels of an embedded object. An embedded object is a copy of the original document that is stored in a container or another OLE document. See Figure GL-8.

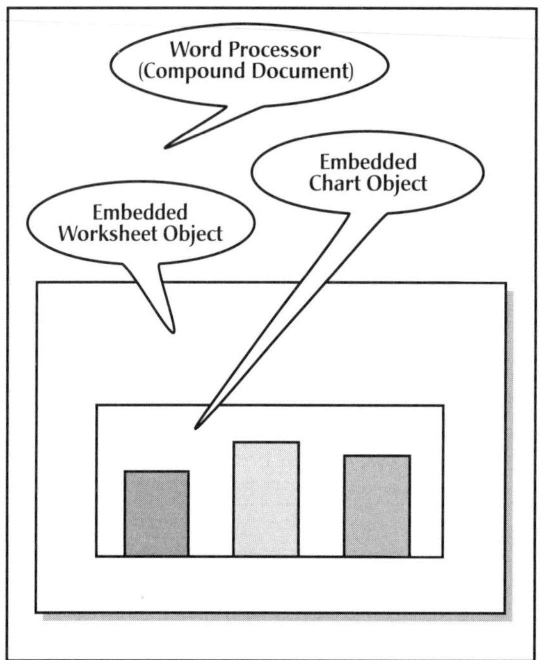

FIGURE GL-8 Multiple levels of document embedding.

Emulation ActiveX™ can do object emulation, a feature of compound documents. The functions COM library functions **CoGetTreatAsClass** and **CoTreat AsClass** are used for this purpose. As an example, I might wish to emulate MyDraw 3.0 with MyDraw 4.0.

Encapsulation Data of an object is encapsulated when it cannot be accessed directly by a client, but only through methods of the object.

Frame adornments Frame adornments occur when an embedded object is activated. Frame adornments can be row or column headers, handles, toolbars, modifying existing menus, adding new menus, or scroll bars that are outside the domain of the object. These adornments may temporarily obscure neighboring objects. Editing of an embedded object will not affect the title bar of the top-most container.

Free-threading A synonym for multi-threading in Windows NT 4.0. The apartment model prevailed before Windows NT 4.0 where each COM object was limited to one thread.

Full server A full server runs stand-alone and by definition is a local server in that it does not run in the process address space of the client. Excel is a good example of a full server. A full server that is also a remote server supports the concept of a tiered architecture. An example is a remote server supporting business rules, with common business functions in the next tier and the client interface in the final tier.

GUID A unique 128-bit value used for object identification.

Iadvisesink The **IAdviseSink** interface occupies a rather unique position in the COM architecture. It was the first asynchronous interface. All other interfaces are synchronous except for **IAsyncMoniker** and the **IConnectionPoint** advisory mechanism. The **IAdviseSink** notification mechanism requires the client to implement **IDataObject::DAdvise** and **IOleObject::Advise**. In-process object and handlers can optionally implement **IViewObject::SetAdvise**.

IadvisesinkEx **IAdviseSinkEx** inherits from **IAdviseSink**. Containers implement this interface to receive notification of changes in the view status of a contained object.

IAdviseSink2 The **IAdviseSink2** interface inherits from **IAdviseSink**, adding the method **OnLinkSrcChange** to the contract. This method handles a change in the moniker of a linked object which avoids overloading the **IAdviseSink::OnRename** implementation.

IasyncMoniker The presence of this interface indicates asynchronous binding.

IbindCtx Access to a bind context. This interface provides information to an object about a particular moniker binding operation. Bind context parameters are passed to many methods of **IMoniker** and other functions related to monikers.

Ibinding Provides methods that the client of an asynchronous moniker can call to control the progress of bind operations. An asynchronous moniker calls the client's **IBindStatusCallback::OnStartBinding** method to provide the client with a pointer to the **IBinding** interface.

IbindStatusCallback Clients requesting asynchronous bind operations must expose the **IBindStatusCallback** interface. The asynchronous moniker provides bind information to the client by calling the client's callback interface. This interface also allows the client to pass additional bind information to the moniker. The moniker calls **IBindStatusCallback::GetBindInfo** or **IBindStatusCallback::GetPriority** for additional information after receiving a call from either **IMoniker::BindToObject** or **IMoniker::BindToStorage**.

IclassFactory The interface for creating an instance of an object. **CreateInstance** is the specific method used for object creation. The client originally called **CoGet ClassObject** with the interface IID and CLSID of the new object. The COM library starts the server and returns the **IClassFactory** pointer. The client then accesses **IClassFactory** to create an instance of an object.

IconnectionPoint See connectable objects.

IconnectionPointContainer See connectable objects.

IdataAdviseHolder Methods of **IDataAdviseHolder** create and manage advisory connections between a data object and one or more advise sinks. Its methods are intended to be used to implement the advisory methods of **IDataObject**. Advise sinks receive notifications of object data changes for objects that require notification of changes and which implement the **IAdviseSink** interface. Advise sinks are also usually associated with OLE compound document containers.

IdataObject One of four objects defining uniform data transfer (UDT), the other objects being the **FORMATETC** data structure, the **STGMEDIUM** data structure, and the **IAdviseSink** interface. Specifies methods that enable data transfer of notification of data changes. **IDataObject** indicates at least minimal rendering support for CF_METAFILEPICT.

Idispatch An interface for translating a DISPID to a method call or a property access.

IdropSource See drag and drop.

IdropTarget See drag and drop.

IID An IID is a GUID that uniquely identifies an interface. Each interface must have an IID.

IexternalConnection One of three required interfaces for a DLL implementation, the other two interfaces being **IRunnableObject** and **IOleObject**. This interface is used for silent updates of linked data. It is also used by an external object linked to an embedded object.

Imalloc Task memory allocation. This is not an implementation interface but rather an interface to memory allocation. The recommended interface is **CoCreate StandardMalloc** for standard memory allocator and **CoGetMalloc** for the installed memory allocator.

Imarshal The existence of this interface signals a custom marshaling implementation.

ImessageFilter Called by COM when your application is blocking. **CoRegister MessageFilter** will register your message filter. Provides OLE servers and applications with the ability to selectively handle incoming and outgoing OLE messages while waiting for responses from synchronous calls. OLE messages can be synchronous, asynchronous, or input-synchronized. While the object is processing an asynchronous call, it is prohibited from making any synchronous calls back to the calling object.

Imoniker Exposes moniker functionality. Seven moniker classes are exposed including anti-monikers, class monikers, file monikers, generic composite monikers, item monikers, pointer monikers, and URL monikers. This is where the action starts. **IMoniker::BindToObject** is the workhorse of moniker binding and **IMoniker** is supported by a host of global API calls in addition to the **IBind Ctx** interface. The **IBindCtx** methods are not called directly, but are supported by co-routine to manage the moniker infrastructure. Most implementations of **IMoniker::BindToObject** will require services of the left context object. An item moniker for example, expects the **IOleItemContainer** interface to be implemented on the left context object.

Implementation Inheritance A feature used by languages such as C++ for code reuse. Implementation inheritance is not a feature of COM. A child object inherits a method from the parent object through implementation inheritance, which is not defined outside the address space of the process. The second problem is the "fragile base-class problem" where any change to the base-class can cause erratic or unexpected behavior when the child object executes an inherited method of the base-class. COM supports interface inheritance for code reuses where new methods are combined with existing methods through containment (delegation) or aggregation.

Inactive One of the four states of object presentation, the other four states being active, open and selected. These states apply to an OLE Server object or to an

ActiveX™ component acting in the role of a server object. Embedded objects are indicated with a solid border while linked objects, (which are not embedded and cannot use in-place activation for editing) are indicated by a dashed border. The border will be gray when linked data is not current.

In-place activation A technique used for visual editing of embedded objects. Outside-in activation of an embedded object occurs when the object is double-clicked. Linked objects may be activated in-place but the only operations permitted will be data display or playback and the linked object will open in its own window.

In-Process Handler An in-process handler has only one role, to display an object. It has minimum functionality with no in-place activation, automation, or other features. Quite like an in-process server only with reduced functionality. See Figure GL-9.

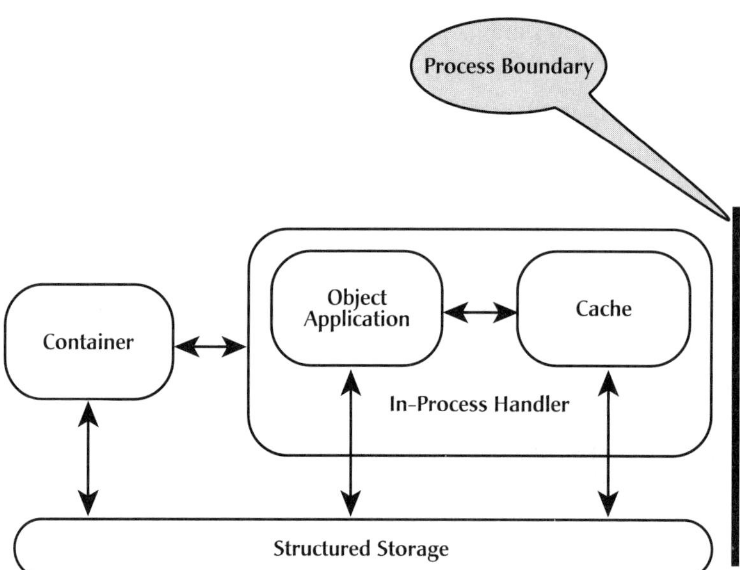

FIGURE GL-9 An in-process handler.

In-Process Server An in-process server is a DLL supporting a client from within the client process address space. This approach removes the overhead cost of inter-process communication. An in-process server supports embedding but not linking.

Inside-out Activation An ActiveX™ (OLE) control is always active and doesn't require activation and is able to process events immediately without activation.

This is different than *Outside-in* activation where the user must double-click the object to activate it. Inside-out objects are indistinguishable from native data.

Interface Inheritance COM only supports interface inheritance. This is accomplished with either containment (delegation) or aggregation. All COM objects use interface inheritance to support the **IUnknown** interface that includes the methods **QueryInterface**, **AddRef**, and **Release**.

IoleAdviseHolder Manages advisory connections of **IOleObject**. The object's container must implement **IAdviseSink**. OLE provides a default implementation of this interface and a custom implementation is typically not necessary.

IoleCache Implemented by object handler and in-process servers. Typical use is not to implement this interface but rather aggregate the OLE implementation whose pointer is available through **CreateDataCache**.

IOleCache2 Inherits from **IOleCache** and allows selective cache updating of those objects created by **IOleCache::Cache**.

IoleCacheControl Maintains the cache and connects the cache portion of this interface to the **IDataObject** implementation on the running object.

IoleClientSite **IOleClientSite** is the linked object's view of the local context. Information includes location and extent of its display site, its user interface, and other container resources.

IoleContainer An interface implemented on the container which will have linked objects (item monikers) or to lock the container for silent updates.

IoleItemContainer Implemented on a linked object. Each linked object must inherit this interface.

IoleInPlaceActiveObject The active object presents the **IOleInPlaceActiveObject** which isn't found by the other interfaces. Consequently, **IOleInPlaceActive Object** supplies its own **QueryInterface** definition. You can think of **IOleInPlace ActiveObject** as only a temporary interface.

IoleInPlaceObject Marks an object as in-place capable.

IoleInPlaceObjectWindowless **IOleInPlaceSiteWindowless** works with **IOleInPlace ObjectWindowless** to implement an environment where an in-place object can be activated without requiring a window or the associated window resources. Small controls do not need a window. It is an extra burden to have a window and the control cannot be non-rectangular within a window. It also prevents a window from being transparent.

IoleInPlaceFrame Container applications use this interface to control the display and placement of the composite menu, keystroke accelerator translation, context-sensitive help mode, and modeless dialog boxes.

IoleInPlaceSite Implemented by container applications and used to interact with the object's in-place client site.

IoleInPlaceSiteEx An add-on interface to **IOleInPlaceSite** which avoids unnecessary screen flashing when an object is activated or deactivated.

IoleInPlaceSiteWindowless See IOleInPlaceObjectWindowless

IOleInPlaceUIWindow A container interface which is used to negotiate border space on the document or frame window.

IoleLink Only implemented by linked objects. The interface through which a container accesses services of the object.**IOleLink** defines functions for managing linked object information. This includes linked source information and the cached presentation data.

IOleUILinkContainer This interface is only implemented by container applications that use the **EditLinks** dialog box.

IoleObject The primary interface through which a linked or embedded object provides functionality to the container. The object application must implement **IOleObject, IDataObject,** and **IPersistStorage** for each type of embedded object it supports. A control implementing IOleObject must be able to manage **Iadvise Sink** when IAdviseSink is supported by the container.

IoleWindow The base class for all **IOleInPlace*** interfaces.

IparseDisplayName Implemented on a custom object to parse a user-readable display name. Compound document applications that support links to embedded documents or pseudo-objects within their documents must provide an implementation of the **IOleItemContainer** interface. This interface is derived indirectly from **IParse DisplayName**. Another alternative is to implement **IParseDisplayName** as part of a class object, which is accessible through the **CoGetClass** function. Monikers that support their own name space with custom requirements for parsing names must implement this interface.

IperPropertyBrowsing Property pages of an object can be accessed with this interface. Required for all objects which a client can browse.

Ipersist The base interface for IPersistStorage, IPersistStream, and IPersistFile.

IpersistFile The **IPersistFile** interface is usually implemented by the object application, but it can be implemented by container applications. It is the mechanism of loading or saving documents to or from disk files. The client application has the responsibility for opening or closing the file. Binding a linked object is the normal use of this interface. This is a link to an embedded object when the application is a container. The object maintains the file in Figure GL-10.

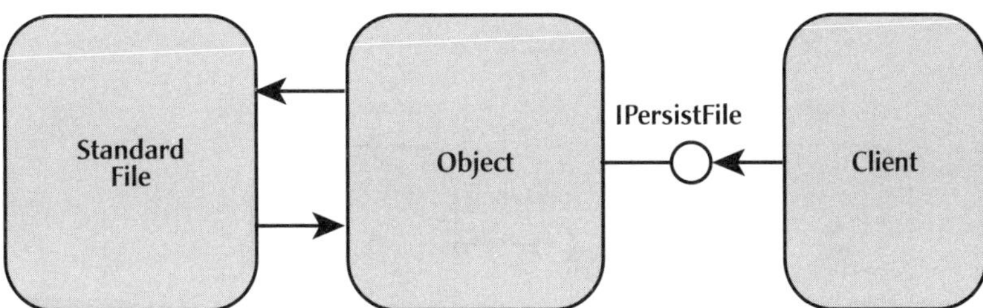

FIGURE GL-10 The object maintaining a file with IpersistFile.

IpersistMemory This persistence service manages shared memory provided by the client application. The interface to the shared memory is identical to the **IStream** interface except that the client is responsible for the persistent storage. See Figure GL-11.

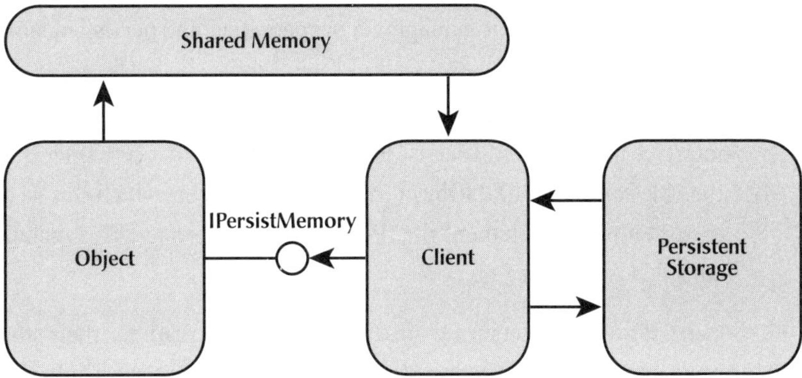

FIGURE GL-11 The client maintaining persistent memory.

IpersistMoniker Objects expose the **IPersistMoniker** interface to obtain additional binding control to persistent data. This interface is used by asynchronous-aware objects. The **IPersistFile, IPersistStream[Init], IPersistStorage** interfaces are returned by **QueryInterface** as part of the **IMoniker::BindToObject** implementation. **IPersistMoniker** does not contain an **InitNew**. Clients wishing an **InitNew** should call **IPersistStreamInit, IPersistMemory,** or **IPersistPropertybag.**

IpersistPropertyBag This is a persistence service where the client stores the data for the object and the object manages the data. Normally the object maintains the data in a structured file, however the client passes data through the **IPropertyBag** interface to the object. Any errors are reported to the object via **IErrorLog.** Typical use of a property bag interface is Visual Basic storing object properties as text strings. See Figure GL-12.

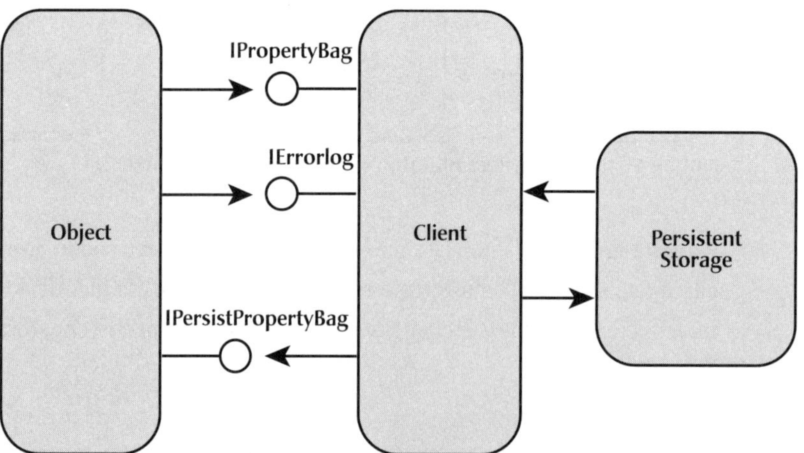

FIGURE GL-12 The client managing a property bag and persistent storage.

IpersistStorage The interface to the structured storage model. The **IPersistSorage** interface inherits from **IPersist.** Embedded objects in a container must implement the **IOleObject** and **IDataObject** interfaces. Any object which *can* be embedded in a container must implement the **IPersistStorage** interface. This includes both embedded and linked objects.

IpersistStream Objects which use a simple serial stream for their storage needs must implement the **IPersistStream** interface. This interface inherits the methods of **IPersist.** Each moniker implementation supports an **IPersistStream** interface.

Embedded and linked component objects of OLE containers must use the **IPersistStorage** interface and not **IPersistStream**.

IpropertyPage The object interface to the actual property page. A different property page object is required for each unique property page within a property sheet. A property page manages a dialog box (modal) which should only display controls for those properties with the property sheet. The page should have the Windows style **WS_CHILD** and should not have a style related to a frame, caption, system menus, or controls.

IPropertyPage2 An extension of **IPropertyPage** which tells the page which property to highlight or to receive focus when the page is activated.

IpropertyPageSite The interface which provides the main features for a property site object. A property page site is created for each property page within the property frame. The property page site provides information to the property page and receives notifications when changes occur. The frame initiates a call to **IProperty Page::IsPageDirty** when a change occurs. The return value is then used to either enable or disable the frame's apply button.

IpropertySinkNotify Implemented on the control container and accepts property change notifications from the OLE control. The object is required to call **IProperty NotifySink** for only those properties marked with the **Bindable** or **RequestEdit** attributes in the object's type information. When properties are so marked the control will call **IPropertyNotifySink::OnChanged** whenever a change occurs or will call **IPropertyNotifySink::OnRequestEdit** whenever an edit request occurs. The exception to these rules is object initialization and object loading time.

IrunnableObject Implemented by DLL object handlers. Enables a container to control the running of a DLL object handler. Differentiates between running and loaded, a state used by some in-process objects.

IrunningObjectTable Manages access to the running object table (ROT), a globally accessible look-up table of each client system. The **IMoniker::BindToObject** process checks the ROT to see if the object is already running. This allows the moniker to bind to the current instance instead of loading a fresh copy.

IstdMarshalInfo Returns the CLSID identifying the handler in the destination process. Not a custom implementation. COM queries this interface when performing standard marshaling.

IspecifyPropertyPage The existence of this interface signals that the control supports properties.

Iunknown IUnknown is the required interface for all COM objects and consists of three methods: **QueryInterface**, **AddRef**, and **Release**. The life of the object is controlled by the reference count that is increments with **AddRef** and decrements with **Release**.

IviewObject Creates and manages an advisory sink connection. This interface enables an object to display itself directly without passing a data object to the caller. **IViewObject** places a representation of the data onto a device context while **IDataObject** places the representation onto a transfer medium. This interface cannot be marshaled since it uses a device context.

IViewObject2 Inherits from **IViewObject** and adds the functionality to return the drawing size.

IviewObjectEx Inherits from **IViewObject2** and provides enhanced, flicker-free drawing for non-rectangular objects and transparent objects. Also supports hit testing for testing for non-rectangular objects.

Late binding ActiveX™ clients doing late binding must acquire the binding information at run time. Dynamic marshaling is required to support late binding.

Loaded Loaded is an object state. The other two object states are passive and running. These states should not be confused with presentation states, which are active, inactive, open, and selected.

Link A link is a feature of a Compound Document. A link has three properties: its type (class), the name of the source data, and its operating basis, which can be either automatic or manual.

Local Server A server running as an EXE in a separate process supporting COM objects on the same machine as the client.

LPC Local Procedure Call. Equivalent to LRPC.

LRPC Lightweight Remote Procedures call (LRPC) or an inter-process communication mechanism (IPC). An IPC or LRPC is used to communicate between processes in the same machine.

Marshaling A proxy packages the data before an RPC or LPC communicates it to the destination object. The stub at the destination unpackages the data for the target object. See Figure GL-13.

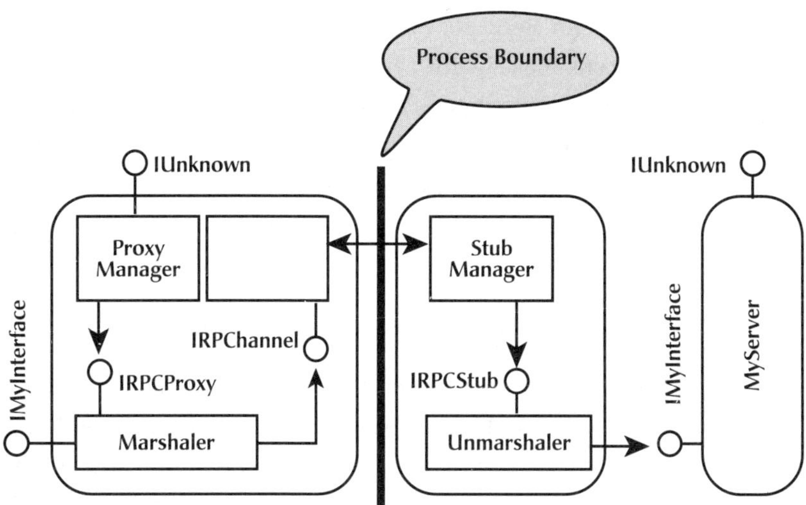

FIGURE GL-13 Using a stub and a proxy for marshaling.

Method An exposed function of an interface.

Mini-Server A local server implemented as an EXE that can only support embedded objects. A mini-server can only run in the context of a container application. Microsoft Chart, Equation Editor, and WordArt are examples of mini-servers. Data for mini-servers cannot be saved to a file.

Moniker An ActiveX™ object that is an alias for the encapsulating of the name, location, and permitted operations of a data item. A moniker can be a simple file name, a URL, or it can be a composite moniker. A moniker is an encapsulation of the interface connection mechanism that insulates a client from connection details.

Multi-threading A synonym for free-threading in Windows NT 4.0. The apartment model prevailed before Windows NT 4.0 where each COM object was limited to one thread.

Native data Native data is required for editing an object while *presentation data* is used by the *default object handler* for rendering the object.

Object Linking and Embedding The OLE prefix was once collectively applied to any technology which used COM. Object Linking and Embedding are now only used when referencing embedded (compound) documents. New technologies based on COM are now grouped under the ActiveX™ banner.

Object States An object state is the relationship between a compound document object, its container, and the application responsible for the object's creation. The object can have three states: *Passive* — the document is closed; *Loaded* — the container is open and the document may be visible; *Running* — the document has been activated and its own window is present in the document which is ready for manipulation. Object states are different than presentation states, which may be *active, inactive, open,* or *selected*.

OCX An ActiveX™ control, formerly known as an OLE control extension or OCX.

OLE An OLE component supports communication. An OLE document supports communication and at least linking and embedding. OLE was formerly known as OLE Documents, the term used for any object that may be embedded or linked in an OLE or ActiveX™ container. The term encompasses objects such as charts, drawings, AVI files, BMP pictures, spreadsheets, or even word-processing text (which is called a document in a different vernacular). Features include visual editing (embedded objects only), drag and drop, nested object support, property inheritance, type conversion, type emulation, extended object layout, management, and adaptable links.

OLE Automation OLE Automation is now called Automation. An application exposes its services (properties and methods) through dispinterfaces for programmability by a client. The OLE Automation Server exposes its components while the OLE Automation Controller manipulates the exposed components.

OLE Automation Controller An OLE Automation Controller is now an ActiveX™ Client. An OLE Automation Controller uses the exposed properties and methods of an OLE Automation Server for programmability. (See *Automation Controller*.)

OLE Automation Server An OLE automation server is now described as an ActiveX™ component acting in the role of a server. OLE Automation objects expose their properties and methods for programmability by an OLE Automation Controller or ActiveX™ Client.

OLE control An object based on COM that utilizes many of the characteristics of OLE Documents such as the concept of a container and a client. OLE controls have the following characteristics.

Events — Fired by the control. Simply the control accessing a method of the control container. OLE Documents do not have events.

Unicode based — OLE controls are 32 bit Unicode based. Unicode is quite expensive in terms of memory.

Properties — The definition of properties is formalized with an OLE control. Properties were vtable interfaces before OLE controls existed. Properties are now defined with property sheets containing property pages managed with a set of interfaces.

Ambient Properties — These are environmental properties of the container and the control adapts to these properties to interface seamlessly. An example is the default background color.

Extended Properties — Support extended properties such as position, size, layout, or automatic headers and footers for displayed pages. There is no limit on these properties and they are specific to the media.

Implementation — Nearly all controls are implemented as in-process servers. Supports object embedding and Automation, but not linking.

OLE Documents See OLE.

OleLoad OleLoad loads a link or embedded object into memory. It invokes the IPersistStorage::Load method, however the complete load task is somewhat complex. Details are available in Chapter 4.

OleLoadFromStream A simple interface with one unique requirement. The object CLSID must immediately precede the object's data in the stream or a NULL is returned as the object pointer. OleLoadFromStream has only two steps and no pointer is returned since the client provided the IID.

OleSave An object is saved in transacted mode into the specified storage object. The object returns error values of the IPersistStorage::Save method.

OleSaveToStream Calls **IPersistStream::GetClassID** to obtain the object's CLSID, writes the CLSID to the stream with **WriteClassStm** and finally calls IPersistStream::Save.

Open Open is one of the four states of object presentation, the other three states being *active*, *inactive*, and *selected*. These states apply to an OLE Server object or to an ActiveX™ component acting in the role of a server object. Embedded objects may be opened into their own window rather than a container window by registering an Open command for the object. The embedded object is completely covered with a hatched pattern indicating that the object is open in another window.

Outside-in activation Outside-in activation requires an action on the part of the user, the double-clicking of any OLE/ActiveX™ control. This is different than inside-out activation where the control is always active and no action by the user is required.

Passive Passive is an object state; the other two object states are running and loaded. These states should not be confused with presentation states, which are active, inactive, open, and selected.

Persistent See persistence service.

Persistence service Persistence is the permanent preserving of an object state with one of the interfaces: **IPersistStream, IPersistStreamInit, IPersistStorage,** IPersistFile, **IPersistPropertyBag, IPersistMoniker,** or **IPersistMemory**. The persistence storage for **IPersistPropertyBag** and **IPersistMemory** are both managed by the client application.

Programmability A feature of Automation where an application defines and makes available to other applications, a set of properties and methods (commands).

Presentation data Presentation data is that data which is rendered by the default object handler. The data may be different than native data, which is used to edit the object.

Primary verb This is the action associated with a double-click of an object. The primary verb is always the first verb in the registration database. The primary action of an embedded document is edit while the primary verb of a linked object may be display or playback.

Proxy A proxy performs the marshaling (packaging of the data) function for a client object. An RPC or IPC is used to communicate the data to the destination, which may be a local server or a remote server. (See *stub, unmarshaling*)

Pseudo-object A pseudo-object is a link to a portion of an object and is a feature of OLE. The most common example is selected rows and columns from an Excel spreadsheet.

QueryInterface A method of the class **IUnknown**. All ActiveX™ objects must support this method and the **IUnknown** interface.

Remote Server A server running on a remote machine. This server must cross a machine boundary and a process boundary while a local server only crosses a process boundary.

Running Object Table A global table maintained by a moniker provider. Binding costs are minimized. Only active (running) objects are in the table. Also known as the ROT table. **IRunningObjectTable** is the supporting interface.

RPC An RPC is a remote procedure call loosely modeled on the Open Software Foundation (OSF) Distributed Computing Environment (DCE) RPC. The primary limitation of a DCE RPC is that it must be synchronous, which can be a limitation for a lengthy database query or for binding an Internet URL.

Root storage The root storage is defined as the outermost **IStorage** object of a compound (structured) file. Compound documents are always saved as children of a root storage object. (See *Structured Storage*.)

Running Running is an object state; the other two object states are passive and loaded. These states should not be confused with presentation states, which are active, inactive, open, and selected.

Save A method of **IPersistStream**, **IPersistStreamInit**, **IPersistStorage**, and **IPersistFile**. The client supplies the stream, storage, file, or property bag identification.

Selected Selected is one of four states of object presentation, the other three states being active, inactive, and open. These states apply to an OLE 2.0 Server object or to an ActiveX™ component acting in the role of a server object.

Embedded objects are indicated with a solid border and there may also be eight sizing handles surrounding the object. You may either edit or play the object. Operations such as playback and display are permitted for in-place activation of linked objects, however editing of linked objects will occur in a separate window.

Storage object Storage objects implement the **IStorage** interface. Compound document storage is always relative to a root **IStorage** object. The analogy to a storage object is a file directory.

Stream object Stream objects are implemented with the **IStream** interface. There is no limit to the number of data streams (**IStream** objects) an object can create.

Structured storage A compound file (structured file) supports the storage of multiple objects. A compound file can be categorized as a file system within a file. Structured storage consists of three objects. A **LockBytes** byte array is managed by the **ILockBytes** interface. The other two objects are a stream object and a storage object. Data is organized with a root storage having multiple storages and streams. A storage may have other storages or substorages and streams with the content of a stream controlled by the client application. Operations to a compound file may be direct mode in that all data changes are saved immediately or data may be saved in a transacted mode until a commit or an undo occurs.

Stub A component of a local or remote server, which provides the unmarshaling (unpacking) of data for a target object. The stub runs in the address space of the receiver and communicates with the sender by an RPC if the receiver is a remote server or by an IPC (LRPC) for a local server. (See marshaling, unmarshaling, or proxy.)

Synchronous call A synchronous function call does not return control to the application until the requested operation is complete. Nearly all OLE 2.0 functions calls were synchronous. This has changed with ActiveX™ on the Internet where the user gets a response before all the data is loaded or rendered.

Synchronous Moniker A moniker which is synchronous and does not have control returned until the binding is complete. This is contrasted with asynchronous monikers which return control before binding is complete. See Figure GL-14.

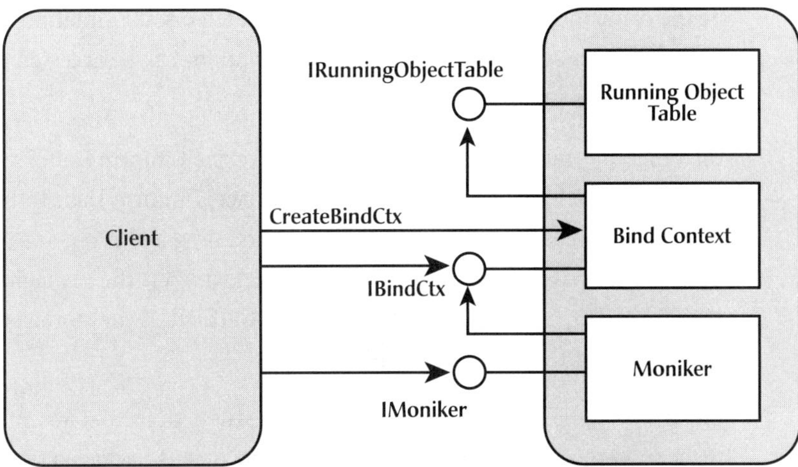

FIGURE GL-14 Binding with synchronous monikers.

Synchronous Call A synchronous call does not return control to the application until the requested operation is complete. Nearly all OLE function calls are synchronous. The notable exceptions are **IAdviseSink** which was the first OLE asynchronous call, **IConnectionPoint** which is a generalization of **IAdviseSink**, and **IBindStatusCallback** used by asynchronous monikers.

Transacted mode One of two modes implemented by the **IStorage** interface, the other mode being direct mode where the data is saved immediately. Transactions are saved in transacted mode until the user issues a commit or an undo command.

Transactions See Transacted mode.

Type A synonym for an object class. An object class has member functions that determine class behavior and object data that is operated on by class methods or functions.

Type conversion ActiveX™ can do object conversion, a feature of compound documents. The functions **OleDoAutoConvert, OleGetAutoConvert, OleSetAuto Convert, GetConvertStg,** and **SetConvertStg** support the conversion of objects.

Type library A type library describes the objects that an application exposes through Automation. A type library can describe one or more objects with information about data types, aliases, enumerations, structures, and unions. These objects can be the component object class (coclass), **IDispatch** or other interface information, and module information. Each of these descriptions can be accessed through an **ITypeInfo** interface.

Uniform Data Transfer Objects that conform to the Uniform Data Transfer (UDT) model will implement the **IDataObject** interface. Uniform Data Transfer is a model for transferring data with the clipboard, drag and drop, or Automation. UDT is comprised of four objects: **IDataObject** which is the managing interface, **FORMATETC** the data format structure, **STGMEDIUM** the storage medium data structure, and the **IAdviseSink** interface.

Unmarshaling The unpacking of data by the stub to a format acceptable by the receiving process is called unmarshaling. The data is packaged (marshaled) by a proxy before being sent to the destination stub for unmarshaling. (See marshaling, proxy, and stub.)

URL Uniform Resource Locator, as in the Internet. A URL is associated with an Internet address such as http:/WWW.Microsoft.COM.

URL Moniker (See Asynchronous Moniker.) A URL moniker is an asynchronous moniker with only small changes. A new data format interface is added on the client side and the generic **Binding** object is replaced with the Transport Protocol object. **BindStatusCallback, IBindCtx,** and **CreateBindCtx** from the asynchronous moniker are still there. See Figure GL-15.

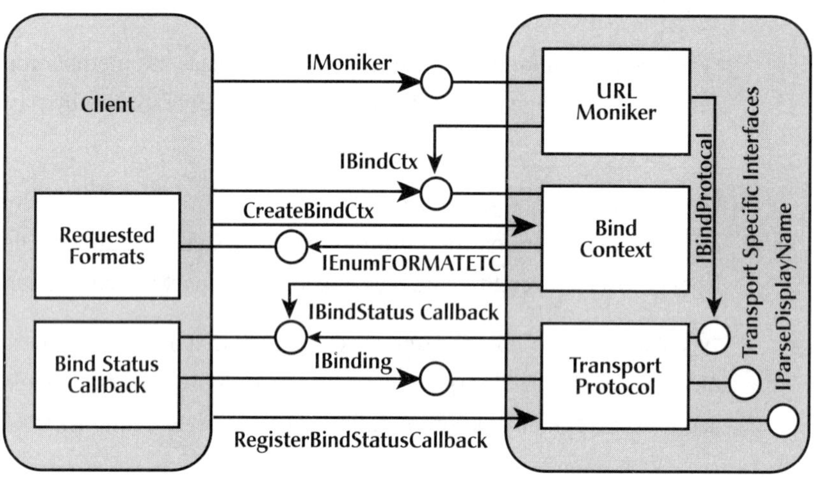

FIGURE GL-15 Binding a URL moniker

UUID A GUID is a synonym for a Universal User Identifier (UUID). The UUID is a component of the Open Software Foundation (OSF) Distributed Computing Environment (DCE).

Vtable (Virtual Table) A vtable is an array of function pointers to methods of an interface implementation. These pointers are not all accessible by scripting tools such as Microsoft Visual Basic or Microsoft Access. (See **IDispatch**, dispinterfaces)

Index

Symbols

Numbers

A

B

Continued

Continued

D

E

F

G

Continued

Continued

Continued

Continued

P

Q

Continued

Continued

Continued

U

Continued

W

X

Z

IDG Books Worldwide, Inc. End-User License Agreement

READ THIS. You should carefully read these terms and conditions before opening the software packet(s) included with this book ("Book"). This is a license agreement ("Agreement") between you and IDG Books Worldwide, Inc. ("IDGB"). By opening the accompanying software packet(s), you acknowledge that you have read and accept the following terms and conditions. If you do not agree and do not want to be bound by such terms and conditions, promptly return the Book and the unopened software packet(s) to the place you obtained them for a full refund.

1. License Grant. IDGB grants to you (either an individual or entity) a nonexclusive license to use one copy of the enclosed software program(s) (collectively, the "Software") solely for your own personal or business purposes on a single computer (whether a standard computer or a workstation component of a multiuser network). The Software is in use on a computer when it is loaded into temporary memory (RAM) or installed into permanent memory (hard disk, CD-ROM, or other storage device). IDGB reserves all rights not expressly granted herein.

2. Ownership. IDGB is the owner of all right, title, and interest, including copyright, in and to the compilation of the Software recorded on the disk(s) or CD-ROM ("Software Media"). Copyright to the individual programs recorded on the Software Media is owned by the author or other authorized copyright owner of each program. Ownership of the Software and all proprietary rights relating thereto remain with IDGB and its licensers.

3. Restrictions On Use and Transfer.

(a) You may only (i) make one copy of the Software for backup or archival purposes, or (ii) transfer the Software to a single hard disk, provided that you keep the original for backup or archival purposes. You may not (i) rent or lease the Software, (ii) copy or reproduce the Software through a LAN or other network system or through any computer subscriber system or bulletin-board system, or (iii) modify, adapt, or create derivative works based on the Software.

(b) You may not reverse engineer, decompile, or disassemble the Software. You may transfer the Software and user documentation on a permanent basis, provided that the transferee agrees to accept the terms and conditions of this Agreement and you retain no copies. If the Software is an update or has been updated, any transfer must include the most recent update and all prior versions.

4. Restrictions on Use of Individual Programs. You must follow the individual requirements and restrictions detailed for each individual program in Appendix D of this Book. These limitations are also contained in the individual license agreements recorded on the Software Media. These limitations may include a requirement that after using the program for a specified period of time, the user must pay a registration fee or discontinue use. By opening the Software packet(s), you will be agreeing to abide by the licenses and restrictions for these individual programs that are detailed in Appendix D and on the Software Media. None of the material on this Software Media or listed in this Book may ever be redistributed, in original or modified form, for commercial purposes.

5. Limited Warranty.

(a) IDGB warrants that the Software and Software Media are free from defects in materials and workmanship under normal use for a period of sixty (60) days from the date of purchase of this Book. If IDGB receives notification within the warranty period of defects in materials or workmanship, IDGB will replace the defective Software Media.

(b) IDGB AND THE AUTHOR OF THE BOOK DISCLAIM ALL OTHER WARRANTIES, EXPRESS OR IMPLIED, INCLUDING WITHOUT LIMITATION IMPLIED WARRANTIES OF MERCHANTABILITY AND FITNESS FOR A PARTICULAR PURPOSE, WITH RESPECT TO THE SOFTWARE, THE PROGRAMS, THE SOURCE CODE CONTAINED THEREIN, AND/OR THE TECHNIQUES DESCRIBED IN THIS BOOK. IDGB DOES NOT WARRANT THAT THE FUNCTIONS CONTAINED IN THE SOFTWARE WILL MEET YOUR REQUIREMENTS OR THAT THE OPERATION OF THE SOFTWARE WILL BE ERROR FREE.

(c) This limited warranty gives you specific legal rights, and you may have other rights that vary from jurisdiction to jurisdiction.

6. Remedies.

(a) IDGB's entire liability and your exclusive remedy for defects in materials and workmanship shall be limited to replacement of the Software Media, which may be returned to IDGB with a copy of your receipt at the following address: Software Media Fulfillment Department, Attn.: *Solution Architectures MCSD Study System*, IDG Books Worldwide, Inc., 7260 Shadeland Station, Ste. 100, Indianapolis, IN 46256, or call 1-800-762-2974. Please allow three to four weeks for delivery. This Limited Warranty is void if failure of the Software Media has resulted from accident, abuse, or misapplication. Any replacement Software Media will be warranted for the remainder of the original warranty period or thirty (30) days, whichever is longer.

(b) In no event shall IDGB or the author be liable for any damages whatsoever (including without limitation damages for loss of business profits, business interruption, loss of business information, or any other pecuniary loss) arising from the use of or inability to use the Book or the Software, even if IDGB has been advised of the possibility of such damages.

(c) Because some jurisdictions do not allow the exclusion or limitation of liability for consequential or incidental damages, the above limitation or exclusion may not apply to you.

7. U.S. Government Restricted Rights. Use, duplication, or disclosure of the Software by the U.S. Government is subject to restrictions stated in paragraph (c)(1)(ii) of the Rights in Technical Data and Computer Software clause of DFARS 252.227-7013, and in subparagraphs (a) through (d) of the Commercial Computer — Restricted Rights clause at FAR 52.227-19, and in similar clauses in the NASA FAR supplement, when applicable.

8. General. This Agreement constitutes the entire understanding of the parties and revokes and supersedes all prior agreements, oral or written, between them and may not be modified or amended except in a writing signed by both parties hereto that specifically refers to this Agreement. This Agreement shall take precedence over any other documents that may be in conflict herewith. If any one or more provisions contained in this Agreement are held by any court or tribunal to be invalid, illegal, or otherwise unenforceable, each and every other provision shall remain in full force and effect.

NO POSTAGE
NECESSARY
IF MAILED
IN THE

BUSINESS REPLY

POSTAGE WILL BE PAID BY
ADDRESSEE
MICROSOFT TECHNET
MICROSOFT CORPORATION
PO BOX 5540
PLEASANTON, CA 94566-9940

Name:

Company:

Address:

City: State: Zip:

Fold here

Fold her

* Purchaser is liable for all applicable sales taxes (US) and GST/HST/PST (Canada). Add the applicable sales tax in the following states: AR, AZ, CA, CO, CT, DC, FL, GA, HI, IA, ID, IL, IN, KS, KY, LA, MA, MD, ME, MI, MN, MO, MS, NC, ND, NE, NJ, NM, NV, NY, OH, OK, PA, RI, SC, SD, TN, TX, UT, VA, VT, WA, WI, WV and WY. In Canada, add a 7% GST. 15% HST will apply if in NS, NB, NF, in lieu of GST. In British Columbia and Ontario, add the PST per your provincial requirements. Microsoft reserves the right to make corrections to tax amounts actually charged, required by law, without notice.

** Please send payment in U.S. currency only. Do not send cash. Make checks payable to Microsoft Corporation. Offer good only in
50 United States, District of Columbia and Canada. Outside the U.S. and Canada, contact your Microsoft Subsidiary or call (925) 275-0826 for local contact information. Offer expires 6/30/00. Orders must be postmarked on or before 6/30/00. Offer is subject to change without notice.

*** 128-bit encryption software is available only to subscribers in the United States, U.S. territories, and Canada. Sorry, we
cannot send 128-bit encryption software outside the US or Canada or to APO or FPO addresses. For additional information see http://www.microsoft.com/exporting/.

my2cents.idgbooks.com

Register This Book — And Win!

Visit **http://my2cents.idgbooks.com** to register this book and we'll automatically enter you in our fantastic monthly prize giveaway. It's also your opportunity to give us feedback: let us know what you thought of this book and how you would like to see other topics covered.

Discover IDG Books Online!

The IDG Books Online Web site is your online resource for tackling technology — at home and at the office. Frequently updated, the IDG Books Online Web site features exclusive software, insider information, online books, and live events!

10 Productive & Career-Enhancing Things You Can Do at www.idgbooks.com

- Nab source code for your own programming projects.
- Download software.
- Read Web exclusives: special articles and book excerpts by IDG Books Worldwide authors.
- Take advantage of resources to help you advance your career as a Novell or Microsoft professional.
- Buy IDG Books Worldwide titles or find a convenient bookstore that carries them.
- Register your book and win a prize.
- Chat live online with authors.
- Sign up for regular e-mail updates about our latest books.
- Suggest a book you'd like to read or write.
- Give us your 2¢ about our books and about our Web site.

You say you're not on the Web yet? It's easy to get started with IDG Books' *Discover the Internet,* available at local retailers everywhere.

CD-ROM Installation Instructions

Each software item on the *Solution Architectures MCSD Study System* CD-ROM is located in its own folder. To install a particular piece of software, open its folder with My Computer or Internet Explorer. What you do next depends on what you find in the software's folder:

1. First, look for a `ReadMe.txt` file or a `.doc` or `.htm` document. If this is present, it should contain installation instructions and other useful information.
2. If the folder contains an executable (`.exe`) file, this is usually an installation program. Often it will be called `Setup.exe` or `Install.exe`, but in some cases the filename reflects an abbreviated version of the software's name and version number. Run the `.exe` file to start the installation process.
3. In the case of some simple software, the `.exe` file probably is the software — no real installation step is required. You can run the software from the CD to try it out. If you like it, copy it to your hard disk and create a Start menu shortcut for it.

The `ReadMe.txt` file in the CD-ROM's root directory may contain additional installation information, so be sure to check it.

TechNet Product Warranty and Support Disclaimer

This program, TechNet, was reproduced by IDG Books Worldwide, Inc. under a special arrangement with Microsoft Corporation. For this reason, IDG Books Worldwide, Inc. is responsible for the product warranty and for support. If your CD-ROM is defective, please return it to IDG Books Worldwide, Inc. which will arrange for its replacement. PLEASE DO NOT RETURN IT TO MICROSOFT CORPORATION. Any product support will be provided, if at all, by IDG Books Worldwide, Inc. PLEASE DO NOT CONTACT MICROSOFT CORPORATION FOR PRODUCT SUPPORT. End users of this Microsoft program shall not be considered "registered owners" of a Microsoft product and therefore shall not be eligible for upgrades, promotions or other benefits available to "registered owners" of Microsoft products.

IDG Books Worldwide License
Agreement included in this book.